The 22nd (Cheshire) Regiment

H.M. King George V.,

The Lord - Lieut. of the County,   Pte. T. A. Jones, V.C.

(Runcorn, 8th July, 1925)

THE HISTORY

OF

THE CHESHIRE REGIMENT

IN

THE GREAT WAR

ILLUSTRATIONS
AND MAPS

BY

ARTHUR CROOKENDEN

COLONEL OF THE REGIMENT

INTRODUCTION.

THE story of The Regiment in the Great War is mainly confined, in this book, to the Official Honours which we won. The incessant trench-holding which fell to the lot of Line Regiments involved continual calls on the courage and endurance of the men. But it seemed best to confine this history to named battles. Among these, are included some notable feats of arms which have, so far, not been officially recognised as Battle Honours. These battles have headings in small type.

Otherwise than might be expected, the war diaries are, generally, of little value in compiling the story of a Battalion in battle. Even if an account is given, it rarely corresponds with the accounts of other Battalions. Such remarks as " there were no troops on our flank " constantly appear, when it is obvious that they really were there.

Brigade war diaries are the worst, and Divisional the best. But these latter sometimes give too good an account of a battle, and are not easy to reconcile with the diaries of lower formations.

As regards Battalion war diaries, the severer the action, the worse the account in the diary. On occasions when a 2nd/Lieut., hardly joined, brings the remnant of a Battalion out of action, he cannot be blamed for not writing up the story. In the first place, he probably does not know that there is such a thing as a war diary. In the second place, he does not know anything of the superior plan and little of the role allotted to the Battalion. On several occasions, when our Battalions suffered most severely, won important objectives, and earned immortal glory, there was no one left competent to tell the tale.

Private diaries were not allowed. But there is no doubt that those who disregard this order provide the Regimental historian with very valuable material.

Throughout the story of infantry, runs the thread of artillery support. Although they may not come into close contact with the enemy, the gunners have as terrible and trying a task as falls to the lot of any. It is a tradition in our service that, as long as infantry require support, the gunners stand to their guns.

This tradition holds gunners to their guns no matter how concentrated or how severe a bombardment may be. Our gunners cannot be driven from their guns, and a battery is only silenced when its servants are all out of action.

If, throughout this story of The Regiment at war, insufficient attention seems to be paid to The Royal Regiment, it is through lack of information and not for want of appreciation of their priceless services.

Major Geoffrey Harding has compiled the chapter dealing with Mons.

The description of the 2nd Battalion's fighting at St. Julien, Frezenberg, Bellewaerde and Loos is due in great measure to the investigations of Brigadier H. R. Sandilands, late of The Northumberland Fusiliers.

Major J. R. Danson, Captain B. W. Corden and Mr. William Courtenay of the 4th Battalion, Captain D. Greville, of the 9th Battalion, and Captain H. Ryalls of the 15th Battalion, have given me much assistance. We are also greatly indebted to Colonel A. C. Johnston, to Colonel Harrison Johnston, and to Captain L. M. Ferguson for access to their diaries, and to " The Oak Tree " for Arthur Greg's diary and for many notes.

The story of each battalion, up to the time it went overseas, will be found in Appendix IV., which was written by Mrs. Hugh Sparling.

Major H. C. Randall and Captain S. Keeling assisted in preparing the Roll of Individual Honours. Colonel H. S. Walker indexed the book.

Though no account is given in this book of the wonderful work done by the ladies of The Regiment and of the County and City, it can never be forgotten. No Regiment can have been better cared for. The supply of comforts to the serving and wounded, work in the numerous hospitals, care of the wives and families left behind, and the steady and efficient supply of food parcels to prisoners of war (which no prisoner will ever forget) were all achieved only by unremitting and self-denying work.

NORTHERN FRANCE

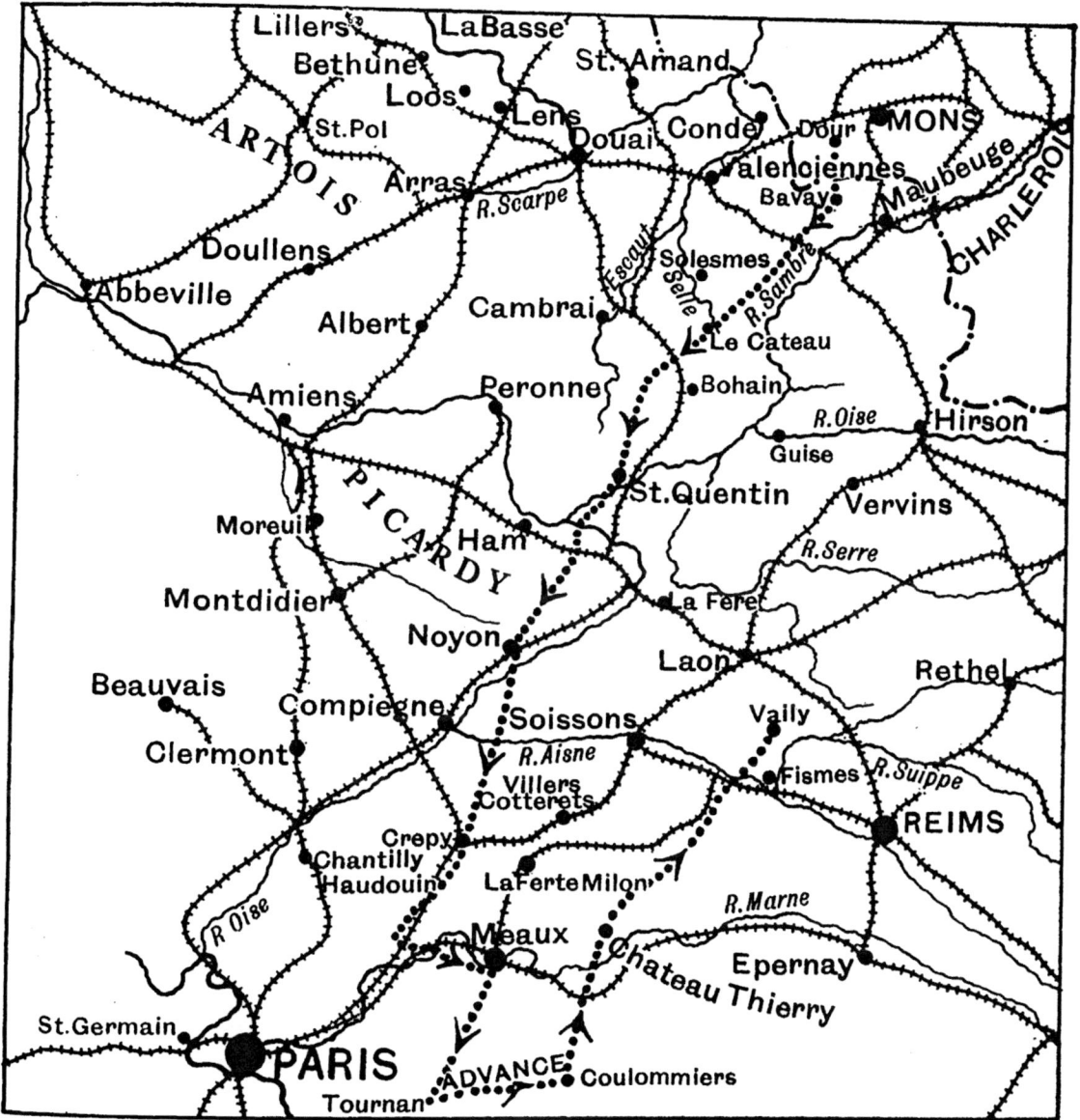

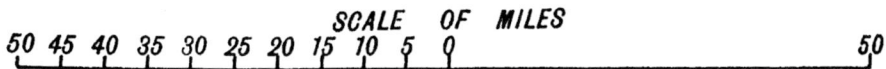

SCALE OF MILES

50 45 40 35 30 25 20 15 10 5 0   50

KEY

〜〜〜 Rivers and Canals   •••▶••• Route of Brit. Troops

+++++ Railways   –·–·–· Boundary

Contents

SHOWING BATTLE HONOURS FOR THE GREAT WAR AWARDED TO THE CHESHIRE REGIMENT

Thirty-eight Battalions were raised, of which Fifteen served in engagements with the enemy

---

GALLIPOLI

NOTE :—*Battles in Brackets are described in the History, but are not official battle honours.*

APPENDICES

THE CHESHIRE REGIMENT
IN THE GREAT WAR

FRANCE AND FLANDERS.

MONS.

Maps p. 18

THE 1ST BATTALION arrived at le Havre at 3-30 p.m. on the 16th August. Brigade Headquarters, the 1/Norfolk, 1/Bedford and 1/Dorset landed in the course of the afternoon and completed the concentration of the 15th Infantry Brigade.

The Battalion spent the night in a rest camp about six miles outside the town, and entrained at le Havre at 11-0 p.m. the following day for an unknown destination.

At Bohain, the news of General Grierson's sudden death temporarily damped the spirits of the officers, who knew of their Corps Commander's reputation, both as a soldier and as a student of the German Army. General Sir Horace Smith-Dorrien was not appointed to succeed him until two days later, and did not reach his headquarters until the afternoon of the 21st August.

Le Cateau was reached at about 8-0 p.m. and there the Battalion detrained. Lieutenant Woodyer, who had developed a bad attack of fever, was admitted to hospital and subsequently invalided home.

The troops rested at Pommereuil, near le Cateau, for three nights while the remainder of the Expeditionary Force completed concentration. The time was well employed in company marches to harden up the reservists. The 1st Battalion was visited in billets by Major-General Sir Charles Fergusson, the G.O.C., and Brigadier-General Count Gleichen, the Brigade Commander. The G.O.C. made a short speech to the men in which he emphasised the gravity of the situation they were likely to have to face, and the necessity for fighting to the last man and the last round.

It is convenient here to recall the plans of the opposing commanders, in order that the course of subsequent events may be made clear.

The German plan was to seize the initiative, move through Belgium with an overwhelmingly strong force, outflank the French by the west, and drive them eastwards towards the Swiss frontier. To accomplish this, their seven armies were deployed between the Dutch and Swiss

A

frontiers. The sixth and seventh armies, to the south, were to pin the French First and Second armies to their ground between Metz and the Swiss frontier, while the remaining five armies, using Thionville as a pivot, were to execute a wide wheeling movement. These five armies were scheduled to reach the line Ghent-Mons-Sedan-Thionville by the 23rd August, and the line Amiens-la Fère-Rethel-Thionville by the 1st September. Finally, while the remainder held their ground, Von Kluck's first army was to sweep down from the north and along the river Seine, to the west and south-west of Paris, and, reinforced by every available division, drive the French eastwards towards Switzerland.

The Belgians, taken unawares, had to stop the German hordes as best they could. Their intention was to check the German advance with one division, covered by the fortress of Liège, while the four remaining divisions, if faced by very superior forces, were to take up a defensive position on the river Gette, screened by the cavalry division.

The French, morally bound to keep clear of neutral Belgium and uncertain of German scruples on the point, were at a great disadvantage. If they waited the development of the German plan, they automatically surrendered the initiative, a policy which was opposed to the peace time training of the army. They therefore decided to launch an offensive at all costs.

The Plan adopted was the now famous Plan XVII., which included attacks by the First and Second armies in Alsace and Lorraine while the Fifth advanced north of Verdun. To the Third army was to fall the task of connecting these two operations and of investing Metz when the time came. The Fourth was to be held in reserve. In the event of the Germans invading Belgium, the First and Second Armies were still to launch their offensives, while the Fourth was to take post between the Third and Fifth armies and advance north-east on Neufchateau with them.

It had been decided that the B.E.F. should concentrate in the Avesnes-le Cateau area and be ready to advance by the fifteenth day after mobilization had been ordered. Thereafter, the force was to operate on the left of the French Fifth army as the situation demanded. The concentration of the B.E.F. was completed in accordance with the peace-time programme, and had been carried out with such care and secrecy that the German Command were in ignorance of the presence of British troops on French soil up to the moment their troops gained contact with them.

It is noteworthy, that in spite of the concentration of vast German forces in Belgium and their subsequent movements, the situation was sufficiently obscure on the eve of the battle of Mons for Sir John French to report in his first despatch, " From information I received from French headquarters I understood that little more than one, or at most two, of the enemy's army corps, with perhaps one cavalry division, were in front of my position, and I was aware of no attempted out-flanking movement by the enemy."

On the 21st August, a further advance was made in a north-easterly direction, Gommignies being reached about mid-day, after a hot march of fifteen miles. Here the Brigade billetted for the night. During the march, the French peasants had given the troops a wonderful welcome all along the route. Their eagerness to force gifts upon the men became almost embarrassing at times and some difficulty was experienced in keeping them clear of the ranks. In return, many men gave their cap badges and shoulder titles, which, later, made identification of units difficult. It had been a hard day for the reservists, who were unaccustomed to carrying a heavy pack, and there were a few stragglers. They were willing to a man and all arrived in billets later, but the heat, together with the weight they were called upon to carry, was too much for their physical capabilities after the comparative ease of civilian life.

The march was continued next morning to Boussu (fifteen miles), by Dour. The pleasant agricultural countryside of the previous day gradually gave place to a more thickly populated industrial area. Once the Belgian frontier was crossed, the difference became more marked, and the inhabitants, too, who turned out to see the troops pass, were of a different type from the courteous French peasants of the preceding days. The road, consisting of uneven pavé bordered by strips of unmetalled track, made marching a painful and tedious affair even for the fittest troops, and, as before, the reservists suffered badly. Several fell out, but all but four re-joined in billets later. The march discipline of the rest was good, organized singing keeping up the morale.

During the afternoon, rumours came through that the Germans were in strength beyond the Mons-Condé Canal, some two miles to the north, which was already held by British troops. Of the 5th Division, the 13th and 14th Infantry Brigades were on the canal line, the 15th Infantry Brigade, in its billeting area, forming the divisional reserve.

The first German gun was heard shortly after noon on the 23rd August, and the sound of intermittent shell fire from the direction of the canal continued for the rest of the afternoon. Von Kluck's army was completing its wheel to the south, the pivot flank being opposite the Mons salient. The shell fire, heard in billets, denoted the first clash of the opposing forces.

The German advance was proceeding according to plan.

The civilian inhabitants in the neighbourhood appeared oblivious of the danger which threatened them, and went to and fro to church in their Sunday clothes, as if in the midst of some peace time field-day. Within twenty-four hours, the same folk were thronging the roads in their move westwards, striving to get beyond reach of the Germans.

About noon on the 23rd August, the Brigade was ordered to dig in on a defensive position which had been selected by the Brigadier that morning, and on which trenches had already been started by the impressed labour of Belgian miners.

The 1/Norfolk was allotted the left sector from Wasmes Station eastwards ; the 1st Battalion was on its right (but thrown back a little in very enclosed country) ; while the 1/Bedford and 1/Dorset occupied some trenches on a high railway embankment further to the east. It was a hopeless position for a force which relied mainly on rifle fire for its defence. There was little field of fire, owing to excrescences such as pit-heads, buildings and innumerable slag heaps, and artillery observation was difficult. But there was no better alternative for miles.

During the night, Lieutenant Matterson (Scout Officer) and a Battalion scout, crossed the Mons-Condé Canal, gained touch with the enemy and brought back useful information.

The Brigadier had visited Battalion headquarters during the day and had informed Colonel Boger that the army was establishing a line of strong points, or " points d'appui," and that the French were about to attack or re-inforce between them. The point is mentioned for it led to some misunderstanding later on.

Next morning, the 24th August, orders came that the Division would stand and fight. The Norfolks and Cheshires were to be in Reserve, on relief.

The 2/Manchester arrived to take over our trenches at about 7 a.m. on the 24th August, and the relief was completed by 10-0 a.m. The Battalion then moved off to Dour Station (Divisional headquarters) just as the German attack re-opened.

This sudden move was bewildering to those who were not aware of the reasons which necessitated it. The entrenching of a position had suggested a stand of some duration, and it is probable that all ranks pictured a fight there to the last man and the last round, as conjured up by Sir Charles Fergusson's speech a few hours before. This must be kept in view in order to appreciate the calamity which later befell the 1st Battalion. It must also be borne in mind that the regulations of the time insisted that, in the event of a retirement being unavoidable, orders for it were only to be issued confidentially to the Commanders concerned. Before the war, in order to foster the offensive spirit, retirement as an operation of war was ignored during training. There was no hint, either at this time or later, that a withdrawal was contemplated, when, in fact, the French had already retired and had left the British Expeditionary Force no alternative but to conform. It was, therefore, in complete ignorance of the true situation that Colonel Boger led the Battalion to Divisional headquarters and reported to G.O.C.

On arrival at Dour Station at 11-0 a.m., Colonel Boger found himself one of several officers who had been summoned to headquarters, among whom was Lieut.-Colonel C. R. Ballard (commanding 1/Norfolk). After some delay, General Fergusson called up Colonels Ballard and Boger, and, having ascertained that the former was the senior, placed the 1st Battalion and the 119th Field Battery, R.A., under his command. The G.O.C. then passed Colonel Ballard on to a staff officer to receive his orders. Colonel Boger had been told to rejoin his Battalion. He was not present while these orders were being given out. The Battalion was then drawn up in " quarter column " on the left of the 1/Norfolk, close by.

Colonel Ballard was not provided with the staff or equipment for exercising command of a detached force, and had, therefore, only two courses open to him. He could make up a separate headquarters by withdrawing personnel from the units under his command, thereby disorganising them, or could exercise the dual function of detachment and battalion commander through his normal battalion staff. The position was aggravated by the fact that most of the signal personnel of battalions had already been withdrawn to form a brigade section. Colonel Ballard chose the latter of the two alternatives.

After a short wait, Colonel Ballard, who, in the meantime, had received written orders through a staff officer, saw Colonel Boger and informed him that the detachment was to take up a defensive position between Élouges and Angre. The orders disclosed the general intention of the G.O.C. to retire south-west, and detailed Colonel Ballard, with his detached force, to act as flank guard. The move to Élouges necessitated a flank march across the enemy's front. " B " Company (Captain Shore), was therefore detailed to act as right flank guard.

The Germans were already to be seen moving along the Mons-Valenciennes road, but they mistook Colonel Ballard's force for their own left wing, which was swinging round south in the direction of Wiheries, and did not deploy or open fire.

The column moved forward with the 1/Norfolk leading. On arrival at the Élouges-Audregnies road, Colonel Ballard distributed his own companies at intervals along it from the Élouges-Quiévrain railway to the colliery. He then met Colonel Boger near the mineral railway bridge and told him to prolong the line to the left of the 1/Norfolk. He added, " You will be all right, our cavalry are in front," or words to that effect. Colonel Boger was left with the impression that haste was necessary and that there was a gap to be filled.

The Germans had by now discovered the presence of British troops on their flank and had deployed from the road to meet the threat. There was, therefore, no time for reconnaissance and Colonel Boger had no alternative but to drop his companies at intervals along the road in the same way as Colonel Ballard had done with the 1/Norfolk. But, by the time he reached the old mill (north of Audregnies), the three companies, then available, were used up.

Acting in accordance with what he concluded was the Commander's plan, Colonel Boger ordered the company commanders to hold their ground at all costs.

The Battalion was disposed of as follows :—" D " Company (Captain Rae Jones) on the right, astride the mineral railway and linking up with with 1/Norfolk ; " C " Company (Captain Dugmore) in the centre ; and " A " Company (Captain Dyer) on the left, covering the junction of the Wiheries-Audregnies and Élouges-Audregnies roads. Later, when " B " Company came in, on completion of its task as flankguard, it was detailed to protect the left flank. To do this, Captain Shore dropped two platoons, under Captain Jolliffe, on " A " Company's left, while he himself, with the remaining two platoons, took up a position on the north-western outskirts of Audregnies.

Here it is necessary to digress, in order to obtain a picture of the state of affairs as far as the rest of the 5th Division was concerned. The 2nd Corps orders to the 5th Division, for the morning of the 24th, were to hold on to its position in order to enable the 3rd Division on the right to get clear. But, at 11-0 a.m., the G.O.C. received permission to retire at his discretion, once the 3rd Division had disengaged. This he did. But hardly had the 13th and 14th Brigades started to withdraw, than reports came in which shewed that his left flank had been uncovered by the retirement of the cavalry and 19th Infantry Brigades from the Montignies-Rombies line, and was threatened by Von Kluck's wheeling movement. General Fergusson had already sent an urgent message to General Allenby requesting the co-operation of the cavalry division in protecting his left flank, and Allenby had responded immediately by ordering the 2nd and 3rd Cavalry Brigades to return to the vicinity of Audregnies. As an additional precaution, the G.O.C. had ordered Colonel Ballard's force to act as left flank guard.

Had Colonel Ballard mentioned the words " flank guard " to Colonel Boger, the situation would have been plain, but he understood that a copy of the divisional orders for the withdrawal, which as already noted, explained the rôle of the two battalions, had been given to Colonel Boger at the same time as he himself had received his own. The position was, therefore, that Colonel Ballard was under the impression that Colonel Boger had all information available when, in actual fact, the latter still believed that the original orders, to hold on at all costs, held good.

As a result of General Allenby's prompt response to General Fergusson's S.O.S., we find the 2nd and 3rd Cavalry Brigades on the battlefield about noon, when Colonel Ballard's force was preparing to meet the enemy. These brigades were disposed as follows :—2nd Cavalry Brigade —18/Hussars in rear of the 1/Norfolk ; 9/Lancers immediately north-west of Audregnies ; and the 4/Dragoon Guards on their left rear. The 3rd Cavalry Brigade took up a position on the ridge south-west of Audregnies, beyond the River Honnelle, and " I," Battery R.H.A. came into action behind the railway to the east of Audregnies.

There was no time for trench digging or for any definite orders to filter down to the rank and file. The sunken road gave some cover, but an adequate field of fire could only be obtained from the open slopes of the fields beyond. Captain Shore's two platoons of " B " Company had more cover than the remainder, but were very isolated. Battalion headquarters was established behind the only cottage on the roadside. There were considerable gaps between companies, and, owing to the slightly undulating nature of the ground, they were unable to see each other, conditions which made inter-communication difficult.

It is hard to imagine a more unfortunate situation than that which confronted Colonel Boger. He had to deploy the Battalion at right angles to the direction of the approach march, and to accept battle on ground which he had never seen before and which was, in some respects, unsuitable for developing the power of his small-arms fire, upon which he depended for security. Corn stooks and slag heaps masked most of the ground, and, besides offering ranging marks to the enemy, added to the difficulty of locating the companies once they had left the road. Communication with " B " Company caused some anxiety, for it could only be reached by the road, much of which was in view of the enemy and under shrapnel and machine-gun fire.

The two Battalion machine guns, under Lieutenant Randall, came into action near the cottage, between " A " and " B " Companies, and created havoc in the ranks of the two German columns which were seen advancing in close order from Quiévrain and the Bois de Déduit. Scarcely had they opened fire than the Battalion's position was located by a low-flying hostile aeroplane, and shrapnel was soon bursting along the whole front. Several casualties occurred, but the shooting was indifferent and most of the shells burst beyond the position.

The 119th Field Battery had come into action in rear of " D " Company and, with " L " Battery, was making excellent shooting at the dense masses of Germans in the distance.

Now that Colonel Boger had time to look round, he satisfied himself that every precaution to meet a frontal attack had been taken. He thought that the Division was holding the line as ordered in Divisional orders received that morning and felt little anxiety.

Meanwhile, seeing the enemy debouching in close order from Quiévrain, General de Lisle (Commander of the 2nd Cavalry Brigade) galloped over to the 9/Lancers, which, as we have seen, were north-west of Audregnies, and instructed the C.O. to deliver a mounted attack northwards in order to take the enemy in flank as he advanced. The 9/Lancers were not slow to take advantage of the opportunity for mounted action and, together with two troops of the 4/Dragoon Guards echeloned in rear, advanced in column of squadrons. They crossed the Élouges-Baisieux road at a gallop and lanced several German scouts in the cornfield beyond.

At first, the Germans mistook them for their own cavalry, but, near the sugar factory, where they were checked by wire, the enemy discovered his mistake and opened fire with nine batteries which were in position north-east of Quiévrain, and brought them to a standstill. Some dismounted, but the majority swung round and retired through the infantry position by way of the railway. At the same time, a squadron of 4/Dragoon Guards galloped down the lane towards Baisieux with a view to making a sortie towards Quiévrain, but they, too, were checked and suffered many casualties. This gallant manœuvre by the cavalry, although procuring no material result, had some moral effect on the enemy and delayed his progress. It was unfortunate that the attack had to be made across the front of Colonel Ballard's force, for it masked the fire of his small-arms and thus deprived him of any co-operative effect.

The diversion created by the cavalry enabled the 1st Battalion to settle down and make certain adjustments to the line. Two platoons, 1/Norfolk, were found to be holding a position near the colliery, in front of the right flank of our position. Captain Jones, on the right, sent two platoons under Captain Rich, to link up with these, and he himself led the remaining two platoons forward and took up a position about three hundred yards west of the road.

Captain Dugmore (" C " Company) had originally sent two platoons forward into a cornfield, retaining the other two platoons in support on the road. Owing to the interval between his left forward platoon and the right platoon of " A " Company, he now ordered Captain Jackson to take the support platoons forward to fill the gap. He himself made his headquarters near Lieutenant Groves' platoon on the right.

The German guns were keeping up heavy shrapnel fire over the whole area and casualties were mounting up. Captain Jackson, amongst others, was badly wounded. " L " Battery and 119th Field Battery were firing with deadly accuracy, in spite of the efforts of the German gunners to dislodge them. The infantry, too, had excellent targets of which they made the most. It was mainly due to the accuracy and volume of this small arms fire that the frontal attack was temporarily held up, the Germans imagining that the position was held by a large force with numerous machine guns.

The 3rd Cavalry Brigade managed to hold up a turning movement further south and thus the German advance was temporarily checked all along the line. The first phase of the battle was now over. The little British force had held up many times its own number.

Shortly afterwards, more German columns (now known to be three

Brig.-General Rivers B. Worgan.

Maj.-General R. D. F. Oldman.

Colonel J. E. G. Groves.

Lieut.-Colonel A. de C. Scott.

battalions of the 36th Fusilier Regiment of 8th Division, IV. Corps) were seen advancing south-east from the direction of Quarauble, three miles south-west of Quiévrain. This should have given warning of a wider turning movement, but Colonel Boger was still under the impression that there were British or French troops on that flank, and did not think the situation particularly dangerous.

The advance of the German 13th Infantry Brigade (7th Division, IV. Corps), on the right of the 1/Norfolk, was beginning to be felt, and by 2-30 p.m., the leading enemy troops were within a few hundred yards of their position. Part of the same brigade were seen advancing on Élouges, and, in a short time, would be behind Colonel Ballard's force. At 2-30 p.m., therefore, Colonel Ballard gave the order to begin retiring. So that there should be no mistake, he sent his Adjutant over to Major Alexander (Commander of the 119th Field Battery) and Colonel Boger, but this officer was killed on the way. Colonel Ballard also despatched messages by cycle orderly at the same time as he sent his Adjutant, but the man was never heard of again. Having sent his orders by two different routes, Colonel Ballard was easier in mind, and felt free to organise his own withdrawal.

Captain Grenfell agreed to use his squadron of the 9/Lancers as rear party, and Colonel Ballard sent another orderly to tell Colonel Boger of this, but he, too, failed to reach his destination. As a further illustration of the difficulty of getting messages through, it may be mentioned that Colonel Ballard had previously sent five messages by orderly to Brigade and Divisional headquarters, but only one of them was received.

The Germans had now found the correct range of the road and were searching it incessantly with both high explosive and shrapnel. Added to this, the approach of the enemy on the flanks enabled him to site machine guns in positions from which cross-fire could be brought to bear upon any target which presented itself. Any movement in our position was greeted by machine gun fire, ever increasing in intensity. Orderlies, who made for the sunken road—the main artery of lateral communication —were either incapacitated while crossing the open, or, having reached it, were caught by the concentration of artillery fire in this awkward defile. Deficient of signalling apparatus, unit and sub-unit commanders were compelled to rely upon orderlies, and, when these failed to pierce the curtains of enemy fire, the hopes of establishing inter-communication were lost.

The 1/Norfolk retired towards Wiheries, but, as it was being shelled, made a detour round the northern outskirts of the village. On his way back, Colonel Ballard came across parties of stragglers which included several dismounted cavalrymen. These told him that the 2nd Cavalry Brigade was retiring to the south and that they believed that the 1/Cheshire was with them. Never at any time did Colonel Ballard doubt that Colonel Boger had received his messages and, indeed, he had taken every precaution to ensure that they got through.

About 2-45 p.m., Colonel Boger became rather apprehensive about the continued movement on his left, and sent a cyclist orderly to Colonel Ballard to inform him of it. This orderly did not return. Nor did three other orderlies who were sent at intervals afterwards. As the 1/Norfolk had already retired, it is probable that these men ran headlong into the German 13th Infantry Brigade, which was advancing from the north, and were shot or captured. About this time, a mounted orderly galloped down the road shouting, " The 2nd Cavalry Brigade will rally behind the wood " (Audregnies), but none of the 1st Battalion who heard this had reason to connect it with a retirement.

On the left flank, the two platoons of " B " Company, under Captain Shore, had been making excellent shooting at the Germans advancing from the Bois de Déduit. A cavalry officer who had retired after being unhorsed during the charge towards Baisieux, bore witness to the accuracy of this fire which, he said, took great effect on the enemy who were quite close to him at the time.

While the 2nd Cavalry Brigade was re-forming behind the Bois d' Audregnies at about 2-30 p.m., several attempts were made by cavalry officers to persuade Captain Shore, with the left half of " B " Company, to retire under cover of the mounted troops. As he had not been ordered to do so by Battalion headquarters, he refused. It was not until 3-0 p.m., when he was given a direct order by a staff officer of the cavalry brigade, that he left the field. When he did retire, and failed to find the rest of the Battalion east of the Bois d' Audregnies, where he had been led to suppose they were assembling, he decided to return to his original position. He was about to do so when he received definite assurance from another officer that the 1st Battalion had retired south-east. Shore then moved off in that direction, and with about seventy men, he eventually found Brigade headquarters, the 1/Bedford, the 1/Dorset, and some details of the 1/Norfolk, and of the 1st Battalion.

It is evident that everyone except the 1st Battalion knew of Colonel Ballard's withdrawal. All assumed that Colonel Boger had received his orders to conform. Actually, it appears that Shore was the only officer who received any definite order to retire.

Captain Jones, with the support Platoons of " D " Company on the right, must have received early news of the withdrawal, either from the groups of cavalry which were retiring through his position or from the left Company 1/Norfolk. Although it is impossible to say, with any accuracy, at what time the various occurrences took place—everyone was too fully occupied to glance at their watches—it seems clear that these two platoons started to retire down the mineral railway about the same time as the two left platoons of " B " Company withdrew from the left flank (3-0 p.m.).

Thus, the outer troops on the flanks had withdrawn unknown to the C.O.

As he had had no reply to his various messages, Colonel Boger knew little of what was occurring on his front or flanks. He had not succeeded in getting into touch with " D " Company on the right or with Shore's two platoons beyond Audregnies. He was still uneasy about the apparently unchecked advance of the Germans beyond the River Honnelle. He decided, therefore, that his best course was to find Colonel Ballard, discuss the situation with him, and obtain his orders.

Accordingly, at about 4-0 p.m., he left his headquarters in charge of Major Chetwynd-Stapylton and moved off up the road towards Élouges. First, he found " C " Company, and, as a strong enemy attack was developing on " A " Company's front, he instructed Dugmore to watch his left. He also warned him that, owing to the continued advance of the German troops on the left flank, a retirement might be necessary.

His conversation with Dugmore made Colonel Boger uneasy about his right flank. Dugmore had indicated the position of the forward platoons of the 1/Norfolk near the colliery, but neither Colonel Boger nor Dugmore knew of the two platoons of " D " Company which were in that vicinity. Colonel Boger was unable to locate the support platoons of " D " Company, which, indeed, had already retired, so he moved off to the right flank to obtain a better view, but he could still find no trace of them.

While on that flank, he came under heavy rifle fire from the direction of the Élouges-Quiévrain railway, which had previously been held by the 1/Norfolk. He retraced his steps. On the way down the road, a cavalry officer galloped past him. Colonel Boger asked if the 1st Battalion was cut off. The only reply was a wave of the arm in the direction of the railway. The assumption was that, in addition to the turning movement on the left, the Battalion was isolated and outflanked on the right. Colonel Boger knew the truth for the first time.

On his way down the road, he came across Sergt. Rothwell and a section of No. 12 Platoon of " C " Company lining a cutting. To these men he gave the order to retire. He also signalled to another group which was crossing the road further south, the direction in which to retire. He followed up the first party himself, but shortly afterwards both he and Sergt. Rothwell were wounded and rendered immobile. The platoon retired under Pte. Jordan. Throughout the day, Colonel Boger had shewn complete disregard of personal danger, and his coolness under fire had been a fine example to those who had come into contact with him.

Captain Tahourdin (Adjutant) who had followed Colonel Boger, lost touch with him when passing an exposed part of the road swept by machine gun fire. In searching for Colonel Boger, he ran into a party of Germans on the railway and was captured.

Meanwhile, as the enemy approached " A " and " C " Companies' position, Dugmore opened rapid fire, causing havoc in the advancing German ranks. The fire control was what one would expect to find on the parade ground rather than the battlefield. But ammunition was running low. Dugmore endeavoured, without success, to get into touch with his reserve supply carried on the company mule, which appears to have retired with the support platoons of " D " Company. This shortage of ammunition, coupled with the continued and ever-increasing enemy pressure, caused Dugmore to decide that the time had now come to move. At about 4-30 p.m. therefore, he passed the order down to retire " individually " from the right. He organized the men around him into two parties. The first he placed under Groves' command and ordered him to retire forthwith, while he himself stayed behind with the remainder.

Groves withdrew to a position east of the Élouges-Audregnies railway and there waited for Dugmore. The second party under Dugmore retired to a bridge on the mineral railway where he could obtain a good view. He ordered his men to line the railway cutting and called up Groves' party to join him. But the field of fire was unsatisfactory, so he ordered Groves to take a few men and make a further bound to a cottage away to the east, while he himself remained with his party to cover their retirement.

Shortly before " C " Company started to move, Rich, with his two platoons near the colliery, had been forced to retire. Pressed in front and outflanked, he withdrew his men yard by yard, disputing every inch of ground. This grim struggle left an indelible mark on the minds of those of " C " Company who witnessed it.

The battle had now taken the form of isolated actions by a number of groups, each working under the orders of the nearest officer or N.C.O.

Dugmore had kept about eight men with him, and these were gradually augmented by a few stragglers, one or two of whom belonged to the 1/Norfolk. The situation by 5-0 p.m. had become definitely worse. The enemy were advancing steadily and nothing could stem the tide. Later, when they crossed the railway to the north of him, Dugmore saw that the situation was hopeless and ordered the men to scatter and get away as best they could. One man, only, evaded capture. Pte. Sharples escaped by driving a derelict transport wagon out of one end of Wiheries, as the Germans came in at the other.

The cottage on which Dugmore ordered Groves to fall back turned out to be an " estaminet," and here he found Rich and the remnants of a platoon of " D " Company. It transpired that Rich and the two forward platoons, with the two platoons of the 1/Norfolk near the colliery, which were also without orders, had retired by platoons in perfect order, steadily fighting their way back. Rich had successfully brought the left platoon in to safety, but the right platoon, under Sergeant Blackwell, which later joined up with the 1/Norfolk platoons, was rounded up by the enemy.

Rich and Groves re-organized their parties, moved off south-east and eventually joined up with Shore and the rest of the Brigade. Their escape was remarkable. They must have squeezed through between the van-guards of the German 66th and 93rd Regiments converging on Wiheries from the north and west.

But No. 9 Platoon, of "C" Company, under Sergeant Raynor, is as yet unaccounted for. Their original position was on the left of the Company, but out of sight of "A" Company. This platoon received Dugmore's order to retire, but, on reaching the sunken road, Raynor and his senior subordinate, Corporal Crookes, were seized with misgivings about the authenticity of the order. They did not therefore retire further but lined the bank on the roadside and opened fire on the enemy advancing in front and on their right.

The shortage of ammunition, now acute, was causing the N.C.Os. considerable anxiety and a further withdrawal seemed indicated. Just as the platoon was about to move off, some troops were seen to their right rear moving southwards. Lieutenant Frost, an officer of the Special Reserve, who was attached to the platoon, volunteered to go and identify them. He did not return. He was seen later by a wounded officer of the 4/Dragoon Guards, "fighting like a demon, having refused to surrender." Although wounded several times, he refused to give in and death alone overcame his indomitable spirit.

Major Chetwynd-Stapylton, now the senior present, did not suspect the danger which threatened the right flank, but was anxious about "B" Company in view of the importance of Audregnies for the security of the left flank.

As no news of Colonel Boger had come in since he had left headquarters, Major Stapylton decided to go out and look for him and obtain his orders. Before doing so, he told Lieut. Campbell to get into touch with Shore, from whom no message had been received, and who, it was assumed, had not left his original position. About 5-0 p.m., Major Stapylton moved off up the road towards the right flank. At a bend in the road, he met No. 9 Platoon which had just started its second withdrawal. On his demanding who had given the order to retire, Sergeant Raynor said that the troops on the right had already gone, and that an order to retire had been passed down. Still doubtful as to the original order, Raynor made his men take up a fire position on the west side of the road. But, on reflection, Major Stapylton called them back and told them to continue their retirement. Stapylton himself returned to Battalion headquarters.

Shortly after Stapylton had moved off, and while No. 9 Platoon was reforming, Captain Jones appeared. It is not clear how he came to be there, but it is probable that, after having ordered his company to retire, and having seen or heard nothing of the rest of the Battalion, he returned, either with the object of getting into touch with Battalion headquarters, or to find out what had happened to his two platoons under Rich.

Having heard the latest information from Raynor, he moved off with No. 9 Platoon, which now left the road and made for the railway. To reach the railway several hundred yards of rising ground had to be covered which was under heavy machine gun fire, and, before the shelter of the cutting was found, the platoon had been reduced to some half a dozen men.

The retirement was then continued down the railway line to the Bois d'Audregnies. Here Raynor himself fixed his bayonet and acted as scout. On leaving the cover of the trees, the party took to a track and, later, to a hedge-bordered lane, which brought them to some enclosed country south-west of Wiheries. Here they ran into the Magdeburg Regiment which was going into bivouac.

Of those who remained, Captain Jones and Hogan were killed. Crookes, who had previously been wounded, collapsed and F. Garrad was mortally wounded. Raynor and Blake were soon rounded up by the enemy after a gallant resistance.

Sergeant Raynor, who had shown great courage and initiative, and who had fought on to the last, was later awarded the D.C.M. His true character is best shown by his own words when Corporal Crookes saw him later in the grip of three Germans, " If I had known you were living I —— well wouldn't have given in."

The door to safety was barred, but a gallant fragment of the 1st Battalion still fought on.

When Major Stapylton reached Battalion headquarters he discussed the situation with Dyer (" A " Coy.). Stapylton thought that Shore's two platoons were still holding Audregnies and hoped to withdraw those who were left in that direction. Dyer agreed that a retirement was inevitable and started to withdraw his men. One of them was wounded coming back and 2nd Lieutenant Elliot gallantly returned and carried him to the road, being shot through both ankles in doing so. He was subsequently awarded the D.S.O.

About 5-30 p.m., having heard that Campbell had been killed, Major Stapylton sent 2nd Lieutenant Spencer-Jacobs, with the left platoon of " A " Company, to link up with Shore's company (he was under the impression that the whole of " B " Company was with Shore). Spencer-Jacobs moved off to the left but could make little progress towards Audregnies. Later, Matterson, who with his scouts had voluntarily attached himself to the two platoons of his old company (" B "), under Jolliffe, was told by Major Stapylton to take his scouts to support him.

At about 6-0 p.m., just as the forward troops of " A " Company had

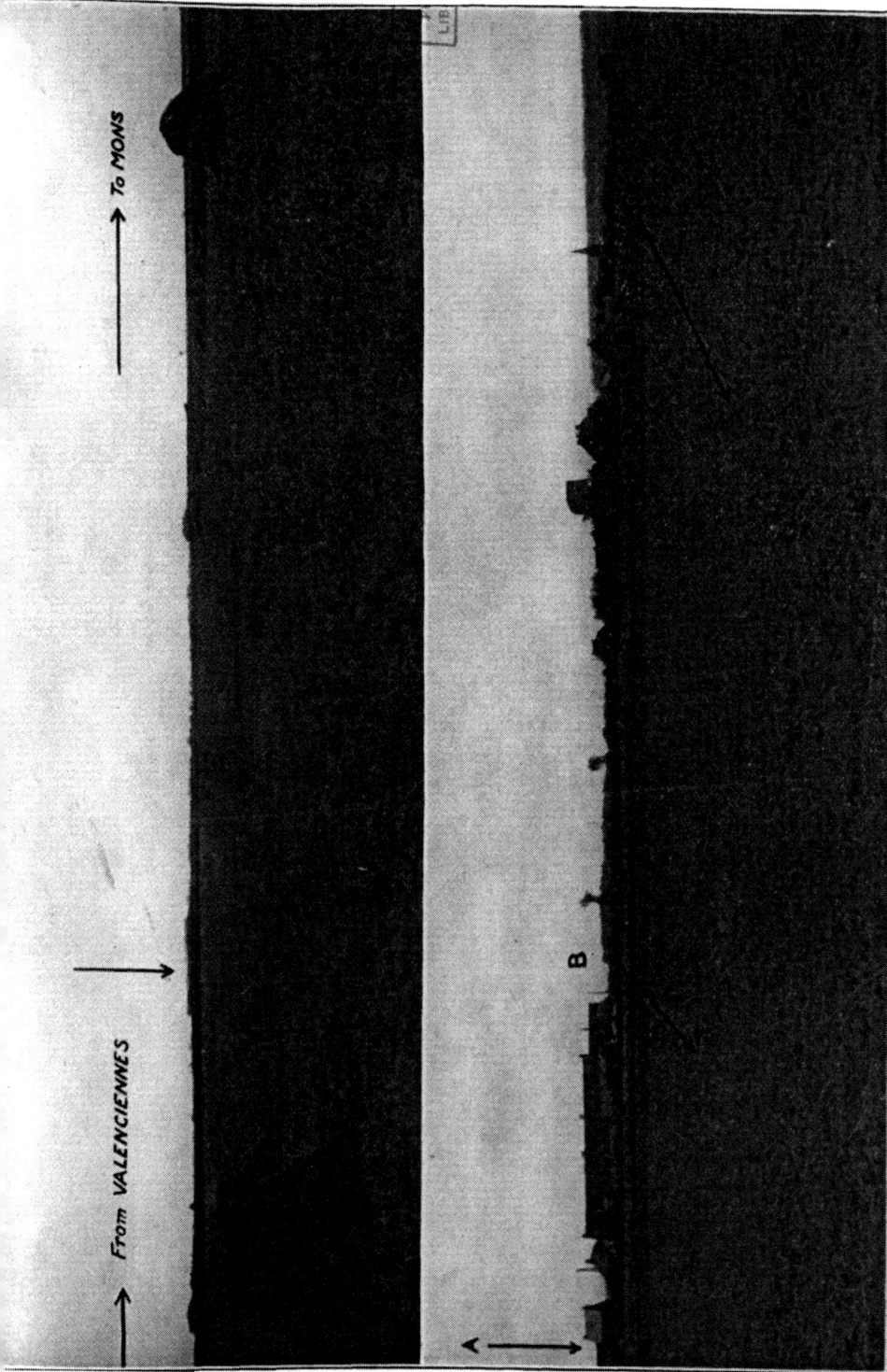

AUDREGNIES, where the 1st Battalion formed the extreme left of the British Army, on 24th August, 1914, in the last phase of the Battle of Mons. The upper picture shows the field of fire from the position held by our left company (B).

The lower picture shows this position as seen by the advancing Germans. A sunken road runs behind the cottages and ruined windmill. The ground contains many hidden hollows.

A. Our final machine gun position. B. Direction of local counter-attack made by some of the 1st Battalion, under Major A. J. L. Dyer, M.C., as a forlorn hope (mostly A and B Companies). C. Direction of charge by 2nd Cavalry Brigade.

been withdrawn, Matterson came in to report that Spencer-Jacobs was held up by the enemy between the two halves of " B " Company. As soon as he received Matterson's report, Dyer drew his sword and ordered the men in the vicinity to " advance (towards the old mill to their left) and enfilade the enemy." He did not know that the Battalion was completely surrounded, and hoped that this manœuvre would relieve pressure on Spencer-Jacobs and enable the remainder successfully to make good their escape.

Captain Massey (second in command, " A " Company), Jolliffe and Matterson joined Dyer, and, together with about thirty men of " A " and " B " Companies, they charged forward, in short rushes, intent on meeting the enemy with the bayonet—a last despairing effort to avert the complete annihilation of their comrades. The result was inevitable. All but Lieutenant Matterson and ten men were shot down. How they escaped remains a mystery.

The forlorn hope had failed.

It is difficult to avoid superlatives in writing of the bravery of these men. Each one of them displayed the traditional attributes of the soldier, courage, devotion to duty and *esprit de corps*, in a marked degree which were only equalled by their loyalty and devotion to their leader. No one who knew Dyer will be surprised at the trust the officers and men placed in him. His singularly quiet and unassuming manner concealed the heart of a lion which beat only for The Regiment.

Nor can the valour of No. 9877 Corporal H. Fleet and No. 9865 Private H. Riley, both of " B " Company, be passed over without special mention. Both men showed utter disregard of danger and acted in a manner worthy of the highest traditions of The Regiment.

Meanwhile casualties were increasing. The fire of the handful of defenders was becoming less effective. The Battalion was now pressed on all sides and no additional effort could have had any effect in delaying the main enemy columns. About 6-30 p.m., every possible line of retreat being now clearly closed, Major Stapylton decided that further resistance meant useless waste of life, and gave the order to cease fire. Forty of the survivors remained unwounded.

Little remains to be written. The 1/Norfolk and 1/Cheshire had forced the leading enemy troops of the IV. Corps to halt and deploy, with the result that the whole Corps was delayed. The 1st Battalion had, single-handed, kept those troops fully occupied for four hours and had, therefore, prevented the whole of the German IV. Corps from pursuing the 5th Division. No fewer than four German Regiments (each of three battalions) were actively employed to encompass the 1st Battalion's position. It is noteworthy that a senior German officer, when checking shoulder-titles later, said, " I have captured a brigade, yet I find nothing but Cheshires."

Colonel Ballard has put the following on record, " I had no intention of sacrificing the Cheshire—but I firmly believe now that the sacrifice saved the 5th Division." General Fergusson corroborated this in his memorandum forwarding his recommendations for awards. He wrote, " It was due to the gallantry of these two Battalions (1/Cheshire and 1/Norfolk) that the division was able to extricate itself."

The rest is best related in the words of the Official History (†) :— " The troubles of the small party that had escaped were not ended on the battlefield. The enemy broke in from Dour during their retreat, and cut off a few of them ; and at Athis only one hundred of them could be assembled. The indefatigable gunners of the 5th Divisional Artillery came into action along the line Blaugies—Athis—Montignies, and again further to the south at Houdin, enabling the survivors of the flank guard to reach their bivouac at St. Waast at 9-0 p.m., utterly worn out by hunger, fatigue and hard fighting, but still unvanquished."

Of the 25 officers and 952 other ranks of the 1st Battalion who had been present that morning, only 7 officers and 200 other ranks remained, many of whom, for various reasons, were not on the battlefield of Audregnies.

* * * *

The Miniature Colour.

The story of the 1st Battalion at Audregnies is not complete without a reference to the Miniature Colour, which was there carried into action.

In 1911, the wives of the officers serving with the 1st Battalion embroidered a miniature of the Regimental Colour, a quarter the size of the original, as a prize for the best shooting company. It was presented for the first time to " F " Company on Meeanee Day, 1912, being subsequently competed for each summer and hung in the barrack room of the successful company, which became the Colour Company for the year. The Miniature was carried on ceremonial parades with the King's and Regimental Colours.

In 1914, the Miniature Colour was won by " B " Company and Captain Shore decided to take it on active service. No. 9461 Drummer Baker, who was with Jolliffe's half-company north of Audregnies, was entrusted with the care of it. As the action developed, Baker, seeing that the situation was hopeless and that capture was inevitable, made for a house in the village and hid it behind some straw under the roof. Hardly had he left the village than he, together with the rest of the survivors, fell into the hands of the Germans.

No. 9865 Pte. Riley, of the same company, was wounded during the action and taken to the local convent for treatment. Riley knew where

† " Military Operations, France and Belgium, 1914." Page 105.

Lieut.-Colonel H. E. Crocker.

Lieut.-Colonel D. C. Boger.

Colonel J. C. Sproule.

Major C. G. E. Hughes.

Baker had hidden the Colour and, through the sympathetic offices of Sister St. Leon, who was nursing him, persuaded Monsieur Soudan, the *Curé*, to accept the responsibility for keeping it for The Regiment.

The *Curé*, together with *Monsieur* Alphonse Vallée, the village schoolmaster, recovered the Colour from its hiding place and removed it to his house. Later, for greater security, he hid it in the church behind one of the choir stalls.

As the war progressed, the Germans became short of war material and made house-to-house searches in the occupied territory, with the object of seizing anything of which they could make use. The *Curé* became apprehensive regarding the safety of the Colour and confided his fears in the Communal Secretary, *Monsieur* Georges Dupont, who promised to conceal it in a bricked-up attic of the local girls' school. This he did, the Colour first being furled and inserted in a length of piping.

There it remained until the end of the war.

The Armistice found the 1st Battalion about twelve miles east of Audregnies, and, on the 17th November, 1918, a Colour-party was sent to Audregnies to recover the Miniature Colour. The Miniature remained in possession of the 1st Battalion until 1927 when it was sent to the Depot at Chester for safe custody, a replica being retained by the 1st Battalion.

*   *   *   *

"The Battalion behaved magnificently in the face of terrible odds and immense difficulties. One could not expect more of them ; they did their duty, and did it thundering well, as I should always have expected from such a gallant battalion, and I am only too grieved that they had such frightful losses. (Signed) E. GLEICHEN." *Gen.*

*   *   *   *

The following letter was written by Lieut.-Colonel D. C. Boger, D.S.O., who commanded the 1st Battalion at Mons, when severely wounded. It was presented to the Officers' Mess of the 1st Battalion by Captain W. G. R. Elliot, D.S.O. :—

Lieut. G. Elliot,   Croix Rouge,
    1st Cheshire Regt.   Wiheries,
                                  Saturday (29 Aug. 14).

Dear Elliot,
    I was so very glad to hear from you. I have been worrying over our left and hoped they had got away, but felt it was impossible. I found on our right the Norfolks had retired or been scuppered and the Germans enfiladed us from the railway and had got almost to our rear. We tried to make away ½ R towards the village just in rear of your left and very

decent order was maintained by Sergts. Meachin, Rothwell and Dowling, but all 3 were wounded and nearly all the men. I was very lucky to be hit 3 times and none serious. Hand by shrapnel and thro' foot and flesh of thigh by bullets. We had no chance, no information and no instructions, except to guard the road and think we did our possible. I pray we may get exchanged when well. I hear Jones, tho' wounded, refused to surrender and pointed his revolver at them. They shot him but left him his arms and the 66th Regt. buried him with mil'y honours and a speech was made at his grave. A very gallant man. So sorry Jolliffe and Jackson were hit badly and for all our casualties, but I think they will say we did our best with both flanks turned.

Yours ever, D. C. BOGER.

There are about 60 here, ours and Norfolks, mostly wounded. I heard Rich and Stewart were killed.

LE CATEAU.

Captain Shore and his company, having been forcibly prevented by a staff officer from throwing themselves into the vortex of the German advance, in the vain hope of rescuing the 1st Battalion, formed a nucleus on which the survivors of the gallant fight at Audregnies could form. As a result, the retreat of our men was less disordered and out of hand than that of many other units. The 15th Brigade, indeed, reached Le Cateau as a formed body, and was further fortunate in being among the lucky ones whose transport rejoined them at this place.

Smith Dorrien's magnificent stand at Le Cateau is so memorable and important, not to say decisive, that it could be wished that the 1st Battalion had taken a more prominent part in the battle. But they had been so severely handled that the 200 odd survivors were too weak to occupy a Battalion frontage in defence, so they were kept in reserve at La Sotiere, near Troisvilles. They endured shelling through a good part of the 26th. When the order to retire reached the 15th Brigade, they formed the rear-guard and withdrew unmolested.

There are numerous records to show that, among the men on this day of Le Cateau, a firm conviction held that relief from the seemingly irresistible German pressure was at hand, either from " masses " of cavalry or from some almost miraculous development of overwhelming French force.

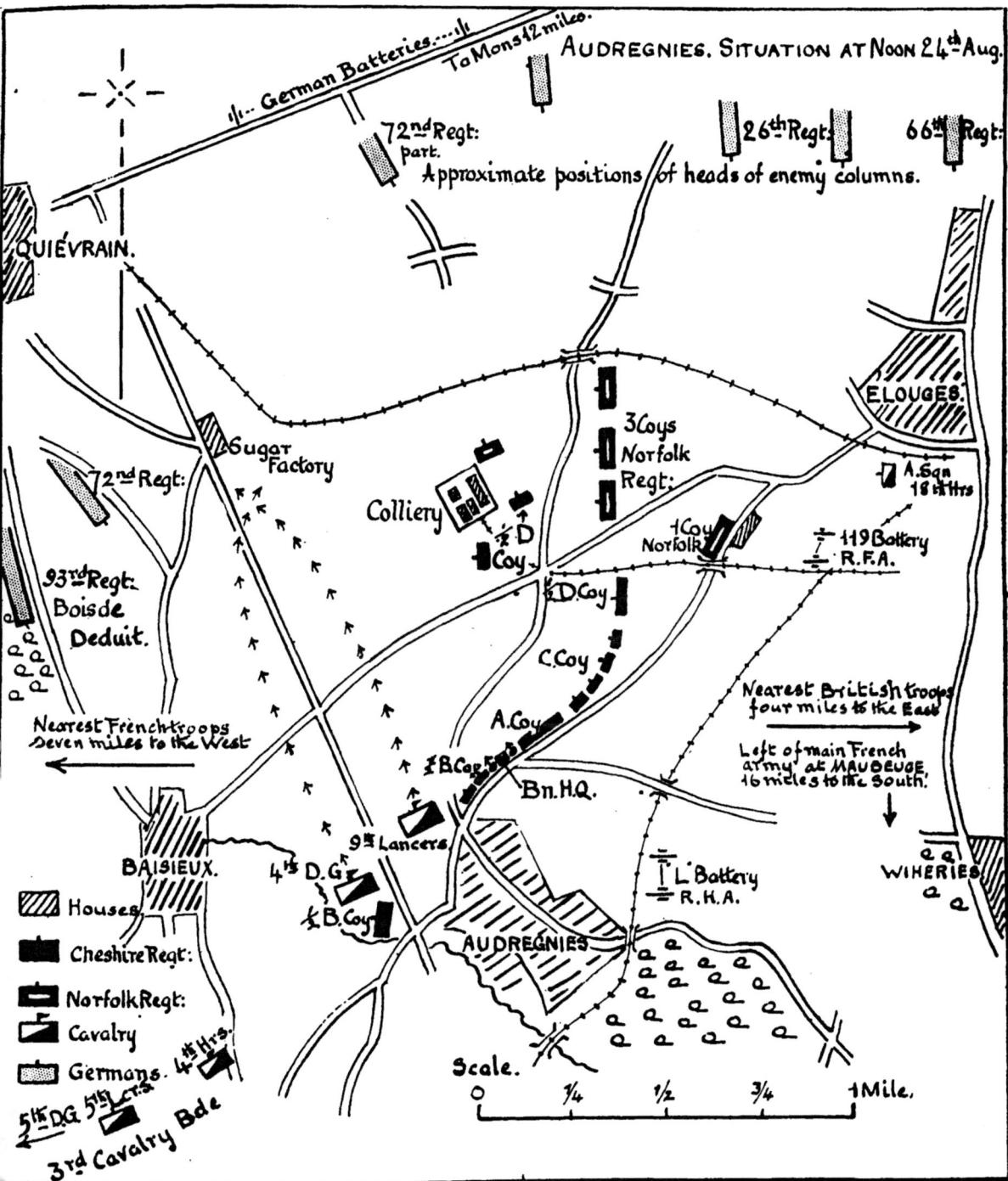

AUDREGNIES. SITUATION AT NOON 24th Aug.

German Batteries...... To Mons 12 miles.

72nd Regt: part.

26th Regt:

66th Regt:

Approximate positions of heads of enemy columns.

QUIÉVRAIN.

Sugar Factory

72nd Regt:

3 Coys Norfolk Regt:

ELOUGES.

A. Sqn 18th Hrs

Colliery

1 Coy Norfolk

119 Battery R.F.A.

D Coy

93rd Regt: Bois de Deduit.

D. Coy

C. Coy

A. Coy

Nearest British troops four miles to the East

Left of main French army at MAUBEUGE 16 miles to the South.

Nearest French troops seven miles to the West

B. Coy

Bn. H.Q.

L' Battery R.H.A.

9th Lancers

BAISIEUX.

4th D.G.

B. Coy

WIHERIES.

AUDREGNIES

Houses

Cheshire Regt:

Norfolk Regt:

Cavalry

Germans

5th D.G. 5th Lct:s

3rd Cavalry Bde

4th Hrs

Scale.

0   ¼   ½   ¾   1 Mile.

SITUATION at 6pm 24th Aug. 1914.

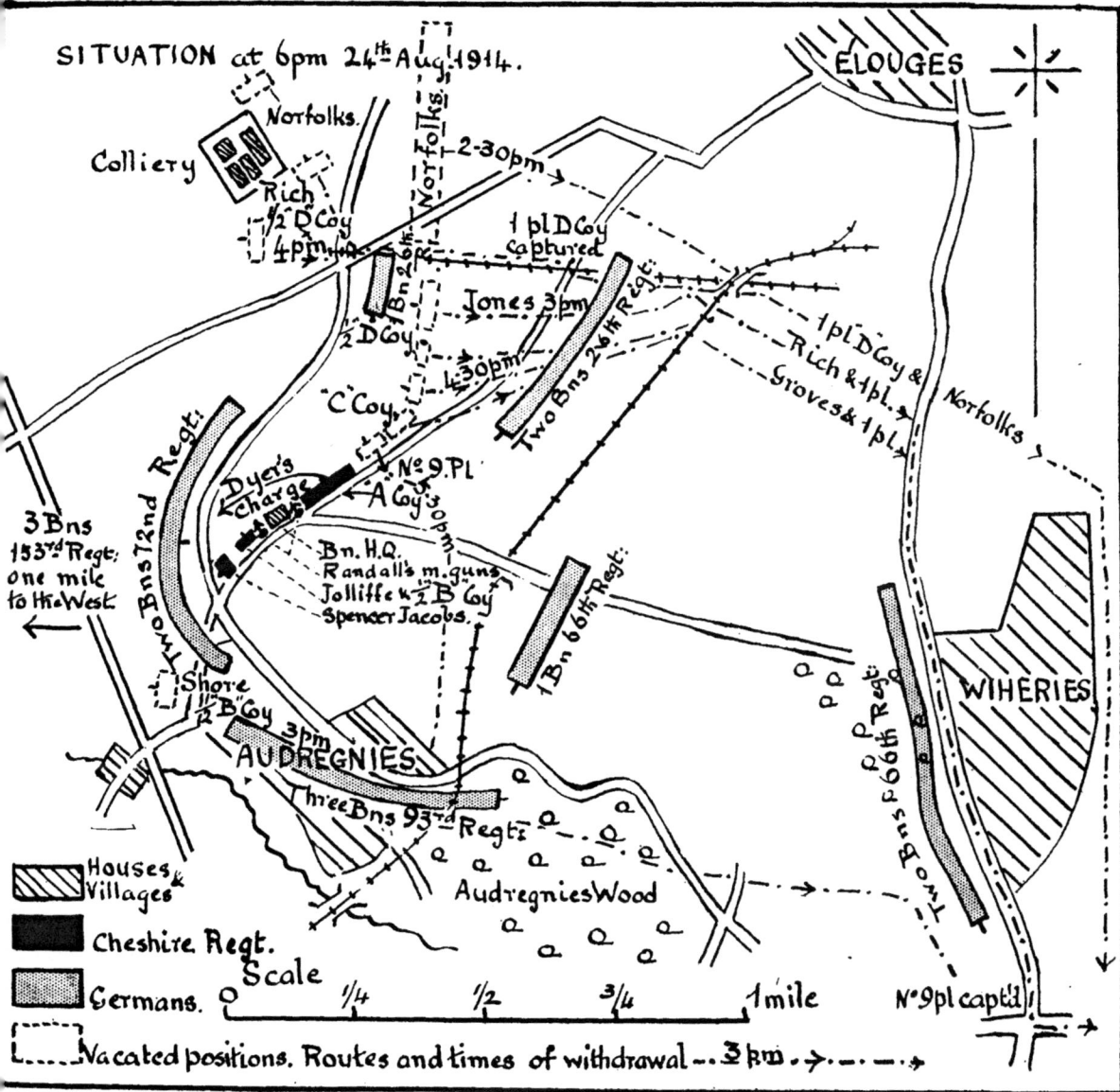

ELOUGES

Norfolks.

Colliery

Norfolks

2-30pm

Rich
½ D Coy
4pm

1 pl D Coy
captured

Bn 26th

D Coy

Jones 3pm

Two Bns 26th Regt.

1 pl D Coy &
Rich & 1 pl.
Groves & 1 pl.

Norfolks

"C" Coy.

4-30pm

Dyer's
charge

No. 9. PL

"A" Coy 5.30pm

Bn. H.Q.
Randall's m. guns
Jolliffe & ½ B Coy
Spencer Jacobs.

1 Bn 66th Regt.

Two Bns 72nd Regt.

3 Bns
153rd Regt.
one mile
to the West

Shore
½ B Coy 3pm

Three Bns 66th Regt.

WIHERIES

AUDREGNIES

Three Bns 93rd Regt.

AudregniesWood

Houses &
Villages

Cheshire Regt.

Germans.

Scale

¼   ½   ¾   1mile

No 9pl capt'd

Vacated positions. Routes and times of withdrawal .. 3 km. ⟶ .—.—.⟶

opp. 18

RETREAT FROM MONS.

Although the retreat from Mons was a disorganized movement, the complete absence of panic made it a not unworthy performance. Indeed, if all factors are weighed, it was worthy of the place which it has on our Colours.

The troops laboured under many disadvantages. More than half the men were reservists who had had no period of training to get them fit, or time to accustom them to the Officers and N.C.Os. who were to command them. Forced marches to the area of concentration had been very trying and at the end of these marches they met the overwhelming masses of an army of high reputation. They then had to undertake a manœuvre which is admitted to be one which tries to the utmost the morale and fortitude of soldiers. The men of our Regiment had, in addition, suffered the severest losses and, what is worse, had seen their Battalion abandoned by the rest of the Allied armies and left to fight it out against hordes of enemy sweeping down on to them from three directions.

During the retreat, our soldiers were never sure of a meal or of a night's sleep. The uncertainty of food and sleep lasted for a fortnight, but at the end of that time, the troops were cheerfully ready to turn and face the fatigues and privation of an offensive. In fact, they never lost their morale and never considered themselves beaten. Not only did the 1st Battalion lose heavily, but the whole of the II. Corps suffered more casualties than the I. Corps.

The Brigade Commander, Count Gleichen, and his Brigade Major, Weatherby, of The Oxfordshire and Buckinghamshire L. I., set an example of coolness and intrepidity which was a constant source of confidence to the troops, and must have had more than a little to do with the comparative regularity of the retreat of the 15th Brigade.

The table on page 20 shows the marches of the 15th Brigade from Le Cateau till they reached the Aisne.

On the 5th September, Joffre's order for the attack, that is for stopping the southward movement and for turning against the Germans, reached British H.Q. about 3 a.m. The intention to assume the offensive was known on the previous afternoon. However, the British army had begun its marches for the 5th late on the 4th, to avoid the heat of the day, and had completed them before the new orders were received. Thus, it occurred, that when the British army began to march North it was some 12 miles further South than Joffre anticipated. This meant a delay of some hours which was going to have considerable effect on the struggle for the heights commanding the valley of the Aisne.

Marches of 15th Infantry Brigade.

		Miles		Date.
Le Cateau	to Ors	4.54	...	18 Aug.
	to Gommignies ...	14.89	...	21 ,,
	to Boussu	14.22	...	22 ,,
	to Paturages	6.79	...	23 ,,
	to St. Waast-le-Bavay	11.22	...	24 ,,
[Battle]	to Le Cateau	20.54	...	25 ,,
[Estrees]	to St. Quentin	23.24	...	26 ,,
[Ollezy]	to Faucourt	11.21	...	27 ,,
	to Pontoise	16.25	...	28 ,,
	to Carlepont	3.15	...	29 ,,
	to Croutoy	10.71	...	30 ,,
	to Crepy	14.62	...	31 ,,
	to Nanteuil	10.84	...	1 Sept.
	to Montge	11.34	...	2 ,,
	to Mont Pichet ...	15.75	...	3 ,,
	to Gagny	16.38	...	4/5 ,,
[starting northwards]	to La Celle	15.75	...	6 ,,
	to Boissy le Chatel ...	9.58	...	7 ,,
	to Charnesseuil ...	8.82	...	8 ,,
	to Bezu le Guéry ...	7.43	...	9 ,,
[not the one mentioned earlier]	to St. Quentin	14.40	...	10 ,,
	to St. Remy	13.10	...	11 ,,
[near Hartennes]	to L'Epitaphe	8.82	...	12 ,,
[on the Aisne]	to La Bigail	10.71	...	13 ,,

Total - 294.30 miles

* * * *

The Turn in the Tide.

' Pile arms, and fall out, we remain here a few hours.' In this prosaic manner ended the historic " Retreat from Mons " as far as The 22nd Regiment was concerned.

The scene was a little orchard on the outskirts of Tournant just on the 18th kilo stone from Paris. The date, Saturday evening, September 5th, 1914.

A little band of dirty, bearded soldiers, mostly capless and without puttees, had wheeled into the orchard, a captain in command.

Not even their best friends would have recognized this little band of tatterdemalions as the 1st Battalion 22nd Regiment, a short fortnight ago one of the smartest and best turned out Battalions in the whole army. Since then, however, their lot had been such as had seldom been endured by soldiers before.

Two hundred and five miles on foot, little food, two battles and several running fights make up a summer programme not calculated to improve either Tommy's appearance or his outlook on life, especially on a Saturday evening.

We were mostly in a very petulant mood, but we soon began to sense something unusual, a sort of vague feeling of optimism pervading everything. Whether it was the sight of " corps troops " who were usually well in advance of us during the retreat, and who this evening did not seem in the usual hurry to continue the rôle, or whether it was the rumour of going to Paris to re-fit, was hard to say. It was difficult to define, yet there was no mistaking its presence, and as we rested in the orchard after a gluttonous feed of chlorinated water and apples, things began to look almost rosy, and we had the feeling, individually and collectively, that better times were in store.

Very shortly, a beautifully clean officer on a very noisy motor cycle arrived with the information that an Ordnance dump was established about two miles down the road, and would issue clothing to re-fit the Battalion. This was glorious news. The writer rattled along in a G.S. waggon to this store of bounteous goodness with a mental note of 240 of everything required.

I think a cynical strain in my character had its inception here, for on arrival I found our dump was waiting, " shared fairly according to strength. That's yours on the left," the Ordnance fellow told me. I believe I received altogether 14 mess tins, 17 pairs of socks, plenty of dubbin but no boots, and one glorious pair of trousers which I got into myself on the way back, and artistically soiled so as not to be too noticeable.

What a disappointing errand it had been! Which would be the best way to break the sad news I pondered. Hints at more coming to-morrow, I eventually decided.

Good kind providence, however, stepped in as usual, for as I drove up I found the Battalion paraded under a couple of apple trees and the C.O. reading out the latest Field Message Order.

I just managed to drop off the wagon and get up in time to hear ' and at sunrise to-morrow, the 5th Division, in conjunction with the remainder of the British Army, will advance to victory, supported by strong French Armies on both flanks. Signed, Charles Ferguson, Lieut.-General.'

It was glorious news—at least it was intended to be—but when I looked round I think I should have been happier if I could have got more trousers."

MARNE.

The turn north began on 6th September and was welcomed with joy by all ranks. The march involved several disputed river crossings, those of the Grand Morin, Petit Morin and the Marne. At none of them, however, was the 1st Battalion involved. They crossed the Marne at Saacy. There was some fighting by the 15th Brigade in an attack on Hill 189 South of Montreuil, of which no account exists.

The British III. Corps met particularly severe opposition at La Ferté Sous Jouarre. By September 13th, the Germans on the front of the British Expeditionary Force had been forced back behind the River Aisne, 50 miles north of where they were on September 6th. The above are some bald facts as regards troop movements during the Battle of the Marne, but, as those know who were present at the battle, the change of morale

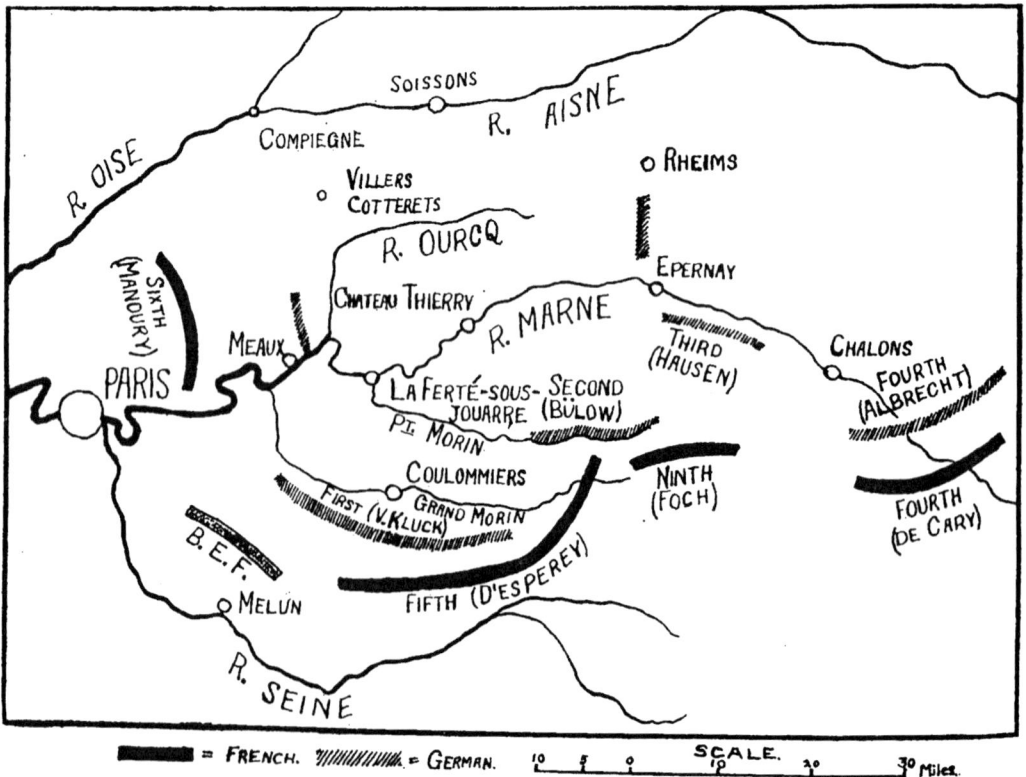

BATTLE OF THE MARNE,

Situation 5th Sept., 1914.

and outlook of the Allies during these seven days was astounding. In place of being hunted, we suddenly became the hunters. Paris was saved and the terrible and mighty German army was in full retreat. How did this miracle happen ?

First, it was due to Gallieni's well thought out plan of assembling fresh reserves near Paris, and his fine judgment in choosing the right moment to turn on the enemy.

Secondly, it was due to Von Kluck closing in on Bulow instead of going for Paris, while German G.H.Q. failed to keep in touch with, and to control the movements of, their flank armies nearest Paris.

Thirdly, the rapid German advance had been an immense strain both on their men and on their administrative services, and they were at breaking point.

Fourthly, it was due to the fine fighting qualities of the British Expeditionary Force and our Allies the French, who, in spite of the wearing retreat that had been suffered, hit out and hit hard on the rebound.

Tactically, the battle was not fought to a finish and the British casualties were small compared to later battles of the war, but strategically its results were so far-reaching that it must be regarded as one of the most decisive battles of the world.

AISNE 1914.

Map p. 25

Under cover of rain and darkness, the 1st Battalion, still under Captain Shore, crossed the Aisne on 14th September, on rafts improvised from wagon bodies wrapped in tarpaulins. These rafts carried 10 or 12 men at each trip. The troops gradually collected on the northern bank and, as soon as it was daylight, advanced across the fields and seized the villages of Missy and Ste Marguerite, which lie at the foot of the Chivres Spur. This spur, running down from the Chemin des Dames ridge to the river, isolated the fighting on the west of it from that on the east, and was the dominating tactical feature of this part of the battle front. It was the key to the local situation and plans were made to capture it.

The 14th Brigade was to attack in front while the 15th, after the 14th had cleared Missy, was to attack the Spur from the south-east.

So far, little opposition had been met, but the rain and mist, the darkness of the country, and the distance back of the guns, they were south of the river because they could not cross it, made it difficult to control the fighting. It developed into a purely infantry battle, in which platoons and sections worked and fought independently at close quarters, almost hand to hand with the enemy.

In these circumstances, the advantage lay with the defence, especially as they had had opportunities of making some simple obstacles.

The troops advanced in full expectation of finding little opposition, but it was not to be fulfilled. The gap in the German front which existed on the left of Von Kluck, opposite our I. Corps, had been filled, only two short hours before the I. Corps attacked, by Von Zwehl's Corps, released from the siege of Maubeuge. This Corps had hurried to the battle by forced marches, 40 miles in 24 hours, and its route was strewn with nearly a quarter of its infantry. But the Corps arrived in time to fill the gap and hold up our attacks. One wonders what might have happened had those precious hours not been lost on the 5th.

It was soon obvious that opposition in force was being encountered. Wire netting held up the 14th Brigade. A further attack was organized with 10 companies from various Regiments of the 14th and 15th Brigades, but this, too, failed. It would seem that our troops were unsettled, not only by the unexpected opposition, but also by the wide stretch of open country in their rear, to say nothing of the river, and also by the thought of their artillery being so far off and its obvious inability to give them any covering fire.

The German preparations for the attack were simple and effective. Trip wires from tree to tree were concealed in the undergrowth. Halfway up the hill, a strong wire fence had been strengthened and adapted to form a barrier, which, running diagonally across the front, led the attackers into machine gun zones of fire, and also caused loss of direction.

Battalions on the left swung unconsciously to the right, and right in front of the Germans there was " the most glorious jumble imaginable." Everyone blamed everyone else and the Germans took full advantage of it all, as may well be imagined. Men fell in every direction, while officers and N.C.Os. strove, by word and whistle, to reduce this chaos to some sort of order. They succeeded, at length, in getting a line taken up, as well as could be done in the dark, through Missy and Ste Marguerite.

The 15th was a day of German attacks on most parts of the front, and here a further attempt on the Spur, led by the Norfolks, began at 8 a.m. By 10 a.m. it had petered out owing to lack of fire to deal with the German artillery. The troops, both firing line and reserves, crowded back into Missy for cover. Unfortunately, a German aeroplane saw the congestion, and it was not long before such a storm of shell fell on the village that it had to be evacuated. This bombardment included the first " Black Marias," 8-in. howitzers, of the war.

Medical arrangements were very difficult, as all wounded had to be man-handled for two miles to the river and then ferried across. The wounded suffered correspondingly. On the other hand, supply wagons drove up to within 200 yards of the Germans and got away safely, crossing the river by a pontoon bridge which had by now been made.

The 15th Brigade recrossed the river before dawn on the 16th.

British troops remained on this front for another three weeks. There were no permanent bridges and the temporary bridges, built with such skill and bravery by the R.E., were not only all under fire, but were also liable to be swept away by flood. No depots or stores could be made on the north bank, and the " carrying " required was terrific. Finally, the artillery was forced to remain on the south bank. It was a most unpleasant front and all rejoiced when the order came to hand over to the French and move north. Every one had had enough of trench warfare, and looked forward to the promise of " open warfare " to which all considered themselves more fitted.

Reinforcements arrived for the Battalion on the 16th September and Major F. B. Young assumed command.

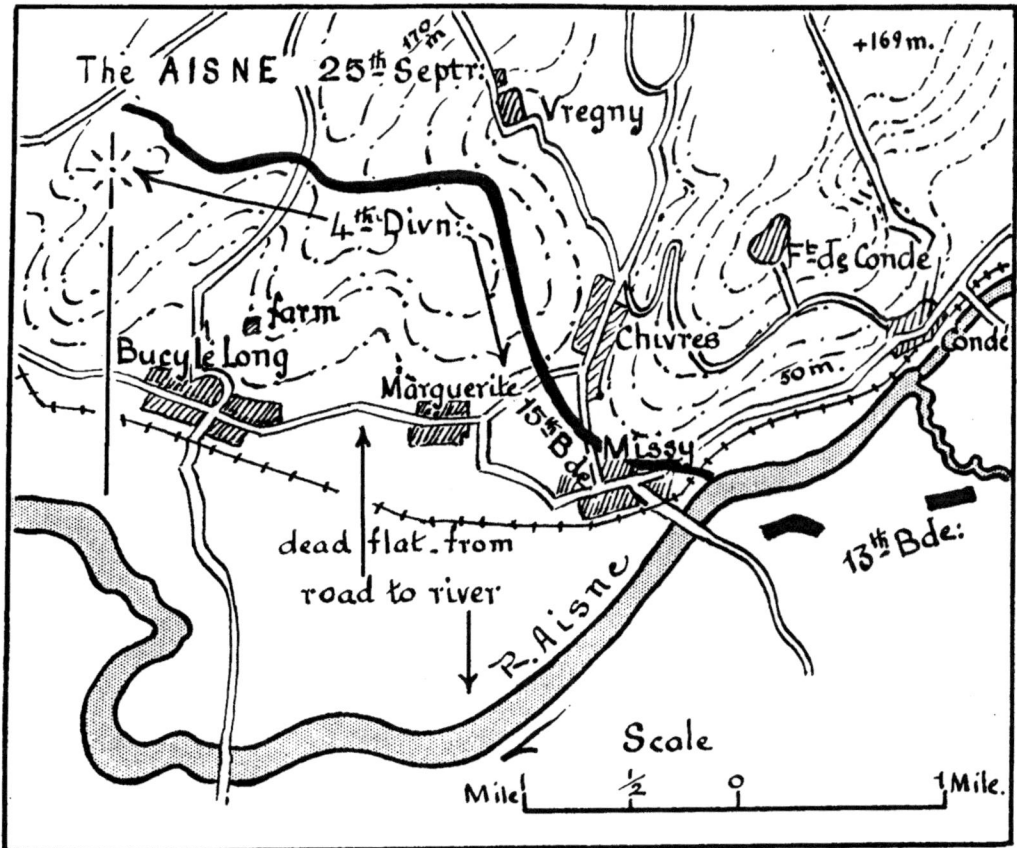

LA BASSÉE. 10th October—2nd November, 1914.

This battle was one of the many engagements which were caused by the " race to the sea," the mutual endeavour of both Allies and Germans to turn their enemy's northern flank.

By 10th October, the French left reached as far north as Vermelles, S.E. of Béthune and the British, pivoting on this, attempted to swing forward, passing to the north of Lille in an endeavour to turn the German right flank.

To the north, the Cavalry made connection with General Rawlinson's force in front of Ypres and with the Belgian Army. Thus, on our side, a thin line of alternate cavalry and infantry reached to the sea.

To the II. Corps (to which the 1st Battalion belonged) was given the task of turning the German northern flank.

The country was extremely flat, but as the soil was rich, farms, orchards, corn-lands and sugar-beet crops were plentiful. There were occasional coal fields. On the whole, but for the dykes and streams which cut up the whole district, the country was not unlike mid-Cheshire. But as soon as the fighting began and trenches and shell holes covered every square foot of ground, the natural and artificial drainage was upset and the country quickly became little better than a morass, which it remained " for the duration." Artillery could only move along roads. Their O.P.s were few, and such high buildings as there were had to be used for observing purposes.

The advance of the Corps was disputed at every ridge, building and watercourse by German Cavalry and Jaegers.

The 1st Battalion marched continuously from the south, from 2nd October to the 7th, when it trained to Abbeville, and thence marched and bussed to Bethune.

It arrived at Festubert on 12th, and went immediately on outposts for the 5th Division, which was holding a line astride La Bassée Canal. During the occupation of this outpost position, Capt. Butterworth was reported missing and six N.C.Os. and men were wounded.

On the 6th October, Major Vandeleur of the Scottish Rifles took over command.

Very early on the 12th October, the Battalion moved off from Béthune in a dense mist to take up a line covering Festubert, with Givenchy on our left. The line to be held was very long and touch was not gained with the troops on the left.

An attack at dawn on 13th was ordered and, as information was poor, it was suggested that the front should be explored with strong patrols during the night. There was a large farmstead, Chapelle St. Roch, part of the village of Rue d'Ouvert, immediately opposite the Battalion front. Two strong patrols were sent out and Major Young went out in support with a half company to try and get a footing in the farm. Major Vandeleur accompanied the party to supervise the direction of the attack.

Before the men reached the farm, fire was opened on them and the whole party charged in and successfully occupied the buildings. They were at once put in a state of defence, and our people, not unnaturally, fully expected that so strong a position would be of great value to the attack at dawn on the 13th. But no attack took place. After fighting during the whole of that day, they found the enemy all round them. The Germans set light to the outbuildings and only a few men remained unwounded. About 10 p.m., Major Young told Major Vandeleur that all the wounded in the cellar were in danger of being burnt alive. As the enemy had now fired the haystacks, a sortie was out of the question. About midnight the gallant little party surrendered.

Major Vandeleur, who was wounded, soon managed to escape, thanks to his knowledge of German. He was the first British officer to get away. He subsequently saw much fighting and was again severely wounded.

Major Young, Captain Harbord, Lieuts. Harrington and Thomas and 55 N.C.Os. and men were captured, and 8 men, other than those captured, were wounded.

Heavy fighting, in drenching rain, took place on the 13th, but why Major Vandeleur's party did not benefit is not clear. After this action, Captain Shore took over command.

The Germans persisted in attacking and shelling both by day and by night, and the Battalion, continually in the trenches, suffered continuous losses.

On the 16th, the Battalion captured its original objective, Rue d'Ouvert, and moved along the Violaines road.

On the 17th, a welcome reinforcement of 3 officers and 248 N.C.Os. and men arrived in the evening, after the Battalion had made a brilliant and successful attack on Violaines which is just north of La Bassée. This attack lasted all day, having begun at 1-30 a.m., it was not until 6-15 p.m. that the village was occupied and entrenched. In the attacks valuable help was given by the D.C.L.I.

During the attack on Violaines, Captain Lloyd was wounded and 7 N.C.Os. and men killed and wounded.

Holding on to its gains in spite of constant attacks, the Battalion made a desperate attempt to secure La Bassée on the 19th, but only succeeded in gaining some 500 yards. Nine men were killed and 2nd Lieutenants Andrews, Sidebotham and Napier and 20 men were wounded.

As the left of the Corps had reached the Aubers Ridge, it looked as if the swing forward might produce valuable results, but alas, this was the high water mark. The Battalion had got nearer to La Bassée than any British or Allied troops were to go for four years.

Reinforcements came up on the German side and on the 20th a great enemy offensive movement was staged, reaching from Arras to the sea. Violaines was heavily attacked, but the attack was repulsed. 2nd Lieutenant Addison was wounded and 27 N.C.Os. and men killed and wounded.

On the 21st, another enemy attempt was made on La Bassée, which was met with heavy shell fire. Capt. Mahoney was mortally wounded, 3 men killed and 16 wounded.

The attacks were continually renewed, and the position of the II. Corps, and especially of its foremost detachment, the 1st Battalion, was rapidly becoming untenable, but the II. Corps stood fast on the line of Violaines.

Violaines.

On the 22nd October, our companies were disposed as shown on the map, " D " Company being engaged in digging trenches, protected by the usual covering party. The Germans managed to rush " D " Company, owing to the covering party giving insufficient notice, and the Company fell back to the second position, shown on the map.

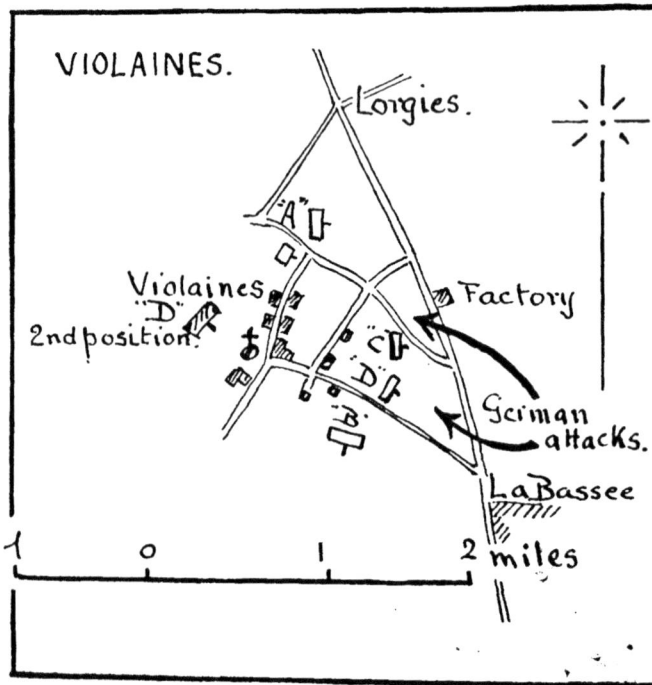

This exposed " C " Company which fell back in line with " A." As there were no troops on either flank, the Battalion was further enfiladed and forced to withdraw.

Captain Shore and 2nd/Lieut. Leicester were captured. Captains Rich, Hartford and Forster, and 2nd/Lieuts. J. A. Greenhalgh and Noel Atkinson were killed or died of wounds in German hands. 2nd/Lieut. Atkinson was a well-known golfer. His father, Vicar of Audlem, put up a monument to his son and his comrades in Violaines civil cemetery. Under the terms of the endowment, this cemetery is visited every two years by an officer of The Regiment.

Captain Rich had displayed great gallantry and coolness in every action from Audregnies onwards.

We lost over 220 N.C.Os. and men.

2nd/Lieuts. Pogson and Stalker brought the Battalion out of action.

The Brigadier wrote : " The surprise was obviously due to insufficient covering parties, not far enough out. But it is probable that, in any case, the large number of the enemy would eventually have compelled retirement."

After this action, the Battalion practically ceased to exist. An officer of another Regiment commanded and only one other officer was fit for duty, but such as it was the Battalion remained in the trenches digging and suffering casualties. The men were utterly exhausted and it was hard to keep them from lying down and sleeping in the so-called trenches they had dug—mere muddy ditches.

ARMENTIÈRES. 13th October—2nd November.

On the 28th, the First Battalion was sent to the 14th Brigade to assist in repelling the attack on Neuve Chapelle, which gives us the Battle Honour of Armentières. 2nd/Lieut. Woodhead was wounded and other losses amounted to 20 killed, wounded and missing.

During October, the Battalion had seven commanding officers and at the end of the battle of La Bassée it was commanded by the Adjutant, Lieut. T. L. Frost, with the Quarter-Master, Sproule, as his Adjutant.

Lieutenant T. L. Frost was a descendant of the Miller of the Dee, and a son of Sir John Frost, five times Mayor of Chester. Except for the Quarter-master, Sproule, he was the last of the officers who had landed with the First Battalion.

YPRES 1914.

Map p. 54

The next series of battles is known as the First Ypres. Although names are given to periods of fighting, it is not possible to describe them as battles. It was a period of continuous, prolonged, ruthless encounter, hardly interrupted at night. Our troops had no rest. They were out-numbered, out-gunned and opposed by a determined, skilful and im-placable enemy. The fighting was largely individual. The casualties were so heavy that units lost their identity and were roughly grouped under Brigadiers. The troops fought in shallow trenches and shell holes, and in terrible weather conditions. In addition to wound and death casualties, they suffered from frozen feet and knees and from rheumatism. Repulse of German attacks was a daily commonplace and receives hardly any mention in the war diary. Hourly shelling, to which no reply was possible owing to shortage of ammunition, passes without comment also.

" To give a true picture of the long hours of patient, stubborn resis-" tance, there should be mention in every page of bursting shells, of " blown-in trenches, hunger, fatigue, death and wounds." (Official History).

Only at night could supplies be brought up and wounded removed. As soon as dusk fell, Ypres was crowded with vehicles passing in and out.

The Regiment lost more men in the Ypres salient than on any other front.

Up to the 10th November, the front was unusually quiet. The First Battalion had moved up to Ypres on the 7th and was holding trenches just south of the 6th kilometre stone on the Menin road.

Between the 5th and 10th, Captain G. B. Pollock-Hodsall, of The Suffolk Regiment and 2nd/Lieut. G. R. L. Anderson were killed while gallantly heading a counter-attack against some Germans who had pene-trated our front. Twenty-five prisoners were taken, but we lost 36 N.C.Os. and men killed and wounded. No drafts had arrived since Violaines, so it was with very considerable difficulty that the Battalion held the 350 yards of front allotted to it.

NONNE BOSSCHEN. 11th November.

Map p. 54

This battle marked the final attempt of the Prussian Guard to break through to Ypres. They fought under the eyes of their Kaiser in this supreme effort to drive the " contemptible British Army " into the sea.

At 5-30 a.m. on the 10th, " the most terrific fire that the British had yet experienced broke out." The First Battalion diary records the bare fact, and goes on to say that " the enemy appeared to be massing in a wood south of our position, but our shells scattered them, and they were easily repulsed by our rifle fire, with heavy casualties to them." Our fire did much damage to enemy attacking the Gordons on our flank.

Other troops had more severe fighting, and the break through of the Prussian Guard was only checked by the gallantry of three weak Scots Battalions called the 1st (Guards) Brigade, and The King's Regiment and the Duke of Wellington's Regiment.

* * * *

The close of the battles of Ypres was a period of continuous shelling, of readjustments of the front which caused unnecessary casualties, of the misery of cold, of wet, of mud and of cold food. It petered out into a long spell of the unrelieved tedium known as trench warfare. The German Minnie (mine thrower) made her unwelcome appearance, with her large and particularly objectionable shell.

Although the actual fighting was not so severe as later on, this tour of the trenches was as unpleasant as any of the first two years. It was the beginning of trench warfare, without any of the amenities which were afterwards introduced. There were no sandbags, no communication trenches, no shelters of any kind, no cooking, though Sproule managed to get tea to the trenches every day. The rum ration, two or three times a week, was the only solace the men had. It was most uncomfortable.

On the 14th of November, we lost Lieut. H. R. Stables, Royal Fusiliers, killed and 2nd/Lieut. E. Glan, wounded, as well as 30 N.C.Os. and men killed, wounded, or missing. Between the 5th and the 20th of November, that is during this period in the Salient, the 1st Battalion lost 35 killed, 99 wounded and 65 missing.

On the 21st, the Battalion was relieved and went to Locre. The Brigade war diary records, on 24th " Cheshires only 230 strong, suffering very much from swollen feet and knees and rheumatism, but none from chest complaints, or colds, or coughs. But they cannot get their boots on after the march in and many are quite crippled."

Only three officers were present at duty when the Battalion left Ypres and went to Locre.

On the 26th November, the 1st Battalion mounted a Guard of Honour for the Prince of Wales, on the 27th was inspected and congratu-

.lated by General Sir John French, and on the following day by General
.Sir H. Smith Dorrien.   They had certainly earned all the praise they got,
but alas, few who had earned it were present to hear it.

On 3rd December, the Battalion was inspected by H.M. The King.

Reinforcements now began to arrive and by the 17th the Battalion
was sufficiently recovered to be able to go back to the trenches.

*   *   *   *

The severity of the fighting and of the trench conditions in the Salient
necessitated calls on the Territorial Army in training at home.   This
meant destroying the organization of the Territorial Force and the
Cheshire Brigade was one of the unfortunate ones.   Its reward for having
reached a comparatively high state of training, in spite of drawbacks
which have been recorded in the chapter on mobilization, was to lose
two of its stronger Battalions.

The break-up of the Cheshire Brigade, the 153rd Brigade of the
Welsh Division, destroyed many bright hopes which had been enter-
tained of a Brigade at war, wholly officered and manned by men of The
Regiment.

The 6th Battalion was sent to France in November 1914.   They had
the honour of forming part of the escort at the funeral of Lord Roberts
who had died during his visit to the Indian Corps in France.   They were
sent into the trenches, under the 14th Brigade, under the severest conditions.   They were given no preliminary introduction to the severity
of winter fighting in the Ypres Salient and, as is well known, the trenches
were deep in mud and water.

The 5th (Earl of Chester's) Battalion, under Lieut.-Colonel J. E. G.
Groves, followed the 6th in February, 1915.   They, too, were attached to
the 14th Brigade, but were systematically introduced to war conditions
by stages, until they were fit to be entrusted with their own section of
the front.

Troops also began to arrive from India, and the 2nd Battalion
reached France, in the 84th Brigade of the 28th Division, in February
1915.   They immediately went to the front and had " a very hard time
in and around Ypres, attached to the 5th Division."

It is as well to emphasize here the change which had come over
warfare in France between the time the 1st Battalion fought at Audregnies
and when the 2nd Battalion arrived in February 1915.

In place of the heat and drought of summer, the troops had to
contend with cold and wet in the confinement of trenches.   The 1st
Battalion had had full view of their foe and had seen the deadly effect of
their matchless musketry on masses and lines of German soldiers.   The
2nd Battalion was to live for months within a few yards of their enemy
and never to see him.

Colonel B. H. Chetwynd-Stapylton.

Lieut.-Colonel E. P. Nares.

Lieut.-Colonel M. F. Clarke.

Captain D. Greville.

YPRES 1915.

Map p. 54

The 2nd Battalion, in the 84th Brigade, 28th Division, went straight into the Ypres Salient in February 1915 and began at once to experience heavy casualties. On the 16th February, two brothers, Keating, who had worked their way up The Regiment together and had become, one, John, Regimental Sergeant-Major, and the other, George, a Colour-Sergeant, were killed. They had been given commissions in their own Regiment on arrival in England from India. On the same day, another promoted N.C.O., Ward, was wounded.

A few days later, Captain H. G. Turner, one of the cheeriest and smartest officers we have ever had, was killed on a reconnaissance, with L/Cpl. Lloyd and Private Wainwright. They were attempting to locate and report on a sap which the Germans were digging.

During this period, from 22nd February to 6th April, the 84th Brigade was lent to the 5th Division, in which the 1st Battalion was serving.

On the 2nd April, the following letter was received by our C.O. from the O.C. 1st Battalion The Wiltshire Regiment which explains itself :—

" Thank you very much for sending the effects of the late Lieutenant " Hooper. Will you please convey to Sergeant Wynne and Private " Bedda my deep appreciation of and high admiration for their very " gallant conduct in bringing in this officer's body. My Battalion " thoroughly understands the great personal risk that this N.C.O. and " man ran, for which they cannot too highly thank them, and desire to " place on record their sense of their obligation to them for their great " heroism."

An extract from the Brigade war diary gives a side-light on the conditions in which our men were fighting.

" 6th Feb. Everyone is crying out for sandbags in thousands but " very few are obtainable as yet."

* * * *

The 5th Battalion was in the trenches in the area of this battle.

GRAVENSTAFEL. 23rd—24th April, 1915.

Map p. 54

This was the first German gas attack. The Germans, to justify their own use of gas, falsely accused us of using poison gas shells at this time. French Senegalese troops on the British left were selected by the Germans as being most likely to be affected by this dastardly surprise.

Both the 1st, 2nd and 5th Battalions earned this honour. No Battalion was on the front line where the attack began. The First

C

Battalion was in the line to the north of Hill 60, ready to fall back to the Zwartelen switch, should the situation develop unfavourably.

The 2nd Battalion had the very unpleasant role of lying out in the open all day as a reserve to the Suffolk Regiment, suffering losses from fire to which they could not reply.

ST. JULIEN. 24th April to 4th May.

Map p. 54

The 28th Division was occupying a sector north of the Menin road, astride the Ypres—Broodseinde road.

On the 15th April, the 84th Brigade, with the 2nd Battalion, took over the Zonnebeke section.

Hill 60 was a small piece of rising ground some 1500 yards from Zillebeke and north of the Ypres—Courtrai railway. After being in German hands for some months, it was captured by the 5th Division on 17th April. Incessant counter-attacks exhausted the 5th Division to such an extent that the Northumberland Fusiliers were sent up to assist in the defence. While this struggle was in progress, a grave situation had developed to the north.

On 20th April, a heavy bombardment began on Ypres and continued for two days. On the 22nd, under clouds of gas, the Germans delivered a sudden attack on the left shoulder of the Salient, where the line was held by French colonial troops. The French retired and exposed the flank of the Canadians and of the troops of the 28th Division. The reserves of the 27th and 28th Divisions were faced north to fill the gap.

The 2nd Battalion spent a very unpleasant time, suffering from shelling and gassing, waiting for orders. About 5 p.m. on the 23rd April, two companies of the 2nd Battalion with 1½ companies of the Northumberland Fusiliers and a company of the Monmouthshire Regiment were formed into a detachment under command of Major E. M. Moulton Barrett of the Fusiliers. He was ordered to take up a position S.E. of the cross-roads, Zonnebeke—Langemarck and Gravenstafel—Wieltje, halfway between Zonnebeke and St. Julien, in support of the Canadians.

He found this point clear of the enemy and so he advanced to the north of the Hannebeek (north part of the Steenbeke) stream. The Canadians were all but completely exhausted. Reinforcements were sent up by Moulton Barrett. The situation now was that, in a gap of 3 miles between the left of the 2nd Canadian Brigade and the right of the 3rd, were two groups. Moulton Barrett's companies of the 2nd Battalion and one company each of the Suffolks and Monmouths. Further to the S.W., out of touch, was a second group under the Colonel of the Suffolks.

Officers, 1st Battalion The Cheshire Regiment. Taken July 28th, 1915, near Abeele, just before leaving Ypres area for Somme area.

Standing left to right : S. A. Harper, C. T. Cordon, 3rd Wilts (attd.), G. P. Harding, J. R. Moore, J. M. Forsyth, R.A.M.C., W. T. Prout, G. R. Simpson, J. D. Mason, W. R. Easterbrook.

Sitting : G. A. Gleed, J. L. Trevitt, R. N. Greenwood, R. H. Griffiths, J. A. Busfeild, Maj. C. G. E. Hughes (Comdg.), J. C. Sproule (Qr.-Mr.), E. G. Carr, L. M. Hernandez, E. M. Sidebotham.

At dawn on the 25th, the Canadians in front of Moulton Barrett were relieved, and he withdrew his detachment south of the Hannebeek to the position to which he had been originally ordered.

The night of the 25th/26th passed quietly. Moulton Barrett knew the situation was grave, but he did not know that on the 25th the 28th Division had been heavily attacked, and, though they held their ground, that the troops of the 2nd Canadian Brigade had been withdrawn south of Gravenstafel.

Thus, at dawn on the 26th, the left flank of the 28th Division was in a sharp salient, with the Hampshire Regiment, who had relieved the 2nd Canadian Brigade, some 400 yards to the S.W.

South west again, but out of touch with the Hampshire, was Moulton Barrett's detachment. On his left front, was the Durham L.I. in an advanced detached post at Boteler's farm, some 800 yards to the north-west. So that Moulton Barrett's detachment was now in the front line, the 11th Brigade in echelon to their left rear.

By daybreak, the defence had been greatly strengthened. Suddenly a number of Durham L.I. came rushing back, announcing the capture of their position by the Germans. Moulton Barrett withdrew 400 yards and asked for reinforcements. The Germans attempted to assemble for attack, but were dispersed by rifle fire. All their attempts to advance were checked. Moulton Barrett was now wounded. He was succeeded by Captain Auld. He found the detachment reduced to 70 men, out of touch with troops on both flanks, and engaging the enemy at a range of some three to four hundred yards.

On the right, farm buildings on higher ground offered a position from which the detachment could be enfiladed. Auld detached a party under a C.S.M. of the 2nd Battalion to occupy them. Enfilade fire was simultaneously opened on both flanks. The C.S.M. was killed. Further reinforcements came from the Fusiliers and the defence proved adequate. The Germans had missed an opportunity of breaking through a very thinly held line between Gravenstafel and St. Julien.

The resolute stand made by this detachment had led the enemy to believe that it was in far greater strength than was the case.

The position of the 27th and 28th Divisions was very precarious. They were at the head of a salient so narrow as to bring their communications under the observation and close fire of the enemy.

The withdrawal of British troops in the salient on 3rd/4th May marked the close of the Battle of St. Julien. Casualties during this period were 6 officers and 92 men wounded.

*   *   *   *

The 5th Battalion also earned this honour.

*   *   *   *

The 1st Battalion earned this honour through being within the area laid down, in the Ypres casemates as a matter of fact. But the very severe fighting on the 5th, which will be recounted later, did not earn a battle honour.

* * * *

On the 4th May, the 28th Division line was withdrawn and moved to new trenches at Frezenberg with Battalion H.Q., at Potijze. On the 5th, 6th and 7th, the 2nd Battalion suffered severely and on the 6th Captain J. C. Routh was killed. A. B. Stone took over the Battalion on the 6th.

Hill 60.

This is not a " battle honour." As has been already stated, the 1st Battalion was in casemates at Ypres at the beginning of May. They were so short of officers that Colonel A. de C. Scott, Captain Savage and Lieut. Mills had been sent to them from the 2nd Battalion.

On the 4th May, at 8 p.m., the 1st Battalion was called upon to move to the support trenches facing Hill 60. As soon as they reached the open country near Zillebeke Lake, they encountered a heavy shell barrage which, combined with a cloud of gas, persisted till they reached their position. Their gas masks were nothing more than pieces of wadding held over the mouth by elastic. They reached Larch Wood near the railway cutting at 10-30 p.m., and found the Bedfordshire Regiment which had suffered terribly. The Germans had released more gas in the morning, and had recaptured the Hill.

The Battalion was ordered to attack. They cleared Larch Wood and occupied trenches in the wood. In the meantime, attacks by the K.O.Y.L.I. and K.O.S.B. on the Hill failed.

Private Dean, seeing an officer, Captain White, of the K.O.Y.L.I., lying wounded in the open, very gallantly crawled out to him in broad daylight, bandaged his wounds and, assisted by two other men, Smith and Case, got him back safely.

On the 6th, The Regiment suffered a very severe loss when Colonel A. de C. Scott was killed. " Bro." Scott was much loved by all ranks. His abilities were of a scholarly type, all too rare in our service. Captains Woodyer and Savage and Lieutenants Pym and Clay were wounded.

Major C. G. E. Hughes took over command of the 1st Battalion. His courageous example did much to prevent the Germans exploiting the advantage they had obtained by their use of gas. Hughes continued to command the 1st Battalion till September. Officers and men had the greatest confidence in him because he was always up at the tight corner with clear, decided and unmistakable orders.

Further attempts on the Hill were made at dawn on the 7th, but all failed.

Letters from Arthur Greg.

DESCRIBING THE PERIOD APRIL-MAY, 1915.

Eighteen days in a fire trench with heavy engagements only a few hundred yards to our right, and more critical fighting a mile or so on our left, was not calculated to act as a nerve tonic. Our trenches had rocked and swayed under the shock of the six successive explosions that had blown up so many of His Imperial Majesty's Bavarian troops, and had altered the features of what had once been known as Hill 60. We had been the forced spectators of more than one charge up the slopes of that mass of debris. We had been listening for days to the unending shriek of missiles that were angrily hurled over our heads on to the unfortunate town of Ypres. We had heard how the French and Canadians were heavily engaged on our left. We had been warned that at any moment we might have to retire to the ramparts of Ypres. Somehow we felt that everything was not quite as satisfactory as it might be.

And still we were not relieved. We guessed that men were scarce and that what available troops there were, were wanted to try and stem the latest German effort to reach Calais.

At last we heard we were going back to rest. We had heard this so often before that at first not much notice was taken.

When we had started that memorable time we had been assured that it was only going to last eight days and then half of us were going to be allowed to visit " England, Home and Beauty " once more. Towards the end of our stay in the firing line many rather homesick refrains had found voice. There was one that was a great favourite, although perhaps not as patriotic as it might have been. I can only remember the chorus which was :—

        " I want to go over the sea,
        " Where the Allymands can't see me.
        " Oh my ! I don't want to die,
        " I want to go home."

This was significant of our general attitude towards life after a long trip in the trenches. Our joy at departing from the trenches was rather subdued when we heard that we were only going into dug-outs about a mile away instead of billets. But anything in the nature of a change was a relief. After the usual dreadful delays, in which one generally manages to have a sort of glorified game of hide and seek with the various other little detachments of the company, we arrived at our new resting place. The place that had been chosen was the edge of a lake, Zillebeke, into whose slippery sides a good many holes had been burrowed. It was here we were to spend our holiday. Fires could only be lighted with the utmost precaution as no smoke was to be shown. What nightmares those fires were! How we talked of smoke, and dreamt of smoke. We lounged about this rabbit warren all day stamping out a little fire here only to find another huge column of smoke had suddenly risen behind our backs. The soldiers' irresistible longing to "drum up," to make tea in other words, was not easily to be quenched. After crawling into one's own particular burrow after an hour or more's steady lunging and slipping and fire stamping, one nearly always heard that "B" Company's fire was getting too big again—would Mr. So-and-so go and see to them.

At night, in order that our rest might be fully beneficial, we went out for about six hours and dug trenches. These nights out were always enlivened on the way out or coming back by the great game of shell-dodging.

About the fourth day of this blissful rest, the Germans discovered our little warren and shelled us out. That was in the afternoon. As soon as it was dusk, word was passed for our Nonconformist minister who was at that time working with the signallers. He had a busy time that evening although the service was a short one. Shortly after, I was sent for to the C.Os. dug-out. There I found the C.O., the Adjutant and the Second-in-command. The great question was where to go.

Ypres was uninhabitable owing to the perpetual shell fire. There were no more dug-outs anywhere about. It was not a happy moment to search for lodgings. Finally, it was decided that our second-in-command was to go and see if there was any accommodation in the ramparts of Ypres. I was told to take a guide and find out if there were any suitable cellars in a certain disused hospital place. I chose my guide, a man who had been on many solitary little walks with me. After a certain amount of wandering over fields that were still being casually shelled, we saw what we supposed must be the hospital. It was a huge block of buildings, into whose inner recesses it would have taken some time for a stranger to penetrate. We therefore determined to try and find a local inhabitant to act as guide. We tried several houses with no result. Finally, after great hammering, a young Belgian lady appeared more or less clad for the night. She was rather scared as there were still a few shells dropping round and it was just about midnight. But on the whole she seemed extraordinarily affable and obliging. We lent her a few of our superfluous garments and then we started on our voyage of exploration.

The Belgian lady and I walked in front and talked of many things, while my guide remained respectfully behind. We were rather a curious procession, flitting in and out of partially destroyed cloisters which surrounded the courtyard.

We found some gunners in one of the cellars and a number of horses in the outer hall. The gunners were not very pleased at the prospect of some more lodgers arriving, but I told them of our pitiable position on the edge of the lake.

After finishing my mission, I escorted my fair guide back to her abode and returned to report to the C.O. It was not long before the second-in-command returned and gave his report. It was decided that my company was to be one of the two destined for the ramparts. I was secretly rather glad as I did not very much like the idea of living with a battery that was bound to be shelled as soon as it attempted to speak. My guide took the other half Battalion and the Major took " B " and " C " Companies towards Ypres. When we got near the moat surrounding the town, we realized that now the Germans were actually shelling us. By some extraordinary means they knew exactly where we were and followed us with terrible precision. We rushed across the pontoon bridge over the moat, one platoon going while the other crouched on the other side waiting their turn and watching the shells dropping in the moat. My platoon happened to be the first across, and as there was a certain amount of cover under the ramparts, the platoon was left there while the Major and I hastened to find our resting place.

I shall never forget that piece of road from the end of the pontoon bridge to the casemate where we were to billet. It couldn't have been more than 300 yards that we had to go, but there were piles of debris in the road where some house had had its upper story blown off, which all made progress slow. When we started, this bit of street was being heavily shelled by shrapnel and H.E. of all calibres. Bricks and stones were flying about. The noise was exaggerated tremendously by the empty stone buildings.

Shells seemed to drop in front and behind us. We ran hard when for a second there was a lull. We tried to take cover but there was nothing to shelter us except partially demolished houses that were much more likely to fall on top of us than shield us. Having finally reached the building and recovered our breath a little, we both doubled back to bring the platoon along. We had a terribly anxious time covering that piece of road, which they were still shelling fiercely. The first platoon was brought in more or less intact. In due course, the others arrived, some not so fortunate, panting and congratulating themselves on their narrow escapes. This casemate place that had been allotted to us was only a few yards from one of the tallest spires of Ypres. Somebody suggested that there were spies signalling from the top somewhere. A sergeant and I were just going to investigate and had gone a few yards when we heard the shriek of a shell for a fraction of a second. There happened to be a huge gateway quite close ; we each flattened ourselves behind the massive stone posts. It was well we did so as the whole force of the shrapnel burst against the gate, and I felt the stone column shake and many splinters of stone clattered against the opposite side of the street. We were tired and after that escape, we decided that spies or no spies, we would return to our new home.

It was a curious place, this casemate, built into the side of the rampart, so to speak, let into the bank. There was at least ten to fifteen feet of earth above the roof which was of stone and strongly arched. We felt that as long as a 17-inch shell did. not alight actually on our roof we were safe.

There were four compartments ; they could not be called rooms, one in which there were already some R.E., and a few refugees, one which we put aside for officers, and two others which could just hold the two companies with a great squash. A medical officer, had there been one, would hardly have passed the place fit for habitation. It was simply filthy. The men had a dirty stone floor to lie on. They were simply packed—not an inch that was not covered by a prostrate figure. It looked as if they would all have to lie down together and get up together in order to be able to fit in at all. The officers' room was smaller and dirtier if anything. There was one table and a few revolting looking mattresses. We were not particular after three weeks with scarcely any sleep. It all seemed the height of luxury. We even used the disgusting blankets that we found on the floor amongst the other interesting things, that had been left by the previous occupants.

It was just beginning to dawn when we arrived. After pickets and sentries had been posted, it was almost daylight.

We soon discovered that the only daylight that reached the officers' room was through a small grid in the roof. Not much more light penetrated the men's quarters. After a sleep and a meal, two of us thought it would be rather interesting to go and look at the shops. We knew that we were the first body of men to visit Ypres after the precipitate retreat of the majority of the inhabitants. The town was, however, never entirely deserted. We went into various houses whose chimneys were showing signs of life, and in most we found several aged Belgians with long beards and curious little peaked caps. They were generally sitting in a more or less dazed condition in front of their stoves. The windows were generally smashed and often the doors. But they preferred to stay in their old homes rather than flee to the unknown.

We searched many houses for spies. We questioned many. The most likely looking spies either feigned deafness or said they couldn't understand French. Several dilapidated old men, who seemed very interested in our quarters, and who hung about suspiciously, swore that they were " Ze watermen." That meant, apparently, not so much that they emptied their drains into the moat, or drew water therefrom, but that they played about with the level of the water in the moat. Some went so far as to show statements signed by British officers to the effect that they were in English employ.

Some of our men reported that they saw a man on the roof of a house near our abode. We entered with revolvers, searching high and low, and looked into cupboards with far greater precaution than any child ever displayed in playing hide and seek. Our search was fruitless. We had many. Sometimes we found a more or less demented old man drinking coffee and bewailing his fate. He showed us a number of passports, but as it was not necessary for the inhabitants of Ypres to carry a passport unless they left the town, it was difficult to check any suspicious characters.

The shops were most interesting. One only had to climb into the window to find perhaps drawers full of cigars lying strewn about.

We went down the cellar steps of one large cafe well known to us in the more peaceful days of a month before. The cellars were full of every kind of wine, rows of bottles of champagne untouched. The next room had evidently been used by the family as a living room. There were cups and saucers and every sort of kitchen utensil. The adjoining cellar had been converted into a bedroom. I remember this room well.

My friend happened to have a huge boil on his face which he noticed in the mirror. He was so upset that he asked me to operate. We decided to make a halt in this cellar and managed to find some refreshments. I then rummaged about amongst the drawers, full of ladies' garments, till I found some needles and some stuff to serve as lint. The operation was then performed. Just as I was finishing we heard some footsteps coming down the front stairs. We had just time to flee quietly up the back-stairs and so out through the window and into the square. We afterwards learnt that they were some French soldiers searching for refreshment.

Another room we visited was strewn with ladies' clothes and numbers of hats. I chose a wonderful purple velvet one with a large feather, the sort of thing that 'Arriet decks herself in when she meets 'Arry on Hampstead Heath. I remember thinking I looked rather smart in it.

That night some gunners arrived at our dwelling and tied up about fifteen horses outside our front door. We didn't like this much. It was rather annoying wading through horses whenever we went in or out. The men, of course, were only allowed to leave this place at certain times to draw water, under an escort. But even then the horses were a distinct nuisance.

At night we used to go out and dig. Directly the first platoon started, we had to go through the same hail of shell fire, till we reached open country on the other side of the pontoon bridge. The same thing happened when we returned in the small hours of the morning. We were all beginning to feel what an unhealthy spot it was. There simply must be spies directing this fire. But we never caught one red-handed. The second night, nine of the horses were hit, and several killed. We buried all we could in large shell holes immediately outside. The others had to remain as we couldn't move them away. They did not add to the pleasantness of the place, especially as the weather was very hot at the time.

It was after coming in from a particularly hard night's digging just behind the firing line that we were suddenly roused with the alrming news that the Germans had made a gas attack on Hill 60, and had broken through. " B " and " C " Companies had to go up immediately. We only had a few minutes to get ready. We had no time to divide the rations which we had drawn in bulk the night before. We were to go up light, so we left our coats, and heavy things in the casemate. It was not long before the C.O. appeared. " B " Company had to go first with ten minutes interval between each platoon. My platoon was the first to go.

In a few minutes we were ready. It was broad daylight. The guns were firing fiercely. There was a tremendous cannonade in progress. What we all were asking was how far had the Germans pushed through. It was about eight or nine in the morning of May 5th that we started. When we finally emerged on to the pontoon bridge, after traversing that hellish 300 yards, we wondered what was in store for us. We all carried our little cotton wool mouth pads round our necks ready for instant use. At that period that was our sole defence against the gas.

As soon as we were well in the open we extended and proceeded, expecting any moment to be fired on by some concealed Germans. We passed almost under the very guns of one of our field batteries. They were pounding away at high pressure and seemed almost as excited as we were. It was rather a comfort to get past that spot as the Germans were answering their fire with considerable vigour.

After a good many halts, we finally came to the end of that shell-swept two miles of open country. It was piping hot and we were terribly thirsty. The sights we saw on the way up were not calculated to cheer us much. We passed many groups of men dead or dying, some wounded, and all badly gassed. Most of them were writhing in awful agony. The colour of their faces and the noises they made turned our blood cold. We could do nothing for them. We had to push on, leaving them gasping for breath and dying under that pitiless sun. We reported ourselves to the Adjutant of the remains of the Regiment in support. We were told we must go up to the fire trench and work with the Regiment there. Our first business was to clear the fire trenches and communication trenches of all the corpses. My men worked till they nearly dropped. Water was scarce. We tried the puddles at the edge of the railway line. The water was filthy and brown, but it was refreshing. Sometimes we were fired on at close range from somewhere behind. The Germans had broken through and were still breaking through. Nobody quite knew where the next English troops on our left were.

At one time we noticed a number of men dashing down the hill about 70 yards on our left. We thought they were the remains of the Regiment that had been holding the hill, so we held our fire. It was hard to see amid the clouds of dust and bursting shells. It was not long before we realized they were Germans. The artillery of both sides were frightfully at a loss. We were shelled by our own guns. The Germans were shelled by theirs. On the skyline, the crest of the hill, which must have been about 80 yards away, we watched sand bags appearing; we saw shovels wielded by unseen hands hammering them down. Our picked marksmen fired and tried to hinder this work of consolidation as much as possible.

It was about this time that our " C " Company appeared and slowly forced its way through our crowded trench and disappeared to the left where the Germans were. They lost several officers and a good many men in the next two or three hours. I was then told by my new C.O. that I was to go as far along the trench to my left as possible.

We started. Suddenly out of one of the communication trenches one of " C " Company officers appeared alone. He seemed quite cheerful but very tired. He had been doing a little investigation on his own and informed me that if I kept along my present path I should be into the Germans in another 40 yards. ' We pushed on, however. I was in front of the platoon.

The trench had been badly shattered and was lined with that curious yellow colour that spells lyddite. The trench was full of fresh German dead piled over each other. A lucky shell of ours had done its work and slaughtered about 20 Germans. We crawled over these. They were very wobbly and the going was bad. On turning round a traverse a bullet hit the sand bag just beside my face. I looked up and saw a dirty unshaven German staring at me with a rifle in his hand. He was shooting over a barricade. The range was about ten yards. I withdrew and took cover behind a corpse. There were many Mauser rifles lying about and plenty of ammunition. I loaded and peeped over the corpse. We both fired simultaneously and both bobbed down again. It was a weird sort of duel. Neither of us cared much about it. Then, from my prostrate position, I started making a little barricade of my own. My friend behind the barricade had several more shots and so had I, but although hideously close, they did not take effect. This duel must end. It wasn't good enough. I think we both realised this about the same time, as my adversary didn't expose himself any more when I was looking. Meanwhile, my platoon had all come up and were waiting. I passed the word for sandbags to be filled and passed up. In this way I was able to build a sort of barricade. I then withdrew a few yards and piled up what bodies I could with the help of two of my men against the barricade. We had to keep very low as shots came from behind, from the flank and from the front. It was an unhealthy spot, and I didn't like the carpet of Bavarian bodies ; their limbs were so horribly arranged and their shoulders didn't make a firm footing. After leaving some good men near the barricade, I managed to plunge along past men and corpses to the healthier end of the platoon. There I had a smoke and discussed the situation with my platoon sergeant. I bore rather a grudge against the Company Commander of the regiment I had been lent to for having put me in such a filthy spot. None of my men seemed particularly happy about it either.

The first thing was to settle down a bit and see that the men had proper fire positions, and that there was sufficient ammunition. The next thing to do was to find some hand grenades. My sergeant found a box of the jam-tin variety with which I thought I might get my own back on the bearded Hun who mounted guard over the barricade.

On one of the German dead I was lucky enough to find a water bottle full of the most excellent ice cold coffee. What nectar that drink seemed. I didn't stop to think what mouth had last drunk out of that neat little aluminium bottle. It was at this period that I made the biggest blunder of any. I hurled two bombs in quick succession over the barricade. There seemed to be some confusion behind those sandbags in front of me and my men were vastly pleased. It was not long, however, before we got a full dose of those horrid little black grenades that the Germans fling so accurately. For the next half hour or so we had a great duel. Many of my men were unfortunately hit. One can only hope that our jam tins did some corresponding damage on the other side. An officer of the Dorsetshire Regiment had his head blown off just as he was handing me a new box of grenades. I felt very upset as I felt that somehow I was to blame for having urgently demanded more grenades.

After an hour or so, there was the inevitable lull. Both sides were getting tired. By this time it was growing dusk. No one was looking forward to the night. Those Germans were horribly close and greatly out-numbered us. Besides, nobody knew quite how many of the enemy there were behind, and what possibilities there were of our being surrounded. I had sent various orderlies to report on our position. Most of them, I learnt afterwards had been hit on the way. We were told to hold on where we were, if possible. We were then having rather heavy cross fire from the German machine guns. They seemed to know exactly where their men ended and ours began.

As it grew dark there was an ominous lull in the firing that had been so continuous all day. We expected that a large number of Huns might at any time leap over the barricade and engage us in a hand-to-hand fight. Possibly they might hold us on the left, or barricade side, while another party might come up the communication trench in the rear and attack our other flank. By that time I only had about twenty men in the trench, except for one or two more or less useless men who had been partially gassed earlier on in the day. One or two men were sent as sentries down the communication trench that ran direct to the rear from the right of my platoon.

About 8-30, the whole hill was brilliantly lit up by thousands of star shells that were all starting from one point, and this sort of Crystal Palace Show was accompanied by a most extraordinary crackle. Seldom have I seen such fireworks. Our rifle fire or shell fire must have set light to a large store of German star shells. The effect was wonderful and weirdly strange considering the surroundings. During the whole of that memorable night there were not many moments of complete darkness. About nine o'clock our artillery started with renewed vigour. They were pounding the German trenches on our front and left front. The H.E. was well mixed with shrapnel that added its glaring flashes to the other various lights of the night. There was going to be a counter-attack. We wondered what the Regiment would be and where they would start from. We were not left long in doubt. Soon a tall captain in the K.O.S.B. appeared closely followed by what afterwards appeared to be two companies. He told me they were to attack the trenches in front of us and were going to start from my trench at 10 p.m.

At the allotted time, they climbed over the parapet. The order was to go half right. They were met with a storm of rifle and machine gun fire from the hill. Our artillery had not yet stopped and soon their's started. The poor Scots were simply blown back with lead. They started again and went half left. Their wounded were pouring into my trenches. The sounds were terrible, men shrieking, the fierce crackle of machine gun fire, and the cruel shriek of the shrapnel. This was battle. When the next volley of star lights went up there were noticeably more bodies lying out in No Man's Land. Wounded and belated Jocks were still returning, some helping other wounded back or bringing in the body of some comrade. These shattered remains of a fine regiment all found their way back to my already overcrowded trench and its continuation to the right.

About half an hour later the rifle fire to our rear seemed if anything to increase. After a bit, on looking round, we saw a straggling line of dim figures with bright bayonets looming out of the darkness, and coming towards us. Who could they be? When they were nearly on us we noticed the English service caps. I heard an English officer shout " now boys, in at 'em." And they were soon in on us. We worked miracles in the next second or two to make ourselves recognised as friends. It still puzzles me why there was not more damage done.

This was a new mass of overstrained and intensely excited men to cater for. My trench was an absolute inferno. More wounded poured in and most of our field dressings had been given to the Jocks. The uppermost thought in my mind was what a horrible mass to disentangle in all this fearsome noise. The Germans on our left meanwhile were vastly amused. We heard them laughing and shouting. I was quite afraid of an attack at that moment as we could not have put up much of a fight. I had been able to discover no Jock officers and the only officer of the last regiment to arrive was a rather bewildered second lieutenant who had only been up at the front for three days. We divided out the line between us and prepared for the worst, it was not a bright outlook.

Shortly after this, my companion received word that he was to withdraw what remained of his detachment. That cleared the trench a bit. Then I learnt that the Dorsetshire Regiment had retired to rest and that the Jocks had to hold their line. That thinned us out a bit and soon we were more or less comfortable again. It was an anxious night and everybody prayed for dawn as they had never prayed before. In daylight we could at least see what was coming, and there is something very comforting about daylight after the strange artificial lights of the night.

We all felt rather bedraggled the next morning and as we had had nothing to eat for over twenty-four hours, we began to search for food. It's extraordinary what food there is to be found in an average trench, if one only looks for it. Our search revealed some stale bread, and a good many tins of bully beef. This we shared and felt a slight alleviation of our hunger. I then crept into a dug-out down the communication trench for a few minutes snooze, but was soon aroused by a Jock captain who wanted to speak to me. He told me amongst other interesting things that Brigade H.Q. wanted to know if I could blow up the barricade with gun-cotton. I told him I would see if it were possible.

I crept over our own barricade keeping very close to the front parapet. On looking for a second round the corner of a sandbag, I saw for a moment a German head and a rifle at a loophole. They had loopholed their barricade and had made it almost impossible to approach. I withdrew my head and just escaped a bullet. I then rolled back over the barricade with incredible speed and sent a report to the Brigade stating what I had seen and how, in my opinion, it was impossible to destroy the obstruction with gun-cotton.

In comparison to the previous night that morning passed almost uneventfully. My trusty servant at one o'clock came and announced that dinner was served. He was a merry fellow and I went to see what he had produced. He had cut and buttered me some almost clean bread and had opened a tin of beef. It promised to be a good meal, but towards the end, the smell of the corpses was so great that I determined to see if we could not remove them. I was standing on one grey-jacketted fellow and superintending the removal of another when I was conscious of a terrific blow. I went down like a log and was next aware of a loose, horrid and disconnected feeling about the lower part of my face. I was bleeding like a fountain and my mouth seemed full of obstacles. I tried to spit them out and found they were teeth. I remember distinctly some fellow saying in an agonised whisper, " He's had his false teeth knocked out." This annoyed me horribly, as I had always been rather proud of my teeth. My servant then more kind-heartedly than wisely poured the remainder of his water-bottle into my mouth. The water, it afterwards transpired, had been drawn from the moat round Ypres, this at best was nothing more than the town sewer, and as shells had been falling in it like hail for a fortnight, the purity of the water that I received in my wound could not have been very great.

My servant then applied all the bandages and field dressings he could find. I watched his horrified face with interest and noticed that everybody that saw me looked strangely at me. I then stumbled down the trench. I heard the shout everywhere, " Make way, it's an officer." I was at the time in my shirt sleeves with no hat and covered in blood. Some of the Jocks recognised me and said " Its that Cheshire officer that's got hit." I heard everything, I noticed everything, especially the looks on people's faces.

It was not long before I arrived in a very shaky condition at a big dug-out that was serving as a dressing station. The roof was low and I had to kneel. Even the doctor looked horrified when he took off the bandages, and quickly bandaged me up again, giving me some morphia. I sat against the wall of the dug-out and found that the man lying at my feet had been hit in the arm and kicked me violently in his writhings.

At last they injected me with more morphia and I began to feel easier and happy.

At one time I thought I should not live as I was bleeding so furiously. I thought it a pity that one more so young should have to go. I then thought that if I did recover I should be so disfigured that no lady would ever look at me again, and this depressed me horribly. I remember writing my fears on a bit of paper and showing them to the C.O., who came to see me. He smiled and was very kind.

I was then asked if I could walk and said I thought I could. Two of the Company stretcher-bearers helped me along, I had one arm round each of their necks. My servant brought up the rear with my pack and odd things. We had the best part of a mile and a half to cover along the railway line which was still being shelled. I did not mind that now a bit. I was not for stopping now I had once started. I had to have a good many halts on the way. One of the stretcher-bearers, an old friend of mine, kept consoling me that I was safe on the way to Blighty, and it would be a long time before I ever saw Belgium again. He meant well but I was not duly impressed with his arguments.

When the farm was finally reached I had to lie on some straw for two hours before an ambulance came. It was then getting dark. The journey in that shaking ambulance was too awful and seemed interminable. At last the car slowed down and finally stopped.

After lying out on a stretcher in the garden, waiting my turn to be examined, they took me into a crowded room, placed me on a table, and redressed me and gave me an anti-tetanus injection.

I was then returned to the stretcher in the garden.

My faithful servant was as tender and solicitous as any nurse but he could not do much. I lay out there for most of the night, but was at last put into another ambulance which was more of a torture than the first, as my face was growing stiff.

It was not till next morning, Friday, May 7th, that I reached Bailleul and a bed. From that time till I reached England I was treated with every care and possible attention, and was, in spite of all, deeply grateful once more to have reached civilisation.

   . . . .

Arthur Greg was killed with the R.F.C. in 1917.

FREZENBERG. 8th to 13th May, 1915.

Map p. 54

The name Frezenberg stands for the 2nd Battalion's chief share in the Second Battle of Ypres. Supreme issues were at stake, comparable only with those at other great crises of the War, such as the Marne in 1914 and Bapaume in 1918. Behind our gassed and shattered lines, had the Germans only known, lay nothing to prevent their capturing the Channel Ports.

The sector of the Front held by the 28th Division was North of the Menin Road, from Frezenberg to Mouse Trap Farm. The line to be held was nothing more effective than narrow trenches three feet deep, hastily constructed, with little wire, no communication trenches, and little or no overhead cover. It was not a line in which to meet a heavy attack, yet the Allied plan required it to be held, because the success of the French and First Army attack further South would be seriously prejudiced if the Salient were to require reinforcement.

In continuation of their plan to break through to the Channel Ports which the Germans had begun at St. Julien, they attacked, on the 8th May, the 27th and 28th Divisions astride the Menin and Frezenberg roads with three Corps, two of which attacked the 28th Division. The attack was supported by as heavy a bombardment of shell and gas as weapons and technique of that period could produce. Our men were protected against the effects of gas by an issue to each Battalion of 200 cloth bands to be worn across the mouth !

At day-break, a pitiless hail of destruction from a far larger number of guns than our artillery could hope to silence, from North, North-East and South-East began, and continued till the trenches and troops were battered out of shape and sense. Then the German Infantry came on. They were met by the shell-racked survivors with the greatest bravery, but with such numbers the Germans could not be denied.

The 2nd Battalion, to the command of which Major A. B. Stone had succeeded on the 6th, had two Companies in the front line and two in support, with Head Quarters in between. The Suffolks were on our right and the Monmouth on our left. The 83rd Brigade on the right of the 84th were attacked at 8-30 a.m. and again at 9-0. Their front was exposed to enfilade as well as to frontal fire, but it was only at the third attack at 10 a.m. that their front gave way.

Continual attempts of the Germans, supported by artillery, on the front of the 84th Brigade were held up by the Battalions of the Brigade. The gap left by the 83rd Brigade made it clear that the 84th Brigade was in a very critical position.

Reinforcements sent forward were mowed down by shell fire before they could reach their destination.

About 1 o'clock, our men and the Suffolks were over-run and a similar fate befell the Monmouth some time later. The left Battalion, the Northumberland Fusiliers, held on gallantly till dark. When they were about to withdraw they were wiped out by a sudden bombardment followed by attack from all sides, and the Battalion went down in a blaze of glory in the most stubborn and gallant hand-to-hand fighting.

Three Companies of the 2nd Battalion were wiped out, but the fourth fought on and preserved a semblance of order as it withdrew. The losses were very severe.

Major A. B. Stone was killed. His loss was one which the Regiment could ill afford. His cheerfulness in all circumstances, his humour, his devotion to his subordinates and his splendid courage made him one of the best loved men we have ever had. His death, coming so soon after that of his life-long friend and comrade Colonel A. de C. Scott, who, as already told, was killed at Hill 60 with the 1st Battalion, made our loss doubly severe.

Captain C. W. Hayes-Newington, Lieut. H. M. Chaplin and 2nd/Lieut. P. C. Nosworthy and 2nd/Lieut. S. F. Smith were also killed. Three other officers and 200 men were wounded and 182 were missing including R.S.M. Want.

The Battalion was brought out of action by 2nd/Lieut. T. Roberts, he and 2nd/Lieut. T. S. Newell being the only surviving officers. Only 32 men drew rations on this evening.

D

The fighting was very severe and at close quarters. Owing to the heavy casualties, no satisfactory account of what happened can be obtained. The only deed of heroism which has been recorded is the bravery of 2nd/Lieut. Moorshead. As Signal Officer he maintained communication with Brigade Head Quarters in the terrible circumstances already described, laying and maintaining his lines under heavy shelling. He was wounded while crawling forward to watch the counter-attack of the Connaught Rangers. This and other counter-attacks intended to regain our lost line, did not succeed in getting further forward than Verlorenhoek.

At the end of the Battle, though the 28th Division had lost its positions, a line was held across the gap behind the Verlorenhoek Ridge by Wieltje to Mouse Trap Farm.

The remnants of the Battalion were temporarily placed under command of Colonel T. O. Marden, of the Welch Regiment, a former 22nd officer, who had left us on promotion in 1898.

Later, they formed part of a composite Battalion with what was left of the Northumberland Fusiliers, the Suffolk and Monmouthshire Regiments under Major Toke of the Welch.

The following account of Frezenberg is from " From Private to Major " by Major J. Hawke who was a Corporal in the 2nd Battalion at Frezenberg.

" One sunny afternoon, the Battalion moved out of St. Jean . . . . In front, the country looked as quiet as Lincolnshire. Then someone from the horse lines galloped up . . . ' The Germans are using gas. . . . Bullets are falling in St. Jean. The Canadians are rushing up. They're splendid.'

At a leisurely pace, the Battalion went forward to a field at Frezenberg. From the left, a thin yellow cloud drifted towards us. ' Gas,' said an officer, ' it won't hurt—too dispersed.' One or two said it made their eyes smart ; most of the Company sniffed hard, just to see what it was like. . . .

At places in the front line, we were only twenty paces from the enemy. . . . Five men of Kitchener's Army shared a dug-out with me. They were all elderly men who had left good homes and safe jobs to fight for their King and Country. They had twenty-three children between them. . . . It must have been irksome for them to be ordered around by a little whipper-snapper like me. Their steadiness and coolness put me to shame many a time. Not one survived this tour of Ypres. . . .

Things were rather chaotic after the fall of the Frezenberg position. At one time, a number of Germans were calmly walking along the road to Ypres and they had not much more than a mile to go—just as though they were on manœuvres.

Unfortunately for them, . . . a number of our machine guns . . . did some accurate shooting at two thousand yards. We paid for this next day. . . . For two hours we crouched at the bottom of the trench, pressed against the side. Hot metal flew at all angles. Dug-outs went sailing into the air. The ground trembled. Trenches tumbled in. . .

When night fell, there were no companies or platoons—merely a number of men in those trenches, not more than seventy of the Battalion."

*   *   *   *

The 5th Battalion were in trenches near the Comines Canal, in the area of this battle.

BELLEWAERDE.   24th and 25th May.

Map p. 54

Both 1st and 2nd Battalions gained this honour.

At dawn on the 24th May, the 85th Brigade was gassed and turned out of its trenches. The 2nd Battalion, under Capt. S. R. Barton, was, in consequence, ordered at 5-45 a.m. to the General Head Quarters line which crossed the Menin Road at Hell Fire Corner and ran North to Potijze. They reached a point East of Vlamertinghe at 9-25 and began to prepare their mid-day meal. Unfortunately, they were ordered forward before they could eat it. All the Battalions of the 84th Brigade were very weak, having been only partially made up to strength with drafts of young officers and raw men after the terrible day of Frezenberg. What men they had were immature, inexperienced and untrained, and the officers were in much the same state. There were very few N.C.Os. All ranks lacked training and discipline.

They moved forward, dinnerless, at noon, across country south of the Roulers Railway.

In the front line, were the Northumberland Fusiliers and the 2nd Battalion, our left being on the Railway, the Fusiliers directed on Wittepoort.

The actual attack started at 5 p.m. There had been no chance of cooking food and the men were all tired and famished, besides being without experience. Direction and cohesion were soon lost, but a few men got within 200 yards of the German line and dug themselves in. In the meantime, the 80th Brigade had come forward in support and overshot the G.H.Q. line, where they had been ordered to " rendez-vous." A new plan was made in which two Battalions of the 80th Brigade were to co-operate with what was left of the 84th. The Plan never had any chance of success, as it could not be communicated to the troops (who were —a Brigade diary admits—completely exhausted), and by now the Northumberland Fusiliers had been completely wiped out. The Battalions of the 80th Brigade were driven back and retired behind the line of the 84th Brigade, which hung on till it was relieved on the night of the 25th/26th. Six officers were killed, Captain C. R. Andrews, Lieuts. J. E. Gresson, T. Roberts, H. H. Nicholson, W. H. M. W. Dawson and R. M. McGregor. Our C.O., Captain Barton, and nine other officers were wounded and 279 men casualties.

This counter-attack may appear futile and unnecessary, but it is not possible to say what might have happened had the attempt not been made. The Official History says " in the evening of the 24th May the German Fourth Army issued orders that operations should be stopped. The German Battalions were quite worn out and had suffered nearly as many casualties as the British."

*   *   *   *

The 1st Battalion, holding a line in front of Zillebeke from Hill 60 to the North, carried out " demonstrations " to support an attack in the Hooge area. Enemy shelling was heavy and German retaliation with minenwerfer was worse.

Bellewaerde closed the Second Battle of Ypres.

*   *   *   *

An incident worth chronicling was the meeting of two brothers at this period in the trenches.

Towards the end of April, Captain Nares' Company had been in reserve in the " Tuileries " and then relieved Captain Woodyer's Company, our right front line company. After the relief was complete and they were cementing the relief in the usual manner, Woodyer remarked to Major Nares " By the way, your brother is in the next trench and wants to see you." When time permitted, Nares went along to see the Company of the East Surreys on the right. He saw his brother and they arranged to meet for tea at his dug-out on the following day. But there was no tea for anyone next day. After a hurricane bombardment, the Germans attacked Hill 60 on the Sector held by the East Surreys. The bombardment extended over the whole of our Company Sector and we also were expecting attack. After the East Surreys had repulsed the attack and things had quietened down after dark, Nares went along to see how his brother had fared. He found out where his dug-out had been after considerable difficulty, but his Company had been relieved as they had had such heavy casualties that evening. He ascertained, however, much to his relief, that his brother was one of the few officers of his Battalion who had survived that day. Only five officers out of 25 who went up to the line with the East Surreys came out unhurt 36 hours later.

*   *   *   *

On 30th June, the 1st Battalion had been 41 days in the trenches. How this was regarded can be judged from a laconic remark in the 1st

Battalion War Diary. " News of relief received with general incredulity
by the men, who have to-day completed their 41st consecutive day in
the trenches, and have come to look upon them as their normal residence."

During the whole of this tour, the Battalion had three companies
in the front line and support trenches, and one in reserve in the
" Tuileries," just outside Zillebeke. The reserve company used to do
four days there and then relieve the forward companies in turn, so that
each company did 12 days up and 4 in reserve. Although the line was
comparatively quiet during this long tour, there were frequent " busy "
periods, and every morning and evening, the Germans used to carry out
a hate with " Minnies " which did a lot of damage to our trenches and
caused many casualties. The moral effect of their terrific detonations,
after 40 days of it, was considerable. Snipers were also very active
during the whole of the time and caused many casualties, but, in this
department, we gave as good as we received. The trenches were very
open and innocent of traverses and parados. Often, Captain Busfeild's
coolness in sitting in a breach made by a Minnie, smoking his pipe, had a
very steadying effect on the men while they hastily repaired the damage.

The weather throughout the tour was, luckily, perfect. It was during
this tour that the first Zeppelin reached England, and returned over our
heads early one morning.

On the 5th July, the 1st Battalion was complimented by Sir Charles
Fergusson on the state of the trenches handed over to the 138th Brigade.

Some idea of life in the trenches in these days can be gathered from
the following two extracts from the War Diary. What is here described
went on daily for weeks at a time, and it is not surprising that mention
of such occurrences was gradually dropped.

" At 7-30 a.m., a large portion of the parapet of 47 trench was blown
in, destroying the telephone dugout and causing several casualties, afterwards ascertained to be 6 killed, 6 wounded and 2 missing. Regimental
sappers spent the day repairing the damage, the work being completed
by nightfall."

" Heavy musketry fire heard to the N. at 1-30 a.m. At 5-30 a.m.
48 trench was hit by a " Minenwerfer." The top of the parapet was
blown down, the machine gun blown from its emplacement in the parapet
on to the parados, and 3 gunners were practically buried. They were
extricated unhurt and the parapet repaired. The machine gun was not
damaged and was removed to a new emplacement in one of the rifle pits.
All day a heavy bombardment was carried on by the enemy on our
trenches, and was particularly evident between 3 p.m. and 6 p.m., when
the approaches and surrounding country were also heavily shelled."

*   *   *   *

Three months' rest on a quiet front gave the 2nd Battalion the time and opportunity to recover from the shattering losses of April and May and to become a well organized unit before facing the last ordeal that they were to endure on the western front.

*   *   *   *

By this time, the old Army may be said to have gone. The men of the New Armies and Territorial Force now took up the struggle and the two, New and Old, never met.

An incident in the 1st Battalion in the Spring of 1915.

" Not long ago, when taking over our trenches, we found that the Mining Officer had, in our absence been indulging in an orgy of " blowing." The Mining Officer is a rabid enthusiast whose home is in a dark and inaccessible cave. Here, surrounded by his clay-covered minions, he concocts his nefarious schemes for blowing up our parapets, and blocking our trenches with sandbags. Incidentally he also wages underground warfare against the Germans. He occasionally emerges, but only to dive anew into one of his numerous burrows. He is rarely visible except when arrested as a German spy, or, when appearing to announce the progress of some evil deed of his own or of the enemy's.

On this occasion, he certainly had not been idle ; the smiling field had been changed into a gaping chasm, the valley had become a miniature mountain range. Our parapets were flat. He consoled us, however, by assuring us that the Germans had been circumvented.

The German may have been baffled underground, but the new hill gave him an opportunity of stepping round to our trenches and dropping a few hand grenades into them. The damage was not great, but the indignity of the thing rankled, our self-respect was shattered ! That the German should get the better of us was not to be thought of, something must be done and done quickly.

Then Sycamore planned his sap.

Soon after dark, 40 men were hurried up, and they dug as men will dig when every inch of depth makes them safer from bullets, and when the German is less than a hundred yards away.

A cunning trench soon wound its sinuous way round our young Vesuvius, ending in a little pocket, invisible from the front, but which gave a view into the crater below.

In this pocket two men sat waiting all night. A second and yet a third night they waited, Sycamore hanging around, watching over his sap like a mother over her infant.

The company shared in the enthusiasm, a retaliatory bombing attack on the Germans, eliciting only the mildest interest.

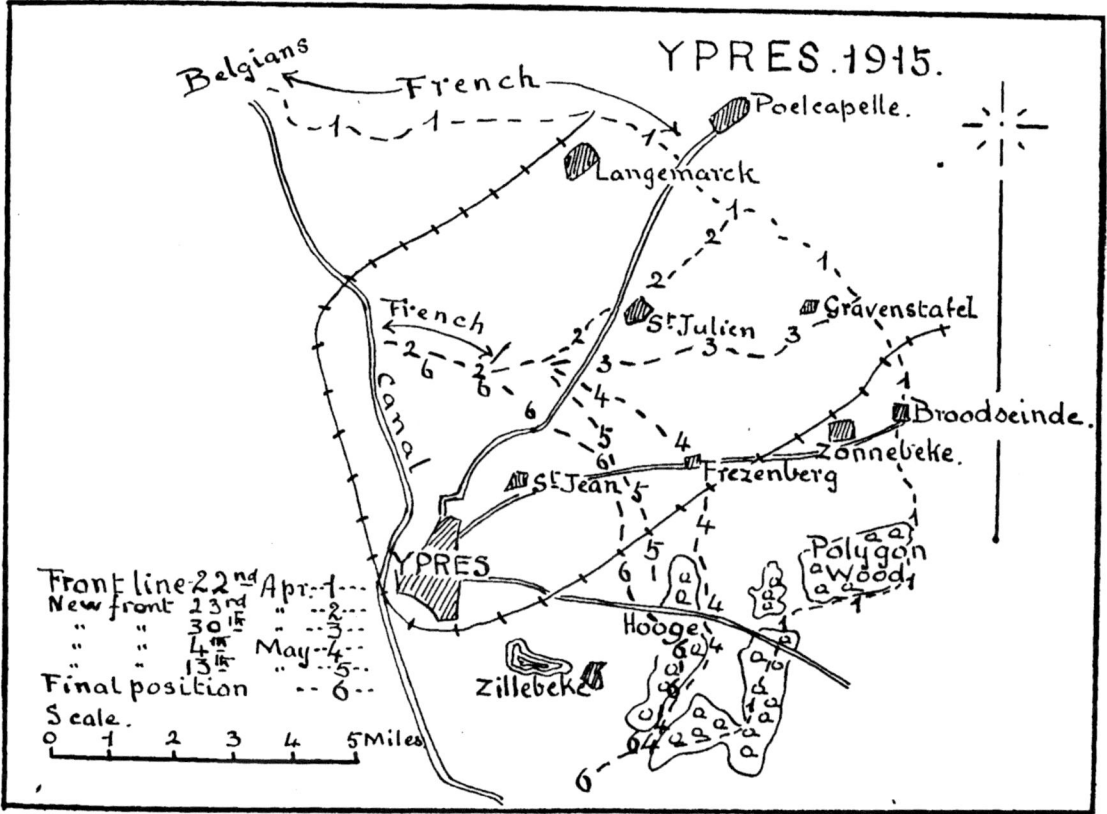

YPRES. 1915.

Belgians
French
Poelcapelle.
Langemarck
French
St Julien
Gravenstafel
Broodseinde.
Zonnebeke.
St Jean
Frezenberg
Canal
Polygon Wood
YPRES
Hooge
Zillebeke

Front line 22nd Apr. ---1---
New front 23rd --- ---2---
  "   "   30th --- ---3---
  "   "   4th May ---4---
  "   "   13th --- ---5---
Final position --- 6 --
Scale.
0   1   2   3   4   5 Miles

opp. 54

At last the expected happened. The watchers at the end of the sap saw below them a number of crawling figures intent on repeating their performance of a few nights before.

Then we let them have it ! Bomb after bomb was thrown into the crater, making it look like a volcano in active eruption. The patrol was well nigh annihilated, the surveyors beating a hasty retreat, so we were left in peace to the end of our turn in the trenches, and we had well paid back the German's previous efforts. Sycamore's Sap had restored our self-respect ! "

LOOS.

Map p. 57

This battle was intended to result in the capture of the German positions from Loos to the La Bassee Canal.

The British attack, opening with success at many points, was held up by the evening of the 25th September.

On the extreme left of the attack, immediately South of the La Bassée Canal, the 2nd Division had had the misfortune, owing to a change of wind, to be overwhelmed by their own gas, and their attack failed completely. On their right, however, the 9th Division had achieved a remarkable success. From a slag heap, known as the Dump, in rear of the German front line, the enemy had observation over the whole of the Rutoire plain which lay between the British front line and Vermelles. To protect the Dump, the Germans had constructed a projecting work, strongly mined, known to us as the Hohenzollern Redoubt, a map of of which is in the text.

Early on the 25th, the 26th Brigade of the 9th Division had carried the Redoubt and gone forward as far as Haisnes, 1,200 yards further East. Owing to their exposed flanks, and in spite of reinforcement, these advanced troops were driven in.

The 84th Brigade, in which was the 2nd Battalion, meanwhile was moving forward, by bus and march route, to a position in reserve at Béthune. Heavy fighting continued for the recovery of the Dump during the 26th and 27th. On the 28th, an attack at dawn was driven back and in the afternoon the 85th Brigade made another attempt with no better success. At nightfall, the British front line was still in the Hohenzollern, but the enemy had footings in Big and Little Willie.

The close and desperate fighting on this day and on those which were to follow can be taken as an outstanding example of trench warfare, and for which the Germans were better prepared than we were. They had more and better bombs and many more machine guns. The close hand-to-hand fighting, the congestion in the shallow trenches, the break-down in the means for removing wounded, made it impossible to follow the progress of the battle or to ascertain the local situation. Often orders were issued by Divisional H.Q. for a position to be captured which had been won and, at such heavy sacrifice, that it had been lost again before the orders arrived !

Fighting continued on the 29th, and under constant bomb attacks, the 85th Brigade held fast. Through the incessant bombardments, the trenches had by now become unrecognizable.

The 84th Brigade was ordered into the line on the night 30th September/1st October in relief of the 83rd Brigade. The Northumberland Fusiliers and the 2nd Battalion were in the front line in the Southern portion of the Hohenzollern Redoubt, and adjoining trenches. The 2nd Battalion was to occupy the west face. No opportunity was given to reconnoitre the trenches or even the way up to them. The communication trenches were very narrow and deep and most complicated for newcomers.

When the 84th Brigade was trying to move in, three disorganized brigades were using all available means of leaving the front line, and Central Alley, which had been allotted to the Fusiliers and ourselves, was a funnel into which poured to the rear scores of wounded and leaderless men from many units.

The loss of the Brigadier and Brigade Major of the 85th Brigade at the outset of a difficult and confusing situation handicapped the troops very seriously. Throughout the operation, the great difficulty was the movement of troops along the trenches. Parties arriving at the wrong places, and having to retrace their footsteps, found the places allotted to them occupied by other troops. This hampered and delayed all preparations for offensive movements. To keep the troops supplied with water, bombs and food, required the ceaseless employment of large fatigue parties. These parties took many hours to come and go and so the troops in reserve got little rest.

On this day, the 2nd Battalion had received its first issue of Lewis guns, in the use of which Lieut. Cole and four men had had some elementary instruction. The guns were taken into the line. Trenches, so full of dead, and so knocked about that they averaged only 18 inches in depth, were taken over from the Royal Fusiliers. Part of this line was a piece of the German second line, about 300 yards long and terminated at each end by a barricade, on the other side of which were Germans. The trenches were taken over under a fairly stiff barrage of shelling from guns, minen werfer and hand grenades. Many men had been lost through machine gun fire on the way up.

In these circumstances, it is not surprising to learn that the Battalion had hardly finished taking over, about 9-30 a.m. on the 1st, when it was found that the Germans were occupying a portion of the line allotted to the Northumberland Fusiliers on our right, near the point of junction of the Hohenzollern Redoubt and Big Willie. When this report reached Divisional H.Q., howitzers were turned on to the point and on all communication trenches leading to it from the German side. The Northumberland Fusiliers attacked, but in spite of every effort, did not succeed in turning the Germans out. Bombing continued all day, and towards evening our men began to establish some superiority.

On the night of the 1st, an attack was ordered, on the " Chord " by us, and on Little Willie, on our left, by the Welch. At first, it was thought that we had captured the Chord, but daylight showed that we had not. The fact is that the Chord was unrecognizable even by day and still more so by night among the maze of trenches and ditches with which this area was covered. Although Major Roddy had reported the state of affairs and advised making no further attacks, there is no doubt that Brigade

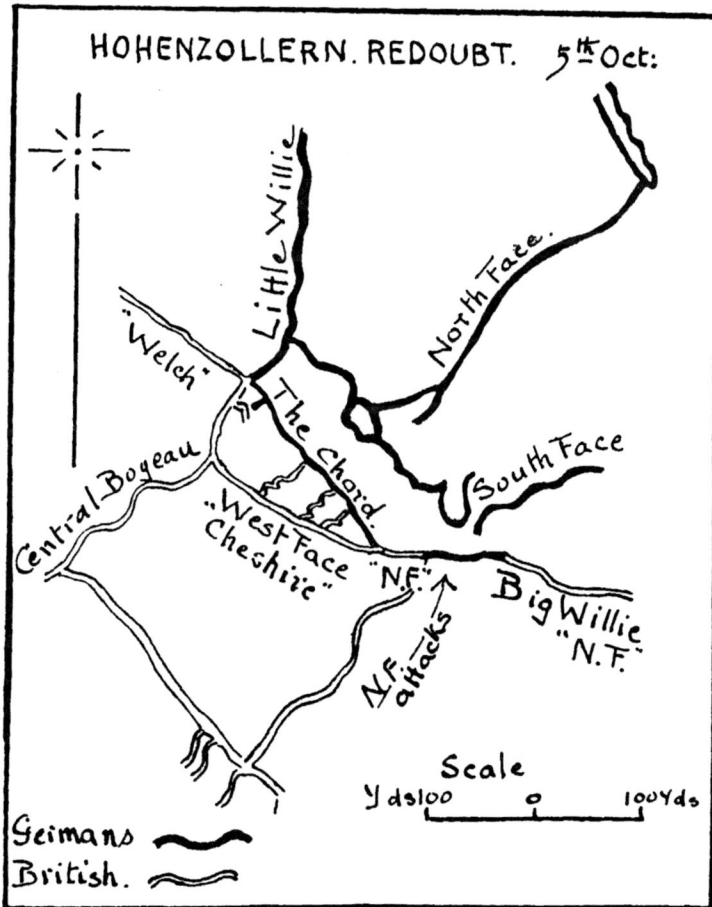

and superior head-quarters entirely failed to realize the conditions in and around the Redoubt, and ordered attack after attack in a way that can only be described as ruthless and senseless. The troops were bombed all day, and although there were officers and men in this maze of trenches, they were completely disorganized, and mixed, mainly owing to the heavy loss in officers and senior non-commissioned officers. It was beyond the power of human endeavour to collect and sort them out for an organized attack. However, all through the 2nd, in the most gallant way, our men, Northumberland Fusiliers and Welch delivered individual bayonet and bomb attacks in their efforts to dislodge the Germans and to comply with orders.

One of the many plucky deeds performed during this fighting was the way Lieut. Cole, Sergeant Rimington and his section served their Lewis gun. During an enemy attack, the gun, fouled with mud, jammed, and the section were all killed, Lieut. Cole persisted in his efforts to clear the gun, but was himself, too, finally killed.

After nightfall, the Suffolk Regiment made an attack on Little Willie, but was heavily repulsed. The only thanks they received was a demand to rally and attack again. This was beyond human endurance and was not done.

On 3rd October, the Germans attacked all along the line of the 84th Brigade, but were repulsed except on the left where they gained a footing. Our men put up a wonderful resistance. All our bombers were killed. A bayonet counter-attack, led by Major Roddy, was met with a hail of bombs and driven back to the British front line. Brigade H.Q. ordered fresh attacks but this was quite out of the question, having in view the exhaustion of the individuals and the congestion in the trenches. It was quite clear to anyone who visited the front line that further attacks were not feasible, even by fresh troops, until the congestion of wounded and dead had been overcome. Nevertheless, another attack was ordered, and gallantly carried out by the East Yorkshire Regiment and one company of the K.O.Y.L.I. early on the 4th. This attack, too, failed, at great loss of life, and confirmed the judgment of Major Roddy which he had given in a report to Brigade H.Q. on the evening of the 1st.

Later in the morning, the Germans swung in a surprise attack on the left of the 84th Brigade, drove through the Welch, and swept down on our men in their trenches. Our war diary says " The enemy broke through " part of the trench occupied by the Welch on our left flank and advanced " with great rapidity, throwing hundreds of bombs, their bombers being " supported by machine guns and rifle men. The attack came as a " complete surprise."

Our line was driven back till the Germans were held up by " C " Company of the Northumberland Fusiliers at their block at the end of Big Willie.

On the night of the 5th/6th October, the Brigade was relieved by the 2nd (Guards) Brigade. The relief took 13 hours of daylight, although ample time was given for reconnaissance by officers, the trenches cleared of all obstacles to movement, and all arrangements most carefully organized. This shows, in some measure, the impossibility of the demands made on men of the 28th Division during the previous five days.

Our casualties were very heavy. Six officers, the Adjutant Major A. Rowland Hill, Captain F. L. Lloyd, Lieuts. S. Cole, D. C. B. Brien, W. E. Hartley and M. McGregor, and 43 men were killed ; 7 officers and 153 men wounded, and two officers and 166 men missing, of whom none were ever recovered.

The survivors had all but reached the limit of human endurance. This phrase is often used, but it is, unfortunately, justified. The unpreparedness of England in 1914 threw on a handful of her willing servants a burden which demanded the most extreme exertions of which the human frame is capable. Their bodies were sustained by their spirit which rose superior to all trials and dangers.

* * * *

In this battle, the first of our New Army Battalions made their appearance under fire, the 9th Battalion in the 58th Brigade of the 19th Division and the 11th Battalion in the 75th Brigade of the 25th Division.

The 58th Brigade, whose Brigade Major was Major H. S. Adair of The Regiment, attacked on 25th September against Rue D'ouvert, North of Givenchy and reinforced the attack of the 9th Welch Regiment, but was held up by uncut wire and machine gun fire.

Captain Symons particularly distinguished himself in bringing in wounded from the wire during the night and three men won the D.C.M.

* * * *

The 11th Battalion held the line near Ploegsteert Wood.

* * * *

The 2nd Battalion now left France and went to Salonika.

* * * *

R. D. F. Oldman, of The Norfolk Regiment, commanded the First Battalion from September '15 to July '16. He was succeeded by W. H. G. Baker, an Indian Cavalryman, who remained with us till July '17.

* * * *

The 5th Battalion are made Pioneers.

In consequence of earning a high reputation as diggers and as constructors of field works, the 5th Battalion was appointed Pioneer Battalion to the 56th (London) Division, in course of formation. The following order was issued by the Brigadier :—" In saying farewell to the 5th Battalion Cheshire Regiment, which is leaving the 14th Brigade and being formed into a Pioneer Battalion, the Brigadier places on record his very high appreciation of the excellent work of the Battalion since it joined the Brigade. The conduct of the 5th Cheshires both in the field and in billets has been exemplary, and the fact that they have been selected for formation into a Pioneer Battalion is proof of the excellence of their work."

A Pioneer Battalion has a dual rôle to play, namely, it must be capable of taking the part of Infantry of the Line as well as being capable of carrying out engineer duties, either by itself or in conjunction with the Royal Engineers. Its chief work is that of Field Engineering, and it is only in emergency that it is called upon to act as Infantry. The work carried out is almost entirely battle zone work, and its great object in all offensives is to help towards the successful exploitation of an attack, which largely depends upon the speed and skill with which communications (roads, bridges, tracks and tramways) are repaired or constructed. The movement of reserves, the advance of artillery, the supply of ammunition for the guns, the getting forward of supplies of food, water and ammunition to the infantry, as well as reliefs and the evacuation of the wounded are largely dependent upon the rapidity with which communications are restored and new tracks and routes constructed. Its object is not to " make " roads or communications in the ordinary sense of the word, but rather to make such means of progress temporarily passable as quickly as possible, leaving the subsequent permanent improvement to troops in rear. One of the most important duties in this connection is that of road reconnaissance, which demands speed and accuracy. It is vital to the successful organization of engineering operations and is one of the tasks which was frequently allotted to Pioneer officers.

These duties, especially trench construction, repair and wiring, were very arduous. Being in the battle zone, they had to be carried out in nearly every case at night. They involved long and trying marches up to the site of work and back, frequently under shell fire, as the approach areas were always the subject of the enemy's artillery attention in the evenings. Finding their way and setting out the work in pitch darkness, when the site was only described by a map reference, demanded a high standard of training and skill on the part of officers and non-commissioned officers.

The heavy loss in officers of the 5th Battalion shows how dangerous pioneer work was.

Officers, 1st Battalion, on the Somme, 1915.

Standing, left to right: Richardson, Gleed, Dr. Forsyth, Harding, Sproule,

Sitting: Baker, Clarke, Oldman, Patteson.

A First Battalion Raid.

Map p. 62

On the night of the 6th/7th of December, 1915, a party of the First Battalion carried out a raid south of Mametz, which was afterwards regarded as a model of its kind. It is not possible to describe the many small raids which took place, so this typical sample must answer for all.

The Battalion had recently done 42 continuous days in the front line at Ypres, and had suffered severely. Colonel R. D. F. Oldman, of the Norfolk Regiment who had just taken over command, ordered that a raid should be carried out to improve morale. The raiding party was led by Lieut. G. P. Harding, who was the Battalion bombing officer. It consisted of two other officers, Lieuts. Harper and Richardson and 50 men. Both these officers were very stout men in a tight corner. It was lucky for Harding that they volunteered to serve under him, as both were his seniors.

The section of German trenches to be attacked was chosen from air photographs and by personal reconnaissance. A convenient gap in the German wire, used by their patrols, was discovered at the end of a sap leading to the main trench. This sap is shown on the map. While the Battalion was out of the line, a plan of the German trenches was spit-locked out and the raid carefully rehearsed. Brigade and Divisional H.Q. tried to insist on artillery preparation, but Harding, backed by Oldman, refused this and secured instead that a " box barrage " should be put down behind the German lines, after the raid had begun, so as to prevent the arrival of German reserves.

On the night of December the 5th/6th, Harding did a final reconnaissance, made certain of the gap in the German wire and discovered an empty sniper's post at the end of the sap nearest our lines. Thus, everything possible was done to secure the success of the raid.

The raiding party was divided into three detachments ; an advanced party under Harding, a supporting party under Harper and a reserve party under Richardson. At 1-45 a.m. on the 7th, the advanced party left our parapet in single file and reached the sniper's post without being discovered, in spite of a Verey light sent up by the enemy. The men had been trained to keep still in such an event, and their steel helmets, which they were wearing for the first time, looked like lumps of mud.

The sniper's post was found to contain two men and was bombed. One of them got away and Harding pursued him into the German trenches. His men did not understand that they were to follow him immediately and waited by the gap. As he came back towards them, after being away for some time, he was taken for a German and two bombs were thrown at him ! Luckily, he was not hurt and led the whole party into the main trench marked " C " on the map, which was full of glue-like mud. Some of the men were posted as a " stop " at " D " and the rest turned to the left, killing two Germans at " E " and taking a prisoner at " F." Further on, three dug-outs were bombed and another " stop " placed at " G."

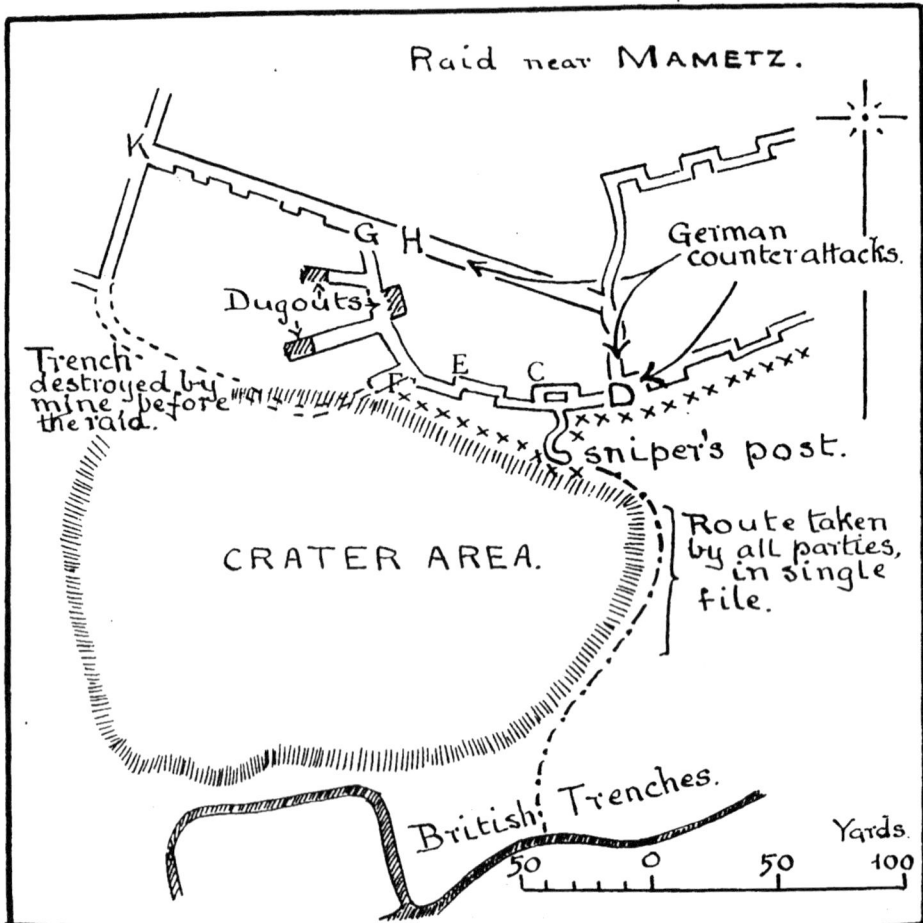

Raid near MAMETZ.

Meanwhile, the second party, under Harper, had arrived at the gap, reinforced the " stop " at " D " which was being hard pressed, and advanced with it to where a communication trench came in from the left. Harper then took over from Harding at " G " and bombed on to " K," leaving a stop at " H." Harding returned to look after the first stop.

"Ham Sandwich."   "R.M."   "Tube."

Men of the First Battalion. Somme, Winter 1915-16.

First Battalion.

Piccadilly Street, Longueval.   Somme, 1916.

By this time, grenades were running short and the Germans were thoroughly aroused.

As a prisoner had been obtained, Harding ordered a withdrawal. This was safely carried out, all being back in our lines by 3-5 a.m. The casualties were two officers very slightly wounded, one man severely wounded, who subsequently died, and five men slightly wounded. Ten Germans were definitely accounted for, as well as an unspecified number killed in the dug-outs and in the attacks on the " stops " at " D," " H " and " K."

On arrival at our trenches, Harding was met by Major Stone of The Norfolk Regiment with two officers and 50 men, all volunteers, who had come to take the places of our men, so that they could go back to rest billets, a very welcome and friendly act.

A feature of this raid was the excellence of the artillery co-operation. This was controlled by Colonel Oldman himself from the top of a ladder. The raid had a marked effect on the morale of the Battalion, so it was in every respect successful. All Commanders from the Army Commander (Allenby) downwards came next day to express their congratulations in person. Lieutenant Harding was awarded the Military Cross, the first awarded to The Regiment. Corporal Moore, Privates J. Keating and S. Bland were given the D.C.M. Curiously enough, Harding's bar to his M.C. was awarded in the final gazette.

Corporal Moore deserves a special word of praise on account of the first-rate example he always set of courage and cheerfulness. He was not detailed for this raid but managed to arrive before the end !

Among the N.C.Os. on the raid was Case, for so many years, after the war, Provost Sergeant of the 2nd Battalion.

THE BATTLES OF THE SOMME, 1916.

Map p. 96

The situation of the Allies in May, 1916, was such that it appeared that the offensive, which had already been decided upon in principle, could not be postponed beyond the end of June.

The object of this offensive was three-fold, to relieve the pressure of the Germans on Verdun, to stop further transfer of troops from the German Western front to act against the Russians, and to wear down the strength of the German troops.

Preparations were on an elaborate scale, and during the months which preceded the attack, the troops wore themselves out in digging assembly and communication trenches, cable trenches, and dug-outs; in collecting vast dumps of ammunition, of material and of warlike stores of all kinds; and in building miles of railways and trench tramways. All this time the " line " had to be held and, most important of all, tactical training of the new levies had to be carried on.

The Germans were holding the life-preserving high ground, which our lack of tactical skill had allowed them to seize all down the front from the sea to Switzerland. The vital advantage of " observation " which high ground confers had, in our pre-war training, been obscured by the mist of academical argument. So, in this, as in most other battles of the war, the tactical objective was the " observation " line. The ridge in dispute formed the watershed between the Somme on the west, and the rivers flowing towards Belgium on the east and north. The German position was on the plateau. Its forward edge overlooked the Ancre and the Somme. In order to secure the observation forward, it was necessary for us to secure the line Morval-Thiepval, whence the ground sloped down towards the north-east. The Germans had neglected no artifice to strengthen their hold on this valuable feature. The defences were arranged in three main systems, one only partially constructed, each consisting of several lines of well made trenches, well provided with bomb-proof shelters, and with dug-outs of a depth which gave complete protection from the heaviest shell. Differing from our conception of trench lines at that time, the German trenches resembled a net work rather than lines, the trenches being connected backwards and forwards with communication trenches, made like fire trenches, by means of which " switch " lines could be made to localize attacks which had penetrated the front line. As regards their dug-outs, we had imagined nothing to compare with these wonderful shelters 30 to 40 feet below ground. Here the Germans sat under the heaviest bombardment, ready at the first sign of slackening of fire to rush up the numerous exits and man whatever parapets or shell holes the bombardment had left of their original trench.

In and between the enemy trench systems, every topographical feature, every knoll, village or wood, had been converted into a fortress. Weapons were sited, not only to sweep approaches and their wire, but also their own trenches in case they should be lost.

To these difficulties must be added the Somme mud, which increased in stickiness as shelling and rain gradually churned up the whole area. In the late autumn, distances had to be reckoned in mud rather than in time.

The official account says " The material means available for attack in July, 1916, were notably inferior to those developed in the following spring. The number of guns and howitzers was, in particular, inadequate to cope with so deep and wide an objective presenting so many targets. Their fire was necessarily so dispersed that many strongpoints and machine gun posts were never touched. There was an entire lack of gas shell (which was to become the most potent factor in preparing an assault) except for the almost negligible quantity fired by our Allies' 75-m.m. batteries. In quality, too, both the artillery weapons and ammunition were indifferent. . . . Some of the ammunition was not only defective but dangerous."

Our troops passing over the battlefield saw for themselves the quantity of " dud " shells which our guns had fired. Nevertheless, the quantity of ammunition supplied was so enormous and had been so rapidly made as to make a proportion of bad stuff no great marvel. During 1916, the weekly output of Mills' bombs rose to 1,400,000, and during the year, 127,000 tons of high explosive and 50 million filled shell were provided.

While " the new guns and new ammunition were woefully defective," the tactical methods of the infantry proved faulty, and the very bravery of the troops caused unnecessary losses. It has been suggested that had our men been quicker across no-man's land, and less calm, less well-disciplined and less overloaded with stores, bombs and ammunition, the Germans might have been over-run before they could get their small-arms to work. This is what the man meant who said " The battle of Somme was lost in three minutes." Had we only realized it, it was a race for the parapet between the attackers from their trenches and the defenders from their dug-outs.

On 1st July, the German morale was quite unshaken, and whether the New Army could have competed with the trained German, had open warfare been the result of success on that day, is a matter for speculation.

The tactical results were disappointing. The XIII. Corps had taken Montauban. The XV. Corps had taken Mametz, and isolated Fricourt. The III. Corps had captured and held the German front line between Fricourt and La Boisselle. It was on this front that our 9th, 10th, 11th and 13th Battalions were employed. The X. Corps had captured the

E

nose of the Leipzig salient, but only held one other point in the German front line north of Thiepval. The VIII. Corps failed to hold its capture of the German trenches on the front Beaumont Hamel to Serre. On the extreme left, in the VII. Corps, the 56th Division, with which was our 5th Battalion, failed to maintain its successful penetration of the whole of the German first system.

The casualties were 57,470 on the first day, respresenting the fine flower of the best Army the nation could produce. The official account says " The losses sustained were not only heavy but irreplaceable." Fortunately, it was to turn out that the effects of the Somme were felt even more severely in the German Army than in the British. . . . The Somme battle destroyed most of what remained of the old German Army, so highly trained in peace time.

Although a " break-through " was not made, the wider, strategical results hoped for from the battle were achieved. After four months of relentless effort, Verdun was relieved, the transfer of German troops to the East was stopped, and most important of all, the German morale was broken and never recovered. After the Somme battles, the Germans never hoped for victory. On those bloody fields, the old German army was wiped out. The German nation was aghast at the fearful loss suffered by the troops.

Lastly, it must be considered what would have been the effect of the German thrust in 1918, if it had started from the German front line of 1916 instead of from the Hindenburg Line, to which the Germans retired in 1917 as a result of the Somme fighting.

The battle began on 24th June with a terrific artillery " preparation " of the German positions, from Montauban, where we joined the French, to Serre, and at Gommecourt. One thousand five hundred and thirteen guns plastered the enemy trenches, cut his wire, destroyed his earth works and, it was hoped, wrecked his morale. It seemed to onlookers of this week's bombardment, that there would be nothing left to attack. Patrols reported the enemy's wire well cut and his trenches unrecognizable. It was, consequently, anticipated that the advance would be almost unopposed, anyhow as far as the first trench system. But we had reckoned without those deep dug-outs and their high-couraged and well-disciplined occupants.

Only on the right, as has been said, where we had the help of the French heavy artillery, was the victory complete. Elsewhere, as the general advance began at 7-30 a.m. on 1st July, a storm of machine gun, shrapnel and rifle fire swept our ranks and barely half the men survived to reach the German front line, where they killed, wounded or captured every German in it. Here the advance stopped. The courage and steadiness of our New Army Battalions, whose baptism of fire this was, advancing under as terrible a fire as had ever been loosed in war, was beyond praise, and forced the admiration of the Germans.

In view of the meagre success of the first day's operations, it is doubtful if the attacks should have been carried on. Subsequent operations were planned on a less ambitious scale, but in the early days of July, were often undertaken with insufficient time for reconnaissance, for the issue of orders, for arrangements for covering fire, and even for the movement of the troops.

As the battle progressed, the weather got worse, and the mud became an obstacle to movement which few of the higher staff ever appreciated at its proper value.

The strain on the British was very great, although, in general, they maintained their ascendancy. Coming, as most did, into the Somme battle for their first experience of active modern warfare, officers and men entered on an ordeal which tried them to the uttermost. The capricious weather subjected all to extremes of heat and dust, rain and mud.

The infantry was often committed to bitter trench fighting, and nearly every advance above ground had to reckon with machine guns. Trenches were dug under persistent machine gun fire, and material was carried forward through heavy barrages.

ALBERT. 1st to 13th July, 1916.

Map p. 96

The first portion of the Somme is called Albert.

On the whole front of attack only one Cheshire company went over with the first wave at zero, 7-30 a.m., on 1st July. This was " A " Company of the 5th Battalion (Pioneers of the 56th London Division) attacking Gommécourt on the extreme northern flank of the British Army. The company was split up among the attacking Battalions of the 169th Brigade, with the task of constructing strong points.

This attack had a wide no-man's land to cross, no less than 800 yards. It would have been double this, but for a fine piece of work by the 5th Battalion some days earlier in making a new jumping-off trench.

" A " Company lost all its officers and 130 men.

" C " Company had a similar task with the 168th Brigade, but orders miscarried and the company remained inactive.

" B " Company, under 2/Lieut. J. D. Salmon, had the task of removing barricades and making trench bridges as the attack progressed, and carried out all its tasks. The total casualties were 2nd/Lieuts. F. A. Davies, P. B. Bass and G. S. Arthur, and 43 men killed. Five officers and 154 N.C.Os. and men were wounded.

* * * *

On 1st July, the 9th Battalion, 58th Bde. of 19th Division, was in reserve to the attack on La Boisselle.

After the comparative failure of the original attack, the 58th Brigade was ordered to attack at night, at 10-30 p.m. The C.O., Colonel R. B. Worgan, was sent for to Brigade H.Q. at 7 p.m., and the Battalion meantime was directed to the old British front line, from Locknagar to Inch Str. After getting his orders, Colonel Worgan hurried to the front, as there was no time to lose. But he found no trace of the Battalion. The trenches were not only very much knocked about, and full of dead and wounded, but were also being heavily shelled. Eventually, he found Captain Ward, with " D " Company, who explained that the Battalion had been delayed by finding the communication trenches full of wounded. Colonel Worgan told Ward to remain where he was and then went ahead to find the remainder. From wounded men he learnt that some 60 unwounded were holding the crater where a 600-lb. mine had been fired just before zero on the 1st July, and some 200 more, with two or three officers, holding a part of the German front line—all belonging to the 34th Division. Realizing the importance of holding on to our gains, he sent " D " Company to reinforce the crater. On further search, he found Lieut. C. F. King with portions of two companies near Bécourt Wood, and he sent him also to the German trenches alongside the crater. It was now 9-40 p.m., too late to carry out the original plan of attack, especially as the remainder of the Battalion was not to be found. So, after reporting personally at Brigade H.Q., Colonel Worgan returned to the front line and ordered consolidation to be put in hand at speed. The scene beggars description. Every shell-hole held a killed or wounded man. The whole area was littered with all the debris of a battle, with equipment, clothing, timber, stores, and dud shells.

At 2-30 a.m. on 2nd July, a telephone message from Brigade H.Q. ordered the C.O. to prepare to attack at once. Although the Battalion was very scattered and not easy to get hold of, Colonel Worgan had them assembled in the old German front line ready to attack, in 20 minutes. But the trenches were found to be too crowded and some men were withdrawn. It was not till 4 a.m. that definite orders came. The Battalion was to attack La Boisselle and to bomb through it, clearing all dug-outs. It was pitch dark, deathly quiet, no shelling, no machine-gun bursts, and no Verey-lights.

At 4-30 a.m., the Battalion went over the top under its own covering fire, and charged across the open for the German support trench. Some of the men used a Russian sap to get forward, till it was blocked with wounded. A deep and wide, and unexpected communication trench held up the advance. Bombers were sent right and left to clear a way forward. It was terribly difficult to keep direction in the dark and among this maze of trenches. Captain T. L. Jackson, killed later in the day, and Lieut.

C. F. King, wounded, were invaluable in leading and organizing the companies.

At 8-30 a.m. on 3rd, the advance had gone as far as the strength of the Battalion warranted, some 300 yards short of La Boisselle. Consolidation was put in hand, and only then did Lieut. C. F. King go to have his wounds dressed. At the end of the day, Lieut. E. Watts was the only officer left with the C.O.

At 2-45 a.m. on 4th, further orders were received to continue the attack in conjunction with the 57th Brigade on our left and the 9th Welch on our right. By 3-45 a.m., no touch had been gained with either flank, so our men started bombing along saps towards the Germans. Attack over the top, without troops on our flanks, and without covering fire would have been impossible. The ground was swept by German machine-gun fire, and four rows of uncut wire protected their front.

During this attack, a small party was detached to bomb a post, but the party was driven off and one man was left wounded and prisoner. He was taken down into a dug-out where there were twenty-five Germans. There he remained until a commotion overhead and the explosion of a bomb at the end of the dug-out told him that the British were advancing again. He was quick to act. He seized a bomb in one hand and a revolver in the other, and under this threat his captors more or less cheerfully consented to become the captives. His comrades found him in charge of twenty-five Germans when they started " mopping up."

These bombing parties, under Lieut. Watts, progressed till stronger parties of German bombers attacked and drove them back. At this point, Captain G. G. Symons, who had been kept back to replace casualties, came up and did splendid work in organizing and inspiriting the defence. The position was held till 3-30 a.m. on the 4th, when the Battalion was relieved. It was, certainly, cruel luck on the C.O. and his Battalion to be thus pitchforked into action in such impossible circumstances. We can be proud of the magnificent spirit and determination which they displayed.

*   *   *   *

The 25th Division had one Cheshire Battalion in each Brigade. The 7th Brigade had the 10th Battalion, the 74th the 13th, and the 75th the 11th.

This Division came into the Somme area on the 30th June/1st July. Its splendid Commander, General E. G. T. Bainbridge, had the mortification of seeing his Division used up and destroyed piecemeal unde-other Staffs. The result was that the first appearance of this magnificent fighting Division gave little indication of what it soon afterwards showed it could do.

*   *   *   *

The 11th Battalion was the first in action, attacking Thiepval from the direction of Authuille, under the 32nd Division. Without going into all the details, it is sufficient to say that the 75th Brigade was sent into action under as bad conditions as the 9th Battalion on the same day. Their Brigadier had taken the utmost pains to get all arrangements as cut and dried as the short notice allowed. But late in the evening, the Corps Commander, who earlier had heard and approved the whole plan, sent for the Divisional Commander. It took the latter an hour to go, and an hour to return with a new plan. It was not till 12-30 a.m. on the 3rd that Brigade H.Q. got it. Zero was to have been at 3 a.m., so the Brigadier protested. Corps H.Q. agreed to a three-hour postponement of infantry, but not of the artillery, attack ! The 11th Battalion, under Colonel R. L. Aspinall, struggling through heavily shelled communication trenches, packed with wounded moving out, on stretchers and walking, were hours late.

They received no fresh orders, could not identify the rendezvous, objectives, nor find other troops. Practically every battery telephone wire was cut. The orders for the barrage for the new attack had to be carried by runners, who, in the darkness and congested state of the trenches, could only travel slowly. Most of the batteries did not receive their orders till half way through the preliminary bombardment for the 3 a.m. attack. For the later attack, only half the necessary ammunition was available. It is easy to understand now why the artillery support was so poor. It need hardly be said, that the gunners were as desperate about their inability to help the infantry as the latter were at not receiving support. But without notice, without reconnaissance, without ammunition, what could the artillery do ?

Matters were made worse by a terrible catastrophe at Brigade H.Q., which lost 40 of its indispensable personnel from shell fire, while new orders were actually being drafted.

However, an advance was made with little artillery support, with the calm deliberate courage which our New Armies always showed. The only reason for the attack, or indication that an attack should be made at all, was the fact that our people saw the 8th Border Regiment moving and went too.

They were met by a withering fire of machine guns, under which they walked forward till the Battalion simply melted away. Colonel Aspinall was killed. Every Company Commander was a casualty. The Adjutant, Captain Hill, of the Suffolk Regiment, with great energy and bravery, got the survivors back to the starting line.

On the morning of the 4th, no organised body of men existed, " one simply ran about no-man's land collecting men here and there." On this day, Private Marsden and about 60 men reached the enemy front line and established themselves there. They were withdrawn after dark.

Battle of Albert.   Scene of the successful British attack on La Boisselle (19th Division).
Taken from the British front line trench immediately after the assault on 3rd July, 1916.
In the foreground is the original British front line and the crater formed by the explosion
of a mine before the advance took place.

Destroyed German trenches at Ovillers, looking towards Albert, July, 1916.

Of 20 officers and 657 men who went in to the attack, few answered the roll on the 6th. Including those who had been left with the details, only 6 officers and 50 men remained. They spent a miserable night in pouring rain. A draft arrived. Thus reinforced, they made another attack on the 8th, a fine warm day.

On this day, the 8th, the Battalion advanced in two parties, one led by the new C.O., Evans of the South Lancashire Regiment. He was soon knocked out by a shell splinter. The companies he was leading went astray. Eventually, the Adjutant, Captain Hill, having found that one of the trenches from which the attack was to start was held by the enemy, tried to arrange to attack this first. He was, in the end, given command of the 8th South Lancashire Regiment, his own two companies, and the 78th Trench Mortar Battery, and told to attack. There was no artillery support. The attack failed.

During this fighting, about 60 of our men joined the Highland L.I. in Leipzig trench, but all who reached the enemy line were either killed or captured.

How could these attacks succeed without any reconnaissance or any artillery support, when the original attack, with every advantage that adequate preparation and military skill could contrive, had failed? That these attacks were ordered at all shows how little the higher commanders and their staffs were alive to the true state of affairs.

———

Special order by O.C. 11th Battalion.

"The Commanding Officer wishes to convey his congratulations and thanks to all ranks for their splendid work and determination under most trying circumstances in the recent fighting. The cheerfulness and willingness of all ranks, although thoroughly tired, were worthy of the highest praise. The loss of Colonel R. L. Aspinall, D.S.O., and so many other gallant comrades of all ranks is very great."

* * * *

The 10th Battalion was in the trenches from the 2nd to the 15th of July, the latter part of the time in front of Ovillers. They had a very sticky time, but made no attack till the 12th. On this day " C " Company captured a trench which protected the right flank of the attack of the 14th/15th July. See " Bazentin."

* * * *

The 13th Battalion, commanded by Colonel L. H. K. Finch, was employed, on the 7th July, under the 12th Division against Ovillers. Jumping-off trenches had been contrived from the newly-won German trenches in La Boisselle. These trenches formed a salient in the German line and our attack ran parallel to the British and German fronts, the Germans still holding trenches flanking the line of advance from La Boisselle to Ovillers. The village was below the crest from the front, but was in view from our starting line.

It had been arranged that the attack should be protected by smoke and by an intense barrage. But there was no smoke and our men thought the barrage particularly feeble. It is probable that, as the wind dropped, the smoke rose at once. Our advance, being thus unscreened, drew heavy artillery fire. This fire, together with machine gun fire from front and flanks, stopped the attack about half way to Ovillers. The Loyal North Lancashires on our right lost heavily, the loss in officers being particularly severe. The 13th Battalion lost eight officers killed, Major J. C. Metcalfe, Captain and Adjutant W. E. Davy, Captain F. G. Hall, Lieutenants Fitzroy Somerset, H. F. Stevenson, D. A. Stewart, 2nd/Lieuts. A. E. Cotton and C. M. Bellis. Colonel Finch and eleven other officers were wounded. 243 N.C.O.s and men were killed or wounded.

*   *   *   *

Order by Corps Commander.

" On their withdrawal from the line after eleven days' hard fighting, the G.O.C. wishes to express to all ranks of the 25th Division his appreciation of their gallantry and devotion to duty, and congratulates them on the final success of their efforts."

BAZENTIN. 14th to 17th July, 1916.

Map p. 96

In this battle, the 25th Division was used as a whole under its Commander, General E. G. T. Bainbridge.

The preliminaries of the battle included some excellent staff work. Three thousand men were assembled in the dark and formed up within 500 yards of the enemy, without confusion, and undiscovered. Our control of no-man's land was complete. No hostile patrol or raid interfered with the assembly.

The attack started at 5-30 a.m. on the 14th July " at the earliest possible moment after receipt of orders." " Attack started under very heavy fire which meant crawling." The slope to the German trenches was swept by small arm fire and immediately our men appeared, a German counter-attack was made on our right flank. This attack reached our starting trench and had to be bombed out. On the left, the attack nearly reached the German trench, but was mown down by machine gun fire and withdrew with heavy loss. Attempts then made to bomb up a trench leading towards the Germans were much hampered by shell fire, which so damaged the trench as to make it untenable.

* * * *

During the 14th, the 10th Battalion was nearly destroyed by shell fire. Notwithstanding this, under a full moon, supported by no artillery, the Battalion made two attacks, one at 11-0 p.m. and one at 2-50 a.m. on the 15th, for which the 8th Battalion Loyal North Lancashire Regiment carried material. " C " Company, under G. L. Lowry, by now reduced to 29 strong, fought magnificently in a bombing attack on the flank.

In the first of these attacks, a good many men reached the enemy trenches, but not in sufficient order or numbers to maintain their position. The loss in officers was severe. The second attack, mainly by bomb, in which the 8th Loyal North Lancashire Regiment and some Lancashire Fusiliers combined with our men, nearly reached the objective. But it was now beginning to get light and machine gun fire became more effective, so the C.O. reluctantly withdrew the remnant, 100 men, back to the starting trench. The result of these heroic efforts made the capture of Ovillers possible, but the absence of any mention of artillery support makes one wonder how anyone expected these attacks to succeed. The new armies seem to have been trained almost too mechanically, or they would hardly have gone on in such conditions.

During the period 3rd to 15th July, five officers were killed, Captain N. C. R. Merry, Lieuts. G. F. Oliver, A. E. Hampson and S. H. Thrift, and 2nd/Lieut. R. Walter. Three officers were missing and seven wounded. 38 N.C.Os. and men were killed, 72 missing, and 276 wounded. Most of these casualties occurred on the 14th and 15th.

* * * *

The 13th Battalion also attacked Ovillers again on the 16th at 1 a.m. and did well, till, finding themselves unsupported, they withdrew. On being reinforced by fresh troops, they went forward again and succeeded in dislodging the defenders from a strong position, and in capturing the survivors.

They lost three officers and 27 N.C.Os. and men.

Waterlot Farm.

Map p. 96

About the middle of July, the Somme offensive had reached a critical stage. The salient with its apex at Delville Wood was too narrow an area in which to deploy large bodies and, being open to bombardment on both sides, invited a German counter-attack. It was at this moment that the 16th Battalion was sent into the line.

This was the first appearance of the Bantams. On their way up, they passed the First Battalion of The Regiment, who cheered them on their way with the " Quickstep."

The position to be held lay between Guillemont and Delville Wood.

A patrol sent towards Guillemont on the 16th actually penetrated the village, which would seem to show that the Germans had left it. The information never got back, or the village might have been occupied and much subsequent bloodshed saved.

On the 17th, the 16th Battalion was ordered to take over from the Camerons, with one company, two Lewis gun " nests " in front of Water-lot farm.

Lieut. H. D. Ryalls, whose company, " W," was to man the posts and intervening ground, made reconnaissances to see if relief could not be made in daylight. Lieut. R. MacLaren, who accompanied Ryalls, was hit, and died of wounds. To German rifle and machine gun fire, was added shelling, so it was decided to relieve the posts at night.

The company sat under heavy shelling all day waiting for dark. It kept in close touch with Battalion H.Q. by the devoted work. of Private Hoare and other runners and signallers.

Just as " W " Company was about to start, about 9-30 p.m., a great German attack began on Delville Wood. Movement was out of the question. The sound of shells going overhead was like the flight of birds migrating, and the noise of their crashing and rending was awful. The Wood itself must have been a most terrible place.

About midnight, the storm quietened down and " W " Company went up to the farm. Two platoons were detailed for the north-west, and two for the south. From the farm, light railways ran to Guillemont, and the posts, about 300 yards apart, were connected by cuttings.

One of the platoons was led by a Cameron guide into Guillemont, but came out again. This confirms that the Germans had left it. But again, this information was not passed back.

The platoons at the south post worked all the rest of the night improving these German trenches and making a block on the right, the flank of the British Army, with the French left, being some half-mile away.

Pioneers began work on a communication trench and a section of the Machine Gun Corps also arrived.

Posts of 3 or 4 men were distributed along the cutting.

Lieut. R. P. Scholefield was in command of the north post, and had dug a fresh line, which was to be a " surprise " for the Germans.

At 9 a.m. on the 18th, the Germans began an intensive bombardment on the cuttings and on the farm. The new posts, dug well forward of the farm, got no shells at all, except our own " shorts." Both the 16th Battalion and the 15th in Bernafay Wood, suffered severely.

This went on till about 2 p.m., when the bombardment increased

Somme, 1916. First Battalion going " over the top."

First Battalion.
Mametz Sector. Relief in progress.

Maricourt, Somme, 1915.
A First Battalion M.G. showing first method of using M.G. against aircraft.

in severity, and was " something to remember." At 3 p.m., the Germans came over. They were checked by rapid fire, but, pushing machine guns out on their flanks, they came on again, till they reached the embankment of the cutting. Leaving a party to watch the right flank, Lieutenant Ryalls led a counter-attack across the open and, after two or three minutes desperate rough and tumble, drove the Germans back. Our men followed them up with fire, until they, in their turn, were forced to leave the cutting and return to their posts.

The two platoons on the left withheld their fire till the Germans were almost on top of them, and then let fly. The Germans were completely surprised and fled. Lieutenant Scholefield was wounded and died later.

These platoons were supported by fire of Camerons and " X " Company, who engaged Germans coming out of Delville Wood on the left.

Privates Lowe and Campbell particularly distinguished themselves in carrying messages to and from Battalion H.Q.

German guns now began to find the two posts of " W " Company and to cause casualties. But, in the nick of time, reinforcements came up under Lieutenant Millington, with a supply of bombs and S.A.A. and two more Lewis guns under Sergeant James.

The Germans attacked again, but this time the cutting was strongly held and the Germans were driven back. More reinforcements were sent up from " Y " Company, in time to meet a third German attack. This attack coincided with an artillery barrage and quickly died away.

Up to this time, our losses at the Farm were about 80. The German losses can only be estimated at between 600 and 700, mostly caused by Lieutenant Scholefield's half company.

Systematic German shelling all next day, the 19th, caused as many casualties as we had lost on the previous day. A shell hit Battalion H.Q. R.S.M. Giles, Lieutenant A. C. Styles and the Orderly Room Sergeant were all killed, and the Adjutant, Captain Johnston, severely wounded.

This small operation was extremely well conducted. The tactical dispositions and the bravery of the men defeated all German attacks. The Battalion worked together as one man. Every message was anticipated, and reinforcements allowed nothing to stop them getting forward. Food, S.A.A. and bombs arrived at the right time, though a water cart was blown up on its way forward.

Many rewards were given, among them the C.O. Colonel Browne-Clayton and Lieut. Ryalls won the D.S.O., Private Bruce, the undaunted ubiquitous C.O's. runner, who " took over " Battalion H.Q. when it was hit, received a well-earned D.C.M. Another runner, who did fearless work, was Private Saballa.

The Company, well backed by the rest of the Battalion, had held a position of vital importance at a critical moment.

DELVILLE WOOD. 15th July to 3rd September.

Map p. 96

In this period, the 5th Division was attacking the German line between Delville Wood and High Wood in order to capture Longueval.

Attacks were made on the 20th and 23rd July. On the 27th the main attack was made by the Norfolk and Bedfordshire Regiments. This attack was carried out in the form of a series of methodical advances from point to point, under cover of artillery barrages. It was preceded by a two-hours' bombardment.

While the main attack was going on, the 1st Battalion carried out a separate operation on a German strong point about the existence of which some doubt reigned. We were really attacking a map reference. The attack was made in three parties, under 2nd/Lieuts. Prout, Duckworth and Barthelemy. There was some misunderstanding about the timing of the covering barrages, in spite of which Prout's and Duckworth's parties made gallant attempts to reach their objectives. They were met by cross fire from machine guns at High Wood and Longueval which our artillery had not reached. Nearly all the men were killed, and both officers. None were ever seen again. A party sent in support was forced to retire. Colonel M. F. Clarke was wounded. Although the Battalion objective was not reached, an advanced post, protecting the left flank, was established.

Heavy fighting continued all day, and, by evening, all communications were broken by the intensity of the hostile fire.

On the night of the 28th/29th July, the 1st Battalion, which was in Brigade reserve S.E. of Mametz, moved up across Caterpillar Valley and occupied the northern and western edges of Longueval. Companies moved independently and the Battalion, with the exception of Headquarters, had reached their positions before the usual barrage came down on the south edge of the village. Battalion Headquarters, however, had to pass through this barrage, and it was with the greatest difficulty that the Headquarter's dug-out, said to be at the cross roads by the church, was eventually found. This barrage died down as suddenly as it had begun, but started again about 04.00 hours on 29th and continued intermittently all day, eventually setting fire to the Headquarter's dug-out which was evacuated amidst the bursting of boxes of Mills' grenades stored at the entrance.

On the night of 29th/30th, the 13th Brigade relieved the 15th Brigade and the Battalion withdrew into Divisional reserve near Mametz. Our casualties had been very heavy. On withdrawal from Longueval, our strength was under 300 of all ranks.

* * * *

The only dug-out available for a Regimental Aid Post was in view of the Germans, on a well-defined road leading towards the front. Stretcher bearers were wiped out by 5.9's. Casualties could not reach the Aid Post. Our Medical Officer, J. M. Forsyth, consequently went forward to aid them. Forsyth was with the First Battalion from February, 1915 till July, 1918. He was a lion-hearted man for whom no place was too dangerous if there were wounded to be attended, or a good snapshot to be obtained ! He had a keen sense of humour and was most even-tempered. He loved the Battalion and all ranks loved him. He refused to leave us many times, but in July 1918 was compelled to go to a Field Ambulance, worn out by his devoted labours. He won a Military Cross and bar. After the war, he became a medical missionary and died in harness.

* * * *

The Division was relieved by 17th Division and moved back, the transport by road and the remainder by train to Hangest, marching to Laleu, for a rest and refit. Every officer and man was given 48 hours' leave to go to one of the adjacent coastal places and all were thankful of this opportunity to forget what they had been through.

Reinforcements arrived shortly, many of them men who had been drafted from Yeomanry regiments at home. This had been made possible by an amendment to the Army Act, by which men could be posted to any arm or unit where they were most required. In future, Battalions were to receive men from a pool formed by recruits and reinforcements from units whose recruiting areas were contiguous. It was felt that this would des-troy " esprit de corps " but, given the opportunity to get the Battalion together in a rest area, these men soon became one with the unit.

The Yeomanry who came, after the first period of the Somme offen-sive in 1916, found themselves suddenly dismounted from their horses and called upon to do intensive training to fit themselves for trench warfare. Once they realised that there was no alternative, they soon learnt the work and made excellent reinforcements.

Later, to meet the demands for men trained in bombing and Lewis gun work, the " Bull Ring " was instituted at the Base Reinforcement Camps. Here, every man was put through an intensive course of training before being sent up to his unit which, under the stress of active operation, had no time to undertake the training of specialists.

A vivid account of the impressions of a C.O.
on the Somme, July 1916.

The Commanding Officer lay curled up in a niche in the parapet dozing fitfully. With the aid of a button stick and a toothbrush, his batman, Webb, had pinned an oil sheet in front of the niche to screen him from the vulgar gaze of the fatigue parties passing to and fro. Still, with all these advantages, sleep didn't come easily, for all night long the noise of a thousand distant guns rolled and swelled like the breakers on a rocky shore. While heavy projectiles overhead rumbled to their distant objectives, and high velocity guns spat at the trenches in front.

Force irresistible and terrific seemed everywhere supreme. The stupor that comes half of sleep and half of sheer exhaustion soaked into his brain and left it free to wander in the fanciful realms of dreamland. He seemed to be standing in a railway junction in Hell, where express trains ran amuck at incredible speed unguided by human hands. Sooner or later, there must be a collision ! And then ! Crash !

" That was a near one," thought the C.O. now thoroughly wakened, as he drew the screen aside and looked out at the glimmering dawn. " Time to be getting up."

After tying up his puttee strings he walked a few yards to another niche in which a very long young man had packed himself and was snoring contentedly with his head pillowed on his steel helmet. " Time to get up, R——," he shouted. " We must be going up to our Battle Headquarters."

The young Adjutant uncurled himself slowly and blinked stupidly at the C.O. " I think I must have been asleep, Sir," he murmured. " No need to apologize, I only wish I could have slept through all that din," said the other.

" Cup of tea, Sir," shouted a cheerful voice from a further corner, and a muddy soldier hurried out with two steaming mugs, followed by two plates of delicious eggs and bacon.

" I don't see how we could get through this war without tea," said the C.O. " and rum."

Then together, as day was breaking, they worked their way up the trench to the battle position, followed by the orderlies and signallers.

The way was not hard to find, and there were landmarks on the route ; here a dud shell, there a smell, and further on still was that which had been a man. It was lying down as in life, but the face was blue and unpleasant to look on.

They walked past and said nothing, but the thought must have been uppermost in all their minds that many of the Battalion would be like that one before the day was over.

Arras, 1916.
Comm. trench, showing effect of direct hit on a tree.

Brickstack Sector, 1917.
Camouflage tree, with one of our men.

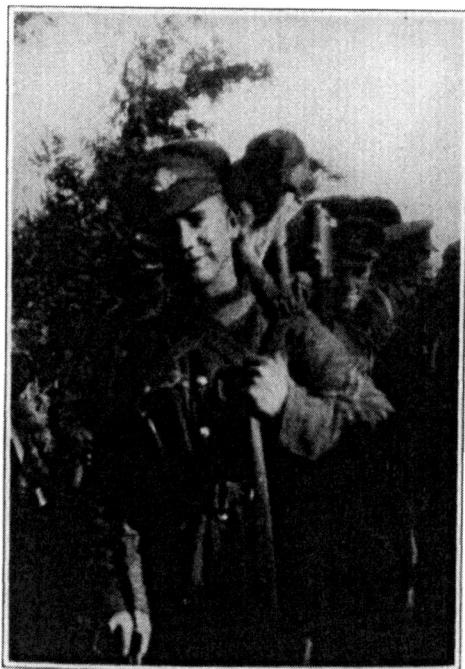

1917.
Men of the First Battalion on the move.

Brickstack Sector, 1917.
The front line, typical Cheshire Soldiers.

" Here we are, Sir," said R——, as they arrived at a higher bit of ground. " I am afraid the machine gunners have placed themselves on our right, so we may get it rather hot here."

" Never mind, too late to change now. How quiet and peaceful it all seems ! "

" Ten minutes to six now," said the Adjutant.

They waited and looked at their watches, and at six exactly, hell was let loose. All the guns that England could mass together opened on the German lines.

Then the enemy answered, and the orderlies crouched lower in the trench. " That was a near one," said the Adjutant. " There's someone groaning, must have been hit. I'll go and see."

A minute later, he returned. " It's all right, Sir, one of the orderlies. He's only winded. I've made him lie down. He will be all right presently."

But the C.O. hardly heard him. He was gazing through his field glasses, and peering through the smoke and haze to where his front line lay. Something was going wrong with the barrage, and he feared it was being brought down on his own men.

There was another burst not far away. He felt a smart tap on the side of his head, and put up his hand, and felt a little bit of shell embedded deep in the flesh.

" Stretcher Bearer," called the Adjutant swiftly. And a stretcher bearer came running up with iodine and a first field dressing, while the C.O. dictated messages to the front line Companies and to the Brigade Headquarters.

" I am fed up with waiting here," said the C.O. at last. We haven't had a word back from companies. I think I shall go up myself and see what is happening. You stay here and carry on."

" Very good, Sir. I shall expect you back in about an hour, I suppose."

" R—— ! " shouted the C.O., and immediately from some recess in the trench emerged a little active man, the C.O's. orderly.

The C.O. and his orderly R—— moved down the hill along a battered trench, running across the open bits, and resting where there was cover, until at last the trench led out on a sunken road.

Just then a burst, and then another on the side of the road. " Quick, Sir ! " shouted R——, " There's a barrage coming down."

The C.O. leapt into a hole by the side of the road, Roberts leapt into another, and then the barrage came down in earnest.

As the C.O. leapt, he missed by a bare inch the leg of a young officer who was reclining awkwardly in one corner. He was wounded in the ankle.

Sitting up opposite him was the Company Commander.

" Only just in time, Sir," he said, " two seconds later, and that shell would 'have done you in.   Have a cigarette ? "

And then they talked and exchanged information, till the C.O. said " Well, I wanted to get along the whole line, but I don't see how I can now.   I simply must get back to my battle position."

" Well, good luck, Sir, the barrage seems to have shifted a bit, but it doesn't look too safe now."

" R——, I'm going back."

" Sir ! Coming Sir ! "

The journey back was harder work.   Running up hill is heavy work at the best of times, but is worse still when the ground is pitted and scarred with shell holes, and when arms and equipment must needs be carried.

The rushes became shorter, and the rests longer, and the shell bursts became more frequent.

What is the matter !   What has happened !

The C.O. was sitting in a battered trench, with a heavy pain in his chest, every limb trembling as with a palsy.   There was silence all round. Blood in front of his eyes.   His head felt like a boiled potato   .   .   .

He had been hit, he felt sure by a shell, but was he alive or dead ? Was he wounded, and, if so, where ?

" Roberts," he shouted.   But no answer came.   Again he shouted, but could hear nothing except from time to time a little tinkle, that sounded like the clang of a bell.

" How strange to have church bells on a battlefield ! "

" Something must be done."

His shaking hands tried to mop his eyes, and shift the bandage on his head, but they couldn't do it.

Then he felt his legs.   They seemed all right, anyhow.

He stood up, and was glad to find that he could walk, and now he was able to peer through the film of blood that obscured his sight, and saw a mound of earth beside him where a trench had been.   " R—— is buried" flashed across his mind—a machine gun post is just round the corner —I must get help."

Up he got, feebly, at first, but gaining strength, as he went on, though still shaking all over.   It was strangely silent but for the tinkling of the bells ; yes, there were the machine gunners at their post, but dead, all dead.   He picked his way over the bodies, and pushed on as in a dream, and was hardly surprised to find another post of corpses further on.

Then suddenly he came on his old battle position.   Judging from the expression on his Adjutant's face, he must have looked an unpleasant sight, as he sank down on the firestep gasping " Roberts must be buried. .   .   .   Can you send someone to dig him out."

Captured German pill-box " Gibraltar." Pozieres, 20th September, 1916.

Battle of the Ancre. Serving coffee to wounded. Hamel, November, 1916.

POZIERES. 23rd July to 3rd September.

Map p. 96

Our 6th Battalion was in the trenches in front of Thiepval during this period and so earned the honour for this battle which was mainly concerned with the fighting for Mouquet Farm.

*   *   *   *

Our 10th, 11th and 13th Battalions were also fighting in this area during August without taking part in any set-piece attack.

About this time Sergeant G. Marsden and Pte. P. Moore of the 10th Battalion performed a very brave act in bringing in a wounded Corporal of the 1st Wiltshire Regiment in daylight.

*   *   *   *

The reason why the 25th Division wear a red horseshoe with a blue bar as a distinguishing mark is that the Colonel of one of our Service Battalions at the Battle of Pozières picked up a German horseshoe which he handed to the G.O.C. who from that time adopted the horseshoe as the distinguishing mark of his command.

GUILLEMONT. 3rd to 6th September.

Map p. 83

This Battle is, as far as we are concerned, an attack on Falfemont Farm. It was preceded, and the arrangements and orders very much assisted, by an extremely valuable and well-planned reconnaissance carried out by our 1st Battalion. This reconnaissance located enemy strong points and machine gun posts, and captured some prisoners. No doubt such reconnaissances are very valuable, but whether raids merely for the purpose of capturing prisoners were justified is not so clear.

The trenches were now in a terrible state, knee-deep in mud. A good deal of work was necessary to make an attack from them possible.

Leaving billets on 24th August, the 1st Battalion moved up by train to Mericourt. There they found two Divisions of Cavalry, hoping for the eternal G in GAP. After one night here, they relieved our 15th Battalion in trenches near Carnoy.

Preparations were now in hand for a combined attack by French and British troops, the objectives being Combles, Ginchy, Flers and Le Sars.

Fighting for Guillemont had been going on for over a month. It was hoped, that, merged in the bigger offensive, the main object of which was to widen the salient to the north, Guillemont would fall.

Our junction with the French was in the valley running from Harde-

F

court to Combles. The French left was completely overlooked by the high ground between Combles and Guillemont, still in German hands.

On this high ground, was Falfemont Farm. The French insisted on this being captured before they began their advance.

Tanks were to be employed further north. It was hoped that the Cavalry might break through to Bapaume.

The 13th Brigade was detailed to make the attack on Falfemont Farm, three hours before the main zero hour on 3rd September. The 1st Battalion which moved into Chimpanzee trench immediately north west of Hardecourt on 1st September, was detailed as immediate reserve under the orders of the Commander of the 13th Brigade. When moving across the valley, S.W. of Hardecourt, the Battalion was heavily gassed, but luckily had no casualties.

The attack on Falfemont Farm by the 13th Brigade was launched at 9 a.m. on 3rd September and failed at the outset, as the French, who had undertaken to supply the artillery support, had failed to do so. The 1st Battalion was immediately ordered up to reinforce the 13th Brigade front line. From Chimpanzee trench to the front line, they had to cross the forward slopes of the hill N.E. of Hardecourt, in full view of the enemy and under heavy shell fire. A barrage of 5.9's was playing on the valley south of Angle Wood. Companies were, therefore, ordered to move independently, adopting the most suitable formation, " A " and " C " Companies moving on the trenches occupied by the 13th Brigade immediately N.E. of Angle Wood, whilst " B " and " D " went into trenches W. and N.W. of Angle Wood.

On our arrival at the position, we found the front line trenches crowded with men of the 13th Brigade. All the while, heavy shelling was in progress. Gradually, the units were sorted out and the 1st Battalion took over the front line, the men of the 13th Brigade being brought back to the reverse slope of the hill N.E. of Angle Wood. During the night of the 3rd/4th, the 13th Brigade was withdrawn and the Norfolk Regiment came in on our right, whilst the Bedfordshire Regiment continued the line on the left, to a point opposite Wedge Wood.

Though Falfemont Farm remained in German hands, the main attack had been fairly successful. Guillemont had been taken and the French had occupied the high ground north of Maurepas. In the 1st Battalion, casualties had been fairly light in spite of the heavy shelling.

At 12 noon on the 4th, orders were issued by 15th Brigade for an attack on Falfemont Farm by the Norfolks on the right, 1st Battalion in the centre and the Bedfords on the left. The attack was to take place at 3 p.m. that day. " A " Company on the right and " C " on the left were ordered to attack the Farm and the trenches immediately north of it. " B " and " D " Companies were to move forward in support and occupy the trenches from which " A " and " C " had assaulted. The

Norfolks, on our right, were also to attack the south side of the Farm. The Bedfords were to attack the German trenches immediately south of Wedge Wood.

The attack by the Norfolks and " A " Company failed, owing to heavy machine gun fire. Capt. Francis White, of " A " Company, was killed with many of his men, as they left our trenches. Captain White was from our 6th Battalion, a first-rate officer, much liked by all ranks.

On the left, the Bedfords and " C " Company succeeded in entering the German trenches to the north of the Farm. Lieut. Gwynne-Jones, of " C " Company, who particularly distinguished himself during work

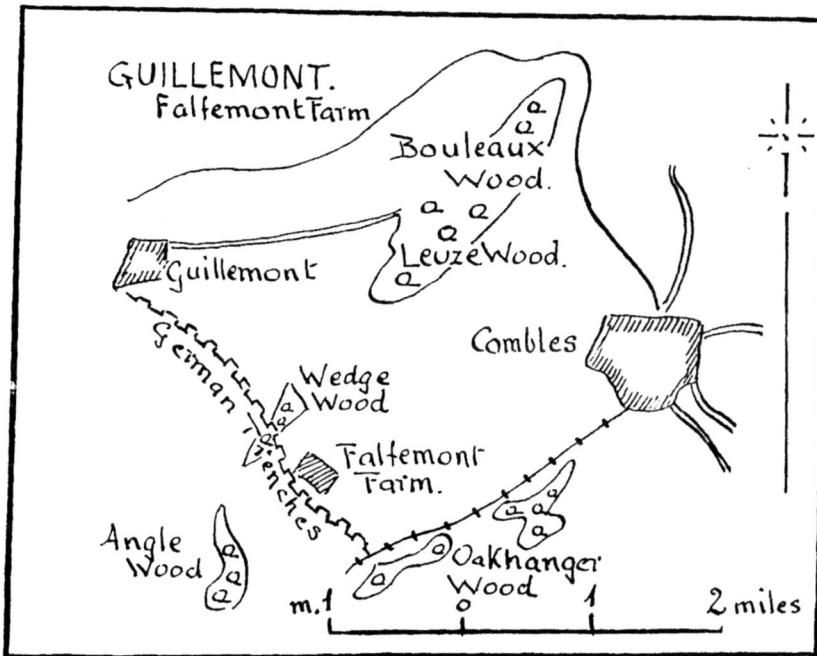

on patrol, led a bombing party which, assisted by the Bedfords, eventually gained a footing in Falfemont Farm. By dark we had at last won the position but at very severe cost. Lieut. Gledsdale especially distinguished himself by his organization of the defence of the Farm against counter-attack. Capt. Gleed, of " D " Company, was very severely wounded and died later. He had come out with the Battalion as orderly room sergeant in 1914, and his loss was deeply regretted by all ranks. In addition, six other officers were wounded and five W.Os. missing. Only some 280 men remained untouched. The Germans, too, had lost heavily, whole machine gun detachments being killed at their posts.

The 5th passed off quietly except for some shelling and towards evening the French could be seen advancing up the valley towards Combles which place, however, was not taken until some three weeks later. To the north, the 95th Brigade had advanced into Leuze Wood and the Bedfords and ourselves held the high ground from Falfemont Farm to the Leuze Wood.

This brilliant success was the second of two prolonged and successful offensive movements by the 15th Brigade since they came into the Somme battle. Numerous congratulatory messages were received by the Division and Brigade for the troops.

FLERS COURCELETTE. 15th to 22nd September.

The 1st Battalion " very worn out and wet " was holding the line on the right of the attack on the Flers-Courcelette line, getting ready for the next advance.

* * * *

From the 9th Battalion War Diary.

My dear Colonel Dauntesey,

I much regret that I have not found an opportunity of personally thanking the gallant lads of your Battalion who brought a lot of our wounded in with such bravery on the 25th September. Where acts of heroism were so frequently performed on that day, it is now difficult to particularize, but Captain Mackenzie mentioned 2nd/Lieut. Jones, Privates Callf and Johnson. I shall be much obliged if you will convey to them this poor appreciation of their gallant conduct.

Wishing you and your gallant Battalion the best of luck in the future, and that the good feeling between your Battalion and mine may always continue and increase.

Yours very sincerely,

C. H. Young, *Lieutenant-Colonel*,

Commanding 9th (S.) Bn. The Welch Regt.

MORVAL. 25th to 28th September, 1916.

Map p. 87

A general attack by the British and French Armies was contemplated for 25th September. The main British attack was to be made N.E. towards Bapaume with a view to making an opening for the Cavalry. The French were to attack from Rancourt towards Sailly-Saillisel. On the right of the British attack, was the 5th Division which had already had much hard fighting and suffered heavy casualties. In fact, we only had 10 days in which to refit since the strenuous fighting near Falfemont

Farm. This was recognised by the higher command, who, however, were anxious to make as extensive an attack as possible. It was, therefore, decided that the 5th Division on the right, with the 6th and Guards Divisions should attack the line Morval-Lesboeufs. If this attack was successful, we should gain good observation for any further advance and would assist the French to pinch out Combles which would be surrounded on three sides.

The attack was to be in three stages. The first objective was the German front line, at the bottom of the valley between Ginchy and Morval. This task was allotted to the Bedfordshire Regiment.

The second objective was the German support line, half way up the slope to Morval. This task was given to the Norfolk Regiment. The third objective was to be captured by the 1st Battalion, it was the eastern edge of Morval. The final objective, allotted to the Royal Warwicks, was a line from which observation could be obtained on Sailly- Saillisel and Le Transloy.

The attacks were to take place at fixed intervals. The time between the attacks was to be occupied by getting battalions into position to go forward with the barrage. Three tanks were to follow the attack to assist in mopping up the German trenches S.W. of Morval.

Assembly trenches had to be sited and dug at night. They were extremely well made and the labour of making them was well spent.

At 12-55 p.m., the Norfolks, led by their Colonel, captured their objective ; then the Bedfords and then our 1st Battalion, under a creeping barrage, reached the western edge of Morval at 2-42. Pushing rapidly through the village they reached the eastern exits at 2-55 and pushing out parties to secure their flanks, began consolidation. The Royal Warwicks passed through our lines in due course to the final objective.

Whilst the line was being consolidated, a certain amount of sniping caused some casualties. Private Jones lost an old comrade from this cause and set out to stalk the snipers. This he did successfully and came back to our lines with some 100 prisoners whom he had caught in some partly made trenches and a dug-out, about 150 yards from our own position. He was awarded the Victoria Cross. The citation follows.

His Majesty The King has been graciously pleased to award the Victoria Cross to :—

11000 Pte. Thomas Alfred Jones, Cheshire Regiment :—

" For most conspicuous bravery. He was with his company consolidating the defences in front of a village, and, noticing an enemy sniper at 200 yards distance, he went out, and, though one bullet went through his helmet and another through his coat, he returned the sniper's fire and killed him. He then saw two more of the enemy firing at him, although displaying a white flag. Both of these he also shot. On reaching the enemy trench he found several occupied dug-outs, and single-handed, disarmed 102 of the enemy, including three or four officers, and marched them back to our lines through a heavy barrage. He had been warned of the misuse of the white flag by the enemy, but insisted on going out after them."

Contrary to expectation, this attack on Morval and Lesboeufs had gone through without a hitch and our line had been advanced some 2,000 yards, whilst what was regarded as the main attack further north had not progressed as anticipated. In fact, seeing no opportunity in this direction, the Cavalry were ordered back into reserve. Opposite Morval, there was no doubt that the German line had been completely disorganised. Bodies of men could be seen hurrying back towards the Sailly-Saillisel—Le Transloy road, and a battery was observed galloping out of action from a position about a mile N.E. of Morval. Had the Cavalry been available for action on this front, there is little doubt that we could have reached Le Transloy and perhaps Bapaume. As it was, Le Transloy was not captured until a month later.

As a result of the capture of Morval on the north, and of Saillisel to the east by the French, Combles fell without the necessity for a direct attack on the town.

The whole operation was a great feat of arms, well planned, well executed and well supported by artillery. Mutual co-operation which had been so lacking in the earlier Somme battles, made a welcome reappearance and contributed to the success of the advance.

*   *   *   *

Our 5th Battalion earned the same honour. They dug a trench on the 19th to protect the left flank of the Morval position, and on the 25th September consolidated the ground won by the 56th Division in Bouleaux Wood, from which a view of the valley between Morval and Combles could be gained.

*   *   *   *

"The heavy fighting in Delville Wood and Longueval, the attack and capture of the Falfemont Farm line and Leuze Wood, and finally the storming of Morval, are feats of arms seldom equalled in the annals of the British Army. They constitute a record of unvarying success which it has been the lot of few Divisions to attain, and the gallantry, valour, and endurance of all ranks have been wholly admirable.— RAWLINSON."

*   *   *   *

This ends the story of the 1st Battalion as far as the " Somme " is concerned. On relief, the 1st Battalion moved to the Citadel, north of Bray and thence by train to S.E. of Abbeville. Though the Somme battle continued well on into the winter months, they had seen the last of it. The Division had established a fine record and had accomplished every task given to it. Needless to say, the 1st Battalion had their full

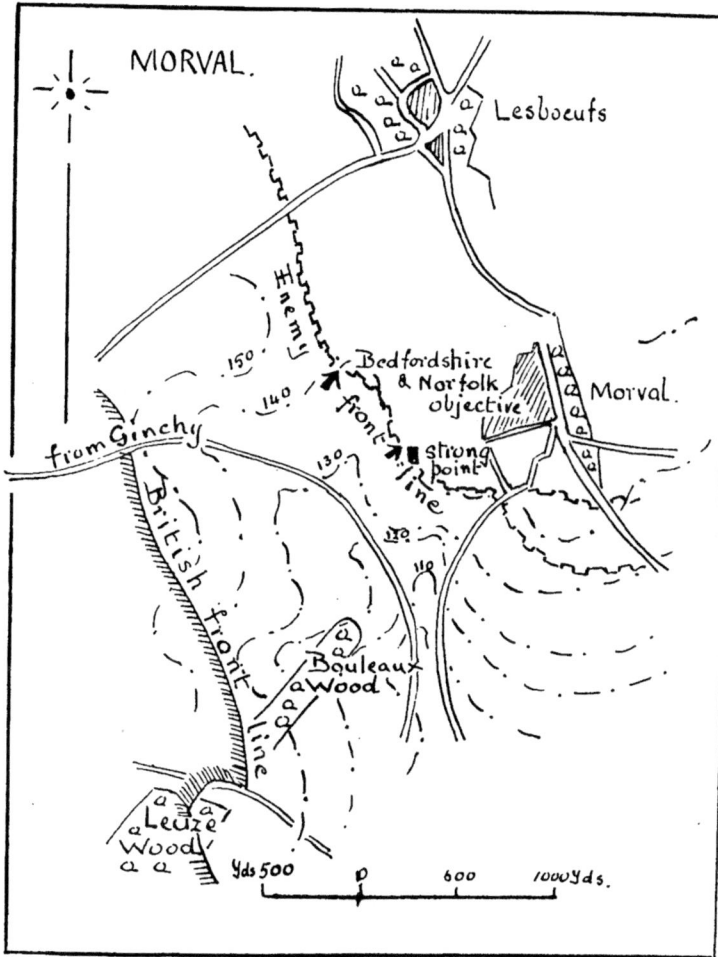

share of the reputation gained by the Division and also their quota of the losses that had been suffered. They had taken part in three separate operations, and their losses in killed, wounded and missing had been about 20 officers and over 1,000 soldiers. After each action, they had received large reinforcements, many of the men having no connection with the county, but all had united to maintain the reputation of The Regiment.

All through the periods when the Battalion was in the front line, supplies had to be brought up each night. This entailed long journeys over broken ground in the dark, frequently through heavy shelling. Never once did our transport fail us, and a large amount of praise is due to the transport officer, Lieut. Jasper Bruce and his staff for the way in which they carried on. Few realized what a strain these nightly journeys entailed, and how the morale of the Battalion would have suffered, had supplies not been available.

Jasper Bruce paid his own passage from Canada. He joined the 1st Battalion in 1915 and served with it till the Armistice. He died of influenza in a Base Hospital in 1919. Throughout the war, his transport, with himself at their head, never failed to find the Battalion every day, whatever the conditions. He was a splendid officer, and all ranks thought the world of him.

THIEPVAL. 26th to 28th September.

To assist the main attack on the Thiepval Ridge, on 26th, the 118th Brigade made a feint attack by smoke, in the area north of Hamel. Our 6th Battalion raided the enemy trenches in conjunction with this attack. Under cover of a barrage, they crossed no-man's land at 9 p.m. and rushed the enemy trenches. A fierce fight ensued. While the covering party on the enemy parapet kept the enemy at bay in face of heavy machine gun fire, another party attempted to clear the enemy trenches. The trenches were found to be blocked with "knife rests" and loose wire. All the German garrison were killed or driven off, and our men withdrew with some difficulty, with a loss of 12 men.

LE TRANSLOY. 1st to 18th October.

Map p. 96

Operations were undertaken during October to secure a line from which the main Le Transloy system would be attacked at a later date. The first objective was to drive the Germans from the western crest of the ridge and the second to secure a position on the eastern crest giving observation over Le Transloy.

The following description of the condition of the ground in the Somme area is taken from the Rifle Brigade History.

"By this time the weather had become very bad. The attacks

Digging a communication trench through Delville Wood.

which followed in quick succession must be regarded much as the struggles of a man, who, having waded into a bog, is plunging and floundering to clamber out on to firm ground beyond. The French had a definite tactical objective in the high ground of Sailly-Saillisel, which enfiladed the British line, but when that had been gained the Allies can hardly have expected to progress much further."

" The tanks were already useless on the treacherous ground. The men employed in the assault stumbled exhausted into their assembly positions, and, at zero, slithered and slipped, staggering under the weight of their equipment, through sludge and water in their effort to keep up with the barrage. The dash of the September battles was irrevocably gone. But the winter was fast approaching, and it seemed to be worth any sacrifice to get out of that awful mud before it came. None but the Fourth Army came to within striking distance of the Le Transloy line, and they would break through once again on a wide front and find themselves in open country."

Perhaps what was insufficiently appreciated was, that in the existing conditions of warfare, the open country was a mirage, that with each successive advance must inevitably recede farther and farther away. By virtue of the contending artilleries, they took their mud with them. Unless there could be a break through of such a depth as to penetrate beyond the shelled area, there would be no escape from it. And unless the enemy could be kept on the run, there was equally no escape ; for directly the line halted, the mutual bombardment would be resumed and the mud would reappear. Meanwhile, the immediate problem was to get within striking distance of Le Transloy.

The British front line now ran just east of Morval—Les Boeufs—Guedecourt.

*   *   *   *

The attack began at 1-45 p.m. on 7th October. One company of our 5th Battalion was with the 168th Brigade on the right, and one with the 169th Brigade on the left. The battle raged for 48 hours with very little progress.

The 5th Battalion had had a very strenuous five weeks in September, and during the period of this battle, digging trenches and constructing strong points. The most famous of these works was a trench called Gropi (Groves' Pioneers) about a thousand yards long, in front of Boule-aux Wood. The Corps Commander considered it a perfect example of a battle trench. It was dug in one night, within about 100 yards of the Germans.

In this period, 2nd/Lieut. W. F. Smith was killed..

ANCRE HEIGHTS. 1st October to 11th November.

Maps p. 92, 93

This battle was undertaken to gain the ridge running from just south west of Martinpuich to the high ground north of Thiepval, which was crowned by the Schwaben and Stuff redoubts.

The capture of this ridge would give us the observation over the Ancre Valley and Grandcourt.

Thiepval had been captured, but not the top of the ridge.

On the 9th October, our 10th Battalion made a single-handed attack on the Stuff redoubt under Colonel A. C. Johnston. The attack started in the southern portion of the redoubt, which was in our hands, and was intended to capture the remainder.

The 10th Battalion moved up by platoons and relieved the troops holding the front line by 10-15 a.m. on the 9th. A hot meal was issued. By 12-35, when an intense artillery fire opened on the enemy trenches, every man was in his place. The barrage was rather " over " the enemy trench. Under its cover, the Battalion formed up in no-man's land and advanced in excellent style, keeping good direction and not bunching.

Thanks to the splendid leadership of 2nd/Lieuts. Wilson and Hills, the advance of the first wave was so rapid that our men were in the German trenches before their men had time to man the parapet and get their machine guns to work. On the right, the enemy put up a poor fight. On the left, a bombing party rushed a strong point where there were several deep dug-outs, from which many Germans were emerging. A mélèe ensued. Many Germans were killed in the open or in dug-outs. Five officers and 100 men were captured. Some very fierce bombing and a determined bayonet charge under 2nd/Lieut. Hills ensued before the enemy blocks, some way up the two communication trenches leading away from the Redoubt, were captured, these being the second objectives.

A block was then made here to protect the left flank, but was twice destroyed by our own artillery fire. The third wave, led by Captain Simmons, materially assisted in the capture of the second objective.

By this time, all communication with our Artillery had been cut, and increasing German pressure with bomb and rifle drove our men back some 50 yards.

All the time, enemy shelling was severe on the communication and support trenches, making the supply of bombs and ammunition very precarious.

At about 4-30 p.m., the enemy brought up a minenwerfer and under cover of its fire and of a heavy artillery barrage, made a counter-attack which was successfully driven off. The gallantry and energy of two artillery subalterns of the 58th Field Brigade, 2nd/Lieuts. Taylor and Touse, did much to maintain protective artillery fire and to defeat the counter attack.

The situation quietened about 7 p.m., but a fresh counter-attack in the night was repulsed.

A company of the 1st Wiltshire Regiment was invaluable in carrying bombs and stores during the whole action.

*   *   *   *

Extracts from diary of Colonel A. C. Johnston who commanded the 10th Battalion at this time.

8th October. The weather seems to be dead against us, and we woke up in the morning to find it pouring with rain. About 9 a.m. we got orders postponing our attack, and, almost immediately after we were told that we should again be relieved in the trenches by the 8th Loyal North Lancashire Regiment. It is extraordinarily bad luck, everything was ready, the men tuned up to it and quite ready to go over. However, we went back to some excellent dug-outs near Ovillers, where the men were able to be quite warm and comfortable, which was what I wanted for them particularly, as it was a wet night. Having settled them in comfortably, I got a message about 8 p.m. to my dismay, to say that we had got to do the attack at 12-35 p.m. next day. I was certainly not going to disturb the men now that they were comfortably settled in, but, of course, it meant trudging all the way up there in the mud next morning, doing a relief, making final arrangements without much margin if anything were to go wrong, and then doing the attack.

9th October. A great day, and the Battalion has covered itself with glory. Started off from our dug-outs about 8 a.m. and relieved 8th N. Lancs. without a hitch by 10-30 a.m. Had arranged for a hot meal to be brought up for the men at 11 a.m., and went round the trenches, had a talk to the men, and gave final instructions to the officers. By 12-20 p.m., everything was ready, and all the men in their places. Our " heavies " had been shelling one or two trench junctions behind the German front line intermittently during the morning, but otherwise had been quiet. At 12-35 p.m., we put an intense barrage on to the German front line, on to their communication trenches leading backwards, and on to neighbouring trenches on our flanks. Stokes mortars conformed to the artillery barrage. Heavy artillery shelled German dug-outs behind, and places where the enemy was known to keep his supports. Our machine guns covered our flanks, and swept the German communication trenches with overhead fire. At the same moment, our fellows climbed out of our trenches and formed up in No-man's land. For a moment I was a bit anxious, as our barrage, instead of being on the German front line, was over it, so that there was really no reason why the Germans should not man their parapet. I counted six or more of their sentries standing up and firing at our fellows, but fortunately their firing was wild, and none of our chaps were hit. The men were splendid. There was no faltering. They went straight over without bunching or losing direction, and were in the German trench before they could get their machine guns into action. It turned out that the trench had not been damaged by our bombardment.

Aeroplane observers, who watched the attack from above, reported that it was the best carried out attack they had seen, and people who watched it through their telescopes from behind, all remarked how well the men went over, and said that it was quite a model of how an attack should be done. On the right, the enemy put up their hands at once, but on the left where fortunately I had thickened our line in anticipation of some trouble, there was quite a lively " mix-up," and some 40 Germans were killed at this point alone, besides those bombed, burnt and buried at the bottom of their dug-outs. The whole of the Stuff Redoubt was in our hands, and, so far, at trifling cost.

After three minutes, our barrage began to roll back, and our third wave passed over our first objective, kept close up to the barrage, and assaulted the next line we had got to take ; not at all an easy task, but here, too, everything came off with complete success. Point 80 on the right was gained after a momentary check, more Germans were killed and

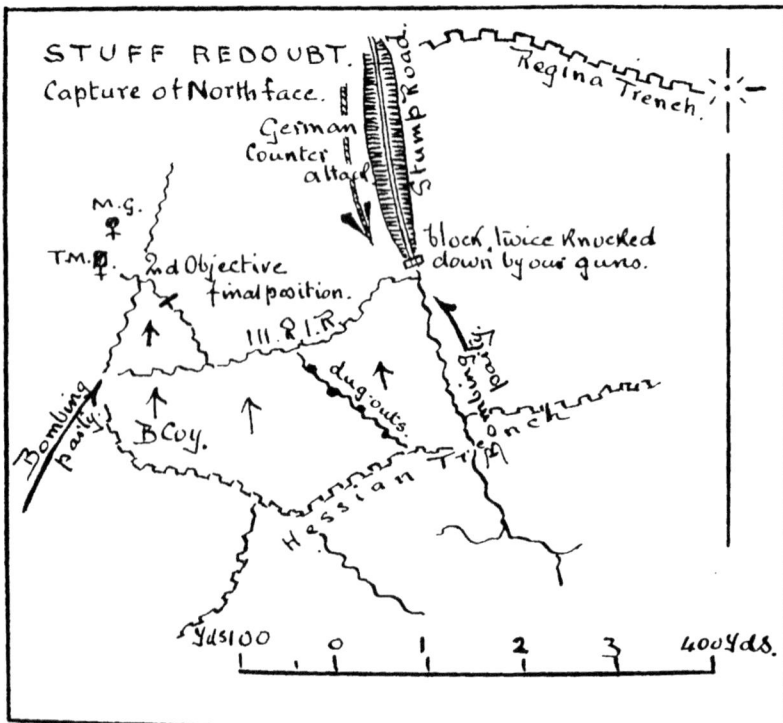

captured, some big dug-outs crowded with enemy were bombed and burnt out, and a block was made across Stump Road about 80 yards in front of Point 80. On the left, also, we did considerable execution but the Germans here were in great strength, and a tremendous fight ensued which lasted for about two hours.

As long as we had a good supply of rifle grenades, we were able to keep the Germans back, but they with their egg bombs and stick bombs could out-throw our fellows, and eventually we had to come back about 50 yards. The Germans had put on a good stiff barrage all this time, and there was a good deal of confusion and difficulty in getting bombs, ammunition and sandbags into the captured trenches. Communications to the rear were cut past repair, and the smoke and flashes made visual signalling impossible, so that one would get no help from the gunners at short notice. Another difficulty was that I had exactly one officer only, above the rank of 2nd/Lieutenant, who had as much as a few days' experience in the trenches, fortunately he was not wounded till 7 p.m. I went round the trenches at 3 p.m. Had wanted to go before but had been ordered by Bde. H.Q. to remain at my Battalion H.Q. Had a lively

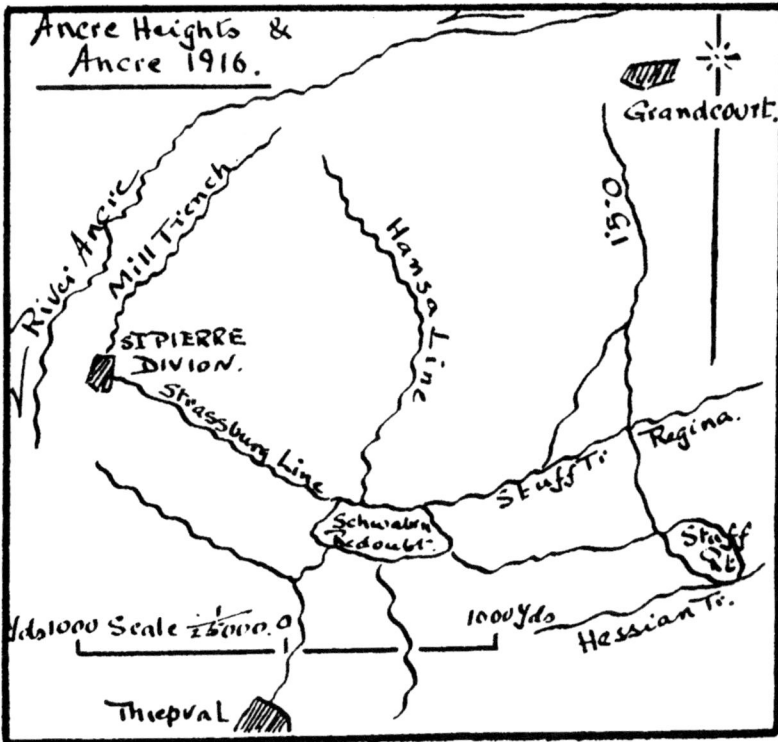

Ancre Heights & Ancre 1916.

walk, but was able to buck the men up, and find out all I wanted to know.

The German shelling was getting more severe and about 5 p.m. they put down a tremendous barrage. They were obviously going to counter-attack, and probably this time against my right. I, therefore, sent the remainder of my fourth company up to Point 80, where they arrived just at the right time. The enemy counter-attacked alongside of and up Stump Road and we had a bad moment when three officers got knocked out. However, the men were splendid and easily repulsed the attack with rifle and Lewis gun fire. The enemy were not finished with yet, and at 6 p.m. they put down another stiff barrage, and attempted another counter-attack. This time our artillery were able to assist, and the counter-attack was nipped in the bud. Lack of communication was a great trouble throughout. We had to see the first counter-attack through entirely by ourselves. We suffered a lot of casualties, and eventually had to abandon our advanced barricades in front of Point 80, owing to the fire of our own Gunners which we could not get them to lengthen.

After about 7 p.m., things began to quieten down a bit, though we had a good deal of trouble from a minenwerfer in front of our right, and there was shelling intermittently throughout the night. However, the men worked well. Went round and saw them once or twice, and day dawned with our being firmly established in the captured trenches, the Germans having apparently for the present, given us best.

We had lost one officer killed, 2nd/Lieut. W. Hunter, 8 officers wounded, 137 N.C.Os. and men killed, wounded or missing, but I do not know that that was very heavy when one considers how much we had done. We had captured the whole redoubt and the trenches beyond it, and killed certainly 70 or 80 Germans, exclusive of those killed or burnt in their dug-outs, or of casualties from our shelling. We had taken 120 prisoners, ... and the men behaved splendidly throughout, and there were many acts of great gallantry.

10th October. . . . It was a treat to see the men coming back with a grin from ear to ear, with German helmets and other souvenirs hanging all over them.

The Worcesters, 1st Battalion, gave the 10th Battalion a rousing cheer as it passed on its way back to rest.

*   *   *   *

On the 14th October, our 6th Battalion took part in an attack on the Schwaben Redoubt by the 37th Division. The Battalion was in reserve, but two platoons reinforced the Cambridgeshire Regiment and lost 3 officers and 14 N.C.Os. and men.

*   *   *   *

On 21st and 22nd of the month the 25th and 39th Divisions attacked Regina trench.

This attack was carried out under a barrage starting at 12-6 p.m. The troops had by now gained confidence in barrages and moved forward close under it. The enemy's wire had been effectually cut and was no obstacle.

The only one of our Battalions in the front line was the 13th which advanced in three waves and took its objectives without much difficulty, though the casualties were severe, 12 officers and 198 men.

*　　*　　*　　*

The 11th Battalion was split up, one company was attached to the 8th Border Regiment, one company was " carrying " for the two assaulting Brigades, and two companies were holding Hessian trench.

Some of the men of the 11th Battalion, attached to the 8th Borders overran the objective and got ahead of the barrage. In consequence a gap occurred at the point of junction of the Brigades, and here the enemy held out for some time. In the end the enemy post was taken and its defenders all killed or captured ; a large dug-out holding 150 men was afterwards found at this point.

*　　*　　*　　*

The 10th Battalion was also " carrying " and had one company garrisoning Stuff Redoubt.

*　　*　　*　　*

Our 9th Battalion also earned this honour by being in the area at the end of October and 1st November. But beyond the fact that the mud was " thigh deep," no mention is made of any action in their own or the Brigade War Diary. In fact, their Brigade-Major (*not* Major Adair, who by now had become G.S.O. 2) hardly records any movements, except his own, in the Brigade War Diary.

ANCRE. 13th to 18th November.

Map pp. 93, 96

The attacks in this battle were made in less unfavourable conditions than were those on the right flank near Le Transloy.

On the greater part of this front our trenches now, in November, looked down on an enemy in low lying and water-logged valleys.

If a surprise attack could be made, the Germans in front of the III. Army, to the north, might be taken in flank.

The Butte de Warlencourt marked the limit of progress of the right flank. Thence, the line ran through Stuff trench and Regina trench—north of Thiepval—to St. Pierre Divion, and thence it ran north unchanged since 1st July.

The condition of the ground has already been described. To make movement at all possible, duck-board tracks were laid from Thiepval to the assembly area. The trenches had been so shot about and damaged by weather that even in daylight it was hard to locate one's position or even to say whether one was in a trench or not. Fifteen yards a minute was the fastest that could be calculated on. Evacuation of wounded was almost impossible. Men had to sit down and pull their legs out of the mud.

The Fifth Army was to attack Grandcourt—St. Pierre Divion—Beaumont Hamel.

Our 6th Battalion (39th Division) was formed up in the Schwaben redoubt ready to advance in four lines, part of the main attack.

Zero was fixed for 5-45 a.m. The darkness was accentuated by a thick fog which lasted till 9 a.m. and caused some confusion on the left of the attack which moved forward under an excellent barrage. Our 6th Battalion and the Black Watch were the culprits owing to loss of direction.

The attack of our 6th Battalion down the Strassburg Line being interrupted by loss of direction, they missed their objective. However, the Adjutant, Lieut. Naden managed to re-organize them and they captured their objective, Mill trench, along the banks of the Ancre, by 8-30 a.m.

Captain R. Kirk, M.C., who led the leading wave, was killed, as also was Captain W. R. Innes and Lieut. Morrison. The total casualties were 167.

North of the Ancre, although Serre again resisted all attacks, Beaumont Hamel was captured.

*   *   *   *

On 18th April, an attack was made on Grandcourt on both sides of the river, in which the 9th Battalion took part. They started in reserve to the 19th Division, but as the situation was still obscure in the afternoon, the Battalion was ordered to make an attack. The order was given to the Colonel, R. B. Worgan at 2-30 and by 4-30 his arrangements were complete. The Battalion moved forward in artillery formation with orders to deploy on reaching the crest of the ridge near Stuff trench.

The going was very bad and a thick fog came down before the Battalion had reached the starting line. After passing Stuff trench, direction was lost, and there were no landmarks to pick up. The mud was deep and clinging, and when Lucky Way was reached, our barrage began and the companies immediately realized their mistake in direction and wheeled

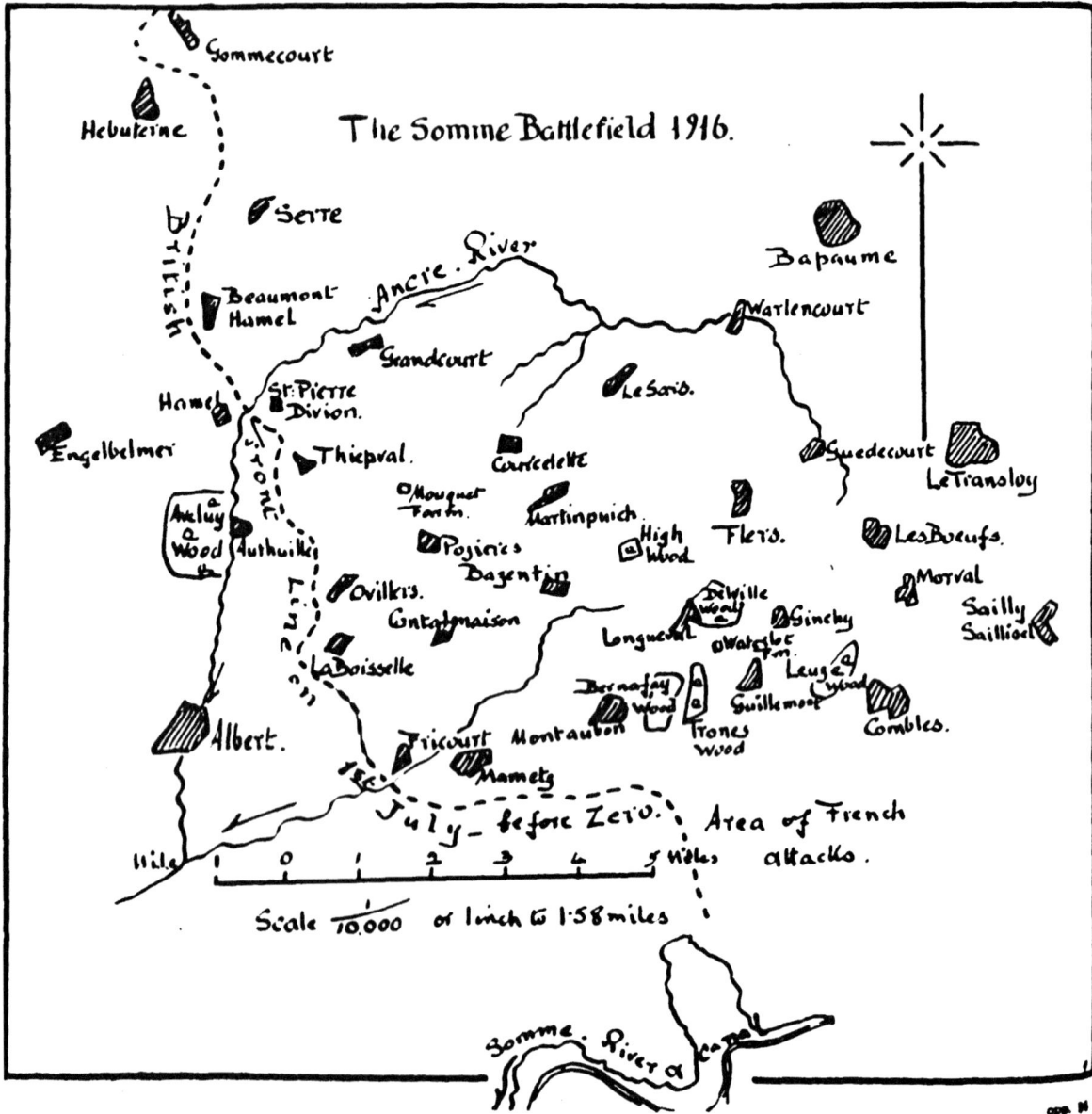

The Somme Battlefield 1916.

Scale $\frac{1}{10,000}$ or 1 inch to 1.58 miles

to the right to overtake the barrage a very fine piece of work. It was now dark and many men were lost in the mud and darkness. Eventually, four officers and a handful of men charged O.G. 1. The enemy drove them off with bomb and rifle. Meantime two platoons on the left, working alone had bombed a dug-out and captured a machine gun. But the enemy counter-attacked strongly and this party was driven back.

A third detachment reached the Ancre and was thence directed to their proper area by the 6th Battalion, who had reached Mill trench, as already related.

*   *   *   *

Raid in Flanders carried out by 10th Battalion on 17th February, 1917.

The raid was first discussed on 7th February when Colonel A. C. Johnston was given the idea at Brigade H.Q. He decided to pick 70 men from each of three companies. Training was begun at once. The trenches to be attacked were marked on the ground near Romarin, and every man was taught his exact rôle. Very careful reconnaissances were made of the German line to locate every detail of the ground to be crossed, and of the German defences. Meantime, the German trenches were systematically shelled and lanes were cut through their wire. The ground was hard with frost so the usual difficulty of mud was not encountered.

Colonel Johnston's diary :—" 15th Feb. Busy morning in the trenches, went back in the afternoon and saw my raiders practising. They are a splendid lot of men, and it is a real treat to see how keen they are. It is particularly refreshing when one remembers that these men, are no enthusiastic novices who don't know what they are going in to but all are old soldiers, who have been through the Somme and other big fights. Most of them have been wounded, and they all know well the inferno that they are entering. Yet they are all in tremendous fettle and are just itching to go over. The officers are the same and one feels proud to be commanding such men. I wanted about ten more men, and called for volunteers this morning from these three companies, and could have got 50 if I had wanted.

16th Feb. We have now made an awful mess of the German wire, and patrols report the right point of entrance good.

17th February. Up early and relieved to find it not raining (the ground had been frozen, but unluckily it began to thaw on the 16th). The raiders arrived in good time, drew their bombs, and assembled in the front trenches according to plan, without a hitch, about 20 minutes before zero. So they did not have long to hang about before the attack,

G

which is always a trying time. Was in the front trenches myself to wish them luck, after which I took post in the front line between the two parties, with one of the Battalion snipers, so that if we saw any German snipers, or machine guns, we could pick them off.

At 10-40 a.m., our hurricane bombardment began on the front to be attacked. Howitzers, and heavy guns turned on to known machine gun positions, and strong points, other heavy guns fired on German batteries, while 60 pounders and machine guns swept all the German communication trenches which they would be likely to use. The barrage under which we went to form up was not as thick or as accurate as it should have been. It was a bit behind instead of on top of the German trench. However, it kept the enemy's heads down, and our fellows were able to climb out of our trenches, get through our wire, and form up in three waves without being troubled.

They went across quite well . . . . I saw the left party reach the German trench, and the right party get to the German wire. Thinking all was well, I made my way back to Battalion Battle H.Q., where I was supposed to be. Arrived there, I heard that the right party had failed to get in owing to the wire being uncut. Apparently, it had been much knocked about, but not properly destroyed as erroneously reported. The right party held on for three or four minutes in the hope that the left party might be able to help them. They got badly knocked about by machine gun fire, till a very gallant Lewis gunner, standing up in the wire, emptied the whole of a magazine into the loophole and knocked the German machine gun out. The German trench was found to be packed. Our fellows bombed them, and undoubtedly knocked a good many over. As it was impossible to get through the wire, the right party withdrew. On the left, we got into the German front line. Killed 35, apart from those in nine dug-outs, full of Germans who refused to come out, and who, therefore had to be bombed with fumite bombs. "C" Company, for the German support line, went over in splendid style. They reached the support trench, which they found much battered by our artillery and full of dead Germans. Owing to the failure of the right party, they got badly pinched, and suffered a lot of casualties from machine guns on both flanks. The withdrawal was carried out very well, but our artillery was disappointing and did not keep the German machine guns down, and these cost us a lot of casualties."

The raid was a failure owing to the wire being reported cut on the right. Our losses were 40 killed and 60 wounded. We accounted for about 100 Germans exclusive of those killed by artillery fire, but it was a pity that the men who were so keen and who behaved so well did not have a better chance.

" Interim " trench work. The 1st Battalion in Flanders.

In March 1917, the 1st Battalion took over a new sector near Cambrai from a battalion of the 21st Division. Here they found that the German snipers had got the upper hand. It was unsafe to show a head anywhere and there were no snipers' posts in our lines. Lieut. Lee, the sniping expert, and his men, quickly got to work to build snipers' posts. Meanwhile, any form of activity on the part of the German was answered by severe rifle grenade fire. Once our snipers could get to work, they had instant success, one German sniper, wearing a camouflaged suit, being shot whilst lying out in their wire, from where he had been sniping at us. In a few days there was no more trouble from the Hun and all was quiet, which illustrates the truth of the maxim that offence is the best means of defence. In the Ferme-du-bois sector, our snipers had another success, accounting for the Commander of the 6th Bavarian Division which was opposite us.

During the whole of this winter, the Battalion was very short of establishment, all reinforcements being diverted to units on the Somme. As a result, the front was often very weakly held, and they had to resort to a system of defended posts along the front line. Frequent patrols moved from post to post, to ensure that none of the enemy gained a lodgment in the vacated portions of our trenches. This did not always prove sufficient, and other units had instances of small patrols being seized by enterprising Germans, who had entered an unoccupied trench unobserved. To guard against this, the Battalion adopted the tactics of making " No man's land " their own. Throughout the night, patrols were out between the lines which prevented the Germans sneaking across to our trenches. There is no doubt that constant patrolling of the enemy's front line gives more protection at night than does any number of sentry posts, however alert they may be.

Throughout this winter, which was an exceptionally cold one, the usual precautions were taken against " trench feet " and when in billets, every effort was made for the men's comfort, hot baths and frequent changes of clothing being provided. Leave home was opened and everyone, who could, availed themselves of the opportunity to visit England once more.

After the winter of 1914, it was always possible to deliver one hot meal a day to the trenches, as well as tea. Sproule put the food in hay-packed containers to keep it warm. Clean socks went up every night. Old jam tins, filled with grease and a wick, enabled the troops to cook tea for themselves, a dry issue of tea being made for the purpose.

On returning to rest each man got a hot bath, a change of clothing and a good hot meal.

ARRAS. 1917.

This honour covers the battles fought in the spring of 1917.

British G.H.Q. hoped that this would be the final and decisive campaign of the war. It was an attempt to complete that overthrow of Germans, which, it was believed, only the winter had prevented on the Somme. But, however well intentioned the plan, the methods of the Somme remained. It was not realized that these methods had failed.

*   *   *   *

The 5th Battalion, formed into a Special Reserve Brigade with the Field Companies R.E. of the 56th Division, was in position in support of the infantry on the night 27th/28th March in the Bailleul neighbourhood. An attack was beaten off by the infantry who fought magnificently with great grit and determination.

*   *   *   *

Arras Caves.

The Arras caves were used a good deal by the 5th Battalion at this period, and an account of them will be interesting.

The houses of Arras not only have cellars, but, below their cellars, excavations of great antiquity, locally called " boves," of some depth, from which stone was quarried for building. These excavations have been connected at some time and lead to a series of vast caves below the suburbs of Ronville and St. Sauveur. During the war, these caves, cleared and improved, were fitted with electric light and gave accommodation for large numbers of troops. They were most useful for the assembling of troops before an attack. The main passage had a light railway in it for trucks. At the west end, passages led into the sewers of Arras, and at the other, a long passage led to the trenches, some 1,200 yards from the town.

The caves were damp, smelly, gritty, and unhealthy. Great care had to be taken to protect them from gas. At times, heavy shells knocked down lumps from the roof and some parts became unsafe and were barricaded off. Cooking was a difficulty and water was unobtainable. In spite of this, the caves were used a good deal and Divisional bands used to give concerts in them.

A Typical Dressing Station near Arras.

VIMY. 9th to 14th April, 1917.

Map p. 105

The 1st Battalion advanced with the Canadians in their attack on the Vimy Ridge on the 9th April, and passed through them till brought up by the strongly-fortified position of La Culotte.

On 13th April, the 1st Battalion moved to Carency and was placed at two hours' warning. Early next morning, orders were received that the Battalion was to take over from 12th Canadian Brigade on the summit of Vimy Ridge, immediately east of Souchez. The Battalion Commander went forward to reconnoitre, leaving orders for the Battalion to rendezvous immediately S.E. of Souchez at 4 p.m. that evening. On arrival at Brigade Headquarters, the Brigade Commander suggested a personal reconnaissance, and the party proceeded to the top of the hill, only to find that the Germans had withdrawn and that the Canadian Brigade was following them up. Eventually, the Canadian front line was discovered, established in German trenches at the foot of the ridge, and to the east of Givenchy and Givenchy en Gohelle. Here two of our airmen, one with a broken leg and the other with a broken arm, were picked up. They had been brought down on the morning of the 9th and had been left there by the retiring Germans. They were carried back and both recovered from their injuries.

The problem now was how to get in touch with the Battalion, as orders had meanwhile come from the 15th Brigade that this forward line of trenches was to be occupied. There was nothing for it but to go back over the ridge and give them orders where to go.

On returning again to the east of the ridge, it was found that the Germans had withdrawn some distance and touch with them had been lost. During the interval, the Canadian Brigade Commander and his orderly had been strolling about in " No man's land " and had been wounded in attempting to stalk a German machine gun in the Bois de Hirondelle.

Just as it was getting dark, the Battalion arrived and was deployed in the German trenches east of Givenchy. As touch with the enemy had been lost, it was decided to push forward a line of outposts towards La Culotte. Orders to this effect were given and the Brigade informed.

Outposts were eventually established astride the Givenchy—La Culotte road and about half way between the two places, when a pre-emptory order was received from the Brigade to withdraw to the line which we were originally ordered to take over. By the time this withdrawal was completed, it was almost daylight, and at this moment, an order was received that the Battalion was to act as advance guard to the Brigade, moving via La Culotte on Lens. Practically none of the officers had any experience of this form of manœuvre and only after very strenuous work by the Battalion staff, was the unit ready to advance at the appointed time. All went well until nearing La Culotte, when they came on a line of German trenches, heavily wired and fully manned. Machine gun fire was also opened from houses in rear, and no further advance was possible. The 1st Devons on our left, were also held up and here they remained the whole day. In the afternoon, an unfortunate incident occurred. A party of the Devons coming up from the rear, mistook our Battalion Headquarters for a party of the enemy and opened fire on them. Our R.S.M., who had only just come out from home was killed.

There was now nothing for it but to organise the line and dig in, which was done on a line N.W. and S.E. about 400 yards west of La Culotte. Further attempt at an advance was impossible, as no close artillery support could be obtained. Shelling and the weather had combined to make the roads over the Vimy Ridge impassable, and all wheeled traffic had to move north of the Ridge by Angres. Here, the congestion was very bad. It was several days before any field artillery was in position in front of the ridge. Meanwhile the troops relied on 60 pounders for any artillery support required.

Later in the month, Second Scarpe, a " set piece " attack, failed to capture the La Culotte position, so it is not surprising that our casual advance, just related, failed.

* * * *

During the time Baker was in command of the 1st Battalion, two ladies of Chester, Miss May and Miss Alice Gore, embroidered a beautiful flag for the Battalion. The flag was carried for some time till a sudden concentration of transport wagons made in a hurry in the dark, took it from us. All efforts made to trace it and recover it failed.

FIRST SCARPE. 9th to 14th April.

The First and Third Armies were to break through the Hindenburg Line. The frontage allotted to the 56th Division was to the north west of Neuville Vitasse.

The attack was made in atrocious weather, but was quite successful.

* * * *

The 5th Battalion (Pioneers) was now employed clearing roads through Achicourt to Neuville Vitasse. Owing to the rapidity of the advance, road clearing demands were very heavy and meant hard work for the pioneers.

SECOND SCARPE. 23rd and 24th April.

This attack has already been mentioned. It was an attempt by the Canadian Corps on the Thelus—La Culotte line.

The 1st Battalion had very hard work preparing for the attack, carrying supplies, and building tracks.

The battle was fought in snow and torrential rain. The 1st Battalion was in reserve, but the reserves were so exhausted by their preliminary work that all " carrying " was done by " dumped personnel," known at other times as " B " teams.

Lieut. Bruce, our transport officer, especially distinguished himself, as did his Sergeant, Smith. Smith was the ideal Transport Sergeant. Whatever the conditions, he always managed some shelter for his animals. So, they were always fit. This contributed in no small measure to the satisfactory working of the transport services. Smith himself was always cheerful and ready to take his share of any dirty work that was going.

The German position was exceptionally strong and successfully withstood the attack, thanks largely to the very heavy belts of wire which our artillery was unable to cut.

Our casualties were over 100 officers and men in the period 9th to 24th.

THIRD SCARPE. 3rd and 4th May.

On the 3rd May, a simultaneous attack was made by the Fifth, Third and First Armies on the high ground east of Bois du Sait, St. Robart and Chensy.

The 5th Battalion had a strenuous time consolidating and improving advanced trenches in this unsuccessful attack.

Two companies repaired the Arras—Cambrai road, which had been badly damaged by shell fire.

In the preparation for these battles the 5th Battalion lost 2nd/Lieuts. N. P. Sandiford and R. Smallwood.

OPPY. 28th June. An " Action " in the Third Scarpe.

Map p. 105

The object of this attack was to move the enemy from a position in front of Oppy Wood, from which he had observation over our lines, and was limited to the German front line system.

Only eight Battalions took part, and on that account it is a rather unusual " honour." The Battalions were our First Battalion, the 1st

Norfolk, 1st Bedford and 16th Royal Warwicks of the 15th Brigade, and four Battalions of the 95th Brigade. All units were very much below strength.

Preparations for the attack included making by the Cavalry Division Pioneer Battalion four long communication trenches across the Vimy Ridge totalling some 10,000 yards in all ; improving existing trenches and making new forming-up trenches ; making dummy trenches to disperse the enemy's fire ; and lastly, detailed instruction and practice of the assaulting troops over a taped training course.

The artillery was to carry out steady destructive bombardments on the whole Corps front, and to obliterate portions of the enemy trenches from which he might interfere with the attack. Wire-cutting and active counter-battery work was carried out for five days. It was arranged that during the assault every hostile gun should be engaged, if only by one gun or howitzer.

Heavy flanking machine gun fire was arranged to bear across the front of the captured trenches after the objectives had been gained.

Stokes guns were to fire a smoke screen to hide the left flank of the attack.

Daily reconnaissances by infantry and aeroplanes, and practice over dummy trenches were carried out for a week before the attack. Troops were equipped as lightly as possible.

Other preparations for the attack included the dumping of all necessary supplies, reserves of water in petrol tins, ammunition, and bombs, well forward, in order to save the men a long carry when moving into the assembly trenches. The wisdom of this was well illustrated as, when the Battalion moved in on the evening of 27th June, all these etceteras were carried forward from the dumps within an hour. On the other hand, the unit on our right had not arranged for similar dumps and their men were carrying stores right up to within an hour of zero. Zero hour was fixed for 7 p.m. on 28th and the men had a long and weary wait throughout the day.

The 95th Brigade attacked on the right, and on the 15th Brigade front, the four Battalions attacked in line, each on a two company front, in this order from right to left—16th Royal Warwickshire, our 1st Battalion, 1st Norfolk, 1st Bedfordshire.

The enemy appears to have realized that an attack was intended, for the crowded assembly trenches were heavily shelled, and some 200 casualties caused in the two Brigades. This did not affect the nerves of the troops, for the assault was launched with great dash and vigour under a perfect 18-pounder barrage.

So quickly did the infantry move that the enemy barrage, which opened in three minutes, fell on practically empty trenches.

The objectives were rapidly secured, and consolidation begun. At 7-30 p.m. a thunderstorm broke with great violence, accompanied by lightning and torrential rain. This seriously interfered with the work and soaked everyone to the skin.

Consolidation under cover of advanced posts was practically complete by mid-day on the 29th, three communication trenches had been made. Of our casualties, 60% were " walking " wounded, and, in all, amounted to 3 officers and 50 others, mostly wounded.

The operation was a simple one. Both flanks were adequately protected, ample time allowed for preparation, adequate covering fire arranged, careful staff arrangements made, and provision made for rapid consolidation. Such preliminaries should always ensure success in cases where a definite and limited objective is in view.

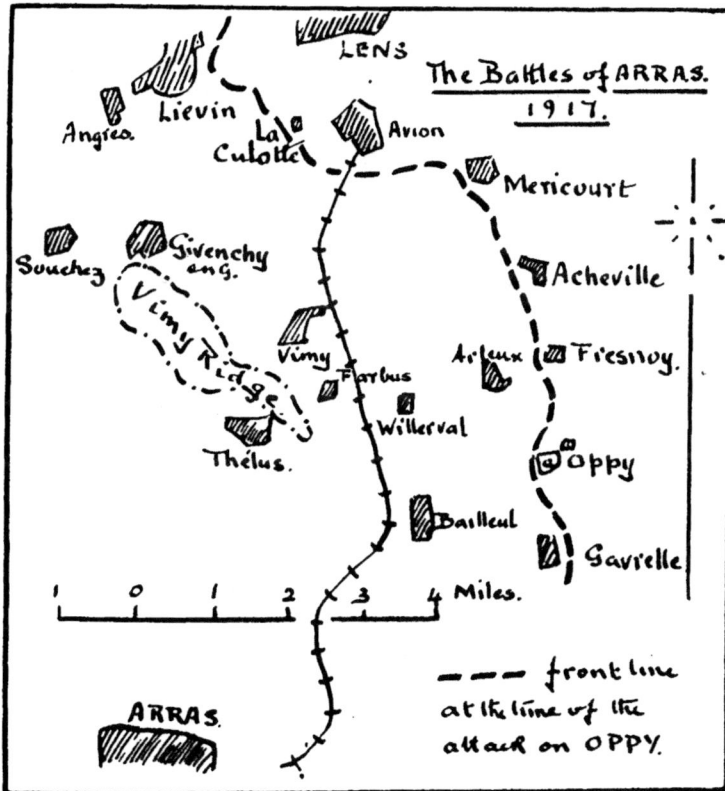

The Battles of ARRAS. 1917.

--- front line at the time of the attack on OPPY.

MESSINES. 7th to 14th June, 1917.

Map p. 109

The battle of Messines was a preliminary move in a plan to occupy the belt of high ground which runs from Armentieres to Dixmude, and which overlooks the Ypres Salient.

A glance at the map shows how possession of that part of this high ground which runs from Wytschaete to Messines, not only gave the Germans observation over the roads and tracks leading forward from Ypres, but also enabled them to fire into the backs of the defenders of the Salient's trenches.

The general plan was to begin at the south end of the high ground and work northwards. Thus, the axis of the Messines attack diverged from the German lines of communication and, however successful, could not affect the German position in France. This battle, then, was one with a limited objective, and there was no question of a " break-through." It was, strictly, a siege operation. The Germans had fortified the ridge with two separate trench systems, each consisting of front and supporting trenches with switch lines and wire, and they also had a series of supporting trenches on the reverse slope of the ridge. In all, in the depth to be traversed by the troops, there were no less than nine distinct lines of trenches to be captured. These lines were grouped in the plan of attack, and subdivided into " objectives," coloured on the maps. The hour at which troops and barrages were to reach, or to move on from, each objective was laid down.

Across the Wulverghem front from which our Battalions started, ran the valley of the Steen-Beek, a little rivulet which flows into the River Douve. From our lines, it was not possible to see into the bottom of this valley, and so the possibility of uncut wire always existed, in spite of the great efforts of our artillery to cut it.

Our men had to advance down the slope to the brook, cross the bottom reasonably dry at this time of year, and then climb the opposite slopes, heavily protected, not only with trenches, but also with several fortified farms, woods and specially constructed strong points.

The preparations for this attack had been in hand for a long time, and were continued up to the very eve of the battle. These preparations included road-making, water supply and storage, tramways, magazines, dressing-stations, aid posts, shelters of many kinds, crossings over the Douve, bomb-proof telephone exchanges, engineer store dumps, ration dumps, tunnelled H.Q. for Brigades, less " protected " Battalion H.Q., concrete report centres, miles of communication and assembly trenches, many artillery headquarters, command posts, shelters for gun crews, trench mortar emplacements, machine gun emplacements and thousands of yards of cable trench, dug seven feet deep.

During the whole period the infantry worked with the technical troops, interspersed with periods of duty in the trenches. All were working against time, and all benefited from the inspiration of their great commander, Plumer. Thanks to this, and to genuine hard work by the troops, assisted by admirable staff work, the task was completed in time.

One of the best pieces of work was the construction by the 7th Brigade which included our 10th Battalion, of a front line assembly trench. Although it was only 150 yards from the German front line, it was dug four and a half feet deep, in three hours, on the night of the 30th/31st of May.

During this period of preparation, artillery and machine guns kept the wire " open," and trench mortars kept up a destructive fire on all enemy organizations, trenches and wire, and constant raids were made by the infantry. On the 16th of May, for instance, the 13th Battalion raided the enemy, when two officers were wounded, 2/Lieut. Jones, The Welch Regiment, and 2/Lieut. Malone. Again on the 24th of May, Captain Moir led a large raid of 120 men with 2/Lieut. D. P. Dunkley. On neither of these raids were any Germans captured, but identifications were secured.

But the key-factor in this battle was the great line of mines, twenty in number, distributed along the front of attack beneath the German trenches. These mines had been " laid," that is to say dug with incredible skill, in the face of very active counter-mining by the Germans. It required not only skill on the part of the tunnellers, but determination on the part of the Army Commander who had to decide whether to risk discovery, or to " blow " a mine which the enemy counter-mines might discover. In one case, the German counter-mine was within 18 inches of ours.

Only one mine had to be " blown," leaving nineteen for " the day." These mines held 600 tons of explosives, and required 8,000 yards of galleries. As well as this, a formidable array of guns, amounting to one gun to every 7 yards of front, was assembled to support the attack.

The plan of attack was based on leap-frogging. The 7th and 74th Brigades attacked with two battalions in front line which, on reaching their objectives, were to be passed by the two rear battalions. Similarly, the 75th Brigade was to pass through these latter and move on to the final Divisional objective. The Divisional front was skilfully planned to narrow down from 1,260 yards at the start to 700 yards on the top of the ridge. The assembly was carefully arranged and timed and took place without a hitch.

In this great battle, we were represented by four Battalions. Three of them, the 10th, 11th and 13th were in the 25th Division and attacked under the orders of the Anzac—Australian and New Zealand Army Corps—just North of Messines. The fourth was the 9th Battalion, in the 19th Division, which attacked just north of Wytschaete. The areas in which they attacked are shown on the sketch map.

Starting on the right, the 25th Division was in the Wulverghem Sector. The 13th Battalion, in the 74th Brigade, commanded by Colonel L. H. K. Finch, went over the top at zero, under cover of the terrific explosions of the mines, and of a hail of steel from 250 British guns of all calibres. This Brigade had the greatest depth to pass, some 2,000 yards.

There was a slight ground mist. As our mines went off and barrage fell, a line of light from the simultaneous discharge of enemy S.O.S. rockets sprang into view and extended for six miles from North to South, a very peculiar and striking spectacle. The troops moved forward in a gathering cloud of dust and smoke from the explosions of mines and shells, as well as from mist and gas.

The 13th Battalion swept over the first German trenches and the leading companies, " C " and " D " (Lieut. Pigott and Captain Thomas), reached the second line, their objective. Some direction had been lost, but Colonel Finch, arriving with the leap-frogging companies, " A " and " B " (Lieut. Gilderall and Captain Moir), led them forward to the Battalion objective.

* * * * *

The 10th Battalion, under Major J. B. Howell, M.C., Colonel A. C. Johnston having had the mortification of being retained with the " B " teams by Division H.Q., started in the second wave of the 7th Brigade and reached their final objective without much loss. On the way, their left company (Captain S. F. Morgan), captured and passed Hell Farm, but the second wave were counter-attacked from Hell (Lenfer) Wood. Both these places are on the left of the area marked on the map. A grim struggle ensued, in which our men gradually gained the upper hand, and killed or captured all the German defenders of the wood and the farm.

* * * *

In the meantime, the 11th Battalion, in the 75th Brigade, under Colonel W. K. Evans, D.S.O., left their assembly positions at 6-50 a.m. to attack the most distant of the Division's objectives. They secured them quickly, but pushing on too keenly, an officer and some men of the 11th Battalion found themselves attacking Despagne Farm. The officer suddenly realized that he was ahead of our barrage. It was too late to do anything but get the men into shell holes and await the storm. It came and fell in all its terrible fury, but the bulk of the little party were lucky enough to live to tell the tale.

Thanks to the excellent arrangements made by the Staff, and to the energy of carrying parties, material for consolidation, as well as food and water, was rapidly on the spot, and was promptly used to make counter-attack as difficult as possible for the Germans. The position gained was, in short, consolidated, and none too soon, for at 1-45 p.m. a strong counter-attack by a German battalion from the Blauwepoort Beek was beaten off mainly by rifle fire of the 11th Battalion and a platoon of the 8th Border Regiment. The opportune arrival of boldly handled sections of machine guns was of very great help.

The casualties were :—

13th Battalion.—2 officers and 29 others killed, 4 officers and 132 others wounded.

10th Battalion.—1 officer and 26 others killed, 7 officers and 14 others wounded.

11th Battalion.—3 officers and 43 others killed, 8 officers and 170 others wounded.

* * * *

It is impossible to omit reference to the artillery. Their programme was, as can well be imagined, most carefully arranged to suit the estimated rate of progress of the infantry. So skilfully had this been done by the Divisional Commander, General E. G. T. Bainbridge, that no alteration

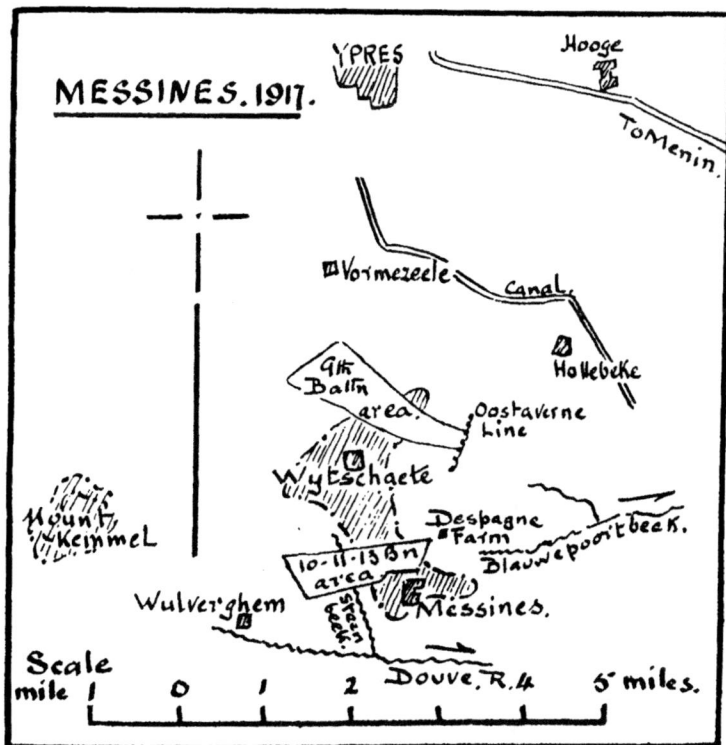

MESSINES. 1917.

was required by the infantry during the whole battle. Standing barrages moved forward in such a way that all Germans within 1,500 yards of our infantry were kept under continuous fire. These standing barrages remained till " relieved " by the arrival of the " creeping " or " rolling " barrage, and then moved on to their next task.

To augment the normal means of getting supplies of all kinds forward to the fighting troops, a pack transport company was formed in the Division, in five convoys. All did excellent work. One of them was under Lieut. Green of the 13th Battalion.

As has been shown, the capture of each objective was carried out with few casualties, but the subsequent shelling of our newly-won lines was amazingly and unexpectedly accurate. Carrying and working parties also suffered heavily. The enemy guns took a heavy toll of life in the days following the assault.

*   *   *   *

We must now turn to the left flank of this great attack where the 9th Battalion (19th Division) was also earning its laurels. The 58th Brigade had two lines to capture. Like the rest of the force, the 19th Division took their full share in all the fatiguing preparations for the attack, and the 9th Battalion had dug an assembly trench, laid out and organized by Lieut. J. G. Wood. The Battalion had paid daily visits to a full scale model of their objectives on the ridge.

Arrangements similar to those of the 25th Division for gun, machine gun and trench mortar fire were in force on this front.

Under Colonel R. B. Worgan, the 9th Battalion went over the top at 3-10 a.m., " A " and " B " Companies leading, into the cloud of dust, smoke and debris caused by the mine explosions, blown in their faces by the east wind. Some sections lost direction, and gaps were filled from the second wave.

Passing through the troops which had captured the first German lines, the leading companies reached their objectives at 4-50 a.m., where many Germans were killed or captured. There was a two-hour halt here, which was spent in " consolidating," an imperative necessity, and in reorganizing the platoons.

At 6-50 the advance continued, following the rolling barrage. The sun had driven the morning mist away and the Battalion reached its final objective in bright sunshine.

Almost at once, the 57th Brigade passed through. Rations, water and material were brought up by the Regimental Sergeant-Major and the trench made safe against attack. During the afternoon, the Battalion moved forward to a line near Oostaverne. 2nd/Lieut. F. B. Gadsden was killed and 34 men, and 3 officers and 120 men were wounded. At nightfall a heavy artillery strafe fell on the front line, but, somehow, the Battalion was undamaged.

During the ensuing days enemy artillery increased in intensity and caused casualties.

Although outside the period of the battle, two excellent reconnaissances on the 18th must be mentioned. They were made by 2nd/Lieuts. Colvin and Read, and located the new German positions on this front.

* · * * *

The actual capture of the position on the 7th had taken one hour and forty minutes. In the words of the Commander-in-Chief's despatch "The position assaulted was one of very great natural strength on the defence of which the enemy had laboured for nearly three years. The excellent observation from this position had ensured him ample warning of our intentions."

"The sight of the battlefield after the battle, its utter and universal desolation stretching interminably on all sides, its trenches battered out of all recognition, its wilderness of shell holes, debris, tangled wire, broken rifles and abandoned equipment confirms the opinion that no troops, whatever their morale and training can withstand the fire of such overwhelming and concentrated masses of artillery as were brought against the Germans. With a definite and limited objective and sufficient artillery support, complete success can be reasonably guaranteed" (official report 25 Div.)

Although the story of our own Battalions only has been told, the battle was a perfect example of co-operation of all arms and services to a common end.

Four Battalions of The Regiment engaged in a comparatively small front, and in so successful an operation, made this one of the red-letter days in the story of The Regiment. Their dash, discipline and determination could not have been bettered by any troops.

Our total casualties in The Regiment were 7 officers and 132 men killed, and 22 officers and 436 men wounded.

YPRES, 1917.

Map p. 125

After Messines, a long pause of two months ensued while preparations for the remaining attacks were made. As had been the case before the Somme and Messines, preparations for the offensive were on a vast scale, and while they called for the highest skill on the part of the Staff, which was generally forthcoming, they also made demands on the courage and physical energy of the troops which led to complete exhaustion.

These preparations could not be concealed from the Germans who made characteristic counter-preparations. In this district, owing to water lying so close to the surface, mined dug-outs were out of the question. The Germans held their line, therefore, lightly, in a series of disconnected posts, strongly supported by concrete pill-boxes for machine guns, while the remainder of the men were held back ready for counter-attack.

Among the preliminaries of the Ypres offensive was a raid carried out by 4 officers and 130 men of the 6th Battalion with an R.E. demolition party, on Caliban trench, just north of Wieltje. This took place on the night of the 4th/5th of July. It was preceded by " wire cutting " with 106 fuzes, that is with fuzes which burst immediately on impact, so that the whole force of the charge is expended in the air, and thus " cuts " wire among which it falls.

There were two broad bands of wire, and all ranks of the raiding party satisfied themselves, by patrolling, that satisfactory gaps existed in both bands.

Just before zero, an enemy patrol advanced but was driven back by our scouts and caught in our barrage.

The raid went over in two waves, under a barrage, and as the barrage lifted on to the enemy support trench, the first wave was in the first trench. Four prisoners, the survivors of the garrison, were despatched to our lines under escort.

At zero+6 the artillery lifted off the support trench and formed a box barrage, while the second wave rushed the support trench.

After doing all the damage they could with explosives, the party withdrew at zero+35.

The raid was very much assisted by a feint attack on the left, where wire had also been cut and kept open. The enemy artillery put down a really heavy barrage in our lines after the attack. One officer was killed and nine men were wounded. In the subsequent bombardment, four men were killed and 12 wounded.

The raid was a great success and earned much credit for the Battalion and its C.O., Colonel W. H. Stanway, D.S.O., M.C., and Captain J. Lee, who commanded the raiding party. Every man knew his task thoroughly and the enemy trenches by heart. It was quite a model raid, and secured valuable information.

Two Military Crosses and four Military Medals were awarded.

PILCKEM. 31st July to 2nd August.

Map p. 124

The 6th Battalion (118th Brigade) followed the attack, moving N.E. from Wieltje on St. Julien, in reserve to their Division. About 10 a.m. they passed through the leading troops on a line beyond the Hannebeek, including St. Julien.

The advance proceeded steadily in a terrific downpour of rain, and passing through St. Julien, the 6th Battalion captured the final objective, known as the Green Line, some 1,100 yards north-east of St. Julien. Patrols were pushed forward to Tirpitz Farm about 300 yards on, occupied it, and formed a defensive flank.

Unfortunately the troops on our right had not advanced with us, and had been held up short of St. Julien. Consequently, a large gap appeared on our right. The enemy were not slow to take advantage of this, and an attempt was made to turn our right flank, causing us many casualties. Simultaneously, a number of the enemy in front, who had surrendered, took new heart and picked up their rifles. A hand to hand combat of a desperate nature followed. Our men were fighting not to be cut off; the Germans to save a desperate situation. On top of all came down a heavy German barrage. A heavy German counter-attack developed from the north on the Battalion on our left, the Hertfordshire Regiment, which having lost all its officers, was forced to withdraw. A gallant counter-attack by the Cambridgeshire Regiment held up the Germans, and gave our men a chance of withdrawing. The whole line fell back slowly, fighting stubbornly, to the St. Julien line, along the east bank of the Beek which was reached by about 5 p.m.

Heavy shelling marked the rest of the evening in which our guns, owing to the general confusion, caused us many casualties.

The casualties were very heavy. Captain Jack Lee, M.C., Lieuts. G. Cowpe and W. E. Rogers were killed, and 193 men killed or missing; 12 officers and 269 men wounded.

Captain Frank Naden brought the Battalion out of action. He had played a conspicuous part in the attack.

*   *   *   *

The 25th Division (10th, 11th and 13th Battalions) was in II. Corps on the right of the Fifth Army attack. Its objective was Zonnebeke. The Division was in support to the 8th Division, moving on the left of the Corps along the line of the Ypres-Roulers railway.

The two leading Brigades followed up the attack—that is the 7th (10th Battalion) and 75th (11th Battalion) while the Battalions of the 74th Brigade (13th Battalion) were held ready for any work that might be required by the Chief Engineer.

H

The attack did not progress beyond a line on the western slope of the Westhoek ridge, where the 7th Brigade took over the line.

After the battle, the 75th Brigade similarly took over the line on the left of the 7th up to the Roulers railway.

*   *   *   *

The story of the 10th Battalion in the battle of Pilckem, from Colonel A. C. Johnston's diary follows.

31st July. " Zero for the great push was at 3-50 a.m. Suddenly, as if by a wave of a magician's wand, hundreds of guns began to roar, captive balloons were hoisted in every direction, the sky became full of aeroplanes which seemed to arrive from all corners of the horizon, light trains steamed up full of troops, bodies of infantry began filling up all the emergency routes, mounted troops trotted up towards the front, lorries in streams noisily made their way along the roads. R.E. and Pioneers began moving up with all their tools and paraphernalia . . . . We were busy ourselves issuing bombs and tools, and getting ready to move forward. At 6-30 a.m., we heard that the first two objectives had been gained on the whole Army front. Soon after, we started to move up to our forward assembly area at Halfway House. This entailed going along a track through our guns. The noise was simply deafening, and some of our recruits were rather terrified by it. However, we got along all right and were lucky not to have to go through much German shelling. The orders were for the whole Brigade to be crammed into tunnels. I was pretty certain that there was not room for all and, as we were the rear Battalion, I saw there was not much chance for us. Fortunately, I knew this area very well, and took the law into my own hands by putting three companies into some neighbouring trenches, where they were very comfortable. They got in before the shelling on Halfway House began. This shelling caught some of the men trying to get into the tunnels where the congestion was awful. I lost two officers and two sergeants here. We halted here some hours, and it was obvious that the attack on the front near Hooge was not going well. Further north, things were going excellently, but the weather looked ominous. About 5-30 p.m., we got orders to relieve the 24th Brigade (8th Division) on the West Hoek and Bellewarde ridges to-morrow. It had now begun to rain steadily. I went up past Bellewarde lake to the 2nd Northamptons whom I was to relieve. The ground was already very slippery, a mass of crump holes, and in an awful state generally. The attack had gone well up to a point, but machine gun fire from the right flank had eventually held up the advance. The Germans had few men in their front system, so the casualties and prisoners were less than had been hoped. Hardly had I got back to Halfway House, than I was sent for to Brigade H.Q. The corps were nervous lest the 8th Division should be driven off the Bellewarde ridge. They, therefore, ordered a Battalion to be sent up to lie out in the open on the reverse slope of the ridge, not to go into the trenches on the ridge, and not to be used for anything. It was to wait till the 8th Division had been pushed off the ridge, and then it was to counter-attack the Germans off it—what an order! We were to be within 150 yards of the 8th Division, but were not allowed to help them till the position was lost, though we were to counter-attack up a steep slope, through a good deal of wire, and over nothing but a wide expanse of slippery crump holes. Prior to this attack, the Battalion would be lying out in the open, under an intense barrage from which they would have no protection. However, it had got to be, and my Battalion was " for it." It was now 11-30 p.m., pitch dark, the whole country a mass of slimy mud and obstacles. No one in the Battalion except myself and one other had ever seen the ground before. I went on ahead with an orderly in the pouring rain, and though I knew every inch of the ground, was unemcumbered with equipment, and had a stick to help me along, I found some difficulty in finding my way. Owing to the mud, it took me over two hours to get there, a distance of only a mile. When I got there, the 24th Brigade did not want us. However, the order had to be carried out. Waiting for the Battalion to arrive, and wet to the skin, I slithered about looking for any old German dug-out to shelter in, but without success. Tried several times to shelter in a hurdle lean-to in the wood near the lake, but was always getting shelled, and eventually had to content myself with walking up and down in mud up to my knees in a vain endeavour to keep warm, with my clothes soaked, and with the rain trickling down my neck. The worst night I have ever known.

1st August. The Battalion began to arrive about 3-30 a.m. The men were fearfully done up, having been slithering about in the dark all night, wet to the skin, and carrying a lot of extra weight. I felt very bad at having to line them out in the swamp, and put them in little groups in crump holes, most of which were deep in water. There was a little shelling, and being out in the open, we began at once to have casualties. About 7 a.m., to my great relief, I was told I could relieve the 2nd Northamptons right away. But it was not going to help us much, as they were holding new, half-dug trenches, which the rain was fast filling, or making them crumble to nothing. The relief was quickly over, and I made my H.Q. in a German concrete machine gun emplacement on the Bellewarde ridge. The rain continued to pour, and there was a good deal of shelling. About mid-day, the Germans started to bombard us heavily, and kept it up for the rest of the day. We had an awful time. There was no cover for the men. Trenches were soon non-existent, or became wet ditches in which men often sank up to their waists, and it often took six men to pull one man out of the mud. The Germans had got the range to an inch, had direct observation on to us from our right, and plastered the area incessantly with crumps, whizz-bangs, and 4.2's. Our casualties mounted rapidly. There was no cover, all one could do was to spread the men out in crump holes to minimize casualties. In these circumstances, the men are apt to crowd together. It was when I was going about shaking them out that I got hit, though only slightly. First I was knocked off my feet by a bit of shrapnel, which fortunately only went through my boot and sock, and badly bruised my ankle. About 20 minutes later, I got a small piece of shell in the left hand which the doctor extracted. My poor fellows had an awful time, and many wounded sank in the mud, and were drowned in it before assistance could reach them, or before they were discovered. One officer, who had practically sunk in the mud out of sight, was found only half an hour after I had been speaking to him. We had about 200 casualties in the day, and besides this, there were men dropping from cold and exhaustion. The stretcher bearers could not compete with the number of casualties, and, in many cases, it required about 6 men to carry a stretcher, as each man sank into the mud at least up to his knees, and most of the men were too done up to be able to carry the weight.

As it got dark, the shelling gradually subsided, but not so the rain, which fell incessantly. We got rations up with difficulty, but cooking was out of the question. The men had just to make the best of things, and spent the night in the mud, often up to their waists. Fortunately, we managed to get some rum which warmed them up a bit.

2nd August. The rain still continues and conditions are as bad as I have ever known. We get shelled at intervals, and, as there is no cover, we are still having a good many casualties. The powers that be are continually warning us that the enemy means to counter-attack us. In the present state of the ground, I doubt if they could attack.

The Battalion was relieved in the early morning of the 4th August, and moved back to Halfway House. Though it was only a mile, it took the men all their time to get back. Even here, the mud round about was so deep, the tunnels and dug-outs so water-logged, and the filth and smells so bad, that it was no real rest for the men. The Battalion went back to Vancouver Camp on the 5th.''

The 10th Battalion lost 2nd/Lieut. W. G. Hastings and 53 men killed and missing, and 10 officers, of whom 6 remained at duty and 140 men wounded.

* * * *

The 11th Battalion lost Captains R. Mallinson and G. E. Martin, 2nd/Lieuts. G. W. Watson, T. C. Morgan and R. Duncanson killed and 136 men killed and wounded.

* * * *

During this period, but outside the area officially assigned to " Pilckem," the 9th Battalion (19th Division) took part in an attack in the Wytschaete area, towards Hollebeke. The whole Division was on a three-battalion frontage.

The 9th Battalion was in rear of the whole Division and took no active part in the fighting, but took over front line trenches on the 2nd where conditions were very bad in every respect, mud, shelling and cover. The 9th Battalion had made a successful raid on Junction Buildings on 17th on the Wytschaete front.

* * * *

When we speak of reserves it is well to visualize what being in reserve in this type of warfare meant.

As shelling and rain gradually churned up every yard of progress, the task of supplying the advanced troops with food, water, material for consolidation, and ammunition, assumed colossal proportions, and had to be borne by troops in so-called reserve. They themselves not only were liable to be called on to fight, and as often as not were so employed, to stem a retreat, to fill a gap, or to exploit a success, but were invariably required to take over the line and endure heavy punitive shelling, to allow the attacking troops to withdraw and recoup.

So, when we read of such or such a Battalion being in reserve during an attack, we must not imagine them sitting behind a haystack on Salisbury Plain, but picture, rather, their ceaseless journeys in clinging and slippery mud, through mazes of communication trenches, crowded with wounded, and sometimes with beaten soldiers, carrying heavy loads, soaked to the skin, and enduring at every turn shelling purposely intended to hinder their progress.

At other times, we can picture the reserves digging for dear life, in order to get some cover against the fury of bullet and shell with which the tenacious German was certain to support his inevitable counter-attack.

This aspect of " Reserves " is emphasized, because, without their gallant labours, many a successful attack would have lost all its gains.

West Hoek. 10th and 11th August.

Map p. 124

An incident in the Ypres area was an operation carried out by the 74th Brigade in which our 13th Battalion was engaged on the 10th and 11th August, but which was not awarded a battle honour. It was, however, so successful, that a full account of it is warranted.

The object of the raid was to improve the observation to the East and South East, in other words, to complete the capture of the West Hoek ridge.

The left of the Brigade was on the Roulers railway.

It rained incessantly the whole day. The 13th Battalion, under Colonel L. H. K. Finch, advanced at 4-25 a.m. in four waves. The first wave reached the objective without much difficulty, after capturing an enemy strong-point. The fourth wave was to push through to a covering position, which was to be held until the original line had been consolidated. But, unfortunately, it was caught in heavy shell fire and reached the covering line with only 1 N.C.O. and 14 men. The right flank was reinforced by parties of the 7th Bedfordshire Regiment from another division. A gap was caused by the heavy casualties on the left which was not closed till after dark. Meanwhile, evacuation of Glencorse Wood by troops on the right laid the right flank of the 13th Battalion open to fire from snipers and machine guns. Hostile artillery failed to pick up the new Brigade line except in the case of our 13th Battalion. However, consolidation was pushed on under cover of posts in front.

Counter-attacks were made throughout the day and night, which were mostly annihilated by machine gun and gun fire.

At 11-23 the O.C. 3rd Worcestershire Regiment took over command of the 13th Battalion whose C.O., second-in-command and all senior officers had become casualties.

Very fine work was done by the machine guns supporting the 13th Battalion. Some of them were in action for 30 hours, up to their waists in water, enduring heavy shelling and sniping.

Supplies were carried up for the attacking troops by other Brigades with the greatest difficulty.

The total casualties of the Battalion were 2nd/Lieut. P. B. Silcock killed, 10 wounded, including Colonel Finch and Major Nares, 106 men killed or missing and 266 wounded.

The tactical importance of West Hoek ridge is fully brought out in Haig's despatch of 25.12.17. para. 44.

"During the night of 31st July and on the following days, the enemy delivered further counter-attacks against our new line, and in particular made determined efforts to dislodge us from the high ground between the Menin Road and the Ypres-Roulers railway . . . . In this he completely failed."

.   .   .   .

"A week later (than 3rd Aug.) a successful minor operation carried out by English troops (18th and 25th Divisions) gave us complete possession of West Hoek."

General view of devastated area, showing wrecked transport.
Westhoek Ridge, 26th October, 1917.

Machine gunners manning shell-holes, Passchendaele, 14th November, 1917.

The Battalions were composed of 50% recruits, who had joined since Messines, who had worked hard to turn themselves into soldiers. (Bde. Report p. 10).

    *   *   *   *

The 10th and 11th Battalions were also employed in the area of this operation " carrying " and being in readiness to support the attack.

The success of the attack was the subject of a special order from II. Corps, 14th Aug. 1917.

LANGEMARCK. 16th to 18th August.

Map p. 124

The 11th Battalion moved from Dominion Camp into Ypres in readiness to help the 8th Division who had been severely handled in an attack on the 16th.   But the Battalion was not called on to fight.

    *   *   *   *

The 5th Battalion was employed on 16th carrying material, and constructing and wiring strong points for the Brigades of the 56th Division attacking Glencorse Copse and Polygon Wood.   The night was a terrible one, the ground being so cut up by shell fire and the mud so deep and tenacious, that movement was almost impossible.   Hostile shelling was so intense that little constructional work was feasible.   The companies returned in the early morning, quite exhausted.   2nd/Lieut. F. Newton was killed, 2nd/Lieut. K. D. Rees died of wounds. 2nd/Lieut. H. S. Burt was wounded, 3 men killed and 38 wounded.

MENIN   ROAD. 20th September.

The 6th Battalion was in reserve to the 118th Brigade.   The front of this attack by the Second Army was from the Ypres-Comines Canal to just south of the Ypres-Roulers railway.

One company of the 6th Battalion, under 2nd/Lieut. W. D. Riley, attacked in the afternoon under orders of the 41st Division, and succeeded in gaining with great gallantry its objective, a German strong-point near Basseville Beek.   Here it held on all night.   In the morning it was found that troops on both flanks had failed to come into line, and flanking fire from both sides compelled the company to withdraw.

    *   *   *   *

The 9th Battalion, under Colonel J. A. Southey, " A " Coy., Captain H. E. Quayle, " B " Coy., Captain R. D. Tonge, " C " Coy., Captain J. G. Wood, and " D " Coy., Major W. H. Jones, formed part of the 19th Division.

The Division attacked, in the now normal downpour, on the extreme right of the general attack by Second and Fifth Armies, and its task was to secure the right flank. To carry out this task, Belgian Wood was fixed as their final objective.

The 58th Brigade attacked on the right, and the 9th Battalion was on the left of the Brigade. The Battalion advanced in four lines, all moving forward at once to clear the enemy barrage, and correcting their distances when clear of our front line. They thus escaped the enemy artillery fire, but machine gun fire was very heavy. They suffered heavy casualties, lost touch, and lost the barrage. However, during the pause on the first objective, these points were made good, and the line " mopped-up." But the Welch on our right were held up by a German strong point.

This mopping-up process has not yet been explained. It consisted in clearing the trenches and dug-outs of armed Germans to prevent them using their weapons after the first wave of the attack had passed over them. In the early days on the Somme, it had been thought sufficient to lob a couple of bombs down each dug-out entrance, but this proved inadequate, and measures had to be taken to use enough explosive to block the entrances and exits, or to set fire to the woodwork, and so, in either case, bury the occupants, or to clear them all out, and make them prisoners. The work had to be very carefully and thoroughly done against troops of the class of our enemies.

The advance to the second objective was made as planned. On the right, the only troops required to move were the 9th Battalion, but resistance stiffened, and Potsdam Farm was captured with difficulty. Eventually the objective was secured and touch made with the Worcester- shire Regiment on the left. The Welch were, however, still held up by machine gun fire from Hessian Wood.

2nd/Lieut. Colvin of the 9th Battalion, seeing this, attacked the German dug-outs at the north corner of Hessian Wood with two platoons and so enabled the Welch to reach their objective. But the situation on the right was still not clear, so 2nd/Lieut. Colvin, who had now returned from Hessian Wood, took command of " C " and " D " Companies, whose Captains had become casualties, and withdrew his right flank. Consolidation was pushed on with all speed and wire was put out.

Lieut. Colvin was awarded the Victoria Cross. The official citation follows.

His Majesty The King has been graciously pleased to award the Victoria Cross to :—

Second Lieut. Hugh Colvin.

" For most conspicuous bravery in attack.

When all the officers of his company except himself—and all but one in the leading company—had become casualties and losses were heavy, he assumed command of both companies and led them forward under heavy machine-gun fire with great dash and success. He saw the battalion on his right held up by machine gun fire, and led a platoon to their assistance.

Second Lieut. Colvin then went on with only two men to a dug-out. Leaving the men on top, he entered it alone and brought up 14 prisoners.

He then proceeded with his two men to another dug-out which had been holding up the attack by rifle and machine gun fire and bombs. This he reached, and, killing or making prisoners of the crew, captured the machine-gun. Being then attacked from another dug-out by 15 of the enemy under an officer, one of his men was killed and the other wounded. Seizing a rifle he shot five of the enemy, and, using another as a shield, he forced most of the survivors to surrender. This officer cleared several other dug-outs alone or with one man, taking about 50 prisoners in all.

Later, he consolidated his position with great skill, and person-ally wired his front under heavy close-range sniping in broad daylight, when all others had failed to do so.

The complete success of the attack in this part of the line was mainly due to Second Lieut. Colvin's leadership and courage."

This attack had been rehearsed. In fact, all the troops taking part in it had done two full dress rehearsals. They were also kept as fresh as possible, and not worn out by digging, and other preparatory work. The result was that many headquarters and cable routes were incomplete, and there was insufficient cover for reserves against enemy counter-preparation fire. However, the policy of keeping the men fresh certainly paid in this case.

In each Brigade, a senior Battalion Commander went forward to a commanding position in the front of attack from which he could judge the whole tactical situation, and he was given power to use reserves without consulting the Brigade Commander. One might, however, think that this was the Brigade Commander's duty and place. If someone else is to command his reserves, it is not very clear what purpose the Brigade Commander serves in the battle.

The Battalion lost 2nd/Lieut. J. H. McKeever and 43 men killed and missing, 5 officers and 111 men wounded.

Conditions in the Salient in October.

The month of October was marked by continuous rain and strong wind. The operations of 4th and 26th were particularly affected by the bad weather which made the work of the contact planes almost impossible. The ground on the sides of the streams became impassable, and several cases occurred of men being lost in the mud.

Towards the end of the month, the tracks forward to the front line were so bad as to make the task of carrying, and reliefs, increasingly difficult, and incredibly exhausting.

The construction of plank roads across this morass was constantly impeded by shell fire, and duck-board tracks had to be renewed daily. On one day, 70 direct hits fell on a plank road between Zillebeke and the front line.

During the last 10 days of October, artillery and infantry suffered from phosgene and mustard gas shelling, which was chiefly directed against battery positions, Brigade and Battalion H.Q., and duck-board tracks.

The enemy counter-battery work was often intense, and a large number of heavy and field guns were put out of action. The enemy also carried out a regular programme of back-area shoots.

*   *   *   *

During this period, the 6th Battalion was employed in the front line facing Gheluvelt, or rather in the scattered line of half-fortified shell holes which represented the front line and which had to be linked up with each other, and connected with the rear by communication trenches, very heavy work at any time under continuous shelling, but much more so having in view the condition of the country.

POLYGON WOOD. 26th September to 3rd October, 1917.

The 1st Battalion came into the area of this battle on 3rd October near Sanctuary Wood in Divisional Reserve. Twelve men were killed and 18 wounded on the first day. One officer was wounded and 12 men were killed and 33 wounded on the next.

*   *   *   *

In this same battle, the 6th Battalion was in support of leading Battalions of the 118th Brigade in an attack on German positions extending about 1,000 yards south from the Menin Road.

2nd Lieut. Hugh Colvin, V.C.

At 5-50 a.m., the Brigade advanced to the attack. The artillery barrage was no less than 1,000 yards in depth.

Rapid progress was made, except on the right where the going was very boggy. Companies of the Battalion were used piecemeal to reinforce the Black Watch.

BROODSEINDE. 4th October.

Map p. 124

The Second Army began the third phase of its offensive on the 4th October. The 5th Division had to capture the Spur south west of Reutel (Polderhoek) to protect the flank of the Army.

The honour was earned for us by the 1st Battalion in the same way as that for Polygon Wood. They were in reserve in Sanctuary Wood suffering an average of 12 killed and 40 wounded daily from shell fire.

The 1st Battalion was destined to exploit the success of the 95th Brigade, but, as success was not obtained, it had to endure, as patiently as it could, the inevitable shelling of reserve positions.

POELCAPPELLE. 12th October.

The 6th Battalion was employed under the 2nd Anzac Corps daily from 5 a.m. to 5 p.m. for five days on the very exhausting and unenviable task of supplying working parties at Hell Fire Corner, Potijze.

PASSCHENDAELE. 26th October to 10th November.

Map p. 124

The Second Army resumed its offensive on 26th October, the object being to create a strong flank for the British battle front.

The 5th Division was ordered to capture Polderhoek. The attack was made by the 13th Brigade, the 15th, with the 1st Battalion, being in line on the left.

Polderhoek Chateau was occupied by two Battalions of the Warwickshire Regiment, but owing to lack of support on the right, was eventually evacuated, but the troops brought back 100 prisoners.

This concluded the service in France of the 1st Battalion for a while, and they thankfully withdrew to the comparative peace of the Italian front.

Under every condition of weather and modern warfare in twenty-eight named battles, and innumerable days of trench warfare, they had set an example to The Regiment of courage, discipline, and cheerfulness which can never be surpassed.

*   *   *   *

The following appreciation of our First Battalion was written by our Scottish Medical Officer, the gallant Forsyth.

"Except in the retreat of 1914, this can be said of the First Battalion of The Cheshire Regiment, they only once failed in an objective and they never lost a trench. Falling out on the line of march was a crime unknown, sudden death was the only excuse accepted. "Trench feet" was as great a crime as "cold feet." There are no recorded cases of either. Grousing was never heard in the line, but very frequently in billets. If you wanted to see a real Cheshire grin, in mud, sleet and a heavy barrage, all you had to say was "Rum." Mud was the worst enemy of the men, but it never defeated them.

Daily rations never failed to reach the front line, barrage or no barrage ; hot meals at least once a day.

During the whole war, the Battalion was never out of the line for any period exceeding one month, and once held a sector for 42 days without relief, (See page 54, Ypres, 1915) and without a bath ! "

*   *   *   *

The 15th and 16th Battalions, in the 105th Brigade, attacked on the 22nd on the British left, their objective being the road running west from Colombo Ho, the 16th under Colonel B. C. Dent, and the 15th under Colonel H. P. G. Cochrane. The 16th Battalion was in the front line of the Brigade and the 15th in reserve.

The night of the 21st/22nd was bitterly cold and rain fell heavily. The men were perished. Unfortunately, rum and tea, which had been provided, did not reach the Battalion. The enemy kept up a strong barrage fire all night.

At 5-30 a.m., the advance started. The state of the ground can be imagined when it is learnt that the pace of the barrage was 100 yards in eight minutes. The whole ground was one mass of shell holes, each containing about a foot of water. Even at this slow pace, the troops had

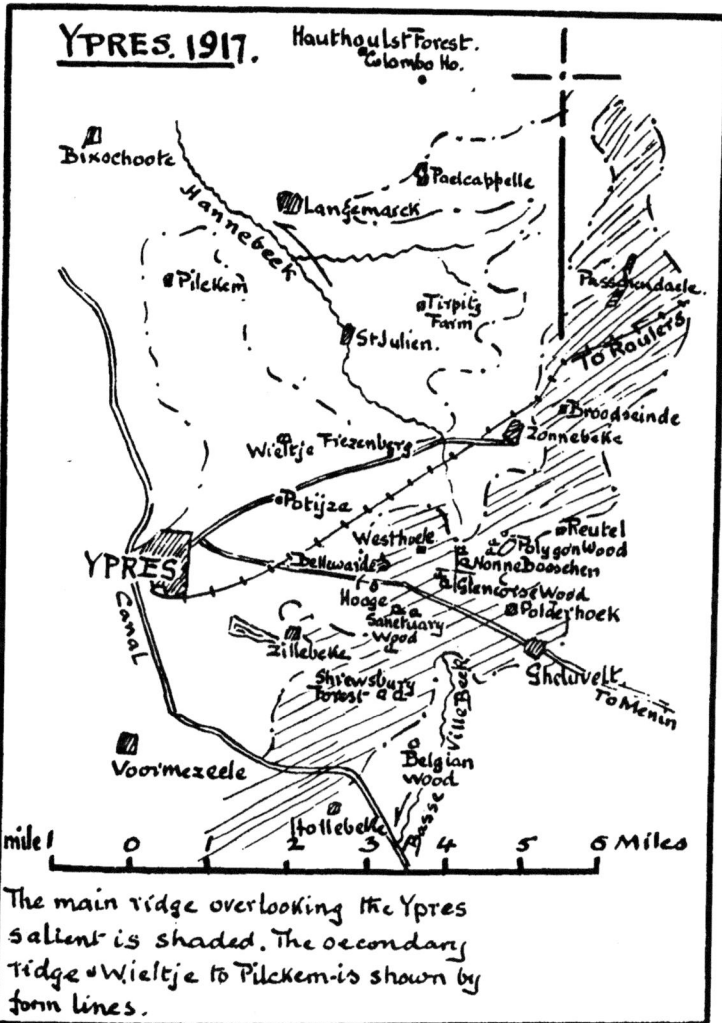

YPRES. 1917.

The main ridge overlooking the Ypres salient is shaded. The secondary ridge Wieltje to Pilckem is shown by form lines.

the greatest difficulty in keeping up with the barrage. Still, the objectives were reached. Then began a long day's struggle, dealing first with unconquered pill-boxes—concrete machine-gun posts—and enemy counter-attacks. However, most of the original gains were successfully held, and the Battalion was relieved by the 15th. This Battalion had to deal with more counter-attacks and was very much harassed by low-flying aircraft. But they held on to their line and repulsed all attempts to drive them back.

The 15th Battalion lost 22 killed and 75 wounded and the 16th a total of 9 officers and 327 men.

CAMBRAI. 20th November to 7th December, 1917.

In this great battle, the 5th Battalion was our sole representative. During November, the 5th Battalion was employed on widening the main Cambrai road by corduroying the north side from Beugny to Boursies. It was evident that something was in preparation, but no news of an attack leaked out till the 16th. No additional camps had been constructed, no guns had registered, and secrecy had been maintained. The 56th Division on the extreme left, made a feint attack in which dummy tanks, dummy figures and smoke were largely used.

On the 21st, two companies of the 5th Battalion were engaged in clearing the main road by circumventing craters by corduroy diversions, and in bridging trenches cut across it.

By the 24th, the enemy was much more active and Boursies had to be evacuated.

On the 30th, after they had beaten off very heavy German counter-attacks, the 5th Battalion sent H.Q. and 3 companies to reinforce the 169th Brigade and one to the 168th,.

During this period, gas casualties were very heavy, " A " Company having as many as 50.

SOMME, 1918.

This name covers the six battles of the German offensive which began in March, 1918, and which was only stopped at Villers Bretonneux. Had the enemy gone any further, the railway junction of Amiens would have been under hostile shellfire, and the junction between the English and French armies would have been cut.

Owing to the disorganization caused by the rapid retreat of the British and Allied troops in the German offensives of 1918, in Picardy, in Flanders and in Champagne, the Battalion war diaries of the period are very poor records indeed.

ST. QUENTIN. 21st to 23rd March, 1918.

Map p. 134

St. Quentin is the name given to the first of the battles of the German offensive in Picardy, when the Allied line was pushed back to Villers Bretonneux and strained to breaking point.

The country over which the fighting took place had been the scene of the Somme battles of 1916, and was a waste of wire, trenches and shell holes.

The troops had not recovered from the exhaustion of the offensives of 1917 at Arras, at Messines, at Ypres, and at Cambrai, in none of which had it been found possible to " break through " the German line, and throw off the fetters of trench warfare. Whether the troops were ready for open warfare, or sufficiently well trained for it, is another question.

Reserves had not been adequate to fill the ranks, and divisions had been reduced in strength by one battalion in four, and the three remaining had not been fully reinforced.

In addition to this, the Fifth Army, at any rate, was holding a very extended front. Considerable skill and forethought was necessary to make the best defensive dispositions having regard to all these factors, exhaustion, deficiency of men, and wide frontages. The problem was sufficiently well solved on certain portions of the front, but not on others. Rear lines had been partially dug, but in single lines, not in " systems " with front and supporting trenches, and not garrisoned, so that retiring troops as often as not overlooked them, instead of holding them.

The attack was not unexpected. Staff rides and tactical exercises without troops, had been held to rehearse possible counter-attacks.

*   *   *   *

Two Battalions, the 10th and 11th, represented The Regiment in the first onslaught, both in the 25th Division. The disappearance of the 13th Battalion marks the re-organization already mentioned. This fine Battalion had the mortification of losing its identity. On the other hand the 10th and 11th Battalions were proud and glad to welcome members of a Battalion which had proved itself second to none in a first-class Division.

When the storm broke and the British front line was driven in, the 10th Battalion, under Colonel W. T. Williams, was in reserve in camp at Achiet-le-Grand, Captain J. H. E. Dean, M.C., " A " Coy. ; Captain S. Cheetham, " B " Coy. ; Lieut. R. E. Huffam, " C " Coy. ; and Lieut. G. H. G. Gadson, " D " Coy.

On the 21st, at 6 a.m., the Battalion was ordered to Fremicourt, whence it moved on to the " Army line " which ran from Beugny to Behagnies, and occupied about 1,000 yards of front. Before daylight, the line was deepened and strengthened, and a series of posts, 100 yards apart, were dug as a support line. Two companies held the front line, and two the support.

During the morning of the 22nd, the Battalion was subjected to intermittent shellfire.

About 5 p.m., the troops in Vaulx withdrew under strong attacks, came into the Army line and were taken charge of and reorganized by officers of the 10th Battalion.

A quiet night followed.

On the 23rd, about 9-30 a.m., the enemy attempted a surprise attack on the left, which broke down under our rifle and machine-gun fire.

At 3-15 p.m., after an hour and a quarter of terrific barrage fire, an enemy attack in four waves developed. Not a single German reached our trenches. The attack was repeated later with the same result which was all the more creditable to our men, as, owing to the failure of the signal lights, we had no artillery support.

During the night of the 23rd/24th, the enemy dug himself in in front of our line, while our people replenished their ammunition, and harassed the enemy with trench mortars.

* * * *

The 11th Battalion (75th Brigade) under Major E. R. S. Prior, D.S.O., M.C., moved from Bihucourt about 9 a.m. on the 21st to Favreuil, and on to a point east of Beugnatre. About 5-30 a.m. on the 22nd, it was ordered to occupy a position near Chaufours Wood, and the road running south from Morchies, which it did, after making a short attack with the assistance of some tanks.

This sounds all very normal, but the fact is that confusion reigned. The Battalion " came under the orders " of no less than five Brigade Commanders in this 24 hours.

Heavy casualties were caused by enemy shelling.

When the troops retired from Vaulx on the left, " D " Company remained in the Morchies trenches till they were withdrawn at 7-30 p.m.

This order failed to reach two of the companies and they were never seen again.

About 8 a.m. on 23rd, the enemy renewed his attacks. North of the Bapaume-Cambrai road they were held up, but south of it our Divisions were pressed back, so the 11th Battalion formed a defensive flank facing south east along the main road.

Retirements of troops on the right and left, and an order to retire which came from the rear, made withdrawal seem inevitable. However, five commanding officers met and decided to remain in position. This they succeeded in doing till about 5-30 p.m., when further withdrawals compelled them to go, and the Battalion went to Beugny, whence it was withdrawn to the " Army line " near Sapignies.

All through the day, these Battalions were withstanding the massed attacks of the enemy, and inflicting very heavy casualties with rifle and Lewis gun, suffering themselves also very severely, especially from low-flying aeroplanes.

On this front three British Divisions were opposing the thrust of eight German Divisions.

The evening of this day, 23rd March, marks the end of the battle of St. Quentin.

BAPAUME.   24th and 25th March.

Map p. 134

This battle continues that called St. Quentin.

On the morning of the 24th March, the 10th Battalion was still holding the " Army line " after repulsing many attacks.

At dawn, signs of another attack were seen, but no enemy action took place. Unfortunately, many casualties were caused, and two of our posts were destroyed by our artillery.

At 2-45 p.m., it was observed that troops on the right were retiring, but no Battalion of the 7th Brigade retired till the order came from Brigade H.Q. When it did come, the withdrawal, though under heavy fire, was conducted in an orderly manner.

A line east of Beugnatre was then ordered to be held, but before it could be occupied, the enemy came on in masses, so the leading companies fell back on the supports. Firing and retiring slowly, and losing heavily, the Battalion fell back to Favreuil. By now the Battalion was thoroughly disorganized. All the company commanders and many other officers had become casualties. A remnant was collected at Bihucourt, and marched to a camp near Bucquoy.

The Officers, 1st Battalion, under Hugh Sparling, in March, 1918, with General W. H. Anderson.

The remnant of the 11th Battalion took up a position about 1-30 p.m. on the 24th, east of Sapignies, where the trenches were full of men of many different Divisions. The day was quiet. During the night, the Brigade was relieved and the Battalion went N.W. of Grevillers, whence it joined the Brigade near Gommecourt, having lost 17 officers and 419 men.

At 7-30 a.m. on the 25th, the 10th Battalion moved forward to slit trenches east of Logeast Wood.

During the afternoon, heavy fire was directed on our position, and later it became evident that the enemy was closing in on our right flank.

After much consultation with the C.O. of the 1st Battalion Wiltshire Regiment, the C.O., Colonel W. T. Williams, decided to hold on. We did so till, 9-30 p.m., when further withdrawals on our flank decided us to conform. The Brigade marched off in good order across country to Achiet-le-Petit, and thence by road to Gommecourt.

*　　*　　*　　*

On the front to which the 19th Division was in reserve during the weeks and days prior to 21st March, many signs had made it evident that a big attack was impending. Like other Divisions, the 19th had carried out tactical exercises to practice the re-capture of certain localities in event of their being lost. Our 9th Battalion was in this Division.

At 4-40 a.m., on the 21st, our " counter-preparation fire " began. This means artillery fire on enemy forming-up places, gun positions, roads and tracks. At 4-50, hostile " drum " fire of terrific intensity fell on our forward trench system, which was rapidly over-run by the enemy.

At 7 p.m., on 21st, the 19th Division made a counter-attack from Velu on Doignies, which was only partially successful. This attack was carried out by the 57th Brigade, which, in the end, withdrew to the Beaumetz-Morchies line.

At 10-45 p.m. on the 22nd, the 56th Brigade was ordered to occupy a line south of Beugny, and the 9th Battalion went to a rendezvous at Delsaux Farm, which they reached at 1-15 a.m. on the 23rd. The trenches there were at once improved and deepened. Stocks of bombs and small arm ammunition were collected. The night passed quietly, but, during the 23rd, enemy aircraft were very active, visibility being excellent. Their artillery kept up a desultory but persistent fire.

As the day wore on shelling increased in intensity, and towards evening became very heavy.

During this day, the whole line was heavily engaged and had it not been for the gallant defence of Beugny by the 9th Welch, the whole line must have been driven back.

Late in the evening, lorries moved all stores of value back to Pozieres,

J

The night 23rd/24th was quiet, but in anticipation of attack, our artillery began " counter-preparation " at 5 a.m. on the 24th. Soon after this hour, the troops holding Beugny began to withdraw. This was expected and was in accordance with orders received.

After a barrage on the 9th Battalion and its fellows in the Brigade, lasting from 9 a.m. to 10-45 a.m., the enemy attacked in mass, and we lost our front line trench, and Delsaux Farm. But the Battalion rallied in the support line, whence Captains A. D. Milner and F. A. Palmer led a counter-attack. The lost trench was gallantly re-taken and heavy casualties were inflicted on the enemy. Unfortunately, " A " Company lost all its officers.

At 2 p.m., orders were received that the Battalion was to conform to withdrawals on the right.

In the early evening, orders were received to withdraw west of Bapaume, where the 9th Battalion attempted to organize a single line in some old trenches and endeavoured to re-inforce their ranks with stragglers from other units. This was difficult owing to the extreme darkness of the night, which led to much confusion. Before it was properly completed, orders were received for a further retirement to a position just south of Grevillers. This move was completed by about daylight on the 25th, but satisfactory dispositions to resist attack had hardly been completed, when the Germans suddenly opened attack on the north flank of the Battalion. There was some higher ground on that flank and the enemy had been able to get machine guns into position there and to enfilade our line, before sending infantry in a frontal assault on our positions. Our leading companies were withdrawn under cover of fire from Loupart Wood, by crawling to the extreme right (south) of our position and then utilising the cover afforded by a partially sunken road.

The enemy pressed boldly on and forced our withdrawal, which was general with the troops on either flank, to the line Miraumont—Achiet-le-Petit. The enemy's boldness is illustrated by the following two incidents. German infantrymen on coming under close range rifle fire from the British troops had " gone to earth " and shown a disposition to return whence they came. The German O.C. Battalion evidently recalled them all and paraded his Battalion in mass in full view of the 9th, but out of rifle range. Through glasses, he and his officers could be seen riding round the Battalion presumably giving them the length of his tongue. To their chagrin, our people could not get in touch with the artillery.

They were very soon to get " in touch " with some artillery, as soon afterwards a German battery gallopped up in full view of our men and came into action against them. Through glasses one could see the guns being loaded and fired, and there was time to warn the men before the shell burst in their midst.

J I

This went on for about half-an-hour, but, with the exception of the first shell or two, caused very few casualties.

During the night of the 25th/26th, a German N.C.O. who walked unarmed into the rear of our line was captured. He had come from further on the right where their line was much advanced, had lost his direction and got behind our lines. During this night, the retreat was continued under orders and the 9th Battalion were put in reserve about Sailly au Bois. In the afternoon of the 26th, while en route for Sailly, they had their first meal for nearly two days, no rations having been received on the 24th or 25th.

Billets were found in and around Sailly which was reached about dusk, and everyone went to sleep utterly worn out. The Battalion transport was still in Hebuterne and in the early hours of the 27th a small German advance party caused consternation by suddenly opening fire on them. The party was, however, driven back by the details and the the Australians, who, by now, had relieved the Brigade.

On the 27th, the Battalion was withdrawn to Souastre (two miles north of Sailly), on the 28th to Famechon (four miles west), and on the 29th to Candas (a further seven miles west), where it entrained after a very trying experience. In seven days, the Battalion had lost 14 officers and 355 N.C.Os. and men.

As far as the 56th Brigade and our 9th Battalion were concerned, there was, during this retreat, no panic of any sort. The men were quite willing to halt and fight, but as the troops on their right were falling back, and as the difficulty of getting orders to them made them uncertain as to their correct action, they fell back slowly, and in good order. Once they received definite orders, and came into contact with officers who knew the situation, they fell into line and dug themselves in at once.

*   *   *   *

As far as the 10th and 11th Battalions, in the 25th Division are concerned, it is enough to repeat the words of their commander, General Bainbridge, written on 28th March :—

"I wish to record my appreciation of the work of the Division during 21st to 28th March. During this period, all ranks and all units have proved themselves to be men of the finest quality, men of whom England may well be proud."

"It is not too much to say that no unit of the 25th Division retired without an order, and that, when ordered to do so, they retired with reluctance, refusing to credit that the order applied to them."

*   *   *   *

The 15th Battalion was in the Ypres Salient when the German blow fell on the Somme on the 21st of March. The 35th Division was sent for on the 22nd and entrained for the Somme.

After marching 8 miles to the station by night, and a 12-hour railway journey, the troops marched 14 miles from Méricourt L'Abbé by Suzanne to Méricourt. The march took place at night, along roads congested with transport of every description, with retiring troops and with civilian refugees, all spreading the wildest rumours of the enemy's success. The Brigade pushed on three miles more to a rendezvous, where it was hoped to give them rest and food before going into action in relief of worn-out troops. But at the moment of their arrival, tired troops from the front came streaming back saying that the Hun was on top of them. So there was nothing for it but to move against the enemy, and the 15th Battalion went straight into a spirited counter-attack about 11 a.m. on the 24th, against the high ground known as the Cléry ridge. Advancing in splendid order, they recaptured the ridge, suffering serious casualties. After a morning of sharp and fluctuating fighting, they established themselves more than a mile from their starting point.

The 15th Sherwoods attacked alongside our 15th Battalion, with a big gap between, and share the glory of this admirable action.

Each Battalion consisted of only three companies, the fourth having been kept to unload the train.

As was always the case, the Germans did not let matters rest, and both Battalions were desperately counter-attacked with high explosive gas shell, rifle and machine-gun fire, and grenades, the Sherwoods losing two companies after holding out to the last.

The two forward companies of the 15th Battalion, " Z " and " X," though completely surrounded by the enemy, owing to the gap between them and the Sherwoods, held up the German advance all day, and succeeded in fighting their way out, taking many wounded with them, when they were ordered to withdraw about 5 p.m. Casualties were very heavy, and the Battalion lost its Colonel, H. P. G. Cochran, D.S.O., the Adjutant, Captain V. G. Barnett, and Major H. F. Le Mesurier, M.C.

The enemy must have lost heavily, for he came on in mass, and gave wonderful targets to rifle and machine gun. In repelling these attacks, the Canadian Motor Machine Gun Company gave incalculable assistance.

The retirement was steadily carried out to a line running north from the river at Curlu, with the 15th Sherwoods on our left, and the North Staffords in support at Maricourt. Immediately on arrival here, an attack was made on them but was easily driven off. So heavily had the enemy been punished, that the new line was not attacked during the night. The Battalion remained on outpost much strengthened and encouraged by the arrival of "W." Coy. at 11 p.m. Major H. Johnston, D.S.O., succeeded to the command of the Battalion.

On the 25th, the outpost line was pushed back, but two companies of the North Staffords, assisted by accurate and heavy artillery fire, almost regained the original line.

Towards mid-day, the enemy broke into Maricourt, and were only ejected after heavy fighting, but the 15th Battalion, with the Sherwoods and Royal Scots, maintained their ground.

At 1 p.m., a mob of retiring troops of all Divisions was stopped by the Commander of the 105th Brigade, Brigadier-General Marindin, hastily organized and placed in position.

That night, 25th/26th, when it was hoped to relieve our people, the relieving troops did not arrive, and further orders to retire were received. The Brigade had to withdraw under fire, and march five miles to the Bray —Meaulte road. This was carried out in perfect steadiness, but on arrival there, it was too cold to rest, and the men had to walk about to keep warm.

An outpost line covering Bray was occupied by 3 a.m. on the 26th, which was duly attacked about 10 a.m. All attacks were repulsed, the Battalion suffering heavy loss. At 3 p.m. they were again ordered to retire, when they marched back through an artillery barrage, to the Ancre, east of Morlancourt.

Morlancourt presented the now familiar spectacle of hopeless congestion, civilian carts, guns, tanks, transport, wounded soldiers, civilians, and leaderless men, all struggling westward.

Here it was found that the Battalion transport with food, blankets, and great coats, had been sent across the river. The only rations procurable were some biscuits, the remnants of a dump made for the retiring troops, which naturally had been mostly eaten by those who first passed that way. However, by some means or other, the officers succeeded in getting the men some hot food, the first hot meal they had had since leaving Ypres.

During this period, many orders were received by the Brigade Staff from superior authority, which would have meant further counter-attacks by exhausted if willing troops, to say nothing of shortage of food and ammunition. We can have nothing but praise for the tenacity and equanimity of the Brigade Commander, whose skill and judgment had contributed so much to this brilliant episode.

A definite order was now received to hold the line Bray—Albert, so General Marindin, after protest, ordered a counter-attack by the North Staffords, supported by the 15th Battalion, on the ridge east of Morlancourt.

The order was cancelled by 35th Div. H.Q., but too late to stop the North Staffords, who were, however, skilfully withdrawn from the very dangerous position, which had been foreseen by the Brigade Commander.

For the next four days, the west bank of the Ancre was held.

During the whole of this period, the Brigade was never forced out of any position by the enemy. All withdrawals were effected in consequence of orders received from superior authority. There was no stampeding, and no men left their posts without orders—a very fine performance.

The 15th Battalion lost 3 officers and 52 others killed, and 15 officers and 385 others wounded and missing, in this fighting.

ROSIÈRES. 26th and 27th March.

This is the third battle of the great German March attack, and the name is given to the fighting between the Ancre and the Somme.

The 6th Battalion was at rest on the 21st and on the alarm being given, was sent on the 22nd of March to dig, and occupy, a switch line to run through Longavesnes, some 13 miles N.W. of St. Quentin.

Retirements of the Fifth Army reached in succession Peronne, Clery, Herbecourt,

On the 25th, the 6th Battalion was in action with the 66th Division at Flaucourt.

On the 26th, the enemy attacked Herbecourt, his planes, it was said, shooting up their own infantry to hurry them on !

In this battle, the 118th Brigade (6th Battalion) made a counter-attack on Framerville, of which no details are available.

Flank attacks caused further retreat of the 39th Division and, by the 27th, the Battalion was swamped in the general mass of fugitives from many corps. What was left of the 118th Brigade was formed into a composite Battalion, which eventually pulled up the enemy at Aubercourt.

On the 31st, the composite Battalion moved back by lorry, after making a gallant counter-attack on Wiencourt (not on map) from Cayeux, under Colonel E. T. Saint of the 1st Cambridgeshire Regiment. The men were very tired but moved most gallantly under heavy machine gun fire, and drove back the Germans, killing many and taking many prisoners.

LYS. 9th to 29th April, 1918.

Map p. 142

This name, Lys, covers the second phase of the German Offensive of 1918, in Flanders. The lie of the land affected the fighting very much and it will be as well to give a short description of the chief features.

Eastwards of a line drawn roughly from Arras to Calais lies the Flanders plain, bounded on the north-west by the sea, and on the south-east by the canals joining Lens, Lille, Roubaix and Courtrai, and by the River Lys, between Courtrai and Ghent.

The German Offensive
in
Picardy . 1918.

The flatness is almost complete, but is broken by a range of hills which, from Mount Cassel in the west, runs eastward to Mont Des Cats, Mont Noir, Mont Rouge and Scherpenberg, to Mount Kemmel. At this latter point the ridge changes direction, runs northward and becomes much lower, until passing east of Ypres, through Wytschaete, Gheluvelt and Passchendaele, it merges finally into the plain again near Dixmude.

Mount Kemmel is ten miles south-west of Ypres, at the apex of the angle formed by the two arms of the range. Lying at the eastern end of the hills which dominate the country south and north, it threatens the flank of any force advancing south of it towards Hazebrouck, or north of it past Ypres. The capture of the hills was, therefore, of the utmost importance to the Germans, if they wished to drive us towards the coast. So, it was the principal objective of the German armies on this front.

The battles resolve themselves into two periods, one from the 9th to the 18th April, and the other from the 25th to the 29th.

The first period brought the Germans up to the Kemmel ridge, and in the second they captured it, only to find that their bolt was shot and that they had neither the energy nor means to make further headway.

On each occasion of a major attack, fog favoured the Germans, and in the initial attack they were opposed by Divisions which had withstood the great onslaught on the Somme, and which had been sent north to rest.

It can be fairly said that the success of our troops in this series of battles was due as much to the skill and tenacity of the Generals and Staff as to the bravery and stubbornness of the Regimental officer and man. They fought well as always, but in the bewildering succession of withdrawals, Regimental officers and men lost their bearings, and though willing and ready to fight, and by no means feeling beaten or disheartened, did not know where best to go. It was the coolheaded steadiness of the higher leaders which over and over again prevented the enemy from completing our destruction.

It is not possible from the war diaries of this Lys period to describe the action of individual Battalions.

The story will therefore be told by days rather than by Battalions. Besides Lys, the battle honours won by us in this period are :—

ESTAIRES. 9th to 11th April.

MESSINES. 10th and 11th April.

HAZEBROUCK. 12th to 15th April.

BAILLEUL. 13th to 15th April.

KEMMEL. 17th to 19th April and 25th and 26th April.

SCHERPENBERG. 29th April.

The 19th and 25th Divisions, containing, it will be remembered, the 9th Battalion, and the 10th and 11th Battalions respectively, had come up to the Messines front for a rest after the strenuous fighting in the German Offensive on the Somme in March.

On this front, the defence was organized in two lines of " posts," with a third continuous trench line as reserve. Five hundred yards in rear was another system, only partially dug, called the " Corps line."

9th April.

The 9th Battalion was in Brigade Reserve at Gibraltar Camp.

No intimation of any possible attack had been received, till, on the 9th, the enemy advanced, over-ran the Portuguese near Festubert close to the La Bassee Canal, and attacked the British positions at Armentières and Givenchy. Precautions were taken on the front of the Corps to which the 19th Division belonged.

The front line ran roughly north and south, through Hollebeke, west of Warneton, to Armentières. The 25th Division was in the same Corps, and our 11th Battalion was in line opposite Deulemont. The 10th Battalion was in reserve s.w. of Ploegsteert Wood.

Late on the 9th, the 9th Battalion was sent to Nieppe, Colonel G. K. Fulton in command, with Captain D. Greville as Adjutant and Captains J. Naylor and H. J. Dresser, " A " Company ; A. W. Barnes, " B " Company ; A. R. Walton, " C " Company ; and Lieut. V. E. Humphries, " D " Company.

10th April.

At about 5-15 a.m., under cover of a thick fog, the enemy attacked with eleven divisions on the Corps front, a superiority of 5 or 6 to 1.

By 6-30 a.m. the right Battalion of the 75th Brigade (25th Division) had been driven in. In the rapid on-rush of the enemy, the front and support posts were over-run and their garrisons never seen again.

The 11th Battalion was forced, by the pressure coming from the south against its right flank, to fall back to west of Ploegsteert. At 8 a.m., the Battalion reported that the enemy was in Ploegsteert.

By 8-30 a.m. the enemy had taken Armentières.

At 10-15 a.m. the 9th Battalion was transferred to the 25th Division, and ordered to occupy a line north-east of Nieppe. This was successfully accomplished by about 2 p.m.

By this time the enemy had penetrated Ploegsteert Wood, and were taking the troops supporting the 9th Battalion in reverse.

In the meantime, the 11th Battalion was in the front line of the 75th Brigade, and on the left flank. The hostile attack began about 6 a.m. mainly round the left flank, and quickly penetrated to the rear of Battalion " H.Q." where Colonel G. Darwell was wounded. Major E.

Prior, D.S.O., M.C., took over command. The Brigade on the right, and the right of the 75th Brigade, were now falling back, but the 11th Battalion held on to their line, although isolated on both flanks, till an order came directing the occupation of a line astride the Romarin-Ploegsteert road near Regina Farm. This was done in good order, and the 11th Battalion thus found themselves close to, and on the left of, the 9th Battalion.

Here the 11th Battalion found that the enemy had penetrated Ploegsteert Wood and was moving against the village of Ploegsteert.

The hostile flanking movement on the left was still in progress, and to check it a counter-attack was ordered about 3-50 p.m. against Ploegsteert.

This attack took place about 5-30 p.m., and two companies of the 10th Battalion co-operated in it by driving south from Ploegsteert Wood.

As already stated, the 10th Battalion had been in reserve at the start of the battle. At 7-15 a.m., it was ordered to send three companies to the south end of Ploegsteert Wood, but the enemy was found to be already in it. Later, thanks to the energy and tactical skill of Colonel Fulton, the 10th Battalion, with the 1st Wiltshire Regiment, succeeded in making an orderly withdrawal, and occupying, a line near St. Ives in prolongation of the line of the 75th Brigade. An attempt was made by one company about 3 p.m. to clear Ploegsteert Wood, and two companies co-operared as already stated in the 5-30 p.m. counter-attack. Both flanks of our Battalions were now in the air, the 75th Brigade being at the apex of a salient in the British line.

11th April.

During the 11th, the German attack centred on the IX. Corps (19th and 25th Divisions), and gained the top of the Messines ridge and Hill 63.

The Army Commander (Plumer), felt himself forced by pressure on the right flank to order the troops to fall back to the line Steenwerk—Neuve Eglise—Wulverghem—Wytschaete.

At 5-45 a.m. on the 11th, the enemy made a breach in the 75th Brigade front. The 9th Battalion was on the south of the breach and withdrew, while on the north of it, the remainder of the 75th Brigade, including our 11th Battalion, formed a defensive flank facing south. The 9th Battalion, much worried by machine gun fire from near Romarin, had to fight its way back to a line west of Romarin. The capture of this machine gun post with 14 Germans by 2nd/Lieut. Strong, of the Border Regiment, with some of his own men and some of ours, was an especially fine and valuable piece of work. Many unrecorded acts of gallantry took place during the day's fighting, which was very severe.

During this time, the 9th Battalion earned special praise from the Brigade Commander for the invaluable service it had rendered in keeping touch with both flanks during a very difficult withdrawal, and for the way it had kept Brigade " H.Q." informed of its progress.

The German penetration on the 11th, quickly widened into a gap of some two miles into which German machine guns were boldly advanced.

To return to the 10th Battalion, the evening of the 10th found them also in a pronounced salient along the north edge of Ploegsteert Wood, holding a very extended front of some 2,000 yards.

At 12-30 p.m. on the 11th, 7th Brigade H.Q. ordered the 1st Wiltshire and the 10th Battalion, both now in the catacombs of Hill 63, to retire as soon as practicable. It was the first intimation of danger on this day which they had received. Colonel L. H. K. Finch, of The Regiment, temporarily Commanding the 4th North Staffords, who had come to 10th Battalion H.Q. to get information, rang up Brigade H.Q. and, it is said, agreed with them that withdrawal should begin at 5 p.m. Somehow there was a misunderstanding and the impression was left that the Battalions on Hill 63 were to hold out to the last.

The enemy attacked, and one company of the 10th Battalion made a gallant effort to relieve the situation on the St. Yves spur by a counter-attack, but it was all in vain. The catacombs were surrounded, and only individuals succeeded in fighting their way back to a position west of Neuve Eglise, where a 7th Brigade Composite Battalion, under Major A. Reade, M.C., was formed.

A party which had been previously detailed by Colonel Finch to give covering fire from Hill 63, while those in the catacombs withdrew, had to endure there a terrific machine gun barrage. These men did wonderful work, keeping the enemy off Hill 63 till nightfall. By dark, the hill was surrounded, but they managed to retire under cover of darkness.

The first orders received by this Composite Battalion were to take up a position in rear of Bailleul with a view to counter-attacking that town. Later in the night, at 2 a.m., it was sent to a position on the Ravelsburg. The fighting was very fierce, but it was this position which held up the enemy. The enemy sent forward patrols who fired Verey lights to show the way. But these patrols were promptly attacked and their efforts annulled.

12th April.

At daylight, the position was as follows. The 75th Brigade was holding from Papot—via Lampernisse Farm—west of Romarin—and thence northwards. The 9th and 11th Battalions were both close to Papot.

The 10th Battalion, or what was left of it, was in the Ravelsburg line.

The 25th Division was again attacked, the 75th Brigade with the 9th Battalion being the only Brigade in the front line. Snipers began work the 9th Battalion at daylight, from Lampernisse Copse, but no attack in strength was launched till 2 p.m. By 4 p.m. the 9th Battalion was being pressed back, and the companies were withdrawn to a position at Kortepyp.

13th April.

By the morning of the 13th, the IX. Corps was facing south, protecting the high ground which runs from Kemmel to Cassel.

The fighting on this day, in which the 9th, 10th and 11th Battalions were involved, was very confused. The Germans attacked heavily, once more covered by fog, and elements of the 75th Brigade were driven back across Ravelsburg, to be collected and reorganized by the ever-watchful Generals and Staff at Crucifix Corner, where the 7th Brigade Composite Battalion was already in position.

14th April.

At 4-30 a.m. the German barrage started, and their infantry advanced against our position at Crucifix Corner, and began to fight their way up-hill in spite of the fire of the 7th Brigade Composite Battalion and of the Battalions of the 75th Brigade.

The fighting here, in which the 1st Wiltshire Regiment bore its full share with our men, was of the most heroic character against great odds, and after many days of continuous exertion. Our men not only kept their formation but made a magnificent counter-attack led by Major A. Reade, M.C., in which machine guns and 100 prisoners were captured. It seemed to our men as if they were fighting in a hollow square with the enemy practically all round them. It was a magnificent exhibition of unquenchable determination. Major Reade was rewarded with the D.S.O.

However, in spite of all this, the enemy made another attack preceded by a heavy bombardment, at 4-30 p.m., which also was driven off, thanks largely to a splendid protective barrage put down by the artillery. The situation was safe for the night, which passed quietly.

Unfortunately the gallant and able Commander of the 9th Battalion, Colonel G. K. Fulton, was killed. Captain Dresser took command of the Battalion till the arrival of Major J. A. Busfeild.

15th April.

The 9th Battalion rejoined its Brigade and took over the Kemmel defences. It suffered casualties from hostile shelling on 16th and 17th, and on the 18th beat off an attack. On the night 18th/19th, it was relieved by the French.

16th April.

By this date, the remnants of the 7th and 75th Brigades had been amalgamated into the 7th Composite Brigade, consisting of two Battalions under command of the 34th Division, and went to Mont Noir in Reserve.

19th to 24th April.

From the 19th to the 24th April there was a pause in the fighting and nothing occurred beyond minor actions. The ranks were filled up and reorganised as far as reinforcements allowed.

The Germans had failed in their attempt to break through the northern flank of the Ypres Salient, and also had failed to capture the vital line of hills of which Kemmel formed the key.

25th April.

On this day, the 25th Division was transferred to the French 2nd Cavalry Corps and the 19th Division to the XXII. Corps. Kemmel had been lost and the French arranged for its recapture by the French 39th and British 25th Divisions.

On this morning, the three Infantry Brigades of the 25th Division were training, digging and reorganizing, in the Poperinghe-Proven area.

At 11-25 a.m. Division H.Q. was warned of the impending attack, and working parties were recalled.

At 4-45 p.m. a warning order for the attack under orders of the 2nd French Cavalry Corps was issued, but the situation was so obscure that patrols had to be sent out to locate friend and foe.

Orders from the Corps came in bit by bit with constant alterations. In the end, the plan was roughly as follows.

The two divisions were to attack on either side of the Reninghelst-La Clytte road. The 47th Division was to protect the left flank.

26th to 29th April.

The attack was ordered to begin at 5 a.m. on the 26th. Objectives, boundaries, starting points were altered almost hourly up to midnight 25th/26th and, in the end, the objective was a line running from Linden Hoek to La Polka. The jumping-off line was the Kemmel Beek. Thus, from the map it can be seen that the troops would have to make a half wheel to the right after leaving the starting line, a sufficiently difficult task with fully trained troops. Owing to the inexperience of the officers in the reconstituted Battalions, the Commanding Officers of the Brigade decided to lead their Battalions, to ensure that direction was maintained.

The 74th Brigade was on the right, the 7th on the left and the 75th in reserve.

Shortly after dark on the 25th, the weather turned wet, and by midnight the rain was falling in torrents which made the going very heavy.

There had been no reconnaissance. There was no touch with the 39th French Division on the right.

At 3 a.m. the Brigades advanced, soaked to the skin. The fog was thick, but the barrage was thin, so thin in fact, that the Germans mistook it for mild harassing fire and put down no S.O.S. barrage in reply. But for this, the attack could hardly have started in worse conditions.

The French Division came to a standstill by 8-15 a.m.

The 10th Battalion, under Major A. Reade, was on the left of the 25th Division. Owing to the fog, the 7th Brigade lost touch on both flanks, and suffered from machine gun fire from the right rear owing to the failure of the French to advance west of the La Clytte-Kemmel road, and although it reached its objectives, the rear companies suffered from pockets of the enemy which had not been "mopped up." Hostile fire now opened from the right rear. Meantime portions of the Division, including some of our men, had entered Kemmel village.

The 74th Brigade found themselves some 2,000 yards ahead of the French and their right entirely exposed. Owing to the heavy mist, the enemy failed to take full advantage of this error. It was, however, realized, that when the fog lifted, the position would be untenable, so both leading Brigades withdrew to their original line at 8-50 a.m. The 10th Battalion lost 5 officers and 180 men. Of the three commanding officers of the 7th Brigade, two were killed and Major A. Reade very seriously wounded.

This operation does not sound a great success, though objectives were reached and many prisoners taken, but the decision to withdraw was, in the circumstances, obviously a wise one, and difficult for the Divisional Commander to make. On the other hand, it will be agreed that it reflected great credit on the Commanders and Staffs as well as on the Regimental Officers and men when the conditions in which it was undertaken are remembered. The Division had in less than twenty hours, collected its men from working parties and other duties, withdrawn its " B " teams, fed its troops, marched more than eight miles to a position of assembly, through a country subjected to considerable shelling, pushed out patrols to clear up a situation which was unusually obscure, advanced to its jumping-off line, carried out a counter-attack over nearly 3,000 yards of difficult country under impossible conditions, and reached its objectives, although the men comprising the Battalions had for the most part only just joined as reinforcements, and very few senior officers were left to lead them.

The Brigades of the 25th Division held the La Clytte line in turn, till, on the 29th, when the 75th Brigade was holding the position, a heavy bombardment, mainly of gas, began at 3 a.m., and continued till 5 a.m. German troops massing for attack were dispersed at 5 a.m., and again at 5-15 a.m. by fire of all arms.

Thus ended a very valiant period in the story of the 9th, 10th and 11th Battalions.

AISNE.   27th May to 6th June.

Map p. 150

The Great German offensives of March and April, 1918, had been directed almost wholly against the British front, and had cost us some 250,000 casualties.   Many Divisions were almost wiped out, and the state of the 25th Division, an account of whose furious and continued fighting has been given, can be imagined.   It had lost no less than 10,941 in the Lys battles alone.   A period on a quiet front was imperative, to enable the Battalions to absorb and train the drafts of imperfectly trained recruits and equally new officers with which their depleted ranks had been filled, to refit and to rest.

So, the 25th was one of the Divisions selected to be sent south to the French Sixth Army to have a rest on the Rheims front.

The defences on this front consisted of two zones, each to be held to the last, which seems an odd arrangement.   The second line was not an organized trench system.

The German preparations for a surprise attack on the Chemin de Dames were very skilfully concealed and were assisted a good deal by many thickwoods untouched by war, behind their front.   They were completely successful.   A great mass of men and guns was assembled without interference.

On the day before the attack was to be launched, two Germans were captured who announced the impending attack.   The British reserves were consequently moved into position, the 25th Division into the second position.   The 7th Brigade took up a line between Chalons le Verguer and Boufferingeux and the 75th Brigade thence to Concevreux.   The 74th Brigade was at Muscourt.   Our 10th Battalion was in the 7th Brigade, the 11th in the 75th Brigade.

In the early hours of the 27th, a bombardment fell on front and support lines, on gun positions, headquarters and other vulnerable points, which is generally agreed to have been the heaviest, most terrible and most destructive of the war.   The enemy was over the infantry and past the gun line almost before the alarm could be given.   By 10 a.m., the support line, held by the 74th and 75th Brigades, was in action, with no artillery to help it, save for an improvised battery of six guns, which came into

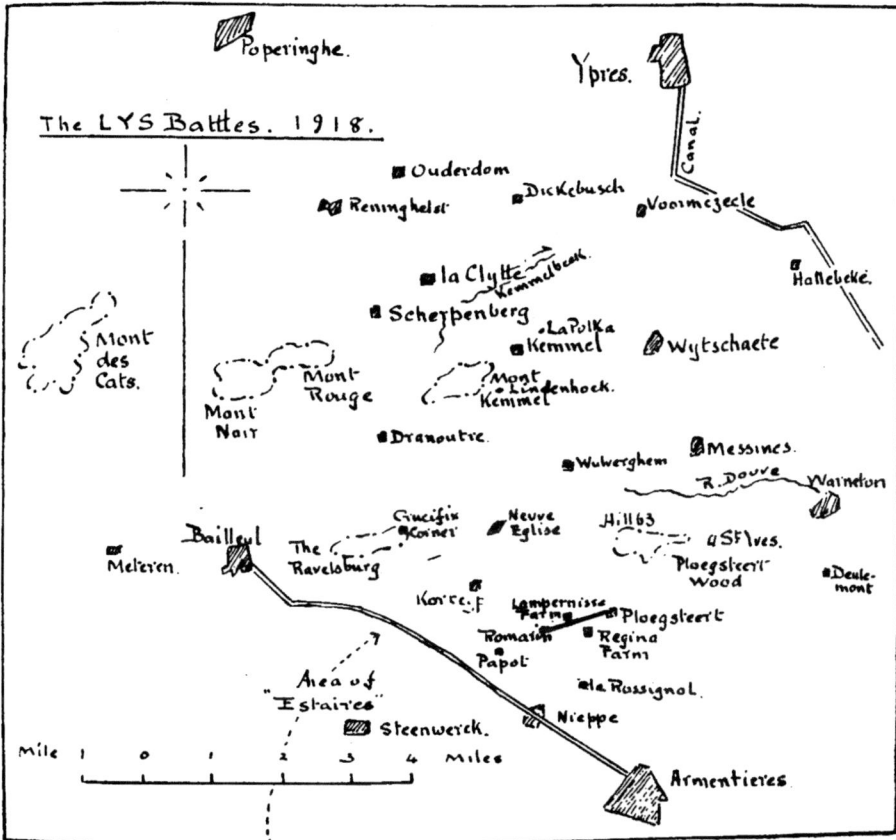

The LYS Battles. 1918.

opp. 142

action at Guyencourt about noon. One artillery brigade remained more or less intact supporting the 21st Division and 7th Brigade.

After a pause, to bring forward their guns and to reorganize their infantry, the Germans moved forward against the second position about 1 p.m.

This position had not been prepared for defence. There were some old trenches, dug during the operations of 1917, but no regular trench system. Officers of the 25th Division had not reconnoitred the ground, so each brigade had to settle, as it arrived, what line it would take up.

On this front, the river Aisne and the Aisne canal (Canal Lateral) ran in separate channels, the former north of the latter, at varying distances from it, the intervening space being covered with high grass. Both river and canal are unfordable, but the French had made as many as 50 bridges across both.

So anxious was the French Army Commander not to lose the forward position, that authority for destroying these bridges had not been delegated other than to the Corps Commander and that only for those east of the Miette. It is obvious that the difficulty and time to be spent in securing his approval for destruction meant that the bridges could not be destroyed in time to be of any value in an emergency, such as actually occurred. In one case, an R.E. Major, Major E. C. Hillman, took upon himself the responsibility, and managed to destroy, with severe casualties to his men, some 10 out of 19 bridges, but the action was of inestimable value to our troops.

The Germans seized the other crossings and thus avoided a good deal of delay, which a more reasonable delegation of authority would have certainly caused them.

By 1 p.m., the 74th Brigade, with a two-mile gap on their left flank, where they "joined" the French, were out-flanked, and withdrew to the line Meurival-Beauregard Farm.

By 3-15 p.m., the enemy had broken through the 75th Brigade on the right of Concevreux, and the 11th Battalion was driven out of Roucy, and retired to the ridge 1 mile south of Ventelay, where they were in touch with the 74th Brigade.

A gap now opened on the right of the 75th Brigade, owing to one Battalion of the 75th retiring south-west to Rouvroy, and one of the 7th to Chalons le Verguer. A German Division pushed unopposed into the gap, and entered Guyencourt and Bouvancourt.

The withdrawal of the 75th Brigade became imperative, and this was ordered at 9 p.m. This involved the 74th, and both Brigades withdrew to the ridge north of Montigny with severe losses. The right of the 75th Brigade was now out of touch with the 7th Brigade. Colonel E. Prior, D.S.O., M.C., of the 11th Battalion, was wounded.

*　　*　　*　　*

The 7th Brigade, now under 21st Division, was in its place by 1 or 2 p.m. At this hour Boufferingeux was held by the Brigade and the 21st Division line from Cormicy to Cauroy. Behind this line the 10th Battalion held Chalons le Verguer.

By 3 p.m., the garrison of Cormicy had withdrawn. At 5-30 p.m. Boufferingeux was lost and, soon after, two companies of the 10th Battalion were sent to prolong the left on the Cormicy-Guyencourt road, but they could not stop the German outflanking movement. Retirement was necessary and the Brigade withdrew to Pevy during the night. The 10th Battalion lost their Colonel, E. C. Cadman, who was killed by low-flying aeroplane machine gun fire.

At dawn on the 28th, the line ran from the French at Hermonville across the Pevy Spur, a thin disjointed line with many gaps, with no touch on the left, and with little or no artillery support. On the immediate left, the French had been driven across the Vesle at Magneux.

By this time both the 10th and 11th Battalions had disappeared, and their remnants which could be assembled were made into the composite Battalions with which the Lys battles had familiarized us.

Without artillery support, these battalions yielded to the German attack. The Germans reached the high ground overlooking Pevy, turning the flank of the 7th Brigade. Successive retirements to the Trigny-Pouilly Ridge, the line Branscourt-Vandeuil, ended across the Vesle, on the night of the 28th.

During this night, the French evacuated Soissons, thus leaving the Germans in a huge pocket stretching down to the Marne.

*   *   *   *

The 6th Battalion were transferred to this Division from the 38th. They arrived by train in the Fismes area at 7 p.m. on the 27th May, and were attacked in the train by aeroplanes, bombs, and machine guns. An enemy outpost picquet was seen, and a party went from the train, attacked and captured the picquet and brought them into the train. The train then ran back through the French outposts to Fère en Tardenois where the Battalion bivouaced. Had the Germans not fired at the train, they could have captured the whole Battalion. Later, the Battalion continued its journey by rail, and detrained on the Marne at 2 a.m. on the 29th. It went straight into action in front of Vente Wood near Augny and suffered heavily from shell fire.

The 6th and 11th Battalions were temporarily amalgamated on the 17th June.

*   *   *   *

On the 29th May, the 19th Division, the Division in which was our 9th Battalion had been in action continuously since 21st March, as already related. Finally, at the end of May, completely worn out, and with ranks filled with recruits, they were moved to Chalons sur Marne for a complete rest. They enjoyed a few days bathing in the canal and river, and some " Paris " leave was granted. When the storm burst and " Big Bertha " began to shell Paris, the Division was bussed during the night of the 28th/29th to Chamuzy, whence they marched to a position on the line Faverolles-Lhéry, their left flank being in the air.

Officers with the 9th Battalion on arrival at Chaumuzy on 28th May, from training camp at La Chaussée where they had gone after the fighting in the Salient were : Major W. W. S. Cunninghame, C.O. ; Captain R. H. Griffiths, 2nd in command ; Captain D. Greville, Adjutant ; Captain E. F. Thurgood, " A " Coy. ; Captain S. A. Alexander, " D " Coy. ; Lieut. S. R. Broome, " B " Coy. ; Lieut. G. W. Day, " C " Coy. ; Lieut. T. C. Gibbs, I.O. The strength of the Battalion was 21 officers and 560 men.

The 9th Battalion was in reserve to the 58th Brigade at Sarcy, its own Brigade being, it will be remembered, now the 56th. Having come by bus, the Battalion was without its transport, which did not arrive till the 31st.

Fighting, ill-described in the war diaries, in which the 9th Battalion was not involved till the afternoon, took place all day on the 29th, and at the end of the day the 19th Division, and remnants of the others, held a line along the east side of the Les Vautes-Rosnay road—Treslon—Bouleuse Ridge—Lhéry—Augny.

In the evening the French 1st Cavalry Corps took over command.

On the 30th the Germans attacked the Lagery-Lhéry line successfully. By 1 p.m. the troops had retired, leaving the 9th Battalion on the high ground north-west of Sarcy. With machine gun and rifle fire they repulsed an attack made on them about 5 p.m.

Hard fighting on the right resulted in the capture of two Battalions of the 58th Brigade, the survivors of which joined the 9th Battalion.

Retirements from the Bouleuse ridge left the 9th Battalion in front of the general line, so they withdrew through the high corn to the high ground south of Sarcy, at 8-30 p.m.

On the 31st, the leading companies of the 9th Battalion had a quiet morning, but an uncomfortable one. Attack was certain, but it was most difficult to select, organize and dig a defensive position owing to the standing corn.

About mid-day, German artillery and machine guns opened on the Battalion. They had excellent observation of our positions from the high ground immediately south of Sarcy, and west of the Sarcy-Chambrécy road, on to which their infantry had got opposite to the French on our

K

left, and also from the high ground south-east of Lhéry. Their fire grew in intensity until mid-afternoon, when the left of our front in the valley was a perfect inferno of high explosive and machine gun fire, against which our hastily-improvised cover was useless. Most of the officers were killed or wounded. In particular, we lost Capt. Thurgood and Lieut. Gibbs, both excellent and conscientious officers whom we could very ill afford to lose.

By 3-15 p.m., the position had become utterly untenable. The remnants were personally withdrawn by Colonel Cunninghame, who carried out his reorganization mounted, in full view of the enemy. He rode about the valley in complete disregard of his own safety, in the endeavour to keep the Battalion an organized and disciplined body.

Having successfully done this, Colonel Cunninghame, still mounted, led the Battalion forward in a north-westerly direction to attack and recapture the heights west of the Sarcy-Chambrécy road, from which we were suffering so much small arm fire. Near a farm, about ¾ mile north of Chambrecy, his horse was killed, riddled with machine gun bullets. He himself, wounded in more than one place, remained till the Battalion had successfully been established on the objective.

Extract from a letter 1.2.35 from General Sir G. D. Jeffreys who commanded the 19th Division at the time :—

"The account in question hardly does justice to the great gallantry of Colonel Cunninghame, 2nd Life Guards, who had only a few days previously taken over Command of the Battalion. He rallied the Battalion when it was falling back in comformity with some troops on its flanks, re-organized it and led it forward again to the attack. He was mounted the whole time until his horse was killed, and his action was described to me by his Brigadier as being 'exactly like a whipper-in turning hounds.' I have always regretted that I did not recommend him for the V.C., which I believe I ought to have done. As it was, he got an immediate D.S.O. He was so badly wounded that he never was able to come back, but his brief command of the Battalion was a blaze of glory."

This success brought some relief to the remainder who were able to regain a portion of the lost ground.

The 9th Battalion had lost so heavily that it was numerically incapable of holding a front, of something approaching a mile, astride the valley running from Sarcy to Chambrécy, with its left "in the air" and a gap on its right between it and the next battalion. Trouble soon came from the left and our men were driven down the steep slope on to and across the Sarcy-Chambrécy road and finally had to retreat on to lower portions of the crest of the Mont de Bligny. This small hill was a very com-

W.Os., Staff-Sergeants and Sergeants of the "Butterfly" Battalion (9th).

manding position, as it slopes fairly steeply towards Sarcy on the north, and even more steeply to west and east. Moreover, these steep slopes were pasture land and, unlike the valleys which were cloaked in high standing corn, gave excellent fields of view and fire. South of the summit there was cover from view, so that communication could be kept up with the rear by dropping down to the Chambrécy-Bligny road and then into the Bois d'Eclisse.

It reflects great credit on our signallers that during all these operations from 31st May to 6th June, the Battalion was continuously in touch with Brigade H.Q. by field telephone, except for short periods, at repeated intervals, when the line was blown to pieces.

The 2nd Wiltshire Regiment now reinforced the 9th Battalion and succeeded in regaining a position on the high ground, which prevented the enemy seeing into the Chambrécy valley.

Casualties in the 9th Battalion up to 31st May were Captain E. F. Thurgood and 2nd/Lieut. J. H. Swift killed, twelve officers wounded and missing ; 14 men killed and 69 wounded.

On this day the Germans attacked the junction of the 56th and 57th Brigades, and proceeded to roll up the line. However, the 8th Gloucestershire Regiment, after a preliminary reverse, regained their line. In spite of this, withdrawals on the left forced the 19th Division to withdraw to a line running southwards from the western outskirts of Bligny. After this, there was no permanent loss of ground, but a brilliant episode remains to be recorded.

The days from 2nd to 5th June were spent in consolidating the ground held, and in organizing formed bodies out of the remnants of the 8th, 21st, 25th and 50th Divisions.

The digging was done under continual interference by the Germans, in every form, harassing gun and small arm fire, and raids. It was only the magnificent tenacity of our men, assisted by the excellent field of fire, that kept the Germans at bay. They gave us no rest, day or night. Our patrols were always meeting German parties creeping up under cover of darkness, and generally got the better of them. Prisoners were hard to get, as the Germans did not wait when attacked.

On the 6th, the 19th Division line was held by the 56th and 57th Brigades. The 6th Battalion was in support of the 57th Brigade.

At 3 a.m. on this day, the Germans bombarded the position, and sent in a heavy attack on the Montagne de Bligny or Mont de Bligny. The summit was held by the 9th Battalion, who held up the enemy attack for some time. But the Germans captured the village of Bligny from the French, who withdrew into the Reims Wood. The Mont de Bligny is quite bare and so our men were exposed to fire from Bligny.

The position of Mont de Bligny was vital to the Allied line, because from the top there was a view well into the rear of our front up the valley of the Ardre, commanding all our battery positions.

The position was critical and it was decided to withdraw the front troops who were suffering very heavily, to the line of the Chambrecy-Bligny road, and to organize a counter-attack, which should include the village. This withdrawal took place under as orderly conditions as could be expected.

Lieuts. Clarke and Berry attempted an immediate counter-attack, but it made no headway, so our men hung on to the line of the road, some little way below the crest.

Brigade H.Q. now ordered the 4th K.S.L.I. to retake the summit. On their way forward, along the Chambrecy-Bligny road, they came under very heavy and murderous shell fire which scattered the Battalion and caused heavy casualties. The remnants, some 200, pushed forward with great gallantry and reached the position held by the 9th Battalion. Both Battalions, or rather their remnants, and some men of the 8th North Staffords, advanced to recapture the summit. The 9th Battalion was in the centre, the K.S.L.I. on the left and about one company of the North Staffords on the right.

The position was gallantly assaulted at the point of the bayonet. The flank troops, K.S.L.I. and North Staffords, were held up, but led by Lieuts. Clarke and Berry, Wright and Lees, the 9th men went on and retook the summit. This established our right and centre, but a pocket of the enemy held out on the left, in spite of two counter-attacks under 2/Lieut. C. H. Jones, of the Welch Regiment. Captain R. H. Griffiths at length led an attack which was successful, but the position could not be called secure till Bligny was recaptured, which was accomplished some two hours later.

The German troops engaged belonged to three Divisions against one French and one British, which had been through all the fighting in the Lys battles.

The 9th Battalion was warmly congratulated by the French and received many French decorations.

This action is mentioned in Haig's despatch of 21.12.18, para. 10 :—
" Though the enemy's attacks continued persistently for some time longer, and on 6th June culminated in two determined attempts on the important position known as the Montagne de Bligny, which commands the valley of the Ardre, all these attacks were definitely stayed."

" Throughout this long period of incessant fighting, against greatly superior numbers, the behaviour of all arms of the British forces was magnificent."

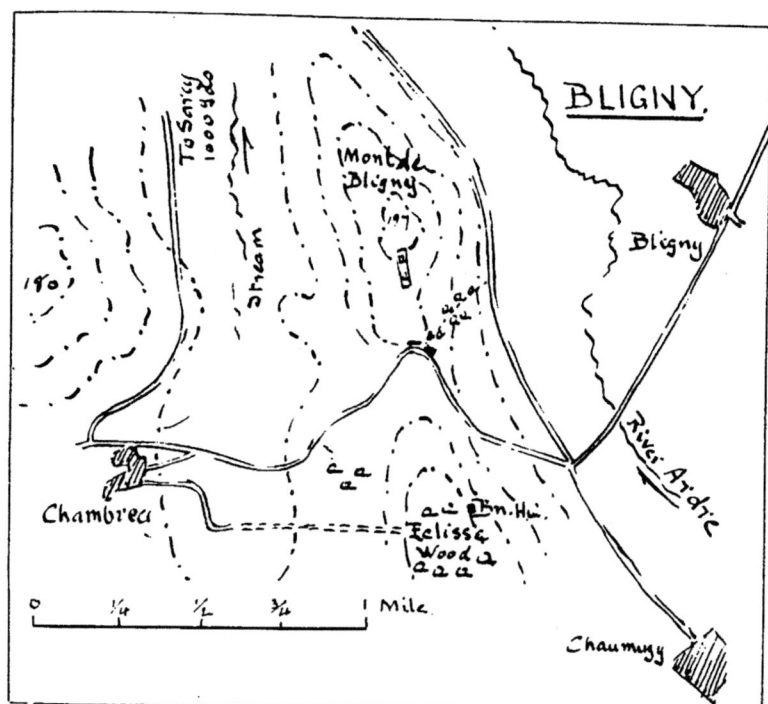

Extracts from letters dated 1st Feb. and 20th Feb. 1935, from General Sir G. D. Jeffreys who commanded the 19th Division in 1918 :—

" The whole Division fought extraordinarily well in these operations, but there were two days on which the 9th Battalion Cheshire Regiment particularly distinguished themselves. One was in the counter-attack made on May 31st, by the Battalion under the command of Lieut.-Colonel Cunninghame, and the other on the 6th of June in the advance and counter-attack upon the Mont de Bligny. On the latter occasion the 9th Battalion was holding the Mont. It completely repulsed the first attack, but after a fresh and very severe bombardment the Germans made a further attack on the hill at about 11 o'clock and captured the summit. The 9th Battalion made an immediate counter-attack, but failed to capture the summit.

" The 1st/4th K.S.L.I. were then ordered to counter-attack and capture the hill. As they went forward they carried with them the 9th Battalion Cheshire Regiment, and the two Battalions captured the summit of the hill, which was never subsequently lost by us.

" The K.S.L.I. get the main credit for this achievement and there is no doubt that the successful counter-attack was in the main their work. It is, however, distinctly stated in my diary—and my recollection confirms this—that the 9th Battalion Cheshire Regiment went forward with them and had, at any rate, a share in the success of the counter-attack.

" The K.S.L.I. were rewarded by the French with a Croix de Guerre for their performance. I think, however, there was little difference between what they did and what the Cheshires did in that particular action. It certainly was a brilliant feat of arms."

From the 1st to the 7th June, the 9th Battalion lost 5 officers and 231 men. On the 7th June, only four officers survived and remained with the Battalion. On the 19th June, the 10th Battalion was temporarily absorbed by the 9th.

MARNE, 1918. 20th July to 2nd August.

SOISSONAIS OURCQ. 23rd July to 2nd August.

Maps p. 151, 153

The 4th and 7th Battalions had come from Palestine into the reconstituted 34th Division. With all the rest of the infantry of the Division, they had had no experience of war as waged in France, except in one respect, this was no great drawback, as open warfare was expected. The one exception was that they knew nothing of gas. So, they were slow to recognize gas shelling. This caused casualties which troops accustomed to gas would have avoided.

Before they went into action in France, it had not been possible to send more than a small proportion of the men home on leave. Many of the men who were killed in this fighting had been abroad on service for over 18 months without seeing their families.

The Battalions reached France in June. Soon after this, the Division was transferred to the 30th French Corps.

On account of its experience in open warfare, French G.H.Q. had asked for this Division to assist in these operations, which were to storm the ridge dominating the whole country-side between the Aisne and the Ourcq, and so bite off the big salient which the German attacks in May already described, had driven into the Allied front.

On the 18th of July, the 10th French Army attacked the west side of the German salient, north of Soissons, and drove the enemy back some

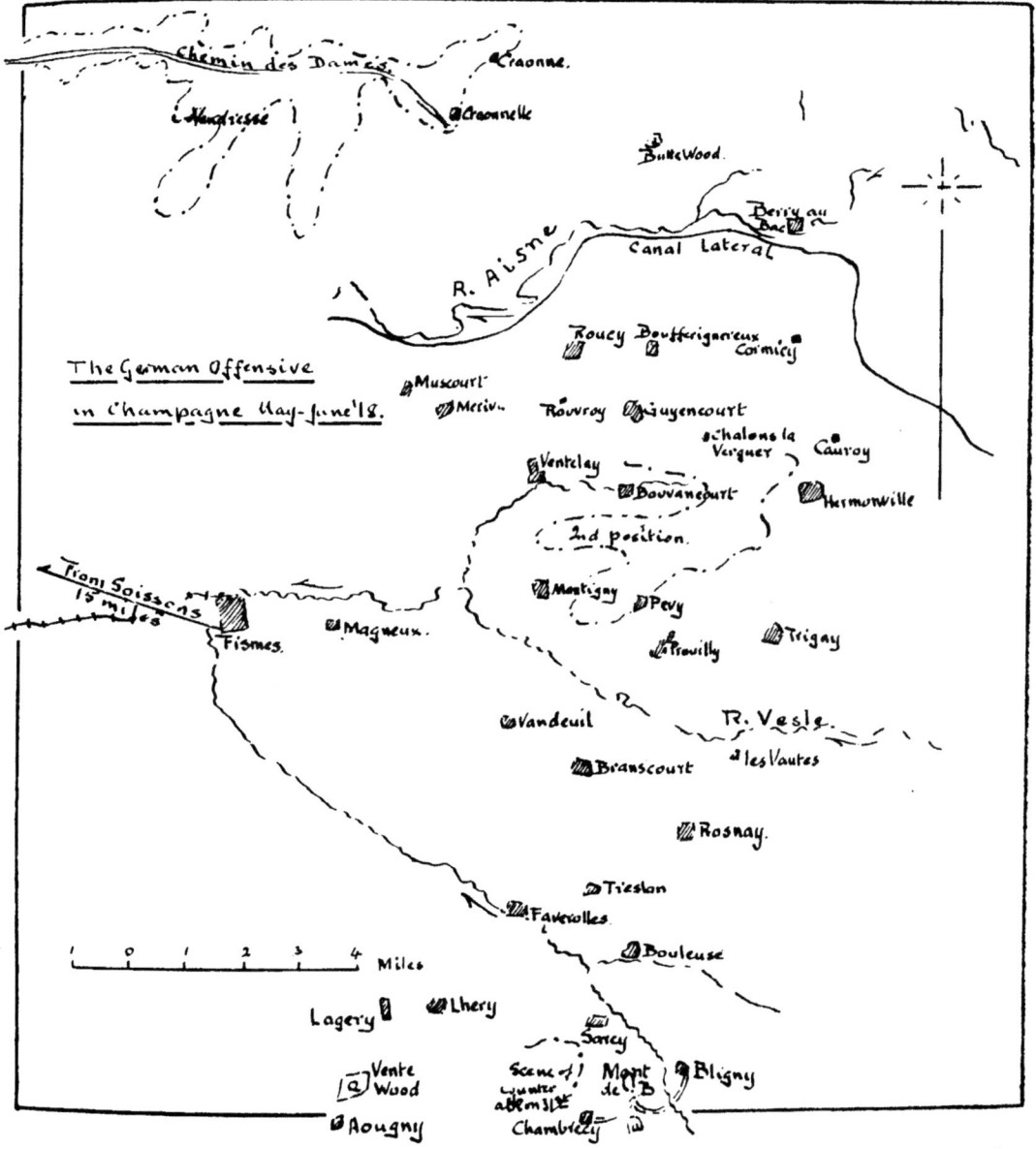

The German Offensive
in Champagne May–June '18.

Chemin des Dames

Craonne.
Neuwiesse
Craonnelle
ButteWood.
Berry au Bac
Canal Lateral
R. Aisne
Roucy Boufferigenieux
Cormiey
Muscourt
Meriw.
Rouvroy Guyencourt
échalons la Varquer
Cauroy
Ventelay
Bouvancourt
Hermonville
2nd position.
Montigny
Pevy
From Soissons
13 miles
La Provilly
Trigay
Fismes.
Magneux.
Vandeuil
R. Vesle.
les Vautes
Branscourt
Rosnay.
Treslon
Faverolles
Bouleuse

1	0	1	2	3	4	Miles

Lagery
Lhery
Sarcy
Scene of
Counter
attack 31st
Mont
de l'B
Bligny
Vente Wood
Chambrecy
Aougny

opp. 150

five miles, taking prisoners and guns. The 34th Division was to take part in the exploitation of this victory.

Orders on the 21st to relieve a French Division in the line, near Parcy Tigny, were quickly followed by orders for an attack to take place on the 23rd.

The 34th Divisional history says " In the most favourable circumstances, this would have been difficult for any troops. But, for a newly constituted Division, composed of troops which had not yet been in action in France and which had just completed a trying move by rail, bus and march route, it was a severe test. The country was entirely new.

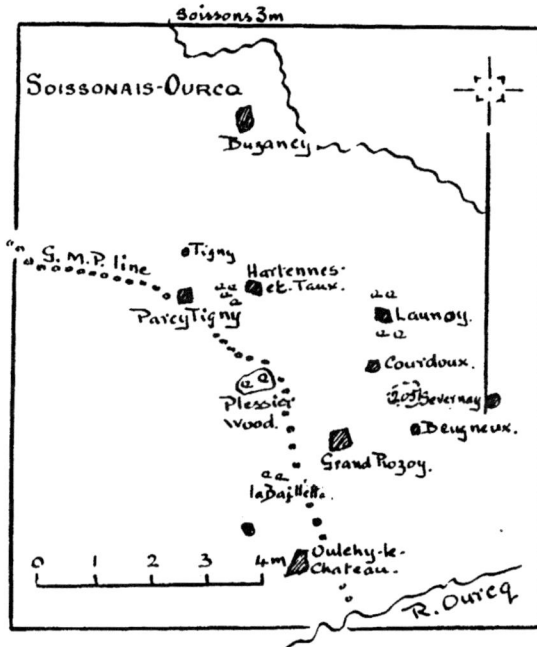

There was no time for reconnaissance. There were no organized trench systems on either side. The enemy's positions were never more than approximately known till they had been captured. To all these difficulties, were added those inseparable from acting for the first time with foreign troops."

On the 23rd July the Division advanced on Launoy with two French Divisions, while other French troops made turning movements round the woods on either side of that place.

The country was looking its best. The battlefield was a stretch of fields of ripe corn, surrounded by glorious forests.

The plan was for the 7th Battalion to take Reugny Wood, and then for the 4th Battalion to pass through and secure Hartennes.

The advance was planned to begin twenty minutes after a rocket signal, but the message reached the signal station late, and even then, when the rockets did go up, they were not visible to the troops. However, orders were received in sufficient time by telephone and wireless.

Owing to the standing corn, the advance of the 7th Battalion was difficult to control, and Lewis guns had to be fired from the hip. After gaining some 1,200 yards under heavy machine gun fire, they were held up, owing to the failure of the French to capture Tigny. The companies instinctively moved into dead ground and here dug in, suffering severe casualties from shell, gas and machine guns.

During the night, the line was advanced and our two Battalions were in touch with each other and with the French.

On this day the 4th Battalion lost 4 officers and 276 others and the 7th Battalion 180 of all ranks, including Captain Thomas Furnell, who died of wounds. He had been with the Battalion since mobilization, and had gained his rank by keenness and hard work. Both Battalions were heavily shelled on the 24th by our own guns.

On the 25th, the enemy was kept alive by very active patrolling, and by continual pushing forward of small parties from trench to trench and by the construction of forward strong points.

On the night of the 27th/28th both Battalions were relieved by the French. On the next night, the Division concentrated in the Baillette Wood, prior to launching an attack on Beugneux and Grand Rozoy. The Brigade (102nd) was in Reserve.

As soon as the main attack was held up, which became evident about 10-50 in the forenoon, the Brigade was ordered to outflank Beugneux by the west, and then to push on to the original objective.

Preparations took till 2-30 p.m., when the attack began. The 4th Battalion moved to fill a gap caused by French withdrawals on the left. Shelling was heavy and snipers in Grand Rozoy were very troublesome.

A German counter-attack delayed the advance, and the troops were halted and reorganized in the G.M.P. line (Government Militaire de Paris— outer Paris defences).

The French took Grand Rozoy on the 30th.

On the 1st August, the advance was resumed. The 4th Battalion and 1st Herefords had the task of following the attack, and holding a spur south east of Bucy Le Gras, to cover the advance of the 12th French Division.

The 4th Battalion, carrying out their tasks in a way that earned the warmest praise of the French Generals, reached a line just south of the Beugneux-Courdoux Road. But they suffered a very great loss.

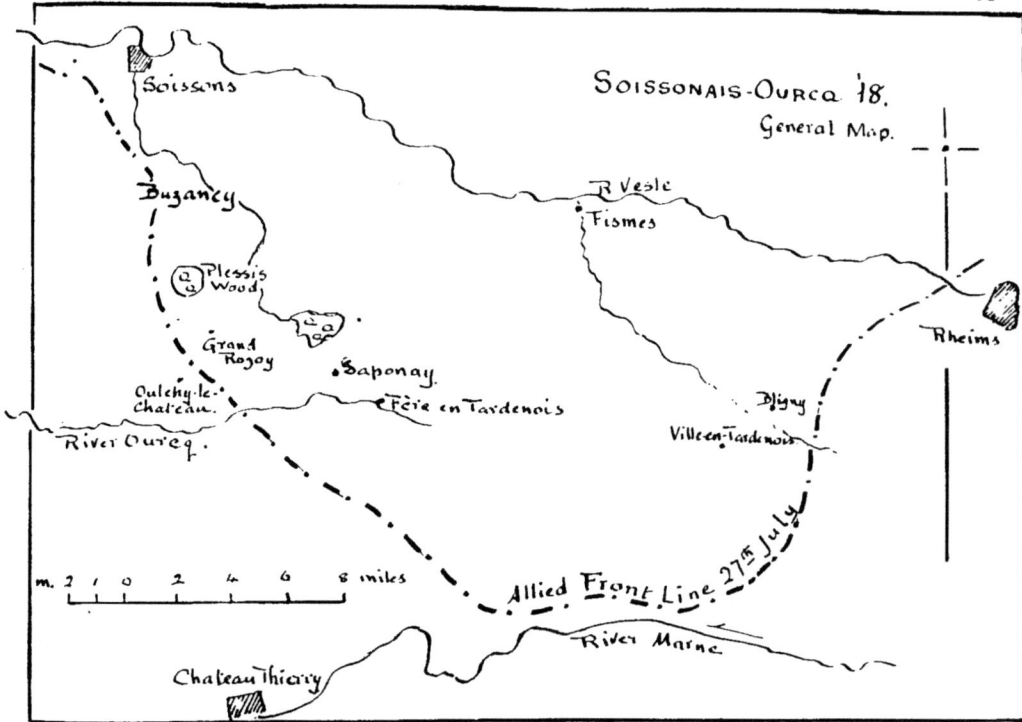

SOISSONAIS-OURCQ 18.
General Map.

Their gallant commanding officer, Colonel G. H. Swindells, was killed. He had commanded the 4th Battalion since October, 1914, when he was transferred from the 7th Battalion. With the exception of a short break recovering from wounds received at Suvla, Swindells had been at duty the whole war. In peace, he had been one of the keenest and most studious officers in the Cheshire Brigade. In war, he earned the devotion and affection of all who served under him.

A further advance of some 4,000 yards was necessary to command the valleys on either side of the hill 192, whence the Germans could get observation into Severnay.

However, the Germans had had enough, and began to withdraw on the 2nd August.

A feature of the operations was the splendid work done by signallers and runners. The French were most appreciative of the work of the Division and bestowed decorations promptly and handsomely on our troops.

SECOND SOMME. 1918. 21st August to 3rd September.

This name covers the battles of the advance in Picardy, "Albert" and "Bapaume." The 1st Battalion was the only one of ours engaged.

ALBERT. 21st to 23rd August, 1918.

On the 8th August, 1918, Haig struck his first great blow in the counter-offensive, with the object of freeing the Paris-Amiens railway. The 3rd and 4th British Armies, assisted by General Debeney's French Army on their right, attacked east of Amiens, and by the 11th August, 22,000 German prisoners and 400 German guns were in British hands, and a large area of ground had been re-captured.

The 1st Battalion detrained from the Foret de Nieppe area on the 14th August at Frevent (north of Doullens), and then marched by easy stages to Bayencourt, where they arrived on the 19th August, ready to take part in further operations by the 3rd Army, which were designed to cut off a large force of Germans in the Ancre Valley.

The front to be attacked was a glacis-like slope from Bucquoy to the bottom of the valley and a similar slope up to the railway. The valley on the right of the attack was cut up by banks and old trenches. There was also a trench running the whole length of the hill about half way up. The valley had many machine guns in it, which could sweep the whole front of attack. Above all, there were three lines of wire west of the railway, in which gaps had to be found, and it was in looking for these gaps that many casualties to officers occurred.

Amongst the officers present with the Battalion at this time were :—
Lieut. Colonel E. L. Roddy (Commanding), Major M. F. Clarke, D.S.O. (2nd-in-Command), Major H. S. Walker, Major J. A. Busfeild, D.S.O., Captain C. H. Horsley, M.C. (Adjutant), Captain E. J. Groves, D.S.O., M.C., Captain R. W. Mills, M.C., Capt. and Qr. Mr. J. C. Sproule, M.C.

On the night of the 20/21st August, the Battalion marched to its assembly position west of Bucquoy, being guided into position by officers and men of the New Zealand Division, who were holding this part of the line. Their staff work was quite admirable.

The 37th Division was to take the first objective, the 15th Brigade the second and third. The 1st Battalion was, with the 1st Norfolks, destined for the third objective, the railway line S.E. of Achiet-le-Petit.

Starting just before dawn, under a very heavy barrage, the infantry advance began in pitch darkness and a heavy ground mist, which made co-operation and maintenance of direction very difficult.

Bucquoy and the second objective were swiftly taken, hostile outposts being completely taken off their guard, and offering little resistance.

Meantime, the 1st Battalion and 16th Warwickshire had followed the advance, moving by compass bearing with great difficulty.

A pause of half-an-hour on the second objective allowed the 1st Battalion and the Warwicks to form up for their attack on Achiet in perfect order.

The advance then began, with the Hood Battalion of the Royal Naval Division on our left. As we had passed beyond range of our artillery, and none had been pushed forward, there was no artillery support, but six tanks moved with us. It was now broad daylight, but the fog still held and a road led straight on to the objective.

Achiet was captured without very heavy casualties by " A " and " B " Companies, which, with " C " Company, pushed on through the village to the final objective, the railway line. " D " Company was left to mop up a large number of prisoners, a battery of artillery, and many machine guns.

As the Battalion debouched from the village, the fog lifted and the leading companies under Major Busfeild and Captain Groves, came under very heavy machine gun fire from beyond the railway and from both

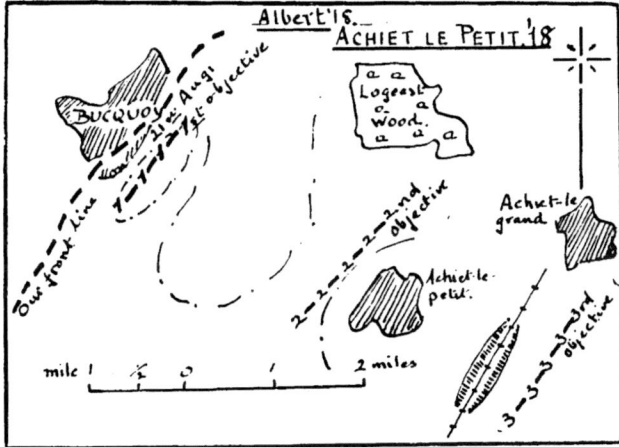

flanks. But this did not stop them from fighting their way up the hill reaching the railway, and holding it. The tanks had moved round to the left of the ridge, but most of them were knocked out before they could support the leading companies.

Patrols were pushed forward at once some 600 yards ahead. It was now found by Major H. S. Walker at 8-50 a.m. that touch had been lost with the Royal Naval Division on the left, and it was also learned that the Royal Warwickshires were ahead of troops on their right, the others having lost their way in the fog.

Within 15 minutes of the Battalions reaching their objectives, the usual determined counter-attack was made, mainly on the left flank, and was successfully repulsed.

It was now realized that the two Battalions were some 500 yards ahead of any other troops, and that the enemy was working round the left. " A " and " B " Companies withdrew slowly to the high ground west of the railway, and defensive flanks were made on the left by Major Busfeild's company and on the right of the Royal Warwickshires by Captain Ferguson's company. The trench running along the face of the hill was occupied as a front line.

This retirement was carried out under very heavy machine gun fire from three directions.

Lieuts. R. J. Jolley, McGuire (attached) and Postells (attached) were killed. Major Busfeild and six other officers were wounded.

The Battalion went into action 600 strong and lost no less than 300 killed and wounded on this day, three officers being killed and eight wounded.

The Battalion was relieved in the evening.

BAPAUME.   31st August to 3rd September.

Map p. 134

Here the enemy was now fighting carefully staged rear-guard actions in which machine guns played a decisive part, in so far that they were the principal obstacles to our progress. The ground was terribly battle-scarred and had already been fought over twice.

On the 2nd September, the 1st Battalion took part in the capture of Beugny.

The village was known to be strongly held by the enemy, a previous attack by another Division having failed.

The assembly was difficult. Shortness of time, and vigilance of the enemy had made previous reconnaissance impossible. So the advance was planned to make the best of a heavy barrage.

A barrage began at 5-8 a.m. on our right which brought down a heavy retaliatory barrage on our assembling companies, whose own barrage was not due to begin till 5-51 a.m. This caused us many casualties, especially among officers and non-commissioned officers. However, when our barrage fell, it was excellent. In spite of this, the left of the Battalion met very considerable opposition and was held up before reaching the village, but the right company, under 2nd/Lieut. J. D. Pinguey, reached the village and the 1/Norfolks, under Major H. S. Walker, of ours, reached the final objective, the high ground beyond the village.

During this day, Private Jones, V.C., won his D.C.M.

The result of the day's fighting was that Beugny was nearly surrounded.

Major J. A. Simmons.

Lieut.-Colonel C. F. King
(whilst temporarily with the 9th Welch Regt.)

Destroyed German Trenches at Ovillers, looking towards Bapaume Road, July, 1916,
showing Dug-out Entrances.   Q. 4,045.

The left of the Battalion consolidated a position near Delsaux Farm, which had been the scene of severe fighting by the 11th Battalion in the spring.

The enemy withdrew a considerable distance during the night.

At the end of the fortnight, out of twenty-five of the original combatant officers who had taken part in the first day's fighting, only four remained.

* * * *

The following account of Bapaume '18 is from Captain L. I. L. Ferguson's diary.

" Friday, 30th August, 1918.—The Division are side-slipping to the left for this show. On reaching Achiet-le-Grand, we formed up in column of Brigade, marching forward for about 4 miles, where we had a long halt. A number of prisoners passed us. They all looked very " done up." We moved from this position in " Artillery Formation " of half-platoons and soon came under shell fire, but it was not heavy and we did not suffer. We halted just under a ridge with the Beugnatre-Vaulx-Vrancourt Road running along it. This road was getting badly strafed and we got the order to " dig in." It proved a rotten position, for lines of our field guns " pull-in " all around. So, after digging for an hour, we were withdrawn and told to " dig-in " again. But, before we had time to start, we again advanced to a position 400 yards behind Beugnatre, with Battalion H.Q. taking up a position on the right of Sapignies, about one mile behind us. We had a very good position, " C " and " D " Companies in the front line, " A " and " B " Companies in support. We found a few old trenches in which, when cleared of dead, it did not take us long to get cover.

Sunday, 1st September, 1918. Col. Roddy explained that orders had arrived for an attack at dawn, also that officers coming up would not be here in time to take over, so that we were to carry on.

The plan was for the 1st Battalion to move up to-night at 8 p.m., capture the village of Beugny as a first objective, then advance about two miles to Delsaux Farm. Operation orders would be issued later. Zero hour was not yet fixed. We had to hurry back to our companies as we had little more than an hour to fix up the men with everything for attack.

We heard that a big draft of reinforcements were just behind but had been marching all day and were too tired to take part in the show. The companies were all very much below strength, nor had we had the time to organise the sections. Operation orders prescribed Beugny as our objective.

By 8 p.m., it was quite dark and we moved off to a line which we had never had time to investigate. The attack was timed for 5-15 a.m. Guides met us on the Vaulx-Vrancourt road informing us that their battalion had only gone in the night before to hold the line, that they had had a rough time and had had a big number of officers and men killed during the day. We had not gone far when a halt was called and word passed back that the front guides had lost the way. This was made more alarming by enemy night planes hovering over us and dropping tons of bombs on the right and left. We had to retrace our steps and after about an hour we got on the right path. After about a mile, we came to a crowded trench which we were informed was the front line. The officer in charge did not know much about the lie of the land. He was only a junior. His Company Commander had been killed during the day. He informed me that the village of Beugny lay about 500 yards away in the direction a quarter right but they had been keeping under cover all day, as it was unsafe to move in the trench. After getting settled in, I went and saw Captain Bathurst on my right. I found him in a shelter with C.S.M. Wager and he was also very worried over his very indefinite orders. He was unable to find troops on his right and he had sent out a patrol under Lieut. Squires to look for these but with no result, as they soon got fired on by the enemy. We had scanty idea of our true position, so we agreed to send a message by runner to Battalion H.Q. informing them of the situation and also saying we would advance at 5-15 a.m. if we received no fresh order. No fresh order did arrive nor were we visited by anybody during the night.

Collecting my Company H.Q. in two small recesses, all was ready for the advance by 4-50 a.m., " B," " C " and " D " Companies being in front line and " A " Coy. in support. My company officers were Lieut. Munro and Lieut. Dampier-Bennett. I had given them and my N.C.Os. all the instructions I could on the very scrappy information I had myself received. Just at this moment, a very urgent after-order arrived to the effect that we were only to go to the first objective unless we had a Brigade order to advance. This, I discovered afterwards, was caused by the Australian Division on the right refusing to go further than their first objective, because during all the recent attacks, G.H.Q. have asked troops to advance an unreasonable way, causing very heavy losses between the first and second objectives, owing to lack of artillery support. To-day, the attack is to be conducted without tanks. Also a new experiment is being tried by sending over field guns with the infantry at zero hour. The dawn was getting later and 5-15 a.m. was a quarter of an hour later than the usual British zero hour during the past ten days. At 5 a.m. the enemy guns opened on our trench and in less time than it takes to write had just about blown us to hell. Great big shells fell right into the trench, causing at least 50% casualties before we started. We also got sneezing gas, and liquid fire was mixed up with the H.E. I was uncertain what order to give, or rather how to give it, but it was certain if we stopped in the trench till 5-15 a.m. none of us would be left to do the attack. I noticed " B "

Company on my left leaving the trench, so I called to those who could hear me to get out and lie in " no man's land " till time was up. I saw them all start. Shells were now falling like hail and I saw a number of fellows blown to bits including two officers' batmen, who were just near me in the trench. A wounded runner came and gave me the Company roll, telling me it was from C.S.M. Smith who was wounded. I was just mounting the parapet followed by my servant, two runners and signallers, when we were caught by a shell and I next found myself sheltering in the trench with my runners either dead or badly wounded beside me. One fellow, I think he was a Lewis gunner, was lying on top of me and was able to talk. He told me a shell had just caught the back of my H.Q. Section and that I had jumped back into the trench. As I now felt better, I came to the conclusion that I was only suffering from shock, but soon found I was sitting in a pool of blood and my leg seemed stiff. The trench was a shambles and I could see at least twenty killed all around my position. Suddenly, six or seven Huns came creeping along the trench and I at first thought we were being attacked, but on my covering them with my revolver they at once informed me they were prisoners. I lay still for half an hour but then decided to try and make my way back as I was becoming faint.

" As I heard later, the facts were that our chaps only got 500 yards and never entered the village that day. Only 18 of " C " Company returned and poor Munro was killed. He was an excellent fellow and from the day I took over the Company I was always pleased with his good work. Only two officers in the fighting companies got through the day, both belonging to " A " Company who were in support."

* * * *

Captain Ferguson was wounded on September 2nd as described above, operated on at No. 2 General Hospital on September 3rd, invalided home on September 17th and saw no further service in France. He rejoined the 3rd Cheshires at West Hartlepool and was demobilised in March, 1919.

The Battalion got into Beugny, as far as a sunken road running north from the centre of the village. There, they were held up and, later, repulsed a counter-attack, as already stated.

ARRAS. 26th August to 3rd September.

This name covers the battles preliminary to the attack on the Hindenburg Line—" Scarpe '18," and " Drocourt-Queant line."

The 5th Battalion represented The Regiment and was engaged in Scarpe '18.

SCARPE. 26th to 30th August, 1918.

The 5th Battalion's work included sinking wells in the bed of the Cojeul river, as there was some doubt as to the sufficiency of the water supply in this area. They also had a great amount of road-making, but luckily the weather was fine and dry.

HINDENBURG LINE. 12th September to 9th October.

This name covers the battles fought to gain the Hindenburg Line, the strongest fortified line which had ever been constructed, protected by masses of wire, and designed with all the skill which the experience of four years of war could command.

The two battles in this series in which any Battalion of The Regiment took part were the " Canal du Nord " and " Cambrai."

CANAL DU NORD. 27th September to 1st October, 1918.

Map p. 162

This battle, which involved crossing the canal, as well as tackling strong fortifications with wide fields of wire, was as pretty a manœuvre as any in the war. In place of a general attack on the whole front, part of which was marshy, the Canadians crossed the Canal south of the main Arras-Cambrai road and spread out fanwise. The 11th Division crossed behind them and turning northwards took over the northern part of the ground. Then the 56th Division, to which our 5th Battalion belonged, crossed at the same place and went up between the 11th and the Canal. The 5th Battalion was now commanded by Lieut.-Colonel W. A. V. Churton.

The 5th Division was acting as a pivot to operations of the Corps on their left, in the general attack on the Canal du Nord. The immediate task of the Division on the 27th was to capture Beaucamp village and Highland ridge. The 15th Brigade was to form a defensive flank to the right, once these objectives were captured. The enemy facing us was the Jaeger Division, one of the best German divisions in the field.

The 15th Brigade started from a line of trenches facing Beaucamp, the 1st Battalion being on the left. The attack started at 7-52 a.m. on the 27th, but in spite of great gallantry of the Royal West Kent Regiment, the 13th Brigade, on the left of the Division, was held up.

Lieut.-Colonel H. Johnston.

Lieut.-Colonel H. Smyth.

Lieut.-Colonel W. H. G. Baker.

Colonel L. H. K. Finch.

In the meantime, the 1st Bedfordshire had reached their objective, and captured many prisoners. The village of Beaucamp was cleared by one company of the 1st Battalion, under Lieut. Lockett, after severe close quarter hand-to-hand fighting.

A gap was now driven between the 13th and 15th Brigades by German bombing parties. So two companies of the 1st Battalion were sent up to support the company holding Beaucamp, and two platoons of the right company went to support the 1st Bedfordshire. Little more was done on the 27th. On the 28th, the 1st Battalion and the 1st Norfolk were ordered to advance to the Villers Plouich-Gouzeaucourt railway. This was successfully accomplished by 6 p.m. On the 29th the advance was continued in face of strong resistance, the 1st Battalion being in reserve.

On the 30th, the 1st Battalion and the 1st Norfolk were again in front. The objective was the Gonnelieu ridge. This meant breaking through the front and support trenches of the Hindenburg system, and capturing the high ground overlooking Banteux and the canal crossings. There was an immense amount of wire and many trenches to cross. It was supposed to be the strongest fortified line ever constructed.

The night was very wet and very dark, and, again, reconnaissance of assembly positions had not been possible owing to hostile machine gun fire. The attack started at 04.00 hours on the 30th, and was entirely successful. The withdrawal of the enemy was just forestalled. The success of the attack was mainly due to the H.E. barrage which guided the troops to their objectives.

The liberties taken in various ways during these battles, such as assembling and advancing without reconnaissance, are a measure of the demoralization which had by now set in among the German troops.

*   *   *   *

The 5th Battalion was employed making canal crossings on zero day. The orders for this work had been worked out by Major N. B. Ellington, M.C., with the greatest care, and to this the success of the Battalion's operations was largely due.

The Battalion moved forward behind the Canadians and, east of Baralle, encountered artillery and machine gun fire. They passed through the infantry and reached the eastern edge of the village. A boldly-handled Lewis gun patrol, under Lieut. G. H. Williams and Sergeant Cruikshank, drove the enemy from the west bank and by 12 o'clock bridging was begun.

L

CAMBRAI. 8th to 9th October, 1918.

The 9th Battalion was in the area of the battle, at Graincourt.

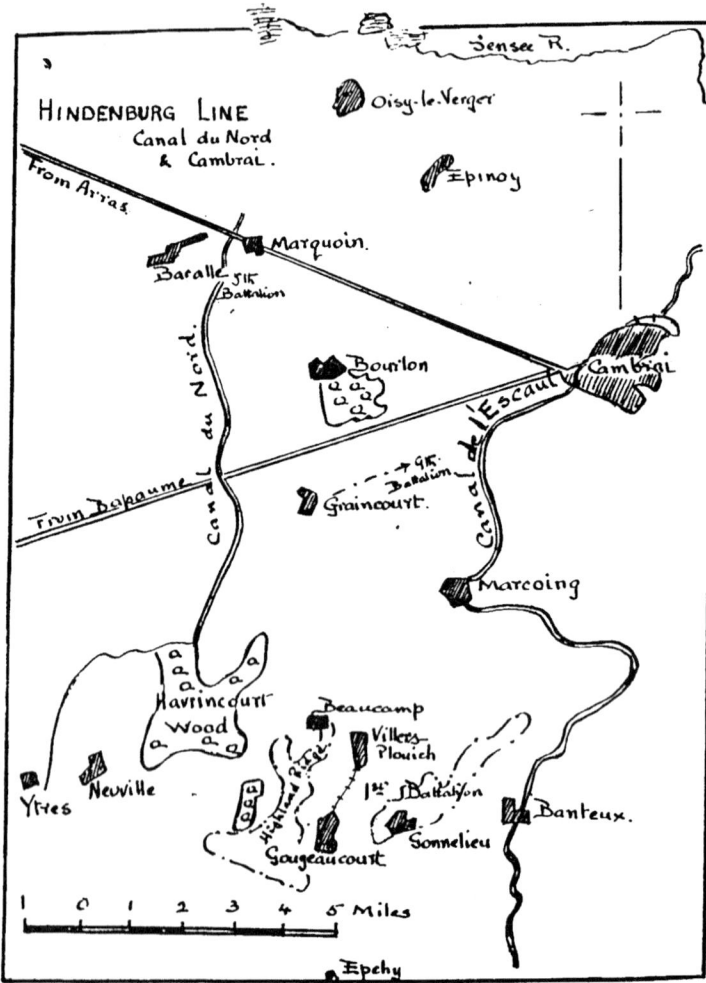

Hindenburg Line

YPRES, 1918. 28th September to 2nd October.

This, the final battle of Ypres, was the result of the successes following the advance of the 4th Army from Villers Bretonneux, the capture of the Hindenburg Line, the crossing of the Canal du Nord and the capture of Cambrai.

*   *   *   *

On the 20th September, " C " Company of the 6th Battalion, under Captain H. Cooke, attacked a German strong point which formed a small salient in our line near Wulverghem.

In forty minutes the raiding party had advanced four hundred yards, captured the salient with fourteen prisoners and a machine gun and gained very valuable information.

The Corps and Divisional Commanders both went up to the line to congratulate the Battalion.

*   *   *   *

Prior to the date of this battle honour, the 4th and 7th Battalions in the 34th Division had reoccupied Mount Kemmel on the enemy's withdrawal and advanced as far as the Messines-Wytschaete ridge.

This ridge was the first objective in the operations to free the salient, and fell without difficulty, as the Germans were withdrawing all along this front.

*   *   *   *

During September 1918, the 15th Battalion (105th Brigade) was in and out of the line south of Voormezeele between the Canal and the western edge of Zillebeke lake.

The Battalion distinguished itself by a series of well-conducted daringly-executed strong-patrols, by which the enemy's morale was kept subdued and which furnished prisoners and information. In this work, Lieuts. H. C. Mann, H. V. Shaw and W. G. Stott, who unfortunately was killed, particularly distinguished themselves. The Battalion runners, Ptes. Olley, Kay and Houghton, are especially praised in the war diary for carrying messages to the front companies by day, as the telephones were under direct observation of the enemy and were constantly cut by shell fire.

The front here was lightly held by the enemy and this accounts for the necessity of constant and bold patrolling to keep in touch with his movements.

On the first day of the attack, the 15th Battalion was in reserve, but on the 29th, passed through the leading troops of the Brigade to attack Zandvoorde.

They lost their way in the mist, and instead of approaching Zandvoorde from the north west, came at it from the west and suffered severely from machine guns on the extreme point of the Zandvoorde Spur.   However, an enveloping attack from the north-west by the 15th Sherwood Foresters, cleared the opposition away.

In the end, the enemy's strong occupation of the Gheluwe Switch brought the whole advance to a standstill till the guns and administrative units could be moved forward.

*   *   *   *

The 23rd Battalion, under Colonel A. E. Churcher, with Major R. E. Druitt as 2nd in command, was in the 121st Brigade of the 40th Division.

The Brigade was in the line near Pont de Nieppe (Armentières) at the start of the offensive of 28th September.

Progress in the south, enabled the 40th Division to advance to the Scheldt without very much difficulty.

COURTRAI.   14th to 19th October, 1918.

Map p. 166

The 4th Battalion, under Lieut.-Colonel Godfrey Drage, D.S.O., took up a position in an open trench and German pillboxes near Gheluwe for two days prior to the night of the 13th/14th, ready to assault.

Captain Angas, with his own (" A ") Company and " C " Company, under Lieut. Oakes, started well under the barrage with some loss of direction owing to gas, smoke and wire, but, as the light improved, this was corrected.

Assisted by a captured interpreter, Captain Angas' companies pressed on across the Gheluwe-Menin road close to Menin.   2nd/Lieut. Stafford here shot down two German machine gunners who were getting their guns into action.

About 110 prisoners were rounded up and several guns captured in Cou Cou, Job and Query farms.

2nd/Lieut. Stafford continued to do excellent work during the night and following day, pushing forward posts and making strong points as opportunity offered.

Menin was captured and passed on the 15th.

There was a good deal of trouble in crossing the Canal.   The Battalion Pioneers made a raft and in spite of very gallant attempts by 2nd/Lieut. Leech, 2nd/Lieut. Herbert and 2nd/Lieut. Jenkins, the enemy managed to prevent our men crossing in numbers, though 2nd/Lieut. Jenkins actually got across with two men.   The enemy fire was heavy and accurate.

Lieut. Montague, M.C., did extremely good work.   His patrol was the first through Menin early on the 15th.   He skilfully organized and held a strong point on the far side for thirty hours against machine gun attack.

Some 136 prisoners and some field guns were taken by the Battalion.

The casualties were 2nd/Lieut. E. W. Herbert killed, 2 officers wounded and 163 others killed, wounded or missing.

*   *   *   *

During this period the 7th Battalion was commanded by Captain R. D. Flunder, D.S.O., Colonel H. L. Moir, D.S.O. having been wounded at the end of September. The leading companies advanced on the right of the 4th Battalion. Although suffering somewhat from hostile strong points not touched by our initial bombardment, they reached both their objectives up to time. A thick fog allowed a good many of the enemy to escape in spite of the energy of the patrols. Our casualties were 3 officers, 117 others.

*   *   *   *

In this attack, 14th October, the 6th Battalion started in reserve to the 21st Brigade. The Battalion crossed the Lys in the afternoon and established themselves beyond it.

*   *   *   *

The 15th Battalion, under Colonel H. Johnston, took part in this battle in the area to the north of where the 4th and 7th Battalions were fighting.

There were no trenches in this area and the enemy resisted very stoutly.

On the first day, the Battalion captured its objectives as well as many guns and prisoners. The men fought with the most admirable vigour and pluck, and literally brushed aside the by no means inconsiderable opposition.

After two days' rest, the Battalion was called upon to attack, but the Germans were now on the run and masses of civilian refugees made fighting difficult.

*   *   *   *

In the area south of Courtrai, the 4th Battalion, under Major E. W. Morris, was in another attack on the 24th, just east of the Courtrai-Bossuyt Canal, when 2nd/Lieut. Stafford again especially distinguished himself by his bold leading and tactical skill in the capture of Autryve.

2nd/Lieut. Rouse continued to command " B " Company for three hours after being shot through the thigh, and to make clear and useful reports on the situation.

The Battalion cleared the whole front of the Canal from Knocke southwards and gained the final objectives on the Scheldt by dusk the same evening.

*   *   *   *

During the night previous to this attack, the 7th Battalion cleared the park of Bossuyt Chateau, and made two very gallant but unsuccessful attempts to cross the Canal at locks 3 and 4. They eventually succeeded in doing so in the afternoon of the 25th October, joining hands with the companies of the 4th Battalion which had moved round to the S.E. face of Moen village.

During October, the 4th Battalion lost 14 officers and 297 others.

*   *   *   *

On the 14th of October, the 15th Battalion was on the right of the 35th Division attack to secure crossings over the Lys between Menin and Courtrai, near Bisseghem.

The advance was difficult owing to the objective being diagonal to the line of advance and to the length of the attack (7,000 to 8,000 yards) making it impossible for the artillery to cover the whole advance without shifting their position. But objectives were reached like clockwork, in spite of a thick white mist.

Attacks were continued on the 15th and 16th, but the Lys was not crossed till 19th, when Marcke was captured and bridges made. Further moves were rapidly organized and energetically carried out. The advance of the 35th Division was the subject of congratulation by the Corps and Army Commanders on more than one occasion, but there is no particular episode concerning the 15th Battalion which need be chronicled.

They crossed the Scheldt on the night of the 9th November, and by 11 a.m. on the 11th, portions of the Division had advanced another 23 miles and could claim to have captured the crossings over the Dendre before hostilities came to an end. The 15th Battalion reached Audenhove. Their casualties were 37 men killed and 7 officers and 177 men wounded.

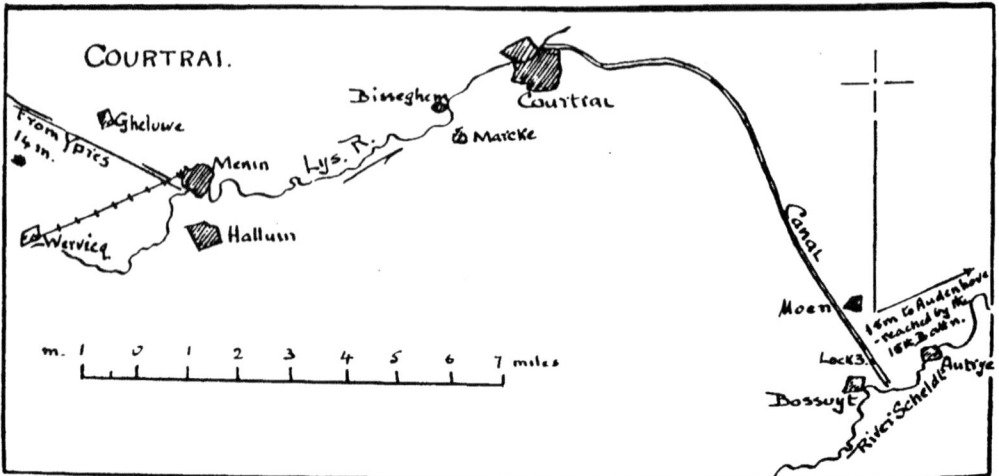

SELLE, 17th to 25th October, 1918.

Map p. 168

After the loss of the Hindenburg Line, the German retirement became fairly rapid, as their next prepared line of defence was a long way further east.

The 5th Division marched by Masnieres (S. of Cambrai) Caudry and Inchy. The dotted line on the map shows the 1st Battalion's movements. During this advance, the Division was not in touch with the enemy, and were only following up some miles in rear of the advanced troops. This country was no longer devastated by war, no shell holes pock-marked the fields, villages were whole and inhabited by civilians, and when the Battalion billetted for the night, it was no longer a case of crawling into a hole in the side of a trench, but of really comfortable billets, and in some cases even the luxury of a real bed.

On the night of the 16th/17th October, the great battle of the Selle river began, in which the 1st, 3rd and 4th British Armies took part.

The 1st Battalion, commanded by Lt.-Col. M. F. Clarke, D.S.O., attacked and captured Beaurain. They reached their assembly position early on the night of the 16th. There was no cover and they lay out all night in the open on top of the hill overlooking the village.

The Germans had by this time lost so many of their field and heavy guns, that they usually made a practice of placing their guns so far back, that they could only just about reach the most advanced infantry posts, and were quite unable to reach our battery line, except with long range high velocity guns.

As early as 2 o'clock on the morning of the 17th, a British barrage opened up on some part of the huge battle line, and a Corps near the Battalion began firing a barrage. The German guns immediately put down a counter-barrage on our unfortunate infantry, who were lying out in the open without cover. The 1st Battalion suffered heavily during the night on this account, and from a heavy barrage which was put down on the assembly position.

The advance began at 3-20 a.m. through a heavy enemy artillery and machine gun barrage. The German infantry came out of their positions to meet our attack.

The 1st Bedfords were on the right, the 1st Battalion on the left and the 1st Norfolks in reserve.

A number of officers quickly became casualties, Captain G. B. Lockett, 2nd/Lieuts. W. N. Stubbs and H. May. Lieut. L. E. Davies took his company straight through to the objective in a manner deserving the highest praise. Lieut. J. Bland mopped up a sunken road full of Germans, and 2nd/Lieut. B. F. Morris with three men of " B " Company rushed a M.G. nest. All four were wounded. 2nd/Lieuts. S. R. Phillips and L. O. Kitchingman pushed on with their own platoons and remnants of others, and held on alone to the final objective in touch with the 42nd Division, till the 1st Norfolks came up. The Germans withdrew and the Battalion was relieved by fresh troops.

The attack was expected and prepared for by the Germans who had orders to hold on to the last. Our casualties were 2nd/Lieut. W. N. Stubbs killed, 5 officers wounded, 34 men killed and 172 wounded.

The British battery lines during this battle were a most amazing sight. Owing to the front having narrowed very considerably during the advance, batteries were crammed in almost everywhere and the guns were practically wheel to wheel all along the front. It was an awe-inspiring sight and made a great impression on the German prisoners. One German officer was overheard to remark that he was not surprised that Germany was losing the war now that he had seen the British batteries. If we suffered from the German artillery, what must have been their experience under ours ?

*   *   *   *

The 9th Battalion, 56th Brigade, was in reserve at St. Aubert, in an attack by the 19th Division on the ground east of the Selle river.

SELLE and SAMBRE
THE FINAL ADVANCE. 1918.

VALENCIENNES. 1st and 2nd November, 1918.

The 9th Battalion moved in pursuit by Cagnoncles, Haussy and Sommaing. The Germans were on the run, but still putting up stiff rearguard resistance.

SAMBRE. 4th to 7th November, 1918.

Map p. 168

The last operation order of the war for the 1st Battalion was issued by H.Q. 15th Brigade on the 4th November. It ordered the 1st Battalion to assemble at Jolimetz with the object of exploiting the success of the 1st Bedfords across the Sambre canal.

The 37th Division began an attack on the western edge of the Forêt de Mormal at 5-30 a.m. on the 4th. They met with very stout resistance. Although the enemy was in retreat, the difficulty of passing through the forest and keeping organization, made it advisable to leap frog the Battalions.

At 5-30 a.m. on the 5th, the 15th Brigade moved forward following up the advance through the forest. The 1st Battalion leap-frogged over the 1st Bedfords and, after an exceedingly arduous march, reached the eastern outskirts of the forest. The roads were very heavy through continuous rain, and they had been very cleverly demolished at road junctions and brook crossings, which compelled detours through the fields. This made transport useless and S.A.A. as well as Lewis guns had to be carried by hand.

The 1st Battalion pushed on to Pont-sur-Sambre and arrived there by 9-40 p.m., a few minutes after the last German had left. A very fine performance considering that the march through the forest in the dark had to be by compass. They were, however, received with heavy shell fire. This position was consolidated and patrols went forward down to the river. No attempt was made to form a bridge head on the far bank by Bde. H.Q. order.

Patrols were sent to the river at dawn on the 6th, but could accomplish nothing owing to the heavy machine gun fire.

The 15th Brigade was ordered to cross the river by the Quartes bridge.

During the whole afternoon, the Brigade front and La Porcquerie was heavily shelled, and any movement towards the river was met with heavy machine gun fire.

Major B. M. Cloutman, R.E., made a most gallant reconnaissance of the Quartes bridge and successfully cut the leads of the demolition charge under close fire. A platoon of the 1st Battalion, with two light mortars, was ordered up to prevent the enemy repairing the leads. However, the troops arrived too late to prevent the bridge being blown up. It was now decided to proceed with the original plan of building a bridge. By 6 a.m., the bridge was complete and two companies of the 1st Battalion went across and made good the line of the railway. The 95th Brigade took over the line and the Battalion billetted in Pont-sur-Sambre. Our Casualties were 2nd/Lieut. F. H. David killed and four men; one officer and 39 others wounded.

* * * *

The 9th Battalion went into the line in front of Sommaing on 2nd/3rd November.

The enemy having withdrawn, the two leading companies pushed forward to regain touch. They came under fire from machine guns near Jenlain. In spite of this the ground was consolidated and patrols went forward while reserve companies and Battalion H.Q. moved up. The whole front was subjected to a severe bombardment. A platoon of the 9th Battalion managed to get into Jenlain. This made the enemy withdraw and the left company was in consequence able to establish itself beyond the north edge of the village, and the right company to reach the railway which ran through the village. All these movements were carried out not only under hostile but also under " friendly " artillery fire.

On the 4th, the attack on Jenlain was resumed under a barrage, which again caused some casualties to our men. Realizing that the right flank of the Division was exposed to enfilade fire from the southern portion of Wargnies-le-Grand, one of our company commanders mopped up the village and attacked and captured a machine gun nest, as well as a number of prisoners.

On the 7th, the 9th Battalion took part in an attack by the 57th Brigade on Bellignies.

All objectives were gained, but the war diary had a great deal to say about our artillery barrage which made the attack " a very difficult and dangerous proceeding."

This engagement is called the Passage of the Grande Honnelle, the name of the river west of Bellignies. Our casualties were nine officers wounded, 12 N.C.Os. and men killed and 132 wounded.

* * * *

The 5th Battalion was engaged in this battle, its energies being concentrated on repairing the widespread damage done to the roads by the Germans, sufficiently well for horse transport to use them. The Battalion gained great credit for the speed with which they cleared the débris of a viaduct over the river Honnelle which the Germans had blown up.

* * * *

The Armistice in France.

The Armistice, bringing hostilities on the western front to an end, began at 11 a.m. on the 11th of November. Cheshire Battalions did no more fighting, but there was a Cheshire Brigade with the Army of Occupation on the Rhine.

On December 3rd, the King, the Prince of Wales and Prince Albert paid a visit to Le Quesnoy. The King left his car at the gate and walked up to the square. He was cheered all along the route, and the 1st Battalion gave him three hearty cheers when he reached the square, where they were formed up. After the mayor had read an address and the mayor and councillors had been introduced to him, the Miniature Regimental Colour of the Battalion was brought up for his inspection, and he made enquiries as to its origin, loss and recovery. He appeared much interested in it, and whilst congratulating the Battalion on its recovery he said that he trusted it would never be lost again. He then went to the ramparts to see how the town was captured, and on returning to the square was cheered again and again by the soldiers of the garrison who happened to be there at the time.

The final pursuit of the Germans back to our starting point at Mons was begun by the crossing of the Canal du Nord. It then continued through Flanders (Ypres), Artois (Selle) and Picardy (Valenciennes). This inspired the compiler of the official list of battles to quote from Chaucer :

"With him ther was his sonne, a young squyer

" . . . .

"of twenty yeer he was of age, I gesse,

"and he had been some time in Chivalrye

"in Flaundres, in Artois, and in Picardie."

ITALY.

The 1st Battalion left the French front on the 12th December, 1917, under Colonel M. W. Halford, M.C., of the Gloucestershire Regiment. General W. H. Anderson and Colonel A. Crookenden visited the Battalion on its way through France and found they knew no one except Sproule, the Q.M., who stuck to his post through the whole war and finally brought the cadre to Chester.

It is difficult to say how much The Regiment owes to the Quartermaster of the 1st Battalion, Major J. C. Sproule, M.C. He, and many men in the same position, went right through the war as Quarter-masters. They saw hundreds of young N.C.Os. whom they had trained and taught all they knew, become commissioned officers. Their work debarred them from many of the honours to be acquired by actual fighting. Yet it is due to these men that the Regular Battalions of our Army never lost their distinctive quality. By 1917, the personnel of a Regular Battalion was exactly the same in officers and men as the New Army and Territorial Battalions. Yet, one could always tell a Regular Battalion, in or out of the line. This maintenance of prestige and esprit de corps was, and must have been, due to the Quarter-masters, because there was no one else to carry on the tradition.

Of Sproule himself, it is impossible to say too much. No Battalion was better served by its Quarter-master than the First Battalion. Clean clothes, dry socks and other creature comforts, and at least one hot meal every day were always produced at the right time. Sproule always took his turn in bringing the transport to the Battalion at night. He and Bruce, the transport officer, did more than can ever be told for the morale of officers and men. It was the regularity of their services, in any and all conditions of weather, or of enemy action, that made their work so valuable.

Before going into the line in Italy, Colonel E. L. Roddy returned and took over command.

Two companies and H.Q. took over trenches on 10th February, after a very pleasant seven weeks of marches, football matches and some mild training. It was a very much-needed change from the severity of the fighting in France, from which all ranks benefited enormously.

A patrol went out on Meeanee Day and brought back one live prisoner to celebrate the occasion.

One officer and two men were wounded during February, and three killed and six wounded in March.

The Battalion's period of peace came to a sudden end on 4th April, when they entrained to return to France.

From a diary :—

"Saturday, 15th December, 1917—Such a beautiful morning. I roused myself at 6 a.m. as we were nearly due at Marseilles and I wished to see as much of it as I could, but we arrived before I was ready and after a short halt we moved on. The day was so delightful and warm we decided to spend the day on the open forage flat, having a picnic on the hay. This idea was a happy one and those who were present will never forget this view of a land of palms and bamboos and a blue Mediterranean, a contrast indeed after the trenches of Flanders."   L.F.

Lieut.-Colonel J. A. Pemberton.

Lieut.-Colonel H. Backhouse.

Major Wm. Hodson.

Lieut.-Colonel G. H. Swindells.

GALLIPOLI.

SUVLA. 6th to 21st August, 1915.

Map p. 175

This Battle honour stands for our share in the disastrous " side-show " of Gallipoli.

The 4th and 7th Battalions left England in the middle of July with the 53rd Division, not sorry to leave behind them the memory of the muddled and wasted months which are briefly described in appendix IV. Their destination was unknown, except that it had a warm climate. The vessels carrying the Division were neither in convoy, nor escorted. All lights were doused at 7-30 p.m., so there was nothing to do after that hour but to go to bed. As no one had any idea where they were going, it was not possible to study maps or to make any study of local conditions.

On reaching Alexandria, the first joke of this end of the war, which made a whole ship laugh, was an embarkation officer, in shorts with enormous spurs, clanking along the quay. However, he had the last laugh, as he removed all our transport and would have taken cooking pots too had not a more determined person intervened.

Moving hence in all secrecy, the Division found itself in Port Said and although six days were spent there, the troops were not taken ashore for a much-needed march. Late on 4th August, the ships pushed forth once more into the blue, and sailed it for three days till they reached Mudros harbour. Eventually, on the 8th, at nightfall, the ships anchored off a black and unknown coast, on which the only sign of life was the ceaseless rattle of musketry and the winking of signal lamps. Naval officers came on board and ordered instant readiness to disembark. They added that nothing was to go on shore except what the troops stood up in. This order was disobeyed, and ammunition and cooking pots were carried off by the men of one ship. The troops sat on the decks in marching order all night, waiting for the promised landing vessels. These vessels, known as " beetles " from their rotund appearance and projecting cranes, which looked like horns, came at dawn, and it was then seen that the ships were in a bay enclosed on the north by the sharp jagged spur of a high rocky boulder-strewn hill. This hill ran inland, and curving away to the south, shut in a broad, flat valley covered with scrub. The capture of the formidable hill barrier was the principal objective of the landing force, yet its name, Tekke Tepe, which should have been branded on the consciousness of every officer and man, through "orders," was never even mentioned.

On the south of the bay, a conical hill, Lala Baba, kept guard over the beach and beyond it, along the coast, a sandy plain ran to meet the rugged spurs running down from the southern end of the wide circle of hills, where the Anzacs were pouring out their life blood in the effort to hold on to a mile of precipitous crags. In the middle distance could be seen foothills of the main range, later known as Chocolate, "W," and Green Hills.

To an observer on Lala Baba, the whole country-side lay spread out like a map. Immediately in front was the dry bed of the Salt Lake, a large flat surface which emphasized the imposing circle of the hills which formed the background of the picture, and which separated Suvla from the Dardanelles.

Even after landing, the troops did not know where they were till the Brigade Clerk, Q.M.S. Fred Weston, found a case of maps on the beach, broke it open, and disclosed the fact that we were at Suvla Bay! He handed each officer a map as the Battalions filed along the top of the low cliffs, to seek cover from the shrapnel on the western slopes of Lala Baba.

The military situation at this juncture beggars description. The 10th and 11th Divisions had landed two days earlier, and had been severely handled by the enemy and poorly directed. Commanders and staffs, officers and men, all showed marked signs of having reached the limit of endurance. An atmosphere of indifference, laissez-faire and chaos was the result, which was inimical, if not fatal, to action even by fresh troops.

The hearts of all sank as they realized the conditions in which they were to go into battle. They had no ammunition except what they carried, no transport, no artillery. It seemed incredible.

On landing, the 53rd Division, though soft after three weeks on board ship, and tired after a sleepless night, was still perfectly capable of sustained effort, and anxious to acquit itself well in this, its first experience of war.

The Brigade Major of the 159th Brigade, Captain Arthur Crookenden, of The Regiment, went up the hill to see the state of affairs. He saw the Salt Lake covered with wounded men coming back to the beach, each escorted by two or three of their comrades. There was a little shelling, and some distant rifle fire. He told the G.O.C. that the Brigade could capture the distant objective if an hour's law was granted for a talk with the officers with map and compass on the top of Lala Baba. But no! Hurry was the order of the day! He objected, was threatened with arrest, was given a verbal order to send two Battalions to "report to General —— in the bush." He refused to bear such an order, and the G.S.O. himself took it to General Cowans, commanding the 159th Brigade. The 4th

Battalion and 5th Welch moved off gallantly across the Salt Lake towards Chocolate Hill in " artillery formation " under shrapnel fire, through streams of men retiring, suffering some casualties, and grumbling that they had been given better orders for a Saturday afternoon bun-struggle in Birkenhead Park.

Later, another General Staff Officer of the 53rd Division produced an order for the remainder of the Brigade, written on a corner torn from an Army Book 153—" Attack the Turks " and added verbally " Report with two Battalions to General —— in the bush." To find this man the Brigade Staff and Brigadier General advanced ahead of the two remaining Battalions, extended to 250 paces ! Eventually the left-hand man found him. No orders or information could be obtained from him when he was found.

It was difficult to know what to do. In the thick scrub, nothing was apparent but a steady and heavy rifle fire from the neighbourhood of Sulajik farm. It was a case for reconnaissance and deliberate planning. However, the 7th Battalion at length received orders to advance against a distant point when the only obvious fact was that it was strongly held, and had already held up all the rest of the troops in that neighbourhood.

The 4th Welch was also ordered to advance, but Brigadier General Cowans refused to allow it to move, and wisely kept it under his control.

Night fell with three Battalions of the Brigade " lost." The order by which the Brigade was placed under the 11th Division on this day must be recorded. The 53rd Division is placed under the 11th Division

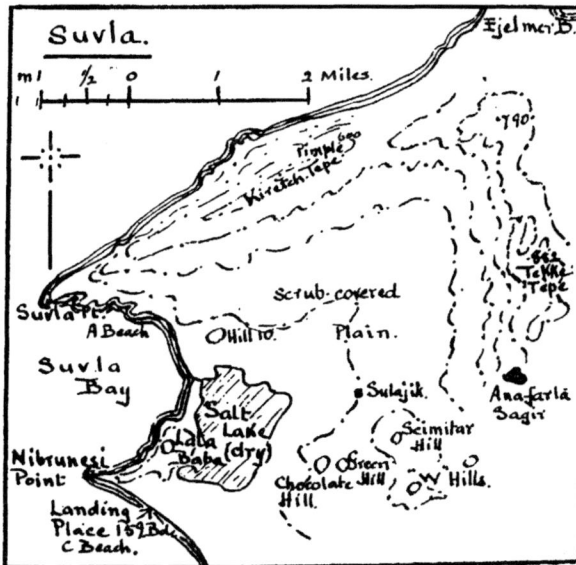

and " can be used in such way that it will be possible to re-assemble them in the evening." Comment is needless.

The Brigade Major spent the night, mostly behind the Turkish lines, trying to find his missing Battalions, and succeeded only in finding part of the 7th Battalion. On again reaching Brigade H.Q., about 3 a.m. on the 10th, he found an order had arrived for an attack at 6 a.m., which involved leap-frogging by a Brigade which had last been seen in Bedford. Boundaries and objectives were described from a map, and included such easily recognizable points as the crossings of tracks with contours ! It was pitch dark, and it should also be remembered that the Brigade had no transport of any sort, no arrangements for ammunition supply, no medical arrangements except the doctors' haversacks, no tools, no food, no water, nothing but what they stood up in, and a few odd boxes of ammunition carried by the men. There was no artillery. The artillery " support " was provided by the 15in. guns of the " Queen Elizabeth " which, it was said, would protect the left flank. Hidden in the bush, the Brigade flank would not have been visible to an aeroplane, still less could an observer on a ship five miles away tell where it was.

At 6 a.m., portions of the 7th Battalion, followed by the 4th Welch, advanced a few hundred yards, till they reached a trench full of men of various Brigades and Corps. Here all halted, and nothing would make them face the steady stream of bullets which swept over their heads. A machine gun in Sulajik farm fired uselessly in the general direction of the Turks, but otherwise the troops seemed dazed and at the end of their tether, as indeed most were.

During the afternoon, an order from the beach directed a general advance at 5 p.m. It was obeyed by a few brave men of the 159th Brigade led by their Commander, General Cowans. But these were soon killed, or wounded and left to perish in the bush, which by now was burning fiercely. The survivors reached a bank some 200 yards ahead, from which they were driven by a counter-attack, while the men in the packed trenches behind looked on.

Water was short, but available. There were wells in many places, but all were under fire and needed earthworks to protect the users. But the 53rd Division had no tools, and it is likely that the other Divisions had none either.

The whole action was a nightmare of indecision starting at the top, and spreading its evil effects through all ranks. The opposition was not negligible, but even without artillery support it was within the capacity of a combined effort by well-led troops to overcome. As it was, individual Brigades attacked Major Willmer's (the German Commander) well-held position one after another, whereas had all attacked at once on a wide front and under a plan, the small Turkish garrison of " W " and Green Hills must have been forced to withdraw.

Movements were at all times hampered by the impossibility of finding out what the plan was. The higher Staff not only refused all help and information, but made it clear that they had none to give.

The 4th Battalion lost nine officers killed, seven wounded, and twenty men killed, 117 wounded, and 289 missing. Major T. A. Prentice, Captains G. R. Taylor, A. H. Bazett, G. R. Wilson, Lieuts. F. R. Danson, A. G. Nicholson and T. V. Anthony, 2nd/Lieuts. J. S. G. Burrell and S. W. T. King were all killed.

The 7th Battalion lost 9 officers wounded, 2 missing, 18 men killed, 145 wounded, and 286 missing.

Among the officers evacuated was Colonel H. Backhouse. He was lost some weeks later when the S.S. Persia was torpedoed, on his way back to the 7th Battalion.

The 4th Battalion did not rejoin the Brigade till the 11th. It had reached Chocolate Hill and remained in front of the 11th Division.

Later, a trench line was selected by a S.O. from G.H.Q. which was found to be enfiladed from Kiretch Tepe, so the line was swung back and the troops dug in on the line which was held till the evacuation in December.

On the 12th and 13th, envoys from the higher command arrived looking for " gaps," and enquiring whether the troops were standing fast. The 7th Battalion showed the gap between themselves and the 10th Division to be three yards, and the two Cheshire Battalions were as steady and calm as ever in spite of the handling they had experienced. They kept their heads and contributed in a greater measure than has ever been acknowledged to prevent a major disaster. The fact is, chance of success had almost gone when the 53rd Division arrived. A well-planned attack on Tekke Tepe by the Division as a whole might have succeeded, but it was not to be.

The wise course after the 10th was immediate evacuation, but more useless loss was to take place before our failure was acknowledged.

SARI BAIR. 6th to 10th August, 1915.

The 8th Battalion won this honour for us. The 8th Battalion left England on 26th June, 1915, under command of the Hon. Heathcote Drummond Willoughby. They landed on V. Beach at Helles and had a quiet month " breaking in." A month's rest at Lemnos was followed by the attack at Anzac, where the 13th Division was to assist the Australian and New Zealand Army Corps. The 40th Brigade, to which the 8th Battalion belonged, was broken up. During the battle of Sari Bair, the 8th

M

Battalion was attached to Light Horse Brigades of the Australian and New Zealand Army Corps. They were employed in trench duties during these days, and lost a number of men; 9 officers and 66 men were wounded, and 2 officers and 77 men missing.

SCIMITAR HILL.

The 4th, 7th and 8th Battalions won this honour, but they did no more than hold trenches on the flank of the gallant but hopeless attack of the splendid 29th Division. Hundreds of men of the five Battalions of the 29th were lost in this unavailing attempt to win a minor success.

The 7th Battalion lost one officer and 26 killed and 14 officers and 249 wounded and missing.

The Evacuation of Suvla.

From Anzac, the 8th Battalion had come with the 13th Division to Suvla in August. A period of trench warfare came to an end in December, in the great storm, after which this part of the peninsula was evacuated.

The storm was very violent. During it, a relief was taking place. Next morning the plain was covered with dead, dying and half frozen men of the relieving Brigade. Dry nullahs became swift torrents, down which poured through our lines dead Turks and a considerable quantity of Turkish war material. Our casualties were very heavy and provided an opportunity of getting rid of a number of men under peace conditions.

The evacuation was organized in this way. All casualties were first removed by hospital ship. Of the 53rd Division, some 2,000 went in this way.

This having been done, all the rest of the troops were taken off by night until 10,000 remained at each of three areas, at Anzac, at the south side of Suvla Bay and at the north side of Suvla Bay. The 13th Division held the line in front of the south side of Suvla Bay.

On the night of the 18th December, 5,000 troops were removed from each sector without a hitch. Bivouacs on the beaches were occupied by skeleton formations. Fires were kept burning at the usual cooking places.

The " beetles," coming to fetch the troops, came too early. The Turks saw them, but drew the wrong inference. They assumed that reinforcements were arriving. So, on the 9th, the Turks gave the beaches as good a strafing as they had ever had, in fact, better, because the Turks had a supply of newly-arrived 5.9in. howitzers. A pier in the bay from which half the south side troops were to embark was nearly hit. But no

M I

Suvla Bay and Suvla Point from the South side of the Bay.

harm was done as the areas were only occupied after dark. The whole terrific " hate " only wounded one man.

This long day at length drew to its close with every sign of rising wind, which, if it got too strong, might make evacuation impossible.

After dark, the troops began to embark in batches at 2½ hour intervals. A small force was left to hold the front line till the last possible moment. It came straight back to the pier from the front.

At 4-15 a.m., General Maude, who commanded the 13th Division, with General Marshall who was in charge of the embarkation arrangements and his G.S.O. (Crookenden), came to the pier head to satisfy himself that all his men were safe. The rear guard, men of the 8th Battalion, stood on the cliff above the pier. After making his G.S.O. (Hildyard) inspect the men with a torch to see if they had all got their packs on, Maude told the officer to count the men. He reported thirty-nine, but added that all were present. The correct number was forty, so Maude told him to count again. He produced the same result. The party would never have got away at all if an exasperated voice had not called out from the dark, " The fellow isn't counting himself."

There was a full moon, a slight haze and a flat calm, ideal conditions in spite of the weather prophets. Casualties were far less than on a normal night.

The operation was lucky in more ways than one, for the original idea had been that a rear guard of 4,800 men should be left for 24 hours in a position close to the beaches. From this position, there would have been no escape. Wiser counsels prevailed in time.

The 13th Division went direct to Cape Helles to assist in the evacuation there.

On the last night, 8th January, the 8th Battalion occupied the Eski lines which ran from Artillery Road to Gully Ravine, and embarked direct from the front line without casualties.

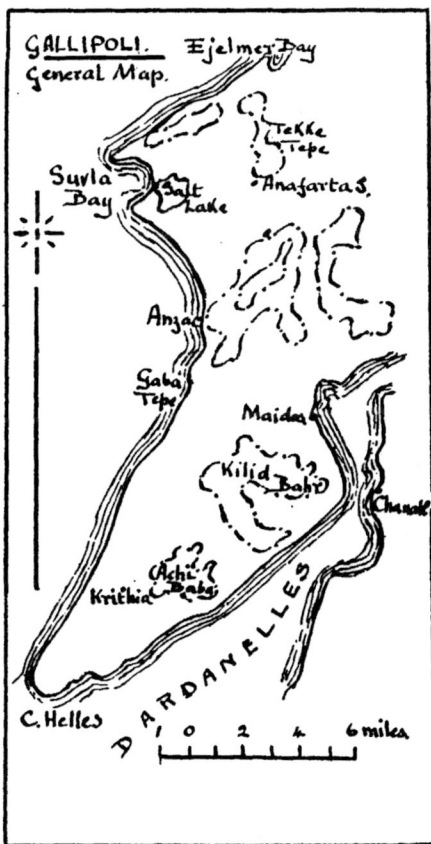

GALLIPOLI. General Map.

PALESTINE.

GAZA. 26th and 27th March, 1917.

Map p. 194

Towards the end of January, 1917, the 53rd Division, which had marched across the desert from the Suez Canal during the previous few months, found themselves at railhead, at that time El-Arish.   A few days later they advanced some 10 miles northwards to cover the further construction of the railway towards Palestine.

For the next six weeks the railway advanced at a rate of about one mile a day, and the covering troops advanced by bounds to new positions as necessary.

About the middle of March, the 159th Infantry Brigade, which consisted of our Fourth and Seventh Battalions, and the 4th and 5th Welch Regiment, were out of the line " resting " near Rafah.   Actually, they were engaged in the uncongenial task of sinking wells among the sand hills near the coast.

Rafah itself is a small village of little importance except for the fact that it stands upon the boundary between Egypt and Palestine, and also upon the only practicable road between these two countries.   It is also on the edge of the desert, which stretches from this point to the Suez Canal.

During this period, the Commanding Officers (Colonel G. H. Swindells, 4th Battalion, and Colonel H. M. Lawrence, 7th Battalion) and Company Commanders made frequent reconnaissances towards Gaza with the Australian mounted troops and it therefore came as no great surprise when the Division was ordered to move forward to Khan Yunis on the 24th March.   Gaza at this time was little more than an outpost held by a detachment on the flank of the Turkish line of communication.   It had been decided to capture Gaza by a " coup de main."

Khan Yunis lies some six miles north of Rafah and is a considerable native village surrounded by orchards, the hedges of which consist of prickly pear cactus, which is almost impenetrable.   In the village, there is a very deep well of good water and also the ruins of a rather fine Crusader's church.

The night of the 24/25th was spent in an almond orchard, the trees of which were in full bloom.   No movement was permitted except after dark, as there were rumours that enemy aircraft were about.

On the 25th, the Brigade moved on to a position near Deir El Belah, starting in the late afternoon, and arriving after dark after a short march of five miles.

Their Drums and Fifes were with the 4th Battalion and, on moving from Khan Yunis in column of route, the possible presence of enemy aircraft having apparently been overlooked, were playing as usual. About a mile outside the village they had to pass the Divisional Commander, and the Staff appeared to be quite annoyed that the " Drums " should be playing when there was, as they described it, a " war on."

During the evening the men lay in a hollow getting colder and colder, as no lights or fires were allowed. Eventually orders were received to be ready to move off at midnight.

It is of interest to recall how the troops were clothed and equipped at this time, as this has some bearing on the subsequent operations.

First, it must be remembered that most of them had been out in a fairly hot climate for some 18 months or more, and so were not likely to be affected much by the heat in March. Moreover, they had recently marched across 150 miles of soft desert, and had never had more than one gallon of water a man a day *for all purposes*. So any lack of water was more easy to bear than had been the case at Suvla Bay. The clothing consisted of ordinary tropical kit, helmet and khaki drill shorts, but as the nights were very cold, serge jackets were retained. Full equipment was carried, but no greatcoats, and each man carried 200 rounds of S.A.A. and one additional day's rations for the battle.

There was no regimental wheeled transport, all water and cooking utensils were carried on camels, and each company had seven mules for the four company Lewis guns.

These transport arrangements were in some ways a nuisance. Camels are slow movers. On the other hand, they do not mind being shelled, and, while it was often difficult to get rations, water and reserve S.A.A. up when they were wanted, in no case was a convoy stampeded by enemy shell fire or bombing.

As to the mules, they were a definite advantage over wheeled transport, as the guns could be brought much further forward on mules than would have been the case if they had been carried on limbers.

The town of Gaza lies some two miles from the Mediterranean sea, and about 4½ miles north of the Wadi Ghuzze. (A wadi is the bed of a stream). This latter, in March, is a wide dry water course with a sandy bed and steep mud cliff banks. Into it run a large number of smaller wadis, all with steep sides. There are pools of water in various places in the bed of the main wadi, and fresh water can be obtained almost anywhere by digging down a few feet.

The Wadi, near its mouth, runs almost due east and west and along its south bank there is a low range of hills which become sandy on the sea coast.

Immediately north of the Wadi, and about one mile from its mouth, is a low hill Tel-el-Ajul, the site of ancient Gaza, and between it and the sea is a stretch of very soft sand hills. To the eastward of Tel-el-Ajul runs the main road from Egypt to Gaza. This road runs up a shallow valley on the edge of the sand hills. Immediately to the east of the road is a low ridge running N.E. toward Gaza, then a valley, then another higher ridge, the Es Sire Ridge, and a further valley, beyond which lies the Burjahye Ridge. The valley between these last two ridges, which was subsequently known as Happy Valley, ends at some mud cliffs at Mansura Ridge, about 2½ miles S.E. of Gaza.

North-west of Mansura the ground is very open, falling away to a slight valley, the Wadi Mukademe, before rising gently to a ridge crowned with cactus hedges immediately east of Gaza. At the south end of this ridge is a detached and very conspicuous hill called Ali el Muntar, from the top of which a magnificent view of the surrounding country, including Gaza, can be obtained. This is the hill up which Samson is stated to have carried the gates of Gaza.

On the south, west and north-west of Ali el Muntar, are a large number of gardens, surrounded by cactus hedges, and which, at this time, were intersected by Turkish trenches. This difficult position was well named the Labyrinth.

The troops taking part in the battle consisted of the Australian and New Zealand Mounted Division (less one Brigade), the Imperial Mounted Division (less one Brigade) and the 53rd Division, all the above being under the command of General Chetwode.

The total artillery used at the first battle consisted of six 60 pounders, sixteen 4-5in. Howitzers, and sixty-four 18 pounders, but the 53rd Division's attack was supported by the fire of six 60 pounders, twelve 4.5in. Howitzers, and twenty-four 18 pounders only.

The rôle of the cavalry was to cut off Gaza from the north, and also to prevent the arrival of enemy reinforcements from the north, north-east and east, while that of the infantry was to capture the town.

The preliminary instructions for the infantry were that the 160th and 158th Brigades should cross the Wadi Ghuzze and proceed towards Ali el Muntar, and Mansura Ridge respectively, while the 159th Brigade with our 4th and 7th Battalions should cross the Wadi immediately behind the 158th Brigade, form up on the north side and await further orders.

The Battalions paraded shortly after midnight, but as Divisional orders had only been issued at 9-15 p.m., they had very little idea of what was taking place.

No maps were available, except such sketches as could be hastily drawn in Army Book 153.

The night was dark and cold, and although there was only about 3 miles to cover to arrive at the Wadi, there were very frequent delays, largely caused by the 158th Brigade losing their way and being about an hour late at the Wadi. Eventually, however, we got across and, as ordered, halted on the high ground immediately north of the Wadi.

Shortly afterwards a thick fog rolled up from the sea and, as it became light, it was impossible to see more than a few yards. At about 7-30 on the 26th the fog began to clear, but still no orders to move came, and it was not until 9-30 a.m. that orders were received for the Brigade to proceed forthwith to Mansura Ridge.

During this period all was quiet and apart from an occasional rifle shot from the direction of Gaza, there were no signs of any enemy activity.

About 10 a.m. the 159th Brigade was actually on the move towards Mansura Ridge and while the distance was only some 3 miles, it did not arrive at the destination until about noon, as the Brigade had to advance up Happy Valley in artillery formation owing to a certain amount of hostile shelling.

Meanwhile the infantry attack had been ordered to begin at 11-50 a.m., the 160th Brigade's objective being the Labyrinth and south slopes of Ali el Muntar and that of the 158th Brigade the east slopes of Ali el Muntar. There was accordingly a large gap between the Brigades when the attack started, but they joined up later.

On arrival at Mansura, the 159th Brigade received orders to join in the attack, the tasks being to seize the high ridge running north from Ali el Muntar, and to guard the right flank of the 158th Brigade.

The Brigade attacked on a two-battalion front. The 1/5th Welch on the left and our 4th Battalion on the right.

As the attack had already started and had got 1,000 yards ahead, there was no time for reconnaissance, and the Brigade was pushed out at once. In fact, in order to catch up, a large amount of doubling was necessary.

The 1/4th Welch were in support and our 7th Battalion were in Divisional reserve, still behind Mansura Ridge.

The 4th Battalion attacked on a two-company front, with "A" on the right and "B" on the left, with "C" behind "A" and "D" behind "B."

As soon as they left the shelter of Mansura Ridge, they came under fairly heavy shrapnel fire which made it necessary to advance in artillery formation. Shortly after, as the enemy machine guns were becoming active, they had to extend.

A very great initial difficulty was that the attack was at right angles to the line of march and so the Battalions had to change direction from north-east to north-west. As the 4th Battalion were on the outer flank of the Brigade, they had further to go than the others, and had difficulty in keeping up. In addition, as will be described later, a gap appeared between the left of " B " Company and the right of the 5th Welch.

There was no artillery forward observation officer at the assembly position, partly because the Brigade had moved so far and so fast that no wire could be laid. Consequently all communication with the guns had to be by runner or galloper, and the result was that the objective, a cactus hedge, crossing the Beersheba road, was not shelled, and the advance was more costly than it need have been. Throughout the battle, artillery fire was inadequate because the field guns remained at Mansura, and were out of range. " Co-operation " was not.

The 4th Battalion, after deployment, found itself on a gentle, grassy slope running down for about a mile to a small wadi, the Wadi Mukademe, from which point the ground rose gradually to the top of the ridge east of Gaza. This ridge was crowned by cactus hedges which were Turkish position. On the left of the ridge was the clearly defined hill of Ali el Muntar, upon which our shells were bursting. To the right front, a line of telegraph posts showed the line of the Gaza-Beersheba road, and further to the right again was a slight rise called Clay Hill.

There was no cover except in the bottom of the Wadi Mukademe and the troops were in full view of the enemy's position. As the advance continued, the enemy machine gun fire became more and more effective from the enemy left, and casualties occurred.

As the 4th Battalion advanced, it was clear that they were losing touch with the 5th Welch on their left, either because the latter were edging in towards Ali el Muntar, from which point the greater part of the enemy fire was coming, or because the 4th Battalion had not wheeled round enough when the change of direction took place. The left of " B " Company was aiming for the point where the Gaza-Beersheba road crossed the ridge near Clay Hill, whereas the right of the 5th Welch were apparently making for a gap in the ridge just north of Ali el Muntar. This gap was subsequently known by the delightful name of Delilah's Neck. Noticing that there would be a space of about 400 to 500 yards between the Battalions, Lieut. Danson edged out with the leading platoon of " D " Company to fill it up. Eventually the whole of " D " Company followed.

By this time, the enemy fire was becoming heavy and effective, the advance had to be continued by short rushes.

Movement forward became painfully slow and a great deal of ammunition was fired against the cactus hedge, from which the enemy's fire was very heavy, although there were actually no Turks to be seen. Gradually the firing line, composed of all units of the Brigade, got to within about 200 yards of the enemy.

At 3-30 p.m., the 7th Battalion was thrown into the fight on the left, to support the 5th Welch, and at long last some field guns, the 21st Field

Brigade, moved forward. This support had immediate effect, but it was not till the guns began to shell the cactus hedge, which marked the enemy front line, effectively that the position could be assaulted. Then the Welch and 7th Battalion stormed the outlying portions of the citadel, and the 4th Battalion captured Clay Hill.

Although, according to the official History of the Palestine Campaign, Ali El Muntar was captured by the 5th R.W.F. and 5th Welch Regt., at 3·50 p.m., actually it was captured by a very mixed bag of about 70 individuals, and including officers and men of the 4th Battalion.

Quite a number of prisoners were taken at Ali el Muntar, among them several Austrian gunner officers. They had probably been observing from the hill, and evidently did not expect to be captured as they had on their best uniforms, complete with medals.

Ali el Muntar itself was very strongly fortified, with a row of trenches round the bottom, a second row about half way up and a final row on the top. The hill itself is very steep, and at that time was crowned with a sheik's tomb and a few trees. During the subsequent few months these disappeared. The hill had been used as an O.P. and the view from it was most extensive.

On the north side of the hill, about half way up, was a trench dug back into the hill, with a dug-out behind it. This trench could not be seen from the front, as it faced the flank, and owing to the steepness of the hill it was about 10 feet deep, a few feet from the entrance. Across this trench, and about four feet from the entrance, was a steel plate with a hole in it for the muzzle of a machine gun. This gun had evidently been trained on the front of the first cactus hedge, along which it could fire for about 400 yards.

Very fortunately for the attackers, one of our 4.5 howitzer shells had dropped right over the hill and had got a direct hit on this trench, thus putting the gun out of action. Though the troops did not get very much support from the artillery during the battle, they certainly blessed them for that lucky shot which probably saved a great number of lives.

Ali el Muntar was the key to the Turkish position and while there was a good deal of promiscuous firing from all sides for some little time after its capture, and although our 60 pounders did their best to blow our men off the hill for a short period, things gradually became quiet and the hill was put into a state of defence.

By now the 7th Battalion were coming up, their place as Divisional reserve having been taken by the 161st Brigade. They eventually took over Ali el Muntar and consolidated the position.

The men were immensely pleased with their success. They felt that the failure of Gallipoli had been avenged.

Efforts were now made to re-organize the troops, but everyone was very tired and very thirsty. A pool of water, full of tadpoles, provided a welcome drink for some of the 4th Battalion. No orders came for a move. Dusk came on. Outposts were put out towards Gaza by individual Company Commanders.

There was complete silence from Gaza, and hardly a shot was fired. The cries of the wounded lying out in the open could be heard but it was almost impossible to do anything for them as it was most difficult to find them in the darkness, and they were scattered over a wide area. In spite of the almost superhuman efforts of the stretcher bearers and others, it proved to be impossible to collect them all and unfortunately a number were subsequently taken prisoners by the Turks.

During the early part of the night a certain amount of S.A.A. came up, and Lewis gun magazines were refilled. In the withdrawal later, their added weight was a great disadvantage, although all took a turn with them.

The only other matter which gave a certain amount of interest at the time was the appearance of some Australians from Gaza. All troops had had strict injunctions not to enter the town, but these Australians had apparently got detached from their unit north of the town and had come straight through. As friendly troops from the direction of Gaza were not expected, they were very lucky to have got through our line without being shot, though from their language when challenged, it was clear that they were not Turks.

At about 8 p.m. on the 26th, or soon afterwards, to the amazement, indignation and wrath of all ranks, a withdrawal of the infantry began, starting on the right.

The Brigade bivouaced on the Mansura ridge, and remained there till the afternoon of the 27th. With chagrin, the troops watched the Turks re-occupy the ridge which had been so gallantly won the day before.

Towards dusk, the march back to the Wadi Ghuzze was resumed.

That march was a nightmare. Our Battalions were the last to move and marched down the sandy bed of the Wadi, running down Happy Valley until it joined the Wadi Ghuzze until finally they emerged near the Cairo road. The troops were terribly depressed by this incomprehensible retreat. The night was very dark and it was impossible to see. The bed of the Wadi was soft and its course very winding. There were constant checks. Everyone was very tired and most of the men were asleep as they marched, and at every check, bumped into the man ahead. At one point a company commander fell asleep on his horse and promptly fell off, causing a mild diversion.

On one occasion they lost their way and proceeded for some hundreds of yards in the wrong direction towards the Turkish position, before the guide found out his mistake. While he was trying to find the right track, the whole 4th Battalion went to sleep.

Eventually, however, at about 2 a.m. on the 28th, they reached the high ground south of the Wadi Ghuzze, overlooking Red House. They had only covered about 7 miles, but the conditions were so bad that it seemed much further.

So ended the first Battle of Gaza. Between 5 p.m. on the 25th, when they left Khan Yunis, until 2 a.m. on the 28th, when they arrived back over the Wadi, the Brigade had marched between 25 and 30 miles, pushed the Turk out of his position captured, Gaza, and also dug two lots of trenches. All felt that though the battle was for some reason a failure, the responsibility did not rest with the troops engaged, and they were, in fact, very proud of themselves.

In considering the reasons for the failure of the Desert Column to capture Gaza on the 27th March, we may begin by dismissing the official explanation—the fog. It was held that owing to the delay of several hours which resulted therefrom, the time available for attaining the objective was so curtailed that night fell before the task was accomplished, and a withdrawal to the Wadi Ghuzze was rendered necessary, partly because the Turkish relieving force was approaching from the east, and partly because the horses had to be watered. But, in fact, the fog, which lasted about four hours, entailed far less than four hours' delay as the infantry continued to advance throughout its duration, if at a slower pace ; whilst for the mounted troops, whose advance under their own skilled guides across the open country lying to the east of Gaza, was screened from hostile observation, the fog was a positive advantage.

Likewise we may dismiss the minor causes adduced. It is true that General Dallas took several hours to reconnoitre the position, when in fact the order for the attack could quite well have been dictated from the map. It is true also that delay occurred in moving up the 159th Brigade. But incidents of this nature were only to be expected with troops taking part in their first battle since the fiasco of Suvla Bay, and do not suffice to account for Gaza remaining in Turkish hands, if not at nightfall, at any rate next day.

For the real causes of the failure we must go deeper and start further back. As few troops were employed as possible, owing to water and transport difficulties, so the 52nd Division was immobilized at Rafa, and was not available in the event of unforeseen emergencies. Gaza had to be taken by a " coup de main " or not at all.

It thus resulted that when the infantry advance proved slower than had been anticipated, there were no reserves available to impart fresh impulse.

Secondly, the operations were planned to repeat the successes of Magdhaba and Rafa, where detachments beyond reach of immediate support had been brilliantly " snapped " by the Anzac Mounted Division and Camel Brigade. But the parallel was far from exact. Gaza was a much harder nut to crack than either of the other two places, and the

Turkish General Reserve was known to be occupying an area which began again eight miles away at Huj. Actually there were no Turks on the march westwards of Huj until after 4 o'clock, an inexplicable delay in marching to the sound of the guns that far more than offset any delay which our operations suffered owing to the fog.

Thirdly, no steps were taken to prevent the arrival of the Turkish General Reserve, beyond throwing out a few squadrons which had little or no power of resistance. At least the whole of the Camel Brigade, which had about twice the rifle strength of a Mounted Brigade, should have been thrown across the Huj-Gaza road and ordered to dig in.

Finally, in spite of all the mistakes that were made, there was no need to withdraw the mounted troops at nightfall. The Turkish relieving force was still six miles away and could have been prevented without difficulty from advancing far in the night. The horses could have gone without water for a few hours more. But south of the Wadi Ghuzze, where both Eastern Force H.Q. and Desert Corps H.Q. remained throughout the fight, the Commanders took the cautious view, with the result that a battle, which the troops by their gallantry had already won, was converted into a defeat.

In these operations, the 7th Battalion lost four officers, J. A. Clayton, N. R. Foster, G. P. Gregg and J. O. Laybourne, 12 N.C.Os. and men killed, and 175 wounded. One officer was missing. The 4th Battalion had fewer losses, six men killed, nine officers and 96 men wounded and 10 missing.

GAZA. 17th to 19th April, 1917.

Map p. 194

On the 17th April, the second attack on Gaza was made. The Turks had naturally used the three weeks peace which had been granted them to improve their defences. There was no continuous trench line, but redoubts crossing their fire commanded all lines of approach. The garrison of the place and neighbouring defence works was steadily increased. It was clear that a deliberate attack, well supported by artillery, would be necessary.

The attack was planned to be delivered as an eastern attack on Ali el Muntar and the Beersheba road, and a western attack by the 53rd Division, west of the Rafa-Gaza road, to capture the defences between Gaza and the sea on and behind Samson Ridge.

The task of the 159th Brigade was to capture the line to Sheikh Ajlin, on the shore, after the capture of Samson Ridge. Very heavy casualties were incurred in the capture of the ridge. Sheikh Ajlin was reached, but owing to enfilade fire from the high ground to the east, no further advance was possible. The losses in the 4th Battalion were 18 men wounded and 21 missing. In the 7th Battalion, 7 men were killed and 17 wounded.

*   *   *   *

Here follows an account of the First and Second Battles of Gaza, written by a lance-corporal, Mr. William Courtenay, in his book "Airman Friday." Mr. Courtenay later became an officer in the R.F.C.

"I had by now some seniority in my company.

In my own platoon I was, at Gaza, the only surviving private soldier of the 1914 roll call. The rest were all men who had either not served at Gallipoli or who had joined the battalion after the War broke out.

In this condition of seniority I was given a stripe and became an acting lance-corporal (unpaid) which was as high as I ever rose. . . . . .

When at last we stopped to man the Turkish trenches and to fire after the retreating figures, I suggested to my platoon sergeant, Charles Parr, that I might take two men with me and reconnoitre down the Beersheba road—for we were close to it—with a view to reporting whether the enemy were really retreating into Gaza. This was readily agreed to. Incidentally I was determined to search for water whatever the risk. Thirst had been my chief enemy that day.

With two men I tripped over the trenches, followed the line of retreating Turks, and wandered down the road which, with its high hedges of cactus hid us from view.

Hardly had we walked a few hundred yards down it towards Gaza when we were startled by shell-fire.

A shell burst in a cactus hedge just behind us. Though we did not know it, we had wandered in front of the gun-fire from our own artillery whose gun teams had no knowledge of how far the Turks had retired. In the distance I could see figures hurrying and mounting horses preparatory to moving out of Gaza. On the right-hand side of the road we came to a villa with a garden. With great caution we entered. It seemed untenanted. In the garden on a line hung several blankets. We forgot our thirst for the moment ; forgot the official nature of our duty, and fell on the blankets to divide them between us. We had slept the last two nights under heavy dew. We were determined to be rolled up this night in warm blankets.

While we were busily engaged in this task a door in the villa suddenly opened and out ran two German or Austrian officers with their belts and revolvers in their hands. They wore grey uniforms with red facings, not unlike the uniforms of our own pre-war glory. (The 4th Battalion wore grey full dress uniform).

They looked startled when they saw us and without waiting bolted down the steps of the house towards the town. I raised my rifle and fired at them, but no doubt an excited and unsteady aim, coupled with the fact that the rifle sights had been fixed for more distant work, caused the shots to fall over their marks.   However, the men ran as fast as their legs could carry them and we deemed it wiser to reconnoitre the house than to follow them.   We crept round the back with rifles and bayonet ready and through a chink in a tall wide farm door (into which a smaller door was built) we could see grey figures hurrying hither and thither in a big yard.

Without more ado I pushed the small gate open followed by the two men with me, yelled " Hands up ! " and presented my rifle in menacing attitude at the line of troops.

They were Austrian soldiers.   With one accord they formed two ranks and threw up their hands with an alacrity which almost made me laugh.   It was so amusing.   Had they wished they could easily have turned on us, but they did not know whether there were others behind us.   This was fortunate.

While I held them up and the two privates with me did likewise, I was not quite sure of my next move.   What did the text-books say an acting Lance-Corporal (unpaid) ought to do in these circumstances ? Here we were with about thirty prisoners and only three of us to deal with them.

One youth in khaki at one end of the front row spoke some English. He was a Greek.   Wringing his hands above his head he beseeched me not to shoot him.

Instead, I decided first to search the prisoners for arms or useful documents.   While my two comrades continued to hold them up I went round each rank taking a sword from one (which I slung round my waist) ; a revolver from another (which I slung round my neck), and some fine Zeiss glasses from a third which I also found space for somewhere on my already overloaded person.   All their pocket-books were then taken and stuffed into my pockets.

At this point I remembered our thirst and calling to a peasant who was evidently employed at the house and who stood shivering with his wife behind the soldiers, I demanded water.   There was a cool well in the centre of this courtyard.   He produced a jug and we all three drank a jugful of lovely, cool, pure water ;   bathing our faces and hands in it, letting it trickle down our shirts and necks to seek added refreshment and finally thoroughly soaking our hot but empty water-bottles.   When they were quite cool we filled them.

I decided to take the prisoners back with me.   We lined them up and marched them out.

As I was leaving I saw a small black bag on a table.   It looked for all the world like the small leather gladstone the country doctor used to carry. In that, I fancied, must be plans for the battle, or may-be for the whole war. They might be of use to our side. I decided to take it.

I must have appeared a comic spectacle for the chinstrap of my topee was hanging down one side of my face. My cheeks, chin and upper lip were green with grass mixed with the water I had smeared over them. I was loaded with pack and rifle ; with sword, revolver and field-glasses hanging round my neck and waist ; while the disengaged hand carried the little black bag ! With all this " arms, clothing and equipment " I struggled out of the house into the open.

Then we remembered the precious blankets and took these also as we left the front garden.

Twilight was now falling. It was about 5-30 p.m. We retraced our footsteps down the Beersheba road making for the open country.

As we emerged from between the cactus hedges where we could be seen, a hail of bullets spat at us from machine guns in the trenches lately occupied by the Turks. It was our own side firing on us. They could see the grey-clad figures and evidently feared a counter-attack. I ordered the column to lie down. But it was too late. One of the prisoners was hit by a bullet which passed through one leg and out through the other.

Darkness, which falls quickly, soon encompassed us. I felt so confident that our own troops would be in Gaza during the night, that I deemed it advisable to march my prisoners to the rear, hand them over, and then return to my unit.

Gaza had been ours for the asking. I had seen that with my own eyes, for I had seen the Turks retreating through the town as fast as they could go.

Over the battlefield of the morning and the afternoon we trudged amid the groans of the wounded and the still forms of the fallen.

At length we reached the camp and were halted by a sentry who nervously fired point blank at me till I cursed him, telling him the name of my regiment. Fortunately he missed. The Brigadier-General came out of his tent. It was our Brigade Headquarters in the field. The late Brigadier-General J. H. de B. Travers, C.B., asked me whom I had brought. I reported to him what had happened. " Good boy ; good boy," was all he said.

He gave me about fifty bedraggled Turks and three or four slightly wounded men as escort and with the whole column I started off wearily for Divisional Headquarters some miles farther back.

When my task was safely accomplished I fell down to the ground exhausted ; but before I could sleep I felt I must examine my treasures. Many contained much writing in German and some Turkish paper money.

Finally I opened the little black bag to which I had clung tenaciously all through the night. Instead of the plans of the war, as I fondly imagined, all that the bag contained was a neat array of socks and handkerchiefs, for all the world as if they were the week's luggage of a suburban commercial traveller which his wife had carefully packed at the start of his week's tour away from home ! In disgust I flung them over the desert.

I slept soundly till reveille when all the odd details including me were roused and paraded, sorted out into our respective regiments, and marched back to join our units.

Imagine my surprise when I found the whole of our 159th Infantry Brigade packed together at a point not far from where we had started the previous day's advance. I could not understand it. Why was not the British Army in occupation of Gaza ? The explanation was simple. Of course we ought to have been there. The Turks had retired. The generals on the spot had considered our force was too weak to face the expected and customary counter-attack.

So we retired also. When the Turks discovered this during the night they returned and by next morning had reoccupied all their original positions. The day's operations had been wickedly wasted. The indecision of the generals on the spot had lost us the day. The Battalion withdrew to Mansura Ridge.

That night orders came to retreat still farther and the Turks being in no condition to follow us, we retired through the night down the Wadi Ghuzze until we emerged near the old Cairo road. We were so tired on this forced march back through the night that it was dangerous to lie down each hour when we halted for ten minutes. To do so meant risking instant sleep of a deep nature and a struggle to get up which, with loaded packs, could only be accomplished by literally climbing to a standing position with the aid of one's rifle. Most of us slept even while we marched.

I was surprised to learn a few weeks later that for my part in the capture of the men at Gaza I had been awarded the Military Medal.

It transpired that we had actually captured the Headquarters of the 53rd Turkish Division—the same numbered Division as our own. The Divisional General was captured by the Australian Light Horse.

After a month's rest to lick clean our wounds we went into action on April 19th to fight the Second Battle of Gaza. On this occasion we fared worse than in March. The Turks had had a month in which to strengthen their defences and to bring up heavier guns. The advantage of surprise was lost. Even the introduction of a couple of tanks, something quite novel to the Turks, left them cold. They put one out of action between our lines and theirs, which meant that for weeks afterwards until the autumn campaign opened we had nightly patrol-work to do in searching this tank in case the Turks got there first and made a machine gun post of it."

An Incident of the 2nd Battle of Gaza.

" In the early part of 1917, the British Forces were in position in front of the ancient city of Gaza. They had gained a victory on March 26th, when they had captured Ali el Muntar, the great hill dominating Gaza, but the cost had been so heavy that a retirement had to be made until the force could be re-organized and a fresh attempt made. I was commanding a section of the 159th Coy. M.G.C., most of the officers of which had come from the 7th Battalion of The Cheshire Regiment at the time, and we received a draft from the base to replace casualties. They were all likely looking lads, and amongst them was a Lance-Corporal, by name Duffy. He was an Irishman from Liverpool, but, contrary to what might be expected, he was a most unwarlike fellow. He spoke in a thin piping voice and seemed afraid to order his men about. His knowledge of the the machine gun was, to say the least, elementary, but his enthusiasm was undoubted. He seemed a queer mixture, but as our own range-taker was at the time having a bullet removed from his knee-cap, we gave Duffy the job. He soon became fairly proficient and followed me wherever I went. Then, on 19th April, the second big attempt on Gaza was made.

We were detailed to cover the advance of the 7th Battalion of the Cheshire Regiment who were to advance along the coast and occupy the high ground and mosque of Sheikh Ajlin. The ground was very difficult from a machine gun point of view, as no cover was to be had anywhere, but after doing a lot of crawling on our stomachs we got two guns in position on the left of the line—that was on the sea side, and two guns on the right where cover could easily be obtained. Of the guns on the left, one was actually on the shore, and the other behind a mound about two feet high on the top of the low cliffs. This gun was speedily made the mark of enemy snipers, of whom there were many, and from the higher ground they could easily pick off anyone who moved away from the scant shelter of the mound. Three casualties in quick succession among ammunition carriers brought home to us the seriousness of our position. In order to get even this scant cover we had been compelled to get slightly in advance of the Cheshire Regiment's left, and ammunition at the gun was getting short.

About 700 yards to our right front was a low cactus hedge which appeared to be a regular sniper's nest, and, by lying on the side of the mound, we could see, through glasses, several signs that the surmise was correct. We determined to give the place a good strafe, so I rolled down to the foot of the mound and ordered Lance-Corporal Duffy to take the

N

accurate range. He crawled to the side of the mound and I gave the N.C.O. in charge of the gun his instructions. I glanced up to see if Duffy had the range and to my horror he was lying flat on the top of the mound in full view of the enemy, carefully taking the range ; I yelled " Come down you————fool," but it was too late. There was a rattle of machine gun fire, bullets screeched overhead and thudded into the mound and Duffy rolled down, carefully holding the instrument, or what was left of it. He had thirteen wounds in his head and shoulders—five from bullets and the rest from pieces of the instrument which had been driven into him. Fortunately, he was not vitally hit and we did the best we could for him. It was impossible to get him away from the gun position and equally impossible for stretcher bearers to get up to him. We stayed in the same position for three hours, and we never heard a word of complaint from Duffy who was lying exposed to a broiling sun. The first words he spoke were " 700 exactly, Sir," and his taking of the range was so accurate that we strafed the hedge well and truly and had the satisfaction of finding, later in the day, five perfectly good Turks turned into amateur cullenders. After three hours we managed to assist Duffy on to the beach and had to leave him again. Ammunition could now be brought up and the first message brought up from Duffy was that he hoped the Barr and Stroud was not badly damaged, and the ammunition carrier added that his chief worry was that I would be cross with him for breaking the instrument. The second message consisted of his iron rations, which he said he would no longer require, and an apology for having to leave before the action was over. Then later in the day it became possible, by keeping close to the cliff, to get to the rear. The last message came up that he wished the officer and all the section the best of luck. It was impossible to spare anyone to go back with him, and the gallant fellow started off alone. After he had crawled for half-a-mile, some stretcher bearers spotted him and offered him a lift. His reply was typical : " I laid up on that ———— hill for three hours and you couldn't come for me, and you can keep your ————stretcher now." He made his way for another mile, alone, with five bullets in his body and eight other wounds, before he found a dressing station. When he found one he stood up, walked in, saluted the M.O. in charge and fell down in a dead faint.

Then followed a trip in a camel cacolet and a journey to the ambulance train at Port Said, 150 miles away. Here, an immediate operation was declared necessary and his right arm was removed at the shoulder. For medical reasons of some kind, no anæsthetic could be administered and the poor fellow was perfectly conscious while the operation was being performed. When it was over he thanked the doctor and nurses for their kindness and asked if he might have a " gasper." He was subsequently invalided out of the army, and I am glad to say that we have been able to find a suitable position for him in civilian employment."

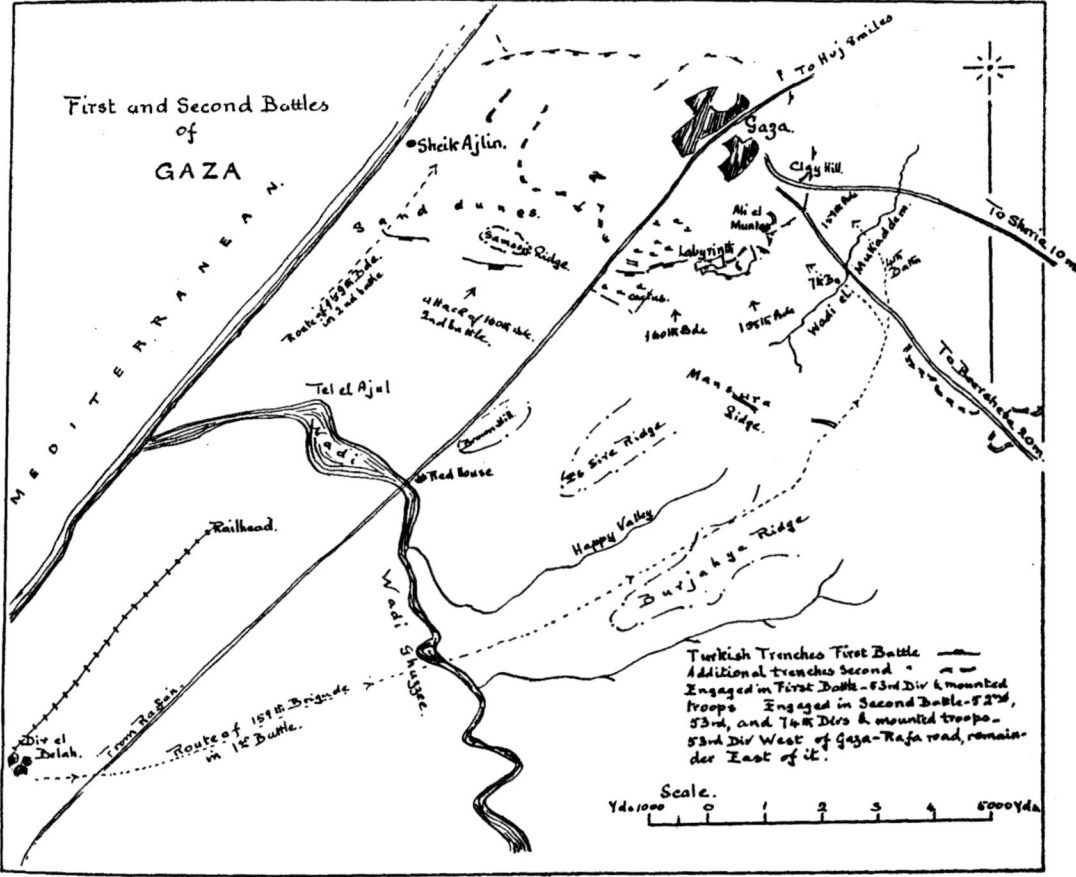

First and Second Battles
of
GAZA

MEDITERRANEAN

Sheik Ajlin.

Sand dunes.

Samson Ridge.

Route of 159th Bde.
in 2nd battle.

Attack of 160th Bde.
2nd battle.

Tel el Ajul

Wadi

Red House

Burnin

Railhead.

From Rafa

Div el
Belah.

Route of 159th Brigade
in 1st Battle.

To Huj 8 miles

Gaza.

Clay Hill.

Ali el
Muntar.

Labyrinth.

159th Bde.

cactus

158th Bde.

7th Bde.

155th Bde.

Wadi el Mukaddem

To Sherie 10 m.

To Beersheba 20 m.

From Khan

Detn

Mansura
Ridge.

Es Sire Ridge.

Happy Valley.

Burjabye Ridge

Wadi Shuggee.

Turkish Trenches First Battle ————
Additional trenches Second — — —
Engaged in First Battle—53rd Div & mounted
troops   Engaged in Second Battle—52nd,
53rd, and 74th Divs & mounted troops—
53rd Div West of Gaza-Rafa road, remainder East of it.

Scale.
Yds.1000   0   1   2   3   4   5000Yds

opp. 194

GAZA.   27th October to 7th November, 1917.

Maps p. 208

After the failure to capture Gaza at the 2nd battle on the 19th April, there was no more serious fighting until the autumn.   During the summer the force was re-organized, and General Allenby was sent out from France as G.O.C.-in-C.

During August, the 53rd Division was withdrawn from the line to Belah, a mile or so south of the Wadi Ghuzze, and about the same distance from the sea, to undergo intensive training for the forthcoming operations.

At this time of the year the country, which in the spring is green with crops and grass, is burnt up and there is no sign of vegetation other than a few fig trees.   The soil itself is light and the passage of troops very soon cuts the surface up, resulting in clouds of choking dust.   After the rains, this dust becomes thick mud, making transport movement almost impossible.

Training at this time was carried out by day and night, and much practice was given in night marches.   The water ration was cut down, and no man was allowed to drink until after his return to the bivouac area.   This, in the heat of summer, when marching in clouds of dust, was a real hardship, but it proved its value later when the water supply failed north of Beersheba.

During this period the Commanding Officers and Company Commanders made numerous reconnaissances towards the Wadi el Sheria and Beersheba.

The third attempt on Gaza was planned on a more ambitious scale than the first two, and included Beersheba.   This meant dealing with a front of some 30 miles.   On the west lay Gaza, near the sea, by now converted into a well-wired, well-dug, strong modern fortress, offering no prospect of success to a frontal attack.   Thence, eastwards, the defences consisted of a series of field works, mutually supporting as regards gun fire, if not by small arm fire.   These positions ended at Tel Es Sharia.   Then came a gap of about 14,000 yards, about 8 miles. The defences of Beersheba covered the last four miles.

The country beyond the Wadi Ghuzze was an arid roadless desert so that the most careful and thorough organization was necessary to ensure a minimum provision of ammunition, food, and above all, of water for the force, not only for the attack and assault, but also for maintaining a rate of pursuit which would ensure inflicting a very severe blow on the enemy.

The plan of attack was to feint in front of Gaza and the enemy right centre, and to make the main attack by the XX. Corps and mounted troops on Beersheba ; thence to attack Tel es Sheria, based on the water at Beersheba, without which further advance was impossible.   Indeed, if the water supply at Beersheba could not be captured in a single day there would be no alternative but to return to the starting point. This question of water governed all the operations, tactical and strategical. The official history says (p. 19) " Time after time in the days to come the Desert Mounted Corps was faced by the problem of whether to allow a beaten enemy to withdraw and re-coup or to founder invaluable horses by continuing the advance without water." The sufferings of the animals from this cause hardly bear thinking about.

Every possible ruse was employed to make the enemy think that the main attack would be made on Gaza. One of the simplest, which had, however, probably the greatest effect, was the preparation of a staff officer's portfolio, containing mock agenda for a conference at G.H.Q., indicating that the main attack would be made on Gaza, with many other items to make it appear genuine. This portfolio was taken out by the staff officer on patrol. Allowing himself to be chased by the Turks, he pretended to be wounded and dropped the papers. They were picked up and carried to Turkish H.Q. and had a very marked effect on their preparations.

On the night of the 24th, the 53rd Division (XX. Corps), which included the 4th and 7th Battalions, came up to the Wadi Ghuzze between Hisea and Shellal. The infantry had a very trying and long march, requiring careful reconnaissance and leading, and although they were " done," the Welsh and Cheshire men had no thought but to make their point. In the 159th Brigade, only four men were admitted to the ambulance.

On the morning of the 29th, the 53rd Division was holding an outpost line running from El Baggar to the Wadi Esh Sharia and covering the left flank of the Corps. The other divisions, 60th and 74th on their right, were facing Beersheba, while the mounted troops were preparing to move further to the east. All movement was by night and done without a hitch, thanks to admirable Staff work and skilful leading by the young officers who acted as guides. During the day, the troops remained hidden in the bottom of the wadis, suffering severely from the heat. A paragraph from the official history gives a vivid picture of the scene.

" Hardly had dusk screened the land from view when the whole area swarmed into life like a stirred ant-hill. From Shellal the labourers hastened along the railway east of the Ghuzze, stripped off the brown camouflage which screened their uncompleted work, set about plate-laying and the screwing up of the pipe-line. Regiment after regiment of Australians, New Zealanders and Yeomanry, rode south-eastward, till by 30th October there were 12,000 men and as many horses at Asluj and Khelasa. Closer to the enemy's front advanced the infantry divisions. Huge columns of camels, having picked up the loads stacked ready for them in long rows, filed out across the Ghuzze almost in silence, to dis-appear in the dust raised by their own feet. The supply tractors ground their way forward, the lorry columns, railed up from Cairo, were at work ; half a dozen wheeled divisional trains marched with their burdens. Each column had its allotted route, not necessarily on an existing track ; for movement across country was not much more difficult in the light of a moon nearly full. The transport column of the Desert Mounted Corps alone from Tel el Fara on the night of the 28th was six miles long. By midnight vast clouds of dust hung over the teeming plain. But by dawn all was still once more."

On the night of the 28/29th, the Brigade was pushed forward to cover the construction of the branch railway to Karm, and on the following night an outpost position was taken up on the forward slopes of the Wadi Hanafish opposite to the Turkish Rushdi system of trenches. By the morning of the 30th, the 53rd Division was dug in on this line. It held a line of hastily entrenched posts on a front of some seven miles, to secure the left flank of the Corps. It was also to be prepared to attack the Turks if they retreated from Beersheba towards Gaza. The main infantry attack was on that part of the Turkish line south of the Wadi es Saba.

Advancing with the utmost gallantry, magnificently supported by our guns of all calibres, the 60th Division had actually carried the whole of the enemy's first line by half past eight in the morning, and by two o'clock in the afternoon the two attacking divisions had swept over the enemy's second line. The 74th Division then swung to their left and took all the enemy works to the north of the Wadi es Saba. Meanwhile the cavalry had worked their way round to the north east of the town to cut off the escape of the enemy, and captured some 1,300 prisoners and eight guns. The town itself was entered by the cavalry just after sundown, and the water supply which was essential to the later operations was secured.

On the 1st of November, the 53rd (Welsh) Division moved to the north of Beersheba and was soon in touch with the enemy in the mountains in front of Towal Abu Jerwal. On this day the 4th Battalion marched 20 miles and no men fell out. The advance of the 53rd was apparently a great surprise to the enemy who hurriedly collected portions of four divisions to oppose them. The task of this Division from now until the final breaking of the Turkish centre on 6th November, was to hold off this large enemy force, an object which could only be attained by continuous fighting under very difficult conditions.

The hill country into which they had now penetrated was very different to anything which had previously been encountered in Palestine. Instead of soft sand or hard earth, which soon disintegrated into fine dust, they found barren stony country, intersected by deep wadis at the south end of the central ridge of the Judean hills, which runs north and south with only one break from Dan to Beersheba.

Further north it may be likened to the back bone of a flat fish, the centre bone being the ridge up which the only main road in the hills runs from Beersheba through Jerusalem to Nablus and to north, and its side bones the ridges, intersected by deep wadis, running east and west to the Jordan valley and Dead Sea on the one hand, and to the fertile maritime plain on the other.

This central ridge, which rises to 3,000 feet near Jerusalem, gradually decreases in height as it goes south, and the last few miles, just north of Beersheba, is very broken with wadis running east, south and west in a most bewildering manner. It was in this country that the action of Khuweilfe took place.

Owing to the necessity of building up a sufficient forward reserve of ammunition and supplies, and to the fact that a bad khamsin (hot wind) blew steadily for three days, the second phase of the operations could not be undertaken until six days after the capture of Beersheba.

Meanwhile the XXI. Corps had captured the whole of the enemy's first line at Gaza, and were inflicting heavy casualties on the garrison by continuous bombardment and in the repelling of many counter-attacks.

The second phase had as a main objective the water supply at Sheria which involved the capture of the Rushdi system of trenches, and was to be carried out by the 10th, 60th and 74th Divisions. At the same time the 53rd Division was to attack Tel el Khuweilfe and protect the right flank of the XX. Corps. In the main attack everything depended on the progress of the 74th Division on the right, which had as a task the capture of all the enemy trenches on the east of the railway. These were strongly held by the enemy and bristled with machine guns and, in addition, the attack had of necessity to take place over very open ground. The 74th, however, though only after very heavy fighting, captured all their objectives, taking many prisoners. With their right flank secured, the 60th and 10th Divisions quickly stormed the main system.

The 60th Division then captured the water supply at Sheria and the 10th Division took the Hareira Tepe redoubt.

On the 7th, a gap was ready for the cavalry. To this result, due directly to the attacks of the 74th, 60th and 10th Divisions, the resolution with which the 53rd Division beat off the enemy attempts on the right flank contributed in no small degree.

The enemy evacuated Gaza and mounted troops were sent off in pursuit.

The operations of the 53rd Division on the right flank began on the 3rd of November, when the Division advanced in two main columns, the 159th Brigade on the left.

It is almost impossible to ascertain exactly what took place in this

Ali el Muntar from Munsura Ridge.   2nd Battle of Gaza.

Wadi Ghuzze, 1918.

battle, which lasted from the 3rd until the 6th November. As has been seen, the ground in this district is extremely broken and no large scale maps were available. Indeed the map in use, 1/250,000, had been prepared by Kitchener and Condor in 1882, and while it was very accurate, it was not contoured, and minor features, though of great tactical importance, were not shewn ; added to this, much of the fighting took place at night.

In these circumstances, it is not altogether surprising that the published accounts are not very detailed, nor do they in many instances agree with each other.

The weather was hot and the men suffered severely from thirst. The Brigade, moving on Ain Kohle, had several skirmishes with the enemy.

The Division attacked Tel el Khuweilfe on the 4th November. The 159th Brigade had the secondary task of capturing Ain Kohle, but with only one battery to support it was unable to get forward. The position was not captured in spite of the efforts of the other two brigades and the yeomanry. But this costly attack had prevented the enemy from withdrawing any troops, or guns, to deal with the main attack.

During this period, a khamsin was blowing, and everyone suffered greatly from thirst. The advance had commenced with all troops carrying two full water bottles, but such were the transport difficulties that in some cases 48 hours elapsed before further supplies could be brought up. In addition, units were very scattered and in some instances were in such exposed positions that supplies could only reach them by night.

As an example of the difficulty of keeping touch in this particular district, it may be mentioned that during the battle a party of Turks got in between the left of the 160th Brigade and the right of the 4th Welch and the 4th Battalion, and sniped advanced Divisional Headquarters. It was impossible to get at them and, eventually, they were dispersed by an 18-pounder which was with great difficulty man-handled into a position from which it could deal with them.

Hence forward, the 53rd Division was to have the task of protecting this flank and preventing the enemy coming through the hills from Hebron while the main force moved by the coast roads. As the Commander-in-Chief said—" our prospects of success now depend on the valour of the 53rd Division." The casualties in these operations were :—4th Battalion, six men killed, two officers and forty-eight men wounded. The 7th Battalion lost one officer and two men killed, and two officers and twenty-one men wounded.

Congratulatory Messages.

4th November.

To 53rd Division.

Please convey to troops of your Division how much I admire their staunchness in gaining and holding their positions and impress on them the importance of the task entrusted to them of guarding our right flank.

From General Chetwode.

6th November.

To General Mott.

I congratulate you and your troops on admirable success of your efforts and troops' gallant conduct. You have drawn enemy into the very position required to facilitate success of main operations of 20th Corps. Your operations have given us most favourable prospects of success which now depends on the valour of the 53rd Division. General Chauvel adds his congratulations.

From Commander-in-Chief E.E.F.

6th November.

To 53rd Division.

I cannot sufficiently express my admiration for the dash and gallantry with which 10th, 60th, 74th carried out their attack to-day. I would wish them to know how much they owe to the staunchness of the 53rd Division who have for 3 days and nights withstood repeated attacks by superior forces and to the cavalry who have held the gap. I heartily congratulate all ranks.

From General Chetwode.

4th November.

To all Brigades 53rd Division.

I take this opportunity of thanking my brigadiers and every officer and man in this Division for their steadfast loyalty and ready response to the call of duty. All ranks have surpassed themselves under conditions of the greatest physical strain of fighting and long marches which I have been obliged to impose on them to carry out the role assigned to me, namely to protect the flank of their comrades in the main army in its advance on Sheria. The privations of all have been my constant anxiety in conducting these operations.

I consider that the fire support given to the infantry by the artillery under Lieut.-Colonel Walker is worthy of the highest praise, and I feel sure I am expressing what the infantry wish to say in conveying to the gunners the best thanks of their comrades in the infantry.

Kindly convey these messages to all ranks.

From General S. F. Mott, Commanding 53rd Division,

Operations leading up to the CAPTURE OF JERUSALEM,

8th November to 9th December, 1917.

Maps p. 298

From the 8th November until the end of the month, the troops of the 53rd Division remained in the Khuweilfe area to protect the right flank of the Force. The pursuit was now transferred to the coastal plain on the line Huj to Esdud. This required all available transport, so that the 53rd Division was, for the time being, immobilized.

The character of the hill country formed a great contrast to the fertile plain. In place of orange groves, vineyards and cultivation, were barren and boulder-strewn ridges, separated by narrow valleys. There was occasional cultivation on terraces, and in the bottoms of the valleys. It is a hard, barren, stony country. One fairly good road ran from north to south through Nablus, Jerusalem and Hebron to Beersheba. Water was scarce, being mostly rain water stored in rock cisterns.

During this period reconnaissances towards Hebron were carried out, and the infantry spent much time improving the main road running north and clearing up the Khuweilfe battlefield.

On the 19th, the weather broke. There was heavy rain for two days, and the temperature dropped considerably. The troops were still dressed in khaki drill shorts, serge jackets and steel hats, but all spare clothing had been left behind at Belah, and the troops had a very uncomfortable time with no chance of a change of clothing. In addition, the boots began to give trouble. They had been on sand or soft ground for about two years and, although they had marched the whole way from the Suez Canal, boots appeared to last indefinitely on the soft sand.

As soon as the rains came, however, coupled with stony ground in the hills, the boots gave way, stitches, which had been weakened by wear in the sand, broke, and the soles came off the boots. On the march up to Dhaheriye at the end of the month, many men had to use their puttees wrapped round their boots to keep the soles on. Before the final advance to Jerusalem, however, a small quantity of new boots were received and the worst cases were re-shod.

Some idea of the difficulty of maintaining this detached force in the hills will be gained from the supply arrangements.

The supplies of the Division during their advance along the hills came by railway to Karm. They were then carried by " caterpillar " tractors to Bir Abu Irqaiyiq, thence drawn by mules along the old Turkish railway to Beersheba, thence by lorries to Hebron, and finally delivered to the troops by camel.

EL MUGHAR. 13th November, 1917.

Though this battle is one of our Honours, neither the 4th nor 7th Battalions were actually engaged in it. But they are included in the troops engaged because it was only the presence of the 53rd Division, moving alone up the hill country through Hebron on Jerusalem, that enabled the main advance to continue along the coastal plain, unmolested on its right flank. The account of what this Division did is very meagre in the war diaries, and its essential and admirably performed task has been overshadowed in the histories, by accounts of the fighting in the plain.

JERUSALEM. 7th to 9th December, 1917. 26th to 30th December, 1917.

Maps p. 208

The attempt to capture Jerusalem, without bringing it into the zone of operations by cutting it off from the north, having failed, it was now decided to attack it directly from the west. In this plan the 53rd Division moving up from Hebron was to co-operate by covering the right flank of the attack and threatening Jerusalem from the south. The 158th Brigade was left behind to guard the road back to Beersheba.

On the 3rd December, the 159th Brigade moved from Burj El Bemareh to Dilbeh by Ed Dhaheriye.

On the 4th, the Brigade was three miles south of Hebron, and on the 5/6th, the 7th Battalion took up an outpost position three miles north of that town.

On the morning of the 6th, the 7th Battalion, under Colonel H. M. Lawrence, moved, acting as advanced guard to Mott's Detachment, as the force north of Beersheba was now called. In the evening, the line ran through Beit Fejjar, a total advance of 23 miles.

At dawn on the 7th, the 7th Battalion moved against Sherifeh, a strong hill held by the Turks and, assisted by the 4th Welch, captured the hill by 7 a.m. Meanwhile, the 4th Battalion, under Colonel G. H. Swindells, were advancing on the right of the main road, conforming with the movements of the 7th Battalion. During the day the weather broke again, and fog or mist descended on to the hills and blotted everything out, though occasionally Jerusalem, or rather the Mount of Olives, was to be seen in the distance through breaks in the clouds. Bethlehem lay about two miles away directly in front, and enemy artillery could be seen in action, shelling the main road. But our guns could not reply, as orders had been given that no fighting was to take place in the immediate vicinity of Bethlehem or Jerusalem.

The night of the 7/8th December is not likely to be forgotten by those who were unfortunate enough to be in the hills that night. The state of the roads prevented all transport movement, and no rations could be delivered. Off the main road there was a sea of mud and, though mules and donkeys could move with difficulty, no other form of transport could move at all. The main road had been much improved by the Germans, and had been very well engineered up the steep hill sides. The stone of the district is, however, soft lime stone, and as the wheels of the German lorries were, in the absence of rubber, tyred with iron, the roads had become terribly cut up, and by now were a soup of liquid grey mud, full of pot holes. Teams of artillery horses came down wholesale on the slippery roads, and blocked the traffic. Camels' legs splayed out and split the poor creatures at the quarters, and many of their Egyptian drivers died of cold. There was no shelter. The driving rain beat down unmercifully. Everyone was wet through, cold and miserable.

Thinking that he had come up against the main Turkish defences of Bethlehem (and influenced by the failure of the transport), General Mott decided to wait till next morning before resuming the advance.

Next morning, enemy shelling on the road began to be very troublesome, but General Mott did not like to reply, in face of instructions to respect at all costs the Church of the Nativity and Rachel's Tomb.

On the morning of the 8th December, the 4th Battalion were withdrawn to the main road and, on arrival, found the previous day's rations waiting for them. These, for the first time for some weeks, consisted of bread and fresh meat. As the bread was soaked with water, and there was no dry fuel, they remained hungry.

On the 8th, the line was advanced somewhat, but the Turks were still holding Bethlehem, and were shelling the troops and main road with 5.9's and 77 M.M. guns, and a number of casualties were sustained.

During the night of the 8th, the Turks withdrew from Bethlehem, and the 159th Brigade passed along the main road west of the town in the early morning of the 9th, some three hours after the Turks had left. The road had been blown up in places, and the advance was slow, but by mid-day the 4th and 7th Battalions arrived at Mar Elias, with the remainder of the Brigade on the main road as far as the outskirts of Jerusalem and joined hands with the main army which had moved eastwards from the coast. Here they swung round and took up an outpost line facing due east from Mar Elias to Jerusalem.

On this day Jerusalem surrendered. The casualties between the 3rd and 9th December were : 4th Battalion, 9 men killed, 2 officers and 61 men wounded. 7th Battalion, 1 officer and 3 men killed and 2 officers and 35 men wounded.

CAPTURE AND DEFENCE OF JERUSALEM.

9th to 29th December, 1917.

Map p. 208

On the morning of the 9th December, the 159th Brigade were on the line of the Jerusalem-Bethlehem road, facing about east from the walls of the city to Mar Elias, in the order 5th Welch, 4th Welch, 4th Battalion, 7th Battalion. During the day the Brigade was ordered to cover Jerusalem from the north and north-east and advance down the Jericho road.

Jerusalem stands some 2,600 feet above sea level, and is surrounded by hills a few hundred feet higher, except at the south-west, where the valley of the Kedron falls away steeply to the Dead Sea. Jerusalem stands at the head of this valley, one branch of which separates the Mount of Olives from the east of the city, while the other branch, the valley of Hinnom, runs round the south of the city.

The ground south and south-west of the city is broken by steep-sided, deep valleys, and there are no roads running east from the Jerusalem-Bethlehem main road. Thus, to get to the Jerusalem-Jericho road from the south, one must go right round, or through the city and on to the Mount of Olives, which lies east of the city.

In order to carry out the plan, the 4th Welch went round the west and north of Jerusalem and attacked the Mount of Olives, where they were held up. The 5th Welch were accordingly sent to assist, by the south and east of the city, but they were held up by the deep valleys, and only got forward after considerable delay. In the meantime the 4th Battalion captured some high ground east of Mar Elias, from which fire could be brought to bear on the Jerusalem-Jericho road. The 7th Battalion were held in reserve and, in the evening, provided the guards on the gates of Jerusalem.

On the 10th, the 4th Welch occupied the Mount of Olives, but the Turks still held the ground to the east of it.

On the 11th, the 4th Welch occupied Aziriyeh (Bethany) and the 4th Battalion Abu Dis, taking some prisoners.

On the 12th and 13th, the line remained in approximately the same position. On the 14th, the 7th Battalion, who had been finding guards in Jerusalem, advanced through the line held by the 5th Welch and seized a ridge, in the face of heavy enemy fire. On the same day, a post held by the 4th Battalion (Bullocks Post) was raided by the Turks, but was subsequently reoccupied by the Battalion.

On the 16th, the 4th Battalion were withdrawn to Bethlehem. On the 17th, the 7th Battalion attempted to capture Ras Ez Zamby, but were unsuccessful. It was captured by the 160th Brigade on the 21st.

About the 23rd, the weather broke and there were heavy falls of rain accompanied by high wind, and the weather became very cold.

On the 24th, the 4th Battalion were moved up to Sir John Grey Hill's house on the Mount of Olives. This house, which now forms part of the Jewish University, stands right on top of the ridge and from it the view is magnificent. To the north can be seen ridge after ridge, culmimating in the high ground round Tel Asur (captured on the 9th March), to the west lies Jerusalem, and to the south-east the Dead Sea. A few hundred yards south-east along the ridge, stands the German hospice, later used as XX. Corps. H.Q.

This house was in full view of the enemy, but strangely enough it was not shelled, even during the attacks which took place a few days later.

Christmas Day was a hopeless day of sleet and driving rain. All the valleys became full of water, and the roads deep in mud. Owing chiefly to the weather conditions, there was very little activity during the day.

On the 26th, in the evening, the 4th Battalion were relieved by the 7th R.W.F. and went back to billets in the Convent of Notre Dame de France in Jerusalem.

On the night of the 26th/27th, the Turks attacked to recapture Jerusalem, but without success. On the divisional front, the chief attacks were on White Hill, and Zamby and though the Turks managed to capture the former, they were shelled off and it became for the moment no man's land.

During the day, the 4th Battalion were " standing to " ready for action if necessary and in the late morning two companies were sent up to the west slopes of the Mount of Olives to make a new road for the artillery limbers. Owing to the heavy rains of the preceding few days, it was quite impossible for wheeled vehicles to travel across country, quite apart from the fact that the ground was intersected with walls. The guns, or rather howitzers, were in position just behind the German hospice on the Mount of Olives, and the only road along which ammunition could be brought ran right along the top of the hill and was therefore in full view of the Turks. The task therefore, was to break down walls, and make a new track lower down the hill.

Near by was the hospice, the tower of which was being used as an O.P., and strangely enough the Turks did not shell it, probably because it was German property. From the top, a most wonderful view of the battle could be obtained, and every movement of both sides could be clearly followed. Observers on the tower saw a Turkish force, which had massed in the bottom of a wadi, preparatory to launching an attack on Zamby, caught in the fire of our howitzers, and almost completely wiped out.

On the 28th, it appeared that the Turkish attack was losing its power and the 159th Brigade was put in on the left of the 158th Brigade to join up with the 60th Division, as the latter advanced. During the day, the 4th Welch reoccupied Ras Eztawil, and the 7th Battalion a ridge further north.

On the 29th, the Turkish opposition died away and they were in full retreat. The 4th Battalion left Jerusalem at 1 a.m. and during the day occupied in succession Hizmeh, Jeba and the high ridges beyond without very much difficulty.

As a result of these operations the Turks, instead of recapturing Jerusalem, found themselves 6 miles further away. Jerusalem was now out of range of artillery fire.

From a letter :—

" The Mount of Olives makes the most wonderful observation post in the world. Although three thousand yards away I could see every detail of the fighting. The objective was the ridge known as the Wall, a rocky escarpment projecting six or seven feet above a saddle between two hills. The attack at this part was made by troops from Cheshire.

" As they came into view, a burst of machine-gun and rifle fire showed that the enemy was alert. The Turks could be seen lining the ridge and pouring a rapid fire into the steadily climbing infantry. The small projecting plateau was the first objective, and when within a few yards of the top the gallant lads charged and gained the crest, the late Turkish occupants of which could be seen scattering beyond and finally dropping behind the Wall."

JERICHO.

The 4th Battalion was within the area of the Jericho operations, but were not engaged in the battle.

TELL 'ASUR.   8th to 12th March, 1918.

Maps p. 208

At dusk on 6th March, the 7th Battalion (Col. H. L. Moir) moved out from Rummon Rise to occupy Nejmeh by dawn, followed by the 4th Battalion who were to remain in support at Kilia. The 7th Battalion accomplished a very fine performance. After a long and trying march over most difficult country intersected by deep ravines and the precipitous wadi Dar Jerir, both objectives were reached, the enemy outposts being entirely taken by surprise and driven off both hills.

The next operation was carried out by the 4th Battalion (Major E. W. Morris) on the right flank of the army, on the 8th and 9th March.

View illustrating the nature of the country between Jerusalem and Jericho.

The objective was the clearing of the narrow ridge running north-west from Munatir to the neighbourhood of Kefr Malik. On each side of this ridge were deep inaccessible wadis, so wide that the high ground to the east was only just within rifle range, while the slopes of Tel 'Asur itself to the west, on the other side of the wadi Dar el Jerir, the nearest of which was being attacked by the 4th and 5th Welch, was out of rifle range altogether. These wadis limited the frontage of the attack in some places to about five hundred yards.

From the position occupied at Kilia, a branch of the wadi Dar el Jerir had first to be crossed. This as well as Morris Hill 2224 (the saddle connecting Nejmeh and Munatir) was reconnoitred on the night 7/8th March by an officer's patrol. This party found that the only footpath from Kilia down to the bed of the wadi was impracticable for loaded mules which necessitated the Lewis guns and ammunition being man-handled during the advance on the following night, the mules being sent by a detour with orders to try and join up with the Battalion after daylight.

The 4th Battalion moved off just after dark on 8th March. The advance had to be commenced in single file and it took some six hours, in this formation, to cross the wadi and climb Morris Hill where it was possible to form up and deploy. The 7th Battalion at Nejmeh were to be responsible for the protection of the right flank.

It was still pitch dark when the Turkish post on the top of the hill opened heavy rifle fire, which, however, went well over the heads of the attacking companies. The advance was now quickened, although, as the men were tired and out of breath, progress was still comparatively slow. However, for the last seventy or eighty yards, a somewhat breathless charge with fixed bayonets was organised. The enemy did not wait to try conclusions hand to hand.

As the summit was reached, it was just beginning to get light and the Turks could be seen retreating along the ridge to a low rocky hill, 2595 east, about half a mile distant. " A," " B " and " D " Companies had become somewhat mixed up in the last advance, but " C " Company was intact and was at once ordered forward to seize the position to which the enemy was retiring. They encountered considerable rifle and machine gun fire, but advanced with great dash, sections only halting long enough between rushes to regain their breath. Artillery support was not available as there had been insufficient time to give the supporting battery the precise target, maps being unreliable for this purpose. Overhead Lewis gun fire support was given by the remaining companies and the position was carried, but at the cost of a good many casualties, including two officers wounded.

While this attack was in progress, the remainder of the Battalion, crowded behind the summit of Munatir, came under fire from 77 m.m.

guns to the north and enfilade fire from a machine gun on the other side of the wadi, on the right or eastern flank. As it was quite impossible to get across the wadi to the high ground on which the enemy gun was posted, a couple of Lewis guns were told off to deal with it. This Turkish machine gun inflicted numerous casualties, among whom was Captain G. Sidebotham.

The position captured by " C " Company was reinforced, consolidated and extended to include 2595 west. Pear Hill, 2628, a bare stony mound, named from its shape and from an orchard in blossom at its foot on the southward side, was swept by machine gun fire from Rock Park, but posts were established just behind the crest.

The next position occupied by the enemy was Rock Park.

Supported by the fire of the pack battery and a section of the 159th Machine Gun Company, which, owing to the inaccessible nature of the country, had only shortly before been able to get to the front, the 4th Battalion pushed home the attack on Rock Park. The enemy put down a 77 m.m barrage just in front of Pear Hill, but too late, for our men had just crossed. As usual, the Turks hung on to the position until the last minute and then made a hurried retreat under cover of the trees in the orchard. The position was handed over to and consolidated by the 7th Battalion at about 17.00 hours.

In this battle the 4th Battalion lost Captain G. Sidebotham and 2/Lieut. L. G. Hutchinson (attached), and five men killed and four officers and 35 men wounded ; the 7th Battalion five men killed and one officer and 29 men wounded.

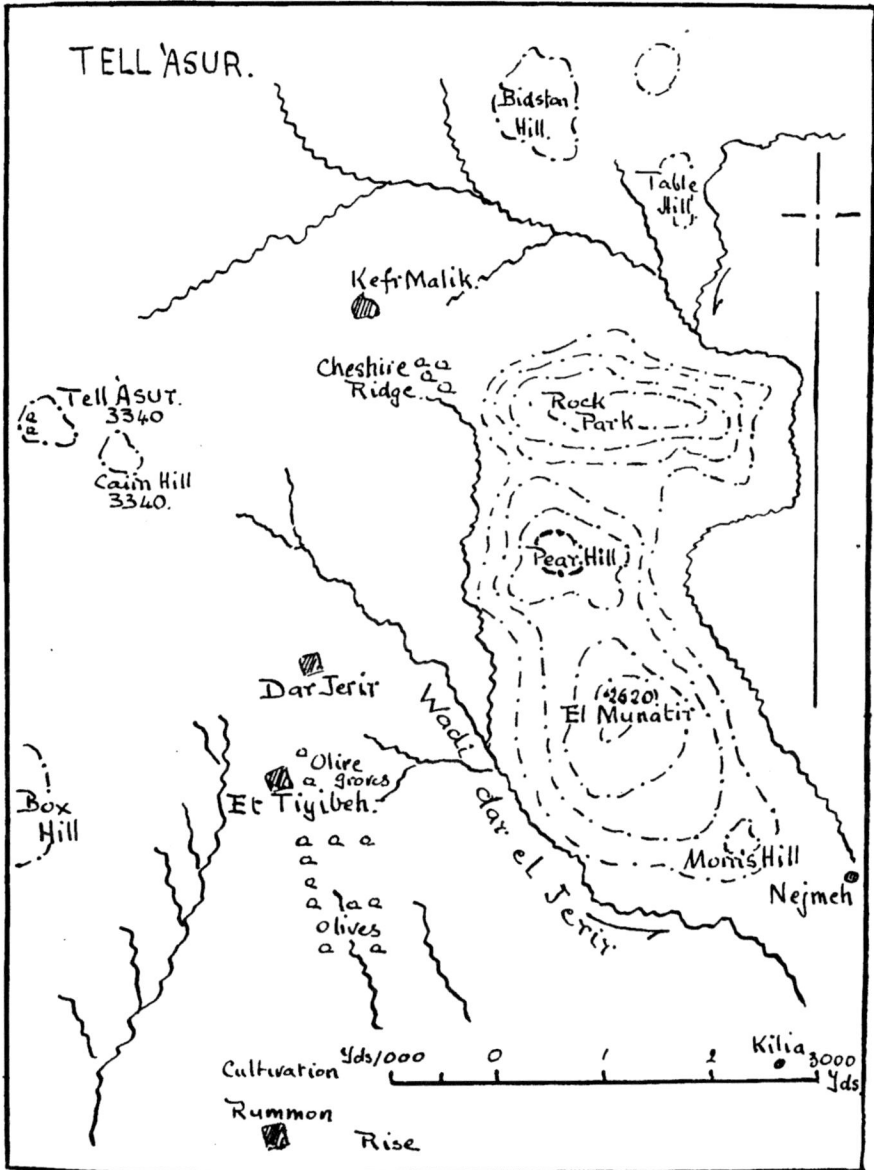

TELL 'ASUR.

Bidstan Hill.

Table Hill

Kefr Malik.

Cheshire a a
Ridge. a

Rock
Park.

Tell Asut.
3340

Cairn Hill
3340.

Pear Hill.

Dar Jerir

(2620)
El Munatir

Box
Hill

Olive
a groves
Et Tiyibeh.

a a a
a
a
a a a
Olives
a a

Wadi dar el Jerir.

Mom's Hill

Nejmeh

Cultivation   Yds/000   0   1   2   Kilia   3000
                                                            Yds
Rummon
Rise

opp. 208

Palestine Campaign

Gaza to Jerusalem

Jericho

MEDITERRANEAN.

Jerusalem

Mar Elias.

Beit Jala.

Bethlehem

El Mughar.

Junction Stn.

Sherifeh.

Beit Fejjar.

Esdud.

Hebron.

Dilbeh.

Burj el Beigaveh.

Ed Dhaheuye.

Huj.

Tel el Khuweilfe.

Ain Kohle.

GAZA

Sheria Position

Teleo Sheria

Hareira Redoubt.

Rushdi system.

Tel Abu Jerwal.

Wadi Sheria

Wadi Hareira

Beersheba.

Telea Saba.

Turkish trenches

Khan Yunis.

Shellal.

Karm Stn. (2 shouti)

Wadi Khuslfe

Scale.

Miles 5 4 3 2 1 0   5   10   15 Miles

Tel el Fara.

El Bajjar.

Wadi es Saba.

Rafa.

To Asluj 4 m.

Khelasa.

opp. 208

MACEDONIA.

Map p. 211

The British Government sent troops to Salonika in conjunction with the French, to support the Serbians. The troops arrived in insufficient force and too late. The result was that it was impossible to withdraw those already landed, but on the contrary they had to be reinforced.

The Serbians were wiped out, until they succeeded in reorganizing their army. They played a decisive part at the end of the war on this front.

Expecting an attack on Salonika by Bulgars and Turks, supported by two German Divisions under Von Mackesen, the Salonika force started a formidable system of entrenchments about ten miles from the town, the flanks resting on the sea. This started on Christmas Day, 1915, and the whole force British, French, Italians and Serbs, worked at it with the greatest energy for two months.

No attack came off, and in the spring of 1916, reconnaissances and roads were made for an advance against the Bulgars who had a strong position in front of, and on, the Belashitza mountains.

In the spring of 1916, Colonel H. Smyth took over command of the 2nd Battalion. A Manx company joined about the same time.

In the summer, the whole force moved forward some 60 miles from Salonika. There were five British Divisions. The 28th, to which the 2nd Battalion belonged, moved to the line of the River Struma. The 12th Battalion went to the Doiran front.

In July, 1916, a French force of a cavalry and infantry Brigade advanced some ten miles beyond the Struma, but was attacked by the Bulgars and driven back over the Struma with considerable loss. The 84th Brigade, to which the 2nd Battalion belonged, was brought up to cover the French retreat, and the Bulgars halted and entrenched themselves some two miles from the Struma, which was held by our troops partly on one side of the river, partly on the other.

Thus, except for an occasional raid, from the autumn of 1915, until November 1918, the 2nd and 12th Battalions were constantly employed on making outpost positions, reserve works, roads, and bridges.

They had much to do to preserve their health under the varied climatic conditions. The winters in Macedonia were bitterly cold, with heavy snow and rain, while the summers were excessively hot, and liable to heavy thunder storms which put rivers in spate and washed away camps and horse lines.

The hardships of the 1916-17 winter were increased by the submarine campaign which caused a shortage of rations and canteen stores. The troops felt this all the more from having been weakened by malaria during the summer.

This loss from malaria was the outstanding feature of the Salonika

O

campaign. What useful military purpose the campaign fulfilled need not be discussed here, but the Germans called Salonika the British internment camp. One wonders what effect the men and stores squandered here and in Gallipoli would have had if they had been employed in France.

The Struma valley must be one of the most unhealthy places in the world. To sleep on the low swampy ground without elaborate precautions means, to the western European, at the best, a sharp attack of malaria of a malignant form. The 2nd Battalion at Lozista was probably in the worst place in the valley. They had no mosquito nets and no gloves, or other protection and practically no quinine. In three weeks, at this plague-spot, the Battalion lost 700 men, 400 of whom never rejoined. Men attacked by this disease dropped unconscious as if they had been shot. These casualties were as honourably earned as any in action. It was no fault of the regimental officers or men that they were incurred.

The 12th Battalion did a good raid in the Ardzan area in October, 1916, inflicting severe casualties and earning a D.S.O. for Captain W. H. Barff and an M.C. for Lieut. F. A. Ninis.

On April 17th, 1917, the 12th Battalion moved to D. Sector, a line completely commanded at every point by the Bulgarian positions on the "P" ridge and the famous Grande Couronne. The latter deserves a word to itself. Grande Couronne was the name given to a cone-shaped hill immediately to the west of lake Doiran. By tunnelling through the apex from the rear, the Bulgarians had made an observation post such as only occurs in the dreams of artillery observers. From its narrow window, could be seen the whole of our position, laid out like a map. No movement could have escaped the observer's notice, and except

Group of Officers of the 12th Battalion in the Balkans.

O I

for an attempt at blinding with smoke shell on suitable occasions, no action was possible against this prince of observation posts. The ships in Salonika harbour, 40 miles away, could be counted, and the arrival of reinforcements known long before they reached their destination. On October 9th, the Battalion returned to Horseshoe for a further front line tour lasting 25 days. During this period the enemy artillery was extremely active, and few important places in our defences escaped a heavy bombardment. Following a three days' bombardment, the Bulgar made a determined attempt to re-capture the hill P. $4\frac{1}{2}$, and an interesting little encounter took place. Previously, by joining up our new defences with the enemy old ones, a trench ring was formed round the summit of the hill, and the rear trenches were used as support trenches. By nightfall on the 23rd November, the wire and trenches on the front side of the hill were smashed beyond repair. As soon as it was dark, the front trenches were filled with loose wire, a double apron fence was run across the reverse slope of the hill, and the support trenches manned. At midnight, after an intensive bombardment, a strong attack was made on this work, and, as was anticipated, a surprise awaited the enemy. The front trench filled with wire upset their organization, and after reforming and charging over the crest, they blundered into the new entanglement and were shot at five yards' range from the support trench. The enemy left dead and

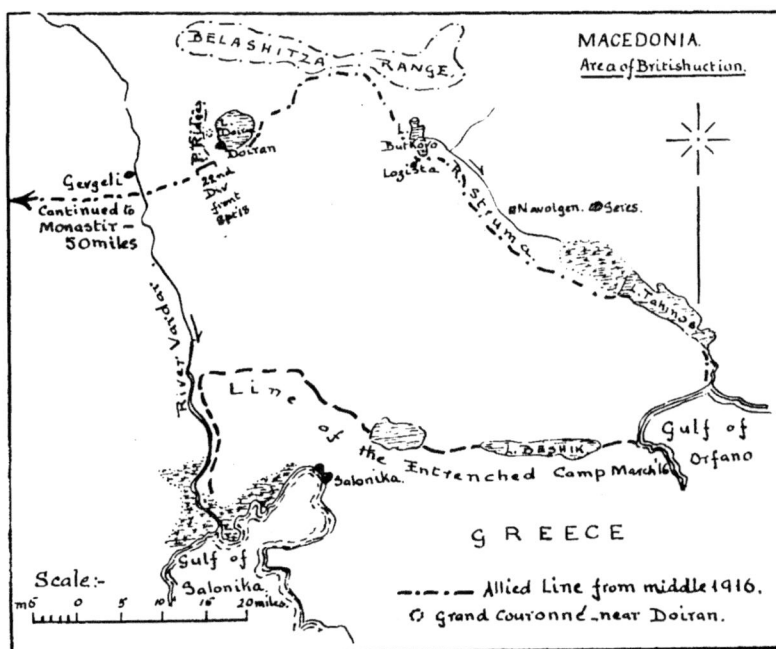

prisoners behind. Our casualties were 3 killed and 14 wounded. For this little action, the post commander, Lieut. C. H. Vigors (killed September 1918) received the Military Cross. An amusing incident was the arrival at P. 4½ an hour after the attack had failed of a Bulgarian " runner." This man was the bearer of a message from the regimental commander to the officer commanding the attack. He had evidently had a sticky journey over the rocks through our barrage. He could speak some English and when told that his officer was dead and that he was a prisoner, remarked, " That is splendid, thank God I shall not have to run back."

STRUMA. 30th September to 4th October, 1916.

Map p. 211

In September, the 7th Bulgar Division attacked the position on the Struma held by the 84th Brigade and two Battalions of the 27th Division. The strength of the 84th Brigade was only 2,000, owing to malaria, and the Battalions of the 27th Division were not much better off. The Bulgar Division was 20,000 strong. The attack failed with 5,000 casualties to the Bulgars.

A Yeomanry Brigade, with some horse artillery, was ordered to follow up the Bulgars, who were retiring in confusion, but the yeomanry were driven back by artillery fire and could not advance. On the same day, before the yeomanry advance, two companies of the 2nd Battalion (Captains Cuff and May) attacked and captured the entrenched village of Navoljen, taking eighteen prisoners.

On the failure of the yeomanry advance, the 2nd Battalion was ordered to follow up and locate the Bulgars. The other two companies crossed the Struma in the night, and the Battalion moved forward at daybreak covered by a battery of field artillery, crossing the plain and coming into contact with the Bulgar rearguard some six miles from Navoljen. The scouts, under Lieut. Beckett, and two companies under Captains King-Smith and May, got in touch. One scout was killed. The Bulgars were retiring up the Belashitza, apparently in panic, and Colonel H. Smyth, Commanding the 2nd Battalion, with characteristic energy, wired to the Brigade that he thought it possible to capture the pass if the remainder of the Brigade would support him.

An answer was received that supply arrangements would not permit an advance of this nature, and directing the 2nd Battalion to retire with the information gained. A great pity and a great opportunity missed!

In a few days, the Bulgars, finding they were not pursued, came back to the foot of the hills, but not so far forward as before.

DOIRAN. 24th April to 9th May, 1917.

Map p. 215

The 12th Battalion was in the area of this battle, but beyond moving companies forward to support the attack and suffering casualties from shell fire, took no active part in the fighting.

A Second Battalion Raid. 20th December, 1917.

At dawn on the 20th December, 1917, two companies of the Second Battalion, commanded by Captain King-Smith, with a detachment of the 506th Field Company R.E. and supported by " A " and " C " Companies on the right and left respectively, raided Butkova Dzuma.

The Bulgars occupied a line on the north side of the valley and the Battalion a line on the south side. The two lines were about three miles apart, with the Butkova river flowing between.

It was discovered by observation, that the village was occupied by one company of Bulgars.

The raiding party assembled in Butkova, in our lines. After tea and rum, the raiders moved off in column of route, and crossed the river at 4-20 a.m. Moving through high grass, and marching by compass, they reached the various land marks without difficulty.

At 6-35, the party passed between two posts, previously located, and could hear the garrisons talking. A certain amount of difficulty was experienced in crossing the ditch and hedge. As the rear company were getting through the gap in the hedge, the enemy opened fire on them, but there were no casualties.

After crossing the railway, the raiders turned west and deployed along the embankment. Fire was opened on them without effect. Enemy who were encountered were killed or captured, unless they ran away.

Three green Verey lights was the signal to move towards our lines. As our men passed through the village many more Bulgars were met, all of whom were captured, almost without resistance, including the Company Commander.

In spite of a barrage put down by the enemy on the west and south sides of the village, our men were all clear of it soon after 8-0 a.m.

It was estimated that thirty Bulgars were killed. One officer and fifty-two men were captured. Our losses were two officers and eleven men, all slightly wounded. Our casualties were chiefly caused by a trip bomb, during the withdrawal.

Captain King-Smith was awarded the Military Cross, and Sergeant Glover and Corporal Toyne the Military Medal.

A month later Butkova Dzuma was again raided, from the west

instead of from the east. This raid was equally successful except that one man was killed. Captain King-Smith who was wounded won the D.S.O. About forty Bulgars were killed. No prisoners were taken.

DOIRAN. Pip Ridge, 18th to 19th September, 1918.

Map p. 215

The military situation on the Struma was one of stalemate for nearly two years. Neither side was strong enough to make any move. To have advanced across the plain without capturing the mountains which dominated it to the north and south would have served no useful purpose and would merely have placed the troops in an unfavourable tactical position, as well as exposing them to malaria.

On August 8th, the decision was made by the Higher Command to put into operation the plan of the Serbian strategist Voivode Mischitch. Put briefly, this operation was a powerful surprise attack on the Serbian front to be delivered where initial success would place the Allies in dominating positions within measurable striking distance of the enemy's chief communications. It was hoped by adopting this plan to separate the Bulgar forces in the Vardar valley from the Bulgar forces round Monastir, and to cut the road and railway running down the Vardar valley. One of the factors for success of this plan was that no reinforcement of the enemy could be permitted. Therefore, to pin the enemy to his ground it was necessary to attack his most important positions everywhere, make him use up his local reserves, and at all costs prevent any movement towards the Monastir front at the critical time. On the front held by the British troops, the " P " Ridge, " the strongest natural fortress in Europe," was of predominant importance, and it was well known to both sides that the fall of the " P " Ridge would be immediately followed by the invasion of Bulgaria and the cutting off of the Bulgar troops operating west of the Vardar river.

The attack began on September 15th and by the night of the 16th six Serbian divisions and one cavalry division were pouring through the gap made on the 15th, and the action was extending right and left with great rapidity. Pushing on with incredible speed, the Serbians reached the Vardar valley on September 21st. The Bulgarian army was cut in two, one of his main lines of communication had gone and defeat stared him in the face. Before this point was reached, the British made their contribution to the final debacle. No single enemy battalion must be allowed to move westward to the ever-widening gap in their front and one more attempt on the pitiless bullet and shell-swept slopes of the " P " Ridge was ordered. After four days preliminary bombardment and wire cutting, the 66th Infantry Brigade, led by the 12th Battalion, attacked the Ridge.

On skyline, " Pip " Ridge seen from the South-west.   Running down the centre with a
track alongside is Vladaja Ravine.   To the left with trenches over it is Pioneer Hill.   On
the right is La Tortue and in the foreground immediately below is Junction Hill.

The 12th Battalion left Pillar Hill, just off the map showing the enemy trenches, at 12-45 a.m. on the night of the 17th/18th September, and moved along the mule track through Doldzeli village and on to Jackson's ravine, where the front line was.   A few men were wounded by shrapnel from shell bursting about the Doldzeli ravine, otherwise the assembly took place without incident.

At " zero," eight minutes past 5 a.m., the Battalion advanced to attack the formidable whale-backed ridge several hundred metres high with practically a knife-edge crest, and from which the ground fell away on each side at a very steep gradient.   On this account the preliminary gas bombardment had very little effect.   Furthermore, our artillery was unable to make any impression on the phenomenally strong dug-outs and galleries, which the enemy had made on each successive rise of the ridge, and which in many cases were covered with as much as twenty feet of concrete.

The 66th Brigade had to attack the end of this long spur named P. Ridge, and to capture the successive well-fortified and wired knolls which rose steadily from P 4½ to P. 1, the highest.

The name Pip came from the word Piton, a French word meaning knoll or knob, and which they had used when they held this front.

It is difficult to imagine a more formidable task than that which faced the 12th Battalion, provided the enemy were stout fighters and well armed.

" A " Company carried P. 4½ by 8 a.m. after overcoming considerable resistance.   The right platoon, under 2/Lieut. R. P. Jervis, met some

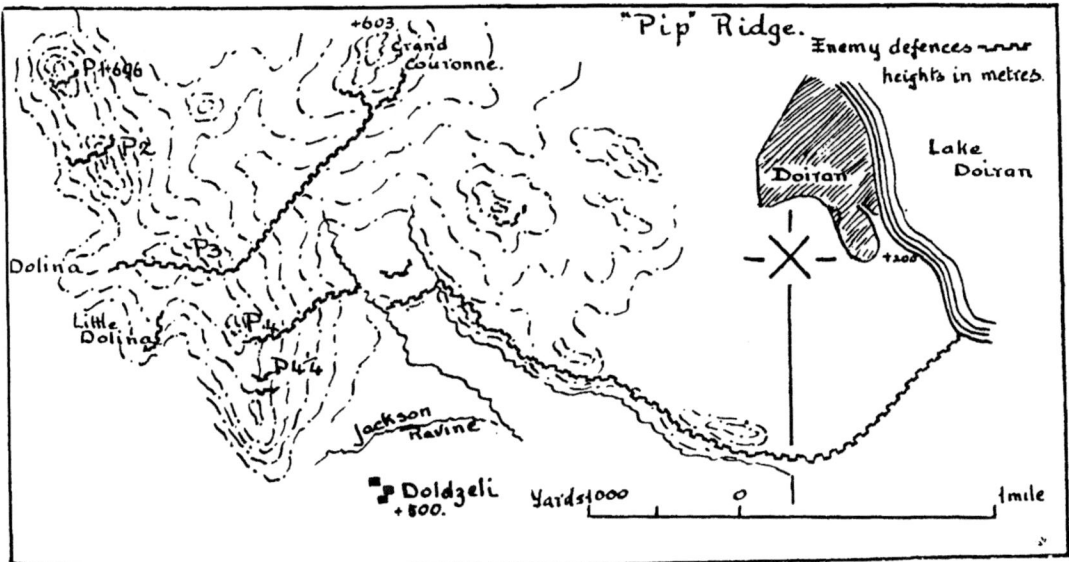

forty of the enemy coming out of a large dug-out on the right of this work. Severe hand-to-hand fighting ensued in which at length all these men were killed, except for two prisoners. The dug-out was bombed and set on fire. This opposition delayed the attack and Colonel Clegg-Hill led the remaining three companies forward to attack the next ridge, P. 4. This advance was checked by an explosion, either of a mine or of a bomb dump, which caused many casualties and some confusion. At the same time very heavy machine gun fire, a barrage from trench mortars and from a *flammen-werfer* (flame thrower) opened from the western end of P. 4. As a result, the companies began to lose the barrage and consequently, when they reached P. 4, they found the enemy manning the trench, ready for them.

About this time, a bullet burst the tank of the flammen-werfer and it blew up.

In face of very heavy fire, the companies pressed on. " A " Company penetrated the centre of P. 4, " B " and " C " Companies stormed the western portion of the work, but " D " Company was held up on the eastern side.

Colonel Clegg-Hill was now wounded and assisted to a shell hole where he was bandaged.

Meanwhile the enemy had mounted a number of machine guns at the western end of P. 4 and in the shell holes below it, and opened a close range enfilade fire along P. 4, whilst trench mortars put a heavy barrage down on P. 4 as well.

However, portions of " B " and " C " Companies swept on to the attack of P. 3, but the enemy had by now occupied Little Dolina and the men attacking P. 3 were annihilated, So severe a cross fire swept the column between P. 4½ and P. 4 that nothing could remain alive in the area.

The 12th Battalion had ceased to exist. 2/Lieut. L. Richmond did well to withdraw the 50 or 60 survivors to Jackson's ravine, where the remnants of the Brigade were reorganized.

The Bulgarians abandoned the position on 21st September.

The casualties suffered by the Battalion, which went into action on September 18th very weak in numbers, were :—

KILLED.

Lieut.-Col. The Hon. A. R. Clegg-Hill, D.S.O.	Capt. A. Morris.
Capt. F. A. Ninis, M.C.	Capt. C. F. W. Marsh.
Capt. C. H. Vigors, M.C.	2/Lt. T. F. Sampson.
Capt. E. F. Sellars, M.C.	Capt. A. La Barte Clarke, R.A.M.C.

WOUNDED.

Lieut. S. B. F. Spencer	2/Lt. E. A. Canning	2/Lt. F. Barrett
2/Lt. E. M. Stuart	2/Lt. F. E. Sidaway, M.C.	2/Lt. E. Stockton, M.C.
2/Lt. C. E. Shuttleworth	2/Lt. T. Meredith	2/Lt. R. W. F. Poole.
	2/Lt. R. P. Jervis, M.C.	

N.C.Os. and Men :—Killed, Died of Wounds and Missing, 144 ; Wounded, 130.

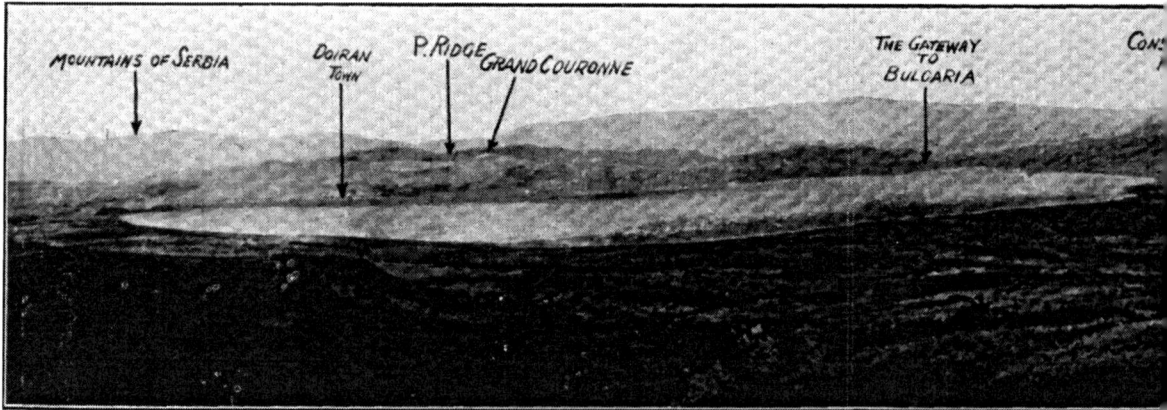

Lake Doiran from the South-East showing Doiran town, the P. Ridge, Grand Couronne, the Gateway

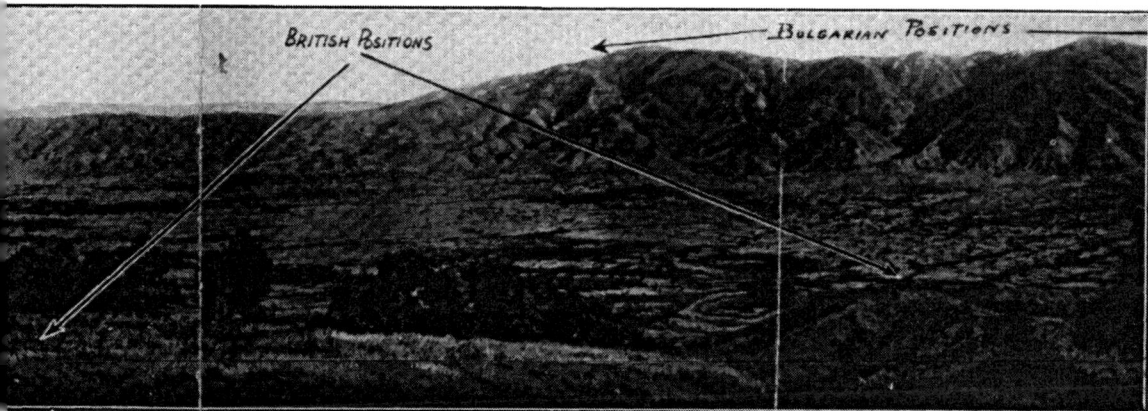

BRITISH POSITIONS   BULGARIAN POSITIONS

Range (the Ramparts of Bulgaria).   The small black dots in the Plain are large trees.

The Battalion was brought out of action by the only surviving unwounded officer, 2/Lieut. L. Richmond, who was awarded the D.S.O. for his gallant conduct during and after the assault. By September 23rd, the Bulgarian Army was in full retreat and was being actively pursued by other units of the British Salonika Force. After a period of rest and re-organization, the 12th Battalion, under Major S. Watson, M.C., marched to Stavros, arriving there on October 19th.

For their gallant conduct, the Battalion was awarded the Croix de Guerre by the French. It is kept in the Depot Mess.

The 2nd Battalion, under Major W. B. Durrands, was in the area of this battle, but saw practically no fighting.

GENERAL ORDER No 125.

"The General Officer Commanding-in-Chief, Allied Armies of the Orient, mentions the following regiments of the British Army in an Army Order :—

12th Battalion Cheshire Regiment.

A marvellous Battalion, which has shewn the finest qualities of courage, enthusiasm and endurance.

On the 18th September, 1918, gallantly led by Lieut.-Colonel Clegg-Hill in person, it rushed to the assault of a strongly fortified position, shewing a magnificent spirit of self sacrifice. In spite of a cross fire from artillery, trench mortars and machine guns, and of the loss of its Commanding Officer, who fell mortally wounded, the Battalion continued to advance, making light of its heavy casualties, and thereby giving a glorious example of heroism, and maintaining the loftiest traditions of the British Army.

(*sgd.*) FRANCHET D'ESPEREY, *General,*
Commanding-in-Chief of the Allied Armies."

* * * *

In considering the utility of the Salonika force, it must be remembered that they brought the war to an end by defeating the Bulgars, and the Turks, by advancing on Constantinople through Bulgaria and Western Thrace. The collapse of these Allies of Germany, followed by that of Austria, put an end to Ludendorff's idea of prolonging the war into 1919.

It was the constant pressure of the Allies which pinned the Bulgars to their ground and prevented them reinforcing their right flank, which enabled the Serbs to succeed.

MESOPOTAMIA.

Map p. 219

The British Government had very large interests in oil in Persian territory at the head of the Persian Gulf. A large portion of the oil fuel for the navy comes from these oilfields.

Shortly after the outbreak of war with Germany, in 1914, the authorities became anxious about this oil supply and the question of its protection was very seriously considered. The conclusion arrived at was that no troops could be made available for the purpose and the First Lord of the Admiralty (Mr. Churchill) noted in a Naval Staff Paper " We shall have to buy our oil elsewhere. The Turk can be better dealt with at the centre." So, it appears that the Government were reconciled to the loss of this supply or were, at any rate, prepared to make shift without it. About the same time, the Military Secretary to the Secretary of State for India produced a memorandum entitled " The rôle of India in a Turkish War." In this document, he expressed the opinion that a Turco-Arab coalition would be a very serious danger to India. He recommended that a force should be sent from India at once to the head of the Persian Gulf to protect the oilfield and, incidentally, to notify the Turk and Arab that we meant business. The date of the memorandum was the 26th September, 1914. It was apparently seen by Lord Kitchener, the Secretary of State for War, but the opinion of the General Staff was neither asked for nor given in the matter. However, it so frightened the Secretary of State for India (Lord Crewe) that on the same evening he wired to the Viceroy that India might be called upon to furnish a Division for service in the Persian Gulf. So we see a State department apparently about to start a private war of its own. The warning telegram was followed up in the course of a few days by another, ordering India to send a Division and to dispatch the 1st Brigade at once. The authorities in India were rather at a loss to know what it was all about. They knew the destination of the troops, but very little else. On receipt of the order to start the troops off, India sent the following wire to the Secretary of State : " We assume you are sure the advanced Brigade is strong enough for its purpose. We cannot judge without knowing its instructions and objective. Do you intend that we should manage the Expedition or do you mean to run it direct from India Office ? "

This elicited the information that the troops were to occupy Abadan (Abadan island, near Mohammerah), to protect the oil tanks there and the pipe line to the wells. They were also to show the Arabs that we intended to support them against the Turk. Further, India was to manage the campaign, but the Secretary of State would define the objectives. The pipe line extended for 130 miles inland.

This was the beginning of the Mesopotamian Campaign. It was started as a private enterprise of a Department of State without any reference to the requirements and resources of the nation as a whole. No attempt was made to obtain the advice of the experts as to the conduct of the operation. No warning was given to the experts that part of the forces earmarked for their disposal were being withdrawn ; no enquiry was made from the people who had to do the work, whether they were able to do it or not. An ill-considered objective was chosen, for the

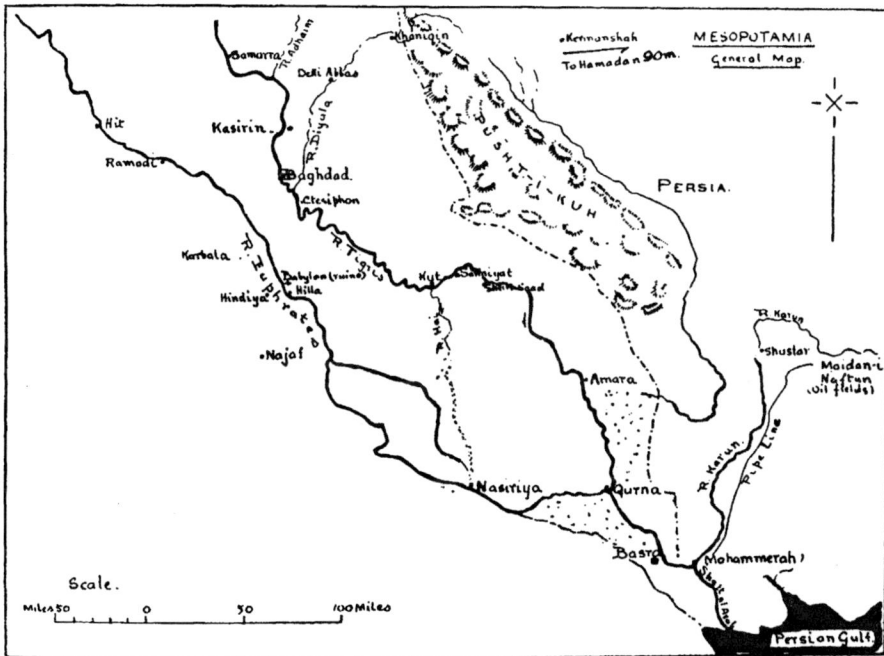

attainment of which no proper plan was made. Such was the start, and it will be agreed that it did not promise well.

A sort of " Mass Direction " was instituted. The " Mass " consisted of the Secretary of State for India, the Military Secretary to the Secretary of State, the Viceroy, the Commander-in-Chief India, and the Finance Member of the Government of India. They had no co-ordinated method of control, but worked together or individually, by official wire or *private* wire, as they thought best. The G.O.C. Mesopotamia received instructions from all. The only one who was quite consistent and had a definite line to which he stuck through thick and thin was the Finance Member. Knowing his own mind, he got his way.   At the end of 1916, he was able to boast proudly, at the Government council meeting, that the only vote upon which he had been able to effect a saving was the Military Vote. To attempt to run a campaign on these lines was simply asking for trouble.

The trouble came in full measure.   Nobody, unless he was actually there to see, would believe that our men could be called upon to suffer such hardships as they did.   However, the operations struggled on. Their scope was altered from time to time, always in the direction of extension; first Abadan, then Basra, Kurna, Amara, Kut, Baghdad. The force was gradually increased to two divisions and some cavalry. At first, a large measure of success was attained, and it was the only bright spot in all our theatres of war at this time.   But these early successes were a snare.   They gave the impression to the controlling authorities that everything was all right and that a cheap victory was to be gained.   Further, it made the soldiers shut their eyes to much that was wrong and, in short, take chances.

Much was indeed wrong.   India was supposed to maintain this force.   She could not do it.   She had not the necessary material.   She could not provide transport on a sufficient scale either for land or water. In fact, she was short of everything in the way of supplies.   This was the direct result of the tremendous power which the financial authorities had obtained since Lord Kitchener had left India.   Further, she had to supply other forces, in East Africa and Egypt, while she had a frontier campaign going on as well.   She had no plant to produce material, even if raw material could be found.   The force, originally never intended to exceed one division, had been sent out without base organizations of any sort. Nobody with the force knew how to set about organizing a base, or at any rate it was not done.   While the Turkish resistance was light and he was on the run, we scratched along somehow.   That we were able to do so at all was chiefly due to certain British mercantile firms, like Strick Scott, Lynch Bros., and one or two more.   These firms provided practically the whole of the river transport by which the troops were carried and supplied.   But when the tide turned and the Turk reinforced this front, he gave us a good beating, drove us back a hundred miles or so, and locked up a very considerable portion of our forces in Kut.   Then the shoe began to pinch.   Reinforcements began to stream into Basra, where a state of complete chaos existed.   For instance, a number of officers were sent from India to reinforce British units ; nobody knew anything about them ; there was no accommodation, no orders, no anything.   They disposed of themselves as best they could and most of them got in the first river steamer they could find, without orders, went up stream and joined the first units which would accept them.   They got up because they were in ones and twos, but the reinforcing troops could not do this.

There was nothing to carry them. Troops could not march owing to floods, and even if they had gone up by march, they could not have been supplied. It is a fact that on no less than three occasions, when important general actions were fought in the attempt to relieve Kut, there were present in Basra 12,000 fighting men and a number of guns which could not be sent up to take part in the fighting for lack of transport. The troops at the front could barely be supplied. To get some idea of the situation one has only to read of the terrible sufferings of the wounded after the battle of Sheikh Saad, all due to insufficient preparation.

In the middle of 1916, General Maude was appointed to take command of the army in Mesopotamia. As soon as he had made suitable arrangements on the Tigris, he moved his Hd. Qrs. to Basra, and there, for four months, the work of organizing the base and base services went on at high speed under his personal direction. Pressure was brought to bear on him by the Home Government to begin an offensive, but he firmly refused to move one step until his backward areas were completely in order. When these were working, Hd. Qrs. were moved forward. He was now able to make his fighting plans, secure in the knowledge that all behind him was well, and that he could be supplied fully and regularly. It was from this time that fortune took a turn in our favour and never looked back.

TIGRIS.

Attempts to relieve Kut, 4th January to 24th April, 1916.

Map p. 219

The 8th Battalion, under Captain F. H. C. Wilcox, reached Mesopotamia with the 13th Division on the 28th of February, 1916. They had taken part in the evacuations at Suvla and Helles as already recorded. Men who had landed at Suvla were veterans by now and few of them were left in the ranks. The Battalion had been filled up with drafts, many of whom were now seasoned and bronzed, but they had had very little training and there was a pronounced shortage of young officers and of experienced non-commissioned officers. Of the officers who had been with the Battalion in August only three arrived in Basra, besides the Quartermaster, J. Murphy, who worthily filled this key post throughout the war. It is fitting here to pay tribute to that body of regular soldiers who, not only in our Regiment, but throughout the infantry, kept the flag of *esprit de corps* flying no matter how the personnel of a battalion changed. At the very end of the war, regular battalions could always be distinguished as such, and there can be no doubt that this preservation of their character was due to the man who was " always there," the Quartermaster. New Army Battalions, such as the 8th, were lucky to get an old

Regular Sergeant-major as their Quarter-master, and to imbibe from him the steadiness and cheerfulness of the regular.

The 8th Battalion arrived in Mesopotamia, or Mespot as they called it, at a moment when hope of relieving the garrison besieged in Kut was almost gone. The great attack on the Dujaila (or Es Sinn) position had failed through too rigid adherence to the plan of attack, itself open to criticism on the ground of rigidity and over-caution on an occasion when it would have been justifiable to take a risk. This failure was one of a series of reverses, the like of which the British Army had never before experienced.

But as long as any smallest chance of relieving Kut remained, it had to be tried. The 8th Battalion spent a month training under Colonel W. W. B. Gover, a regular officer of The Regiment.

Action of Fallahiya.

It was decided to make the next effort on the northern, or left bank of the Tigris. A river's banks are called right or left as they appear to one facing down stream. The first Turkish position, and apparently the only one on this side, was that at El Hanna.

Saps had been dug to within fifty yards of the enemy's wire, ample artillery was available, and we were able to bring fire to bear on the Turks from both flanks. The 13th Division had rehearsed the attack, during its month's training, over full scale dummy trenches. Every battalion, every company, knew its task thoroughly.

On the 5th April, the 8th Battalion passed through the leading Brigade to the attack of the 3rd Turkish line. But the Turks had gone and the Battalion found itself advanced guard to the Division moving into the "blue." Nothing could be seen of the enemy but gradually fire was felt on the left flank, and Colonel Gover changed direction in this direction, the Battalion covering a front of some 2,000 yards. After moving forward some 300 yards, the enemy fire became heavier, and after advancing a further 300 yards by short rushes, the Battalion halted and dug in. They were quite unsupported. Here they remained till dark, when they were relieved by the 38th and 39th Brigades. Our losses were Captain H. Delves Broughton, Captain C. W. Boote killed, seven officers wounded; 28 men killed, 170 wounded and seven missing.

After a bombardment, the 38th and 39th Brigades made a night attack, which was successful. The Turks were driven back to a position at Sannaiyat with one flank in the river and one on the Suwaikiya marsh as before. So we were no nearer Kut. An attack made in daylight on this position by the 7th Division was defeated with terrible loss.

General view showing old trenches at Qurna, Mesopotamia.

Second attempt on Sannaiyat.

On the 9th of April, the 13th Division made an attack on Sannaiyat. But the plan was too wooden. After advancing the 600 yards ordered, the Battalion charged, as planned. After running until the men could run no more, they reached no trenches and only drew a hail of small arm fire. A short halt to re-organize and a second charge brought no success. Only 2nd Lieuts. Tierney and King, and a few very active men actually reached the Turkish trenches, only to be shot down. Our losses were heavy. Lieuts. John Cullimore and R. B. Turner, 2nd/Lieuts. G. W. King and H. S. Tierney were killed, several officers wounded, seven men killed and fifty wounded, and sixty-four missing.

Operations from the 6th onward were much hampered by the marsh overflowing, flooding our trenches and those of the Turks. On the 11th, a violent thunderstorm preceded a waterspout and hurricane on the 12th. The left bank became impassably waterlogged and operations were moved to the right bank.

Action of Bait Isa. 17th and 18th April.

Map p. 225

This position might have been occupied when the troops withdrew from the unsuccessful attack on the Dujaila (or Es Sinn) position, but was not.

The 8th Battalion relieved the forward Battalions of the 3rd Division early on the 18th April and were continuously engaged in strenuous trench warfare till the 19th May, with one day's rest for a wash and brush-up in a rest camp on the 7th.

After a third attack on Sannaiyat by another Division on the 22nd April, Kut fell. The total casualties in the Battalion during the month were, including sick, eighteen officers and 355 men.

On the 19th of May, the Turks evacuated the Es Sinn position, but held on to the trenches covering Kut in the Hai bridge-head on the south and in the Khadairi Bend on the north. They also still held on to the Sannaiyat position.

Further military operations were prevented by the heat. The troops were worn out with diseases, dysentery, cholera, and boils. Vegetables were not to be had. The temperature was 130 degrees in the tents. The casualties from heat in occupying the abandoned Es Sinn position were very heavy. By the end of August, the 8th Battalion mustered only 8 officers and 279 men.

A long period of training at Amara under Colonel J. W. Ley of the North Staffordshire Regiment, now followed, and continued till December.

During this time, drafts arrived and by the end of November the Battalion was 732 strong, Colonel Gover had returned from hospital and all ranks were ready for a renewed offensive.

KUT AL AMARA.   1917.

Map P. 225

By December 1916, General Maude's energy and skill had furnished the force with everything needful for a successful advance. The base and lines of communication were properly organized. The units were reinforced, re-equipped and trained, their morale and efficiency were restored.

The offensive began by a march on the Hai by the 3rd Corps, the 13th and 14th Divisions, while a bombardment kept the enemy quiet in his Sannaiyat position. It should be noted that the Hai flows out of, and not into, the Tigris.

The 40th Brigade crossed the Hai at Atab about 8 a.m. on the 14th December, dug a line of trenches on the east bank and were then withdrawn.

On the 20th December, the 40th Brigade made an unsuccessful attempt to force a passage at the Shumran Bend, in daylight. Rain now stopped all operations for a fortnight.

The Turkish position in the Khadairi Bend was captured on the 19th January, after much hard fighting, by the 9th Brigade. Our guns could now shell Kut and the Hai defences.

Capture of the Hai Salient.   25th January to 5th February, 1917.

The 8th Battalion was in reserve when the 40th Brigade successfully attacked the Hai salient on the east bank, on the 25th January. The troops were strictly ordered not to go beyond the Turkish first line.

On the west bank, the 39th Brigade was not so successful, in spite of very great gallantry.

On 1st February, the 40th Brigade made a further attack on the east bank of the Hai, the 37th on the west bank. The 8th Battalion led the way, captured their objectives, the Turks' 2nd line, and then bombed outwards on both flanks until they had won the whole line between the Tigris and the Hai. 165 prisoners were captured, but a lot more Turks, who were coming to surrender, were mistaken for a counter-attack by another battalion and driven back by fire.

Our casualties were one officer wounded.

After relief on the 2nd, the Battalion was sent across to the west bank. They had no fighting but had to endure a good deal of shelling, and " overs " from the rifle fire aimed at the front trenches.

On the 15th, the 8th Battalion took part in an attack on the west bank which proved to be the last effort in this period of trench scrapping and digging. The enemy surrendered "en masse" and the Hai salient was ours. Unfortunately, Colonel Gover was very severely wounded, half his skull being blown off, but he is still alive and well in 1937. Two other officers were wounded, Four men were killed and 33 wounded.

Colonel H. E. Crocker, of the Essex Regiment, the 2nd in command, succeeded to the command.

On the 16th, a terrific thunderstorm with hail, flooded camps and trenches, just too late from the Turks' point of view.

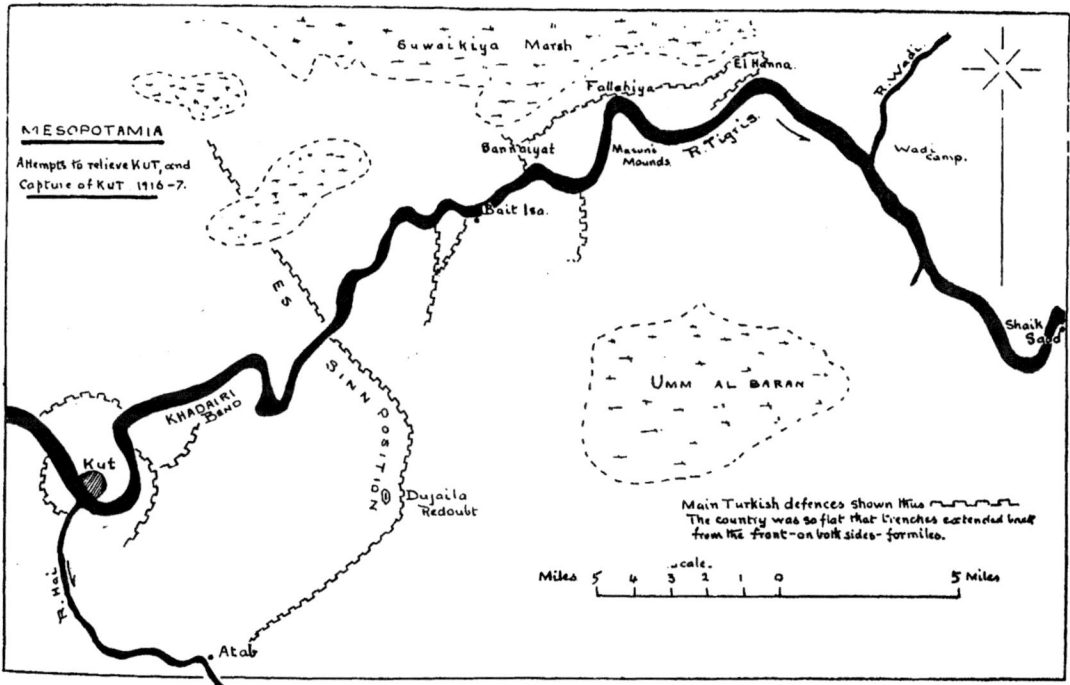

MESOPOTAMIA

Attempts to relieve KUT, and Capture of KUT 1916-7.

Main Turkish defences shown thus. The country was so flat that trenches extended back from the front—on both sides—for miles.

Scale. Miles 5 4 3 2 1 0   5 Miles

This country was certainly a terrible one to fight in. The following extract from "The Long Road to Baghdad" gives some idea of the conditions.

"The barren acres in front of us, often strewn with more debris of munitions than blades of grass, were only a weariness to us when we possessed them. It is hard to conceive the staleness of this kind of fighting, and the dead monotony of Mesopotamia as a field of war. There was no longer the incentive of the garrison of Kut. This year it was only a series of ditches in a mud flat; furrows in an infinity of caked clay leading nowhere as far as the man in the trench could see, for we had forgotten the hope of Baghdad. Each day we attacked a new ditch, and each ditch became the grave of the inheritors of the green fields of England—buried in this barren soil. One could not keep depression at arm's length sometimes when the glamour of war had faded. One knew how tired of it all men were. . . . . There were few signs of tiredness, none of collective tiredness among the troops who fought in the Hai Salient."

Among the many difficulties of campaigning in this pestilential country that of " mirage " must not be forgotten. Mirage is an optical illusion caused by the waves of hot air rising from the ground. Objects seen through this are distorted in an amazing way, and the imagination working on these distorted mirages produces extraordinary results. Flocks of sheep look like columns of infantry, with gaps occurring and being filled up, and mounted officers riding up and down the column. Men walking appear 20ft. tall, and mounted men appear to be in the air. Tracts of dry land look like water, and objects out of direct sight appear reflected through the mirage. In such conditions, observation of artillery fire, and reconnaissance by scouts became impossible.

Between the 20th of January and the 31st, the 40th Brigade dug seven-and-a-half miles of fire and communication trenches, besides wiring and consolidating four miles of captured trenches. It was all done in the open, but every man who fell digging saved many lives which would have been lost by advancing across the open.

*   *   *   *

Two more desperate affairs were necessary before the Turks could be got to leave hold of this area. The first was the forcing of the passage of the Tigris at Shumran, the second the capture of Sannaiyat. The first was the work of the 14th Division, Gurkhas, Norfolks, Hampshires and Burma Sappers on 23rd February. The second was the prize of the 7th Indian Division, who had faced this formidable position since April, 1916. The position was taken on 23rd February.

The Turks' rearguard was well handled. On the 25th, the 13th Division took up the pursuit. The passage of the Diyala by the Lancashire Brigade was an epic of gallantry which has never been surpassed. In order to assist them, it was arranged that the 8th Battalion in the " beetles," or armoured motor launches of the Gallipoli beaches, was to be run ashore on to the Turkish trenches facing the river, and to rush the position. But one of the launches grounded on a sand bank and the engines of the other broke down, and our men were lucky to get out before the Turkish guns found them. The crossing was secured without our aid.

P I

BAGHDAD. 11th March.

Operations for consolidation of the position. 14th March to 30th April, 1917

Map p. 229

When the force, or such part of it as was available, entered Baghdad, the fighting was by no means over. There were still four objects to achieve; to pursue and complete the rout of the 18th Turkish Corps on the Tigris ; to seize the railhead at Samarra ; to fall on the flank of the 13th Turkish Corps which was falling back from Hamadan by Kermanshah in front of the Russians ; and lastly, to control the inundations of the Tigris and Euphrates. By pursuing these objectives we automatically blocked the paths of any possible Turkish offensives down the valleys of the Tigris, Euphrates, or Diyala. Of these four objects, perhaps the most vital was the control of the inundations. Baghdad could be flooded out in the rainy season and all movement stopped.

The 8th Battalion, under Colonel Crocker, had some minor scrapping with the Turks in clearing the immediate neighbourhood of Baghdad. They captured a couple of barges with several hundred rifles, and assaulted and took the villages of Khan Jadida and Kasrin (25 miles north of Baghdad). As already mentioned, the 13th Turkish Corps was moving west to join up with their 18th Corps on the Tigris. Owing to the revolution in Russia, the Russian pursuing army came to a standstill for want of food and ammunition. In consequence, two of our Brigades were sent to attack this Corps. But they were driven back and the 13th Turkish Corps crossed the Diyala and swung south-west towards its friends on the Tigris.

This junction was prevented at the action of Dogame (Duqma) on the 29th March, when the 13th Division drove the 18th Corps back to the line of the Shatt el Adhaim, while the Cavalry Division held off the 13th Turkish Corps at Delli Abbas. In this battle, which took place on a marl plain, as hard and flat as a billiard table, the 8th Battalion was in reserve.

Ishan Bey, the Commander of the 13th Turkish Corps, now made efforts to force his way into the plain from his base in the Jabal Hamrin Hills. News of this move came on 10th April, on the eve of an attempt to force the passage of the river Adhaim. The attack was postponed, and to support the cavalry watching the exits from the Jabal Hamrin, the 39th and 40th Brigades were at once sent across the desert, marching all night, to a point on the Sindiya light railway, about 5½ miles from Chaliya, some twenty miles in all. The 8th reached this spot about 5 a.m., and were at once sent forward in the front line on the right flank. A change of direction was ordered, but the left Battalion did not conform, and a gap of some 1,000 yards was caused. This was filled by reserve platoons. Owing to a threat to the right flank, other reserves were sent there, and the whole Battalion was thus deployed in the front line. The Turks had been entrenched near Delli Abbas, but they left their trenches and came on in long waves. The battle was an encounter battle, both sides racing for a small hillock which was the only rising ground in the neighbourhood. Our men reached the crest first and lay down to shoot. Their steady fire, supported by the guns, soon checked the Turks, who gradually drew off as we gained fire superiority. They fell back in the first instance a few hundred yards and later to a position some 6 miles away.

Our casualties were six officers wounded, ten men killed and 54 wounded. Colonel Crocker was also wounded but remained at duty. Major T. Mitchell died of wounds later.

The Turks were pursued for five days, by the end of which time they had disappeared into the hills.

The troops suffered a good deal from the heat and lack of water, to say nothing of a maddening swarm of locusts hopping incessantly over everything. Lying out in a " cat-scratch " all day in these conditions, in thick serge clothes, was most trying, and even after the battle, rest and sleep was almost an impossibility.

Our Adhaim flank was now clear. The Shatt el Adhaim was forced on the 18th of April by the 38th Brigade, with a loss to the Turks of some 1,200 prisoners.

Affairs on the Shatt el Adhaim. 30th April, 1917.

Maps pp. 229, 231

The 13th Turkish Corps, collected in some miraculous manner after its defeat on the 11th April, leaving a containing force at Delli Abbas, moved down the Shatt el Adhaim in an attempt to save Samarrah. By some great marching they reached the defile where the Shatt emerges from the hills but were too late to stop our crossing of the Adhaim or the capture of Samarrah on the 24th April. They were attacked in position at Dahuba by the 38th Brigade, on the 24th, and driven back to another position close under the Jabal Hamrin range where they waited attack. The position was a strong one covering some seven or eight miles of front, with a splendid field of fire over the open plain.

The main attack was made on the night of the 29th/30th April. The 38th Brigade was to threaten the enemy's left, while the 35th Brigade attacked the " Boot " on the west of the river. The 40th Brigade attacked in the centre, the 8th Battalion on the left and S.W.B. on the right in front line. Our men advanced across the bare plain under the protection of an artillery barrage, and a screen of smoke and dust. They drove the Turks from their trenches, suffering few casualties. The enemy seemed surprised and retired behind Adhaim village. The ground in front of the village was very much broken by deep nullahs running down to the river. This, combined with the rapid advance, caused some disorganization in the companies, but the men pressed on into the village under a storm of rifle and machine-gun fire, and drove the Turks out with bomb and bayonet. Both Battalions, the S.W.B. and the 8th, swept on, missing the Turkish second line and strong points, where they had been ordered to halt and consolidate. Colonel Crocker was severely wounded early in the action and his Adjutant, 2nd/Lieut. S. W. H. Welsby was killed, which may account for the failure of the Battalion to stick to the plan of attack. Anyhow, the Battalions, by now much intermingled, reached the enemy's gun line and captured some 800 prisoners.

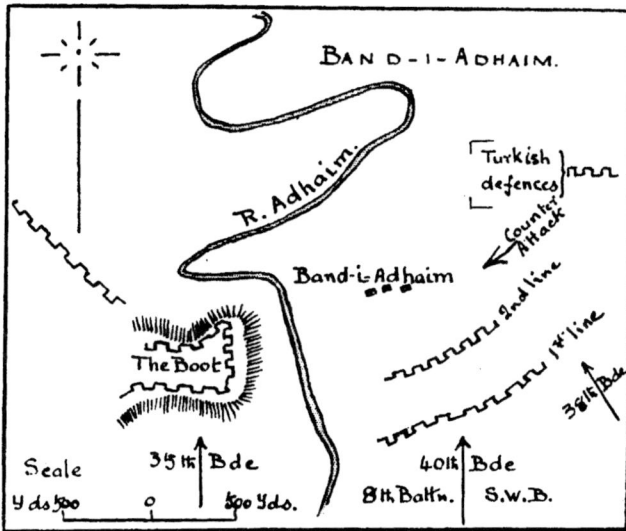

Captain Marr, of the Machine Gun Corps, attempted to restore some order, but before he could accomplish anything a sudden and terrific dust storm swept over the field. No one could see anything, nor could people at the back realize what was happening to the two forward Battalions, by now two miles ahead of their supports. Telephone communication was broken and the chain of command no longer existed.

The Turkish Commander, Ali Ishan, was quick to seize his opportunity. Pouring in a heavy enfilade fire from the " Boot," he sent in a smashing counter-attack of 2,000 men, hidden by the dust, right across the front of the 38th Brigade, which, it will be remembered, was advancing on the right. Our guns could see nothing and could not help. A bloody hand-to-hand struggle took place behind the screen of dust. The Turks regained seven of their guns and more than half the prisoners. Thanks to a brilliantly-handled Lewis gun, the Turks were held up long enough to enable our men to get back to the Turkish second line where General Lewin had brought forward the machine guns of the rear Battalions when he saw the leading companies overshoot their objective. The Turks could not get forward from the village, out of which they were soon shelled when the dust storm subsided.

By midnight the battle was won and the Turks were in full flight.

Our casualties were Lieut. S. W. H. Welsby killed and five officers wounded; 24 men killed, 44 wounded, and 58 missing. Considering that the strength of the Battalion going into action was only 247, their loss of 131 men made the engagement one of the bloodiest in this theatre of war.

The punishment the Turks had received broke their morale and the bulk of their 13th Corps disappeared.

The heat was terrific. The men were still in serge clothes. The thermometer stood at 110 degrees in the shade. Constant dust storms parched the throat and filled the eyes and ears. Well might General Maude write in his dispatch :—

"But as conditions became more trying, the spirit of the troops seemed to rise and to the end of this period they maintained the same high standard of discipline, gallantry in action, and endurance which had been so noticeable throughout the army during the operations which led up to the fall of Baghdad."

Second action of Jabal Hamrin. 18th to 20th October, 1917.

Map p. 231

The 8th Battalion, now some 800 and more strong, having been reinforced by many men who had served in France with the 5th and 6th Battalions, took part in the mobile operations against Turkish detachments in the Jabal Hamrin country.

General Maude's death on the 18th November was a real sorrow to the troops. They had in him the high confidence which thoroughness in preparation and skill in leading always inspires.

Third action of Jabal Hamrin. 3rd to 6th December, 1917.

Map p. 231

The 8th Battalion, starting from Delli Abbas, led the attack on a final attempt to clear the Jabal Hamrin district of Turks.

Beyond the severe cold, water froze in the water bottles and snow was lying on the hills, the operations were not too arduous.

8th Battalion in the Jebel Hamrin returning to camp after a combined drive
through the hills at the end of 1917. Taken in a dust storm.

8th Battalion crossing a bridge over the Tahwila Canal.

8th Battalion road making in the Jebel Hamrin near the Nahrin River during
the summer, 1918. This road formed the main line of communication
to the rest of the 40th Brigade echeloned to Kifri.

Kirkuk Operations.   Action of Tuz Khurmatli.
25th April to 24th May, 1918.

In these operations, Colonel Crocker had his own column consisting of the 8th Battalion, half a squadron of the 12th Indian Cavalry, a section of a mountain battery, and a small R.E. Cable Section.   This column bore a decisive part in the battle of Tuz Khurmatli (near Kifri) in which several small columns, boldly handled, rounded up outlying detachments of Turks.

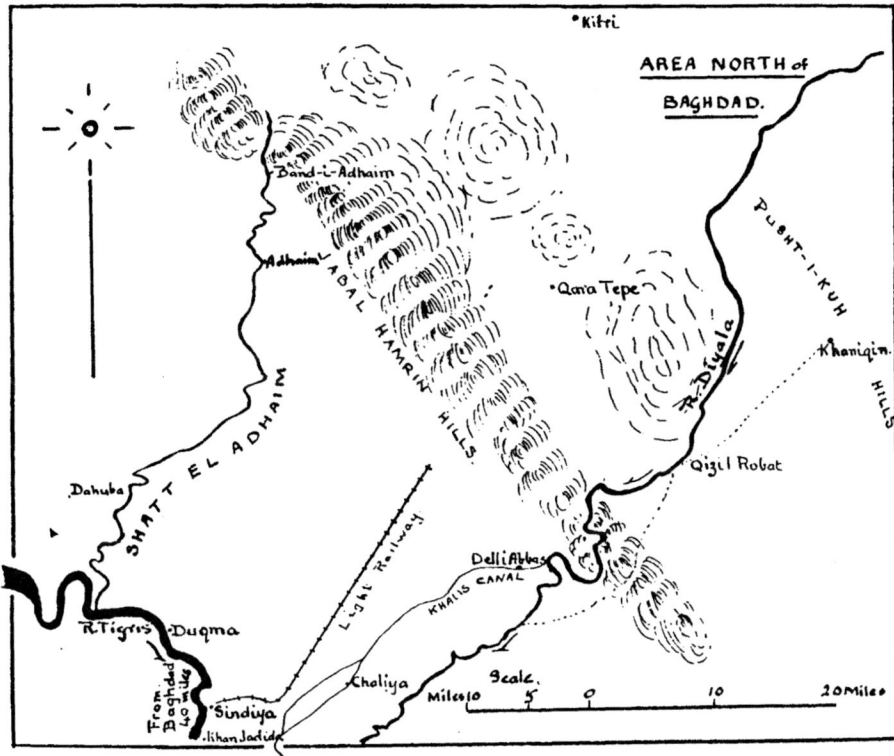

Appendix I.

The Regiment's Roll of Honour

Killed in Action,   Died of Wounds,   Died of Disease,
1914 — 1919

Officers ▪ ▪ ▪ ▪ ▪ 378

W. Os., N.C. Os. and Private Soldiers

1st Battalion	1259	11th Battalion	672
2nd Battalion	521	12th Battalion	204
3rd (Reserve) Battalion ...	66	13th Battalion	636
Depot	36	14th Battalion	12
1st/4th Battalion	357	15th Battalion	519
2nd/4th Battalion	2	16th Battalion	371
4th (Reserve) Battalion ...	20	17th Battalion	10
1st/5th Battalion	296	18th Battalion	7
2nd/5th Battalion	7	19th Battalion	13
5th (Reserve) Battalion ...	2	20th Battalion	12
1st/6th Battalion	587	21st Battalion	2
2nd/6th Battalion	6	22nd Battalion	1
6th (Reserve) Battalion ...	1	23rd Battalion	57
1st/7th Battalion	295	24th Battalion	2
2nd/7th Battalion	6	223rd T.F. Depot	2
8th Battalion	408	1st Garrison Battalion ...	18
9th Battalion	713	2nd Garrison Battalion ...	20
10th Battalion	900	3rd Garrison Battalion ...	2

Eight Thousand Four hundred and Twenty
whose names are recorded in their Regiment's Roll of honour
which is ensbrined in the Cenotaph erected in the memory of
General Sir hastings Anderson, K.C.B., and of his father
General David Anderson, both Colonels of this Regiment.

*The Cenotaph stands in our Regimental Chapel of St. George
in the Cathedral Church of Chester.*

"And all the Trumpets Sounded for them on the Other Side"

The Roll of Honour

OFFICERS.

Abell, John Lloyd Williams Howard, Capt.
Aldersey, Mark, 2/Lt.
Anderson, Archi. John Scott, 2/Lt.
Anderson, Gerard Rup. Laurie, 2/Lt.
Andrews, Charles Raymond, Capt.
Anthony, Thomas Vaughan, 2/Lt.
Armitage, John Basil, Capt.
Arthur, George Stuart, 2/Lt.
Ashworth, Edgar, 2/Lt.
Aspinall, Robt. Lowndes, Lt.-Col., D.S.O.
Atkinson, Henry Noel, 2/Lt., D.S.O.
Austin, Edward Garrard, 2/Lt.
Austin, Edgar William, 2/Lt.
Austin, George Frederick, 2/Lt.

Bailey, John William, 2/Lt.
Backhouse, Henry, Lt.-Col., T.D.
Barnes, Arthur William, Lt.
Barton, George Rawson, Capt.
Bass, Phillip Burnet, Lt.
Baskett, Roger Mortimer, 2/Lt.
Bates, Ernest Harold, 2/Lt.
Bazett, Arthur Hugh, Capt.
Beck, Chas. Brough. Harrop, 2/Lt.
Bell, Norman, 2/Lt.
Bell, Robert Stephen, 2/Lt.
Bellis, Cecil Magnus, 2/Lt.
Bennett-Dampier, John Tud., 2/Lt.
Berry, Bernard, Lt.
Biddulph, William, 2/Lt.
Blackaby, Arthur, 2/Lt.
Blain, Charles Victor, 2/Lt.
Boote, Charles William, Capt.
Bostock, Joseph, 2/Lt.
Brierley, Roger Christian, Lt.
Brien, Desmond Cecil Bagge, 2/Lt.
Brookes, Percy, 2/Lt.
Brocks, Archibald William, 2/Lt.
Broughton, Hugo Delves, Capt.
Brown, Richard Stanley, 2/Lt.
Bruce, Jasper, Lt.
Brundrett, George Fredk., 2/Lt.
Bullock, Charles Sidney, 2/Lt.
Burrell, John Stamp Garth., 2/Lt.
Burrows, Arthur Cecil, 2/Lt.
Bushe, Gervase Gray, 2/Lt.

Cameron, Colin Neil, Capt.
Campbell, Charles Arthur, Lt.
Carpenter Cedric Theo. Arundel, Lt.
Carswell, Henry Bradshaw, Capt.
Casson, Thomas, M.C., 2/Lt.

Chandler, James Cook, 2/Lt.
Chamberlain, Geo. Herbert, 2/Lt.
Chaplin Hum. Marmaduke, Lt.
Chattaway, Philip Spencer, 2/Lt.
Cholmeley, Roger James, Capt.
Clark, Egbert Douglas, Lt.
Clarke, David, 2/Lt.
Claye, Geoffrey Woolley, Lt.
Clayton, John Arnold, 2/Lt.
Clayton, Wm. Ernest Albert, 2/Lt.
Clegg-Hill, The Hon. Arthur Reginald, Lt.-Col., D.S.O.
Cobbold, Edgar Fran. Wanklyn, Lt.
Cooke, Charles Taylor, Capt.
Cole, Leslie Stewart, 2/Lt.
Cotton, Arthur Edward, 2/Lt.
Cotsworth, John Henry, 2/Lt.
Cowpe, George Bleazard, Lt.
Crew, Denis-Merville, Lt.
Crowther, Norman, 2/Lt.
Cullimore, John, Lt.
Curry, William Gordon, 2/Lt.
Curtis, Thomas Britt, 2/Lt.

Dale, Frank Cottrell, 2/Lt.
Daniels, James, 2/Lt.
Davey, Wm. Aubrey Carthew, 2/Lt.
David, Edward Harold, 2/Lt.
Davies, Idris Powell, 2/Lt.
Davies, Frank Arnold, 2/Lt.
Davies, Hugh Frederick, 2/Lt.
Davies, William Edward, 2/Lt.
Davy, William Edward, Capt. and Adjt.
Dawson, Walter Henry Mountiford Westropp, 2/Lt.
Danson, Francis Rudolph, Lt.
Dean, John Henry Ellis, Capt., M.C.
Denyer, Horace Frederick, Lt.
Dewar, Harold Ernest, 2/Lt.
Dickin, Albert Edward, 2/Lt.
Dickinson, Colin Jas. Henry, 2/Lt.
Dodd, Herbert, 2/Lt.
Dodd, Stanley Preston, 2/Lt.
Done, Robert, Lt.
Downes, Arthur Chernocke, 2/Lt.
Dowse Wm. Arthur Clarence, Lt.
Dresser, Harry Jex, Capt. (A/Major)
Duckworth, Bernard, 2/Lt.
Dunlop, Launcelot Lindsay Brook, 2/Lt.

Earle, Charles Edward, Lt.-Col.
Earle, Walter Colby, Capt.

Easterbrook, William Reginald, Lt.
Edwards, Edward Ernest, 2/Lt.
Edwards, John Kelvin, Lt.
Ellerton, Charles Fleetwood, Capt.
Elliott, James Dunsmore, 2/Lt.
Ellis, Douglas, Wilmshurst, Lt.
Evans, William Ashton, 2/Lt.

Ford, Kenneth, George Haslam, Lt.
Foster, Charles Clifford, Lt.
Foster, Norman, Rae, Lt.
Forster, Lionel Archibald, Capt.
Fraser, Harold Reginald Drummond, Lt. (A/Capt.), M.C.
Fraser, Victor Murray Drummond, 2/Lt.
Frost, Kingdon Tregosse, Lt.
Frost, Thomas Lawrence, Capt.
Fulton, George, Koberwein, Capt. (A/Lt.-Col.), D.S.O.
Furnell, Thomas, Capt.

Gadsdon, Frank Bannatyne, 2/Lt.
Gamon, Sidney Percival, Capt.
Gardiner, Ellis, Hubert, Lt.
Gell, Philip, 2/Lt.
Gibbs, Thomas Charles, Lt., M.C.
Girod, Milton, 2/Lt.
Gledsdale, Irving, Lt.
Gleed, George Alfred, Lt.
Goodwin, George, 2/Lt.
Goss, Hubert John, 2/Lt., M.C.
Gosse, Robt. Buch. Wilkes, 2/Lt.
Gosset, Claude Butler Gosset, Major
Gough, George Henry Waldron, Lt.
Gould, Arthur, 2/Lt.
Grace, Joseph, 2/Lt.
Gray, Cyril Seaton, 2/Lt.
Green, Gilbert Pitcher, 2/Lt.
Greenhalgh, James Arthur, 2/Lt.
Greg, Arthur Tylston, Capt.
Greg, Robert Phillips, 2/Lt.
Gregg, George Philip, 2/Lt.
Gresson, John Edward, 2/Lt.
Greswell, E. W., Lt.

Haddon, Thomas, Capt.
Heath, Geoffrey, Capt.
Hall, Frederick Grainger, Capt.
Hampson, Alfred Eric, 2/Lt.
Hamilton, Ronald Millie, 2/Lt.
Hand, Maurice William, Lt.
Hanford, Albert William, Lt.
Harper, James, 2/Lt.

Harris, Frank, 2/Lt.
Harry, Alfred Edward, Capt.
Hartford, Hugh Leving St. John, Capt.
Hartley, William Edwin, 2/Lt.
Hartill, John Harry, Capt.
Hay, J. M. Lt.
Hayes-Newington, Chas. Wetherell, Capt.
Heron, Ernest Stewart, Lt.
Hesketh, William, 2/Lt.
Hill, Arthur Rowland, Major
Hodson, Edward Hutchinson, Lt.
Holding, James, Capt.
Holmes, Wilfred Bertram, 2/Lt.
Holmes, Duncan McPherson Studdert, 2/Lt.
Holmes, Vernon Raines, Lt., M.C.
Howes, Harold Edward, Lt.
Hughes, John Norman, 2/Lt., M.C. and Bar
Hunter, Archibald, 2/Lt.
Hunter, William, 2/Lt.

Innes, William Robert, Capt.

Jackson, Thomas Leslie, Capt.
Joice, Philip Sidney, 2/Lt.
Jones, Ernest Rae, Capt.
Jones, George William, 2/Lt.
Jones, Thomas William Allen, 2/Lt.
Jolley, Robert James, 2/Lt.

Keating, George, 2/Lt.
Keating, John, Lt.
Kennedy, R. B. C., 2/Lt.
Kenyon, William Douglas, Capt.
Kerr, Daniel, Lt.
Kidd, Claude Bernard, Capt., M.C.
King, Gordon Wick, 2/Lt.
King, Sydney, Wm. Thacker, 2/Lt.
Kirk, Richard, Capt., M.C.
Kneath, David John, 2/Lt.

Lacey, Edred Severs, 2/Lt.
Langdon, Wilfrid Max, Capt.
Lawrenson, Ray. Fitzmaurice, Lt.
Laws, Selwyn Vernon, 2/Lt.
Laybourne, John Oscar, 2/Lt.
Lee, Jack, M.C., Capt.
Lees, William Henry, 2/Lt.
Leigh, Herbert, A/Capt.
Lester-Smith, Henry, 2/Lt.
Leftwich, Nigel George, Lt.
Lloyd, A., Lt.
Lloyd, Frank Lewis, Capt.
Loder-Symonds, Robt. Fran., Capt.
Logan, Edward Townshend, Lt.-Col., D.S.O.
Longster, William Ernest, 2/Lt.

McArdle, Peter Paul, 2/Lt.
McCall, Robert Alfred, 2/Lt.
McCullagh, Edwin Samuel, 2/Lt.
McCullough, Robert James, 2/Lt.
McGregor, Marcus, 2/Lt.

McGregor, Ronald Malcolm, 2/Lt.
McKay, Ernest, Lt.
McKeever, James Holden, Lt.
McLaren, Robert, John, Capt.
McLaren, Robert, 2/Lt.
Mahony, Frederick Henry, Capt.
Maitland-Addison, Arthur Creighton, 2/Lt.
Mallinson, Richard, Capt.
Malone, William Adolph, 2/Lt.
Manning, John Carlton, 2/Lt.
Mansfield, Harold, 2/Lt.
Maquire, Maurice, 2/Lt.
Marsh, Chas. Fredk. Wm., A/Capt.
Martin, George Ernest, Capt.
Mathews, Arnold, Lt.
Maxwell, Henry, 2/Lt.
Melland, Edward Guy, Lt.
Melling, Harold, Lt.
Merry, Norman Cuthbert, Capt.
Metcalfe, John Chaytor, Major
Miller, George Frederick, 2/Lt.
Miller, James, Lt.
Miln, George Gordon, Capt., M.C.
Milner, Archi. Donald, Lt. (A/Capt.)
Molyneux, Benjamin, Lt., M.C.
Moore, John Rushton, Lt. (A/Major), M.C.
Morgan, Thomas Cyril, 2/Lt.
Morris, Arthur, Capt.
Morris, Leslie Tounsend, 2/Lt.
Morrison, Robert Cecil, 2/Lt.
Moss, Charles, Capt., M.C.
Mountain, Cyril Robt. Wightman, 2/Lt. (A/Capt.)
Moyes, Alexander Barclay, Lt.
Munro, Alexander Douglas, 2/Lt.
Murray, Thomas, Capt.
Musker, John Henry, 2/Lt.

Napier, Henry Edward, Brig.-Gen.
Napier, Maurice Alexander, Major
Naylor, John, 2/Lt. (A/Capt.)
Newell, Matthew Banks, 2/Lt.
Newell, Thomas Stanley, 2/Lt.
Newson, Norman, A., Lt.
Newstead, Rupert Randolph, 2/Lt.
Newton, Frederick, 2/Lt.
Newton, Henry Joseph, 2/Lt.
Newton, William John, Major
Nicholson, Alan Grifford, Lt.
Nicholson, Hugh Hathorn, 2/Lt.
Nicholson, Huntly Warwick, Lt.
Nicholson, Richard Le Brun, Capt. (A/Major), M.C.
Ninis, Francis Aubrey, Lt.(A/Capt.), M.C.
Noble, Archibald, Francis, Capt.
Norris, Fredk. George, 2/Lt.
Nosworthy, Philip Chorlton, 2/Lt.

O'Brien, William Vincent, 2/Lt.
O'Callaghan, James, 2/Lt.
Oliver, Edward Cole, 2/Lt.
Oliver, George Frank, 2/Lt.
Owen, Herbert Morris, 2/Lt.

Owens, Edward, 2/Lt., D.C.M.

Page, Dudley, Alfred, 2/Lt.
Parker, Wm. Brabazon Hallowes, Lt.
Patterson, Charles Cox, Capt.
Peake, Arthur, Lt.
Petty, Eric Bateman, Lt.
Phillips, Ivor John Douglas, Capt.
Pickersgill, John Henry, Lt., M.C.
Pickering, Charles Leigh, Lt.
Potts, Charles, 2/Lt.
Powell, Ernest Arthur, 2/Lt.
Prentice, Thomas Alfred, Major
Proctor, Frank Goodheart, 2/Lt.
Prout, William Thomas, 2/Lt.
Pumphrey, Hubert, 2/Lt.

Radhill, P. J., Lt.
Read, William Lister, Capt., M.C.
Rees, Kenneth David, 2/Lt.
Reynolds, Eric Hindle, 2/Lt.
Rhodes, Chas. Fredk. Stanley, 2/Lt.
Rhodes, Gerald Rudolph, Lt.
Rich, William Suttor, Capt.
Rigby, Douglas Marshall, Lt.
Rimington, Ernest Cameron, Waterfield, 2/Lt.
Robbins, John Laurence, Lt.
Roberts, Robert James, 2/Lt.
Roberts, Thomas, 2/Lt.
Roberts, Thomas Wilson, 2/Lt.
Robertson, Herbert Neville, 2/Lt.
Rogers, William Ewart, Lt.
Routh, John Cyril, Capt.
Rowe, Harvey Wilfrid Warwick, Lt., M.C.
Rowley, Gerald, Capt., M.C. and Bar

Saltmarsh, John Henry T., 2/Lt.
Sampson, T. F., 2/Lt.
Saniford, Noel Pendlebury, 2/Lt.
Scholefield, Richard Powell, 2/Lt.
Schultz, George Edward, Capt.
Scott, Arthur Blake, 2/Lt.
Scott, Arthur de Courcy, Lt.-Col.
Scott, Clarence Trebor, 2/Lt.
Scott, Kenneth Wm. Laing, 2/Lt.
Scott, Samuel Lackland, 2/Lt.
Seel, Horace Arthur, 2/Lt.
Sernberg, Allan, Capt.
Shaw, Bernard Hudson, 2/Lt.
Shaw, Rowan, 2 L/t.
Sheard, Geoffrey, Senior, 2/Lt.
Sidebotham, Gerald, Capt.
Silcock, Percy Bryan, 2/Lt.
Simcock, Gilbert Alexander, 2/Lt.
Simpson, Eric Hadley, 2/Lt.
Simpson, George Ricardo, Lt.
Small, Dudley Francis, Capt.
Smallwood, Reginald, 2/Lt.
Smith, Sydney Ferrar, 2/Lt.
Smith, Wilbraham Fremantle, 2/Lt.
Somerset, Fitz Roy Aubrey, Lt.
Sproston, Frederick, Alvin, 2/Lt.
Stead, Geoffrey Henry, Lt., M.C.

Stephenson, Claudius, Capt.
Stevenson, Henry Fitzroy, Lt.
Stewart, Douglas Alexander, 2/Lt.
Stone, Arthur Brabazon, Major
Storrs, James Parker, 2/Lt.
Stott, Frank Gordon, Lt.
Stringer, Gerald Moffatt, 2/Lt.
Stubbs, William Norman, 2/Lt.
Styles, Alfred Cornwall, Lt.
Sweeney, Gilbert Martin, 2/Lt.
Swindells, Geoffrey Hillier, Lt.-Col.

Tapp, George Norman, 2/Lt.
Taylor, Archibald McMillan, Capt.
Taylor, Arthur, Lt.
Thrift, Sydney Henry, 2/Lt.
Tierney, Herbert Stanislaus, 2/Lt.
Thurgood, Ernest Fuller, Capt.
Trayes, Frederic Kenneth, Jackson, 2/Lt.

Turner, Herbert Guy, Capt.
Turner, Roger Bingham, Lt.
Tyson, William Noel, Lt.

Vance, Chas. Richard Griffin, 2/Lt.
Vernon, Fredrick Travis, 2/Lt.
Vigors, Charles Henry, Capt,. M.C.

Wainwright, Harry Arnold, 2/Lt.
Walford, Alfred Sand., Lt. (A/Capt.)
Walker, Arnold Henry, Lt.
Walker, Basil Scarisbrickle, 2/Lt.
Wallis, Noel Veder, 2/Lt.
Walsh, Geoffrey Christian Lansdale, 2/Lt.
Walter, Raymond, 2/Lt.
Warwick, Wm. Robt. St. Clair, 2/Lt.
Watson, Charles John, Lt.
Watson, Geoffrey William, 2/Lt.
Watt, John Vade, 2/Lt.

Webb, Denys Stubbs, 2/Lt.
Welch, Richard Sydney, 2/Lt.
Welsby, Sydney, Walter Humfrey, 2/Lt.
White, Francis, Capt.
White, Gilbert Clement Whit, Lt.
Willmore, William Albert, 2/Lt.
Wilkinson, William Oscar, Capt.
Wilson, George Reginald, Capt.
Wilson, John Victor, 2/Lt.
Winnington, Charles, 2/Lt.
Wolstenholme, Richard Fran, Capt.
Wood, Thos. Leonard, 2/Lt.
Worthington, Ralph, Major
Worth, Thomas, 2/Lt.
Wright, Charles, Lt., M.C.

Yorke, Frederick, Lt.
Young, Leonard Geo. Birmingham, 2/Lt.

OTHER RANKS.

FIRST BATTALION

Adams, Richard, 244962 Sgt.
Aden, John, 67955 Pte.
Ainscough, David, 9622 Pte.
Albinson, Walter, 8999 Pte.
Aldcroft, Herbert, 27612 Pte.
Alleeson, Albert, 7652 C.S.M.
Allman, George, 7461 Pte.
Allman, George, 8568 A/Cpl.
Allman, George, 10521 Pte.
Allman, George Henry, 12269 Pte.
Anyon, William, W/329 L/Cpl.
Archbould, Walter 40244 Pte.
Archer, Thos. Frederick, 9057 L/Cpl.
Ardern, Joseph, 18387 Pte.
Armsby, George, 8994 Pte.
Armstrong, Joseph, 7504 L/Cpl.
Armstrong, Joseph Johnson Talbot, 9578 Pte.
Arnold, Benjamin, 7307 Pte.
Arnold, Joseph, 10014 Pte.
Arnott, Joseph, 6879 Pte.
Asbury, George, 52104 Pte.
Ashcroft, James, 15107 Pte.
Ashley, Richard, 7943 Sgt.
Ashton, Percy, 9007 L/Sgt.
Ashton, Robert, 12166 Pte.
Astles, Fred, 44292 Pte.
Axon, William, 49020 L/Cpl.
Axson, Joseph, 17882 Pte.

Bagan, Peter, 68100 Pte.
Bagley, Thomas, 11705 Pte.
Bagwell, Harry, 11224 Pte.
Bailey, Fred, 12252 Pte.
Bailey, William, 51534 Pte.
Bain, Gordon, 68094 Pte.
Baker, Ernest, 28379 Pte.
Ball, Archibald, 11246 Pte.
Ballagher, George, 9010 Pte.

Bamford, Cornelius, 8251 Pte.
Barber, Arthur, 7250 Pte.
Barber, John William, 10819 Pte.
Barbour, Charles, 51285 Pte.
Barker, Harry, 50508 Pte.
Barnes, Herbert, 9638 Pte.
Barnes, James, 7091 Pte.
Barnes, John, 15669 Pte.
Barnett, James, 6778 Pte.
Barrett, Tom, 265625 Pte.
Barrow, Amos, 10065 Pte.
Bartlett, William George, 7064 Pte.
Bates, Frank, 9339 Pte.
Bateson, Norman, 53878 Pte.
Baum Frederick, 8351 Pte.
Beard, John William, 10103 Pte.
Beard, Joseph, 7211 Pte.
Bebbington, Joseph, 18655 Pte.
Bebbington, Thos. Ed., 7116 A/Sgt.
Bedda, Harry, 6848 Pte.
Beddoe, Percy, 52852 Pte.
Beech, John Willie, 12213 L/Cpl.
Belcher, Hubert, 49737 Pte.
Bell, Hubert, 60526 Pte.
Bellas, Mark, 53876 Pte.
Belshaw, Alfred, 7700 Pte.
Bennett, Francis Thos. 10491 Pte.
Bennett, James, 6283 Cpl.
Bennett, Thomas 25331 Pte.
Berry, Bartholomew, 266657 Pte.
Berry Edgar, 40224 Pte.
Berry, Fred, 12331 Pte.
Berry, Harry, 35280 Pte.
Beswick, Fred, 49029 Pte.
Beswick, William, 13981 A/Sgt.
Bethel, Richard, 266655 Pte.
Bettley, Fred, 10022 Pte.
Billington, John, 11834 Pte.
Birch, James, 9181 Pte,
Birch, Percy, 52182 Pte.
Birch, Walter, 241684 Pte.

Bird, William, 49669 Pte.
Blackhurst, Fred, 18002 Pte.
Blease, Emmanuel, 14524 Pte.
Blinkhorn, Thomas, 67889 Pte.
Boag, Joseph, 11241 Pte.
Bond, James, 50513 L/Cpl.
Bone, William, 7474 L/Cpl.
Boon, Moses, 10120 Pte.
Boote, Charles 9827 Pte.
Boots, John, 11162 Pte.
Bostock, William Henry, 10929 Pte.
Boswell, Edward, 40315 Pte.
Botham, George Albert, 60523 Pte.
Bowen, John William, 52894 L/Cpl.
Bowers, Harry, 52430 Pte.
Bowers, William, 8604 Pte.
Bowett, Ralph, 10174 A/Cpl.
Bradbury, George R., 33483 Pte.
Bradbury, Joseph, 67866 Pte.
Bradley, Luke, 8202 Pte.
Bradshaw, Samuel, 35353 Pte.
Brady, Charles, 36328 Pte.
Brannon Thomas, 24113 Pte.
Brassington, John, 68308 Pte.
Bray, Charles, 10322 Pte.
Brearley, James, 10923 Pte.
Bridge, John Lever, 50512 Pte.
Bridge, Robert, 9330 Pte.
Brindley, John, 24155 Pte.
Brindley, Tom, 49007 Cpl.
Brittain, Thos. Edward, 7215 Pte.
Broadhurst, Harry, 50532 A/Cpl.
Broadhurst, Walter, 60518 Pte.
Brockbank, Walter, 20727 Sgt.
Bromley, William, 13799 Pte.
Brookes, Ralph, 10527 Sgt.
Brooks, Allen, 11036 Pte.
Brooks, James Henry, 14287 Pte.
Brooks, Thomas, 9684 Pte.
Broomhall, John Alf., 25966 L/Cpl.
Broughall, Edward, 66869 Pte.

Brown, Ashton, 8783 Pte.
Brown, Arthur Ernest, 57953 Pte.
Brown, Ernest, 6356 Pte.
Brown, George, 18099 Pte.
Brown, James, 27648 Pte.
Brown, Samual, 10507 Pte.
Brown, Simeon, 36855 Pte.
Brown, Thomas, 9744 Pte.
Brown, William Bowden, 53748 Pte.
Browne, George William, 6469 Pte.
Brownhill, David, 7402 Pte.
Brownhill, William, 15741 Pte.
Bruckshaw, Harry, 12278 Pte.
Buchanan, Alexander, 9549 Pte.
Buck, Edmund Brown, 62813 Pte.
Buckley, Arnold, 25674 Cpl.
Buckley, Herbert, 17713 Pte.
Bullock ,William, 6771 Pte.
Bumford, Ed. Luther, 72008 Pte.
Burford, David, 16571 Pte.
Burgess, John, 243251 Pte.
Burgess, Josiah, 9424 Pte.
Burgess, Sam, 36918 Pte.
Burguine, John, 9356 Sgt.
Burke, James, 52011 Pte.
Burke, Patrick, 33550 Pte.
Burkill, John, 10238 Pte.
Burkhill, Samuel, 10266 Pte.
Burnes, Clifford Geo., 40202, Pte.
Burns, John, 10060 Pte.
Burns, John, 11375 Pte.
Burns, William, 8977 Pte.
Butler, Joseph Ernest, 24637 L/Cpl.
Byrne, John, 10088 Pte.
Byrne, William, 9060 Pte.

Cadman, Isaac, 10213 Pte.
Caine, Leonard, 12805 Pte.
Calvert, Arthur, 60538 Pte.
Calvert, Larry, 53882 Pte.
Campbell, William, 26405 Pte.
Carney, John, 11767 Pte.
Carr, William, 10452 Pte.
Carroll, James, 9339 A/Cpl.
Carter, Charles Cedric, 70094 L/Cpl.
Carter, Fred, 49340 Sgt.
Carter, John Lawton, 7472 Pte.
Carter, Thomas, 9484 Sgt.
Carter, Walter, 10337 Pte.
Carter, William, 25784 L/Cpl.
Carter, William, 40230 Pte.
Carter, William, 70083 Pte.
Cartlidge, Albert Edward, 8406 Pte.
Cartwright, Frederick, 51327 Pte.
Carty, Augustus Leo, 10811 A/Cpl.
Caton, Richard Gren., 49122 Pte.
Cave, Harry, 50514 Pte.
Cave, William Hy., 58092 Pte.
Chadwick, Charles, 10890 Pte.
Chadwick, Charles Ed., 35231 Pte.
Chadwick, Fred, 9948 Pte.
Chadwick, Harry Shaw, 35474 Pte.
Chadwick James, 9393 L/Cpl.
Chadwick, Thomas, 26257 Pte.
Chantler, Richard, 7388 Pte.
Chapman, John Edward, 244974 Pte.

Chapman, Luke, 12262 Pte.
Chapman, Philip, 50653 Pte.
Charlesworth, John 7548 Pte.
Chatterton, Clarence, 49034 Pte.
Cheadle, William, 32218 Pte.
Chesters, Frederick, 10185 L/Cpl.
Chilton, Jack, 12137 A/Cpl.
Christian, Robt. Edward, 26386 Pte·
Clague, Walter Douglas, 33776 Pte.
Clark, Henry, 20239 Cpl.
Clark, Richd. Francis, 10164 Pte.
Clarke, Edward, 7812 Pte.
Clarke, Harry Cyrel, 12283 Pte.
Clarke, John, 7432 Pte.
Clarke, Walter, 6227 Pte.
Clayton, Fred 9034 Pte.
Clayton, John Henry, 27829 Pte.
Clayton, William 10375 Pte.
Cliffe, John, 13313 Pte.
Clough, Ernest 17649 Pte.
Clowes, William Clive, 70101 Pte.
Cohen, Harry, 9998 Pte.
Colbert James, 10120 Pte.
Colley, Frank, 70019 Pte.
Collier, John, 33509 Pte.
Collins, Frank, 10816 Pte.
Collins, Richard, 53880 Pte.
Collins, Thomas, 25815 Pte.
Coltman, William 8331 Bdsmn.
Comboy, Michael, 10304 Pte.
Conlon, David, 49008 Pte.
Connell, Edward, 25229 Pte.
Connolly, John William, 10112 Pte.
Conroy, Matthew, 10912 Cpl.
Consil, Frank, 10935 Pte.
Conway, Peter, 12219 Pte.
Cook, Harry, 17945 Pte.
Cook, Henry Laskey, 70072 Pte.
Cooke, Thomas, 6023 L/Cpl.
Cookson, William 12254 Pte.
Cookson, Wm. Farrington, 10791 Pte.
Cooper, Charles, 52108 Pte.
Cooper, Charles Henry, 266049 Pte.
Cooper, David, 49035 Pte.
Cooper, Edward, 266219 Pte.
Cooper, Ernest, 10572 L/Cpl.
Cooper, Fred, 26872 Pte.
Cooper, James Henry, 8217 Pte.
Coops, Frank Nevel, 8676 Sgt.
Coote, Harry 9417 Pte.
Cope, William, 49036 Pte.
Coppock, Gerald, 8069 Pte.
Cordall, Archibald Kay, 65639 Pte.
Cordiner, John Wm., 36700 Pte.
Corker, Bertie, 51551 Pte.
Corrigan, Joseph, 6117 Pte.
Cotterill, John James, 9788 L/Cpl.
Cotterill, Eli, 70100 Pte.
Coward, Norman Nicholson, 60536 Pte.
Cowcill, Frederick, 24771 Pte.
Crawford, Samuel, 9437 Sgt.
Crawford, William, 51538 Pte.
Crawley, Frederick, 10083 Pte.
Crisp, James, 10126 Pte.

Critchlow, William, 49299 Pte.
Cronan, Stephen, 9743 Pte.
Cross, John, 10163 Cpl.
Cross, Thomas, 24055 Pte.
Crow, James Henry, 50691 Pte.
Cryer, George Cecil, 53905 Pte.
Cummings, John, 10258 Pte.
Cunnah, Robert Ellis, 49739 Pte.
Curran, Edward, 9046 Pte.
Currie, Gordon, 49033 Pte.
Curtis, Thomas Bagnell, 60539 Pte.
Cusick, Christopher, 27213 Pte.

Daggers, Joseph, 24452 Pte.
Daglish, Jos. Bucknall, 28334 L/Cpl.
Dale, John William, 10610 Pte.
Dale, Sidney, 8540 Pte.
Dalinsky, Barnett, 49295 Pte.
Dalzell, John, 11039 Pte.
Daniel Charles Henry, 11145 Pte.
Darby, John 11165 L/Cpl.
Darbyshire, Albert, 11926 Sgt.
Davenport, Samuel, 10821 Pte.
Davidson, John Archi., 68631 Pte.
Davidson Robt. George, 49744 Pte.
Davies, Alfred, 52703 Pte.
Davies, Edward, 17569 Pte.
Davies, Fred, 49746 L/Cpl.
Davies, Fred. Horace, 52119 Pte.
Davies, George, 10111 Pte.
Davies, Harry, 10423 Pte.
Davies, Harry, 23268 Cpl.
Davies, James, 49749 Pte.
Davies, John Hugh, 53760 Pte.
Davies, Samuel, 6236 Pte.
Davies, William, 10344 Pte.
Davies, William, 16497 Pte.
Davies, Richard, 28393 Pte.
Davison, Ernest, 68412 Pte.
Dawson, Alfred William, 11202 Cpl.
Dawson, Edward, 60548 Pte.
Dawson, George, 6816 Pte.
Deakin, Samuel, 9428 Cpl.
Deakin, William Henry, 11066 Pte.
Dean, Ernest, 266596 Pte.
Dean, Harry, 24117 Pte.
Dean, Peter, 10325 Pte.
Dedman, James, 53890 Pte.
Deeks, Walter, 8755 Cpl.
Dennis, Thomas, 9951 Pte.
Derby, Ellis, 8936 L/Sgt.
Derbyshire, James, 10574 Pte.
Devaney, Roger, 6150 Pte.
Devenport, Alfred, 25315 Pte.
Diamond, Paul, 18583 Pte.
Dingle, Ernest, 49329 Pte.
Dixon, James, 7831 Pte.
Dobson, Charles, 10444 Pte.
Dobson, Harry, 6426 Pte.
Dobson, James, 58218 Pte.
Dodd, Cecil, 45943 Pte.
Dodd, Frank, 1684 Pte.
Dodgson, Samuel, 6203 Pte.
Doggett, Vincent, 14973 Pte.
Dolan, Thomas, 12033 Pte.
Donegan, Martin Jos., 10649 A/Sgt.

Dootson, Robert, 60545 Pte.
Douglas, William, 9962 Pte.
Dowd, Harry, 8540 Pte.
Doweli, Frederick, 6184 Pte.
Dowling, Patrick, 9037 Sgt.
Downs, William, 35929 Pte.
Doyle, John, 6027 Pte.
Duckworth, Herbert, 49576 Pte.
Duddy, Joseph, 7550 Pte.
Dunn, James, 8539 Pte.
Dunn, William, 10579 Pte.
Dunning, George, 8534 Pte.
Dunning, Walter, 11557 Pte.
Dutton, Horace, 60549 Pte.
Dykes, Charles Peter, 50575 Pte.
Dykes, Reginald, 53894 Pte.

Eames, Owen, 52099 Pte.
Earp, Alfred Harold, 10049 Pte.
Easton, Peter 31934 Pte.
Eastwood, Allen, 10746 Pte.
Eaton, Albert, 12086 Pte.
Eaton, Edward, 9156 Pte.
Eaton, George, 26135 Pte.
Edge, James, 53765 Pte.
Edge, William Alfred 9708 Pte.
Edwards, Albert, 10364 Pte.
Edwards, Alf. Charles, 202045 Pte.
Edwards, Edward, 7680 L/Cpl.
Edwards, John Richard, 53766 Pte.
Edwards, John William, 21867 Pte.
Edwards, Richard, 51517 Pte.
Edwards, Richard, 68089 Pte.
Edwards, Walter John 10322 Pte.
Egerton, George, 26518 Pte.
Eldridge, Charles, 9171 A/R.S.M.
Ellis, William, 7410 Pte.
Ellson, Frank, 265267 Pte.
Emerson, William, 28726 Pte.
Emmett, William, 316129 Pte.
Etherton, Gordon Nor., 51238 Pte.
Evans, Alec, 8172 A/Sgt.
Evans, Evan Gwilym, 67883 Pte.
Evans, Hedley Beely, 60552 Pte.
Evans, John, 10064 Pte.
Eyers, William Henry, 64312 Pte.
Eyres, Thomas, 52097 Sgt.

Fagan, Francis, 6079 Pte.
Fairbrother, Thomas, 26930 Pte.
Fairhurst, Frank, 51592 Pte.
Fairhurst, Joseph, 26530 Pte.
Fallon, William, 9479 Pte.
Faragher, Bertie Alfred, 33752 Pte.
Farr, Charles Ernest, 28399 L/Cpl.
Farrant, Frank William, 7052 Pte.
Farrar, William, 51249 Pte.
Farrell, James, 9397 Pte.
Faulkner, John, 11589 A/Cpl.
Fawcett, Joseph, 8143 Pte.
Fay, James, 12524 L/Cpl.
Fazakerly, Richd. John, 10335 Pte.
Feeney, John, 8036 Pte.
Fieldhouse, Leonard, 10196 Pte.
Fielding, William, 25131 Pte.
Firth, John, 8380 Pte.

Fisher, John Robert, 26120 Pte.
Fishwick, Albert, 26076 Pte.
Fitchett, Richard, 49925 Pte.
Flanagan, John, 5783 Pte.
Flannery, Thomas, 10030 Pte.
Fleming, Wm. Joseph, 28275 Pte.
Fletcher, Joseph Sellars, 14579 Pte.
Fletcher, Vincent, 11971 Pte.
Flitcroft, Harold, 68166 Pte.
Flynn, John, 52009 Pte.
Foley, Thomas, 7114 Pte.
Footsoy, James Robert, 53676 Pte.
Ford Robert, 10859 Pte.
Forshaw, William, 10881 Pte.
Forster, Percy Regd., 36580 Pte.
Foster, John, 5840 Pte.
Fox, Frank Ernest, 8641 Pte.
France, Leonard, 51531 Pte.
France, William, 51560 Pte.
Francis, John William, 7724 C.S.M.
Freeman, Donovan Edgar, 243294 Pte.
Frost, Arthur, 7879 Pte.
Frost, Ernest, 6953 Pte.
Frost, Samuel, 25239 Pte.
Fudge, John William, 25992 Pte.
Fuge, Thomas Robert, 15924 Pte.

Gaff, Michael, 13808 Pte.
Gallagher, John, 19203 L/Cpl.
Gamble, Ernest, 10259 Pte.
Ganner, James, 9578 Pte.
Gannon, Thomas, 11635 Pte.
Gargan, Frank, 9425 Pte.
Garner, Fred, 11704 Pte.
Garrad, Frederick, 10303 Pte.
Garrett, Henry Daniel, 40233 Pte.
Garwood, John Ed., 51299 L/Cpl.
Gash, James Edwin, 10511 Pte.
Gaukroger, John Wm., 6461 Pte.
Gee, David, 12088 Pte.
Gerrard, Frank, 202029 Pte.
Gibbons, John, 12277 Pte.
Gibbons, Walter, 25361 Pte.
Gibson, Thomas, 9349 Pte.
Gildea, James, 242852 Pte.
Gillin, Alfred, 11979 Pte.
Glynn, John, 10278 Pte.
Godsell, William John, 9329 Pte.
Gooch, Edward, 7511 Pte.
Goodall, Edward, 16143 Pte.
Goodier, Sydney, 58265 Pte.
Goodwin, Harry, 28403 Pte.
Goodwin, Thomas, 9690 Cpl.
Gordon, Israel, 49297 Pte.
Gough, Charles, 51432 Pte.
Gray, Arthur James, 8879 Pte.
Green, Charles, 24119 L/Cpl.
Green, Edward James, 9506 Pte.
Green, George, 10223 Pte.
Green, Peter, 9282 Pte.
Green, William, 6288 Pte.
Gregory, Arthur, 14767 Pte.
Gregory, Fred Crossland, 18688 Pte.
Gregory, Harold, 9998 Pte.
Gregory, John, 49042 Pte.

Gregory, Richard, 18048 Pte.
Gregory, Robert, 11912 L/Cpl.
Gregory, Thomas, 51250 Pte.
Griffin, James, 76883 Pte.
Griffiths, Chas.Robt.Henry 8991 Pte.
Griffiths, Jacob, 7597 Pte.
Griffiths, William, 7204 C.S.M.
Griffiths, William, 26432 Pte.
Griffiths, William Phillip, 60561 Pte.
Guest, John, 7673 Pte.
Guy, William, 51533 Pte.

Hadfield, Ernest, 7523 Pte.
Haggerty, John, 9507 Pte.
Halewood, John, 5685 A/Sgt.
Hall, George William, 28024 Pte.
Hall, Robert, 21095 Pte.
Hall, William, 53671 Pte.
Halliday, Thomas, 27567 Pte.
Hallows, Albert, 35776 Pte.
Hallsworth, John, 25806 Pte.
Hallwood, Albert, 68338 Pte.
Hallworth, Herbert, 50464 Pte.
Halsall, James, 33738 Pte.
Hamer, Herbert, 11056 Pte.
Hamlett, Richard, 11554 Pte.
Hammond, John James, 9011 Pte.
Hammond, William, 9268 Dr.
Hampson, Claude, 8789 Pte.
Hampton, Herbert, 7730 Pte.
Hancock, George Wm., 8158 Pte.
Hanson, William, 10582 Pte.
Harding, Joseph, 49361 Cpl.
Harding, Thomas Henry, 9738 Pte.
Hardwick, Albert, 10921 Pte.
Hardwick, Thomas, W/27724 Pte.
Hardy, Albert, 9371 Pte.
Harriss, Gil. Bennett, 24535 L/Cpl.
Harris, John, 28407 Pte.
Harrison, Albert, 241093 Sgt.
Harrison, Albert, 18571 Pte.
Harrison, Albert, 49364 Pte.
Harrison, Alec, 25885 Pte.
Harrison, Charles Cash, 6690 Pte.
Harrison, John William, 8862 Pte.
Harrison, Thomas, 7460 Pte.
Harrison, Thomas, 53060 Cpl.
Harrison, William, 25838 Pte.
Harrison, William, 49049 Pte.
Harrison, Wm. Henry, 65643 Cpl.
Harrop, Fred, 49016 L/Cpl.
Harrop John, 4409 L/Cpl.
Harrop, William, 202143 Pte.
Hart, Hugh, 11504 Pte.
Hartley, Hugh, 49053 Pte.
Hartley, Thomas, 10538 Pte.
Hatton, William, 10134 Pte.
Haughton, John Robert, 9862 Pte.
Havakin, James, 27417 Pte.
Hawkins, John, 6861 Pte.
Hayes, Thomas, 10512 Pte.
Haywood, Samuel, 12026 Pte.
Hazelgrave, Geo. Wm., 51548 Pte.
Hazelhurst, Thomas, 10815 Pte.
Heaps, Richard, 34793 Pte.
Hefferan, Francis James, 9879 Pte.

Hemmingway Percy, 40214 Pte.
Henderson, Thomas, 19222 Pte.
Hennessy James, 8209 Sgt.
Henshall, James, 7491 Pte.
Herrity, Patrick, 8011 Pte.
Hesketh, Charles, 70010 Pte.
Hewitt, Herbert, 7982 Pte.
Hewitt, Thomas, 6932 Cpl.
Hewson, Richard, 10388 A/Sgt.
Hibbert, Henry, 7024 Pte.
Higginbottom, Herbert, 64901 Pte.
Higginbottom, Samuel, 10918 L/Cpl
Higgins, John Henry, 10955 Pte.
Higginson, Thomas, 10023 Pte.
Hilditch, Samuel, 10006 Pte.
Hilditch, Thomas, 10309 Pte.
Hill, Arthur, 10158 Pte.
Hill, James, 8803 Pte.
Hill, William, 8749 Pte.
Hilton, Percy, 10728 Pte.
Hind, Robert Lewis, 10637 Pte.
Hindley, George, 63560 Pte.
Hines, James, 6377 Pte.
Hixson, David John Stanley, 68128 Pte.
Hobson, John, 10944 Pte.
Hockenhull, Harry, 18691 Pte.
Hodgkinson, George, 25208 Pte.
Hodgkinson, Joe, 28406 Pte.
Hogan, Edward, 9696 Dvr.
Holbrook, Geo. Wm. 7579 Pte.
Holden, William, 8269 Pte.
Holder, James, 7290 L/Cpl.
Holebrook, Allan, 202096 Pte.
Holland, David John, 15072 Pte.
Holland, James, 12273 Pte.
Holland, John, 260236 Pte.
Holloway, Fran. Edward, 9858 Pte .
Holmes, William, 9054 Pte.
Holt, Alfred, 10271 L/Cpl.
Honeywell, Thomas, 51296 Pte.
Hood, Harold, 8778 Pte.
Hoole, Samuel, 49048 Pte.
Hooley, Joseph, 76900 Pte.
Hope, Ernest, 244978 Pte.
Hopkinson, Harry, 29530 Pte.
Hopwood, Luke, 7628 Pte.
Horobin, James, 10265 Pte.
Horton, Ernest, 26153 Pte.
Hoseason, Gil. Bruce, 316136 Pte.
Hough, Henry, 7411 Pte.
Houghton, Harry, 7308 Pte.
Houghton Rich. Edward, 9119 Pte.
Houghton, William, 8948 Pte.
Howard, Cephas, 25219 Pte.
Howard, Percy, 26113 Pte.
Howarth, Frank, 70023 Pte.
Howarth, John Wm., 67489 Pte.
Howell, Jess, 23498 Pte.
Howells, Herbert Wm., 8753 Pte.
Hoyle, William, 9648 Pte.
Hughes, Edward, 4829 L/Cpl.
Hughes, Edward, 6759 Pte.
Hughes, Frank, 10552 Pte.
Hughes, James, 25210 Pte.
Hughes, Thomas, 13539 Pte.

Hull, William Henry, 10089 Pte.
Hulse, Thomas, 12945 Pte.
Hummer, Edmund, 60572 Pte.
Humphreys, Harry, 49752 Pte.
Humphreys, Wm. Henry, 50557 Pte.
Humphreys George Charles Edward, 68133 Pte.
Humphries, Percy Ernest, 6410 A/Sgt.
Hunt, George, 7112 Pte.
Hunt, Ralph, 10981 Pte.
Hunt Robert, 9332 Pte.
Hunt, Robert William, 51594 Pte.
Hunt, Walter, 24435 Pte.
Hunter, Harry, 51519 L/Cpl.
Huson, Richard, 6589 Cpl.

Ingham, Thomas, 53621 Pte.

Jackson, Frank Arnold, 10541 Pte.
Jackson, George, 265191 Sgt.
Jackson, John, 8185 Cpl.
Jackson, Samuel, 9564 Cpl.
Jackson, Thomas, 291790 Pte.
Jackson, Walter, 17960 Pte.
Jared, Walter, 17881 L/Cpl.
Jarrett, George, 20017 Pte.
Jeanes, Wm. John, 10440 Pte.
Jefferson, William, 11258 Pte.
Jenkins, Arthur, 6591 Pte.
Jepson, John Edward, 9242 Pte.
Jepson, Noah, 11094 Pte.
Jervis, Collin, 51552 Pte.
Jevins, Herbert, 68246 Pte.
Jinks, Percy, 18259 Pte.
John, Jack, 68123 Pte.
Johnson, Albert, 10109 Pte.
Johnson, Chas. Ernest, 7568 A/Sgt.
Johnson, Frederick, 12271 Pte.
Johnson, Har. Percival, 68248 Pte.
Johnson, Herbert, 51596 Pte.
Johnson, Mark, 36212 Pte.
Johnstone, Walter, 35505 Pte.
Jones, Albert, 49306 Pte.
Jones, Charles, 14095 Pte.
Jones, Chas. Edward, 28291 Pte.
Jones, Cyril, 49759 Pte.
Jones, David, 49238 L/Cpl.
Jones, Ernest, 9653 Sgt.
Jones, Evan, 49767 Pte.
Jones, Fred, 49366 A/Cpl.
Jones, Frederick, 9515 Pte.
Jones, Frederick, 9619 Pte.
Jones, Henry, 9001 Pte.
Jones, Herbert, 8858 Pte.
Jones, Herbert, 7279 Pte.
Jones, John 10200 Pte.
Jones, John, 28808 Pte.
Jones, John Arthur Lloyd, 33148 L/Cpl.
Jones, John Benjamin Stanley, 60581 Pte.
Jones, Johnny, 18733 Pte.
Jones, Jonah, 53782 Pte.
Jones, Joseph, 7451 Pte.
Jones, Owen John, 51595 Pte.
Jones, Robert Charles Garnett, 40260 Pte.

Jones, Robt. Owen, 10056 Pte.
Jones, Stephen, 10167 Pte.
Jones, Thomas, 10969 L/Cpl.
Jones, Thomas, 26265 Pte.
Jones, William, 7833 Pte.
Jones, William, 8019 Pte.
Jones, William, 9799 Pte.
Jones, William Edgar, 9674 Pte.
Jones, William Edward, 25976 Pte.
Jones, William Henry, 1069 Pte.
Jowett, John Edwin, 70029 Pte.
Jowitt, Clarence, 10000 Pte.
Joyce, Peter, 25942 L/Cpl.

Kay, William, 50531 L/Cpl.
Keens, Fred. James, 25236 Pte.
Kelly, Edward, 49066, Pte.
Kelly, Edward, 68320 Sgt.
Kelly, John Edward, 25120 Pte.
Kelly, John Martin, 11666 Pte.
Kelly, Joseph, 9834 Pte.
Kelly, Nicholas, 10389 Pte.
Kelly, Patrick, 315159 Pte.
Kelly, Thomas, 52101 Pte.
Kenrick, Sidney, 27945 Pte.
Kenworthy, George, 10026 Pte.
Kilfoyle, John James, 35022 Pte.
Kilgallen, John, 10632 Pte.
King, Charles Alfred, 7926 Pte.
King, Harry, 25359 Pte.
Kingston, James, 10106 Pte.
Kinsey, James, 26393 Pte.
Kirby, Frank, 25870 L/Cpl.
Kirk, James, 49817 Pte.
Kirkham, Ben. Howard, 243183 Pte.
Kirkham, John, 243269 Pte.
Kitchen, Harold Geo., 10583 Pte.
Knight, Edward, 11516 Pte.
Knowles, John, 49067 Pte.
Knowles, John Rich. 50547 Pte.

Lacy, Samuel, 9956 Pte.
Lafbery, Sydney Thos., 25186 Pte.
Lally, Walter, 10260 Pte.
Larkin, Thomas, 20856 Pte.
Latham, William, 7424 Pte.
Latimer, George, 11271 Pte.
Laurence, Ron. Trevor, 72220 Pte.
Lawson, Ernest, 76863 Pte.
Lawson, Frank, 68080 Pte.
Lawson, Henry, 70033 Pte.
Lawson, Lewis, 70080 Pte.
Lawton, Geo. Henry, 11509 Pte.
Leach, Patrick, 11678 Pte.
Leach, William, 49820 Pte.
Leary, John, 8806 Pte.
Lee, William, 50559 Pte.
Leece, John Henry, 33808 Pte.
Leese, Alfred, 49292 Pte.
Leigh, Thomas, 9342 Pte.
Leonard, Alfred, 7344 Pte.
Leonard, Thomas, 49128 Pte.
Leonard, William, 18588 Pte.
Letton, Frederick John Geo., 53669 Pte.
Le Vesconte, Percy, 51556 Pte.

Lewis, John, 9715 L/Cpl.
Lightfoot, Edward, 8302 L/Cpl.
Lindsey, William, 53061 Pte.
Ling, George, 10161 Pte.
Little, Bruce, 12655 Pte.
Littlemore, Isaac, 11389 Pte.
Lloyd, George, 12110 Pte.
Lloyd, James, 7553 Pte.
Lloyd, John, 20931 Pte.
Lloyd, Wm. Edward, 28748 Pte.
Locke, Albert William, 8847 Pte.
Lomas, Thomas, 72048 Pte.
Long, George, 49068 Pte.
Long, Henry, 7436 L/Cpl.
Long, Walter, 12202 L/Cpl.
Long, Walter, 25311 Pte.
Lord, Lewis, 32010 Pte.
Lorenzoni, Enst. Luigi, 40172 Pte
Lowe, Edward, 6508 Pte.
Lowe, John, 14448 Pte.
Lowe, Timothy, 10539 Pte.
Lucas, Ernest Lionel, 8649 Pte.
Lynchey, John Charles, 33773 Pte.
Lyons, Thomas, 51303 Pte.

Mabey, Arthur, 8444 Pte.
Mack, Alfred, 7721 A/Sgt.
Madden, John, 10367 Pte.
Mahore, Peter, 18769 Pte.
Makin, Thomas, 202031 Pte.
Mallard, William, 40180 Pte.
Mandeville, Joseph, 10313 Sgt.
Manley, Herbert, 10059 Pte.
Manley, James, 9632 Pte.
Mariano, Paul, 25005 Pte.
Marr, James, 49079 Pte.
Marrow, Fred, 8284 Pte.
Marsden, Thomas, 27113 Pte.
Marsh, Edwin, 10102 A/Cpl.
Marshall, Edward, 9881 Pte.
Marshall, George, 52012 Pte.
Marshall, Harold, 72271 Pte.
Marshall, Harry, 60590 Pte.
Martin, John, 266615 Pte.
Martin, John Alfred, 11182 A/Cpl.
Mason, Robert Stanley, 16534 Pte.
Mason, Thomas, 5696 Pte.
Massey, William, 7049 Pte.
Mather, Joshua, 11531 Pte.
Matkins, Jos. Alf. James, 72436 Pte.
Matthews, Chas. Fred, 52127 Pte.
Matthews, Percy, 33786 Pte.
Matthews, Wm. Edward, 49774 Pte.
Matthews, Wm. Henry, 10569 Pte.
May, Wm. Joseph, 260242 Cpl.
McCaffrey, John, 49778 Pte.
McCall, George, 60596 Pte.
McCann, William, 7769 Pte.
McCarroll, Maurice Hy., 32597 Pte.
McCarthy, Frank, 7085 Cpl.
McClellan William, 6830 Pte.
McCormick, William, 49381 Pte.
McCullock, Victor, 9839 Pte.
McDean, William, 7225 Pte.
McDermott, James, 7034 Pte.
McDonald, Harry, 10093 Pte.

McDonald, Joe, 10585 Pte.
McDonald, Robert, 5771 Pte.
McDonnell, Myles, 68233 Pte.
McGarry, Joseph, 5772 A/Cpl.
McGrath, James, 12212 Pte.
McGrath, Wm Henry, W/470 Pte.
McGregor, Charles, 51812 Sgt.
McKay, Charles Anthony, 9289 Pte.
McKay, John, 202093 Pte.
McLachlan, James, 68104 Pte.
McMahon, John, 10187 Pte.
McNaught, Wm. Claude, 50997 Pte.
McPhilemy, John, 50040 Cpl.
McReth, Henry, 8587 Pte.
McVeety, William, 6915 Cpl.
McVey, James, 266199 L/Sgt.
Meachem, George Fred., 53031 Pte.
Measham, Joseph, 34759 Pte.
Meek, William, 49077 Pte.
Meikle, Frederick, 202237 Pte.
Melling, George Arthur, 9785 Pte.
Mellor, Arthur, 8175 Pte.
Mellor, Wm. Albert, 53630 Pte.
Merrifield, Henry, 40266 Pte.
Metcalfe, Thomas, 10447 Pte.
Miller, Herbert, 25868 Pte.
Miller, William James, 33524 Pte.
Molyneux, George, 15993 Cpl.
Molyneux, J. Tarbuck, 11062 A/Cpl.
Moore, Fred, 9872 Pte.
Moore, Henry, 49071 Pte.
Moore, James, 7313 Pte.
Moore, John, 11314 Pte.
Moore, Thos. Jubilee, 12046 Pte.
Moore, William Henry, 6851 Pte.
Morgan, Arthur, 40264 Pte.
Morgan, Percy Lewis, 27100 Pte.
Morris, Frank, 22145 Pte.
Morris, George Thos., 7805 Pte.
Morris, John, 27109 L/Cpl.
Morton, William, 10508 Pte.
Moses, Fred, 27351 L/Cpl.
Mosley, George, 25201 A/Cpl.
Moss, Charles Albert, 8658 Pte.
Moss, James, 26377 Pte.
Moss, Thomas, 11582 Pte.
Moss, William, 45488 Pte.
Mossop, William, 8245 Pte.
Moston, Sidney, 6342 Sgt.
Mott, John William, 6014 Pte.
Mottershaw, William, 12265 Pte.
Mottershead, Harold, 25700 Pte.
Mountford, Thomas, 7317 Pte.
Mulley, Thos. Stone Lewis, 6657 Pte.
Mullins, Alfred, 50560 Pte.
Mullock, William, 10493 Pte.
Mulrooney, Owen, 10682 Pte.
Mundy, Frank, 40178 Pte.
Munro, Hugh, 5943 Pte.
Murphy, Patrick, 31674 Pte.
Murphy, Robert, 9927 Pte.
Murray, Patrick, 9672 Pte.
Mylan, Michael, 8969 Pte.

Nancarrow, Ernest, 11355 Pte.
Navin, John, 51580 Pte.

Naylor, John, 25474 Pte.
Needham, Joseph, 10543 Cpl.
Neil, William, 8326 Pte.
Neild, William Cecil, 16533 Pte.
Nelson, Joseph, 245982 Pte.
Newell, Horace Andrew, 36803 Pte.
Newhouse, Fred, 7435 A/Cpl.
Newsham, William John 10108 Pte.
Newton Geo. William, 10960 L/Cpl.
Nicholson, William, 5259 Pte.
Nicklen, Leonard, 18876 Pte.
Neild, Fred, 49305 Pte.
Nixon, James, 27484 Pte.
Nobbs, Charles, 50567 Pte.
Noble, Harry, 11976 Pte.
Noblett, Edward Wm., 51555 Pte.
Nolan, Henry, 10083 Pte.
Nolan, James, 10379 Pte.
Noon, Patrick, 15582 L/Cpl.
Norbury, William, 16624 Pte.
Norman, Frank, 7699 Cpl.
Norris, Arthur, 44205 Pte.
Nott, George Frederick, 68236 Pte.
Nuttall, Charles, 8610 Pte.

Oakes, Edward, 34968 Pte.
Oakes, John Arthur, 10654 Pte.
O'Berry, Albert, 15875 Pte.
Oddie, James Henry, 9587 Pte.
O'Donnell, John Leo., 8344 L/Cpl.
Ogden, Harry, 6306 Pte.
Ogden, Thomas, 28297 Pte.
Ogden, William Henry, 9840 Pte.
O'Kell, John, 7134 Pte.
O'Loughlin, James, 24985 Pte.
O'Malley, Edward, 8459 Pte.
O'Neil, John, 31826 Pte.
O'Neill, James, 10731 Pte.
O'Neill, William, 49542 Pte.
Onion, Thomas, 244966 Cpl.
Ormes, Leonard, 10085 Pte.
Ormson, Harry, 68238, Pte.
Over, Richard, 10131 A/Cpl.
Owen, John, 10062 Pte.
Owen, Joseph, 8264 Pte.
Owens, Wm. Henry, 26093 L/Cpl.
Pannell, Cuthbert, 9322 Pte.
Park, Joseph Henry, 9545 Pte.
Parker, Alfred, 10267 Pte.
Parker, Charles, 49789 Pte.
Parker, Charles Wm., 51199 L/Cpl.
Parker, James, 24796 Pte.
Parkinson, Frederick, 26779 Pte.
Parkinson, Harry, 28062 L/Cpl.
Parkinson, Joe, 10328 Pte.
Parrott, Edward, 12227 Pte.
Parry, Albert, 17056 Pte.
Parry, Arthur Lloyd, 49786 Pte.
Parry, Joseph Henry, 11215 Pte.
Parsons, Roger, 9065 Pte.
Parsons, Thomas, 7233 Pte.
Pattin, William, 10079 Pte.
Peach, Joseph, 10065 Pte.
Peacock, Frank Stephen, 10175 Pte.
Peake, James Chadwick, 25246 Cpl.
Peake, Walter, 492 87 A/Cpl.

Pearce, Arthur, 10518 Pte.
Pearson, Herbert, 11633 L/Cpl.
Pearson, Thomas, 6986 Pte.
Pennington, William Thompson, 66575 Pte.
Percival, Joseph, 10362 Pte.
Percival Joseph, 10707 Pte.
Perkins, Jack, 49788 Pte.
Perkins, Wm. Edward, 10302 Pte.
Phipps, Edward Thos., 12033 Pte.
Phipson, George, 21774 Pte.
Pickford, Fred, 76896 Pte.
Plant, Harry, 11510 Pte.
Platt, Charles John, 51601 Pte.
Plimmer, George, 9791 Pte.
Plumtree, Harry, 10555 Pte.
Poole, Harry, 6497 Pte.
Poole, John, 10985 Pte.
Postlethwaite, James, 9711 Pte.
Potts, Dexter, 14232 L/Cpl.
Potts, Fred, 30793 Pte.
Potts, James, 9327 Pte.
Potts, James, 49116 Pte.
Powell, Alick, 13145 Pte.
Powell, George, 49087 Pte.
Pownall, Charles, 11815 Pte.
Pratt, Reg. William, 70008 Pte.
Prescott, Frank, 57247 Pte.
Prest, Fred, 51208 L/Cpl.
Preston, John, 31832 Cpl.
Price, Christopher Wm., 11597 Pte.
Price, John Watkin, 8771 Pte.
Pritchard Herb. Francis, 28298 Pte.
Prosser, William, 50391 Pte.
Proudman, Christopher, 7437 Sgt.
Proven, James, 51205 Pte.
Purches, John William, 7270 Sgt.
Pyott, Frederick, 12271 Pte.

Quale, Evan Edwin, 28667 Pte.
Quigley, Bernard, 17647 Pte.
Quinn, Frank, 9793 Pte.

Ralphs, Charlie, 53644 Pte.
Ramsey, Ernest, 51452 Pte.
Ratcliffe, Frank, 49341 Pte.
Rawlinson, William, 8716 Pte.
Rayner, George Wm., 25919 Pte.
Raynor, Fred, 27811 Pte.
Reade, James, 290640 Pte.
Redfern, Joe, 12261 Pte.
Reeves, Henry, 50335 Pte.
Renshaw, James, 52103 Pte.
Renshaw, John Wm., 201977 Pte.
Revell, Joseph, 266218, Pte.
Rice, Owen, 27482 Pte.
Rich, Garnett, 72351 Pte.
Richards, Frederick, 20611 A/Cpl.
Richards, James Bowen, 53642 Pte.
Richards, Thomas, 53643 Pte.
Richards, Wm. Sidney, 51413 Pte.
Richardson, Charles, 12273 Pte.
Richardson, Ernest, 8295 Pte.
Rigby, Albert, 11101 Pte.
Riley, Frederick, 7008 Pte.
Rimmer, Geo. Herbert, 50543 Cpl.

Robbins, Wilfred, 28443 Pte.
Roberts, Ernest, 9220 Pte.
Roberts, Isaac, 7483 Pte.
Roberts, William James, 9993 Cpl.
Roberts, John, 5968 Pte.
Roberts, John, 49793 Pte.
Roberts, Samuel Isaac, 52675 Pte.
Roberts, Thomas, 8824 A/Sgt.
Roberts, Thomas, 52115 Pte.
Roberts, Walter, 12667 Pte.
Roberts, William, 12028 Pte.
Roberts, Wm. Henry, 49795 Pte.
Roberts, William Stanley, 9213 Cpl.
Robertson, Harry, 10340 Pte.
Robinson, Frank, 9469 Pte.
Robinson, George, 45748 Pte.
Robinson, John, 8643 Pte.
Robinson, John Wm., 10581 Pte.
Robinson, Joseph, 9259 Pte.
Robinson, Richard, 11526 Pte.
Robinson, Wm. Alfred, 29716 Pte.
Robinson, Wright, 10711 L/Cpl.
Rogers, George, 67951 Pte.
Rogers, J. Darlington, 15878 Cpl.
Rogers, John William, 9325 Pte.
Rogers, Michael, 8538 Pte.
Rogers, Robert, 15225 Pte.
Rogerson, Thomas, 50978 Sgt.
Roman, James George, 20046 Pte.
Roseblade, Geo. Henry, 64308 Pte.
Ross, Alexander, 9889 Pte.
Rossington, Harry, 7923 C.S.M.
Rousseau, Alexander, 26565 Pte.
Rowland, Edward, 51307 Pte.
Rowland, Walter, 12253 A/L/Cpl.
Rowlands, Jos. Fred., 11807 A/Sgt.
Rowley, Frederick, 18417 L/Cpl.
Rule, Stanley, 9891 Pte.
Rushton, William, 11583 Pte.
Russell, Harold, 33733 Pte.
Rustage, Joseph, 10713 Pte.
Rutter, Cyril, 10282 Pte.
Ryan, Michael, 21906 Pte.
Ryder, James, 9986 Pte.

Salt, Henry, 10413 Pte.
Salt, Joseph, 40199 Pte.
Sanders, Thomas Chris., 11754 Pte.
Sandlands, Charles, 18205 Pte.
Sargent, William, 9487 Pte.
Saunders, Fred. Charles, 34894 Pte,
Scarfe, William Herbert James. 59846 Pte.
Schofield, Harold, 49375 Pte.
Scott, Albert Henry, 17759 Cpl.
Scott, Charles, 11575 Sgt.
Scott, Mark, 10500 Pte.
Scragg, James, 8145 A/Sgt.
Seddon, Charles Henry, 68097 Pte.
Sharp, Arthur, 241338 Pte.
Shaw, Harry, 12481 Pte.
Shaw, Martin, 52471 Pte.
Shaw, Wm. Frederick, 40218 Pte.
Sheen, Martin, 18856 Pte.
Shepley, Samuel, 10568 Pte.
Sherwin, Thomas, 10310 Pte.

Sherwood, Harry, 7063 Pte.
Shirt, Bertie, 25113 Pte.
Shoebridge, Walton Jas., 28458 Pte.
Siddorn, Frank, 34810 L/Cpl.
Sidebottom, Frank, 12263 Pte.
Simpson, Wm. Henry, 10256 Pte.
Slater, Frank Edward, 10195 Pte.
Sleigh, James, 10898 Pte.
Smale, James, 49095 Pte.
Smith, Ezra, 10342 Pte.
Smith, George, 35711 Pte.
Smith, Hugh, 6595 Pte.
Smith, James, 8336 Cpl.
Smith, James Alfred, 7496 Pte.
Smith, John Michael, 68161 Pte.
Smith, Leonard Victor, 10399 Pte.
Smith, Reuben, 10398 A/Cpl.
Smith, Robert, 10019 Pte.
Smith, Wilfred, 70049 Pte.
Smith, William, 8833 Pte.
Smith, William James, 9991 L/Cpl.
Snowdon, Charles, 68190 Pte.
South, Charles, 68263 Pte.
Sparkes, Robert, 10082 Pte.
Sparrow, Henry, 8746 A/Sgt.
Spencer, Frank, 9038 Pte.
Spencer, Henry, 244964 L/Sgt.
Spencer, James, 6637 Pte.
Spencer, James, 76882 Pte.
Spencer, Samuel, 8931 Pte.
Spencer, Thomas, 18563 Pte.
Spiden, George, 40197 Cpl.
Stagg, Edward Charles, 9453 Pte.
Stagg, William, 53647 Pte.
Staniforth, Edmund, 10448 Cpl.
Stanton, Hugh, 11990 Pte.
Stanton, John, 9308 Pte.
Stapleton, Ernest, 24280 Pte.
Stead, George, 10665 Pte.
Stead, William Thos., 10685 Pte.
Stebbings, Leo. Herbert, 40151 Cpl.
Stephens Joseph, 51195 Cpl.
Stephenson, George, 20325 Pte.
Stephenson, William, 51190 L/Sgt.
Stevens, John, 49376 Pte.
Stewart, Thomas, 10162 Pte.
Stockton, John Thos., 18619 Pte.
Stokes, Frederick, 9798 Pte.
Stokes, Leonard, 265323 Pte.
Storey, William, 202057 Pte.
Stringer, Jonathan, 25257 Pte.
Suffler, John James, 53646 Pte.
Sullivan, Dennis, 9519 L/Cpl.
Sumnall, Charles, 9885 Pte.
Sutherland, William, 27702 Pte.
Sutton, Percy Wm., 243221 Pte.
Swann, John, 51220 Pte.
Swann, Joseph, 9160 Pte.
Sweeney, Luke, 7031 Pte.
Swift, Ephraim, 7911 Pte.
Swindells, Thomas, 49101 Pte.
Swinson, George, 8542 Pte.
Sykes, Joseph, 49106 Pte.
Sykes, Rowland Mar., 9973 Pte.

Tait, Harry Albert, 40198 L/Cpl.

R

Tankard, Cecil, 50431 L/Sgt.
Tattersall, James Bray, 15652 Pte.
Taylor, Arthur 8922 Cpl.
Taylor, Ben, 241590 Pte.
Taylor, Bert, 12415 Pte.
Taylor, Bowker, 9748 Pte.
Taylor, Fred. James, 49107 Pte.
Taylor, Harry, 12196 Pte.
Taylor, Herbert, 49346 Pte.
Taylor, Walter, 8891 Sgt.
Taylor, William, 12746 L/Cpl.
Taylor, William, 33771 L/Cpl.
Tedcastle, Herbert, 9995 Pte.
Telford, Albert Edward, 28837 Pte.
Temple, John, 9917 Pte.
Tharme, Albert, 51215 Pte.
Thelwell, Arthur, 12478 Pte.
Thomas, David, 26031 Pte.
Thomas, George, 8386 Pte.
Thomas, George, 10257 Pte.
Thomas, Joseph, 51554 Pte.
Thomas, Wilfred Geo., 53649 Pte.
Thompson, Frank, 8823 Pte.
Thompson, John, 8814, L/Cpl.
Thompson, J. Thomas, 25923 L/Cpl.
Thomson, John, 7001 Pte.
Thomson, William, 10152 Pte.
Thomson, William, 59563 A/Cpl.
Thornley, Albert, 26672 Pte.
Thornton, James, 10495 Pte.
Thorpe, Fred, 8315 Pte.
Threadgold, Wal. Thos., 33507 Pte.
Tipper, Thomas, 6590 Pte.
Titterton, Stanley, 50572 Pte.
Tollis, Ernest, 68331 Pte.
Tomkinson, John, 8817 Pte.
Tomlinson, Fred, 67950 Pte.
Tonge, Sam. Radford, 6973 Pte.
Topping, Herbert, 49581 Pte.
Townsend, Arthur, 10282 Pte.
Townsend, William, 52131 Pte.
Traynor, John, 9927 Pte.
Trent, Edmund, 7606 Pte.
Triggs, Alexander, 11356 Pte.
Tuff, Jonathan, 10164 Pte.
Tunbridge, Harry Henry, 51545 Pte.
Turland, Jack, 8921 Pte.
Turner, Alfred, 7793 Pte.
Turner, George, 25818 Pte.
Turner, Harry, 9808 Pte.
Tushingham, Edward, 10276 Pte.
Tushingham, Harry, 49801 Pte.
Tydd, Alexander, 36326 Pte.
Tye, Thomas, 9892 Pte.

Unsworth, James, 8720 Pte.

Vaughan, Thomas, 7144 Pte.

Venables, Fred, 10058 Pte.
Vickers, John, 12433 L/Cpl.
Waddington, John, 36636 Pte.
Wakefield, Geo. Alfred, 18309 Pte.
Walden, Arthur William Joseph,
	6360 Pte.
Walkden, Wal. Cecil, 244190 Pte.

Walkden, William, 292023 Pte.
Walker, Albert, 68146 Sgt.
Walker, Albert Stephen, 7768 Pte.
Walker, Ernest, 20588 Cpl.
Walklett, Joseph, 7570 Cpl.
Wall, James, 11749 Pte.
Wallbank, John Wm., 50783 Pte.
Wallbank, William, 10903 Pte.
Walsh, John, 45050 Pte.
Walsh, Patrick, 9424 Pte.
Walton Jesse, 24579 Pte.
Walton, Sydney, 49373 Dr.
Warburton, Albert, 8403 A/Sgt.
Warburton, James Wm., 19671 Pte.
Warburton, Joseph, 6135 Pte.
Ward, Harold Bertram, 10025 Pte.
Ward, John Thomas, 10759 Pte.
Wardle, George, 8567 Pte.
Wardle, William, 27168 Pte.
Waring, Richard, 10117 Pte.
Waring, Thomas, 30638 Pte.
Waring, William, 36577 Pte.
Warren, Francis, 7227 Pte.
Weaver, Benjamin, 10683 Pte.
Weaver, John, 25185 Pte.
Webb, David, 6458 Pte.
Webster, John, 40289 Pte.
Webster, Henry Sydney, 53652 Pte.
Webster, Robert, 18476 Pte.
Welsh, James, 11770 Pte.
West, Arthur, 36281 Pte.
West, William James, 51275 Pte.
Westwell, Thos. Henry, 24754 Pte.
Westwood, Joseph, 49370 Pte.
Whaley, Harold, 40288 Pte.
Wheeler, Harry, 8730 Pte.
Wheeler, Robert, 10381 Pte.
Whipp, George Fred., 51258 Pte.
Whitby, Ernest, 68253 Pte.
White, Jonathan, 11133 Pte.
Whitehead, Fred, 53663 Pte.
Whitehouse, Wm. Hy., 51530 Pte.
Whiteley, Abraham, 53658 Pte.
Whiteley, Sam, 7835 Pte.
Whitlow, John, 8097 L/Cpl.
Whittaker, Arnold, 76877 Pte.
Whittaker, Arthur, 15256 Pte.
Whittaker, Fred, 49809 Pte.
Whittaker, John, 17584 Pte.
Whittaker, Samuel, 7257 Pte.
Whittle, Arthur, 11081 A/Sgt.
Whittle, Fred, 70059 Pte.
Wight, John Skeldon, 51322 Pte.
Wigley, George, 10135 Pte.
Wild, Edwin, 9887 L/Cpl.
Wildig, Robert, 10220 Pte.
Wilkinson, Charles, 12103 Pte.
Wilkinson, Daniel, 10608 Pte.
Wilkinson, Holford, 9147 L/Sgt.
Wilkinson, Jeremiah, 7462 Pte.
Wilkinson, Percy, 18222 Pte.
Willers, Robert, 70090 Pte.
Williams, Albert John, 7645 Pte.
Williams, Geo. Edward, 13735 Pte.
Williams, Geo. Joseph, 6976 Pte.
Williams, Harold Morris, 49804 Sgt.

Williams, Henry, 11764 Pte.
Williams, Horace, 8900 Pte.
Williams, Hugh, 10451 Pte.
Williams, Idris Chas., 65863 A/Cpl.
Williams, James, 8820 Pte.
Williams, Rees, 7510 Pte.
Williams, Robert, 49110 Pte.
Williams, Thomas, 25261 A/C.S.M.
Williams, Thos. Fred., 68175 Pte.
Williams, William, 265151 Pte.
Williams, Wm. Joseph, 9937 Pte.
Williamson, James, 10371 Pte.
Williamson, Jas. Albert, 10169 Pte.
Willock, Thomas, 244989 Pte.
Wilson, Arthur, 68182 Pte.
Wilson, William, 10880 A/Sgt.
Winterbotham, Harry, 6800 Pte.
Wise, Stanley, 50542 Pte.
Witkiss, Charles, 10549 Pte.
Wood, Alfred, 49108 Pte.
Woodall, James, 49112 Cpl.
Woodcock, Frederick, 11009 Pte.
Woods, Richard, 18871 Pte.
Woodward, Geo. Henry, 9811 Sgt.
Woodward, Harold, 25232 Pte.
Woodward, John Willie, 15089 Pte.
Woodward, Thomas William Light-
	foot, 8130 Pte.
Woof, Louis, 52072 Pte.
Wooton, Frank Francis, 58012 Pte.
Worrall, John, 24228 Pte.
Worsley, John, 49365 Pte.
Wright, Arthur, 9653 Pte.
Wright, Ernest, 9866 Pte.
Wright, George, 9910 Pte.
Wright, Hugh, 27131 Pte.
Wright, Joshua, 11372 Pte.
Wright, Joseph, 51324 Pte.
Wright, Walter, 35152 Pte.
Wright, Wilfred, 10401 Pte.
Wrigley, Benjamin, 25108 Pte.

Yates, Wilfred, 28113 Pte.
York, John 7249 Pte.

Zugg, Alfred, 12265 Pte.

SECOND BATTALION.

Ainsworth, Leonard, 24129 Pte.
Allen, Edwin, 25153 Pte.
Allen, Frank, 14919 Pte.
Allman, Frank, 9536 Cpl.
Angus, Robert, 9818 Pte.
Archibald, Daniel, 26501 A/Sgt.
Ardern, Fred, 11005 Pte.
Arkwright, John, 28100 Pte.
Armstrong, Oliver, 8732 Pte.
Ashton, James, 12262 Pte.
Ashton, Samuel, 13378 Cpl.
Astles, Alfred, 8379 Pte.
Aston, John, 15188 Pte.
Atherton, Frank, 9102 Sgt.
Atkinson, George, 8821 L/Cpl.
Avison, John Robert, 8658 L/Cpl.

Bagnall, William, 8382 Pte.

Baigent, Wilfred Ernest, 8483 Pte.
Bailey, Leonard, 10226 Pte.
Baines, Samuel, 28084 Pte.
Banks, John, 9839 Pte.
Barlow, John Henry, 8918 A/C.S.M.
Barlow, Samuel, 9075 Pte.
Barlow, Thomas, 26407 Pte.
Barnes, Albert, 9205 Pte.
Barrow, Wilfred, 25482 Pte.
Barry Edward, 25551 L/Cpl.
Bate, John, 18175 Pte.
Baxter, James, 25736 A/Cpl.
Baynton, Sam Harris, 9334 Pte.
Beckwith Albert Edwin, 66301 Pte.
Bedda, Fred, 9259 Pte.
Bell, Thomas, 10383 Pte.
Bennett, Edward, 10939 Pte.
Berry, Charles Enst., 9701 A/R.S.M.
Birtles, Samuel, 11035 Pte.
Blackburn, Thomas, 28081 Pte.
Blackshaw, Robert, 28082 Pte.
Blanton, John, 9170 Pte.
Bleasdale, Arthur, 11214 Sgt.
Blinston, John, 18252 Pte.
Blythe, Frederick, 9723 Cpl.
Boon, Richard, 18287 Pte.
Booth, Joseph, 8851 Pte.
Booth, William, 9930 L/Sgt.
Bowen, Arthur, 28120 Pte.
Bowers, Edward, 9959 Pte.
Boyd, Harold, 9014 Pte.
Bradbury, Jordan, 18426 Pte.
Bradden, William, 10754 Pte.
Bradley, John, 10330 L/Cpl.
Brickell, Thos. Regd., 18732 Pte.
Bridgwood, William, 8414 Pte.
Broadbent, Tom, 9700 Sgt.
Broome, Ernest, 8375 Pte.
Buckley, Wilmot, 25893 Pte.
Buffham, Tom John, 49456 Pte.
Burgess, Joseph, 9982 Pte.
Burke, Michael, 12241 Pte.
Burke, Samuel, 9267 Pte.
Burke, William, 9516 Pte.
Butler, Wm. Patrick, 33826 Pte.

Callaghan, Francis, Pat., 9415 Pte.
Callaghan, John, 9945 Pte.
Callow, William Edward, 28533 Pte.
Campbell, Ricd. Andrew, 25526 Pte.
Cannell, Herb. Ratcliffe, 25160 Pte.
Capper, Frederick, 9697 L/Cpl.
Cardwell, William, 10461 Pte.
Carmen, Henry, 9629 Pte.
Carrier, Wm. Thoday, 25637 Pte.
Carson, Norman, 18268 Pte.
Carter, James, 12522 Pte.
Cartledge, Frederick, 10296 Pte.
Carty, John, 9009 Pte.
Caulfield, Daniel, 11675 Pte.
Chambers, Albert Norris, 25303 Pte.
Charles, Harry, 8886 A/Cpl.
Cherlton, Harry, 9959 Pte.
Cheshire, James, 6769 Sgt.
Childes, Chas. Clifford, 10394 Pte.
Christopher, Thomas, 6540 Pte.

Clare, Stephen, 10953 Pte.
Clarke, Geo. Henry, 26931 Pte.
Clarke, Joseph Percy, 12258 Pte.
Clegg, Thomas, 24391 3 Pte.
Clue, Harry, 9254 Pte.
Clutterbuck, Robert, 25490 Pte.
Coe, Edward, 7656 A/C.Q.M.S.
Coldicott, Harry, 7903 Pte.
Collins, Fred. Arthur, 8853 Pte.
Cooper, Geo. Harold, 25853 L/Cpl.
Corrigan, John, 25486 Pte.
Cousins, George, 8689 Pte.
Cowley, Fred, 28571 L/Cpl.
Cowperthwaite, George, 57211 Pte.
Cox, William, 11040 A/Cpl.
Cresswell, Ernest, 9227 Pte.
Croft, Charles, 24973 Pte.
Cross, Ernest, 10792 Pte.

Dacey, John, 18209 Pte.
Dalton, John, 7212 Sgt.
Dance, Harry Arthur, 9193 Pte.
Davenport, Rodger, 10452 Pte.
Davies, Arthur, 9944 Pte.
Davies, Charles Fred., 8978 Pte.
Davies, John, 9094 Pte.
Davies, John, 9118 Pte.
Davies, Thomas Henry, 28584 Pte.
Dawson, Harold, 26431 Pte.
Dawson, William, 11960 Pte.
Dean, Frank, 12116 Pte.
Dean, James, 12475 Pte.
Dean, Thomas Henry, 9293 Cpl.
Devine, James Thos., 33592 Pte.
Dewsnap, Joseph, 18383 Pte.
Dodd, Edwin, 11828 Pte.
Doughty, Christopher, 9323 L/Cpl.
Downs, George, 18864 Pte.
Doyle, John, 9335 Pte.
Duggan, James, 10745 Pte.
Dunbebin, George, 18549 L/Cpl.
Dutton, Thomas, 8096 Pte.
Dutton, William Henry, 8499 Pte.
Dykstra, James, 10301 Pte.
Dyson, William, 11689 Pte.

Early, William John, 6102 C.S.M.
Eastup, Albert, 18181 Pte.
Edwards, John 26587 Pte.
Elliott, Robert James, 28156 Pte.
Ellis, Edwin, 9149 Pte.
Espley, Richard, 11961 Pte.
Evans, Edward, 7392 Pte.
Evans, George Ernest, 26669 Pte.

Farmer, John Wm., 8350 L/Cpl.
Faulkner, Isaac, 202203 Pte.
Fields, Thomas, 8232 Cpl.
Fitter, Chas. Henry, 8237 C.Q.M.S.
Fleet, Charles, 14056 Pte.
Fletcher, Walter, 18386 Pte.
Foley, William, 8406 Pte.
Freeman, Jesse, 9286 Pte.
Fry, Thomas Henry, 18208 Pte.

Gain, Joseph, 7974 Pte.

Galbraith, Donald, 6076 Pte.
Gallagher, Frank Alden, 25860 Pte.
Gamble Arthur James, 8964 Pte.
Gardner, Arthur, 10419 Pte.
Garlick William, 9238 Sgt.
Gaskell, Robert, 12288 Pte.
Gee, Harry, 8021 Pte.
Gibbons, Austin, 25535 Pte.
Gibson, Edward Percy, 9666 Pte.
Gilbert Thomas, 6833 Pte.
Gilligan, Alfred, 11739 Pte.
Goddard, David James, 9087 Pte.
Godrich, Bert, 9124 Cpl.
Godwin, Joseph, 9176 Pte.
Goley, John James, 8170 Sgt.
Goodfellow, Percy, 25898 Pte.
Goodman, Robt. Stan., 33865 L/Cpl.
Gough, James, 8433 Pte.
Goulborne, William, 24872 Pte.
Gradwell, John, 11262 Pte.
Grant, Wm. Henry, 12217 L/Cpl.
Greatbanks, George, 25924 Pte.
Griffin, William, 12098 Pte.
Griffiths, John, 10597 Pte.
Griffiths, Wm. Arthur, 9697 Pte.

Hackney, Harold, 8556 Pte.
Hall, Alfred, 10564 Pte.
Hammond, James, 14400 Pte.
Hammond, William, 11982 Pte.
Hammond, William, 25915 Pte.
Hamnett, John, 9956 Pte.
Hamond, Chas. Sydney, 33872 Pte.
Hampson, Edwin, 9325 Pte.
Handforth, Frederick, 9228 Pte.
Hands, Charles, 8784 L/Cpl.
Harding, George, 25888 Pte.
Harding, Richard, 9754 A/L/Cpl.
Harper, William, 9300 Pte.
Harris, James, 12398 Pte.
Harrison, Arthur, 9721 Pte.
Haskell, Vincent Froud, 9831 Pte.
Hatton, Richard, 9782 Pte.
Haughton, John Wm., 16626 Pte.
Hayward, Alf. Enst., 8407 A/R.S.M.
Haly, William, 25871 Pte.
Heapey, Ernest, 26398 Pte.
Hearne, William, 8946 Pte.
Hellewell, John, 58326 Pte.
Hesketh Charles, 10587 Pte.
Heywood, Lewis, 10767 Pte.
Heywood Robert, 25547 Pte.
Hibbert, Frederick, 11051 Pte.
Hickson, Clarence, 26097 Pte.
Hickson, Thomas Wm., 8146 Pte.
Higgins, Allan, 9232 L/Cpl.
Hinchcliffe, Christopher, 12306 Pte.
Hinchcliffe, John Wm., 8832 Pte.
Hobday, Frank, 18874 Pte.
Hodgson, Ernest, 66236 Pte.
Hogan, Wm. Edward, 9242 Sgt.
Holland, Thomas, 66215 Pte.
Hollingworth, Joseph, 10087 Pte.
Holt, Clifford, 33387 L/Sgt.
Holt, Herbert, 8715 Pte.
Holt, John Edward, 9258 L/Cpl.

Hoolahan, Joseph, 1411 Pte.
Hopley, William, 12484 Pte.
Hough, Thomas, 8091 Pte.
Hughes, Frederick, 8694 Pte.
Hughes, George, 6483 Pte.
Hughes, George William, 9035 Pte.
Hughes, John, 25751 Pte.
Hughes, Richard, 25263 Pte.
Hughes, Robert, 12291 Pte.
Hulme, Horace, 9091 L/Cpl.
Hutchins, Daniel, 33880 Pte.
Hyde, William, 9915 Pte.
Hynes, James, 26723 Pte.

Ibbetson, Walter, 25489 Pte.
Igo, Patrick, 7082 Pte.
Ince, Harry, 36551 Pte.
Inglis, John Downey, 28612 Pte.
Isherwood, Thomas, 16179 Pte.

Jackson, Thomas, 9742 Pte.
Jackson, Thomas, 10196 Cpl.
Jennings, Charles Wm., 25241 Pte.
Jepson, Fred, 9157 Pte.
Johnson, John, 9314 Pte.
Johnson, Samuel, 8877 Pte.
Joinson, Peter, 9291 Pte.
Jones, Alfred, 25521 Pte.
Jones, Frank, 12541 Pte.
Jones, Harry, 25872 Pte.
Jones, Jack, 25487 Pte.
Jones, Robert Thomas, 5411 Pte.
Jones, Thomas, 11517 Pte.
Jones, Walter, 8768 Pte.

Kane, John William, 10766 Pte.
Kay, John Frederick, 9123 Pte.
Kelly, Joseph, 10764 Pte.
Kelly, Mark, 12139 Pte.
Kent, Herbert Charles, 76328 Pte.
King, George Albert, 28042 Pte.
Kirkham William, 25891 Pte.
Kirkpatrick, Thomas, 7665 Pte.
Kirwin, Dominick, 8727 Pte.
Kitchen, Thos. Barker, 8775 A/Sgt.
Knowles, Harry, 27314 Pte.

Lace, Thomas, 25324 Pte.
Laidler, Joseph, 18579 Pte.
Lamb, Basil Henry, 66253 Pte.
Latham, William, 26913 Pte.
Lauder, Jas. Rowlinson, 18365 Pte.
Law, Gideon, 25726 Pte.
Lawson, Jack Richard, 12276 Pte.
Lawton, James, 25203 Pte.
Lea, John William, 9609 Cpl.
Lee, John Henry, 8685 L/Cpl.
Lee, Leonard, 12030 Pte.
Leeks, Arthur Ernest, 28044 Pte.
Lees, Thomas Rishton, 11742 Pte.
Leigh, James, 8307 L/Cpl.
Le Lacheur Walter, 25354 Pte.
Lester, Joseph, 8148 A/Sgt.
Lewis, Job. 28107 Pte.
Lewis, John, 7153 Pte.
Lightburn Samuel, 15127 Pte.

Lightfoot, Ernest, 11695 Pte.
Lilley, Albert, 18198 Pte.
Lilley, Thomas, 18207 Pte.
Linney, George, 9502 Pte.
Littlewood, Albert, 25270 Pte.
Lloyd, Emmanuel, 24640 Pte.
Locke, George, 11946 Pte.
Lomax, Harry, 28047 Pte.
Long, Joseph, 8856 Pte.
Longworth, Henry, 18101 Pte.
Lynch, William, 6046 Pte.

Macdonald, Thomas, 18229 Pte.
Maddocks, William, 8702 Pte.
Manley, Frank, 9946 L/Cpl.
Mansell, Charles Edward, 9813 Pte.
Marsden, Thomas, 28423 Pte.
Mason, George Wm., 18153 Pte.
Mathison, Fred, 24644 Pte.
Matley, Albert, 17469 Pte.
Mayes, Charles, 9523 Pte.
McBrides, Andrew, 10510 Pte.
McCarty, Wm. Harry, 25854 L/Cpl.
McGee, John, 66217 Pte.
McGowan, Peter, 9591 Pte.
McGrue, Harry, 12598 Pte.
McKay, Herbert, 8005 Sgt.
McMahon, John, 6647 Pte.
Mellor, James Arthur, 12505 Pte.
Mellors, Harry, 28422 Cpl.
Merrils, George, 28429 Pte.
Mewett, Frederick, 8888 Pte.
Miles, James, 9001 Pte.
Miller, Joseph, 28326 Pte.
Mills, James Hartley, 28095 Pte.
Michell, Joseph, 6958 L/Cpl.
Monger, Charles, 8598 A/C.S.M.
Moore, Nathan, 8228 Pte.
Moores, William, 8115 C.Q.M.S.
Moorhouse, Josiah, 11168 Pte.
Morgan, Daniel Thos. 9160 Pte.
Morgan, Frank Wm., 9951 Pte.
Morgan Herbert Matt., 8633 L/Cpl.
Morrison, Duncan, 64684 Pte.
Morton, Thomas, 9050 Pte.
Moxon, Ben. Jefferson, 57218 Pte.
Mullheron, Joseph, 11950 Pte.
Mullineux, William 8064 Sgt.
Munt, George, 9148 Pte.
Murray, Arthur, 25541 Pte.
Mutter, Albert, 26884 Pte.

Nadin, Harry, 25656 Pte.
Nelson, George, 58584 Pte.
Norton, Joseph, 28432 Pte.
Nutting, Walter, 12314 Pte.

Oldham, Alfred, 17312 Pte.
Owen, James, 24655 Pte.

Page, Thomas, 10183 Pte.
Parker, George, 18183 Pte.
Parker, Samuel Cain, 28438 Pte.
Parratt, William, 9497 Pte.
Parry, Arthur, 7949 Sgt.
Parry, Joseph, 25252 Pte.

Patterson, Michael, 10324 Pte.
Pawson, Walter, 57223 Pte.
Pearson, Arthur, 9141 Sgt.
Penlington, Wm. Hy., 315426 Pte.
Pentelow, Fred, 8007 Pte.
Percival, Henry, 9138 Pte.
Pickering, Thomas, 28132 Pte.
Pinder, Joseph, 26030 Pte.
Pitchers, Herbert, 25389 Pte.
Platt, Frank, 9633 Pte.
Platt, Fred, 11072 Pte.
Plover, James Joseph, 28070 Pte.
Porter, George, 8791 Pte.
Potter, Thomas, 11164 Cpl.
Powell, Edward, 12201 Pte.
Powell, Frederick, 8980 Pte.
Prescott, John, 18185 L/Cpl.
Press, Joseph, 24216 Pte.
Price, Robert, 8159 Pte.
Prince, John Edward, 11601 Pte.
Pritchard, James, 9620 Pte.
Procter, Cecil Herbert, 58657 Pte.
Profit, Harry, 9473 Pte.
Pursehouse, William, 315727 Pte.

Quinn, Andrew, 11944 Pte.
Quinn, John Henry, 11020 Pte.
Quirk, William Edward, 28673 Pte.

Randall, Alfred, 25760 Pte.
Randall, James, 25287 Pte.
Randle, Thomas, 28440 Pte.
Rathbone, William, 26216 Pte.
Ravenscroft, Robert, 10345 Pte.
Rawlings, John Wm., 14280 Pte.
Rawlinson, William, 6988 A/Cpl.
Reading, Jos. Ernest, 9645 Bdsm.
Redfern, Arthur, 9755 Pte.
Redfern, Robert, 9330 Pte.
Renney, Alf. Chas. Hart, 26028 Pte.
Renshaw, John Wm., 9434 Pte.
Reynolds, Ferdinand, 28441 Pte.
Richmond, Percy, 28439 Pte.
Ridgway, Walter, 266505 Pte.
Riley, Herbert, 6160 Pte.
Riley, Maurice James, 24793 Pte.
Roberts, Alfred, 8142 Pte.
Roberts, Arthur Samuel, 9080 Cpl.
Roberts, Peter, 13473 Pte.
Roberts, Thomas, 7009 Pte.
Roberts, Wm. Joseph, 33010 Pte.
Robinson, Chas. Edward, 10142 Pte.
Robinson, Thomas, 11753 Pte.
Rogers, Fredk. Leonard, 7802 Pte.
Rothwell, William, 76356 Pte.
Routledge, George, 10965 Pte.
Rowan, John, 10653 Pte.
Rowarth, George Wm., 8336 L/Cpl.
Rowlands, Jesse, 25843 Pte.
Royle, Harry, 10107 Pte.
Royle, John, 12404 Pte.
Royle, Wm. Thomas, 11535 Pte.
Rushton, Jack, 18621 Pte.
Russell, Chris. Vincent, 7526 Pte.

Sadler, Horace, 7602 L/Cpl.

Sansom, Oswald, 28453 Pte.
Sant, Oscar Wood, 26826 Pte.
Sarginson, John, 9702 Pte.
Schofield, Alfred, 12204 Pte.
Schwer, Fredk. Herbert, 5532 Dr.
Scott, James, 28099 Pte.
Screen, Thomas, 10142 Pte.
Scully, John, 6593 Pte.
Sears, Bertie, 9419 Pte.
Senior, George, 14964 Pte.
Sexton, William, 9878 Pte.
Shakeshaft, Percy Ewart, 25463 Pte.
Sharkey, James Thos., 8171 Pte.
Sharples, George, 9896 Pte.
Sharpley, Mark, 10132 Pte.
Shaw, Samuel, 9548 Sgt.
Sheehan, James, 12289 Pte.
Shepherd, Thomas Wm., 9705 Pte.
Shepherdson, Robert, 203303 Pte.
Sherlock, William, 18132 Pte.
Shirt, Charles, 10727 Pte.
Shuttleworth, Walter, 58377 Pte.
Sigston, James Edward, 18330 Pte.
Sills, Arthur, 8537 Pte.
Simmons, James, 28191 L/Cpl.
Simnor, Robert, 15928 Pte.
Sines, James, 9348 Pte.
Skillicorn, J. Bram., 28496 A/Sgt.
Skinner, William, 315434 Pte.
Slavin, Joseph, 9923 Pte.
Smith, Arthur, 12272 Cpl.
Smith, Joseph, 28363 Pte.
Smith, Sydney, 10542 Pte.
Smith, William, 8982 Pte.
Smith, Wm. Henry, 26727 Pte.
Smith, Wm. Henry, 243754 Pte.
Smyth, Michael, 9698 Pte.
Spruce, John Wm. Stan., 12268 Pte.
Stokes, Wm. Fredk., 9989 Pte.
Stubbs, Thomas Hill, 26009 L/Cpl.
Sullivan, Edward, 5481 Sgt.
Sullivan, John, 25849 Pte.
Sweeney, Patrick, 25548 Pte.
Sweeney, Thos. Fredk., 28457 Pte.
Swift, George, 25807 Pte.
Swindells, Cyril Chas., 9055 Pte.
Swinden, James Sydney, 315439 Pte.

Taylor, Frederick, 8962 Pte.
Tharby, George William, 58618 Pte.
Thomas, Arthur, 9808 Pte.
Thomas, Edward, 10613 Pte.
Thomas, Fredk. George, 12021 Pte.
Thomas, William, 28465 Pte.
Thomason, Jas. Albert, 12396 Pte.
Thomason, Wm. Ed., 13916 Cpl.
Thompson, Harry, 9869 Pte.
Thompson, Henry, 10441 Pte.
Thompson, Jack, 25861 Pte.
Thompson, John, 8515 Pte.
Thompson, William, 11959 Pte.
Thomson, Thomas, 9622 Pte.
Toole, James, 12402 Sgt.
Torpey, Thomas, 33269 Pte.
Trundley, Fredk. Wm., 25850 Pte.
Turner, Ephraim, 12370 Pte.

Turner, John, 11053 Cpl.

Upton, Ernest, 18358 Pte.

Varty, John Gordon, 9525 Pte.
Vickers, Harry Ray, 8706 L/Sgt.
Vigden, William, 8802 Pte.

Wainwright, Norman, 8492 Pte.
Waldram, Arthur, 28469 Pte.
Walker, Charles Henry, 9704 Pte.
Walker, Frederick, 8854 Pte.
Walker, John, 25507 Pte.
Walker, Percy James, 25469 Pte.
Walsh, Leonard, 9533 Pte.
Ward, Patrick, 7180 S/Sgt.
Wardle, George, 24303 Pte.
Washbrook, John, 10039 Pte.
Waterman, William, 25181 Pte.
Watkin, Thomas, 8756 A/Sgt.
Watkin, Walter, 25436 Pte.
Weatherley, John, 25766 Pte.
Weaver, Thomas, 8106 Pte.
Weir, Alex. Jas. Stuart, 66257 Pte.
Weir, John, 6907 Sgt.
Welsh, Alfred, 9119 Cpl.
West, Alf. Wm. Harold, 8462 Pte.
Whaley, John Francis, 9261 A/Cpl.
Whalley, Ernest, 9228 Pte.
Wheeldon, William, 25424 Pte.
Wheelton, Fred, 11960 Pte.
White, Chas. Antony, 11006 Pte.
Whitehall, Thos. Walter, 25503 Pte.
Whitehead, Frank, 202636 Pte.
Whitehurst, Joseph, 18272 Pte.
Whittaker, John, 11581 Pte.
Whittaker, Joseph, 7920 Pte.
Wilbraham, William, 26571 Pte.
Wilkinson, J. Holland, 27670 Pte.
Williams, Edward, 11945 Pte.
Williams, Evan, 9820 Pte.
Williams, John, 25558 L/Cpl.
Williamson, Joseph, 8200 Pte.
Winkle, Thomas, 25824 Pte.
Winter, Albert, 10882 Pte.
Wissenden, Leo. Nelson, 9306 Pte.
Wood, John, 8482 Pte.
Wood, Joseph, 6268 Sgt.
Wood, Robert, 18233 Pte.
Wood, William Brown, 12795 Pte.
Woodcock, Geo. Henry, 9510 Pte.
Woodcock, James, 10619 Pte.
Woodhouse, Arthur, 9047 A/L/Sgt.
Woodward, George, 8254 Pte.
Woolley, John, 10239 Pte.
Wrench, Robert, 12578 Pte.
Wright, Arthur, 10708 Pte.
Wright, George, 11943 Pte.
Wycherley, Chas. Spen., 5197 Sgt.
Wynne, James, 8215 A/Sgt.

Young, James, 25456 Pte.
Yoxall, George, 9485 Cpl.

THIRD BATTALION.
Atkinson, Allen, 78622 Pte.

Bailey, Daniel, 77345 Pte.
Bennett, Joseph, 18372 Pte.
Birchall, John, 62789 Pte.
Black, Charles, 59340 Pte.
Bowyer, John, 12280 Pte.
Burch, Alfred, 12053 Sgt.
Burgess, John, 27609 Pte.
Bushell, Evan, 8420 Pte.

Carroll, Edward Henry, 8655 Pte.
Chadwick, Henry, 10478 Pte.
Cooke, Arthur, 77097 Pte.
Cragg, Charles, 62149 Pte.
Critchley, Shadrack, 25196 Pte.

Davies, Fred, 45334 Pte.
Disley, John, 11789 Sgt.
Done, William, 18940 Pte.

Gaskell, Albert Edward, 8924 Pte.
Gregory, Harry, 27397 Pte.

Halton, William Arthur, 35467 Pte.
Hargraves, James, 266051 Pte.
Harrop, Alfred, 17478 Pte.
Haskins, Francis Win., 27909 A/Cpl.
Hodgkinson, Harry, 64780 Pte.
Hopley, Albert, 77248 Pte.
Horan, Thomas, 33071 Pte.
Hurst, Edward, 11318 Pte.

Johnson, Harry, 77087 Pte.
Jones, Alfred, 36906 Pte.
Jones, Ernest Leo, 35525 Pte.
Jones, Samuel, 9334 Pte.

Lebby, Jack, 26962 Pte.
Lee, Charles, 34855 Pte.
Lee, George, 26121 Pte.
Lewis, John Thomas, 36245 Pte.
Long, Alfred, 25895 L/Cpl.
Lucas, George, 33127 Pte.

McDonnell, Thomas, 14956 Pte.
McKean, John Alex., 8493 Pte.
McMichael, Frederick, 45156 Pte.
Melrose, Robert, 77253 Pte.
Moore, Harry, 11203 Pte.

Oldham, James Ward, 16220 Pte.

Parry, Thomas Evan, 35042 Pte.
Pilgrim, Thos. Alb., 8761 C.Q.M.S.
Pritchard, Wm. George, 33409 Pte.

Quayle, John, 33660 Sgt.

Robertson, Donald, 61610 Pte.

Scott, John, 18719 Pte.
Sharpe, Robert, 8233 Pte.
Sproston, Herbert Rees, 81526 Pte.
Stanton, Thomas Wm., 62423 Pte.
Stevenson, Thos., 9211 A/C.Q.M.S.

Taite, John, 15206 Pte.

Taylor, Robert, 10869 Pte.
Thompson, John Wm., 62148 Pte.
Thompson, Joseph, 34152 Pte.
Timperley, Wm. Ezra, 10503 L/Cpl.
Travis, Har. Jardine, 33031 L/Cpl.
Turner, Frank, 19373 Sgt.

Wainwright, Leonard, 33467 Pte.
Whiston, William, 26818 Pte.
Wilkinson, Thomas, 7898 Pte.
Williams, George, 25063 Pte.
Williams, John, 24788 Boy
Wilson, William, 12474 Pte.

8th BATTALION.

Adamson, Frank, 34565 Pte.
Alcock, Arthur, 27174 Pte.
Allman, Arthur, 11553 Pte.
Amsler, Albert Charles, 64516 Pte.
Andrews, Oscar, 10678 Cpl.
Ankers, Noel, 24447 Pte.
Antrobus, Thomas, 24377 Pte.
Arnold, Edwin, 24457 L/Cpl.
Ashall, Peter, 31007 Pte.
Atkinson, Fredk. Wm., 10737 Pte.

Bailey, James, 11039 Sgt.
Barnes, Richard, 24697 Pte.
Baronian, Haron, 33006 Pte.
Bate, William, 11086 Pte.
Bates, George, 9675 Pte.
Battersby, Chas. Burn., 10972 Sgt.
Beacall, Harry Ernest, 12571 Pte.
Beardmoor, Joseph Har., 33421 Pte.
Bell, Donald McAckran, 11717 Pte.
Bell, Thomas, 11716 A/Cpl.
Bell, William, 11288 Pte.
Bennett, Alfred, 10646 Sgt.
Bennett, Tom Hyde, 35457 Pte.
Berrington, Thomas, 24254 Pte.
Berry, Joseph, 26247 Pte.
Birtles, James, 10489 Pte.
Blackburn, John Joseph, 26570 Pte.
Blanton, William, 9140 A/Sgt.
Booth, John Wood, 34753 Pte.
Boothby, Alfred, 24261 Pte.
Bowers, James, 18416 Pte.
Bowyer, Harold, 11590 Pte.
Bowyer, William, 18430 Pte.
Brabenetz, Walter, 12557 Pte.
Bradwell, Frank, 11107 Pte.
Bramhall, Harry, 11030 Pte.
Bramley, Frederick, 58990 Pte.
Brereton, Joseph, 32800 Pte.
Brierley, Frederick, 24426 Pte.
Bristor, William John, 11624 Pte.
Brocklehurst, Harry, 34554 Pte.
Broderick, James, 12463 Pte.
Brough, Wilfred, 24737 Pte.
Brown Ernest, 16231 L/Cpl.
Brown, Harry, 10149 Sgt.
Brown, Isaac, 12065 Pte.
Buckley, Samuel, 34537 Pte.
Bunkall, Joseph, 11411 Sgt.
Burgess, Thomas, 34839 Pte.
Burningham, Ber. Stan., 35252 Pte.

Burns, Eugene, 24587 L/Cpl.
Burrows, Albert, 18213 Pte.
Burrows, Thomas, 35425 Pte.
Bushby, John, 32743 Pte.
Butler, Albert Edward, 10908 Pte.
Byrne, William, 27070 L/Cpl.
Byrom, Thomas, 33329 Pte.

Camble, Jas. Ernest, 17917 L/Cpl.
Cameron, James, 11147 Pte.
Cantwell, Patrick, 11396 Cpl.
Carr, Sydney, 11298 Pte.
Carter, Charles, 11239 L/Cpl.
Carter, Charles Richard, 9875 Pte.
Carter, Thomas, 11467 Pte.
Cartlidge, Ernest, 18674 Pte.
Cartwright, Thomas, 20428 Pte.
Casey, George, 1102 Pte.
Cash, Alex. Robert, 33339 Pte.
Chamberlain, Arthur, 11349 Pte.
Chapman, Thomas, 26735 Pte.
Charmer, Edward, 26233 Pte.
Cheadle, John, 20416 L/Cpl.
Cheetham, Edward, 26212 Pte.
Christopher, James, 10781 Pte.
Clarke, Arthur, 24203 Pte.
Clayton, Harry, 13434 Pte.
Cliffe, Charles, 36453 Pte.
Clowes, Sydney, 11401 Sgt.
Cobbe, Arthur Francis, 18235 Pte.
Conley, Charles, 11053 Pte.
Cope, Leslie, 26036 Pte.
Cork, Benjamin, 27145 Pte.
Counsell, Arthur, 24629 Pte.
Craddock, Alfred Henry George, 31004 Pte.
Cross, Harry, 9244 Cpl.
Cross, William Sanders, 33342 Pte.
Crowther, Fred, 11151 Pte.
Cundiff, Harry, 34678 Pte.
Currie, Joseph Charles, 10600 Pte.

Daniels, Arthur, 32884 L/Cpl.
Davies, Frederick, 64785 Pte.
Davies, Harry, 24018 Pte.
Davies, Harry, 24708 Pte.
Davies, Henry, 26942 Pte.
Davies, John Alb. Pugh, 33396 Pte.
Davies, Sydney, 11429 A/Cpl.
Davies, William, 24646 Pte.
Dawson, Edward, 34557 Pte.
Dawson, Frank, 26780 Pte.
Dean, Francis, 12599 L/Cpl.
Dickens, Frederick, 11574 Pte.
Dobbins, George, 31067 Pte.
Dolan, Thomas, 30898 Pte.
Duffield, Tom, 11213 Pte.
Duggan, Joe, 26864 Pte.
Dunn, Harry, 24058 Pte.

Edwards, Elijah James, 31005 Pte.
Evans, Henry, 24229 Pte.
Fallon, James, 10716 Pte.
Farmer, James Henry, 35223 Pte.
Farnall, Francis Lance., 35502 Pte.
Ferguson, Robert, 11099 L/Cpl.

Fielding, George, 32960 L/Cpl.
Flavell, John Ernest, 36925 Pte.
Fletcher, Edward, 10806 Pte.
Flindle, Percy, 26449 Pte.
Florance, Jack, 9215 Cpl.
Foxey, Harry, 34644 Pte.
Franks, George Crosby, 35404 Pte.
Fraser, William Percy, 10654 Pte.
French, George, 25829 Pte.

Garlick, William, 10652 Sgt.
Garner, Charles, 18340 Pte.
Garside, Curtis Cuthbert, 10861 Pte.
Gaskell, Thos. Richard, 9686 Sgt.
Gathercole, Thomas, 11415 Pte.
Gibbons, James, 18775 Pte.
Gillingham, Joseph, 26239 Pte.
Glover, Ernest James, 12379 Pte.
Goodier, Alfred, 15660 Pte.
Grace, Harry, 35730 Pte.
Grantham, Joseph, 10630 Pte.
Green, George, 27324 Pte.
Green, William, 33430 Pte.
Gresty, Walter Egerton, 25447 Pte.
Griffiths, James, 10695 Pte.
Griffiths, Sydney, 26759 Pte.
Grindrod, James, 34633 Pte.
Groark, William, 11267 Pte.
Guiray, Daniel, 25985 Pte.

Hadley, William Albert, 11508 Pte.
Hague, Frank Oswald, 26692 Pte.
Hall, Louis Ranger, 36278 Pte.
Hallam, John, 10752 Pte.
Hallworth, Walter, 27270 Pte.
Hancock, Thomas, 14054 Pte.
Hardisty, Charles, 58978 A/C.S.M.
Harp, George, 6089 C.S.M.
Harper, William, 11576 Pte.
Harris, Wm. Fernando, 10696 Pte.
Harrison, Harold, 11606 L/Cpl.
Harrison, John, 24199 Pte.
Harrison, Thomas, 31006 Pte.
Harrop, Frank, 12771 Pte.
Hartness, David, 10647 L/Cpl.
Hatton, William, 30627 Pte.
Hegerty, Nathaniel, 26356 Pte.
Herald, Thomas Alex., 30620 Pte.
Herbert, Fredk. Paul, 34946 Pte.
Hewitt, Robert Edward, 32748 Pte.
Higgins, William, 24414 L/Cpl.
Higgins, Wm. George, 9307 L/Cpl.
Higginson, Nathan, 11257 L/Cpl.
Hindle, Percy, 26449 Pte.
Hitchinson, Horace, 64818 Pte.
Hodgkinson, James, 10707 Cpl.
Hodson, Thos. Francis, 33668 Cpl.
Hollahan, David, 10625 Pte.
Holmes, James, 11167 Pte.
Holt, Thomas, 24406 Pte.
Hooper, William, 26836 Pte.
Hopkins, John Wilfred, 32852 Pte.
Horne, Frank, 12024 Pte.
Horner, James, 26282 Pte.
Horrocks, Harold, 24552 Pte.
Houghton, Frederick, 26067 L/Cpl.

Hughes, John James, 18336 Pte.
Hughes, Wilfred, 45944 Pte.
Hulme, Ed. Ardern, 27108 L/Cpl.
Hunt, David, 10612 Pte.
Hunter, James, 44365 Pte.
Hurd, Joseph, 59000 Pte.
Hushin, John, 18251 Pte.

Icke, Samuel, 10697 Sgt.
Illidge, Harry, 16098 L/Cpl.

Jackson, Benjamin, 12328 Pte.
Jackson, Stuart, 10376 Pte.
Janes, David, 14091 Sgt.
Janion, Samuel Harry, 33279 Pte.
Johnson, George, 26993 Pte.
Johnson, James Arthur, 34617 Pte.
Jones, Arthur, 59257 Pte.
Jones, Joseph, 24264 Pte.
Jones, Thos. Edward, 25179 Pte.
Jones, William Allen, 24733 Pte.
Jones, William James, 28038 Pte.

Keene, Edward, 11232 Pte.
Kennerley, George, 34972 L/Cpl.
Kennedy, Henry, 26634 Pte.
Kiddie, Frank, 27248 Pte.
Kinsella, Enoch, 12947 Pte.
Kirby, Tom James, 23395 Pte.
Kirkham, James, 18632 Pte.
Kirkham, Samuel, 25779 Cpl.
Knott, Thomas, 33189 Pte.

Lawless, Michael, 32768 Pte.
Ledsham, Robert James Joseph, 34890 Pte.
Lee, George, 24175 Pte.
Lee, Herbert, 26154 Pte.
Lee, Tom, 11243 Pte.
Lee, Wilfred, 18665 Pte.
Lee, William, 10611 Pte.
Leese, Harry, 11729 Pte.
Lewis, Edward, 59002 Pte.
Lewis, James, 34806 Pte.
Lewis, William, 11377 Pte.
Littler, Reginald, 65011 Pte.
Lloyd, Albert Eardley, 18693 L/Cpl.
Lloyd, Harry, 26468 Pte.
Lloyd, Thomas, 12233 Pte.
Lloyd, Thomas, 33422 Pte.
Logan, James, 33313 Pte.
Lomax, James, 17783 Cpl.
Longworth, William, 28166 Pte.
Lowe, William, 18228 Pte.
Lowthian, Abraham, 15501 Sgt.

Macer, William, 30682 Pte.
Maddock, Richd. Henry, 24208 Pte.
Maddocks, William, 11261 Sgt.
Maddocks, Wm. Edward, 27336 Pte.
Maher, Stephen James, 30130 Pte.
Maiden, Eli, 33455 Pte.
Maloney, Daniel, 59004 Pte.
Martin, Samuel, 24384 Pte.
Mason, John, 10514 Pte.
Mather, Harry, 11683 Pte.

Matthews, James Robt., 10668 Pte.
Mayman, Percy, 34749 Pte.
McColgin, George, 12045 L/Cpl.
McDonald, Patrick, 24601 Pte.
McDonald, Robert, W/735 L/Cpl.
McGrath, Michael, 10648 Pte.
Meakin, Thomas, 24050 Pte.
Meloy, Frederick, 59005 L/Cpl.
Melville, Herbert, 35228 Pte.
Metcalf, Robert, 11383 Pte.
Middleton, Samuel, 11186 Pte.
Millhench, James, 24334 Pte.
Miller, Edward, 59007 Sgt.
Mitchell, John, 243486 Pte.
Mooney, George, 10595 Pte.
Moore, Thomas, 45948 Pte.
Moores, John Foy, 11548 Pte.
Moores, Wilfred, 11310 Cpl.
Morgan, Leo, 35572 Pte.
Morris, John, 35888 Pte.
Morton, George, 27806 Pte.
Mottram, James, 18437 Pte.
Murray, Herbert, 18140 Pte.
Musgrave, Clarence, 14263 Pte.
Myers, Charles, 24665 Pte.

Neville, James, 18725 Pte.
Neville, William, 24181 Pte.
Nevitt, John, 11517 Pte.
Newton, Harry, 26213 Pte.
Nicholson, Leonard, 32803 Pte.
Norman, John, 28333 Pte.
North, Daniel, 32840 Pte.

Ollier, William, 33490 Pte.
Orritt, Robert, 27353 Pte.
Orton, John 59011 Sgt.
O'Sullivan, Francis, 11260 Pte.
Owen, Frank, 18896 Pte.

Pace, Enoch, 10788 Pte.
Palin, William Edward, 17655 Pte.
Parsons, Edwin, 24702 Pte.
Pearson, Frank, 11309 Pte.
Perrin, Samuel, 11223 Pte.
Phillips, Arthur, 18293 Pte.
Phillips, George, 18765 Pte.
Pickering, Ernest, 26744 Pte.
Plant, Joseph, 12390 Pte.
Platt, Samuel, 34594 Pte.
Podmore, Arthur, 26792 Pte.
Pollard, John, 33367 Pte.
Pollitt, Ernest, 12731 Pte.
Poole, Harold, 10369 Pte.
Potter, Arthur, 32749 Pte.
Potts, John, 32785 Pte.
Povall, Edward, 24957 Pte.
Pownall, Ernest, 35350 Pte.
Pownall, James, 11040 Pte.
Preston, William, 45988 L/Cpl.
Price, Alfred, 10979 Pte.
Prosser, Thomas, 28229 Pte.
Proudlove, Edwin, 26577 Pte.
Pursglove, John, 12150 L/Sgt.
Pyke, John, 12691 Pte.

Quaggin, Flet. Doug., 33796 Pte.
Quinn, Andrew, 59014 Cpl.

Railton, Edward, 11909 L/Cpl.
Ralphs, Charles, 35566 Pte.
Rawlinson, Jas. Phillips, 36898 Pte.
Richards, Henry, 32855 Pte.
Richards, Thomas, 10481 Pte.
Richardson, Chas. Fred., 33356 Pte.
Richardson, Harry, 28236 Pte.
Roach, Joseph Holland, 11158 Pte.
Roache, Michael, 10487 Pte.
Roberts, Arthur, 33018 Pte.
Roberts, Arthur, 34661 Pte.
Roberts, David, 10770 L/Cpl.
Robinson, Joseph, 18893 Pte.
Robinson, William, 24555 Pte.
Rogers, William John, 10684 A/Sgt.
Roscoe, Harry, 27115 L/Cpl.
Rothery, Norm. Bern., 45266 Pte.
Rout, Robert, 24045 Pte.
Rowell, Thomas, 28235 Pte.
Rowland, Joseph, 25130 Pte.
Rustomjee, Cecil, 50377 Pte.

Sanderson, William, 26506 Pte.
Sant, Joseph, 3457 Pte.
Saunders, William, 11476 L/Cpl.
Scott, Thomas, Alfred, 59016 Cpl.
Shallcross, Charles, 24732 Pte.
Sharpe, Victor, 24777 Pte.
Shaw, George Lewis, 9108 Sgt.
Shaw, Joseph, 11304 L/Cpl.
Shaw, William, 10919 Pte.
Shaw, William, 11864 Pte.
Sheers, George, 12376 Pte
Shelley, Joseph, 11831 Pte.
Shepley, Samuel, 11055 Pte.
Sherlock, Arthur, 33195 Pte.
Sinker, Fred, 12561 Pte.
Shelly, Edward, 16708 Pte.
Slack, Thomas, 11179 Pte.
Smallman, Wm. George, 25965 Pte.
Smith, George, 34787 Pte.
Smith, George Ernest, 25611 Pte.
Smith, John, W/719 Pte.
Smith, John, 24630 Pte.
Smith, John, 33442 Pte.
Smith, Norman, 33271 L/Cpl.
Smith, Samuel, 11221 Cpl.
Sothern, John, 27542 Pte.
Spencer, Raymond, 10989 Sgt.
Stanley, Robert, 11452 Pte.
Stanley, Walter, 33397 Pte.
Steadman, Alfred, 10615 Pte.
Stockton, George, 44100 Pte.
Stockton, Wm. Henry, 36447 Pte.
Stokes, George, 11144 Pte.
Stott, Harry, 24337 Pte.
Street, Harry, 11831 Sgt.
Stubbs, Frank Broad, 33003 Pte.
Sutton, William, 11070 Cpl.

Taylor, Percy, 28303 Pte.
Taylor, William, 32713 Cpl.
Temple Ed. Stephen, 34951 A/Cpl.

Terry, John Wilfred, 60337 L/Cpl.
Thomas, William, 10784 Pte.
Thompson, Alex. John, 33023 Pte.
Todd, Edward, 28248 Pte.
Torkington, William, 26668 Pte.
Trueman, Daniel, 6416 L/Cpl.
Trueman, Samuel, 7231 C.S.M.
Turley, George, 26125 Pte.
Turner, George Wm., 27322 Pte.
Turner, James, 33661 Sgt.
Turner, Silas, 17875 Pte.
Tydd, John, 26580 Pte.

Vernon, Levi, 17735 Pte.
Vickers, Frederick, 18403 L/Cpl.
Wadsworth, Ernest, 34704 Pte.
Wake, Albert, 18879 Pte.
Wale, Edwin, 10567 Pte.
Walford, Ed. Wm., 11118 R.S.M.
Walker, Frank, 35423 Pte.
Walmsley, John, 26263 Pte.
Ward, John, 24721 Pte.
Ward, William, 33428 Pte.
Wardle, Thomas, 14500 Pte.
Waring, Alfred Edward, 23853 Pte.
Waring, Donald James, 17725 Pte.
Watson, Herbert, 17700 Pte.
Watson, William, 11326 Pte.
Webb, Colin, 9033 L/Cpl.
Whalley, Fred, 35767 Pte.
Whalley, John Wm., 17538 Pte.
Wheeldon, John Henry, 12042 Sgt.
Whitby, John, 27711 Pte.
White, Charles, 34569 Pte.
Wilde, John, 59247 Pte.
Wilkinson, Harold, 11570 Pte.
Williams, Frank, 12384 Pte.
Williams, John, 11540 Pte.
Williams, Richard, 27076 Pte.
Williamson, Richard, 24219 Pte.
Wilson, Francis, 18214 Pte.
Wilson, Thomas, 18677 Pte.
Wilson, Thomas, 36437 Pte.
Wood, George, 33190 Pte.
Woodfine, George, 24306 Pte.
Woodley, Wm. Henry, 32688 Pte.
Woods, John William, 25969 Pte.
Wright, John, 24602 Pte.
Yarwood, John William, 25922 Pte.

9th BATTALION.

Abel Fredk. Cecil, 50938 Pte.
Abraham, Geo. Henry, 72111 Pte.
Adams, Fred, 50221 Cpl.
Ainson, John Sam, 17656 Pte.
Allan, George Henry, 64562 Pte.
Allen, Edwin George, 12352 Pte.
Allen, Sidney, 15011 Pte.
Alloway, Fredk. John, 34188 Pte.
Anderson, John, 24450 Pte.
Andrew Samuel, 49427 Pte.
Andrews, Joseph, 13479 Cpl.
Andrews, William James, 12500 Pte.
Ansell, Harold, 32862 Cpl.
Appleby, Harry, 65691 Pte.
Armitt, George, 244708 Pte.

Arrowsmith, Jas. Cliffe, 50232 Pte.
Ashley, John Thomas, 13509 Pte.
Ashton, Lewis, 36646 Pte.
Aspey, Arthur, 17495 Pte.
Astles, John, 13481 Pte.
Austin, Ernest, 50227 L/Cpl.
Aynsley, John Barnett, 50974 Pte.

Bailey, Harry, 50076 L/Cpl.
Bailey, John William, 51829 Pte.
Bailey, Thomas, 266681 Pte.
Baker, Arthur, 17646 Pte.
Ball, Walter, 50157 L/Cpl.
Bamford, Arthur, 49331 Pte.
Bamford, Percy Newton, 50234 Pte.
Banks, Alfred, 53178 Pte.
Bardsley, Arthur, 15245 Pte.
Bardsley, Wm. Hy., 202108 L/Cpl.
Barker, Edward, 17152 Pte.
Barlow, Robt. William, 52348 Pte.
Barnes, Charles Wm., 36192 Pte.
Barnes, Fred, 315282 Pte.
Barnes, William, 268118 L/Cpl.
Barr, Herbert, 50206 Pte.
Barr, John Ferry, 52259 A/L/Cpl.
Bartley, John Arthur, 13497 Pte.
Basnett, David, 25989 Pte.
Batt, James Cox, 53127 Pte.
Batten, Joseph Marack Harvey, 245963 Pte.
Beadsmore, Fran. Wm., 291954 Pte.
Beard, Joseph, 50359 Pte.
Beare, Charles William, 72184 Pte.
Beddows, Jabez Vin., 18090 L/Cpl.
Bell, Joseph, 51841 Pte.
Bennett, John, 50160 Pte.
Bennett, Walter, 36285 Pte.
Benson, Lawrence, 9992 L/Cpl.
Berry, Edward, 29664 Pte.
Berry, Harry, 49713 Pte.
Best, Robert Tennent, 36496 Pte.
Bettley, William, 17859 L/Cpl.
Bew, Frederick, 22182 Pte.
Bibby, William, 49839 Pte.
Birch, Albert, 14638 A/Cpl.
Bird, Thomas, 12351 Pte.
Bishop, David William, 53176 Pte.
Blackhurst John Reg., 27866 Pte.
Bleakley, Ernest, 12148 Pte.
Bleakley, Walter, 244883 Pte.
Blundell, Thomas, 10862 Pte.
Boulton, Ellis, 18591 Sgt.
Bonfield, Ralph, 51838 Pte.
Booth, Samuel, 49840 Pte.
Booth, Samuel, 202012 Pte.
Bostock, Herbert, 12483 L/Sgt.
Bowden, Charles, 12193 L/Cpl.
Bowden, John, 13506 Pte.
Bowen, William, 923 Pte.
Bower, Fredk. Sefton, 52539 Pte.
Bowker, Alexandra, 11890 Pte.
Bracegirdle, Ernest, 49875 Pte.
Brackner, John Wm., 28384 L/Cpl.
Bradburn, Henry Isaac, 53236 Cpl.
Bradbury, Robert, 49678 Pte.
Bradley, Thomas, 13376 L/Cpl.

Bradshaw, Arthur Ed., 33571 Pte.
Bradshaw, Fred, 29700 Pte.
Brassey, Joseph, 18068 Pte.
Breckin, Alfred, 20739 L/Cpl.
Brereton, George, 12515 L/Cpl.
Brimblecombe, Percy G., 72114 Pte.
Brindley, Geo. Harold, 13445 Pte.
Brook, Percival Claud, 51842 Pte.
Brooks, Arthur, 27925 Pte.
Broughton, William, 49838 Pte.
Brown, Ambrose, 241533 Pte.
Brown, Geo. Ethelbert, 35035 Pte.
Brown, Mager Frank, 50950 Pte.
Brown, Rowland, 33162 Pte.
Brown, Simeon James, 53242 Pte.
Brown, Walter, 17600 Pte.
Brown, William, 12703 Pte.
Bruce, Harry, 49714 Pte.
Bruckshaw, Sydney, 15239 Pte.
Buckley, Edward, 53175 Pte.
Bullock, Joseph, 49841 Pte.
Burchill, David Harold, 30018 Pte.
Burgess, George Gullet, 72128 Pte.
Burgess, Howard, 50152 Pte.
Burgon, Vincent, 67698 Pte.
Burke, James, 50235 Pte.
Burns, Owen Valentine, 200087 Sgt.
Burrows, Frank, 12521 Pte.
Buss, John George, 52224 Pte.
Buswell, Phillip, 49844 Pte.
Butler, Leonard, 50582 Pte.
Butlin, William, 268531 Pte.
Butterworth Joseph, 17821 Pte.

Cadwallader, George, 17216 Pte.
Cannell, Frederick, 35852 Pte.
Cannell, Sydney, 33805 Pte.
Canovan, Frank, 13425 Pte.
Carnaby William, 12359 Pte.
Carsberg, Fred, W/655 Cpl.
Carter, Wm. Francis, 243295 Pte.
Cartwright, Albert, 11776 Pte.
Carver, James Edgar, 53244 Sgt.
Caselli, Henry, 57822 Pte.
Catlow, Samuel, 18794 Pte.
Chatterley, Percival Nor., 51013 Pte.
Chatterton, Arthur, 36823 Pte.
Clarke, Fredk. George, 36843 Pte.
Clarke, Herbert, 72135 Pte.
Clarke, John Edmund, 52346 Pte.
Clarke, Joseph, 51846 Pte.
Clarke, Robert, 27248 Pte.
Clarke, William, 49877 Pte.
Clayton, Arthur, 14900 L/Cpl.
Clayton, Fred, 49683 Pte.
Clayton, Daniel, 50219 Pte.
Cleary, James, 9955 Pte.
Cliffe, James, 34501 Pte.
Cockett, Fredk. Almond, 30458 Pte.
Coe, Leo, 28715 Pte.
Coles, George, 203259 Pte.
Collings, Walter Geo., 72163 Pte.
Connolly, John, 33521 Pte.
Cook, Arthur Fredk., 52294 Pte.
Cook, Edward, 18932 L/Cpl.
Cook, Fredk. Alfred, 51856 Pte.

Cooke, Arthur, 50366 Pte.
Cooke, Walter William, 8073 A/Sgt.
Cookson, Harold, 32535 Pte.
Coombe, George Francis, 53246 Pte.
Coombes, Thomas, 265659 Cpl.
Coope, Frank, 52185 Pte.
Cooper, Herbert, 32582 Pte.
Cooper, Marmaduke, 50238 Pte.
Cope, Collin, 242808 L/Sgt.
Coppenhall, Charles, 12899 Pte.
Corlett, Oscar, 32550 Pte.
Corns, Edward, 14501 L/Sgt.
Cottam, James, 53142 Pte.
Coulman, William, 29908 Pte.
Courtney, William, 17017 Pte.
Couzins, James, 13786 Pte.
Covill, George, 12156 Sgt.
Cozens, Walter Lionel, 53183 Pte.
Cracknell, James George, 52216 Pte.
Craig, Thomas Brown, 50977 Pte.
Craven, John, 265124 L/Cpl.
Crofts, Thomas William, 11720 Pte.
Crone, James, 49879 Pte.
Cross, Harry, 268532 Pte.
Cross, William, 50033 Pte.
Cryer, Herbert, 53181 Pte.
Cullen, James, 12393 Pte.
Cunliffe, John Cooper, 28343 Pte.
Curbishley, Albert, 15609 Pte.
Currie, William, 12293 Pte.
Cuthbertson, William, 20842 Sgt.

Dailey, Herbert, 50054 L/Cpl.
Dale, John William, 266735 Pte.
Darby, Ivor Augustus, 53187 Pte.
Darling, Walter Robert, 52309 Pte.
Darwen, Robert, 51864 Pte.
Davidson, George, W/22 Pte.
Davies, Albert, 32817 Pte.
Davies, Darroll, 49883 Pte.
Davies, Ernest, Ivor Samuel, 53248 Pte.
Davies, Robert, 33167 Pte.
Davies, Thomas, 53188 Pte.
Davies, Thomas Glyn, 53249 Pte.
Davies, William, 266267 Pte.
Dawkins, Frank, 72137 Pte.
Dawson, Henry, 292368 Pte.
Deary, Thomas, 15760 Pte.
Delamere, Harry Gilland, 17183 Pte.
Delve, William Henry, 201958 Pte.
Dewhurst, Preston Flet., 53253 Pte.
Dickinson, John, 12910 Pte.
Dixon, Bert, 57835 Pte.
Dixon, Richard, 266072 L/Cpl.
Dixon, William, 290188, Pte.
Dodd, Leslie, 12091 L/Sgt.
Dooley, Edward, 13016 Pte.
Down, Harry, 72165 Pte.
Downey, Robert, 21937 Pte.
Duckworth, Harry, 52040 Pte.
Dunn, Herbert, Charles, 30378 Pte.
Dunstan, Regd. Thos., 72214 Pte.
Dutton, Archie Clemant, 11786 Sgt.
Dutton, Arthur, 18104 Pte.
Dutton, Joseph William, 12692 Pte.

Eason, Thomas, 40927 Pte.
Ecob, Edward, 58115 Pte.
Edmunds, Henry, 53192 Pte.
Edwards, Edwin, 201980 Pte.
Ellison, William, 33605 Pte.
Ellor, William, 14687 Pte.
Elvin, Thos. Charles, 51867 Pte.
Emery, John, 26148 Pte.
Evans, Daniel, 17095 Pte.
Evans, Rowland, 15598 Sgt.
Exley, William, 45800 Pte.

Fairy, Ernest Jess, 268534 Pte.
Fennell, Joseph, 49966 Pte.
Fewtrell, Edward, 49874 Pte.
Findlow, Alfred, 49611 Pte.
Finnigan, Arthur, 33537 Pte.
Finny, Richard, 12151 Pte.
Fishlock, Albert Edward, 52240 Pte.
Flay, Henry George, 315889 L/Cpl.
Fleet, William, 12752 L/Cpl.
Foote, William, 12698 Pte.
Ford, Joseph, 65770 Pte.
Forrester, John, 28822 Pte.
Forster, James, 7857 Pte.
Forster, William Arthur, 59309 Pte.
Fowles, Ralph, 18116 Pte.
Francombe, James, 17040 C.S.M.
Frazer, Isaac, 52323 Pte.
Frearson, Thomas, 11718 Pte.
Friedrichsen, Emil Jas., 51016 Pte.
Frith, Bertram, 11738 Pte.

Gale, Albert, 53158 Pte.
Gardner, Frank, 28732 Pte.
Gardner, Harold, 53170 Pte.
Gardner, Wal. Highley, 50122 Pte.
Gartland, Bernard, 35305 L/Cpl.
Gerrard, William, 11796 Pte.
Gibbon, Harold, 9854 Pte.
Gibbs, Oliver Stephen, 28280 Pte.
Gibbs, Walter, Edward, 51878 Pte.
Gibson, Harry, 59122 Pte.
Gibson, William Riddle, 52308 Pte.
Gibson, Wm. Shepherd, 23459 Pte.
Gidman, Fred, 7268 Pte.
Gilbride, James, 12494 Pte.
Goddard, Ernest, 12171 Pte.
Goddard, Sydney, 12163 Pte.
Goodall, Alfred, 17599 Pte.
Gooding, George, 72169 Pte.
Goodwin, Frederick, 15247 Pte.
Gorringe, Walter, 12344 L/Cpl.
Gorst, Frank, 12614 Pte.
Gosling, Wm. Thomas, 60296 Pte.
Grant, John Augustus, 53509 Pte.
Green, Albert, 12951 Pte.
Green, Wilfred Henry, 51882 Pte.
Green, John, 11820 Pte.
Gregory, Alfred Edward, 36834 Pte.
Gregory, Wilfred, 12777 Cpl.
Griffiths, David Thomas, 53195 Pte.
Griffiths, James Noel, 34692 Pte.
Griffiths, William, 10622 Pte.
Grundey, John, 27919 Pte.

Hagedorn, Arthur, 20745 Pte.
Halewood, Samuel, 16347 Pte.
Halford, Elliott Glos. 51000 Pte.
Hall, Harry, 17220 Pte.
Hall, Percy James, 72141 Pte.
Hall, Robert, 15479 Pte.
Hall, Samuel, 49723 Pte.
Hall, Tom, 12781 Pte.
Hallam, Frederick, Wm., 35577 Pte.
Hallows, George, 49688 Pte.
Handley, Dennis, 12477 Cpl.
Hankey, Emmanuel, 50169 Pte.
Hardcastle, Ernest, 16345 L/Cpl.
Harding, Bertram John, 18107 Cpl.
Hargreaves, John, 265615 Pte.
Harmon, Richd. Roden, 51891 Pte.
Harris, William George, 51886 Pte.
Harrison, Edward, 12637 Pte.
Harrop, Timothy, 15270 Pte.
Hartley, Basil, 50129 Pte.
Hartley, John, 25178 Pte.
Harvey, Edward, 24565 Pte.
Hassall, Tom, 50126 Pte.
Hatton, Samuel, 11974 Pte.
Hayes, Arthur John, 64184 Pte.
Hayward, Ernest, 12326 Pte.
Hazeldine, Squire, 12101 L/Cpl.
Hazlehurst, Alfred, 17671 Pte.
Heague, Richard, 50231 Pte.
Heamen, Walter, 291666 Pte.
Heathcote, Henry, 14531 L/Cpl.
Hemsworth, Ar. Enst., 10823 L/Cpl.
Henshall, Herbert, 11795 Pte.
Heppell, Wm. Robson, 52329 Pte.
Hewins, Fred, 51005 Pte.
Hewitt, Robert, 51888 Pte.
Higginbottom, Robert, 52263 Pte.
Higgins, John, 241778 Pte.
Hill, Frederick, 45274 Pte.
Hill, Gordon Clive, 64813 Pte.
Hitchins, Fredk. Ben., 245962 Pte.
Hogan, Michael, 28797 Pte.
Hogg, John, 52550 Pte.
Holden, Ernest, 60478 Pte.
Holdsworth, Benjamin, 19663 Pte.
Holliday, George, 49689 Pte.
Holliday, John, 52320 Pte.
Hollinghurst, Percy, 61972 Pte.
Holmes, Arthur, 52253 Pte.
Holyoake, Wm. Rob., 12345 Cpl.
Hornby, Harry, 11135 Pte.
Horsfall, Jackson, 52249 Pte.
Howard, Harold, 15139 Pte.
Howell, Alfred, 50088 Pte.
Hoy, John, 244906 Pte.
Hoyle, Thomas, 244433 Pte.
Hubbard, Henry Vic., 11866 L/Cpl.
Hudson, William, 15981 Pte.
Hughes, Wm. George, 17325 Pte.
Hulme, John Charles, 13917 Cpl.
Hulme, William, 32571 Pte.
Hulse, John, 10924 Pte.
Hunt, Alfred, 33595 Pte.
Hurrell, Edgar Sydney, 72395 Pte.

Ingham, Herbert, 50213 Pte.

Ingram, Roland, 57973 Pte.

Jackson, Albert Daniel, 49895 Pte.
Jackson, Frederick, 36910 Pte.
Jackson, Reginald, 50765 Pte.
Jacobs, Edwin, 67491 Pte.
James, William, 52241 Pte.
Jefferies, Fenton, 293387 L/Cpl.
Jenkins, David, 12938 A/Cpl.
Job, Percy, 53163 Pte.
Johnson, Benjamin, 11783 A/Cpl.
Johnson, Charles, 18562 L/Cpl.
Johnson, John, 26300 Pte.
Johnson, Stan. Inker., 268537 Pte.
Johnson, William, 32623 Pte.
Joinson, Michael, 49690 Pte.
Jones, Abraham Wilson, 53209 Pte.
Jones, David Henry, 10073 Pte.
Jones, Evan Morgan, 53206 Pte.
Jones, Gwilyn Cyrus, 316107 Pte.
Jones, Henry, 12893 Pte.
Jones, Jack, W/1210 Pte.
Jones, John, 16600 Pte.
Jones, John, 36317 Pte.
Jones, John William, 49692 Pte.
Jones, Thomas, 21935 Pte.
Jones, Thomas, 28742 Pte.
Jones, Thomas, 50215 Pte.
Jones, William, 53204 Pte.

Keighley, J. Hy. Manby, 50949 Pte.
Kelly, John, 33622 Pte.
Kelly, Stephen, 17475 Pte.
Kelly, Thomas, 23091 Cpl.
Kemp, William, 12462 Pte.
Kennedy, Andrew, 53144 Pte.
Kennedy, James, 19622 Pte.
Kennerley, James, 50768 Pte.
Kennerley, William, 12813 Pte.
Kent, Frank, 49989 L/Cpl.
Kerrigan, Dennis, 59840 Pte.
King, Harry Davies, 51472 Pte.
Knott, Robert, 18560 Pte.
Knowles, Edgar, 50963 Pte.
Knowles, Thomas, 291841 Pte.

Lally, Dennis, 25004 Pte.
Lamb, Harold, 49695 Pte.
Lambeth, Edward, 12677 Pte.
Larkin, Albert Basil, 72116 Pte.
Latham, Ernest, 50057 Pte.
Leech, Fredk. George, 15381 Pte.
Leech, William, 12511 Pte.
Leech, William, 50218 Pte.
Leigh, Allen, 18919 Pte.
Lever, William, 33559 Pte.
Lewis, Charles Herbert, 50250 Pte.
Lewis, George Henry, 315416 Pte.
Lewis, John Francis, 67614 Pte.
Lewney, Walter, 18899 Pte.
Libby, Richard, 17172 Pte.
Lightford, William, 50964 Pte.
Lingard, Thomas, 266788 Pte.
Littler, Thomas, 12533 Pte.
Llewellyn, Frank Ed., 35256 Pte.
Lloyd, Arthur Lewis, 53214 Pte.

Llyarch, Solomon, 18064 Pte.
Lofkin, Fred, 50131 Pte.
Lomas, Harry, 17618 Cpl.
Lowe, John Arnold, 44142 Pte.
Lowther, Richard, 52354 Pte.
Luke, Arthur Nevill, 62417 Pte.
Lund, William, 52359 Pte.
Lyons, Frederick, 16086 L/Cpl.

Maltby, William Henry, 260047 Pte.
Mansell, John, 45829 Pte.
Marrs, Joseph, 52440 Pte.
Martin, John Hadden Samuel, 52233 Pte.
Martin, Thomas, 33579 Pte.
Mason, William, 49905 Pte.
Massam, William, 50177 Pte.
Massey, George, 49322 Pte.
Maynard, Ernest, 11815 L/Cpl.
McAleavy, Patrick, 50903 Pte.
McCartin, James, 18582 Pte.
McCormack, William, 33642 Pte.
McCrae, Alexander, 52210 Pte.
McDonald, Peter, 30649 Pte.
McGarry, John, 9888 L/Cpl.
McGibbon, Wm. Arthur, 28755 Pte.
McGrail, John, 28700 L/Cpl.
McHugh, William, 12530 Pte.
McLachlan, David William Adams, 64379 L/Cpl.
McNerney, William, 49901 Pte.
Meagher, Dominic, 12444 Pte.
Medlicott, George, 49899 Pte.
Meehan, Thomas, 17443 Pte.
Mellor, Harry, 266666 L/Cpl.
Mercer, Alfred Edgar, 51961 Pte.
Miller, George Fredk., 72193 Pte.
Miller, Thomas, 11176 L/Cpl.
Millward, Abraham, 12825 Pte.
Mobb, William, 40413 Pte.
Molyneux, Geo. Henry, 49697 Pte.
Monks, Henry, 17150 L/Cpl.
Moore, Colin, 27296 Pte.
Moore, George Edward, 50597 Pte.
Moore, Leslie Bernard, 58106 Pte.
Moores, Richard, 17582 Cpl.
Moorhouse, William, 202038 Pte.
Morgan, Arthur, 12138 Pte.
Morgan, Meredith, 53265 Pte.
Morris, Hubert, 65158 Pte.
Morris, Wm. John, 49900 Pte.
Moseley, Harold, 260059 Pte.
Moseley, Harry, 18084 Pte.
Mottershead, Alec, 9216 Sgt.
Mouat, Thomas, 33570 Pte.
Mullock, Sidney, 10178 Pte.
Myatt, Samuel, 36641 Pte.

Naylor, Fred, 13678 Pte.
Neild, Harry, 26034 Pte.
Neville, Michael, 52258 Sgt.
Newcombe, Robert, 51491 L/Cpl.
Newling, Fredk. Ar., 12699 L/Cpl.
Newman, George Harry, 49907 Pte.
Newton, George, 260032 Pte.
Nicholas, Albert, 50147 Pte.

Nicholson, William, 50067 Pte.
Noakes, Fredk. Charles, 40718 Pte.
Nolan, Albert, 35405 Pte.

Oban, Henry, 17491 Pte.
O'Brien, Peter, 9122 Pte.
Oldham, Arthur, 25762 Pte.
Oldham, Marriot, 50476 Pte.
Oldham, Percy, 266696 Pte.
Orr, David, 15228 L/Sgt.
Orton, Arthur, 52342 Pte.

Palmer, Thomas, 13654 Pte.
Parry, Charles, 50179 Pte.
Payne, Richard, 33648 Pte.
Peach, Robert, 18556 Pte.
Peach, William, 268539 Pte.
Pearce, Joseph, 32742 Pte.
Pearson, Joseph, 44123 Pte.
Percival, David, 45145 Pte.
Peters, Sidney, 18553 L/Cpl.
Philbin, David, 266564 Cpl.
Phillips, Godfrey Rees, 53224 Pte.
Piggot, Ernest, 12736 Pte.
Pinnock, John, 17553 A/Sgt.
Plant, William, 16446 Cpl.
Platt, James Ely, 243261 Pte.
Plumb, William, 13659 Pte.
Pollard, William, 15912 Pte.
Poole, James, 14324 Pte.
Potts, George, 49019 L/Cpl.
Powell, Edward, 243625 Pte.
Price, Gwilym, 53270 Pte.
Price, Trevor, 67498 Pte.
Prince, John, 290235 L/Cpl.
Pritchard, Robert, 52276 Sgt.
Prosser, Percival David, 53226 Pte.
Protheroe, George, 17461 Pte.
Purcell, Edward, 45410 Pte.
Pye, Ernest Frederick, 12890 Pte.
Pye, Henry, 67501 Pte.

Quinn, Peter, 17810 Pte.

Rabbage, Andrew Geo., 72195 Pte.
Randall, Frederick, 8968 Sgt.
Read, Jack Stewart, 72101 A/Sgt.
Redhead, Sidney, 74023 Pte.
Redmond, Ed. Cornelius, 33513 Pte.
Rees, Ivor, 66147 Pte.
Regan, James, 26556 Pte.
Richardson, Charles, 15391 A/Cpl.
Richardson, Ken. Joe, 53048 Pte.
Richardson, Peter Reg., 62297 Pte.
Rickus, Thomas, 20508 Pte.
Riddlesworth, Leo., 50230 L/Cpl.
Ridgway James, 12559 Sgt.
Riding, John, 28771 Pte.
Rigby, Charles, 50185 Pte.
Rigg, Richard, 28335 Pte.
Riley, James Edwin, 17643 L/Cpl.
Riley, Thomas, 13763 Pte.
Rimmer, William, 33591 Pte.
Roberts, David, 53229 Pte.
Roberts, Fredk. James, 67647 Pte.
Roberts, George, 17218 L/Cpl.

Roberts, Hugh, 66162 Pte.
Roberts, Trevor Lewis, 66160 Pte.
Roberts, William, 11899 Pte.
Robinson, Charles, 52891 Pte.
Robinson, Stanley, 35044 Pte.
Robinson, William, 66161 Pte.
Robson, Thomas, 66153 Pte.
Roden, George, 18095 Pte.
Rodger, Robert, 33635 Pte.
Rooth, Edwin, 266151 Pte.
Rose, Thomas, 17506 L/Cpl.
Roughley, George, 28774 Pte.
Rowlands, Walter, 62474 Pte.
Rowlinson, Charles, 12582 Pte.
Royle, Edward, 32554 Pte.
Ruffler, Reuben, 13455 Pte.
Rushton, Alfred William Frederick,
    65715 Pte.
Rushton, Barnes, 50775 Pte.
Russon, Sidney, 50996 Pte.

Sargent, Henry Ward, 44329 Pte.
Sayle, John, 50138 Pte.
Schofield, Wentworth, 315349 Pte.
Scott, John, W/373 L/Cpl.
Scott, Richard, 49561 Pte.
Seddon, William, 28775 Pte.
Shaw, George William, 12364 Pte.
Shaw, Herbert, 53272 Pte.
Shaw, John, 50255 Pte.
Shaw, Joseph, 244864 Pte.
Shaw, William, 17337 Pte.
Sheckleston, James, 17514 L/Cpl.
Shepherd, J. Woodruff, 49388 Pte.
Shilling, Percy Clarence, 52196 Pte.
Shine, Daniel, 19600 Cpl.
Shone, Thomas, 11789 Pte.
Short, William Henry, 72150 Pte.
Sillitoe, George, 50136 Pte.
Simmons, Frederick, 72174 Pte.
Simms, George, 67654 Pte.
Simpson, Herbert, 32567 Pte.
Singleton, Timothy, 19008 Pte.
Skelhorn, Samuel, 49704 Pte.
Skinner, Francis Sainsbury George,
    72106 Pte.
Slack, William, 18066 Pte.
Slater, Arthur, 290262 Pte.
Smart, Wm. J. Bevan, 66170 Pte.
Smith, Arnold, 50970 Pte.
Smith, Arthur, 67507 Pte.
Smith, Ernest Braith., 49911 Pte.
Smith, Harry Percy, 11828 L/Cpl.
Smith, Herbert, 18923 Pte.
Smith, James, 65328 Pte.
Smith, Ralph, 52318 Sgt.
Smith, Robert, 16085 Pte.
Snape, Joseph, 64476 L/Cpl.
Snead, George, 12375 Pte.
Sowden, John Richd., 45346 Pte.
Sparkes, Henry, 11141 Pte.
Spencer, Herbert, 12803 Pte.
Spilletts, Walter, W/944 L/Cpl.
Spilsbury, Samuel, 12050 Pte.
Stacey, John, 27462 Pte.
Stafford, Alb. Edward, 268541 Pte.

Stafford, Samuel, 32557 Pte.
St. Clair, Robert, 33637 Pte.
Steel, Albert, 28781 Pte.
Steele, Arthur, 72097 Sgt.
Stephen, Alexander, 16491 Pte.
Stephenson, Thomas, 67662 Pte.
Stevenson, George, 50759 L/Cpl.
Stockton, David, 23147 Pte.
Stockton, Frank, 10775 Pte.
Stokes, William Chas., 67664 Pte.
Stones, William, 65688 L/Cpl.
Suddell, George, 19228 Pte.
Sulch, Harry, 53276 Pte.
Summers, George Baird, 52266 Pte.
Swain, Wm. Harold, 12280 C.Q.M.S.
Symes, Percival Edwin, 72173 Pte.

Taubman, John Henry, 34504 Pte.
Taylor, Fred, 52345 Pte.
Taylor, Joseph Thos., 260053 Pte.
Taylor, Walter, 12672 Cpl.
Teachen, Frederick, 33627 Cpl.
Thomas, Fred, 315176 Pte.
Thomas, Griffith, 12447 Pte.
Thomas, John Henry, 67513 Pte.
Thomas, John, 66177 Pte.
Thomas, Robert, 11771 Pte.
Thomas, William Henry, 17571 Pte.
Thompson, Matt. Peter, 26664 Pte.
Thompson, William, 57893 Pte.
Thornton, Thos. Edwin, 23430 Pte.
Tiddy, Ernest, 49709 Pte.
Tiernley, William, 49873 Pte.
Todd, Arthur Walter, 203238 Pte.
Toft, Joseph, 50071 Pte.
Tonge, James Fray, 67665 Pte.
Tonkinson, Edward, 32569 Pte.
Toop, Ernest James, 65717 Pte.
Turner, Frederick, James Sedgley,
    51014 Pte.
Turner, George Henry, 260055 Pte.
Turner, John, 12869 Pte.
Turner, John Thomas, 33527 Pte.
Turner, Walter, 50761 Pte.

Unger, Harry, 33628 Pte.

Vance, John, 28785 Pte.
Vaughan, Arth. Wm., 28786 L/Cpl.
Vernon, Harry, 12984 Pte.
Vernon, Richard, 9244 Pte.
Vines, Albert, 64610 Pte.

Waddington, Joseph, 17168 Pte.
Wakefield, George, 11743 Pte.
Walker, Ernest, 65006 Pte.
Walker, Reuben, 13478 Cpl.
Wallwork, Robert, 64274 Pte.
Walton, Harry, 24814 Pte.
Warburton, Albert, 12360 A/Cpl.
Ward, Bernard, 9657 Pte.
Ward, Jack, 67683 Pte.
Ward, William, 16080 L/Cpl.
Waring, Thomas, 24064 Pte.
Waring, William, 35504 L/Cpl.
Watkins, Chas. James, 66867 Pte.

Watkinson, John, 45217 Pte.
Watts, Ernest Henry, 292142 Pte.
Watts, Owen, 266189 Pte.
Weaver, Frederick, 50857 Pte.
Weaver, George Henry, 28789 Pte.
Webber, David William, 67691 Pte.
Webster, Thomas, 62294 Pte.
Webster, Wm. Brantford, 45299 Pte
Weston, Frederick, 202006 Pte.
Weston, George, 32928 Pte.
Wharton, Walter, 17602 Pte.
Wheeler, Alfred, 17659 Pte.
Whinnerah, Stanley, 53278 Pte.
White, Charles Henry, 33613 Pte.
Whitehead, Harry, 12172 Pte.
Whitehead, Joseph, 53147 Pte.
Whittaker, Arthur, 201930 Pte.
Whittaker, Joseph, 266535 Pte.
Whittingham, Alfred, 20958 Pte.
Whyat, James, 12581 Pte.
Whynn, Walter, 65699 Pte.
Wilbraham, Leonard, 32632 L/Cpl.
Wilbraham, Thos. Wm., 27568 Pte.
Wild, Alfred, 11698 Pte.
Wild, John Peck, 50144 Pte.
Wilkinson, Harold, 32966 Pte.
Wilkinson, James, 17589 L/Cpl.
Williams, Arthur, 66197 Pte.
Williams, Arthur John, 66863 Pte.
Williams, Bryn Gwynne, 67515 Pte.
Williams, Evan Lloyd, 66192 Pte.
Williams, Geo. Joseph, 49915 Pte.
Williams, Henry John, 72177 Pte.
Williams, Ivor Carlyle, 66193 Pte.
Williams, John, 28792 Pte.
Williams, John, 67676 Pte.
Williams, Joseph William Thomas,
    34392 Pte.
Williams, Robt. Howard, 66194 Pte.
Williams, William, 66189 Pte.
Williamson, George, 11162 Pte.
Willis, Arthur, 18078 Pte.
Wilson, Ernest, 66864 Pte.
Wilson, George, W/194 Pte.
Wilson, James, 53148 Pte.
Windsor, Wm. Arthur, 67687 Pte.
Winship, William, 52335 Pte.
Woodland, Albert Ed., 200696 Pte.
Woods, George Alfred, 44264 Pte.
Woods, William, 33518 Pte.
Woodward, Herbert, 52227 L/Cpl.
Woodworth, John Hy., 50195 Pte.
Worden, John, 45100 Pte.
Worrall, Abraham, 12216 Pte.
Worrall, Thos. John, 11888 Cpl.
Worsley, Fredk. Samuel, 22004 Pte.
Wrigg, James, 18074 Pte.
Wright, George Wm., 51015 L/Cpl.
Wright, James Arthur, 52372 Pte.
Wright, John Henry, 50256 Pte.
Wright, William Henry, 67519 Pte.
Wroe, George, 201997 Pte.
Wyatt, Joseph, 17125 Pte.

Yabsley, Arthur Ernest, 245964 Pte.
Yarwood, Harry, 18502 L/Cpl.

Yarwood, William, 11939 L/Sgt.
Yoxall, William, 17855 Pte.

10th BATTALION.

Abercrombie, James, 60481 Pte.
Adamson, John, 14764 Pte.
Adshead, Walter, 35234 Pte.
Ainsworth, Wm. Jas., 13881 L/Cpl.
Albinson, William, 49425 Pte.
Allen, Ernest, 13075 Pte.
Allman, George, 268147 Pte.
Ambler, Harold, 50581 Pte.
Aynon, George, 62006 Pte.
Archer, Harry, 260004 Pte.
Armitage, Fred Royse, 16898 Pte.
Armstrong, Alb. Henry, 36232 Pte.
Arnold, Charles, 14049 Pte.
Arthur, Thomas, 52413 Pte.
Ashbrook, David, 13879 Pte.
Ashbrook, William, 243690 Pte.
Ashbrook, Wm. Chri., 10900 A/Sgt.
Ashley, Samuel, 17829 Pte.
Ashley, William, 13918 L/Cpl.
Ashmore, Samuel, 34760 Pte.
Ashton, William, 13010 L/Sgt.
Astbury, Henry Fredk., 14960 Pte.
Astles, Samuel, 12921 Pte.
Austin, George, 17888 L/Cpl.
Austin, Harold, 15565 Pte.
Axon, Edward, 14418 Pte.
Axon, Joseph, 14419 Cpl.

Bagley, John William, 52454 Pte.
Bailey, William, 12837 A/Sgt.
Bailey, Arthur Oliver, 50584 Pte.
Ball, Arthur, 26511 Pte.
Ball, Wilfred, 65714 Pte.
Bancroft, Charles, 12786 Pte.
Banks, Arthur, 575 Pte.
Banner, James, 15105 Cpl.
Bardsley, Fred, 12348 Pte.
Bardsley, Robert, 52431 Pte.
Barfoot, John Henry, 53523 Pte.
Barlow, Harry, 11049 Pte.
Barlow, Harry, 49431 Pte.
Barlow, John, 243664 Pte.
Barlow, John Andrew, 44058 Pte.
Barlow, Joseph, 16152 L/Cpl.
Barlow, Wilson, 14927 Cpl.
Barnes, Bertram, 35006 Pte.
Barnes, Samuel, 24610 Pte.
Barnes, Thomas, 12942 Pte.
Barnett, John, 12873 Pte.
Barradell, Geo. Henry, 50633 Pte.
Bartholomew, Jos. Ed., 20187 Pte.
Bartley, Joseph, 59255 Pte.
Bashford, James Chas., 8511 A/Sgt.
Bates, Walter, 50634 Pte.
Bateson, Llewelyn, 14043 Pte.
Baum, William, 291953 Pte.
Bawden, Henry James, 49433 Pte.
Baxendale, Stephen, 242886 Pte.
Bayley, Arthur, 33101 Pte.
Beard, Frank, 34752 Pte.
Beard, Frank, 39895 Cpl.

Beard, Louis, 14085 Pte.
Beattie, James Wallace, 49435 Pte.
Bedford, Cecil, 315567 Pte.
Beech, Thomas, 13054 Cpl.
Bell, Ernest, 49437 Pte.
Bell, John Thomas, 15488 L/Cpl.
Bellfield, Frank, 58124 Pte.
Bellinger, Bernard, 72257 A/L/Cpl.
Belsham, Charles, 33042 Pte.
Bennett, Bert, 26363 Pte.
Bennett, David, 49439 Pte.
Bennett, George.Arthur, 15986 Pte.
Bennett, Thomas, 15657 L/Cpl.
Benson, John Dale, 44025 Pte.
Berry, Charles, 285011 Pte.
Berry, John, 14544 A/Sgt.
Beswick, Albert, 14046 Pte.
Beswick, James Daniel, 13920 Pte.
Beswick, William, 24077 Pte.
Bethell, George, 266198 Pte.
Bexon, Arghur, 291955 Pte.
Bignall, Clifford, 10289 Pte.
Billington, Richard, 36329 Pte.
Billington, William, 36578 Pte.
Billington, William, 260006 Pte.
Birch, John James, 11101 Pte.
Birchall, Charles, 292577 Pte.
Bird, Thomas, 15726 Pte.
Bithell, Harry, 201887 Pte.
Blackburn, Geo. Henry, 33133 Pte.
Blackburn, Joseph, 13024 Cpl.
Blackhurst, Alfred, 16502 Pte.
Blackhurst, Frank, 18003 Pte.
Blank, Archibald, 72262 Pte.
Blease, Harry Buckley, 24684 Pte.
Blything, Albert, 49445 Pte.
Boden, Harry, 241853 Pte.
Boon, Ernest, 28110 Sgt.
Booth, Edgar, 315196 Cpl.
Booth, Frank, 49446 Pte.
Bostock, Thos. Henry, 241453 Pte.
Boulger, James Orrell, 39892 Pte.
Boulton, Robert, 45782 Pte.
Bowers, Wm. Henry, 12123 Sgt.
Bownas, Fredk. Arthur, 49449 Pte.
Bowyer, James, 49450 Pte.
Bracegirdle, Harold, 35600 Pte.
Bradbury Walter, 35009 L/Cpl.
Bradbury, William, 52677 Pte.
Bradley, Richard, 29513 Pte.
Bramhall, John, 36583 L/Cpl.
Bramwell, Joseph, 34907 L/Cpl.
Bramwell, Walter, 49451 L/Cpl.
Brandreth, Robt. John, 39896 Pte.
Branston, George, 49390 Pte.
Bratt, Enoch, 36584 Pte.
Bratt, Samuel, 36113 Pte.
Broadhead, John Chas., 50041 Pte.
Broadhurst, Thomas, 44328 Pte.
Broome, William, 33416 Pte.
Brough, Herbert James, 49452 Pte.
Brown, George, 26628 Pte.
Brown, Lavator, 51936 Pte.
Brown, Robert, 49453 Pte.
Brown, Thomas, 14610 Pte.
Brown, Thomas, 292697 Pte.

Bruce, John, 292028 Pte.
Brunt, William, 33048 Pte.
Bryning, Frank, 49454 Pte.
Buckley, Chas. Henry, 36162 Pte.
Buckley, Isaac, 36166 Pte.
Buckley, James, 13980 Pte.
Buckley, John Wm., 13940 Pte.
Buckley, John, 24223 Pte.
Buckley, Robert, 24614 Pte.
Bunker, Bertram, 14589 Pte.
Burdekin, James, 14350 Pte.
Burdett, Howcutt, 50849 Pte.
Burgess, John, 18844 Pte.
Burgess, Leonard, 9258 L/Cpl.
Burke, Edward, 10746 Pte.
Burns, John, 65778 Pte.
Burslam, Harry, 49457 Pte.
Butcher, Thomas, 52433 Pte.
Byrne, John Patrick, 36149 Pte.

Callahan, William, 292630 Pte.
Camden, Harry, 267017 Pte.
Capper, Frederick, 14325 Pte.
Capper, Peter, 53055 L/Cpl.
Capper, William, 243185 Pte.
Carew, Fredk. Henry, 36725 Pte.
Cargill, Arthur Henry, 50461 Pte.
Carley, Peter, 13083 Pte.
Carlisle, Fredk. John, 49459 Pte.
Carnell, Frank, 58854 A/Cpl.
Carroll, Richard, 17885 Pte.
Cartwright, John, 36040 Pte.
Casey, Andrew, 36382 Pte.
Casey, Thomas, 25175 Pte.
Cashmore, Harold, 265394 Pte.
Cawkwell, Jack, 51944 Pte.
Chadderton, Arnold, 7073 Pte.
Chaloner, William, W/800 L/Sgt.
Chamberlain, Bertie, 50874 Pte.
Charlton, Arthur, 59562 Pte.
Cheshire, Samuel, 15498 Pte.
Clapham, Tom Harry, 20007 Pte.
Clare, Arthur, 33228 Pte.
Clare, Ernest, 15037 Sgt.
Clark, Frank, 64219 Pte.
Clarke, Ernest, 14812 Pte.
Clarke, Fredk. Harold, 50871 Pte.
Clarke, Harold, 290706 Pte.
Clarke, Robert, 13219 L/Cpl.
Clarke, Wilfred Arthur, 33689 Pte.
Clarke, Wm. Edward, 50588 Pte.
Clarkson, Benjamin, 263016 Pte.
Clarkson, Joseph, 50840 Pte.
Clay, John William, 50739 Pte.
Clayton, Charles Thos., 267171 Pte.
Clayton, John, 15051 Pte.
Clayton, Percy Charles, 52406 Pte.
Clegg, Walter, 50465 Pte.
Cliff, Herman, 15021 Cpl.
Cliffe, Charles, 434 L/Cpl.
Clucas, George, 240842 Pte.
Cobden, Harry, 49950 Pte.
Cobham, Wilfred, 50744 Cpl.
Coe, Charles Gordon, 292581 Pte.
Coleman, John George, 51922 Pte.
Coles, George, 291764 Pte.

Collier, Robert, 49858 Pte.
Collier, Thos. George, 51921 Pte.
Collins, John Arthur, 24827 Pte.
Colman, William, 14320 Pte.
Conway, Andrew, 50587 Pte.
Cook, Robert, 13226 Sgt.
Cooke, Ernest, 15017 Pte.
Coombs, Alan, 49385 Pte.
Coombs, Samuel, 13567 L/Cpl.
Coop, Alfred, 50847 Pte.
Cooper, Henry, 49467 Pte.
Cooper, William, 15670 Pte.
Cooper, Wm. Thos., 10244 Pte.
Coote, Jonas, 27657 L/Cpl.
Cope, Thomas, 39889 Pte.
Copeland, Joseph, 49343 Pte.
Corke, Frank, 32988 Pte.
Cottingham, Geo. Eric, 14317 Pte.
Court, Montagu Charles, 8354 Pte.
Cox, Ernest, 17826 Pte.
Cox, Richard, Joseph, 18907 Pte.
Cox, Sydney, 15822 Pte.
Cragg, George, 14045 Pte.
Craig, Ernest, 13986 Pte.
Craven, John, 36013 Pte.
Crook, Harold, 14305 Pte.
Crook, James Albert, 292530 Pte.
Cross, Thomas, 13919 L/Cpl.
Crowton, William, 14346 L/Cpl.
Crump, Charles, 33122 Pte.
Cryer, Charles, 24782 Pte.
Cullen, James Edmund, 25847 Pte.
Curbishley, Oliver, 18649 Pte.
Curzon, Reuben, 18122 Pte.

Dagger, Thos. Henry, 24817 Pte.
Dagnall, Wm. Stewart, 32758 A/Cpl.
Dahmann, Anth. Chas., 36669 Pte.
Dair, Patrick, 13057 Pte.
Darlington, Albert, 13123 Pte.
Darlington, Fred, 15845 Pte.
Davenport, Thomas, 14917 L/Cpl.
Davenport, William, 17785 Pte.
Davey, Bertie George, 51923 Pte.
Davies, George Richd., 45687 Pte.
Davies, Herbert, 49409 Pte.
Davies, James, 49471 Pte.
Davies, Richard, 26575 Pte.
Davies, Simeon, 315314 Pte.
Davies, Wm. Henry, 16510 Pte.
Dawson, Harry Hobson, 44166 Pte.
Dawson, William, 49355 Pte.
Dean, Frank, 35985 Pte.
Dean, Harry, 36774 Pte.
Dean, John Arthur, 243201 Pte.
Dempsey, Joseph, 10887 Pte.
Dennis, Joseph, 49475 Pte.
Dermott, Joseph, 31997 Pte.
Devall, Edward Ernest, 28202 Cpl.
Devenport Wm. James, 14539 Sgt.
Dickinson, Joseph Riley, 26232 Pte.
Dickson, John, 11998 Pte.
Dixon, John Bertrand, 49748 Pte.
Dobson, Frank, 14526 Pte.
Dodd, John, 26427 L/Cpl.
Dodd, James, 64017 Pte.

Dodds, Wm. Vickerman Stevenson, 60504 Pte.
Dolan, Edward, 26555, L/Cpl.
Donnelly, Martin, 49484 Pte.
Dowd, John, 13852 Pte.
Doyle, John, 14857 Pte.
Duddy, Dennis, 14558 Pte.
Duffield, George, 33381 Pte.
Dunlop, Thos. Hume, 36374 Pte.
Dunn, Allen, 49399 Pte.
Durant, George Hugo, 25138 Pte.
Dutton, Charles, 17779 Pte.
Dutton, Thomas Wm., 14861 Pte.
Dutton, William, 14737 Pte.
Dutton, Wm. Arthur, 14047 Pte.
Dye, Walter, 53082 L/Cpl.
Dykins, James Louis, 60468 Pte.

Earlam, Thomas, 36115 Pte.
Eckersley, Robt. Spring., 49392 Pte.
Edbrooke, Hugh Thos., 34851 Pte.
Edge, Walter Thomas, 19469 Pte.
Edwards, Charles, 32108 Pte.
Edwards, Fred, 24575 Pte.
Edwards, Harry, 40545 Pte.
Edwards, John Thos., 16196 Pte.
Edwards, Joseph, 50469 Pte.
Edwards, Timothy, 52943 Pte.
Edwards, William, 11678 L/Cpl.
Ellard, Wm. Herbert, 27773 Pte.
Elliott, John, 245976 Pte.
Ellis, Percy, 26522 Pte.
Ellis, Walter, 36124 Pte.
Elson, Frank, 10875 Pte.
Etchells, Geo. Henry, 18846 A/Sgt.
Evans, Albert George, 49201 L/Cpl.
Evans, James, 35031 Pte.
Everall, William John, 50735 Pte.
Eyres, John, 18345 Pte.

Fail, George, 8292 Pte.
Fairhurst, Ralph, 14048 L/Cpl.
Fallas, Leonard, 35486 Pte.
Fallon, Frank, 16325 L/Cpl.
Fallows, Robert, 13166 Pte.
Farmer, Arthur, 50981 Sgt.
Farmer, Harold, 33477 Pte.
Fenlan, Thomas, 35177 Pte.
Fereday, Archi. Doug., 72264 Pte.
Fern, William, 35564 Pte.
Ferns, Albert, 260014 Pte.
Fewings, Herbert Regd., 72279 Pte.
Fielding, John, 36056 Pte.
Fillcock, Peter, 26038 Pte.
Finley, George, 13421 Pte.
Finnigan, William, 28731 Pte.
Fisher, Edward Thos., 63479 Pte.
Fitzgerald, Joseph Pat., 292383 Pte.
Flaherty, John, 18806 Pte.
Flaxman, Herbert, 35859 Pte.
Fleet, Robert, 52418 Pte.
Fleetwood, John, 25011 Pte.
Fletcher, Albert Robt., 36396 Pte.
Fletcher, Thomas, 241152 Pte.
Flitcroft, William, 292384 Pte.
Foley, Francis Joseph, 72316 Pte.

Forster, James, 13161 Pte.
Forster, George, 35537 Pte.
Foster, Edward, 35559 Pte.
Foster, James, 14238 Pte.
Fowles, George, 33134 Pte.
Fowles, Peter, 13590 Pte.
Foxley, Joseph, 13953 Pte.
Foy, Edward, 243735 Pte.
Frame, Robert, 14429 A/Sgt.
Frankland, William, 40412 Pte.
Freeman, John Edward, 34520 Pte.
French, James Levi, 15079 Pte.
Fretter, Clarence, 292195 Pte.
Frost, Samuel, 16649 Pte.

Gammond, Wal. Clarke, 63290 Pte.
Garlick William, 15470 Pte.
Garner, Samuel Richd., 14710 Pte.
Garrard, Arthur, 14770 A/Cpl.
Gerrighty, Peter, 59637 Pte.
Gerrity, John, 16506 Pte.
Gibson, George Evers, 14014 Pte.
Gibson, Harry, 15512 Pte.
Gilbert, Richard, 52388 Pte.
Gill, Richard, 15801 Pte.
Gill, Robert, 29146 Pte.
Gleave, John Henry, 14732 Sgt.
Goodall, Charles, 14874 Pte.
Goodier, William Ernest, 14825 Pte.
Goodwin, David, 14233 Pte.
Gore, James, 72319 Pte.
Graham, Arthur, 243937 Pte.
Graham, Robert John, 45115 Cpl.
Gresty, James, 44121 Pte.
Gresty, Jonathan, 35292 Pte.
Griffin, Harold, 60506 Pte.
Grimes, Frank, 58275 Pte.
Grimshaw, Alfred, 45342 Pte.

Haines, William, 53097 Pte.
Hall, Bernal, 50649 Pte.
Hall, Ira, 18427 Pte.
Hall, Lewis, 44253 Pte.
Hallam, Frank, 15649 Cpl.
Hallows, Charles, 36195 Pte.
Halls, Fredk. William, 51977 Pte.
Hamilton, Ernest, 15273 Pte.
Hamlett, Charles, 15523 Pte.
Hampson, John, 14542 Pte.
Hampson, Thomas, 25215 Pte.
Hampton, William, 20386 Pte.
Hancock, Arthur, 50479 Pte.
Hancock, Edward Thos., 35277 Pte.
Hancock, Harold, 15132 Pte.
Hancock, William, 6784 A/L/Sgt.
Handley, Thos. Stephen, 51925 Pte.
Hankey, Samuel, 13645 Pte.
Hanlon, Joseph, 36662 Pte.
Hardcastle, Oswald, 24031 Sgt.
Hargreaves, George, 50495 Pte.
Hargeaves, John, 15988 Pte.
Harris, Fred, 52400 Pte.
Harrison, James, 14012 L/Cpl.
Harrison, John Henry, 45702 Pte.
Harrison, William, 15564 Pte.

Harrop, Walter, 14004 L/Sgt.
Haspell, William, 240949 Pte.
Hatton, Alfred, 35515 Pte.
Hatton, Oliver, 12816 Pte.
Hawkins, Charles, 8859 Pte.
Hawkins, John Henry, 36680 Pte.
Hawkins, William, 52341 Pte.
Haycocks, Wm. Henry, 52424 Pte.
Hayes, George Wm., 10152 L/Cpl.
Healy, James, 35534 L/Cpl.
Heaps, Joseph, 13736 Pte.
Heath, Ederton, 35232 Pte.
Heath, Jeffrey, 52387 A/Sgt.
Heatley, Geo. Hudson, 52410 Pte.
Heeler, Joseph Warham, 45522 Pte.
Helsby, Harry, 35698 Pte.
Henry, Hugh, 29286 Pte.
Henry, Peter, 49621 Pte.
Herbert, George Thos., 24728 Pte.
Hewitt, George, 10907 Pte.
Hewson, John 243638 Pte.
Hickson, Thornton, 13115 L/Cpl.
Higgins, John, 11778 Pte.
Hilditch, Harold, 52027 Pte.
Hill, Fred, 35150 Pte.
Hill, Wilson Thomas, 13140 Pte.
Hilliard, Joe, 16782 Pte.
Hinds, George, 23387 Pte.
Hodgkinson, John Wm., 10363 Pte.
Hodgson, Martin, 49402 Pte.
Hodgson, Vincent Ellis, 291678 Pte.
Hodkinson, Charles Wm., 49406 Pte.
Hodkinson, Walter, 12884 Pte.
Holbrook, William, 36325 Pte.
Holden, Harold, 242103 Pte.
Holland, Joseph, 11137 Pte.
Holland, Robert, 13101 Sgt.
Holland, Thomas, 34195 Pte.
Holland, William, 24267 Pte.
Hollingworth, Robert, 60503 Pte.
Holmes, Thos. Walter, 35721 Pte.
Holmes, Wilfred, 36048 Pte.
Holt, Fred, 14609 Pte.
Hope, Samuel, 45236 Pte.
Hopton, Alfred, 50878 Pte.
Horbury, Charles, 26650 Pte.
Horsfield, Ernest, 49979 L/Cpl.
Horton, Harry, 49980 L/Cpl.
Horton, James, 14959 Sgt.
Horton, Wm. Edward, 14967 Sgt.
Houghton, George, 36180 Pte..
Houghton, Percy, 39996 Pte.
Houghton, Thomas, 14196 Pte.
Houldin, Arthur, 35797 Pte.
Howard, Albert, 72461 Pte.
Howells, Bertie, 12210 Pte.
Hughes, Alfred, 10338 Pte.
Hughes, George, 14422 A/Sgt.
Hughes, Thomas, 35717 Pte.
Hughes, William, 36359 Pte.
Hughes, Wm. Robert, 9655 L/Cpl.
Hulme, John, 24567 Pte.
Hunt, James, 15658 Sgt.
Hurst, Thomas Haigh, 36709 L/Cpl.
Hurst, William, 244258 Pte.
Hutchinson, Stanley, 12616 Pte,

Inchley, John William, 50636 Pte.
Ingham, Louis, 10238 Pte.
Inglis Robert, 53103 Pte.
Inions, John, 12653 Pte.

Jacks, Henry, 13910 Pte.
Jackson, Joseph, 18094 Pte.
Jackson, Wm. Henry, 16412 Pte.
Jeffs, William, 14980 L/Cpl.
Jenkinson, John, 65025 Pte.
Johnson, John, 12949 Cpl.
Johnson, John Harold, 18664 Pte.
Johnson, Robert, 13156 Pte.
Jolley, Joseph, 15093 Pte.
Jones, Albert, 50173 Pte.
Jones, Bertie, 17879 Pte.
Jones, Charles Henry, 9958 A/Cpl.
Jones, David, 15816 Pte.
Jones, Edward Evan, W/317 L/Cpl.
Jones, Evan, 59136 Pte.
Jones, George, 36169 Pte.
Jones, Harold, 35386 Pte.
Jones, Harold David, 36273 Pte.
Jones, Harry, 14854 Pte.
Jones, Henry, 15004 Pte.
Jones, Herbert, 15995 Pte.
Jones, Horace William, 16041 Pte.
Jones, Hugh Edward, 10769 Pte.
Jones, Joseph, 24593 Pte.
Jones, Joseph, 32035 Pte.
Jones, Richd. Edward, 17891 L/Cpl.
Jones, Robt. Edward, 49155 Pte.
Jones, Stanley, 13372 Pte.
Jones, Thomas James, 52866 Pte.
Jones, William, 24295 A/Sgt.
Jones, William, 36287 Pte.
Jones, William Henry, 34959 Pte.
Joyce, Frederick, 17774 Pte.
Joynson, Wm. James, W/34 Cpl.

Kay, John, 10770 Pte.
Kearns, William John, W/522 Pte.
Kearsley, Frederick, 33146 Pte.
Keenahan, John, 14859 Pte.
Kelly, John, 13941 Pte.
Kelly, John, 36152 Pte.
Kelly Thomas, 17873 L/Cpl.
Kendrick, David James, 32000 Pte.
Kenna, Thomas, 35180 Pte.
Kenny, Daniel, 242700 Pte.
Keogh, Thomas, 12903 L/Cpl.
Kettle, Albert, 24209 Pte.
Kettle, James, 18371 Pte.
Kettleband, George, 50596 Pte.
Kilburn, John, 32164 L/Cpl.
Kinder, George, 13210 A/Sgt.
King, William, 9611 Pte.
Kirk, Leopold Frederick, 14705 Pte.
Knight, Ted, 24177 Pte.
Knight, Wilfred, 15879 Pte.
Knott, William, 11871 Pte.
Knowles, Albert, 14335 Pte.

Lamb, John, 15144 Cpl.
Lambert, Alfred, 316077 Pte.
Lambert, Charles, 14562 Pte,

Lancaster, Arthur Chas., 8472 Pte.
Lardner, Thomas, 32592 Pte.
Lawrence, Albert, 50839 Pte.
Laws, James, 28347 Pte.
Lawson, James, 34964 Pte.
Leadbeater, James, W/316 Pte.
Leah, George, 266216 Pte.
Leah, Harry, 9760 Pte.
Leather, James, 13137 Pte.
Leather, John, 21965 Pte.
Leech, Joseph, 10108 L/Cpl.
Lees, Samuel, 14688 Pte.
Leitch, Alex. Anderson, 263020 Pte.
Lewis, Harry, 18396 Pte.
Lewis, John, 18886 Pte.
Lewis, William, 15116 Pte.
Liles, Harold Edward, 244940 Cpl.
Little, John, 35848 Pte.
Little, Michael, 10436 Pte.
Littler, William, 36586 Pte.
Lloyd, William Henry, 52396 Pte.
Lloyd, John Wesley, 52425 Pte.
Lloyd, Stephen, 13238 Pte.
Lloyd, Walter John, 72448 Pte.
Lockwood, Clement, 202289 Pte.
Loftus, William, 13015 Pte.
Logan, John, 29545 Pte.
Long, Arthur Hopwood, 50885 Pte.
Lord, William, 49807 Pte.
Loughlin, John, 15518 Pte.
Lowcock, Harold Fielding, 35435 Pte.
Lowndes, John, 26681 Pte.
Lynch, Frank, 15671 Pte.

MacDonald, Archibald, 14761 Pte.
MacMillan, Alexander, 33180 Pte.
Mackenzie, Jack, 35456 Pte.
Maddock, Harry, 35245 Pte.
Mainwaring, George, 13667 Pte.
Maire, Walter, 24608 Pte.
Mallinson, Joshua Percy, 35459 Pte.
Maloney, Michael, 24690 Pte.
Mann, Stanley James, 50637 Pte.
Marlow, James, 36219 Pte.
Marsden, William, 14657 Pte.
Marshall, Fred, 25792 L/Cpl.
Marshall, John, 52956 Pte.
Massey, Benjamin, 50750 Pte.
McCabe, Charles James, W/904 Pte.
McCabe. Leo, 14286 Pte.
McCann, John, 14083 Pte.
McCool Thos. David, 29853 Pte.
McCulloch, Robert, 15938 Pte.
McGarry, John, 25200 Pte.
McLoughlin, William, 50042 Pte.
Mellor, Alphonso, 49382 A/Sgt.
Mellor, Robert, 15575 Pte.
Miller, Alexander, 15894 Cpl.
Milligan, Frederick, 36683 Pte.
Mills, John, 19237 Pte.
Mongon, Owen, 33088 Pte.
Moody, Corbett, 18203 Pte.
Moon, Fred, 12992 A/Cpl.
Moore, William, 25256 Pte.
Moores, Arthur, 14950 Pte.
Moran, Andrew, 15661 Pte,

Morrey, William, 36741 Pte.
Morris, Burt, 50473 Pte.
Morris, Lewis, 25692 Sgt.
Morris, William, 45980 Pte.
Morton, Frederick, 14302 Pte.
Moseley, Arthur, 52398 Pte.
Moseley, Arthur, 242803 Pte.
Moss, Albert, 35267 Pte.
Mould, Cecil, 50882 Pte.
Moult, James, 40544 Pte.
Mountford, George, 20341 Pte.
Mowbray, Fred, 15082 A/Sgt.
Moynihan, Timothy, 53105 Pte.
Munton, Montague, 26676 Pte.
Murrant, Robert, 33728 Pte.
Murray, Alfred, 31947 Pte.

Nash, Frederick, 14548 Pte.
Navin, Edward, 25029 Pte.
Needham, Randolph, 14134 Pte.
Neild, John, 49997 Pte.
Neill, Thomas, 28188 A/Sgt.
Nelson, William, 33150 Pte.
Nevitt, James, 33599 Cpl.
Newport, Richard, 15793 Sgt.
Newton, Walter, 36824 Pte.
Nichols, George Henry, 44337 L/Cpl.
Nightingale, William, 18852 Pte.
Ninnes, Thomas, 14348 Pte.
Noel, Herbert Osmond, 64743 Pte.
Nolan, Robert, 30238 Pte.
Noon, Joseph, 31676 Pte.
Norcross, Frank, 49998 Pte.
Norton, James, 50644 Pte.
Nuttall, John, 27562 Pte.

Oakes, Harry, 36576 Pte.
Oakes, Reginald, 18848 Pte.
Ogden, Charlie, 64252 Pte.
Ogden, John, 35942 Pte.
Oldale, Charles William, 20950 Pte.
Oldham, Henry, 44259 Pte.
Ollerenshaw, Edwin, 35844 Pte.
O'Neill, Ernest, 60509 Pte.
Onions, Albert, 49187 Pte.
Oseman, Edward, 243296 Pte.
Ousey, Frank, 34995 Pte.
Owen, Samuel, 36346 Pte.
Owens, Frank Arthur, 33082 Pte.

Pailthorpe, John, 11970 Pte.
Pantlin, Ernest, 40300 Pte.
Parker, Arthur, 50602 L/Cpl.
Parker, George Charles, 260122 Pte.
Parker, Herbert Joseph, 26415 Pte.
Parker, John, 29748 Pte.
Parnell, George, 9240 L/Cpl.
Parr, William, 52028 Pte.
Parsons, Edward, 50600 Pte.
Paton, George, 64197 Pte.
Paulson, Walter, 50601 Pte.
Payne, Thomas, 34819 L/Cpl.
Pearce, John Henry, 51983 Pte.
Pelling, Frederick, 14836 Pte.
Pemberton, James, 14582 L/Cpl.
Pemberton, Tom, 17775 Pte.

Penlington, James, 49414 Pte.
Pennington, Abraham, 15532 Pte.
Penton, William Robert, 24494 Pte.
Percival, George, 36383 Pte.
Perks, John George, 28149 Pte.
Perks, William George, 21681 Pte.
Phillips, Henry James, 53109 Pte.
Phillips, Moses, 72480 Pte.
Pickup, Thomas, 14000 Pte.
Pimlott, James, 50486 Pte.
Pimlott, John, W/1235 Pte.
Porter, Harry, 52443 Pte.
Postings, Gerard, 14629 L/Cpl.
Potter, James, W/1022 Pte.
Poulton, Richard, 265404 Pte.
Povall, Harry, 40336 Pte.
Povey, Thomas, 36485 Pte.
Povey, Willie Heath, 14008 Sgt.
Prestwich, Fred, 242794 Pte.
Price, Merril, 36044 Pte.
Price, Robert, 15360 Pte.
Price, William, 36433 L/Cpl.
Prince, Ernest, 14721 L/Cpl.
Pritchard, Benjamin, 33606 Pte.
Prytherch, Edwin, 36550 Pte.
Pye, Albert Sydney, 24066 Pte.
Pynn, Frederick, 49408 Pte.

Radley, Victor, 36903 Pte.
Ratcliffe, Joseph, 15549 Pte.
Read, William, 35195 Pte.
Reeves, Geo. Frederick, 14328 Pte.
Reeves, Harold, 33423 Pte.
Reid, Thomas, 15305 Pte.
Revell, John, 30256 Pte.
Reynolds, Ernest, 36337 Pte.
Rhodes, Walter, 18821 Pte.
Rice, Michael, 62034 Pte.
Richardson, Arthur, 244247 Pte.
Richardson, Walter Gar., 24492 Pte.
Ridgway, Henry, 51066 Pte.
Ridgway, Wright, 268184 Pte.
Rigby, John, 32098 Pte.
Riley, Frank, 11128 Pte.
Riley, William, 31566 Pte.
Rimmer, Edwin, W/1035 Pte.
Roberts, Charles Fredk., 33511 Pte.
Roberts, Reginald, 15591 L/Cpl.
Roberts, William, 18833 Pte.
Robertson, Peter, 36210 Pte.
Robinson, Arthur, 34624 L/Cpl.
Robinson, Frederick, 18888 L/Cpl.
Robinson, Frederick, 64343 Pte.
Robinson, Robert, 11161 A/Sgt.
Robinson, Thomas, W/437 Sgt.
Rodgers, Walter, 13095 Pte.
Rogers, Sydney, 49400 Pte.
Rogers, William, 18408 L/Cpl.
Rogerson, Frank, 14675 Pte.
Rogerson, Thomas, 34912 Pte.
Rooney, Samuel, 29771 Pte.
Rowbotham, Ambrose, 25030 Pte.
Rowlinson, Peter, 15803 L/Cpl.
Rowntree, Anthony, 51985 Pte.
Rustage, Samuel, 36592 Pte.
Rutter, John, 14827 Pte.

Ryan, Richard, 36367 Pte.

Saddington, Ben, 50630 Pte.
Sampson, William, 49560 Pte.
Sandham, John Wm., 202043 Pte.
Sanford, Frank, 12417 Pte.
Sattler, William Robt., 52447 Pte.
Savage, Arthur, 14773 Pte.
Savage, Herb. Edward, 292681 Pte.
Schofield, Samuel, 36786 Pte.
Schofield, Thomas, 50477 Pte.
Scholes, Alexander, 26517 Pte.
Scott, Joseph Brayton, 64744 Pte.
Scragg, Arthur, 8998 A/Sgt.
Shallcross, Joseph, 15151 Pte.
Shard, Harry, 15980 Pte.
Sharrocks, Joseph, 14032 Pte.
Shaw, Albert, 13330 Pte.
Shaw, Frank Jubilee, 49422 A/Cpl.
Shaw, James, 14173 Pte.
Shaw, James, 36553 Pte.
Shenton, Robert, 15493 Pte.
Sherlock Ernest Ed., 14924 Sgt.
Shields, John, 58244 Pte.
Shipstone, Percy, 50870 Pte.
Shirt, Sydney, 62303 Pte.
Shore, Albert, 45732 Pte.
Siddle, John Edward, 50836 Pte.
Sidebottom, Harold, 59219 L/Cpl.
Sidwell, Richard, 14974 Pte.
Sinclair, John, 35690 Pte.
Sissons, William Albert, 50641 Pte.
Skelland, William, 24244 L/Cpl.
Skellington, Sidney, 50489 Pte.
Skelton, Joseph, 16919 Sgt.
Skillicorn, Thos. Naylor, 14868 Sgt.
Skillicorn, Wm. Thomas, 14949 Pte.
Slater, Harry, 36237 Pte.
Slater, John Harold, 34243 Pte.
Slattery, George, 22114 Pte.
Smailes, Frank, 34860 Pte.
Smith, Charles, 18422 L/Cpl.
Smith, Ernest, 35993 Pte.
Smith, Fred, 49278 Pte.
Smith, Fred, 202013 Pte.
Smith, George, 11617 Pte.
Smith, Herbert, 50740 Pte.
Smith, James, 10801 Pte.
Smith, John, 21004 Pte.
Smith, John, 24970 Pte.
Smith, Samuel Bell, 24689 Pte.
Smith, Thomas, 14367 Pte.
Smith, William, 72330 Pte.
Snape, Harry Havelock, 14180 Pte.
Snape, Seth, 35364 Pte.
Snelson, Harry, 32644 Pte.
Southern, George, 15526 Pte.
Southern, Thomas, 44284 Pte..
Southern, William, 27221 Pte.
Spargo, Oswald, 51966 Pte.
Speed, Fred, 29556 Pte.
Spencer, Tom, 13720 Pte.
Spilsbury, James, 35282 Pte.
Stafford, Frederick, 16520 Sgt.
Stafford, Harry, 51562 Pte.
Standring, Tom, 265910 Pte.

Stanley, Dan, 28780 Pte.
Stanton, James, 16217 Sgt.
Stanway, George, 14093 L/Cpl.
Stapleton, John, 31957 Pte.
Statham, David, 17828 Pte.
Statham, Ephraim, 21767 Pte.
Steggles, Francis Arthur, 50607 Pte.
Stephens, Alb. Ed., 7714 A/L/Sgt.
Stewart, Jasper Charles, 50604 Pte.
Stewart, John, W/891 Cpl.
Stocker, Geo. Augustus, 51987 Pte.
Storrar, Wm. Edward, 16505 Pte.
Stott, Thomas, 36222 Pte.
Street, Nathaniel, 34929 Pte.
Strugnell, Geo. Herbert, 72252 Pte.
Summerfield, Walter, 35225 Pte.
Sumnall, Richard, 290248 Pte.
Sumpter, Andrew, 35147 Pte.
Sutcliffe, Fred, 72300 Pte.
Swindells, Ernest, 15588 Pte.
Swindells, Joe, 14628 L/Cpl.
Swindells, Sam, 242708 Pte.

Taylor, Frank, 51992 Pte.
Taylor, Henry, 24744 Pte.
Taylor, James, 36701 Pte.
Taylor, John, 14471 A/Sgt.
Taylor, John William, 14070 Pte.
Taylor, Thomas Henry, 35278 Pte.
Taylor, Samuel, 14762 Pte.
Thackwray, John Wm., W/221 Pte.
Thelwall, Fredk. Joseph, 34742 Pte.
Thirlwall, Albert, 14157 Pte.
Thomas, Ernest, 14951 Pte.
Thompson, Leon, W/629 L/Cpl.
Thornley, John, 244238 Pte.
Tilsley, John, 44158 Pte.
Timmis, Fred, 27653 Pte.
Tobin, John 11835 Pte.
Tomkinson, Arthur, 13182 Pte.
Tomlinson, William, 24811 Pte.
Townend, Ernest Walter, 19932 Pte.
Townley, John, 34840 Pte.
Trobridge, John, 8368 A/R.S.M.
Trueman, Fred, 15983 Pte.
Tudor, John Henry, 10431 L/Cpl.
Turner, Edgar, 245969 Cpl.
Turner, William, 14488 Pte.

Unsnorth, Arthur, 13664 Pte.
Uren, Albert George, 16418 Sgt.

Vost, George Clemont, 36208 Pte.

Wainwright, Frank, 18468 Sgt.
Wainwright, Hor. Wm., 292139 Pte.
Walker, Albert, 13591 Pte.
Walker, Alfred, 8060 Pte.
Walker, Herbert, 50642 Pte.
Walker, Joseph, 14649 L/Cpl.
Walker, William Henry, 15480 Pte.
Wall, Charles, 53526 Pte.
Wallis, William, 51930 Pte.
Walton, George Ernest, 35390 Pte.
Wane, Henry, 33572 Pte.
Ward, John, 15106 Pte.

Wardle, Albert, 52876 Pte.
Wardle, Charles Depree, 34812 Pte.
Warrington, James, 14323 Pte.
Warwick, James, 32883 L/Sgt.
Waters, William, 52451 Pte.
Watson, Arthur, 13122 L/Cpl.
Watson, Harold, 60501 Pte.
Watts, Orris George, 53123 Pte.
Weatherby, Joseph, 14497 Sgt.
Webb, James, 21607 Pte.
Webb, Thomas, 241756 Pte.
Weetman, Alfred Ernest, 33163 Pte.
Wells, Gervis, 50646 Pte.
Welsh, Terence, 23140 Pte.
Westerman, George, 16024 Pte.
Westerside, Conrad, 28791 Pte.
Wharmby, Frank, 35478 Pte.
Wharmby, Hubert, 34837 Pte.
Wheatley, William, 51999 Pte.
Whipps, Ernest Harry, 51919 Pte.
White, Edmund, 15762 Pte.
White, Samuel, W/400 Pte.
White, William, 35260 Pte.
Whitehead, Nigel, 13133 Pte.
Wilbraham, Samuel, 24663 Pte.
Wilde, William, 17745 Pte.
Wilding, Harry, 13752 Pte.
Wilding, John, 26851 Pte.
Wilkenson, Alfred, 50467 Pte.
Wilkins, Charles, W/544 Pte.
Wilkinson, Frederick, 13186 Pte.
Williams, David Thos., 315646 Pte.
Williams, Harry, 49363 Pte.
Williams, John, 13167 Pte.
Williams, Joseph, 35501 Pte.
Williams, Joseph Robt., 50492 Pte.
Williams, Percy, 268092 Pte.
Williams, Reginald Thos. 65705 Pte.
Williams, Richard, 241719 Pte.
Williams, Samuel, 27798 Pte.
Williamson, John James, 44026 Pte.
Willis, Fred, 18809 Pte.
Wilson, James, 14181 Pte.
Wilson, James, 45302 Pte.
Wilson, Joe, 35010 Pte.
Wilson, Max William, 53131 Pte.
Winterbottom, John, 14378 Pte.
Wood, Arthur, 14853 A/Cpl.
Wood, Charles Thomas, 9468 Pte.
Wood, Frank, 14443 Pte.
Wood, Frederick, 13849 L/Cpl.
Wood, George, 35830 Pte.
Wood, Maurice, 13426 Sgt.
Wood, Thomas, 13617 Pte.
Woodcock, Ernest, 24275 Pte.
Woods, Edward Irving, 50546 Pte.
Woods, Percy Edward, 51931 Pte.
Woodward, Frank, 11836 Pte.
Woodward, Harry, 13111 Pte.
Wrench, Arthur, 16026 L/Cpl.
Wright, George, 14366 Pte.
Wright, Jacob Robson, 20326 Pte.
Wyatt, James Gladstone, 45070 Pte.
Yarwood, James Henry, 17819 Pte.

Yates, James Edward, 25162 Pte.

Yeoman, Christopher, 65754 Pte.
Young, John Arthur, 15677 Pte.
Yoxall, George, 14242 Pte.
Yoxall, Thomas, 15131 Pte.

11th BATTALION.

Abbott, Thomas, 11470 Pte.
Abrams, James, 17950 Pte.
Adamson, Joseph, 16901 Pte.
Adshead, Oswald, 16988 Pte.
Agnew, George, 16087 Pte.
Alcock Norm. Goulding, 17027 Pte.
Allen, Abraham, 12032 Pte.
Andrew, Ronald, 50712 Pte.
Andus, Alfred, 18075 Pte.
Ankers, George, 243646 Pte.
Annett, Frank, 4890 C.S.M.
Anson, Thomas, 13022 Pte.
Antrobus, John, 18188 Pte.
Appleton, John, 241482 Pte.
Arden, Harry, 15207 Pte.
Arnold George, 24486 Pte.
Arrowsmith, James, 18052 Pte.
Ashborne, Geo. Arthur, 33715 Pte.
Ashton, Ellis, 242898 Pte.
Ashworth, Hudson, 52587 Pte.
Atkinson, Geo. Walter, 24508 Pte.
Avend, Percy James, 72382 Pte.

Babington, Frederick, 23097 Pte.
Bailey, Ephraim, 45874 Pte.
Bailey, Geo. Oakesbury, 18160 Pte.
Bailey, Harry, 13028 Pte.
Bailey, John Thomas, 266841 Pte.
Baker, Francis, 8956 Pte.
Baker, Samuel Thomas, 72352 Pte.
Bancroft, Harold, 10204 Pte.
Banks, Harry, 16849 Pte.
Bardsley, Thomas, 16483 Pte.
Barlow, John, 65657 Pte.
Bate, Arthur, 16542 Sgt.
Bates, Albert, 23162 Pte.
Baxter, Thomas, 16594 Pte.
Beaumont, Charles, 10222 Pte.
Beeley, Herbert, 16994 Pte.
Bennett, Herb. Nelson, 242838 Pte.
Bennett, John, 244034 Pte.
Benson, Frank Percival, 52900 Pte.
Bent, John, 52616 Pte.
Beresford, William, 8869 L/Sgt.
Berry, Richard, 31056 Pte.
Berry, William, 16912 Pte.
Bilbie, George, 50776 A/Sgt.
Birtwistle, Archi. Bilsland, 52586 Pte.
Bishop, Edward Chas., 14990 Pte.
Bishop, Joseph, 24388 Pte.
Bishop, William, 17068 Cpl.
Blackwell, Edward, 24518 Pte.
Boardman, Jacob, 57617 Pte.
Bousfield, Anthony, 24393 Pte.
Bousfield, Rob. Blacklin, 24386 Pte.
Bousfield, Percy, 24396 Pte.
Boon, Arthur, 16995 Pte.
Booth, Eric, 14341 Pte.
Booth, Frederick, 72006 Pte.

Booth, John Wm., 32169 Pte.
Boulton, James, 13717 Pte.
Bowen, Sydney, 285058 Pte.
Bowstead, James, 260145 Pte.
Boyd, Henry, 13821 Sgt.
Boyd, Reginald Geo., 243780 Pte.
Bradbeer, Fredk. Geo., 28375 Pte.
Bradburn, Josiah, 16742 Pte.
Bradbury, Fred, 16700 Pte.
Braddock, Thomas, 16745 Pte.
Bradshaw, William, 241042 Cpl.
Brady, John, 14841 Pte.
Brady, Joseph, 13303 Pte.
Braithwaite, Geo. Wm., 28378 Cpl.
Bramhall, Thomas, 10203 Pte.
Brandreth, Frank, 49943 Pte.
Brenton, Albert Victor, 52748 Pte.
Brighton, Richard, 243050 Pte.
Brimlow, Samuel, 19282 A/Sgt.
Brock, John, 16846 L/Cpl.
Brookes, Frank, 15975 Sgt.
Brooks, Albert, 14557 Pte.
Brooks, George Henry, 50792 Pte.
Brooks, Henry, 74022 Pte.
Brown, Amos, 26337 Pte.
Brown, Frank, 15972 Pte.
Brown, James, 13778 Pte.
Brown, John, 49923 Pte.
Brown, John Duff, 24320 Pte.
Brown, John Edward, 16832 Pte.
Brown, Leonard, 243265 Pte.
Brown, Thomas, 18700 Pte.
Brown, William Ernest, 52626 Pte.
Bruffell, Thomas, 17998 Pte.
Buckley, Charles, 4306 Pte.
Buckley, Herbert, 52700 Pte.
Buckley, Joseph, 10066 L/Cpl.
Buckley, Robert, 15918 Pte.
Buckley, William, 16878 L/Cpl.
Buntin, John, 60522 Pte.
Burgess, Frank, 265985 Pte.
Burns, Christopher, 16603 Pte.
Burrows, Wm. Arthur, 266796 Pte.
Burtenshaw, Richard, 72367 Pte.
Burton, Walter, 52513 Pte.

Cadman, Joseph, 17939 Pte.
Canovan, James, 13612 Pte.
Cartmale, Frank, 52672 L/Cpl.
Case, Walter, 49947 Pte.
Cassen, John William, 285059 Pte.
Casserly, Arthur Pat., 11435 Pte.
Cawley, Thomas, 17989 Pte.
Challinor, Arthur, 16593 Pte.
Chaplin, Louis George, 74022 Pte.
Chapman, Alfred, 14331 Pte.
Cheers, Thomas, 27306 Sgt.
Chesters, George, 24301 Pte.
Childs, Wm. Edward, 267249 Pte.
Clague, Charles Henry, 33744 Pte.
Clarke, George, 18050 Pte.
Clarke, Henry, 14148 Pte.
Clarke, William, 31033 Pte.
Cleary, Michael, 14553 Pte.
Clegg, Thomas, 45636 Pte.
Clement, Sam. James, 50730 Pte.

Clews, John William, 24345 Pte.
Cliffe, Frank, 14473 Pte.
Codd, Alexander, 67368 Pte.
Cole, Thomas George, 263014 Pte.
Coles, Wilfred Douglas, 53703 Pte.
Collette, William, 13189 Cpl.
Collins, William, 52218 Pte.
Colvin, John Wilson, 28556 Pte.
Connor, Thomas, 24493 Pte.
Connor, Thomas, 26602 Pte.
Conroy, William Henry, 16550 Pte.
Cook, Mark Gilbert, 34711 Pte.
Cooper, Ernest Wm., 52697 Pte.
Cope, William, 8187 Cpl.
Cotton, Frank, 20505 Pte.
Cox, Henry James, 53379 Pte.
Cox, William, 17044 Pte.
Coxon, Alfred, 10237 Pte.
Crowther, Thomas, 53491 L/Cpl.
Cullwick Ar. Molineaux, 50795 Pte.
Currin, James Albert, 24649 Pte.

Danvers, Thomas, 243799 Pte.
Darlington, Henry Jas., 24290 Pte.
Darvill, Geo. Henry, 285042 L/Cpl.
Davenport, Samuel, 15862 Pte.
Davey, Harry, 35055 Pte.
Davies, Albert, 15108 Cpl.
Davies, David, 260077 Pte.
Davies, Edward, 24543 Pte.
Davies, Ernest, 72019 Pte.
Davies, Frederick, 266847 Pte.
Davies, John William, 53381 Pte.
Davies, Owen Griffith, 4457 Pte.
Davies, Sidney David, 72094 Pte.
Davies, Thomas, 260071 Pte.
Davies, Tom, 15944 Pte.
Davies, Walter George, 53382 Pte.
Davies, William John, 12104 Pte.
Dean, Charles, 14928 Pte.
Dean, David James, 16875 L/Cpl.
Dewsberry, Jack, 10857 L/Cpl.
Dixon, Edgar, 49480 Pte.
Dixon, James Nathan, 290687 Pte.
Dobson, John Harold, 49481 Pte.
Dodd, Ernest, 24718 A/L/Sgt.
Dodd, Frank, 4393 Pte.
Dodd, Henry, 49482 L/Cpl.
Don, John, 23344 Pte.
Donegan, Thomas, 49924 Pte.
Downing, Albert, 49485 Pte.
Downs, Eli, 16933 Pte.
Downs, John, 52014 Pte.
Doyle, Peter, 29860 Pte.
Draycott, John, 52695 Pte.
Drinkwater, Austin, 34660 Pte.
Duckett, Cornelious, 15186 Pte.
Dunkerley, Harold Ed., 202214 Pte.
Dunn, Frank Matthew, 14010 Pte.
Dunn, Harold, 67418 Pte.
Dunn, Samuel Leonard, 18025 Sgt.

Eades, William, 16744 Pte.
Edwards, John, 16444 Pte.
Edwards, Joseph, 49257 Pte.
Edwards, Leonard, 4285 Pte.

Edwards, Walter Thos. 21505 Pte.
Ellis, Herbert John, 17062 Pte.
Elson, William John, 15191 Pte.
Emmett, William Henry, 53713 Pte.
Emmott, Wilfred, 49865 Pte.
England, Albert Thomas, 53387 Pte.
Evans, Arthur, 267882 Pte.
Evans, John, 53333 Pte.
Evans, Norman, 4579 Pte.

Fabby, Chas. Evan, 14274 A/C.S.M.
Fairbrother, Samuel Disraili, 63672 Pte.
Fairhurst, George, 10320 Sgt.
Farmer, John Herbert, 50789 Pte.
Farrow, Edward, 45406 Pte.
Farrell, William, 72024 Pte.
Farrington, Herbert, 13905 C.S.M.
Farrow, Vincent, 67451 Pte.
Feeley, Daniel, 28728 Pte.
Fisher, Thomas, 16904 Pte.
Fletcher, Joseph, 52707 Pte.
Forshaw, Richard, 16844 Pte.
Freeman, Fredk. Allen, 4171 Pte.
Fretwell, Albert, 74044 Cpl.

Gammon, Clifford Ben., 67484 Pte.
Garner, John, 243716 Pte.
Garnett, Joseph Akister, 21546 Sgt.
Gaskell, George, 14598 Pte.
Gautier, Francis Herbert, 10885 Sgt.
Giles, Joseph, 21548 R.S.M.
Gill, Andrew, 33706 Pte.
Gleave, Lawrence, 50265 Pte.
Goddard, John, 266617 Pte.
Goley, Hugh, 13728 L/Cpl.
Goode, William Thos., 260166 Pte.
Goodier, Samuel, 17047 Pte.
Goodwin, Ernest Robt., W/900 Pte.
Goodwin, John Fredk., 24504 Pte.
Gordon, John, 32705 Pte.
Gough, Geo. Edward, 4413 Pte.
Goulding, George, 18131 Pte.
Grainger, Thomas, 35037 L/Cpl.
Grant, John, 15350 Pte.
Gray, Arthur, 17023 Pte.
Gray, Edwin, 18028 Pte.
Gray, William Peter, 260096 Pte.
Greaves, Percy Gordon, 30393 Pte.
Green, Henry, 49497 Pte.
Green, John, 52656 Pte.
Green, Roland, 12683 L/Cpl.
Greenall, George, 16985 Pte.
Gregory, Charles, 52659 Cpl.
Gregory, Joseph, 16717 Pte.
Gregory, Sydney, 17723 Pte.
Griffiths, Fred, 17974 L/Cpl.
Griffiths, George, 49500 Pte.
Griffiths, James, 9949 Pte.
Griffiths, Jas. Vaughan, 53496 Pte.
Griffiths, Griffith John Glyn, 72027 Pte.
Griffiths, John Howell, 53287 Pte.
Grimshaw, Robert, 58179 Pte.
Grimshaw, Wilfred, 26004 Pte.
Grisdale, Edward, 14364 L/Cpl.

S

Gronow, Arthur, 17053 Pte.
Gudger, Harold Barn., 52599 L/Cpl.
Guest, Ernest, 34715 L/Cpl.
Guy, Thomas Henry, 49154 Pte.

Hall, Albert Victor, 16931 Pte.
Hall, Ebenezer, 74003 Pte.
Hall, William, 20658 Pte.
Hallows, George, 52569 Pte.
Hallworth, Walter, 15110 Pte.
Hamer, Thomas John, 260087 Pte.
Hammond, Percy, 8223 Pte.
Hancock, John Herman, 30990 Pte.
Handrick, James, 16355 Pte.
Hanley, Arthur, 11375 Pte.
Hanlon Patrick, 17029 L/Cpl.
Hanton, William, 50660 Pte.
Hanvey, Ernest, 35307 Pte.
Hardingham, Robert, 50696 Pte.
Hardman, Robert, 243437 Pte.
Hargreaves, John, 243434 Pte.
Harrison, Alfred, 50801 Pte.
Harrison, William, 64141 Pte.
Hartley, Thomas, 17049 Pte.
Harwood, Harry Fredk., 74006 Pte.
Hassall, Thomas, 8513 L/Cpl.
Hawkins, Chas. Osb., 72034 Pte.
Hazlehurst, Thomas, 14198 Pte.
Heath, John, 14277 Pte.
Helsby, Frank Janion, 11031 Pte.
Henshall, George, 7334 Pte.
Henshall, John, 13605 Pte.
Henshall, Thomas, 52592 Pte.
Hepworth, Albert, 266094 Sgt.
Heritage, George, 16711 Pte.
Hetherington, Ar. Wm., 244047 Pte.
Hewison, George, 36102 Pte.
Hibbert, Fred, 49004 Cpl.
Hickson, John James, 49508 Pte.
Hill, Leo Francis, 31061 Pte.
Hilton, Percy, 52678 Pte.
Hinde, Richard, 16099 Pte.
Hitchen, John Joseph, W/285 Pte.
Holder, Frederick John, 53399 Pte.
Holland, Geo. Thomas, 14469 Pte.
Holmes, Harry, 16081 Pte.
Holt, Herbert, 266012 Pte.
Hooley, Harry, 52719 Pte.
Hooper, Alfred Charles, 74005 Pte.
Hooson, Walter, 268373 Pte.
Horton, Arthur, 24013 Pte.
Hough, Alfred, 16941 Pte.
Howard, James, 16722 Pte.
Howarth, James, 25953 Pte.
Howarth, Sam. Stark., 16993 L/Cpl.
Howarth, Walter, 67455 Pte.
Howell, William, 27352 L/Cpl.
Hughes, Arthur Price, 36740 Pte.
Hughes, Joseph, 16693 Pte.
Hughes, Walter James, 53316 Pte.
Hughes, William John, 53479 Pte.
Hulme, William, 14566 Pte.
Hulmes, George, 244905 Pte.
Hulse, Joseph, 16462 Sgt.
Humphreys, George, 49753 Pte.
Hutchinson, Cyril, 65305 Pte.

Hynes, Thomas, 14492 Pte.

Ireland, Kenneth Far., 65625 Pte.

Jackson, Harry, 50268 Pte.
James, Bertie, 53406 Pte.
Johnson, Albert John, 50716 Pte.
Johnson, James, 33379 Pte.
Jones, Evan Joseph, 49516 Pte.
Jones, George, 15578 Sgt.
Jones, Gwilym, 67177 Pte.
Jones, Henry, 11232 Pte.
Jones, Owen, 64619 Pte.
Jones, Robert, 24008 Pte.
Jones, Robert Wm., 1074 L/Cpl.
Jones, William, 24516 Pte.
Jones, William, 49156 Pte.
Jones, William, 53295 Pte.
Jones, William, 53408 Pte.
Jones, William, 67171 Pte.
Jordan, Ernest, 50821 Pte.
Jordan, Henry, 12769 Pte.
Joseph, Llew William, 53409 Pte.
Joyce, James, 17016 Pte.

Kelly, William, 13418 Pte.
Kelsall, Alfred, 13203 L/Cpl.
Kemp, Arthur, 35043 Pte.
Kennedy, George, 49522 Pte.
Kent, Richard, 16824 Pte.
Kettle, Clifford, 15529 Pte.
Killan, Edward John, 49221 L/Cpl.
King, Arthur James, 17025 A/Cpl.
King, Arthur William, 50803 Pte.
King, Israel, 24397 Pte.
King, John, 24316 L/Cpl.
Knighton, Henry Porter, 64932 Pte.
Knowles, Fredk. Albert, 30149 Pte.

Lamb, Ernest William, 28744 Pte.
Land, Ernest, 15695 Pte.
Lane, Fredk. George, 260162 Pte.
Last, Henry Joseph, 50988 Pte.
Latham, Percy, 15358 Pte.
Latham, Thomas, W/27740 Pte.
Latham, Thos. Hodson, 13297 Cpl.
Lavelle, John, 16926 L/Cpl.
Law, Walter Richard, 49139 Cpl.
Lea, William Henry, 52874 Sgt.
Leah, Thomas, 49524 Pte.
Lee, Albert Edward, 24530 Pte.
Leigh, Harold, 14618 Pte.
Lennon, Patrick, 62124 Pte.
Lewis, Charles, 50727 Pte.
Lewis, Evan, 265588 Pte.
Lewis, Hamer, 72051 Pte.
Lewis, Llewelyn Palin, 65750 Pte.
Lewis, Thomas, 16903 Pte.
Lewis, Thomas, 49872 Pte.
Lightfoot, Edward, 17981 Cpl.
Littler, Har. Algernon, 244811 Pte.
Littler, Richard, 62324 Pte.
Lloyd, Fred, 14444 Pte.
Lloyd, Thomas, 4351 Pte.
Long, George, 50665 Pte.
Loughran, William, W/538 Pte.

Lowe, Josiah, 15071 Pte.
Lowe, Willie, 28417 Pte.
Lowick, Sydney Charles, 52543 Pte.
Lowth, Charles, 14634 C.S.M.
Lucas, Percy William, 72221 Pte.
Luff, Arthur, 50697 Pte.
Lunt, William, 12399 Pte.

Maddocks, George, 4038 Pte.
Magall, Owen Arthur Mitchell, 65327 Pte.
Makin, Herbert, 14930 Pte.
Maldon, Arthur, 24522 Pte.
Mansley, Edgar, 67412 Pte.
Manthorpe, Charles, 50666 Pte.
Margetts, Robert, 49529 L/Cpl.
Martin, Henry, 266866 Pte.
Maslin, Alfred, 72353 Pte.
Mason, Herbert, 16694 Pte.
Maxfield, Thomas, 16680 Pte.
May, Geo. John McCallum, 33287 Pte.
May, John, 242879 L/Sgt.
Mayers, John, 52658 Pte.
McCormick, Thomas, 15510 Sgt.
McDonald, Thomas, 52717 Pte.
McGuire, Andrew, 9064 Cpl.
McKee, Peter, 27615 Pte.
McKibbin, Richd. Hen., 32704 Pte.
McLinden, John, 33701 Pte.
McPartland, John, 14432 Pte.
Mellody, Adrian, 16823 L/Cpl.
Mellor, Joe, 44333 Pte.
Mellor, Walter, 59523 Pte.
Mellor, William, 14480 Pte.
Merrall, William, 244569 Pte.
Milarvie, Robert, 18035 Pte.
Miles, Hen. Allen Per., 260173 Pte.
Miller, John, 13051 L/Sgt.
Millington, William, 28294 Cpl.
Minshall, Albert, 49533 Pte.
Mitchell, John, 24259 Pte.
Mitchell, William, 52557 L/Cpl.
Moore, Clement John, 14569 Pte.
Moore, Michael Arthur, 49534 Pte.
Morgan Edgar, 260113 Pte.
Morris, Ernest Edward, 53309 Pte.
Morris, Geo. Benjamin, 16450 Pte.
Morris, John, 49535 Pte.
Morris, Stephen David, 52753 Pte.
Mottram, William, 30279 Pte.
Mould, Matthew Geo., 50698 Pte.
Mulholland, Matthew, 49536 Pte.
Mundy, Clifford, 72397 Pte.
Mycock, James, 49538 Pte.

Nelson, John, 52727 Pte.
Newnham, John William, 243068 Pte.
Newton, Wm. Henry, 244010 Pte.
Nicholson, Henry, 52625 Pte.
Nicholson, Joseph, 200979 Pte.
Nixon, George, 266918 Pte.
Nolan, James Broe, 49927 Pte.
Norton, Fred, 16783 Pte.
Norton, William, 4014 Pte.

Ogden, James, 49541 L/Cpl.

O'Hara, Thomas, 63618 Pte.
Oldham, Fred, 52476 Pte.
Oldham James Arthur, 14131 Cpl.
Oliver, William, 50987 Pte.
Ollerenshaw, William, 67713 Pte.
O'Neill, Frank, 27883 Pte.
Osborne, Thos. Herbert, 16710 Pte.
O'Sullivan, Frank, 10346 Pte.

Ott, William, 39928 Cpl.

Palin, Thomas Henry, 13832 Pte.
Palmer, Wm. Edward, 50809 Pte.
Parker, William, 16902 Pte.
Parr, Charles, 14530 L/Sgt.
Parry, Thomas Bridge, 316132 Pte.
Parsons, Henry Chas. Thos., 53320 Pte.
Partington, Samuel, 67421 Pte.
Peak, Thos. Edward, 13838 Pte.
Pearson, Frank, 17902 Pte.
Peet, William, 49544 Pte.
Pemberton, Geo. Alfred, 18525 Pte.
Percival William, 67426 Pte.
Phillips, George, 12723 Sgt.
Pickering, William, 10320 Pte.
Pickering, William, 14735 Sgt.
Piggott, John, 32869 Pte.
Pimblott, William, 52661 Pte.
Platt, Arthur Hardy, 24528 Sgt.
Pleass, Alfred, 53319 Pte.
Plumer, Edward, 57938 Pte.
Pope, Joseph Edward, 67428 Pte.
Povey, Tom, 67423 Pte.
Powell, Albert, 17975 L/Cpl.
Pratt, Arthur, 24318 Pte.
Preece, Herbert, 50721 Pte.
Price, Charles, 12100 Sgt.
Price, Herbert, 53315 Pte.
Price, John Edward, 285043 Pte.
Price, Thomas, 45725 Pte.
Price, Wilfred, 49549 Pte.
Price, William, 14590 Pte.
Procter, Herbert, 65223 Pte.
Pugh, Alfred, 49163 Pte.

Quinn, Thomas, 243576 Pte.

Radcliffe, Arthur, 35375 Pte.
Ranford, William, 285015 Pte.
Raw, William, 241746 Pte.
Readioff, William, 49552 Pte.
Reece, Edward, 243713 Pte.
Reeves, Charles, 52748 L/Cpl.
Reynolds, Alf. Henry Price, 24417 Pte.
Reynolds, Martin, 244732 Pte.
Richards, David, 52610 L/Cpl.
Richards, Evan Henry, 53420 Pte.
Richmond, Thomas, 53464 Pte.
Ridgway, James Harry, 52747 Pte.
Riley, Arthur, 9941 Pte.
Riley, Richd. Thomas, 16537 L/Cpl.
Riley, Sidney, 17955 Pte.
Rimmer, James Rawson, 13829 Pte.
Roberts, Alfred, 49164 Pte.
Roberts, Daniel, 16552 Pte.

Roberts, Edward, 53342 Pte.
Roberts, George, 30081 Pte.
Roberts, Oscar William, 16574 Sgt.
Roberts, Percy Hylton, 49834 Pte.
Roberts, Wm. Albert, 53325 L/Cpl.
Roberts, Wm. John, 53679 Pte.
Robertson, Albert Gor., 49167 Pte.
Robinson, Austin, 16433 Pte.
Robinson, William, 15475 A/Cpl.
Roe, Percy Victor, 72069 Pte.
Rogers, Arthur, 16536 Pte.
Rogers, Joseph, 16811 Sgt.
Roper, Charles, 50669 Pte.
Rowbotham, George, 52686 Pte.
Rowbotham, John, 49557 Pte.
Rowell, John William, 243746 Pte.
Rowlands, Chas. Wilfred, 15334 Pte.
Rowlands, Richard, 25913 Pte.
Rowlinson, Joseph, 52708 Pte.
Rowson, William Jim, 10886 Pte.
Roxby, Robt. Water., 23305 Pte.

Sampson, Wm. Francis, 21316 Pte.
Samuels, Edward, 14936 Pte.
Sandercock, Her. Clde., 72211 Pte.
Sands, James, 19749 Sgt.
Saunders, Wm. Alfred, 50702 Pte.
Schofield, Ernest, 244513 Pte.
Scott, James, 16346 Pte.
Seddon, Christopher, 35709 Pte.
Seedall, Wilfred, 244540 Pte.
Senior, Fred, 16772 Pte.
Shaw, Jack, 4315 Pte.
Shaw, James, 49564 Pte.
Shaw, Leonard, 17051 Cpl.
Shaw, Neil, 74010 Pte.
Shea, William, 67435 Pte.
Sheargold, Harry, 24391 Pte.
Shearwood, Arthur Ed., 45500 Pte.
Shepherd, John Henry, 24299 Pte.
Sheppard, Ernest John, 244628 Pte.
Simmons, Albert Ed., 24156 Pte.
Simpkin, William, 15773 L/Cpl.
Simpson, John, 45231 Pte.
Simpson, John Fredk., 49566 Pte.
Simpson, Samuel, 19212 Pte.
Sims, Charles, 14493 Pte.
Skelton, William, 29929 Pte.
Sloan, Duncan, 53343 Pte.
Smith, Alfred, 30644 Pte.
Smith, Arthur, 35367 Cpl.
Smith, Arthur Mansfield, 50671 Pte.
Smith, Alex. George, 24533 Pte.
Smith, Herbert, 53683 Pte.
Smith, James, 24078 Pte.
Smith, James, 24467 Pte.
Smith, John, 53327 Pte.
Smith, Percy, 24478 Pte.
Smith, William Lawton, 16838 Cpl.
Souls, Alfred, 21525 Pte.
Southgate, Fredk. Launcelot, 72374 Pte.
Speck, Arthur, 14301 L/Cpl.
Spencer, Albany, 244667 Pte.
Sproston, Robert, 15163 L/Cpl.
Stanley, Daniel, 24461 Pte.

Stanley, John, 24514 Pte.
Stansfield, Richd. Henry, 49171 Pte.
Stapleton, Chas. Wm., 50705 Pte.
Steadman, Frederick, 50819 Pte.
Stephens, William, 53344 Pte.
Stevens, Alfred, 4296 Pte.
Stevens, Frederick, 245984 Pte.
Stockton, Charles, 25242 L/Cpl.
Stokes, Arthur, 15201 Pte.
Stokes, Raymond, 30201 Pte.
Strachan, Ken. John, 50989 Pte.
Stuart, Robert, 52333 Pte.
Stubbs, James, 11552 Pte.
Summerfield, Robert, 25877 Pte.
Sutton, Joseph, 24472 Sgt.
Swain, Thos. Arthur, 13379 Pte.
Swales, Richard, 67443 Pte.
Swan, John, 53328 Pte.
Swan, John William, 11655 Pte.
Switzer, William, 74078 Pte.
Sylvester, Harry, 35376 Pte.

Tate, Herbert, 57264 Pte.
Tate, Percival, 52741 Pte.
Tatler, George Albert, 17962 L/Cpl.
Tatler, Thos. William, 15179 Pte.
Taylor, Harry, 4427 Pte.
Taylor, John, 16868 Pte.
Taylor, Samuel, 14009 Pte.
Taylor, Thomas, 24325 Pte.
Taylor, Wilfred, 14756 L/Cpl.
Thomas, Hiram Rees, 72075 Pte.
Thomas, John, 17949 Pte.
Thomas, William, 45827 Pte.
Thomas, Wm. James, 53329 Pte.
Thompson, Henry, 16252 Pte.
Thompson, Henry, 23384 Pte.
Thorley, Walter, 4490 Pte.
Thorne, Rufus Hamlin, 53432 Pte.
Thornley, William, 11843 L/Cpl.
Timlin, John, 265544 Sgt.
Timperley, Jesse, 14138 L/Cpl.
Timson, Chas. Edward, 50814 Pte.
Tomlinson, Jacob, 12822 Pte.
Tomlinson, Thomas, 52516 L/Cpl.
Tomkins, Wilfred, 57897 Pte.
Tonge, James, 46213 Pte.
Toole, William, 14100 Pte.
Torr, Walter, 50791 Pte.
Tubb, Fredk. George, 74012 Pte.
Turner, William, 19652 Pte.
Turvey, George, 53433 Pte.

Vernon, George, 4468 Pte.
Vernon, Robert, 16847 Sgt.

Wade, George, 22132 Pte.
Wakeham, Fred. John, 245968 Pte.
Walford, Edward, 260176 Pte.
Walker, Alfred, 50707 L/Cpl.
Walker, Stanley, 52489 Pte.
Walker, Thomas, 18039 Pte.
Wall, Oliver, 16591 Pte.
Walters, Harold, 17946 L/Cpl.
Walters, Samuel, 53372 Pte.
Walton, Sidney, 52660 Pte.

Warburton, Fredk., 53694 Pte.
Ward, Robert, 16851 Pte.
Wardle, Joseph, 50199 Pte.
Warrington, Frank, 243711 Pte.
Watson, Sam. Edward, 50811 Pte.
Weaver, James Wilford, 25994 Pte.
Webb, Alfred, 16780 Pte.
Westerman, Geo. Henry, 4424 Pte.
Weston, John, 52690 Pte.
Whitby, Benjamin, 17953 Pte.
Whitmore, William, 50777 Sgt.
Wilbraham, Frank, 4130 Pte.
Wild, George, 52577 Pte.
Wild, Herbert Stanley, 24532 Pte.
Wild Joseph Henry, 11826 Pte.
Wildblood, Enoch, 28253 L/Cpl.
Wilkinson, Arthur, 244767 Pte.
Williams, Edward, 17972 Pte.
Williams, Edward John Terah, 67468 Pte.
Williams, Gil. Henry, 53364 Pte.
Williams, Owen, 67469 Pte.
Williams, William, 27435 Pte.
Williams, Wm. Morris, 24525 Pte.
Wilson, John, 52527 Pte.
Winfield, Frank Edward, 50682 Pte.
Winstanley, Thomas, 24356 Pte.
Wixey, Charles Wm., 53440 Pte.
Wolstenholme, Tom, 244408 Pte.
Wood, Albert, 67465 Pte.
Wood, Edwin Frank, 67459 Pte.
Wood, Emison, 52533 Pte.
Wood, George Wesley, 53368 Pte.
Wood, Herbert Henry, 50673 Pte.
Wood, Samuel, 17014 L/Cpl.
Wood, Samuel, 52750 Pte.
Woodhouse, Chas. Hy., 53737 Pte.
Woods, Joseph, 3524 Pte.
Woollam, John, 14552 Pte.
Woolley, Harry, 16936 Pte.
Worrall, John, 13085 Pte.
Wright, Frederick, 16463 Pte.
Wright, Percy, 19496 Pte.
Wright, Reuben, 53698 Pte.

Yearsley, Thomas, 15227 L/Cpl.
Youds, William, 30042 Pte.
Young, William Henry, W/565 Pte.

12th BATTALION.

Ainscoe, William, 15610 Pte.
Allen, David, 16194 Pte.
Allen, John, 66337 Pte.
Allison, Gordon, 36677 Pte.
Alvey, James, 66371 Pte.

Bailes, Henry, 16296 Pte.
Bailey, John Robert, 15018 Pte.
Ball, John Barsley, 13613 L/Cpl.
Bankes, Jacob, 15301 Sgt.
Barlow, Sept. Harold, 33404 Pte.
Bell, Percy, 13814 Pte.
Bennett, Edward Ang., 243513 Pte.
Bennett, John, 36484 Pte.
Bennett, William, 36477 Pte.
Bent, John, 10901 L/Cpl.

Bentley, Osmond, 35917 Pte.
Birchenough, Walter, 16248 L/Cpl.
Bland, John, 267948 A/Cpl.
Booth, Charles, 34558 Pte.
Bowden, Charles Fredk., 35840 Pte.
Brierley, Walter, 58477 Pte.
Britland, Thomas, 15783 Pte.
Britten, Stanley, 36664 Pte.
Brown, Thomas, 36043 Pte.
Brown, Benjamin, 36208 Pte.
Brown, Robert, 10306 Cpl.
Buckley, William, 16246 A/Sgt.
Burnett, William, 18955 L/Cpl.
Butcher, Thomas, 36766 Pte.
Butterfield, William, 21224 Pte.

Cain, John Thomas, 28498 Cpl.
Cartwright, Frank, 13994 Pte.
Casey, James, 16473 Pte.
Chilton, James, 10346 Sgt.
Clark, John Joseph, 21212 Sgt.
Cleator, Wm. Henry, 28550 Pte.
Clews, John, 16255 Pte.
Cockcroft, James, 16584 Pte.
Collinge, John, 66344 Pte.
Collyer, Norman, 266355 Cpl.
Connell, James Knight, 15231 Pte.
Connolly, John Wm., 13900 Sgt.
Connolly, Thos Howard, 13901 Pte.
Cookson, Herbert, 35191 Pte.
Coppock, Leonard, 24424 Pte.
Corcoran, Thomas, 9899 Pte.
Cowley, Owen, 13512 Sgt.
Culley, James, 14069 L/Cpl.
Curbishley, Ernest, 13886 Pte.

Darlington, Oswald, 15113 L/Cpl.
Davies, Fred Thomas, 18460 Pte.
Davies, Thomas Henry, 13373 Pte.
Dempster, Wm. John, 45966 Pte.
Dibble, Henry Arthur, 40725 Pte.
Didcott, Arthur Edwin, 15931 Cpl.
Didsbury, Walter, 13954 Pte.
Dimelow, John, 13389 Pte.

Edgill, Wm. Bamford, 38206 Pte.
Edwards, Arthur, 18954 Pte.

Faulkner, William, 36205 Pte.
Fitzpatrick, Cornelius, 16112 Sgt.
Foreman, William, 28276 Pte.
Forster, John Condliffe, 35949 Pte.
Furnival, Arthur, 13943 Pte.

Goodwin, Herb. Joseph, 57845 Pte.
Gosling, Robert, 16301 Pte.
Graham, Edmund, 33677 L/Cpl.
Graham, George Fredk., 58506 Pte.
Green, Joseph, 243715 Pte.
Groves, James, 16297 Pte.

Haddock, Terence, 15286 Pte.
Hadley, John, 15347 Pte.
Hall, Walter, 12770 L/Cpl.
Hamer, Herbert, 12768 Pte.
Hammond, David, 45960 Pte.

Hammond, Geo. Hey., 16173 Pte.
Hampson, Herbert, 35480 Pte.
Hancock, Alfred, 18939 L/Cpl.
Hanratty, James, 16277 Sgt.
Harper, Walter, 16214 Pte.
Harrison, John, 18479 Pte.
Heal, Sydney, 13459 Pte.
Henshaw, George, 16474 Cpl.
Hill, Ernest, 13334 Pte.
Hodkinson, Thomas, 45986 Pte.
Holden, James, 45994 Pte.
Horton, William, 36691 Pte.
Howard, Edward, 31000 Pte.
Howarth, Samuel, 15129 Pte.
Hurst, William, 14379 Pte.
Hynch, Joseph Henry, 36312 Pte.

Isaac, John Robert, 13333 Pte.
Isherwood, William, 44387 Pte.

Jackson, Joshua, 16282 L/Cpl.
Johnson, Harry, 15400 Pte.
Jones, Harry, 13930 Sgt.
Jones, Harry, 30996 Pte.
Jones, Leonard, 36216 Pte.
Jones, William John, 36358 Pte.

Kenealy, John, 16218 Pte.
Kennerley, William, 15667 L/Cpl.
Kenyon, Harry, 36215 Pte.
Kewin, Robt. Charles, 28632 Pte.
Kilmartin, William, 16386 Pte.
Kinder, Edwin, 44146 Pte.
Kneale, Robt. Henry, 28638 Pte.
Knott, Ralph, 35967 Pte.

Lawson, Charles, 36679 Pte.
Leech, James, 16060 Pte.
Leigh, Harold, 17487 Cpl.
Littler, William, 13607 Cpl.
Llewellyn, Ernest, 13320 Pte.
Lloyd, William, 58460 Pte.
Loew, Ernest, 16141 Pte.
Lunt, John, 16634 Pte.
Lynch, John Joseph, 15780 Pte.

Maddock, Edgar Arthur, 18519 Pte.
Maddock, Peter, 13190 Pte.
Markworth, Geo. Ed., 28053 Pte.
Marsh, James, 66346 Pte.
Mason, Charles, 66368 Pte.
Massey, Dan, 35748 Pte.
Masters, Arthur Charles, 35594 Pte.
Matthewson, Alex., 14602 L/Cpl.
Mayers, George, 36488 Pte.
McGee, John, 13793 Pte.
Meers, William, 15992 A/L/Cpl.
Mernor, Thomas, 13888 Pte.
Minshull, John, 11627 Pte.
Moon, Henry, 26165 Pte.
Moore, John Fredk., 28652 Pte.
Moran, John Henry, 16279 Pte.
Morgan, Alfred, 66362 Pte.
Morris, John, 58490 Pte.
Morris, Samuel, 18451 Pte.
Moss, James Sherratt, 35869 L/Cpl.

Moughton, Frank, 28655 Pte.
Mulliner, Thos. Victor, 64657 Pte.

Neild, James, 24995 L/Cpl.
Neild, Cecil Jackson, 18477 A/Cpl.
Neild, John, 18949 Pte.
Notley, Walter, 15288 Pte.

Ollerhead, Richard, 15392 Pte.
O'Mara, John, 16018 Pte.
Oultram, Wm. Richard, 64443 Pte.

Parker, Rowland, 58441 Pte.
Parkinson, Frederick, 15296 Pte.
Paul, Charles, 57202 Pte.
Pearson, John, 13081 Sgt.
Pedley, Albert, 14062 Cpl.
Pendlebury, Thomas, 260034 Pte.
Platt, Thomas, 36142 Pte.
Pritchard, John, 16287 Pte.
Proctor, James, 57280 Pte.

Ramsden, Joseph, 10890 Pte.
Reader, James, 25576 Pte.
Reid, Benjamin, 13813 L/Cpl.
Richards, Frank, 50182 Pte.
Ridings, Harry, 266669 Pte.
Riley, George, 18129 Sgt.
Roberts, Edward, W/332 Pte.
Robertson, Thomas, 25336 Pte.
Robinson, Leonard, 58467 Pte.
Rock, Harry, 16308 L/Cpl.
Roughsedge, William, 13151 Pte.
Rushton, Joseph Reg., 33034 Pte.

Salmon, Walter, 35618 Pte.
Sanders, Samuel, 36702 Pte.
Saunders, George, 58504 Pte.
Seagrave, Thomas, 12928 Pte.
Simpson, Gil. Stanley, 57233 L/Cpl.
Staples, Edgar Percy, 36289 Pte.
Stokes, James, 36223 Pte.
Sykes, John Willie, 15282 Cpl.

Taylor, Frank, 58682 Pte.
Thomas, George, W/692 Cpl.
Thomas, Hugh, 16714 Pte.
Tomkinson, Basil, 35214 Pte.
Townley, Charles, 28246 Pte.
Tucker, Ernest James, 66359 Pte.
Turner, Fred Stanley, 26829 Pte.
Turner, Joseph, 16265 Pte.

Walker, Arthur, 35805 Pte.
Wallis, Wm. Stanley, 52623 A/Cpl.
Ward, William Henry, 18472 Pte.
Waring, Thos. William, 36372 Pte.
Waterhouse, Samuel, 13776 Pte.
Watson, Ernest, 14643 Pte.
Wells, Edward Shipley, 34736 Pte.
Westwood, Charles, 18517 A/Cpl.
Whetnall, Edward, 13292 L/Cpl.
Whitehead, Robert, 16068 Pte.
Whitfield, Herbert, 14561 L/Sgt.
Whitley, William Henry, 13606 Pte.
Wilcox, Geo. James, 315949 Pte.

Wilson, Walter, 36871 Pte.
Wood, John, 18483 A/Cpl.
Wood, William, 35782 Pte.
Woodcock, Walter Geo., 13737 Pte.
Woodhouse, Richd. Mel., 24992 Pte.
Woods, Edward, 9835 Pte.
Worsley, John Wm., 13458 Cpl.

Yeates, William Henry, 18825 Pte.
Yeomans, Albert Alfred, 8840 Pte.

13th BATTALION.

Acton, Arthur, W/821 L/Sgt.
Adshead, Arthur, 32540 Pte.
Adshead, Joseph, 15654 Pte.
Aggott, George Fredk., W/837 Pte.
Allen, Tom Barrow, 49223 Pte.
Allen, Wilfred James, W/656 Pte.
Amer, Charles, 35265 Pte.
Anderson, Thos. Harold, W/37 Pte.
Anderton, James, 241502 Pte.
Ankers, William, 24146 Pte.
Anthony, James, 52873 Pte.
Antrobus, Sam, W/834 L/Cpl.
Appleton, Walter, 51030 Pte.
Ardern Walter, 10034 Pte.
Ashpital, James Wm., 50037 Pte.
Aslatt, George, 18057 Pte.
Austin, Thos. Charles, 52857 Pte.

Bailey, David, 35047 L/Cpl.
Bailey, Sidney James, W/228 Pte.
Baines, James, 29233 L/Cpl.
Baker, Charles, 9824 Dr.
Baker, William John, 22044 Pte.
Banber, Samuel, 49938 Pte.
Bardsley, Joseph, 31087 Pte.
Barrie, Wallace, 35565 Pte.
Baugh, Dennis, 17800 Pte.
Bayley, Ernest, 293009 Pte.
Beard, Arthur, 34897 Pte.
Beasley, George Edward, 52065 Pte.
Beech, John, 35514 Pte.
Bell, John Joseph, W/639 Sgt.
Bellis, William, 45750 Pte.
Bennett, William, 26996 Pte.
Benson, William, W/1059 Pte.
Bentley, Edward, And., 49230 Cpl.
Bentley, Ernest, 50907 Pte.
Berry, John William Maudsley, W/1140 Pte.
Bevan, Harold Thos., W/849 Pte.
Bickerton, Chas. Ernest, 27747 Pte.
Birch, Herbert, W/1201 L/Cpl.
Birch, James, 32865 Pte.
Birtwistle, Joseph, 29539 Pte.
Blood, Samuel 52881 Pte.
Blundell, William, W/101 L/Cpl.
Blythe, Enoch, 200540 Sgt.
Board, Geo. Augustus, 7954 Sgt.
Bohan, William, W/925 Pte.
Bond, James, 51058 Pte.
Bosson, Wilfred, 49601 Pte.
Bothan, Chas. Henry, W/539 Pte.
Bowers, William, 243739 Pte.
Bowker, William, 243199 Pte.

Bowyer, Charles, 35115 Pte.
Boyne, Sydney, 13538 Pte.
Bradburn, William, 50029 Pte.
Bradbury, Tom, 50035 Pte.
Bradley, Frank, 35912 Pte.
Bradley, Harry, 26005 Pte.
Bramhall, George, W/590 C.S.M.
Breslin, Frederick, W/541 Pte.
Brightmore, Joseph, 52888 Pte.
Broadhurst, James, 51050 Pte.
Broadhurst, Richard, W/1101 Pte.
Brock, Charles, W/732 Cpl.
Brockbank, Wm. Nich., W/929 Pte.
Brooke, John, 35476 Pte.
Brooke, William, 33391 Pte.
Brookes, Albert Edwin, 36174 Pte.
Brooks, Harold, 52920 Pte.
Brown, Er. Hartshorn, 49234 A/Cpl.
Brown, Francis, W/496 Pte.
Brown, Frederick, W/1203 Cpl.
Brown, William, W/974 Pte.
Buckley, John, 260110 Pte.
Buckley, Thomas, W/714 Pte.
Bunce, Fredk. George, 33823 Pte.
Burgess, Harold, W/1017 Pte.
Burgess, Joseph Stanley, 16118 Pte.
Burke, Thomas, 35025 Pte.
Burke, William, 10686 L/Sgt.
Burns, James, 49596 Pte.
Butterworth, Chas. Aq., 32064 Pte.
Butterworth, John Wm., 51042 Pte.

Cain, George Thomas, 8229 Sgt.
Callaghan, Peter, W/84 Pte.
Campbell, James, W/753 Pte.
Capel, Cecil, 24700 Pte.
Capper, Wm. Edward, W/1096 Pte.
Carefull, John Bird, 50164 Pte.
Carey, Patrick, W/712 Pte.
Carson, John Robert, W/1077 Pte.
Cartlidge, James Aaron, 24116 Pte.
Cartwright, Arthur, 6923 Pte.
Cartwright, John Charles, 32909 A/Cpl.
Casey, John, 52932 Pte.
Cash, John, 29046 L/Cpl.
Caton, William, W/694 Pte.
Chadwick, Samuel, 49953 Pte.
Chadwick, Wm. George, W/573 Pte.
Chambers, John Robert, W/1116, L/Cpl.
Chapman, Jas. Henry, 32657 Pte.
Charleston, Robert, W/27736 Pte.
Charlton, Thomas, 36155 Pte.
Chetwood, Ambrose, W/908 Pte.
Christopher, Alb. Sam., 18980 Pte.
Churchill, Jas. Henry, W/14 Pte.
Clare, Christopher, 45576 Pte.
Clare, Harry, 34664 Pte.
Clarke, Edward, W/259 Pte.
Clarke Harold, W/413 Pte.
Clegg, Albert, 52914 Pte.
Clegg, William, 18971 Pte.
Cliff, Walter, 31106 Pte.
Cliffe, Arthur, 24118 Pte.
Cliffe, Peter James, 266606 Pte.

Clifton, Arthur Percy, 52910 A/Cpl.
Clinton, Arthur, 59048 Pte.
Clough, Frank, 13534 Pte.
Clough, Robert Moss, W/1152 Pte.
Coathup, Andrew, 52045 Pte.
Coley, Samuel, 21729 Pte.
Collinson, James, 24111 A/Cpl.
Condliffe, George Arthur, 51072 Pte.
Cook, Samuel, 29194 A/Sgt.
Cooper, Edgar, W/127 Pte.
Cooper, George, W/748 Pte.
Cooper, Thomas, 28199 Pte.
Copestick, Arthur, 243196 Pte.
Cornes, Harry, 49190 Pte.
Corness, Henry, 50910 Pte.
Cosh, Samuel John, 28198 L/Cpl.
Cottrell, Alfred, 33035 L/Cpl.
Couldrey, John, W/699 Pte.
Coulthurst, Wal. Leslie, 34796 Pte.
Coyle, John, W/1244 Pte.
Crellin, Charles Caesar, 33758 Pte.
Cross, Arthur, 49603 Pte.
Cummins, James, 10331 Pte.
Curran, William, W/175 Pte.

Daly, William Alfred, 24060 Pte.
Darlington, William, 20147 Pte.
Davidson, John, 243244 Pte.
Davies, Chris. Byers, W/504 Sgt.
Davies, David, W/932 Pte.
Davies, David Morris, 52954 Pte.
Davies, Earnest, 14613 A/Sgt.
Davies, Edward Bryan, 49604 Pte.
Davies, George Henry, 52064 A/Sgt.
Davies, Herbert, 49185 L/Cpl.
Davies, Henry Hope, 52052 Pte.
Davies, John, W/29 Pte.
Davies, Leonard, 25272 Pte.
Davies, Leonard Wm., 25158 Pte.
Davies, Thomas, 49256 Pte.
Davies, William, 52074 Pte.
Dawson, Harry, 49957 Pte.
Dayas, Harry Edward, W/1132 Pte.
Deakin, Wm. Nich., W/1033 A/Sgt.
Dean, Joseph Harold, 34540 Pte.
Dearnaley, William, 243877 Pte.
Dennis, John, W/696 Cpl.
Dicker, Edward, W/360 L/Cpl.
Dillon, Andrew, W/343 Pte.
Dilworth, Fred, W/1081 L/Cpl.
Dixon, Harry, 32850 Pte.
Dodd, Albert, 35529 Pte.
Dodd, Frank, W/511 A/L/Sgt.
Dodd, John, 49960 Pte.
Dodd, William, 29161 Sgt.
Dodd, Wm. Thos., W/208 A/L/Cpl.
Donnelly, James, W/340 Pte.
Donnelly, John, 50166 Pte.
Doran, Daniel, 18234 Pte.
Dorchester, Ar. Edward, 52929 Pte.
Douglas, James Bryson, 50905 Pte.
Downes, James, 52898 Pte.
Downs, Joseph, 9922 L/Cpl.
Drayton, John, 240868 Cpl.
Duckers, Thomas, 24162 L/Sgt.
Duckworth, George, 52899 Pte.

Duddridge, Samuel Mark, W/341 C.S.M.
Dudley, Joseph, 49610 L/Cpl.
Dudley, Richard Chas., 49189 Pte.
Dunn, George, W/850 Pte.

Earle, Albert, 27256 Pte.
Eaton, James, W/1010 Sgt.
Eddington, Harold, 49962 Pte.
Edwards, Alfred, 49200 Pte.
Edwards, Lawton, 40866 Pte.
Edwards, Richard, 35270 Pte.
Elliott, Richard, W/701 Sgt.
Ellis, Thomas, W/28 Pte.
Ellis, Walter, W/15 Pte.
Ellison, Frederick, 51049 Pte.
Ennion, Richard, W/903 Pte.
Evans, George, 202036 Pte.
Evans, John, 52837 Pte.
Evans, Thomas Morris, 52053 Pte.
Eyres, Charles, 52901 Pte.

Fabby, Richard, 24063 Pte.
Fagan, Rich. Raymond, 17133 Pte.
Fellowes, William, W/239 Pte.
Fenna, Henry, 24876 L/Cpl.
Ferguson, Robert, 50912 Pte.
Findlater, Alexander, 36763 Pte.
Finn, Michael, 28730 Pte.
Fish, George, 265303 Pte.
Fletcher, George, W/1147 Pte.
Fletcher, Herbert, 26893 Pte.
Ford, Sidney, 52855 Pte.
Ford, Wm. Edward, W/515 L/Cpl.
Forrester, Paul, W/261 Sgt.
Forsey, William, W/816 Pte.
Forster, John, W/229 Cpl.
Forster, Wm. Dickson, 20235 Pte.
Forsyth, Charles, W/151 Pte.
Foster, James Cuthbert, 20820 Pte.
Foxley, Frank Harold, 33000 Pte.
Francis William, W/240 Pte.
Frost, Ernest, 9966 Pte.
Frost, James Arthur, 49612 Pte.

Gandy, George, 33717 Pte.
Gardiner, Harry, 17153 Pte.
Garner, William, 33457 Pte.
Garside, Herbert, 49968 Pte.
Gaukroger, Rowland, 27075 Pte.
George, Francis, W/1142 Pte.
George, Joseph Ernest, W/380 Pte.
Gibson, Thomas, 49614 Pte.
Gibson, Thomas, 50983 Pte.
Gillon, Chas. Francis, W/536 Pte.
Godbold, Henry, 24439 Pte.
Godwin, Ernest, W/156 Pte.
Goodall, Chas. Wm., W/1208 L/Cpl.
Goodall, Richard, 49970 Pte.
Goodger, Fredk. Wm., W/408 Sgt.
Goodwin, Arthur, 52883 Pte.
Gowsell, Thomas, W/591 Cpl.
Graham, James, W/843 Pte.
Greaves, James, 26747 Pte.
Green, Walter, W/1095 Pte.
Green, William, 49188 Pte.

Greenfield, Daniel, 49972 Pte.
Greenwood, Squire, W/27735 Pte.
Griffiths, Albert, 52070 Pte.
Grocott, Frederick, 291214 Pte.

Halford, James, Walter, 51060 Pte.
Halfpenny, Ernest, 15223 Pte.
Hall Wilf. John Arthur, W/757 Pte.
Hamilton, James, 50897 Pte.
Hamlett, Edgar Francis, 10316 Pte.
Hankinson, William, 34682 Pte.
Hannon, Wm. James, W/689 Cpl.
Harding, Albert, 49624 Pte.
Hardy, Herbert Wm., 57618 Pte.
Hardy, John, 13193 Pte.
Harris, George, 35154 Pte.
Harrison, Sam. Edward, 49281 Pte.
Hatton, Henry, 27613 Pte.
Hatton, William, 26013 Pte.
Hayes, Peter, 28735 Pte.
Hayes, William Isaac, 18565 Pte.
Haywood, Geo. Brodie, 59073 Pte.
Healey Fredk. Davenport, W/269 Pte.
Hendry, Robert, 50916 Pte.
Henry, John William, 59049 Pte.
Heywood, John, 16915 Pte.
Higgs, Joseph Habijan, 24167 Pte.
Hill, Edward Thomas, 33533 Pte.
Hill, John 28033 Pte.
Hill, Samuel, 49622 Pte.
Hine, Alb. Wm. Thos., 260111 Pte.
Hitchen, Ralph, 32553 Pte.
Hoban, Thos. Edward, 49590 Pte.
Hockenhull, Joseph, 35568 Pte.
Holdsworth, Fredk. William, 44115 L/Cpl.
Holehouse, Thomas, 50036 Pte.
Holleron, James, 49664 Pte.
Holmes, Fredk. Wm., 11901 Pte.
Holt, Harry, 30746 Pte.
Hoole, Harry, 32659 Pte.
Hooley, Harold, 44154 Pte.
Hooley, John, 243824 Pte.
Hope, John Richard, 52079 Pte.
Houghton, James, 59106 Pte.
Houghton, Thomas, 24686 Pte.
Howarth, Albert, 49619 Pte.
Howarth, John, 49618 Pte.
Howells, Charlie, 52839 Pte.
Hoyle, Thomas John, 29095 Pte.
Hudson, George Arthur, 27972 Pte.
Hughes, James, W/45 Pte.
Hughes, John, W/767 Sgt.
Hughes, John Richd., 52868 Pte.
Hughes, Walter, W/634 C.S.M.
Hughes, Wm. Geo., W/418 A/L/Cpl.
Hulland, Thomas, 59124 Pte.
Hunter, Samuel Charles Denny, 243884 Pte.

Illingworth, Jas. Wm., 24238 Pte.
Inskip, Geo. Fredk., W/282 Pte.
Irwin, Richard, W/782 Pte.

Jackson, George, W/856 Pte.

Jackson, Joseph, 49625 Pte.
Jenkinson, Wm. Royle, W/863 Pte.
Jetson, George, 24178 Pte.
John, David Walter, 260129 Pte.
Johnson, Ben, 18380 Pte.
Johnson, Ernest, 24143 Pte.
Johnson, Frederick, W/889 Pte.
Johnson, Harold, W/505 Sgt.
Johnson, Harry, 13784 Pte.
Johnson, James, W/212 Pte.
Johnson, John Edward, W/255 Pte.
Jones, Edward, W/593 A/L/Cpl.
Jones, Fredk. Duncan, 243197 Pte.
Jones, George Victor, 50038 Pte.
Jones, Henry, W/439 Pte.
Jones, Jenkin, 52094 Pte.
Jones, John, 260106 Pte.
Jones, John Edward, 59042 Pte.
Jones, John Henry, W/628 Pte.
Jones, Joshua John Rich.,W/644Pte.
Jones, Lewin Moston, 51031 Pte.
Jones, Morris, 52043 Pte.
Jones, Percy Walter, 52854 Pte.
Jones, Richard Emrys, 260120 Pte.
Jones, Richard Wm., W/926 Pte.
Jones, Robert Pierce, 59064 Pte.
Jones, Samuel, W/983 Pte.
Jones, Walter, W/1212 Pte.
Jones, William, W/476 Pte.
Jones, William, 25644 Pte.

Keen, Duncan, W/217 Pte.
Kemp, Walter, W/507 Pte.
Kennedy, Leon. Russell, W/667 Pte.
Kerr, Harold, W/806 Pte.
King, Thomas, 18988 Pte.
King, William, 201913 Pte.
Kinrade, Ben. Arthur, 33685 Cpl.
Kitchen, Fredk. Richd., 24379 Pte.

Labrum, Joseph, W/865 Sgt.
Langford, John Ernest, 49666 Pte.
Lawless, James, W/224 L/Cpl.
Leather, Walter, 51075 Pte.
Ledsom, William, W/548 Pte.
Lee, George Thomas, W/587 Sgt.
Lee, Joseph, W/327 L/Cpl.
Lee, Leonard, 11850 Pte.
Leigh, Joseph, 11870 Pte.
Leigh, Richard, 52044 Pte.
Leigh, Samson, 291058 Pte.
Leonard, George, W/1029 Pte.
Lewis, George Henry, W/710 Pte.
Lewis, Joseph John, 9852 Pte.
Lightfoot, Thomas 34705 Pte.
Little John Henry, W/1130 Pte.
Lloyd, Edward, W/180 Pte.
Lloyd, Leslie, 33601 L/Cpl.
Lomas, Harry, 49283 Pte.
Long, Joseph Percy, 59038 Pte.
Long, Walter Ernest, 35546 Pte.
Lumsden, Walter, 266503 Pte.
Luther, Martin, 49210 Pte.
Luty, George William, 30725 Pte.
Lyon, Joseph, 14993 Pte.

Macgregor, Alexander, 50923 Pte.

Maddock, Joseph, 49996 Pte.
Marden, John, 19476 Pte.
Margerison, Arthur, W/198 Pte.
Marley, Thomas, 29301 Pte.
Martin, Joseph, 52085 Pte.
Martindale, James, 50926 Pte.
Mathews, Chas. Herb., 243520 Pte.
Mayor, Fredk. James, 49235 Pte.
McCain, Richard, 29307 Pte.
McCarrey, Henry, W/958 Pte.
McCloone, Bryan, 9682 A/Cpl.
McDonald, Hugh, W/516 Pte.
McDonald, Lewis, 9529 Pte.
McGrory, James, W/253 Pte.
McNally, Jas. Joseph, W/75 Sgt.
McNeil, Robert, W/600 Pte.
McNicol, Robt. Duff, 28178 Pte.
Mealing, Albert, 27679 Pte.
Mee, Fredk. Arthur, W/164 Pte.
Melia, John Thomas, 25650 Pte.
Metcalf, Harry, 19913 Pte.
Miller, Arthur, 243838 Pte.
Mist, Harry, W/487 Pte.
Mitchell, Charles, 19230 Pte.
Moffatt, John, 26882 Pte.
Molyneux, Geo. Wm., 11002 A/Cpl.
Moore, John Corry, 45623 Pte.
Moores, George, 49629 Pte.
Morley, Eric, 19146 Pte.
Morley, James, W/27725 Pte.
Morris, John, 17561 Pte.
Mottershead, Ernest, 52953 Pte.
Mullineux, Alb. Edward, W/237 Pte.
Murphy, Edward, 32589 Pte.
Murphy, George, 52890 Pte.
Murphy, Thos. Patrick, 29314 Pte.
Murphy, William, W/27737 Cpl.
Murray, Charles, 14356 Pte.
Murray, Michael, 15407 Pte.
Mustoe, Philip Joseph, W/553 Pte.

Nash, Ernest, W/690 Pte.
Naylor, William, 35132 Pte.
Neems, Henry Charles, 36308 Pte.
Neild, James Tidswell, 25793 L/Cp.
New, Charles, 26039 Pte.
Norbury, Wilfred, 27438 L/Cpl.
Norris, Robert, W/394 Pte.

Oakes, Samuel, W/281 Pte.
Oakes, Thomas, 10154 Pte.
O'Brien, Thos. And., 32595 L/Cpl.
O'Connor, Martin, 49241 Pte.
O'Kell, Peter, 243796 Pte.
Ollier, John, 33378 Pte.
O'Neill, Matthew, W/267 Pte.
O'Neill, Thomas, W/534 A/Cpl.
Ormerod, Jas. Brooke, 49632 Pte.
Owens, Frank Harley, 52858 Pte.
Owens, James, W/1115 Pte.
Oxbry, Thomas, 21734 Pte.

Pacey, Chas. Fredk., 24764 Pte.
Parker, William, 7333 Pte.
Parkinson, Geo. Hny., W/605 L/Cpl.
Parry, Frank, W/626 Pte.

Parsche, William, 33214 Pte.
Parsons, George, W/89 Pte.
Patrick, Tom, 35788 Pte.
Payne, Geo. Jackson, W/338 Pte.
Pearson, Wm. Henry, 25114 Pte.
Peers, Albert, W/519 Pte.
Peers, George, 11923 Pte.
Peers, John, 59108 Pte.
Pellinger, Herbert, W/195 Pte.
Perrin, Willoughby, 202293 Pte.
Phelan, James, W/792 Pte.
Phillips, Thos. Herb., 260132 Pte.
Pickering, Frank, 52090 Pte.
Pickthall, John R., W/664 A/L/Cpl.
Pickup, Laurence, 49265 Pte.
Pink, John Ford, 5003 Pte.
Plant, Ernest Albert, W/1073 Pte.
Poole, Ernest Henry, W/445 Pte.
Potter, John, W/65 Pte.
Potter, Thos. Herbert, W/952 Pte.
Potts, John, 24548 L/Cpl.
Pownall, Harry, W/1145 L/Cpl.
Pownall, John Chas., W/586 Cpl.
Preece, Herbert, 32919 Pte.
Preston, Robert, 50005 L/Cpl.
Price, Edward Arnold, 260107 Pte.
Price, George, 52885 Pte.
Price, Walter, W1219 Pte.
Pritchard, Alfred, 36722 L/Cpl.
Proudlove, Walter, 35523 Pte.
Pulford, Thos. Geo., W/236 A/Cpl.
Pumford, George, 49244 Pte.

Randles, Wm. Milner, 52848 Pte.
Rayner, Joseph, 52879 Pte.
Redmond, John Pat., W/396 Pte.
Redmond, Peter, W/721 Pte.
Reek, Christopher, 266001 Pte.
Reese, Wm. Arthur, 52860 Pte.
Rhodes, Francis Pat., 49183 L/Cpl.
Richardson, Jarvis, 49250 Pte.
Ridyard, Benjamin, 18994 Pte.
Rigby, Joseph, 33054 Pte.
Roberts, Edward, 33213 Pte.
Roberts, George, W/85 Pte.
Roberts, John, 35194 Pte.
Roberts, John, 52948 Pte.
Roberts, John Hugh, 49672 Pte.
Robinshaw, George, W/27730 Pte.
Rodger, Nor. Guild, W/1071 L/Cpl.
Rodgers, William, 50933 Pte.
Roebuck, Ben, 50932 Pte.
Rose, Sam, 49637 Pte.
Rowe, Frank Woodley, W/638 Pte.
Russell, Alexander, W/707 Pte.
Russell, Charles Henry, 16872 Pte.
Ryder, Herbert, 10740 Pte.

Saxon, Edward, 35557 Pte.
Scheers, Henry, W/674 L/Cpl.
Schofield, Tom, 49277 Pte.
Scott, John, 201871 Pte.
Selby, Frank, W/645 Pte.
Sexton, Robert, 33698 Pte.
Shakeshaft, Henry, W/257 Pte.
Sharpe, Harold Spencer, 49592 Pte.

Shaw, David, 201785 Pte.
Shaw, George, 49642 Pte.
Shaw, Joseph, 24271 Pte.
Sheehan, Jere. Jos., W/871 L/Cpl.
Sheen, Joseph, 32613 L/Cpl.
Shepherd, John, 51028 Pte.
Shore, George Wm., 24091 Pte.
Shore, William, W/1068 Pte.
Sillitoe William, 49640 Pte.
Sinnott, Wm. James, W/760 Pte.
Slater, Harold, 52906 Pte.
Smedley, Robt. Gordon, 50009 Pte.
Smith, Ernest, W/901 Pte.
Smith, Fred, W/1220 Pte.
Smith, Frederick, W/868 Pte.
Smith, Herbert, W/731 Pte.
Smith, John, 4573 Pte.
Smith, Joseph, W/1221 Pte.
Smith, Samuel Thos. 52851 Pte.
Smith, William, 20327 Pte.
Smith, Wm. Edward, W/669 Pte.
Sotorra, Paul, W/716 Pte.
Southern, Edward, 24001 Pte.
Sparrow, Chas. Edward, 49571 Pte.
Speak, Tom, 27029 Pte.
Spencer, Ernest, 52923 Pte.
Stafford, Arthur, 50013 Pte.
Stead, Wm. Robert, 34979 Pte.
Steer, Frank, W/19 Pte.
Stevenson, Arthur, 292136 Pte.
Stevenson, Wilfred, 49572 Pte.
Stewart, Charles, 24869 Pte.
Stock, George, 16886 Pte.
Stokes, Richd. Brinley, 260104 Pte.
Stoneley, George, 243807 Pte.
Storey, Richd. John, 9777 Sgt.
Street, Frank Leslie, 49574 Pte.
Strutt, Francis, W/482 Pte.
Stuart, Gavin Bruce, 50934 Pte.
Sturdy, Charles, 12206 Pte.
Sumner, John Platts, 50039 Pte.
Swift, Sidney, 33370 Pte.
Swindells, John, 49255 Pte.
Swinnerton, Fredk. Wm., 33766 Pte.
Sykes, Frederick, 266463 Pte.

Taaffe, John Thomas, 18554 L/Cpl.
Tandy, Arthur Joseph, 260124 Pte.
Tatton, Herbert, 49181 L/Cpl.
Taylor, Arthur, 45525 Pte.
Taylor, David, 49578 Pte.
Taylor, Geo. Coulson, 200157 Pte.
Taylor, Herbert, 33394 Pte.
Taylor, John, 10391 Pte.
Taylor, Seth, 26799 Pte.
Thayer, Amos, W/630 Pte.
Thelwell, John, W/1149 L/Cpl.
Thomas, Arthur, 10738 Pte.
Thomas, Henry, 23443 Pte.
Thomas, Joseph, 24677 Pte.
Thomason, Thomas, 52895 Pte.
Thompson, Frank, 49245 Pte.
Thompson, James, W/189 L/Cpl.
Thompson, Richard, W/163 Pte.
Thompson, Thos. Henry, 24300 Pte.
Thompson, William, 34595 Pte.

Thornton, Laurence Albert Edward, 12052 L/Cpl.
Tickle, George, 34941 Pte.
Tomkinson, Arthur, 24096 Pte.
Toole, Edward Pat., 21533 A/Cpl.
Trickett, Norman, W/599 Pte.
Truman, Eric Brent., W/456 A/Cpl.
Turnock, Daniel, 24082 Pte.
Tyers, George Archi., 32646 L/Cpl.

Upton, Samuel, W/559 Pte.

Vanables, Alfred, W/378 L/Cpl.
Venables, James, W/162 Pte.
Ventress, Andrew, 50074 Pte.
Vickers, Samuel, 51046 Pte.
Vincent, Jos. Bruce, W/1048 Pte.
Vipont, John, W/381 Pte.

Wainwright, Harold, W/270 L/Cpl.
Wakefield, Denis, 24603 Pte.
Walker, Walter Thos., 9787 Pte.
Walls, George Henry, 49247 Pte.
Walsh, James, 45501 Pte.
Want, Ernest, 201894 Pte.
Warburton, James, 34896 Pte.
Ward, James Henry, W/616 Pte.
Waterhouse, Harg., 291932 Pte.
Watson, Geo. Henry, W/749 L/Cpl.
Weaver, James, W/1061 Pte.
Webster, Harry, 52896 Pte.
Webster, John, W/1080 Pte.
Welch, Thomas, 52067 Pte.
Whalley, Henry, 18970 Pte.
Wharton, Allan John, 50094 L/Cpl.
Whelan, Thomas, 49585 Pte.
Whitby, Harry, W/223 Pte.
White, Arthur, 49659 Pte.
White, Percy, 49662 Pte.
Whitehead, Frank Carr, 32826 Pte.
Whitehead, Rupert, 28142 Pte.
Whitehead, William, 265813 Pte.
Whiteside, Chas. Alfred, W/430 Pte.
Whitton, David, 50904 Pte.
Wilcox, Percy Edward, W/372 Sgt.
Wilday, James, W/647 A/Cpl.
Wilding, James, 49653 Pte.
Williams, Alb. Oliver, W/387 Pte.
Williams, Archie, W/469 Cpl.
Williams, David, 52049 Pte.
Williams, Ernest, W/527 A/Cpl.
Williams, Ernest, 24613 Pte.
Williams, Frederick, W/862 Pte.
Williams, Herb. Wm., 12106 Pte.
Williams, John Henry, W/733 Pte.
Williams, Joseph Hny, 52864 A/Cpl.
Williams, Wallace, W/141 Pte.
Williams, Wm. John, W/1136 Pte.
Williamson, John, 52487 Pte.
Williamson, Leonard, 26741 L/Cpl.
Wills, Robert, 32639 A/Cpl.
Wilson, Alexander, W/399 C.S.M.
Wilson, Richd. Wm., 33723 Pte.
Wilson, William, 49657 Pte.
Wood, Allen, 35460 Pte.
Wood, Edwin, W/598 Pte.

Wood, Ernest, 33093 Pte.
Wood, Harry, 291769 Pte.
Wood, Thomas, W/682 Pte.
Woodfin, Joseph Wm., 243732 Pte.
Woodhead, Joseph, 49587 Pte.
Woods, Bert Robert, W/1122 Pte.
Woods, Joseph, 34804 Pte.
Wooliscroft, William, W/879 Pte.
Worrall, Frederick, 49588 Pte.
Worrall, Peter, 27871 Pte.
Wray, Herb. Wilfred, 24042 Pte.
Wright, Arthur, W/397 Pte.
Wright, Harry, 24253 A/Cpl.
Wright, Vivian, W/898 Sgt.
Wrigley, William, 35287 Pte.

Yarwood, Thomas, 34960 Pte.

14th BATTALION.

Craven, Richard, 36389 Pte.
Eden, William, 35732 Pte.
Goodier, George, 24403 Pte.
Johnson, Fred, 33199 Pte.
Kelly, Patrick, 12849 C.Q.M.S.
Lake, John, 12569 Cpl.
Langhorn, Jas. Isaac, 36031 Pte.
Lloyd, Owen, 11957 A/Sgt.
McLaren, Chas. Henry, 24289 Pte.
Parker, George, 24711 L/Cpl.
Street, Abraham, 36183 Pte.
Wrench, Thos. Henry, 24273 Pte.

15th BATTALION.

Abela, Charles, 19605 Pte.
Acland, Edgar, 21866 L/Sgt.
Adams, Maurice Heath., 241105 Pte.
Alcock, Harry, 25269 L/Cpl.
Allan, Wm. Morton, 20318 Pte.
Alty, Job, 292321 Pte.
Anderson, Edwin Leslie, 51371 Pte.
Anderson, Vic. Albert, 20690 Pte.
Aspin, Jacob, 19521 Cpl.
Aspinall, George, W/435 Pte.
Astles, Clifford, 50286 Pte.
Astles, Harry, 16909 A/Cpl.
Atherton, William, 260227 Pte.
Atkinson, Francis, 22029 Pte.
Atkinson, George, 23139 Pte.
Atkinson, James, 39922 L/Sgt.
Atkinson, John, 45655 Pte.

Bailey, Albert, 13896 Pte.
Baines, Benjamin, 23018 Pte.
Ballagher, Robert, 23057 Cpl.
Ballantyne, John, 51373 Pte.
Ballard, Thos. William, 19492 Pte.
Bamford, Frank, 242829 Pte.
Band, Harry, 58216 Pte.
Banks, Joseph, 292248 Pte.
Barlow, Harry, 63475 Pte.
Barnes, William, 39970 Pte.
Barton, Fred, 58114 Pte.
Barton, Geo. Robert, 23427 L/Cpl.
Barton, Thomas, 44153 Pte.
Bate, Archi. Victor, 19121 Pte.
Bates, Thomas, 67320 Pte.

Bath, James, 45652 Pte.
Beddows, Bertram, 33523 Pte.
Beech, John, 19323 A/C.S.M.
Beet, John, 267928 Pte.
Bellis, Reuben, 52453 Pte.
Bellyon, George, 20127 Sgt.
Benson, Geo. Henry, 19005 Pte.
Benson, Michael Vincent Francis, 19043 Pte.
Bernstein, Harry, 35697 Pte.
Berry, Frederick, 62068 Pte.
Beswick, Frederick, 49675 Pte.
Bibby, William Henry, 41653 Pte.
Bingley, Thomas, 40220 Pte.
Bishop, Stanley Thos., 49735 Pte.
Blackburn, Henry, 19723 Pte.
Bladon, John, 13757 Pte.
Blanchard, William, 267612 Pte.
Bleackley, John, 244677 Pte.
Booth, Thos. Henry, 10009 Pte.
Boothman, William, 267454 Pte.
Boyle, Charles, 260228 Pte.
Bradley, John, 48567 Pte.
Brake, George, 22123 Pte.
Bramwell, Peter, 13314 Pte.
Branscombe, Horace, 19039 Pte.
Breeze, Edward, 41614 Pte.
Britten, Gil. Sidney, 60302 Pte.
Brocklehurst, Wilfred, 76822 Pte.
Brown, William, 20013 Pte.
Brown, Wm. Henry, 58517 Pte.
Bruckshaw, William Harold, 315006 L/Cpl.
Bryan, Albert, 292256 Pte.
Buckley, Charles, 49455 Pte.
Bufton, Alfred Davies, 51657 Pte.
Bulger, Peter, 37006 Pte.
Burke, John, 19876 Cpl.
Burke, Thomas, 265896 A/Cpl.
Burns, Thomas, 19027 Pte.
Butler, Harold, 39923 Pte.

Capon, Oliver, Bert, 20070 Pte.
Carr, Fredk. George, 64176 Pte.
Carr, Harold, 41506 Pte.
Carr, William, 19728 Pte.
Carroll, John, 292997 Pte.
Carter, George, 19641 A/Cpl.
Cartwright, John Thos., 60541 Pte.
Cash, Herbert, 21669 Pte.
Charlton, Joseph, 23093 Pte.
Christie, James Mait., 292259 Pte.
Churcher, Herb. Law., 19863 Pte.
Clarey, Joe, 260189 Pte.
Clark, John, 20328 Dvr.
Clarke, Bernard, 57824 Cpl.
Clarke, Gerald, 26718 Pte.
Clarke, Harry, 19547 Pte.
Clarke, Joseph, 39930 Pte.
Clay, James, 315386 Pte.
Clough, George, 16829 Pte.
Coates, John, 45846 Pte.
Cockerton, Sidney John, 52071 Pte.
Cole, Frederick, 67551 Pte.
Cole, George, 29685 Pte.
Collier, Wm. Henry, 51611 Pte.

Cook, James, 24226 Pte.
Cotton, Richard, 20117 Pte.
Cottrell, Jack Trelford, 40320 Pte.
Courage, George, 51420, Pte.
Court, James Albert, 21631 Pte.
Coventry, Arthur, 67553 L/Cpl.
Cox, John, 19251 Pte.
Crellin, Wm. Henry, 60490 Pte.
Crowe, Wilfred, 23236 Pte.
Cunnah, Benjamin, 19618 L/Cpl.

Dale, Howard James, 20090 L/Cpl.
Davenport, Christopher, 45598 Pte.
Davies, Arthur, 23345 Pte.
Davies, Arthur, 51021 Sgt.
Davies, Evan Thos., 51663 Pte.
Davies, Harold, 40433 Pte.
Davies, Wm. Alfred, 33207 L/Cpl.
Davies, Wm. John, 67561 Pte.
Davis, Stanley Walter, 19038 Sgt.
Deakin, Alfred, 240932 Pte.
Delderfield, Albert, 14135 Pte.
Derbyshire, James, 51737 Pte.
Devitt, Thomas, 23413 Pte.
Dexter, John Roland, 50635 Pte.
Dodd, William, 45029 Pte.
Doran, Arthur Percy, 10476 Pte.
Dowbekin, Harold, 19502 Sgt.
Downs, Wm. Henry, 292702 Pte.
Duckworth, Richd. Ed., 267031 Pte.
Dunning, Fred, 23100 Pte.

Eaves, Joseph, 26162 Pte.
Ecclestone, James, 31096 Pte.
Eckersley, Herbert, 292588 Pte.
Eddings, Tom, 30663 Pte.
Edmonds, Robert, 27137 Pte.
Edmunds, Arthur, 19452 Pte.
Edwards, Alfred, W/687 Pte.
Edwards, Wm. Thomas, 49198 Pte.
Edwardson, Robert, 51620 Pte.
Ellison, Arthur, 202115 Pte.
Elward, Arthur Vincent, 67563 Pte.
Evans, John, 292380 Pte.
Evans, John Victor, 36652 Pte.
Evans, Percy, 51669 Pte.
Evans, Rhys Daniel, 67570 Pte.
Evans, William, 40447 Pte.
Evans, William, 76769 Pte.
Evers, James, 51411 Pte.
Eyre, Thomas Joseph, 27581 Pte.

Fairclough, John Austin, 67363 Pte.
Farmer, John, 30824 Pte.
Fender, Herbert, 10797 Sgt.
Fernihough, Nor. Theo., 67360 Pte.
Fielding, James, 33244 Pte.
Finn, Maurice, 268083 Pte.
Finnigan, Edward, 19004 Pte.
Fitzpatrick, Chris., W/959 Pte.
Fitzpatrick, Joseph, 19552 Cpl.
Flowers, Joseph, 20056 Pte.
Foley, Bernard, 20290 Sgt.
Formby, Robert, 260190 Pte.
Forster, John, 20201 Pte.
Foster, John James, 23007 Cpl.

Foster, John Richard Simpson, 19572 Pte.
Foster, Richard, 23316 Sgt.
Foster Wm. Edward, 315816 Pte.
Friend, Jack, 64149 Pte.

Gandy, Harry, 50376 Cpl.
Garratt, Thomas, 292818 Pte.
Geary, Horace Alfred, 57849 Pte.
Gibby, Price, 40724 Cpl.
Gill, John, 22210 Pte.
Gilroy, Alfred, 19015 Pte.
Gilson, Timothy, 31107 Pte.
Glasstone, Arthur, 19036 Cpl.
Goldman, David, 315819 Pte.
Gomm, Frederick, 29572 Pte.
Goodwin, Sidney, 201996 Pte.
Gore, James, 20458 Sgt.
Gormley, Joseph, 19769 Pte.
Green, John, 260207 Pte.
Green, Thomas, 22166 Pte.
Green, Thomas, 67373 Pte.
Green, Wm. James, 19966 Pte.
Greenlees, John, 20331 Pte.
Greenway, Frederick, 15767 Pte.
Gregory, Walter, 19748 Pte.
Griffiths, Griffith, 67581 Pte.
Gullis, Fredk. Wm., 53552 Pte.

Hague, Robert, 45673 Pte.
Haig, John William, 50247 Pte.
Hall, Arthur, 67586 Pte.
Hall, James, 23053 Pte.
Hall, William, 9252 Pte.
Halliwell, John Herb., 292266 Pte.
Hansbury, Edward, 20041 Pte.
Hargraves, Geo. Wm., 23076 Pte.
Hargraves, Fred, 67391 Pte.
Hargrove, Albert Ed., 52439 L/Cpl.
Harper, Daniel, 19101 Pte.
Harper, Harold, 40311 Pte.
Harper, Wm. Albert, 61954 Pte.
Harrison, John, 19137 L/Sgt.
Harrison, John, 19273 Pte.
Harrison, Walter, 19918 Pte.
Harrop, Harry, 20426 Pte.
Haslam, Thomas, 12440 Pte.
Hassall, Edwin, 53028 Pte.
Hattersley, George, 37085 Pte.
Hawker, Thos. Richd., 37850 Pte.
Haworth, Robert, 62369 L/Cpl.
Haworth, William, 21545 Pte.
Heal, Reginald, 33220 Pte.
Hegerty, John, 19576 Pte.
Herrity, Alexander, 40317 Pte.
Hesketh, Robert, 19742 Pte.
Hewitt, Joseph, 19241 Pte.
Hickman, Thomas, 23287 Pte.
Hill, Horace, 50825 Pte.
Hill, James, 51767 Pte.
Hindley, John, W/272 Pte.
Hitchen, William, 36581 Pte.
Hoare, Robert, 315764 Pte.
Hobson, Herbert, 39980 Cpl.
Hodkinson, Bernard, 53579 Pte.
Hogg, Albert, 33546 Pte.

Holden, Jeremy, 23205 Pte.
Hollies, Oliver, 21676 Sgt.
Holme, Felix, 48693 Pte.
Holmes, Herb. Henry, 51347 Pte.
Holmes, John Wm., 51753 Pte.
Holmes, William, 20004 Pte.
Hope, Ernest, 26934 Pte.
Hopkins, George, 10378 Pte.
Hopkins, George, 15268 Pte.
Hopley, Ernest, 50453 Pte.
Horan, Joseph Henry, 23429 Pte.
Horsfield, William, 10353 Pte.
Hough, Albert, 17825 Pte.
Hough, Thomas, 20339 Pte.
Howell, Henry Walter, 51677 Pte.
Hudson, Alfred, 45772 Pte.
Hughes, Ben, 19806 Pte.
Hughes, Richard, 7071 Cpl.
Hughes, Thomas, 19636 Cpl.
Hunt, Albert Ernest, 8925 Pte.
Hunt, Ernest, 29562 Pte.
Hunt, James, 47708 Pte.
Hurst, William, 60264 A/Sgt.
Huson, Wm. Arnold, 67583 Pte.
Hutchison, Henry, 20319 Pte.

Ingham, Arthur, 32920 Pte.
Ingham, Harold, 49063 Pte.
Irwin, John Fredk., 65482 Pte.

Jackson, Harold, 242141 Pte.
Jackson, John, 64154 Pte.
Jackson, William, 19558 Pte.
Jarvis, Harry, 260185 Pte.
Jefferson, Joseph, 67396 Pte.
Jennings, David Chris., 20077 Sgt.
Jepson, Albert, 45045 Pte.
Johnson, George, 20827 Pte.
Johnson, Samuel, 19887 L/Cpl.
Johnson, Wm. Arthur, 57865 L/Cpl.
Johnstone, Samuel, 15926 Pte.
Jones, Benjamin, 51682 Pte.
Jones, Bertram, 51692 L/Cpl.
Jones, Christopher, 244483 Pte.
Jones, George, 19136 Sgt.
Jones, George Albert, 67600 Pte.
Jones, John Mortimer, 19599 Pte.
Jones, John, 28808 Pte.
Jones, John, 23262 Pte.
Jones, Lloyd, 260194 Pte.
Jordan, Fred, 23066 Pte.
Jordan, Stanley Arthur, 51351 Pte.
Judson, Frank, 15714 Sgt.

Kay, John, 30636 Pte.
Kay, Tom, 67402 Pte.
Keane, Arthur, 19655 A/Cpl.
Keough, James, 22064 Pte.
Kershaw, Harold, 63818 Pte.
King, Norman Thos., 45754 Pte.
Kyne, Albert William, 19874 Sgt.

Lamb, Wm. Henry, 51384 Pte.
Lane, Arthur, 57871 Pte.
Langstaff, John, 19658 Pte.
Leah, Edwin, 62401 Pte.

Leahy, William, 23314 Pte.
Leather, Frank, 19557 Cpl.
Leather, James Arthur, 35248 Pte.
Leatherbarrow, John, 28827 Pte.
Lee Andrew, 40482 Pte.
Lee, Joseph, 52997 Pte.
Leslie, William, 20321 Pte.
Lewis, Griffiths James, 53934 Pte.
Lewis, Isaac, 67618 Pte.
Light, James Sutcliffe, 51402 Pte.
Lightfoot, Joseph, 53574 Pte.
Littlewood, Frederick, 25697 Pte.
Lively, Frank, 27968 Pte.
Livesley, Harold, 19076 Pte.
Lloyd, David, 52058 Pte.
Lomax, John Taylor, 265787 Pte.
Long, John, 53558 Pte.
Longstaff, John James, 52270 Pte.
Lovedays, Bern. Chas., 57980 Pte.
Lowther, Walter, 19877 Sgt.
Lucas, Reginald, 67408 Pte.

Madeley, Walter, 7685 Sgt.
Makinson, Albert, 20039 Pte.
Mallen, John, 52380 Pte.
Marley, George, W/724 Pte.
Marsden, James, 19829 Pte.
Marshall, Alfred, 29674 Pte.
Marshall, Arthur, 244770 Pte.
Marshall, Robt. Douglas, 57882 Pte.
Martin, John Edward, 19935 Pte.
Matthews, Frk. Norton, 15267 Pte.
Maycock, John, 315167 Pte.
McCarthy, Geo. Alfred, 58050 Pte.
McClinchie, Matthew, 20237 L/Sgt.
McDonald, Stanley, W/769 Pte.
McDonald, Thomas, 8266 Pte.
McGann, James Wm., 14064 Pte.
McGowan, William, 65259 Pte.
McHale, James Wm., 40404 Pte.
McNulty, Walter, 51404 Pte.
Middlebrough, Jas. Henry, 19080 Pte.
Millar, William, 20215 Pte.
Mills, Thomas Leslie, 240763 Pte.
Millward, Joseph, 20463 Pte.
Mooney, Harry Alfred, 19860 Sgt.
Morgan, Herb. Ernest, 316061 Pte.
Morgan, Sidney Tranter, 67627 Pte.
Morley, Thomas, 23056 Pte.
Morrey, Reginald, 20952 Pte.
Mottram, Arthur, 13840 Pte.
Moult, John, 30738 Pte.
Muggeridge, Wm. Clifford, 51410 Pte.
Muir, William, 50925 Pte.
Mungeham, Edwin, Geo., 51644 Pte.
Murphy, William, 32603 Pte.

Nash, James, 14774 Pte.
Nethercote, Frederick, 20086 Pte.
Nettleton, Walter, 51795 Pte.
Newbegin, Alfred Wm., 50810 Pte.
Newnes, Thos. Henry, 45512 Pte.
Newsome, Frank, 19900 Pte.
Newton, Chas. Regd., 268546 Pte.
Newton, James, 51630 Pte.
Noonam, James Henry, 50390 Sgt.

Norman, William, 51631 Pte.

Oakes, Ernest, 26349 Pte.
Oates, John, 64088 Pte.
O'Dea, Peter, 51726 Pte.
Oldfield, Frederick, 33629 Pte.
O'Neill, Peter, 241014 Pte.
Ord, Robert, 20307 Pte.
Owen, Pryce, 51375 Pte.
Owen, Robert Edward, 67632 Pte.
Oxley, Stanley, 19978 Pte.

Parfit, Percival Clem., 40299 Pte.
Parker, Albert, 61960 Pte.
Parker, Charles, 10777 Pte.
Parker, Herbert, 45382 Cpl.
Parkes, Samuel, 30006 Pte.
Parkinson, Richard, 52734 Pte.
Parr, Henry, 39989 Pte.
Patrick, Fred, 51778 Pte.
Pearson, Alb. Edward, 20579 Pte.
Pearson, Richard Alex., 201919 Pte.
Pedley, Fredk. Cookson, 49636 Pte.
Pemberton, Wm. Thos., 45971 Pte.
Pettifor, Wm. Ernest, 67638 Pte.
Phillipson, Richard, 19206 Sgt.
Pickles, John Slater, 291946 Pte.
Porter, Harry, 40352 Pte.
Preece, George Wilfred, 25869 Pte.
Prendergast, Alfred, 9571 A/C.S.M.
Price, Charles, 62061 Pte.
Pridmore, Thos. Chesterfield, 51346 Pte.
Prydderch, John Thos., 21374 Pte.
Pye, Herbert, 51632 Pte.

Quinn, John, 19882 Cpl.

Ramshaw, Thomas, 20207 Pte.
Rasburn, William, 19550 L/Sgt.
Retford, Alfred, 292471 Pte.
Reed, Stanley, 57051 Pte.
Rees, Thomas, 67982 Pte.
Relph, Rowland, 19364 Pte.
Rendall, William, 52298 Pte.
Reynolds, Hubert Hry., 37633 Pte.
Richards, David, 51725 Pte.
Richards, Harry, 65540 Pte.
Richardson, William, 19616 Pte.
Richardson, James, 26708 Pte.
Richmond, Frank, 53536 Cpl.
Ridley, Gerald, 50292 Pte.
Riggans, Hugh, 19448 Pte.
Riley, James, 9939 Pte.
Riley, Squire, 39962 Pte.
Rimmer, William, 51708 Pte.
Rivers, Oswald, 60290
Roberts, Donald, 240602 Pte.
Roberts, Percy, 18108 Pte.
Roberts, Samuel, 32519 Pte.
Roberts, William Ellis, 40405 Pte.
Roberts, Wm. Henry, 67643 Pte.
Robertson, David, 21049 Pte.
Rose, Isaac, 26361 Sgt.
Rudd, William, 201806 Pte.
Rushby, William, 52376 Pte.

Rushton, Harold, 19113 Pte.
Rusk, James, 33610 Pte.
Russell, Edward John, 241297 Pte.
Ryan, Joseph, 58094 Pte.

Sabala John, 22125 Pte.
Saven, John Charles, 29625 Pte.
Schofield, George, 40484 Pte.
Schofield, Harold, 291907 Pte.
Sharples, James, 45333 Pte.
Shaw, Thos. Barclay, 44080 Sgt.
Shenton, Frank, 19656 Pte.
Simm, William, 23379 Pte.
Simon, Charles, 20020 Pte.
Skeen, Alfred, 21099 Pte.
Slack, Thomas Wm., 7942 Pte.
Smart, Herbert, 58002 Pte.
Smith, Alfred, 51415 Pte.
Smith, Fred, 23089 Pte.
Smith, Fred, 45670 Pte.
Smith, James, 19083 Pte.
Smith, Joseph, 11347 Pte.
Smith, Robert Wm., 20834 Cpl.
Smith, Wallace, 49570 Pte.
Smith, William, 45965 L/Cpl.
Sproul, Wm. Charles, 20084 L/Cpl.
Stafford, Thomas, 51385 Pte.
Stagles, Wm. Robert, 53566 Pte.
Standing, Richard, 26164 Pte.
Stead, Clifford, 52996 Pte.
Stevens, Herbert Geo., 51700 Pte.
Stevens, James, 20604 Pte.
Sykes, Ernest, 51379 Sgt.
Sykes, James, 52994 Cpl.

Talbot, Walter, 53923 Pte.
Talbott, William, 8473 L/Cpl.
Tate, Harry Ostrend, 200046 Cpl.
Taylor, Herbert, 76840 Pte.
Taylor James Edward, 19673 Pte.
Taylor, James Henry, 19318 L/Cpl.
Taylor, Joseph Wm., 19608 Pte.
Taylor, Samuel, 51703 Pte.
Taylor, Thomas, 12388 Pte.
Taylor, Thomas, 242436 Pte.
Taylor, Walter Elvin, 39920 Pte.
Taylor, William, 20267 Pte.
Tefft, John, 13046 Pte.
Thomas, Evan David, 66172 Pte.
Thomas, Frank, 35168 Pte.
Thomas, Walter Ellis, 40358 Pte.
Thomas, William, 22118 Pte.
Thompson, James, 19519 Pte.
Thomson, James, 20317 Pte.
Thorley, Walter, 23075 Pte.
Thorne, Regd. Price, 58007 L/Cpl.
Thorpe, Percy, 40427 Pte.
Timperley, John Thos., 23285 Pte.
Tittle, Ernest, 59224 Pte.
Tomkinson, Joseph, 50139 Pte.
Tomkinson, Robt. Sum., 32918 Pte.
Tomlinson, James, 18117 L/Cpl.
Toole, Hugh, 36471 Pte.
Towler, Albert Henry, 242598 Pte.
Trueman, Harold, 51723 Pte.
Turner, John, 14734 Pte.

Turner, Theo. Charles, 45819 Pte.
Turner, Thos. John, 53508 Pte.
Turtle, Jos. Hry Deex, 40463 Pte.

Watcher, Ernest, 76842 Pte.
Walker, James, 19827 Pte.
Wallace, James, 19535 Pte.
Walsh, James, 48730 Pte.
Walsh, John Thos. 19897 L/Cpl.
Walton, Fredk. Wm., 23098 Pte.
Walton, Noah, 63623 Pte.
Waring, William, 24112 Pte.
Watson, Chas. George, 19774 Pte.
Watts, Josiah, 38977 Pte.
Weaver, Arthur, 244641 Pte.
Weightman, John, 23045 Pte.
Welbourn, Joseph, 25268 Pte.
Welsh, John, 19059 Pte.
Weston, Ernest, 63831 Pte.
Westray, Charles, 29568 Sgt.
Whalley, Herbert, 243448 Pte.
Whitaker, Enst. Arthur, 40466 Pte.
White Aaron, 24159 Pte.
Whittle, John, 16543 Pte.
Whyte, Charles, 7623 Sgt.
Wilding, Josiah, 19524 L/Cpl.
Wilkinson, James, 23254 L/Cpl.
Williams, Fred, 39959 Pte.
Williams, George, 25580 Pte.
Williams, Joe, 10728 C.S.M.
Williams, John Alfred, 40437 Pte.
Williams, Morris, 19772 Pte.
Williams, Samuel, 27571 Pte.
Williams, Stephen, 17679 L/Cpl.
Wilson, Fred, 19327 Pte.
Wilson, Thomas, 32629 Pte.
Winterbottom, Benj., 52682 Pte.
Woodruff, Ernest, 51488 Pte.
Woollams, Harold, 28065 Pte.
Worden, Harry, 19205 L/Cpl.
Worrall, Alfred, 65486 Pte.
Worrall, John, 34780 Pte.
Worthington, John Wm., 49291 Pte.
Worthington, Stanley, 40351 Pte.
Wright, Ernest Egerton, 51715 Pte.
Wright, James, 33536 Pte.
Wright, Percy Ernest, 23348 Pte.
Wroe, John, 23084 Pte.

16th BATTALION.

Adams, Joseph, 21456 Cpl.
Adshead, Robert, 50293 Pte.
Albiston, Luke, 242800 Pte.
Alderson, Arthur, 27122 Pte.
Ainsworth, Herb. Harry, 63493 Pte.
Aitken, Alexander, 59767 Pte.
Allan, George Wm., 21610 A/Cpl.
Allen, Joseph, 21665 Pte.
Ambrose, Percy Jonah, 57793 Pte.
Antrobus, Samuel, 58260 Pte.
Appleby, George, 20726 Pte.
Armstrong, Arthur, 57787 Pte.
Asher, James Harold, 20525 Pte.
Atherton, Wm. Herbert, 58261 Pte.
Austin, George, 57947 Pte.
Austin, William, 50425 Pte.

Ayre, Thomas, 30136 Pte.

Baker, Leonard, 50295 Pte.
Ball, Jack, 40385 Pte.
Banks, Michael, 26636 Pte.
Barlow, Joseph, 50405 Pte.
Barrett, Alfred Edward, 22046 Pte.
Barton, Harold, 29231 Pte.
Beckett, Ernest Wm., 50347 Pte.
Beckett, John, 29763 Pte.
Bell, Richard, 260202 Pte.
Bennett, David, 57796 Pte.
Bennett, Thomas, 40382 Pte.
Bibbings, Reginald, 40297 Cpl.
Binyon, Samuel, 30796 Pte.
Birch, Harry James, 61964 Pte.
Bird, Hedley, 57811 Pte.
Bird, Joseph, 20891 Pte.
Bird, Sidney, 21003 L/Cpl.
Birdsall, Percy, 51659 Pte.
Bonner, Ernest Harold, 50325 Pte.
Booth, Walter, 241572 Pte.
Bootherstone, Jhn. Thos., 20411 Pte.
Bosson, Frederick, 23218 Pte.
Bourner, George Wm., 19809 Sgt.
Bowen, Thomas, 21668 L/Cpl.
Bowers, John Edward, 29603 Pte.
Boyle, Wm. John, 22134 Pte.
Bradley, Ernest, 58230 Pte.
Bradshaw, Geo. Henry, 61973 Pte.
Brayzier, Basil, 40309 Pte.
Brazil, Fredk. Charles, 21549 Pte.
Brockwell, Fred, 57952 L/Cpl.
Brown, Francis, 21981 Pte.
Brown, James, 23250 Pte.
Brown, John, 20547 A/Sgt.
Bryant, Ernest, 21474 Sgt.
Buck, James Lacey, 20523 Pte.

Calvert, Walter, 21050 Pte.
Canovan, Allen, 26374 Pte.
Carey, James, 51614 Pte.
Catton, Walter, 20809 Pte.
Chadwick, Eadeauf, 21758 Pte.
Chambers, Arthur, 23458 Pte.
Chambers, John Greg., 20858 Pte.
Chorlton, William, 40364 Pte.
Christie, Alexander, 21379 L/Cpl.
Clark, James, 60273 Pte.
Clarke, James, 60271 Pte.
Clutton, Edgar Henry, 50297 Pte.
Clynch, John Edward, 45845 Pte.
Coan, Herbert, 242952 Pte.
Collier, Wm. Hugh, 58223 Pte.
Collins, George Wm., 57829 Pte.
Connor, Henry, 22032 Pte.
Connor, John, 20749 L/Cpl.
Cooke, Alb. Joseph, 22165 Pte.
Cooke, Howard, 12134 Pte.
Cooper, Arthur Regd., 49249 Pte.
Corcoran, Martin, 20920 Pte.
Corr, Joseph, 20930 Cpl.
Corrigan, William, 21329 Pte.
Cosgrove, John Fran., 40361 L/Cpl.
Cottam, Joseph, 266707 Pte.
Cox, Alfred, 60314 Pte.

Cox, Arthur, 290364 Pte.
Craven, Evelyn, 51728 Pte.
Culkin, James, 40325 Pte.

Dacy, John, 19798 Pte.
Dackombe, Robert, 20583 Pte.
Dailey, William, 58256 Pte.
Dalton, Daniel, 21933 Pte.
Daniels, Samuel, 202180 Pte.
Davenport, Herbert, 60275 Pte.
Davies, Albert, 21972 Pte.
Davies, Hubert, 316108 Pte.
Davies, John Edward, 51729 Pte.
Davies, John Joseph, 50246 L/Cpl.
Davies, Thomas, 266339 Pte.
Dawson, James, 21835 Pte.
Day, Owen Samuel, 7953 Sgt.
Dodd, Robert, 40335 Pte.
Dolan, James, 29665 Pte.
Downey, Thos. Edward, 202235 Pte.
Dryden, Walter, 51361 Pte.
Duckworth, Harry, 29641 Pte.
Duncombe, Herbert David William,
  29563 L/Cpl.
Dunkerly, Sam, 60274 Pte.
Dutton, Ernest, 30785 Pte.
Dwyer, Andrew John, 28340 Pte.

Eagles, Richard, 51746 Pte.
Eastwood, Albert, 20677 Pte.
Ellis, Percival, 51356 A/Cpl.
Evans, Robt. Simpson, 61951 Pte.
Evans, Wm. Edward, 52872 Pte.
Farnworth, James, 21445 Pte.
Flint, John, 29703 Pte.
Ford, George, 57844 Pte.
Foster, James Graham, 260182 Pte.
Freeland, Percy Mar., 60276 Pte.
Furay, Thomas, 242479 Pte.

Galliers, Percy, 51672 Pte.
Gardner, John, 61970 Pte.
Garley, Charles, 57963 Pte.
Garner, Gilbert, 21961 Pte.
Garner, Harold, 57848 Pte.
Gater, Frederick, 12970 Pte.
Gibbons, Harry, 23347 A/Cpl.
Gibson, Fred, 51348 A/Cpl.
Gilligan, John, 20443 Pte.
Goostrey, Herbert, 51675 Pte.
Greenhalgh, Ernest, 50044 Pte.
Greenwood, Frank, 8697 Sgt.
Griffiths, William, 64294 Pte.
Grimshaw, Creswell, 26086 Pte.
Grubb, George, 51674 Pte.

Hagger, Fred, 57855 Pte.
Hale, Albert, 49503 Pte.
Hall, Ernest, 45124 Pte.
Hallsworth, Alfred, 23277 Pte.
Halsall, Albert Edward, 18824 Pte.
Hardwick, Walter, 36185 Pte.
Harris, David, 50352 L/Cpl.
Hart, Thomas, 17812 Pte.
Hartley, Horatio Wal., 29861 Pte.
Harvey, George, 57854 Pte.

Harwood, Matthew, 21832 L/Cpl.
Hatton, Joseph, 316049 Pte.
Haw, Henry, 50354 Pte.
Hawthorne, Robert, 61971 Pte.
Hawood, John, 21677 Pte.
Hefferman, Cornelius, 202213 Pte.
Herity, Arthur, 8523 Cpl.
Hickman, Joseph, 21845 L/Cpl.
Hill, Albert, 40334 Pte.
Hill, George Ernest, 21529 Pte.
Hill, Harold, 58164 Pte.
Hodgson, Samuel, 20504 Pte.
Hogg, John, 20620 L/Cpl.
Holden, James, 21925 Pte.
Holt, John, 21502 Pte.
Holt, Peter, 21217 Pte.
Honeyball, Arthur Wm., 20608 Pte.
Horton, Chas. Badham, 51608 Pte.
Houghton, Peter, 260191 Pte.
Howard, Chas. Wal., 51330 A/Cpl.
Huerdine, Joseph Fran., 40316 Pte.
Hughes, Alfred, 29864 Pte.
Hulmes, John, 260184 Pte.
Hurley, William, 20669 Pte.

Ingham, Jarvis, 49668 Pte.

Jackson, Frank, 23201 Pte.
Jackson, William, W/1087 Pte.
James, Walter, 40368 Pte.
James, William Horace, 25841 Pte.
Janes, Fredk. Wilfred, 21818 A/Cpl.
Jenkinson, Norman, 21600 Pte.
Johnstone, Thomas, 21371 L/Sgt.
Jones, Alb. Vic. Dean, 45592 Pte.
Jones, John, 21732 Pte.
Jones, John, 23432 Pte.
Jones, Owen Henry, 44236 Pte.
Jones, Samuel, 40305 Pte.
Judge, Walter Guy, 51350 A/Cpl.

Kay, Eric, 23184 Pte.
Kearton Robt. Bern., 51354 L/Cpl.
Keen, William, 21790 Pte.
Kellett, George, 40314 Pte.
Kelly, Robt. Cecil Ewart, 61977 Pte.
Kent, Alfred, 50445 Pte.
Kinsey, Charles, 316066 Pte.
Kirkham, William, 50355 Pte.
Kissach, Albert Arthur, 51688 Pte.
Knight, Robt. Arthur, 202209 Pte.

Lake, Philip, 21405 L/Sgt.
Lambert William, 40360 Pte.
Lea, James, 29634 Pte.
Lea, Norman William, 50309 Pte.
Lee, Matthew, 20634 Pte.
Legg, George, 20793 Pte.
Leigh, William, 32681 L/Cpl.
Lewis, Thomas, 241584 Pte.
Lincoln, Joseph Bowery, 20717 Pte.
Lowe, Amos, 57876 Pte.
Lowe, Daniel, 23412 Pte.
Lowe, George, 20544 Pte.

Macdonald, Thomas, 20826 Pte.

Maloney, Joseph, 51739 Pte.
Malpas, Harry, 21821 Pte.
Maney, James, 51714 Pte.
Mann, George Bird 20928 Pte.
Mannion, William, 292994 Pte.
Marsh, John, 21777 Pte.
Marsh, John Thomas, 21672 Pte.
Marshall, John, 20930 A/Cpl.
Masterson, Edward, 20903 L/Cpl.
Mather, Joseph, 23132 Pte.
Mayfield, Edgar, 21023 L/Cpl.
McCue, John Joseph, 21984 Pte.
McCullough, William, 40356 Pte.
McDonald, William, 23426 L/Cpl.
McEwan, Dougald, 20554 Pte.
McGregor, Percy, 40310 Pte.
McHugh, Thomas, 29842 Pte.
McKay Charles, 7155 Sgt.
McKeon, John W/405 Sgt.
McKinnon, Hector, 50308 Pte.
McNichol, Malcolm, 21604 Pte.
McVey, Harold, 51025 Cpl.
Mellor, Leonard, 202073 Pte.
Mitchell, Charles Wm., 21169 Cpl.
Mitchell, George, 21135 Pte.
Moore, Sam, 30115 Pte.
Moores, Harold, 45858 Pte.
Moran, Francis, 202234 Pte.
Morris, Edward, 22036 Pte.
Morris, Fred, 60286 Pte.
Morris, Harry Cecil, 51702 Pte.
Morrison, Fredk. Charles, 7655 Sgt.
Morrison, Wm. Reid, 29511 Pte.
Mowbray, John, 13076 Sgt.
Myers, George Wm., 20754 Pte.

Nicholas, Henry, 51645 Pte.
Nicholls, William Vic., 58283 Pte.
Nolan, John, 241493 Pte.
Norton, Alfred, 50314 Pte.
Nuttall, William, 21788 Pte.

Oakley, William, 58170 Pte.
Ogden, William, 60288 Pte.
O'Grady, William, 29606 Pte.
Oldham, James, 9627 L/Sgt.
Ollier, Charles, 58263 L/Cpl.

Padgett, Walter, 19793 Pte.
Palmer, Leonard, 51801 Pte.
Parker, Richard, 51777 Pte.
Parkington, Herbert, 291904 Pte.
Pawley, Albert Ralph, 40322 Pte.
Peacock, John Alex., 50315 Pte.
Pearce, Herbert, 57994 Pte.
Pentland, Claud, 21955 Pte.
Pimlott, George, 201920 Pte.
Poole, George, 291906 Pte.
Pope, Albert, 49214 Pte.
Powell, Patrick, 22035 Pte.
Poynton, Thomas, 58199 Pte.
Price, Edward James, 267684 Pte.
Priestley, George Ernest, 57997 Pte.
Pryce, Percy Lewis, 45833 Pte.
Purtill, Norman, 40357 Pte.
Puzey, Henry, 19000 Pte.

Ramscar, Fred, 40304 Pte.
Randall, Charles Henry, 64200 Pte.
Randles, William, 23155 Pte.
Redford Robert, 316012 Pte.
Redman, Frank Sam., 51358 A/Cpl.
Reeder, Charles, 21363 Pte.
Rhodes, George, 50438 Pte.
Richardson, Charles, 57999 Pte.
Richardson, John, 21383 Pte.
Richardson, Philip, 26685 Pte.
Rigby, Joseph, 292610 Pte.
Riley, George, 27379 Pte.
Rix, Robert James, 20742 A/L/Cpl.
Roberts, Edwin Alfred, 45571 Pte.
Robertson, William, 40393 Pte.
Robinson, Thomas, 21093 Pte.
Robinson, Wm. Francis, 51026 Cpl.
Rogers, Horace, 202249 Pte.
Rose, John, 290591 Pte.
Rourke, Albert, 40354 Pte.
Rowe, Joseph, 34363 Pte.
Rowley, John, 20639 Pte.
Royle, James, 40353 Pte.

Salmon, Ernest, 20406 L/Cpl.
Salts, Fred, 292824 Pte.
Saunders, Charles, 29877 Pte.
Sharratt, Wm. Henry, 8844 L/Cpl.
Shaw, Eric Arthur, 58001 Pte.
Shaw, William 45564 Pte.
Shipp, Thomas William, 52621 Pte.
Sibbert, Fredk. Wm., 20623 L/Cpl.
Singleton, Gerald, 40346 Pte.
Slingsby, Harry, 20590 Sgt.
Smalley, Frederick, 315678 Pte.
Smallman, Thos. Charles, 21562 Pte.
Smith, Ernest William, 200768 Pte.
Smith, Harry, 63562 Pte.
Smith, John, 21867 Pte.
Smith, Leonard, 22181 A/L/Cpl.
Smith, Richard, 58286 Pte.
Smith, Robert, 21635 Pte.
Smith, Robert, 40348 Pte.
Smith, William, 21689 Pte.
Soper, Henry, 21806 Pte.
Souls, Arthur William, 21683 L/Cpl.
Souls, Fredk. George, 21686 Pte.
Southern, Samuel, 26921 Pte.
Speight, James Chris., 19096 Sgt.
Speight, Thomas, 20775 Pte.
Spence, James Wm., 20738 Pte.
Springate, Philip, 30306 L/Cpl.
Stanton, Albert, 30677 Pte.
Steele, William, 19202 Pte.
Stewart, James Lind., 50935 Pte.
Stocks, Harold, 20805 Pte.
Stokes, Richd. Benj., 21720 Pte.
Stott, Matthew, 40398 Pte.
Street, Arthur, 23307 Pte.
Sumner, Arthur, 36110 Cpl.

Tate, Henry Owfield, 292566 Pte.
Tattersall, Miles Wallace, 40321 Pte.
Taylor, Joseph, 21656 Pte.
Taylor, Leonard, 21111 Pte.
Thomas, Edward, 292999 Pte.

Thomas, John Wm., 51610 Pte.
Thomas, Thomas, 51721 Pte.
Thompson, John, 25946 Pte.
Tindall, Joseph Stod., 20828 Pte.
Todd, Robt. George Perrie, 21348 L/Cpl.
Trasler, Wm. John, 58008 Pte.
Troughton, Thomas William, 21110 L/Cpl.
Tull, John William, 21145 Cpl.
Turner, Fred, 50340 Pte.

Underwood, Fred, 58009 Pte.

Venables, Joseph, 45531 Pte.

Wakeman, Fredk. Thos., 29564 Pte.
Walker, Joseph Henry, 28170 Pte.
Wallbank, Henry, 50421 Pte.
Walsh, Daniel Pendleton, 20500 Sgt.
Wandless, Alexander, 21238 Pte.
Ward, William, 50423 Pte.
Warhurst, Joseph, 45453 Pte.
Welch, William, 29750 Pte.
Wellings, Thomas, 290498 Pte.
Westby, Thomas, 26116 Pte.
Whipp, Mark, 30762 Pte.
Whitfield, Sam., 20389 Sgt.
Wilde, Harry, 58248 Pte.
Wilden, Hubert, 21220 L/Cpl.
Wilde, George Robson, 20635 Pte.
Willetts, Harry, 28697 Sgt.
Williams, Rupert, 63367 L/Cpl.
Winfrey, Chas. Henry, 21188 Pte.
Wiswall, Harry, 59764 Pte.
Wood, Harold, 51710 Pte.
Woods, George, 21902 Pte.
Woolley, James Samuel, 44059 Pte.
Woolley, Joseph, 40331 Pte.
Wootton, Harold, 21524 Pte.
Worthington, George, 58174 Pte.
Worthy, Lewis Wm., 21351 A/L/Cpl.
Wrigglesworth, Ernest, 20560 Pte.
Wright, Walter, 202144 Pte.
Wynn, Alexander, 61979 Pte.

Youde, Thomas, 202147 Pte.

17th BATTALION.

Clover, Wilfred, 23234 A/Sgt.
Collins, Justin, 39520 Pte.
Dutton, Hugh, 46726 Pte.
Fleetwood, Thos. Ed., 21343 Pte.
Hennessey, William, 46251 Pte.
Howarth, Arnold, 46955 Pte.
Lackabane, Henry, 41264 Pte.
Lewis, Samuel, 8766 A/Sgt.
Suckley, Wm. Herbert, 22003 A/Cpl.
Whitter, Ernest, 23136 Pte.

18th BATTALION.

Biddle, Robert, 37747 Cpl.
Bowen, Stanley, 56945 Pte.
Carlton, William, 37401 Pte.
Davenport, William, 54604 Pte.
Pill, William James, 37305 Pte.

Sanson, Jesse, 42297 Pte.
Walker, William, 37378 Pte.

19th BATTALION.

Baker, John Thomas, 58043 Pte.
Bird, Thos. William, 38306 Pte.
Clare, James Hatton, 38930 Pte.
Cleminson, James, 39323 Pte.
Fleming, George, 39165 Pte.
Holmes, Stephen, 38471 Pte.
Lythgoe, Edward, 38806 Pte.
Parry, William, 39189 Pte.
Pass, Joseph, 35580 Pte.
Ratcliffe, Wm. Ellis, 39270 L/Cpl.
Topping, Arthur, 39608 Pte.
Whitehead, Orrell, 39631 Pte.
Williams, Frederick, 38553 Pte.

20th BATTALION.

Atkinson, Richard, 57663 Pte.
Baker, Bernard, 41947 Cpl.
Haigh, John Willie, 41245 Pte.
Kelly, Francis, 39853 Pte.
Knight, James, 41557 Pte.
Larter, Vaughan, 46034 Pte.
McDermott, Thomas, 42131 Pte.
Rafferty, Thomas, 57759 Pte.
Steele, Robt. Menzies, 46025 Pte.
Swift, James, 41740 Pte.
Taylor, Reginald, 41975 Pte.
Williams, Walter, 41709 Pte.

21st BATTALION.

Hill, Jonathan, 48531 Pte.
Schofield, Tom, 56429 Pte.

22nd BATTALION.

Thomas, William, John, 54605 Pte.

23rd BATTALION.

Alexander, Rue. Stev., 267669 Cpl.

Bannon, Michael, W/304 Sgt.
Baines, Ernest, 60987 Pte.
Benjamin, Lewis, 53793 Pte.
Brown, Wm. Wheatley, 77652 Pte.
Burke, Thomas, 316299 Pte.
Byron, Frank, 65359 Pte.

Challis, Albert Wm., 68373 A/Cpl.
Charlson, Frederick, 34799 Cpl.
Clarke, Aaron, 60953 Pte.
Cox, Arthur Howard, 63715 Pte.
Crumley, Frank, 65547 Pte.
Davis, Francis, 60970 Pte.
Diamond, Joseph, 65742 Pte.
Dibble, James, 65399 Pte.

Evans, Fred, 292379 Pte.

Fawkner, Albert, 315477 Pte.
Fletcher, Clifford, 77547 Pte.
Fraser, Harry, 316168 Pte.

Gibson, William, 65921 Pte.
Gill, Robert, 77589 Pte.

Gillcrist, Chas. Fredk., 67979 Pte.
Green Edward, 67981 Pte.

Horn, Charles, 77662 Pte.
Hughes, Joseph, 66439 Pte.
Hulme, Arthur, 315029 Pte.

Johnson, Sydney, 61053 Pte.
Jones, John Henry, 315154 Pte.

Kenyon, Thomas, 316324 Pte.

Leader, Albert Claud, 53859 Pte.
Lorenzi, Donald Jas., 263025 Pte.
Marsden, Wm. Ed., 61074 L/Cpl.
Martin, Thomas, 61011 Pte.
McCormick, John, 67983 Pte.
McLean, Robert, 316275 Pte.
Moore, Frederick, 60913 Pte.
Morris, Thomas, 65980 Pte.

Norris, Arthur, 65292 Pte.

Orford, David, 65538 Pte.

Perryman, James, 61070 Pte.
Platt, Frederick, 316310 Pte.
Powis, Arthur, 60959 Pte.

Rees, Harry, 60931 Pte.
Roberts, David Griffi., 315917 Pte.
Rogers, William, 315053 Pte.

Shelley, Willliam, 267695 Cpl.
Stanier, Noah, 244333 Pte.
Stowe, Stephen, 65881 Pte.
Sugden, Walter, 242717 Pte.
Suter, Frank, Thos. Wm., 53791 Pte.
Swaine, Wm. Gledhill, 242450 Pte.

Tarlton, Peter, 315440 Pte.
Trafford, Henry Herb., 315174 Pte.
Tynan, Thos. Patrick, 77555 Pte.

Warburton, John, 65591 Pte.
Weston, John Edward, 65822 Pte.
Wright, Fredk. Richd., 60962 Pte.

24th BATTALION.
Best, John Thomas, 316422 Pte.
Jackson, Fred, 77825 Pte.

THE DEPOT.
Abram, John Thomas, 27688 Pte.
Aimson, Fredk. Wm., 27837 Pte.
Astles, James, 18493 Pte.
Atherton, Thomas Croft, 5811 Pte.

Banham, David, 19580 Pte.
Bannister, Joseph, 30502 Pte.
Bell, William John, 45789 Pte.
Berry Robert, 267346 Pte.
Bowden, William, 11676 Pte.

Carney, Edward, 23385 Pte.

Cooper, Henry, 4477 A/Cpl.
Crayton, Michael Pat., 59488 Pte.

Didsbury, Arthur, 12355 Pte.
Drinkwater, Thos. Berry, 76589 Pte.

Ellis, George, W/302 Sgt.
Exall, Thomas, 46444 Pte.

Fairhurst, Chas. Henry, 5952 Pte.

Graham, David Camp., 25651 Pte.
Gresty Albert Edward, 54289 Pte.

Halliwell, Arthur Enst., 24685 Pte.
Hankey, Thomas, 29281 L/Cpl.
Hannan, Wm. Robert, 20114 Pte.
Hibberd, Harry Herb., 52465 Pte.
Hogg, James, 12546 Pte.

Johnson, Thomas, 64384 Pte.
Keen, Walter, 24922 Boy
Law, Joseph, 12679 Pte.
Martin,Herb.Henry John, 28148 Pte.
Owens, Cecil, 24886 Pte.
Phillipson, Alf. John, 10087 L/Cpl.
Robinson, Chas. James, 7814 Pte.
Shaw, James, 9360 L/Cpl.
Tolson, James, 17194 A/Sgt.
Wilde, Robert, 10582 Pte.
Williams, William, 11163 Sgt.
Winstanley, George, 201455 Pte.

223rd (T.F.) DEPOT.
Lloyd, John, 2099 Pte.

1st GARRISON BATTALION.
Bloor, Aaron, 12321 Pte.
Brooke, Frank, 11712 Pte.
Costello, Joseph, 27087 Pte.
Dean, Herbert, 27436 Pte.
Hall, Peter, 27224 Pte.
Hancock, Owen Sam., 7263 L/Cpl.
Hibbert, Wm. John, 38285 Sgt.
Higgins, John, 11629 Pte.
Horan, John, 29282 Pte.
Jeffs, George, W/1065 Pte.
Lee, John, 29297 Pte.
Ollerenshaw, James, 65848 Pte.
Rixon, Percy Howard, 29334 Pte.
Simm, William, 29351 Pte.
Simmons, John, 29346 Pte.
Slater, William, 40961 Pte.
Ward, Ernest, 29156 Pte.
Williams, Richd. Owen, 39504 Pte.

2nd GARRISON BATTALION.
Clarke, Joseph, 32003 Sgt.
Firth, James William, 61625 L/Cpl.
Forber, William, 31889 Pte.
Greenwood, John, 32095 Pte.
Harrison, James, 31775 Pte.
Heaton, Albert, 292398 Pte.
Jordan, Patrick, 32096 Pte.
Joyce, Joseph, 32094 Pte.

Knowles, William, 26385 Pte.
Lowe, Robert, 202770 Pte.
McGreaves, Joseph, 202617 Pte.
McKeever, Dan. Henry, 31573 Pte.
Mitchell, Thomas, 10190 Pte.
Nicholls, Joseph, 27525 Pte.
O'Shea, Thos. Esmonde, 9617 Pte.
Stanton, Joseph, 60180 Pte.
Thompson, John, 10360 Pte.
Tinsley, William, 31530 Pte.
Walker, John James, 14007 Pte.
Wilkinson, Joseph, 9536 Pte.

3rd GARRISON BATTALION.
Sweeney, Alexander, 31529 Pte.
Venables, Thomas, 25410 Pte.

1/4th BATTALION.
Adamson, James, 49426 Pte.
Akers, Thomas, 1539 Pte.
Alderwood, Alfred, 2191 L/Cpl.
Aldred, George, 201156 Pte.
Anderson, George, 50906 Pte.
Anthony, George, 200881 L/Cpl.
Ashworth, Abraham, 68004 Pte.
Astle, William, 292806 Pte.
Atkinson, Charles, 1682 Pte.
Austin, Tom, 16481 Pte.
Ayre, John William, 2977 Pte.
Ayres, Walter Frank, 202267 Pte.

Barlow, George, 1276 Pte.
Barrett, Fred, 201507 Pte.
Barrow, George, 200193 Pte.
Barry, John 202429 Pte.
Baxter, Joseph, 201421 Pte.
Beckett, Thos. Arthur, 2071 Cpl.
Bell, Thomas Henry, 1911 Cpl.
Belledonne, Leon, 201650 Cpl.
Bennett, Charles, 202508 Pte.
Bernett, Henry, 3178 Pte.
Benyon, Joseph, 18458 Pte.
Berkson, Myer, 1304 L/Sgt.
Bird, Henry, 3001 Pte.
Birss, Charles, 201251 L/Cpl.
Blythen, George, 1605 Pte.
Boden, George, 15525 Sgt.
Boston, Henry, 200523 Pte.
Bowen, Benjamin, 315512 Pte.
Bowen, James, 1470 Pte.
Boyes, Thomas, 67535 Pte.
Bradley, Herbert, 35356 Pte.
Brain, John, 2206 Pte.
Brassey, Albert, 2831 Pte.
Brayne, William, 200796 Pte.
Brockie, John, 200384 L/Cpl.
Brown, John Fredk., 67777 Pte.
Brunsden, George Alfred, 200302 C.Q.M.S.
Buckingham, William, 57803 Pte.
Bull Joseph, 202410 Pte.
Burgess, Geo. Walter, 201582 Pte.
Burns, John Henry, 1049 L/Cpl.
Butler, Edward, 74026 Cpl.
Byrne, Frank, 201468 Pte.
Byrne, John, 2589 Pte.

Cardwell, John, 26018 Pte.
Carey, Michael, 40870 Pte.
Carmody, Dean, 2710 Pte.
Carroll, Edward, 2554 Pte.
Cartwright, George, 200870 Cpl.
Cherry, Charles Fred, 2139 L/Cpl.
Clarke, John, 201037 Pte.
Clarke, Joseph James, 61965 Pte.
Clarke, Joseph, 200194 Pte.
Cohen, Isaac, 77934 Pte.
Collcutt, Geo. Alf., 200016 C.S.M.
Conway, Alfred, 16288 Pte.
Cooper, Donald George Reginald, 200123 Sgt.
Cope, Enos, 202406 Pte.
Cornes, Stanley, 49951 Pte.
Cosgrove, George, 8544 C.S.M.
Cottrell, Regd. Annesley, 2421 Pte.
Cowell, William Henry, 2917
Cox, Albert, 50586 Pte.
Craig, Wm. Roderick, 413 Sgt.
Crosby, Samuel, 200692 Pte.
Crowhurst, Walter, 2374 Pte.
Cummaford, Lawrence, 68025 Pte.

Daly, George, 2341 Pte.
Davidson, Robert, 2482 Pte.
Davies, Albert, 202519 L/Cpl.
Davies, Algernon, 77064 Pte.
Davies, George, 3081 Pte.
Davies, Harry, 202526 L/Cpl.
Davies, Jack, 201447 Pte.
Davies, Nor. Burton, 200222 Sgt.
Davies, Robert Smith, 1619 Pte.
Dean, Harry, 200268 A/Sgt.
Dean, Thomas, 315689 Pte.
Deem, Herva, 315861 Pte.
Dickinson, Frank, 201137 Pte.
Dickson, John Henry, 200654 Pte.
Dickson, William Eric, 201493 Pte.
Dobbing, John, 2605 Pte.
Donbavand, William, 201557 Pte.
Doyle, Thomas, 201282 Pte.
Dray, Ernest, 200596 L/Sgt.
Duffy, James, 63057 Pte.
Duncan, Francis John, 2062 Pte.

East, Edward, 1900 Pte.
East, Robert Naylor, 201479 Pte.
Eccleston, George, 201492 Pte.
Edmonson, James, 40882 Pte.
Edwards, Edward, 201617 Pte.
Edwards, Robert, 2098 Pte.
Edwards, William, 60551 Pte.
Elliott, Wm. John, 68034 Pte.
Errington, Albert, 50958 Pte.
Evans, Francis, 200990 Pte.
Evans, John Thos., 201000 L/Cpl.
Evans, Tom Rees, 66043 Pte.

Fairclough, Robert, 200435 Pte.
Farnworth, John, 68040 Pte.
Fay, Edward, 202431 Pte.
Fitzpatrick, Peter, 201036 Pte.
Foden, Archi. Murray, 1732 Pte.
Foden, Eric Gordon, 200876 Pte.

Forshaw, Arthur, 200291 Pte.
Forshaw, Parker, 200511 Pte.

Gale, Stanley, 200988 Pte.
Garlick Arthur, 266756 Pte.
Glaze, Charles, 60505 Pte.
Glover, James, 66660 Pte.
Gorman, Robert, 2447 Pte.
Goodwin, Harold, 201516 Pte.
Goulding, Ernest, 1373 Pte.
Green, Harold Wake., 1563 L/Cpl.
Greenhalgh, Fred, 267087 Pte.
Greenwood, Frank, 202892 Pte.
Gregory, Albert, 10598 Pte.
Griffiths, Edward, 2002 Cpl.
Griffiths, George, 200032 Sgt.
Grocott, William, 200038 Sgt.

Halewood, Henry, 2299 L/Cpl.
Halsall, James, 241877 Pte.
Harboard, J. Walker, 2171 L/Cpl.
Hardstaff, Ernest, 12774 Sgt.
Harris, Chas. Russell, 243516 Pte.
Harris, Geo. James, 1188 Sgt.
Harrop, John William, 49325 Pte.
Hartley, Arthur, 201740 Pte.
Hawkes, John, 201348 Pte.
Hayes, Sidney, 240427 Pte.
Hazlehurst, Albert, 201067 Pte.
Heilbron, Louis, 40892 Pte.
Hellfritsch, Herman, 201613 Pte.
Herbert, George, 30079 Pte.
Hignett, George, 201657 Pte.
Hignett, Robert, 1652 Pte.
Hill, William Henry, 201380 Pte.
Hird, John Thomas, 2419 Pte.
Hird, Stanley, 2237 Pte.
Hodges, Fred Oswald, 202295 Sgt.
Hodgson, Frank, 201668 L/Cpl.
Holden, Seth, 202545 Pte.
Holebrook Reginald, 201603 Pte.
Holloway, George, 1982 Pte.
Holmes, Wm. Edward, 200515 Cpl.
Hopper, William, 72029 Pte.
Hore, John, 1476 Pte.
Hotchkiss, Albert, 200600 L/Cpl.
Houghton, Olbin, 5303 A/C.S.M.
Houlden, Fred, 66482 Pte.
Hughes, Chas. James, 201435 Pte.
Hughes, Wilfred, 200859 Pte.
Hulston, Ernest, 27835 Pte.
Humphreys, Thos. Jas., 60429 Pte.
Humphreys, William, 1742 Pte.
Hyde, Alfred, 202542 Pte.

Jacklin, Robert, 58117 Pte.
Jackson, Albert, 10516 Pte.
Jackson, Wm. Henry, 200232 Pte.
Johnson, Alfred, 72038 Pte.
Johnson, Frank, 27922 Pte.
Johnston, Fred, 200963 Pte.
Johnstone, Ernest, 201202 Pte.
Jones, Alfred Law., 100102 C.Q.M.S.
Jones, Ashton James, 3116 Pte.
Jones, David, 201016 Pte.
Jones, Ernest Edwin, 65992 Pte.

Jones, Frederick, 200947 Pte.
Jones, George, 13301 Pte.
Jones, Harry, 202925 Pte.
Jones, James, 200977 Pte.
Jones, Richard Henry, 35507 Pte.
Jones, Roger, 1484 Cpl.
Jones, Thomas, 201684 Pte.
Jones, William, 8455 L/Cpl.
Joynson, Samuel, 202551 Pte.

Kay, William, 201408 Pte.
Kelley, Wm. Thomas, 27570 Pte.
Kendrick, Wm. Thos., 201743 Pte.
Kennedy, William, 2289 Pte.
Kent, Edward, 1124 Pte.
Kershaw, Chas. Edward, 1193 Pte.
Kesteven, Harry, 50174 Pte.
Kimber, Hafry, 2049 Pte.
King, Francis, 201314 Pte.
Knight, John, 1598 Pte.

Lawton, Robert, 201291 Pte.
Lawton, Thos. Sidney, 202462 Cpl.
Leeson, John Charles, 2045 Pte.
Lester, Edwin, 200851 Sgt.
Lilley, Walter, 40880 Pte.
Little Thomas, 243720 Pte.
Littlemore, Charles, 243609 Pte.
Littler, Joseph Reeves, 3101 Pte.
Livsey, Harold Smith, 2522 Pte.
Lloyd, Edward, 200180 Pte.
Lloyd, John James, 1691 Pte.
Longson, Jack, 40855 Pte.
Lowndes, Joe, 40879 Pte.
Lucas, Laurence, 1477 Pte.
Lynch, John, 201042 L/Cpl.
Lyon, John William, 67812 Pte.

Maddocks, Edward, 200786 Pte.
Maddocks, Thomas, 1257 Pte.
Mairs, Charles, 50272 Pte.
Marsden, Thomas, 64490 Pte.
Matthews, John Arthur, 50890 Pte.
Mayoh, James, 62887 Pte.
McBride, Bernard, 201681 Pte.
McCabe, Peter, 200507 Pte.
McCartney, Thomas, 8659 L/Cpl.
McCavish, George, 200885 Pte.
McGivern, Henry, 2466 Pte.
McIntyre, George, 1381 Pte.
McKee, John, 51772 Pte.
McLaughlin, John, 201457 Pte.
McMillan, Ernest, 50338 Cpl.
Medlicott, Frank, 201540 Pte.
Melling, Gerald, 200670 Pte.
Merricks, Ernest, 202916 Pte.
Midgley, Francis Edward, 3066 Pte.
Minnis, William, 1330 Pte.
Mitchell, Ewart, 20097 Pte.
Morahan, Maurice Jos., 50311 Pte.
Morgan, Frederick, 1162 Pte.
Morgan, William, 60443 Pte.
Morrey, Arthur, 66591 Pte.
Morris, John William, 201361 Pte.
Morris, Rudolph, 201488 Pte.
Moss, Thomas Maylor, 201386 Pte.

Munro, Alfred, 50838 Pte.
Murphy, William, 200577 Cpl.

Newall, Henry, 1819 Pte.
Nichols, George, 200659 L/Sgt.
Nicholson, John Henry, 36336 Pte.
Nightingale, Ernest, 201586 Pte.
Noble, Albert Edward, 49371 Pte.
Nolan, Anthony, 67753 Pte.
Nolan, James, 200154 Pte.
Norris, Thomas, 67414 Pte.

Oakley, Herbert John, 200555 Pte.
O'Grady, James, 1606 Pte.
Oldfield, Frank, 202423 Pte.
Oliphant, James, 200999 Pte.
O'Reilly John, 201082 Pte.
Ormsby, William, 2467 Pte.
Owen, Arthur, 2804 Pte.
Owen, John William, 40852 Pte.

Parrott, Thos. Towers, 131 Cpl.
Peers, Ernest, 200196 L/Cpl.
Peers, Herbert, 545 Cpl.
Pembroke, Alb. Ernest, 36151 Pte.
Prendergheast, Thomas, 1723 Pte.
Penny, Thomas, 994 Sgt.
Perry, Robert, 202938 Pte.
Perry, Thomas Edwin, 2937 Pte.
Pettit, William, 200649 Pte.
Pleavin, William, 2973 Pte.
Postlethwaite, Robt. Wm., 241821 Pte.
Potts, George Harold, 202544 Pte.
Povall, William James, 3166 Pte.
Povey, Thomas, 12404 Pte.
Pratt, Edward, 12792 Pte.
Prince, George, 920 Pte.

Rae, Joseph, 30316 Pte.
Radcliffe, John, 28485 Sgt.
Randles, John, 200383 Sgt.
Ratcliffe, Wilbye, 201534 Pte.
Reade, George, 62404 Pte.
Reade, Harry, 202421 Pte.
Rhodes, Ernest, 200326 Pte.
Rhodes, Frank, 62974 Pte.
Rhodes, Harry, 2251 Pte.
Robb, Ernest George, 2602 Pte.
Roberts, David, 240981 Pte.
Roberts, Gomer Stanley, 2325 Cpl.
Roberts, Noah, 200390 Pte.
Roberts, Robert, 201101 L/Cpl.
Robinson, Alexander, 420 Cpl.
Robinson, John, 2006 Pte.
Robinson, John, 2033 Pte.
Robinson, John, 20676 Pte.
Rooney, Joseph, 40886 Pte.
Roscoe, Robert, 2762 Pte.

Sadler, William, 200710 Pte.
Saxon, William, 4516 Pte.
Seyferth, Edward Hny., 200898 Pte.
Sheils, Frank, 200082 L/Cpl.
Shenton, George, 53052 Pte.
Sherlock, Wm., Joseph, 201368 Pte.

Siddorn, Alb. Goulding, 200150 Cpl.
Sidebotham, Ryl. Chas., 2243 Pte.
Silverston, Alfred, 20105 L/Cpl.
Simcock, George, 1282 Pte.
Simcock, Herbert, 201530 Pte.
Skinner, Thomas, 291434 Pte.
Smith, Thomas, 200931 L/Cpl.
Smith, William, 200502 L/Cpl.
Snelson, Norman, 40825 Pte.
Soper, Ronald, 200455 Pte.
Spring, Ernest, 7698 Pte.
Starkey, Leonard, 201635 Pte.
Sutton, Percy Alan, 2113 L/Cpl.

Talbot, Abel, 202459 Pte.
Tasker, Charles, 201511 Pte.
Taylor, Ernest, 202844 Pte.
Taylor, Frank, 202415 Pte.
Thomas, Fredk. Per., 1728 Pte.
Thomas, Maldwin, 1698 Pte.
Thompson, Arthur, 201093 Pte.
Tilley, Wm. Edward, 201050 Pte.
Timms, Charles, 16121 Pte.
Topping, Harold, 200717 L/Cpl.
Townhill, Ed. Handley, 45708 Pte.
Tucker, Timothy, 2264 Pte.
Turner, Alfred, 12402 Pte.
Turner, Wm. Herbert, 200663 Pte.

Underwood, Wm. Henry, 1434 Pte.

Venables, Henry, 201638 Pte.
Vickers, Thomas, 266654 Pte.

Wagg, Percy, 52228 Pte.
Watson, Stanley Geo., 2224 Dr.
Watts, Geo. Edward, 64702 Pte.
Weaver, Enst. Arthur, 2242 Pte.
Whelan, Herb. James, 2152 Cpl.
Whelan, Richard, 201095 Pte.
White, Leonard, 11034 Pte.
Whyte, Geo. James, 2867 L/Cpl.
Wiggett, John, 1727 Pte.
Wilding, Leonard, 241171 Pte.
Wilkinson, Geo. Goodess, 15020 Cpl.
Wilkinson, Harry, 14754 Pte.
Williams, Bertie, 1654 Pte.
Williams, David, 1934 Pte.
Williams, Hub. Litton, 1873 L/Cpl.
Williams, Jas. Edward, 133 C.S.M.
Williams, Samuel, 1093 Pte.
Williamson, Harry, 201281 Pte.
Wilson, Henry, 201358 Pte.
Wood, Charles Stanley, 201091 Pte.
Wood, George, 53991 Pte.
Wood, George, 201146 Pte.
Wood, John Arthur, 1239 Pte.
Woodcock, John Wm., 2231 Pte.
Woodward, Harry, 58180 Pte.
Woodward, Robt. Thos., 67739 Pte.
Woolley, Charles, 201519 Pte.
Woolley, Wm. Ernest, 51480 Pte.
Wright, Albert, 1608 Pte.
Wright, Thomas, 2749 Pte.
Wyatt, Henry, 1733 Pte.
Wycherley, Walter, 201313 Pte.

2/4th BATTALION.

Crimes, William Stanley, 243661 Pte
Fisher, Frank Leslie, 2317 L/Cpl.

4th RESERVE BATTALION.

Boardman, Harry, 78895 Pte.
Collier, Stanley, 4140 Dmr.
Gregory, Ernest, 78844 Pte.
Griffiths, William Owen, 201374 A/C.S.M.
Holloway, Hen. Chas., 241030 Sgt.
Hughes, Harry, 78867 Pte.
Johnson, Charles, 13609 A/R.S.M.
Knott, Arthur, 266757 A/L/Sgt.
Lauder, Her. Lightburn, 66677 Pte.
Lea, Tom, 78854 Pte.
Leek, Arthur, 243564 Pte.
McCabe, Thomas, 79409 Pte.
Newport, Arthur, 241479 Pte.
Oakes, Abraham, 290027 Sgt.
Potter, Walter Hughes, 243206 Pte.
Ratcliffe, Joseph, 242144 Pte.
Rushton, Walter, 243683 Pte.
Ryle, John Arthur, 79441 Pte.
Swann, Fred, 265277 L/Cpl.
Waring, Edward, 4271 Pte.

1/5th BATTALION.

Ackerley, Charles, 240081 L/Cpl.
Adkinson, Harry, 486 Pte.
Allen, Sydney, 240341 Pte.
Armitage, John Wm., 4331 Pte.
Armstrong, Harry, 4138 Pte.
Ashley, Edward, 13569 Pte.
Ashton, Samuel, 1981 Pte.
Astbury, Arthur, 1080 Pte.
Astbury, Walter, 3705 Pte.
Atherton, John, 241175 Pte.
Atkin, John, 3421 Pte.

Baker, John, 716 Pte.
Ball, Ernest Victor, 241229 Pte.
Bancroft, Harold, 241424 Pte.
Barber, Harry, 1367 Cpl.
Barton, Thomas, 1701 Pte.
Bates, Stanley, 4952 Pte.
Beatty, Hugh, 3502 Pte.
Beesley, Laurence Chas., 1303 Pte.
Bell, Thomas Henry, 2307 Pte.
Bell, William, 4238 Pte.
Bellis, Harry, 240073 Sgt.
Bennett, Chas. Henry, 240843 Pte.
Bird, George, 241461 Pte.
Birtles, Albert, 1603 Pte.
Birtwistle, William, 4045 Pte.
Blackburn, Charles, 240777 Pte.
Blackburn, Samuel, 1906 Pte.
Blackhurst, John, 3818 Pte.
Blackhurst, John, 241189 Pte.
Blackshaw, John, 1800 Pte.
Blount, Wm. Herbert, 1408 Pte.
Boardman, Edwin, 240063 Sgt.
Boardman, John, 240329 Pte.
Boffey, Norman, 244296 Pte.
Bone, Bern. Andrews, 57804 Pte.

Booth, Wm. Andrew, 243918 Pte.
Bostock, Matthew, 1551 Pte.
Bostock, Samuel, 1738 Pte.
Boulger, John Wm., 1988 Pte.
Bradley, Arthur, 240022 Sgt.
Bradley, Fred, 244231 Pte.
Bradshaw, Albert, 3519 Pte.
Bradshaw, George, 15751 Pte.
Brandreth, Albert, 1094 Pte.
Brandreth, George, 1640 Pte.
Brazendale, Stanley, 1493 Pte.
Broadhead, Frank, 291380 A/Cpl.
Brocklehurst, Reginald, 53081 Pte.
Brocklehurst, Vivian, 1736 Pte.
Brookes, Henry, 1787 L/Sgt.
Brown, Daniel, 4094 Pte.
Brown, Joseph, 244318 Dmr.
Brown, Thomas, 268327 Pte.
Buchanan, Robert, 241099 Pte.
Buckley, William, 2184 Pte.
Budd, Fredk. Arthur, 241448 Pte.
Burton Harold Matt., 268157 Pte.
Buxton, Frank, 4129 Pte.
Byrne, Michael, 1942 Pte.
Byrne, Thomas Peter, 244388 Pte.

Cameron, William, 1699 Pte.
Campbell, James, 240912 L/Cpl.
Carter,Arthur Wm.Henry,52118 Pte.
Carter, William, 241241 Pte.
Cash, Albert, 1628 Pte.
Check, Frederick, 2243 Pte.
Clare, Arthur, 316093 Pte.
Clarke, Arthur, 1779
Clarke, Arthur Edwin, 3123 Pte.
Clifford, John, 1527 Pte.
Cole, William, 1917 Pte.
Comar, Edward, 1752 Pte.
Cook, Albert, 241287 Pte.
Cook, Wal.Hny.Haynes,240559 Pte.
Cooke, George, 244302 Pte.
Cooke, John, 243966 Pte.
Cooke, Thomas, 3246 Pte.
Cookson, Anthony, 28270 Pte.
Cooper, William, 240365 Pte.
Crick, David, 243953 Pte.
Crooke, Frank Cyril, 2357 Pte.
Crowther, Harry, 2104 Pte.
Cutler, Joseph, 244038 Pte.

Dakin, Arthur, 1311 Pte.
Davies, David Alex., 3757 Pte.
Davies, John, 240178 L/Cpl.
Davies, John, 243975 Pte.
Deakin, John, 1524 Pte.
Devenport, Harry, 240789 Pte.
Dewhurst, Alfred, 1661 Pte.
Donovan, James, 1757 Pte.
Duckers, Walter Wm., 244063 Pte.
Dunn, Oswald, 1889 Pte.
Dunning, James, 241095 Pte.
Dutton, Hubert Leslie, 3260 Pte.
Dutton, Neville, 241162 Pte.

Eaton, Arthur Row., 244344 A/Sgt.
Edge, George, 1413 Pte.

Entwistle, Herbert, 1126 Dmr.
Everett, Laurence, 244180 Pte.

Fairclough, Charles, 2237 Pte.
Farnworth, Gil. Kers., 243972 Pte.
Feeney, Thomas, 1534 Pte.
Fishbourne, Thos. Ed., 15524 Pte.
Fisher, Joseph, 240970 Pte.
Fletcher, Robert, 240122 L/Cpl.
Forster, Arthur, 1746 Pte.
Forster, Joseph, 244263 Pte.
Forster, Joseph Wm., 244253 Pte.

Gamson, Arthur, 267581 Pte.
Gayter, Harry, 241137 Pte.
Gibson, Fred, 3012 Pte.
Gilberts, Edward, 1767 Pte.
Goff, James, 1439 Pte.
Gore, James, Henry, 244043 Pte.
Goulding, Thomas, 2728 Pte.
Goulding, Wm. Henry, 267001 Pte.
Green, Sydney Mervin Reginald, 1579 Dmr.
Green, Thomas, 1821 Pte.
Guest, John, 1926 Pte.

Hackney, Philip Shenton, 3885 Pte.
Hague, Joseph, 244049 Pte.
Hallsworth, James, 240371 L/Cpl.
Hamlett, John 241393 Pte.
Hamman, George, 3995 Pte.
Harrison, Chas. Robt., 2176 Sgt.
Harrold, John, 267687 Pte.
Haworth, Tom, 267602 Pte.
Hayes, John Wilfred, 2085 Pte.
Hayes, William, 243588 Pte.
Haywood, Alfred, 15677 Pte.
Hearn, Harry, 3568 Pte.
Heath, Albert, 1574 Pte.
Heywood, John Leon., 240506 Pte.
Hinchcliffe, William, 240123 Pte.
Hinks, Thomas, 4026 Pte.
Hitchen, William, 2154 Sgt.
Hodkinson, Frederick, 240724 Pte.
Holland, Harold, 241247 Pte.
Hopley, John, 241367 Pte.
Hopley, Thomas, 241076 Pte.
Hough, George, 241230 Pte.
Hough, James Henry, 305 Pte.
Howard, Thomas, 15635 Pte.
Howells, Ralph, 244158 Pte.
Hughes, Arthur David, 2291 L/Cpl.
Hunt, Harold, 244370 Pte.

Jagger, Albert, 1898 Pte.
Jellicoe, Stephen, 1559 Pte.
Johnson, William, 44117 Pte.
Jones, David, 244372 Pte.
Jones, Edward, 240390 Pte.
Jones, Fredk. Edward, 1568 Pte.
Jones, George Fredk., 3102 Pte.
Jones, Henry, 2350 Pte.
Jones, Hugh, 1882 Pte.
Jones, John, 2351 Pte.
Jones, Leonard, 244132 Pte.
Jones, Richard, 2079 Pte.

Jones, Robert, 2199 Pte.
Jones, Thomas, 15616 Pte.
Jones, Thos. Batten, 243929 Pte.
Jones, Thomas David, 2367 Pte.
Jones, Thos. Pryce, 240546 Pte.
Jones, Walter, 241364 Pte.
Jones, William Henry, 315531 Pte.
Jones, William Kirkley, 2096 Pte.

Kendall, John Aubrey, 240388 Pte.
King, George Edward, 28634 Pte.
Kinsey, William, 2050 L/Cpl.
Kirkpatrick, Edward, 2392 Pte.

Lake, Henry, 267606 Pte.
Lamb, Charles, 240273 L/Cpl.
Large, Jack, 1820 Cpl.
Lawson, George, 2503 Pte.
Lear, Percy, 266730 Pte.
Lee, Charles, 241324 Pte.
Lees, Harry, 240337 Pte.
Leigh, Peter, 1494 Pte.
Leigh, William Henry, 241357 Pte.
Lindop, Albert, 2041 Pte.
Little, John, 4140 Pte.
Lockley, Thomas, 1263 Sgt.
Lowe, Leonard, 3659 Pte.

Mallalien, Sam, 243977 Pte.
Manley, Alfred, 2072 Pte.
Manton, Frank, 1260 L/Cpl.
Martin, John, 240141 Pte.
Martin, William, 4147 Pte.
Mason, Albert, 53090 Pte.
Mattimore, Leo., 1564 Pte.
Maynard, Samuel, 2384 Pte.
McFeat, Archi. Hood, 241915 Pte.
Meacock, Albert, 241370 Pte.
Meredith, Frank, 2158 Pte.
Miller, Albert, 1904 Pte.
Mills, George, 2030 L/Cpl.
Minshall, James, 240184 Pte.
Moores, Joseph, 241170 Pte.
Morris, Harry, 15566 Pte.
Mounsey, Joseph, 15644 Pte.
Mugan, John, 240736 Pte.

Naylor, Harry, 2305 L/Sgt.
Nicholas, Oswald, 1420 Pte.
Nield, Joseph, 1675 Pte.
Norbury, Frank, 1197 L/Sgt.
Nuttall, Samuel, 241029 Pte.

Oates, John, 1474 Pte.
Oldham Arthur Edward, 1686 Sgt.
Orme, Joseph Edward, 3345 Pte.
Orr, James, 241920 Pte.
Owen, John, 241629 Cpl.

Pagett, William, 1393 Pte.
Parker, Frank Harvey, 244134 Pte.
Parker, John Henry, 15591 Pte.
Parker, William, 1651 Pte.
Parsonage, Robert, 2091 Pte.
Partin, George, 821 Sgt.
Pate, Harry, 45798 Pte.

T

Pate, William Charles, 2752 Pte.
Pearson, Albert, 315296 Pte.
Peers, Frank, 240518 L/Sgt.
Pemberton, Thomas, 241328 Pte.
Percival, George, 3723 Pte.
Perry, Nor. Randolph, 2430 Pte.
Phillips, Abraham, 241128 Pte.
Phillips, Clarence, 2506 Pte.
Pickles, Wilfred, 243941 Pte.
Pierce, Phillip Hugh, 2297 Sgt.
Poock, Fredk. William, 65409 Pte.
Poole, William, 241085 Pte.
Poole, Wm. Morbon, 240321 Pte.
Postles, Henry, 1521 Pte.
Powell, Geo. Thomas, 15551 Pte.
Powell, James William, 4153 Pte.
Prandal, Owen, 2355 Pte.
Preece, Edward Allan, 241284 Pte.
Pybus, Harry, 2024 Pte.
Pye, Albert Edward, 1434 Sgt.

Rackstraw, William, 1920 Pte.
Rafferty, John, 241037 Pte.
Rees, William Albert, 3795 Pte.
Riley, David Paul, 240814 Pte.
Roe, Frederick, 291843 Pte.
Ross, Wm. John Albert, 267699 Pte.

Sanders, John Henry, 2108 Pte.
Shaw, Harry, 240661 Pte.
Shaw, Thomas, 4102 Pte.
Shaw, William, 3072 Pte.
Shirt, James, 3368 Pte.
Shropshire, George, 241436 Pte.
Silver, William, 3161 Pte.
Slater, Harrison, 240801 Pte.
Sloane, Joseph, 1502 Pte.
Stephenson, William, 240805 Pte.
Stockton, Joseph, 244280 Pte.
Stonier, John, 1711 Pte.
Sutcliffe, Herbert, 240257 Dmr.
Sweeney, Frederick, 1647 C.S.M.

Tapley, Harry, 241044 Pte.
Tapley, Samuel, 3576 Pte.
Taylor, Joseph Thomas, 1403 Pte.
Thomas, Harry, 240583 Cpl.
Thomas, Sydney, 1771 Cpl.
Thornber, George, 803 Pte.
Thorp, Harry, 2403 Pte.
Tiddy, Percy Edward, 2328 Pte.
Tippins, Cecil John, 200832 Pte.
Turner, Frank, 1657 Pte.
Turnock, Wm. Ar., 243917 L/Cpl.

Wakefield, John Wm., 3320 Pte.
Walker, Frank, 240094 Pte.
Walker, Frank, 240591 Pte.
Walker, John Wilfred, 430 Cpl.
Walker, Reginald, 244135 Pte.
Walsh, Samuel, 244374 Pte.
Ward, William, 2153 Pte.
Warnock, Alexander, 2113 C.S.M.
Watkinson, Willie Isaac, 4218 Pte.
Wharton, Ernest, 1786 Cpl.
White, Frank, 2667 Pte.

White, George Arthur, 1382 Pte.
White, John Thomas, 240726 Pte.
Whitfield, Harold, 2255 Pte.
Whitney, Herbert, 3015 Pte.
Wilcox, William James, 1720 Pte.
Wilding, Peter, 241205 Pte.
Wilkinson, John Thos., 1436 Sgt.
Williams, Arthur John, 4280 Pte.
Williams, Charles, 1624 Pte.
Williams, Jas. Samuel, 243945 Pte.
Williamson, Joseph, 1670 A/Sgt.
Wilson, George, 3984 Pte.
Wilson, Percy, 2104 Pte.
Wood William George, 15545 Pte.
Worsley, John, 244023 Pte.

Yarwood, Joseph, 1062 Pte.
Yates, Arthur, 1932 Pte.

2/5th BATTALION.

Hogg, Harry Birkett, 2901 Pte.
Holt, James, 242115 Pte.
Jones, Evan, 244504 Pte.
Kenyon, Hubert, 5378 Pte.
Koppinberg, Albert, 5682 Pte.
Sharp, Harry, 241329 A/Sgt.
Taylor, Geo. Caldicott, 3074 A/Sgt.

5th (RESERVE) BATTALION.

Edwards, Thomas, 2800 Pte.
Jackson, Arthur, 4546 Pte.

1/6th BATTALION.

Adams, William, 66000 Pte.
Albert, John, 49857 Cpl.
Alexander, Regd. John, 50202 Pte.
Allen, Jack, 265406 Pte.
Allen, James, 266551 Pte.
Anderson, George, 2826 Pte.
Andrew, Herbert, 265104 Pte.
Antrobus, Frederick, 265689 L/Cpl.
Arnold, Arthur, 267917 Pte.
Ashcroft, Joseph, 268040 Pte.
Ashcroft, Arthur, 268200 Pte.
Ashton, Thomas, 265073 Pte.
Asquith, Alan, 1491 Pte.
Atkin, Fred, 2930 Pte.
Axon, Frederick, 2487 Pte.

Bagnall, Harold, 4311 Pte.
Bagwell, George James, 51495 Pte.
Bailey, Edward, 265873 Pte.
Bailey, Alfred, 3329 Pte.
Bainbridge, Ralph Brad., 4454 Pte.
Baines, Peter, 260181 Pte.
Baines, Thomas, 2291 Pte.
Ball, Alfred, 265329 L/Cpl.
Ball, Joseph, 265823 Cpl.
Balmer, Sidney, 51758 Pte.
Bardsley, Ernest, 3355 Pte.
Barnes, Sydney, 268080 Pte.
Barnett, Frank, 49599 Pte.
Barnett, Harold, 2476 Pte.
Barraclough, Eddie, 51097 Pte.
Beard, Harold, 267790 Pte.
Beard, Joseph, 45701 Pte.

Beard, Walter, 13397 Pte.
Beck, John, 265170 Pte.
Bell, Arthur, 267987 Pte.
Benford, John Edward, 265824 Pte.
Bennett, Edward, 267009 Pte.
Bennett, John, 265884 Pte.
Bennett, Samuel, 267936 Pte.
Bennett, William, 265100 Pte.
Benson, George Thomas, 5424 Pte.
Bentley, Fredk. Geo., 49734 L/Cpl.
Bird, George, 241461 Pte.
Birkenhead, John, 267794 Pte.
Blakemore, Albert Edwin, 9860 Pte.
Blakemore, Harry, 52116 Pte.
Blakeway, George, 15053 Pte.
Blease, Leonard, 265360 Pte.
Booth, Albert, 265297 L/Cpl.
Booth, Joseph, 266028 L/Cpl.
Booth, William, 2916 Pte.
Bound, Faux, 266361 Pte.
Bowden, Jonas, 266372 Pte.
Bowden, William, 265933 Pte.
Bowers, George, 265476 Pte.
Bowers, Robert, 140 Pte.
Box, Charles, 241407 Pte.
Bradbury, Geo. Ed., 266610 L/Cpl.
Bradley, Harold, 265265 Cpl.
Bradshaw, Allan, 2145 Sgt.
Brady, Frederick, 2885 Pte.
Brandreth, Percy, 45662 Pte.
Bredbury James Henry, 265784 Pte.
Breen, Thomas, 15073 Pte.
Brierley, Thos. Wm., 265364 Pte.
Broadhurst, Wallace Chas., 267868 L/Cpl.
Brocklehurst, James, 49615 Pte.
Brocklehurst, John Thos., 3476 Pte.
Brough, Arthur Edwin, 202079 Pte.
Brown, Fredk. Wm., 267972 Pte.
Brown, James, 265200 Pte.
Brown, Joseph Henry, 51098 Pte.
Brown, Thomas, 265107 L/Cpl.
Bryant, Howard, 2506 Pte.
Bryne, Fred, 266609 Pte.
Burgess, Edward, 4276 Pte.
Burgess, Charles, 3600 Pte.
Burgess, James Wm., 15537 Pte.
Burgess, Samuel, 265845 Pte.
Burke, Patrick, 15103 Pte.
Burns, William, 265257 C.S.M.
Buscall, Alfred, 72232 Pte.
Buxton, Sydney, 2891 Pte.

Callister, Robert, 32708 Pte.
Cantrell, Arthur, 268049 Pte.
Carney, James, 1758 Pte.
Carruthers, John, 1436 Pte.
Carter, Fredk. Swaine, 265156 Pte.
Carvell, Samuel, 291957 Pte.
Cawley, Robert, 265037 L/Col.
Cayless, Wal. Seymour, 51136 Pte.
Chaisty, William, 2172 Pte.
Chamberlain, Hny. Jas., 8049 Cpl.
Cheshire, Leonard, 268143 Pte.
Christian, Thos. Arthur, 268149 Pte.
Clare, George, 17805 Pte.

Clarke, Ernest, 265612 A/L/Sgt.
Clarke, James, 11938 Pte.
Clarke, Joseph, 1708 Pte.
Clarke, Samuel Leonard Cooper, 240638 Pte.
Clayton, Ambrose, 265872 Pte.
Clayton, Wm. Joseph, 33073 Pte.
Cleaton, Thos. Richd., 267872 Pte.
Clegg, Harry, 265742 Pte.
Cliffe, Henry, 201565 Pte.
Clough, George, 267873 Pte.
Clough, Stanley, 265495 Sgt.
Colclough, Samuel, 268047 Pte.
Coles, Charles, 50684 Pte.
Comerford, John Joseph, 2061/Pte.
Connor, John, 265822 Cpl.
Cook, Alfred, 267925 Pte.
Cooper, Frank, 266680 Pte.
Corbett, William, 3775 Pte.
Corfe, Allan William, 1489 A/C.S.M.
Corfe, James Henry, 63483 Pte.
Cox, Thomas, 4484 Pte.
Coy, James, 265528 Pte.
Cragen, David, 50956 Pte.
Crates, Harold Leslie, 66011 Pte.
Creswell, Harry, 268048 Dr.
Croft, Frank, 1388 Pte.
Croke, Thomas, 3152 Pte.
Cronin, Timothy, 24484 Pte.
Croppper, Albert, 265408 Pte.
Crow, Ernest, 28392 Pte.
Culley, Herbert, 3478 Pte.
Culshaw, John, 34625 Pte.
Cunningham, John, 268131 Pte.
Curtis, Harry, 241505 Pte.
Curtis, John Benj., 50677 Pte.

Dale, George, 243820 Pte.
Daly, James, 51035 Pte.
Daniel, Samuel 268051 Pte.
Daniels, George, 2220 Pte.
Daniels, Joseph, 24501 Pte.
Darlington, Ralph, 58276 Pte.
Davenport, Enst. Henry, 49478 Pte.
Davenport, William, 34984 Pte.
David, Morgan, 18662 Pte.
Davies, Edward John, 243247 Pte.
Davies, Fredk. Geo., 66021 Pte.
Davies, George, 2173 A/Cpl.
Davies, Joseph Edwin, 49956 Pte.
Davies, Richard, 268225 Pte.
Davis, Thomas, 35085 Pte.
Davies, William, 268042 Pte.
Day, James, 265669 L/Cpl.
Deakin, William, 16439 Pte.
Dean, John 26209 Pte.
Dean, Stanley, 265732 Pte.
Deaville, Isaac, 3937 Pte.
Depledge, Walter, 265675, A/L/Sgt.
Derbyshire, John Wm., 240447 Pte.
Dixon, Robt. Cun., 266082 Pte.
Dobbs, Leonard, 4545 Pte.
Dockerty, Michael, 266510 L/Cpl.
Dominick, Enst. Horace, 4434 Pte.
Downs, Cyril, 265324 Pte.
Downs, Regd. Noel, 66020 Pte.

Duncan, John Henry, 268176 Pte.
Dunkerley, John, 3606 Pte.
Dunnette, Charles, 49486 Pte.
Dunning, Frank, 266431 Pte.
Dutton, William, 32570 Pte.
Dwire, William, 2795 Pte.

Earlam, Arthur, 241401 Sgt.
Eaton, Wilfred, 987 Pte.
Egan, John Patrick, 268054 Pte.
Elliott, George, 268199 Cpl.
Elliott, Richard, 58177 Pte.
Etchells, Joseph, 3972 Pte.
Evans, William, 4110 Pte.
Evans, Edward Hugh, 66040 Pte.
Evans, Isaac, 265497 Pte.
Evans, William, 50427 Pte.

Fairclough, William, 59436 Pte.
Fearn, George, 268105 Pte.
Fenna, Robert, 15106 Pte.
Ferneyhough, Ernest, 268167 Pte.
Fielding, John, 2689 Pte.
Findlow, Samuel, 13061 Pte.
Finn, James, 265012 C.S.M.
Finnerty, Martin, 267910 Pte.
Flowers, Wilfred, 266365 Pte.
Ford, Arthur, 1420 L/Cpl.
Forster, Wm. Arthur, 15000 Pte.
Fox, Harry, 2566 L/Cpl.
Francis, Geo. Stanley, 52124 Pte.
Frearsen, Leonard, 267828 Pte.
Frith, Tom, 265649 L/Cpl.
Fuller, George, 15623 Pte.

Garner, Harry, 2894 Pte.
Garner, Robert, 18559 Pte.
Garside, Frank, 266274 Pte.
Genders, Harold, 51445 Pte.
Gibbens, Vic. Thorn., 51457 L/Cpl.
Gibson, William John, 64013 L/Cpl.
Gledhill, James, 266041 Pte.
Goddard, John, 2117 Sgt.
Golburn, Harry, 267995 Pte.
Gouge, George, 1816 Pte.
Gould, Samuel, 3881 Pte.
Gould, William John, 12301 Pte.
Graham, Harold, 268177 Pte.
Gratrix, John, 265127 Pte.
Gray, Edward, 62063 Pte.
Greenwood, Clement, 50120 Pte.
Gregory, James Henry, 268137 Pte.
Griffiths, George, 268021 Pte.
Groucott, Thomas, 268204 Sgt.
Grundy, Herbert Dyson, 4508 Pte.

Hackney, Thomas, 2588 Pte.
Hadfield, Louis, 2241 Pte.
Hague, Frank, 265220 Pte.
Halford, John Thos., 3284 Pte.
Hall, John, 266504 Pte.
Hallworth, Joseph, 266245 Pte.
Hand, Joseph, 20284 Pte.
Handley, Walter, 265852 Pte.
Hanvey, Leonard, 267832 Pte.
Harris, James, 231 Pte.

Harrison, Charlton Cyril, 2388 Pte.
Harrison, John, 266043 Pte.
Harrison, Joseph, 267930 Pte.
Harrison, William, 2417 Pte.
Harrop, Harry, 265150 Pte.
Hartley, Jas. Edward, 267272 Pte.
Hartley, John, 21231 Pte.
Hartley, Joseph Leigh, 40256 Pte.
Haughton, George, 2249 Pte.
Hayes, Cornelius, 265690 Pte.
Hayes, James, 53043 Pte.
Hayward, Edward, 267834 Pte.
Hazledine, George, 62314 Pte.
Head, Walter Joseph, 268178 Pte.
Heap, John, 265923 Pte.
Heathcote, Frank, 3960 Pte.
Helsby, Charles Harry, 15022 Pte.
Hewitt, Harold, 2293 Pte.
Hewitt, Joseph, 202083 Pte.
Hickton, William, 51720 Pte.
Higgins, Albert Victor, 51099 Pte.
Hillman, Samuel Geo., 267651 Pte.
Hilton, Geo. Whalley, 201985 Pte.
Hind, John, 3895 Pte.
Hindson, Alf. Stanwix, 268059 Pte.
Hobson, Andrew, 50470 Pte.
Hodgkinson, Henry, 28408 Pte.
Holland, Walter Ed., 66074 Pte.
Holliday, Norman, 265633 Cpl.
Holmes, James, 1591 Pte.
Hoole, Herbert, 4357 Pte.
Hopkinson, John, 267836 Pte.
Hopwood, Geo. Arthur, 266011 Pte.
Hornbuckle, James, 4570 Pte.
Horrocks, Arthur, 57652 Pte.
Hough, Albert, 3029 Pte.
Holdsworth, Orlando, 266385 Pte.
Houlton, William, 1406 Pte.
Howarth, Travis, 4515 Pte.
Hudson, John, 2289 Pte.
Hughes, John, 35740 Pte.
Hussey, Thomas, 267838 Pte.
Hynes, Henry, 292786 Pte.

Isaac, John, 265604 Cpl.

Jackson, Ernest, 4482 Pte.
Jackson, Frederick, 268130 Pte.
Jackson, Harry, 2297 Pte.
Jackson, Herbert, 11596 Pte.
Jackson, Herbert, 50106 Pte.
Jackson, John, 1034 A/Sgt.
Jackson, Lee, 265652 Cpl.
James, Alfred Albert, 51902 Pte.
James, Edward Robt., 268144 Pte.
James, Sydney David, 66078 Pte.
James, Tom, 266440 Pte.
James, Wm. Henry, 15005 Pte.
Jenkins, Albert, 51906 Pte.
Johnson, Leonard, 4397 Pte.
Johnston, Edward, 266978 Pte.
Jones, Alfred Gronwy, 52034 Pte.
Jones, David, 267946 L/Cpl.
Jones, Harry, 265672 Sgt.
Jones, Idwal, 66104 Pte.
Jones, John Edward, 1342 Pte.

Jones, Joseph, 268114 Pte.
Jones, Richard, 266380 Pte.
Jones, Thomas, 4637 Pte.
Jones, William, 266661 Pte.

Keighley, Wm. Chat., 266731 Pte.
Kelly, Robt. Joseph, 33735 Pte.
Kellow, Geoffrey, 72396 Pte.
Kenyon, Albert, 62469 Pte.
Kenyon, Samuel, 57102 Pte.
Kenworthy, Joseph, 265402 Pte.
Kind, Fredk. Francis, 63285 Pte.
King, Charles, 265486 Pte.
Kirkpatrick, Herbert, 266816 Pte.
Kivell, Henry, 14494 Pte.
Knott, Robert, 265905 Pte.
Knowles, George, 266499 Pte.
Knowles, Joseph, 268087 Cpl.

Lambert, Geo. Henry, 268221 Pte.
Lawton, Harry, 2781 Pte.
Leach, Henry, 3083 Pte.
Lee, George, 265206 L/Cpl.
Lees, Joseph, 315091 Pte.
Leigh, John, 265155 Pte.
Lesbriel, John, 292880 Pte.
Lewis, Kendrick, 241476 L/Cpl.
Lloyd, Alfred Ernest, 241516 Pte.
Lloyd, Frank, 265122 Pte.
Lloyd, Henry, 50718 Pte.
Lofthouse, Geo. Stanton, 62008 Pte.
Lofthouse, John, 34962 Pte.
Lomas, George, 265248 Pte.
Lomas, Ralph, 266467 Pte.
Longworth, Thomas, 63543 Pte.
Lord, Edward, 1601 Pte.
Lovegrove, Jos. Will., 51916 Pte.
Lovery, Ulic, 10462 L/Cpl.
Lowe, George, 288011 Pte.

Madden, John, 266498 Pte.
Makin, Joshua, 17924 Pte.
Malley, Wm. Henry, 57936 Pte.
Markland, Arthur, 265088 Pte.
Marriott, Arthur, 53307 Pte.
Marsh, William, 15856 C.S.M.
Marshall, Fred, 266419 Pte.
Marshall, James, 1174 Pte.
Mason, Joseph Robt., 266945 Pte.
Mather, Thomas, 1073 Pte.
Matthews, Thomas, 1709 Pte.
Matthews, William, 4026 Pte.
Mayers, Harold, 12001 Pte.
McClellan, Chas. Ratcliffe, 265447 Pte.
McClellan, George, 268309 A/Sgt.
McColgin, James, 5072 Sgt.
McDermott, Thomas, 2549 Pte.
McLaughlin, James, 268116 Pte.
McLean, James, 51170 Pte.
McWilliam, Duncan, 265029 Pte.
Meadows, Joseph, 4348 Pte.
Mealor, Henry, 35493 Pte.
Mealor, Samuel 200780 Pte.
Meikle, William 1858 Pte.
Mellor, William, 3383 Pte.
Middlebrooke, Frank, 2664 L/Cpl.

Midwinter, Wilfred, 2319 L/Sgt.
Mills, John James, 19587 Pte.
Millward, Ben, 265668 Pte.
Mitchell, Geo. Robert, 244746 Pte.
Mitchell, Jas. Berwick, 19177 Pte.
Molyneux, John, 201005 Pte.
Moore, George, 26811 L/Cpl.
Moore, Sydney, 3782 Pte.
Moores, Alfred, 2554 Pte.
Moores, Ellis, 4300 Pte.
Morgan, Ernest, 15033 Pte.
Morgan, Wilf. Austin Hurst, 66121
    Pte.
Morris, Ambrose, 266395 Pte.
Morris, Arthur, 267799 Pte.
Morris, John, 242261, Sgt.
Morton, Ezra, 3449 Pte.
Mullins, Harry, 1647 Pte.
Murphy, Harry, 265596 Pte.

Naden, Arthur Wm., 268212 Pte.
Needham, Gordon, 266242 Pte.
Newsham, Walter, 1779 Pte.
Newton, Allan, 2892 Pte.
Nield, Arthur, 267886 Pte.
Norbury, Albert, 266392 L/Cpl.
Norbury, Ernest, 10612 Pte.
North, James Edwin, 3983 Pte.
Northrop, Herbert, 13029 Pte.
Norton, Thos. Alfred, 45517 Pte.
Notman, Alexander, 4593 Pte.

O'Brien, Fred, 267991 Pte.
O'Brien, Martin, 266366 Pte.
O'Connor, Michael, 267943 L/Cpl.
Oldham, William, 2450 Pte.
Oldham, Wm. Edward, 1690 Pte.
Ollerenshaw, John Jas., 266143 Pte.
Owen, Herbert, 4315 Pte.
Owen, Robert, 66133 Pte.
Owen, Robert, 66135 Pte.
Owen, Robt. Evans, 66134 Pte.
Owens, Alfred George, 66136 Pte.

Pack, John Ernest, 243862 Pte.
Palmer, John Percival Jas., 72222 Pte.
Parker, George, 268215 Pte.
Parmenter, Geo. And., 267693 Pte.
Parry, Edmund Wm., 66138 Pte.
Parsons, Wm. James, 268193 Pte.
Peake, Harry, 58014 L/Sgt.
Peers, John Wm., 62234 Pte.
Phillips, Frank, 267919 C.S.M.
Pickford, Jos. Edward, 3104 Pte.
Pickford, Wm. Robert, 2193 L/Cpl.
Pickup, Cyril, 265482 Sgt.
Pilling, Harold, 51689 Pte.
Pitney, Charles Alfred, 51343 Cpl.
Platt, Charles Fred, 4018 Pte.
Platt, Wilfred, 1562 Pte.
Playfoot, George, 6407 Pte.
Poole, James, 63291 Pte.
Preece, James, 265024 Sgt.
Price, Albert Edward, 66139 Pte.
Price, James, 67834 Pte.
Price, Joseph, 1367 Pte.

Prince, William, 268195 L/Cpl.
Proctor, Edmund, 240757 Pte.
Proctor, Harold, 265898 Pte.
Pugh Bertram, 53063 Pte.
Pugh, Samuel, 15042 Pte.

Ratcliffe, William, 265526 Cpl.
Reid, Albert Victor, 1443 Sgt.
Renshaw, Frank, 265574 Pte.
Rhodes, William, 265576 Sgt.
Richardson, Thos. Har., 52461 Pte.
Ridgeway, Tom, 27497 Pte.
Ridley, Arthur, 1598 L/Cpl.
Rigsby, Joshua George, 53422 Pte.
Riley, Harry, 265865 Pte.
Riley, William, 51717 Pte.
Roberts, George, 268088 Pte.
Roberts, Henry, 2150 Pte.
Roberts, Henry, 31076 Pte.
Roberts, Henry Sam., 240987 Sgt.
Roberts, Wilfred, 266497 L/Cpl.
Robertson, James, 2387 L/Cpl.
Robinson, Arthur, 4554 Pte.
Robinson, Richard, 268024 Pte.
Roebuck, Ernest, 265764 Pte.
Rose, Alexander, 266023 Pte.
Rowbotham, Wal. Norbury 265642
    Pte.
Rowen, James, 3863 A/C.S.M.
Royle, Leonard, 291645 Pte.
Russell, Charles, 265912 Pte.
Ryder, John, 4028 Pte.

Salter, Ernest, 266321 Pte.
Salthouse, Albert, 265286 Pte.
Sandbach, Nathan, 49853 Pte.
Scholes, Frank, 14476 Sgt.
Scott, William, 1182 Pte.
Seddon, Rupert, 1419 Pte.
Sellars, William, 51476 Pte.
Senior, Alfred, 52250 Pte.
Severn, Alb. Edwin, 266956 L/Cpl.
Seville, Joseph, 202230 Pte.
Shackleton, Wm. Henry, 266517
    A/Sgt.
Shakeshaft, William, 35509 Pte.
Shallcross, Thomas, 265714 Pte.
Sharples, Harold, 67446 Pte.
Shaw, Henry, 4019 Pte.
Shaw, James, 2403 Pte.
Shaw, Joseph, 266685 Pte.
Sheard, John, 268012 Pte.
Sheldon, Geo. Clifford, 1207 Pte.
Short, Arthur, 62376 Pte.
Shufflebotham, Andrew Nathaniel,
    266764 Pte.
Siddall, Robert, 267956 Pte.
Sidebottom, Benjamin, 3425 Pte.
Sidebottom, Wright, 266324 L/Cpl.
Simpson, James, 67873 Pte.
Simpson, Wm. Henry, 266980 Pte.
Slack, Thomas, 3438 Pte.
Smith, Charles Walter, 64004 Pte.
Smith, Fredk. Michael, 63286 Pte.
Smith, Geo. William, 18409 Pte.
Smith, Harold, 1592 Pte.

Smith, Isaac, 266280 Pte.
Smith, James, 241667 Pte.
Smith, James, 265687 Pte.
Smith, James, 266549 Pte.
Smith, James Ernest, 3142 Pte.
Smith, John, 267950 Pte.
Smith, Percy Fredk., 33135 Pte.
Smith, Thomas, 51607 Pte.
Smith, William, 34930 Pte.
Smith, William, 265954 Pte.
Southern, Richd. Alex., 292489 Pte.
Southgate, Charles, 266751 Pte.
Speakman, Richard, 265061 Sgt.
Spedding, Arthur, 2731 Pte.
Spicer, Sydney, 18012 L/Cpl.
Spilsbury, Samuel, 265817 Pte.
Spilsbury, William, 265400 L/Cpl.
Sproson, Harry, 265446 L/Cpl.
Start, Frank, 291771 Pte.
Steele, James, 265306
Stonier, Frederick, 267894 Pte.
Stopford, Geo. Henry, 266575 Pte.
Street, John, 266513 Pte.
Stubbs, Fred, 1154 Pte.
Sullivan, John Tim., 61952 Pte.
Sumner, John, 268190 Pte.
Sunderland, William, 265487 Pte.
Surson, James Alex., 29614 Pte.
Sutton, James Wm., 265543 Pte.
Swain, Ernest, 291363 Pte.
Swann, Wilfred, 52751 L/Cpl.
Swindlehurst, 267901 Pte.
Swindells, Harry, 1711 Pte.
Swindells, William, 1461 Pte.
Sykes, Thomas, 58121 Pte.

Taylor, Frederick, 2760 Pte.
Taylor, Fredk. Harold, 21648 L/Cpl.
Taylor, Joe, 265221 Pte.
Tetlow, Charles, 1564 Sgt.
Thomas, Walter, 52698 Pte.
Thompson, Geoffrey Bell, 51174 Pte.
Thorley, John Henry, 2507 Pte.
Thornley, Harold, 266112 L/Cpl.
Thornton, Joseph, 266067 Pte.
Thorp, James Wm., 266100 L/Cpl.
Travis, Robert, 267933 Pte.
Turner, Albert Edward, 266161 Pte.
Turner, Benjamin, 1626 Pte.
Turner, George Arthur, 265720 Pte.
Turner, James Henry, 4198 L/Cpl.

Unsworth, Joseph, 1553 Pte.
Unwin, William Henry, 267898 Pte.
Utley, Fred, 265416 L/Cpl.

Vernon, James, 243641 Pte.

Wadsworth, George, 2207 Sgt.
Wadsworth, Wm., 265500 L/Cpl.
Walkden, Ernest, 267953 Pte.
Walker, Albert, 266639 Pte.
Walker, Ernest, 265253 Sgt.
Walker, George, 50481 Pte.
Walker, Louis Herb., 268171 Pte.
Walmsley, William, 243718 Pte.

Walsh, Owen, 265754 Pte.
Walton, Wm. James, 2330 Cpl.
Want, George David, 2380 Pte.
Ward, Edmund, 1577 C.S.M.
Ward, Edward, 268191 Pte.
Ward, Richard, 15130 Pte.
Wardle, Frederick, 35361 Pte.
Warham, Joseph, 62456 Pte.
Warham, Thos. Percy, 267854 Pte.
Watson, Frank, 51784 Pte.
Watson, James Leonard, 49583 Pte.
Webb, Joseph, 45396 Pte.
Wells, John, 265894 Sgt.
West, Walter, 1405 Sgt.
Whalley, Albert, 265670 Sgt.
Wheeler, James, 265372 L/Cpl.
Wheeler, Thos. Wm., 1062 Sgt.
White, Albert, 243705 Pte.
White, Robert, 3417 Pte.
Whitehead, Wilfred, 266185 Pte.
Whittingham, Arth., 267938 L/Cpl.
Wilcox, Lawrence, 30561 Pte.
Wild, John James, 266097 Pte.
Wild, Joseph, 266552 Pte.
Wilkinson, Edwin, 266048 Pte.
Wilkinson, Richard, 2606 Dmr.
Wilkinson, Wm. Robin., 268224 Pte.
Williams, Albert, 266259 Pte.
Williams, Benj. Wallace, 2803 Pte.
Williams, Evan Jones, 45057 Pte.
Williams, Frederick, 62335 Pte.
Williams, John Henry, W/1129 Pte.
Williams, Percy, 14885 L/Cpl.
Williams, Samuel, 32938 Pte.
Williamson, Walter, 1524 Pte.
Williamson, Chas. Alf., 267900 Pte.
Wilson, George Edwin, 51152 Pte.
Wilson, John Edward, 5252 Pte.
Wilson, Samuel James, 2581 Pte.
Winstanley, Eric, 72081 Pte.
Witherspoon,Rt.Douglas, 68058 Pte.
Wood, Charles, 266671 Pte.
Wood, Thomas, 21193 L/Cpl.
Woodcock, Arthur, 62206 Pte.
Woodhead, Harry, 266383 Pte.
Woodville, Larnall, 15051 A/Cpl.
Woodward, John, 3559 Pte.
Woolley, Charles, 24762 Pte.
Woolley, James, 265565 Pte.
Worthington, Thomas, 24068 Pte.
Wrench, Fred, 241272 Pte.

2/6th BATTALION.

Emery, Lionel Carring., 4235 A/Cpl.
Gee, John, 3645 Pte.
Mawson, John Henry, 267392 Pte.
Parker, Joe, 3783 Pte.
Rowbottom, Frank, 3610 Pte.
Whittaker, Harry, 3243 Pte.

6th (RES.) BATTALION.

Davies, John James, 3185 Pte.

1/7th BATTALION.

Albinson, James, 3208 Pte.
Andrew, Harold, 36228 Pte.

Armstrong, George, 291085 Pte.
Avery, Frank, 291310 Pte.

Bache, Henry, 63079 Pte.
Baguley, William, 2498 Pte.
Bailey, Albert, 291430 Pte.
Bailey, Fred, 76535 Pte.
Bailey, John, 1954 A/L/Cpl.
Bailey, James Edward, 2850 Pte.
Bailey, Samuel, 291654 Pte.
Ball, Mark, 291117 Pte.
Barber, Fredk. James, 60408 Pte.
Barber, Price, 290695 A/Cpl.
Barker, Edwin Jn. Leslie, 40768 Pte.
Barker, James, 290247 Sgt.
Barlow, Frank, 290460 Pte.
Barrow, Frank, 2305 A/Cpl.
Baskerville, George, 290862 Pte.
Bates, Lewis, 40728 Pte.
Bayley James Richd., 293174 Pte.
Beardmore, Ernest, 291370 Pte.
Beech, Walter Ernest, 2533 Pte.
Belfield, John, 290390 Pte.
Bennett, John Thomas, 40780 Pte.
Bennett, Nicholas, 243580 Pte.
Beresford, Arnold, 290495 Pte.
Beresford, George, 291595 Pte.
Birkby,Hodgson Graves,6056 C.S.M.
Blake, Abraham, 2613 Pte.
Booth, Harry, 291000 Pte.
Booth, Zachariah, 291138 Pte.
Boughey, Thos. Yates, 291559 Sgt.
Bowers, James, 290158 Pte.
Bradbury, James, 1902 Pte.
Bradley, John, 3337 Pte.
Braithwaite, Alf. Fredk., 51949 Pte.
Brereton, Wilfred, 290470 Pte.
Briscoe, William, 291313 Pte.
Broadhead, Thomas, 291280 Pte.
Broadhurst, Ralph, 291252 Pte.
Broadhurst, Reginald, 291521 Pte.
Brocklehurst, Ernest, 2808 Pte.
Brown, Ernest, 50613 Pte.
Brown, Joseph, 1376 Pte.
Brown Ran. Cheetham, 291470 Pte.
Brown, William, 2576 Pte.
Broxup, John William, 21113 Pte.
Burgess, Arthur, 290678 Pte.
Burgess, Reginald, 291059 Pte.
Busby, Albert Thomas, 60377 Pte.
Butler, George, 290629 L/Cpl.

Camm, Ernest, 1874 Pte.
Cantrell, Chas. William, 2369 Pte.
Capper, Ernest, 291403 Pte.
Capper, Walter, 291032 Pte.
Carter, Fred, 290802 L/Cpl.
Cartwright, Wm. Hny., 290374 Pte.
Catterall, Fred, 290220 L/Cpl.
Chalkley, Wilfred, 76036 Cpl.
Champ, Norman, 290069 L/Cpl.
Chapman, Jas. Albert, 1823 Pte.
Chappell, Benjamin, 291481 L/Cpl.
Charlesworth, Ar. Jos., 290016 Pte.
Chatfield, Alb. Edward, 290605 Pte.
Cheesewright, Percy, 60378 Pte.

Chilton, Edward James, 29838 Pte.
Clare, John, 14803 Pte.
Cleaver, Harry, 291275 Pte.
Cleminson, Thomas, 293108 Sgt.
Cole, Harry, 290311 Pte.
Collin, James Edward, 40737 L/Cpl.
Collinge, Percy, 267974 Pte.
Collins, James, 290454 Pte.
Cook, William, 2487 Pte.
Cooke, Arthur, 291482 Pte.
Cooper, Frederick, 291209 Pte.
Cooper, John Wm., 291548 Pte.
Cope, Fred, 290272 Cpl.
Coppock, Harold, 290429 Pte.
Counsil, John, 265986 Pte.
Coups, Harold, 738 Sgt.

Dale, John Henry, 2074 Pte.
Daniels, Alfred, 291491 Pte.
Daniels, Charles Henry, 2464 Pte.
Davenport, Henry, 290169 Pte.
Davies, Albert Vincent, 290885 Pte.
Davies, Gilbert Edward, 2781 Pte.
Davies, George, 1272 L/Cpl.
Dawson, Charles, 291167 Pte.
Dobson, Cecil, 290284 Pte.
Dodd, David John, 291107 Cpl.
Dunn, Harry, 291088 Pte.
Dunn, Joseph, 293172 Pte.

Eachus, Richard Wm., 293172 Pte.
Eachus, Richd. William, 2286 Pte.
Elkin, Rowland, 290593 Cpl.
Elvin, Albert John, 76094 Pte.
Farr, Fred, 291093 Pte.
Fawkner, Frederick, 2795 Pte.
Fitchett, John, 91 Sgt.
Foster, Richard, 2629 Pte.
Frearson, Alfred, 267829 Pte.

Gallimore, George, 1720 Sgt.
Gallimore, John, 290804 Pte.
Gannon, George, 290424 Pte.
Garlick, Charles, 291522 Pte.
Gay, Robert, 291404 Pte.
Gibbon, Sydney, 2579 Pte.
Gibson, Joseph Harold, 293119 Pte.
Gilday, James, 206 Pte.
Gill, Charles Albert, 291188 Pte.
Goldthorpe, Harold, 2687 Pte.
Grace, Charles, 293118 Sgt.
Graham, George, 66632 Pte.
Green, Thomas Alfred, 2347 Pte.

Hall, Chas. Harold, 60563 Pte.
Hall, Fred, 291460 Pte.
Hall, Harry, 293158 Pte.
Halton, Frank, 76508 Pte.
Hamlett, George, 17992 Pte.
Hampson, John, 36708 Pte.
Harrison, Gilbert, 2142 Pte.
Harrop, Joseph, 240412 Pte.
Hart, Samuel, 290969 Pte.
Hassall, Arthur, 2997 Pte.
Hawes, Henry, 316152 Pte.
Hazledine, Harold, 3422 Pte.

Hetchells, John, 1467 Pte.
Hewitt, Fred, 76151 Pte.
Higgins, Thomas, 290753 Pte.
Hocking, Thomas Fredk., 260226 Clr./Sgt.
Hodgkiss, George, 291192 Pte.
Hodgson, John, 2388 Pte.
Hodkinson, Thomas, 2598 Pte.
Hodkinson, Walter, 290439 Pte.
Holehouse, Walter, 2080 Pte.
Hollins, Wilfred, 290793 Pte.
Holsey, Horace Arthur, 40777 Pte.
Hooley, Vernon Coates, 2186 Pte.
Horton, Peter, 291893 Pte.
Houghton, Samuel, 290580 Pte.
Hughes, Joseph, 243579 L/Cpl.
Hulme, Thomas, 290909 Pte.
Hunt, Samuel, 947 Pte.
Hunt, Wilfred, 290579 Pte.

Ikin, William, 290511 Sgt.

Jepson, Harold, 290773 L/Cpl.
Johnson, Arthur, 290418 Pte.
Johnson, Frank, 241142 Pte.
Jones, Robert, 293125 Pte.
Joynson, William, 291062 Pte.

Kay, George, 76512 Pte.
Kaney, Thomas, 268086 Pte.
King, Thomas, 241342 Pte.
Knight, Albert, 18810 Pte.

Lawton, Albert, 18810 Pte.
Leah, John, 290653 Pte.
Leech, Fred, 18866 Pte.
Leek, Frank, 291498 Pte.
Leese, Samuel, 290082 A/Cpl.
Leigh, Alfred, 2456 Pte.
Levell, Wm. Edward, 292636 Pte.
Lewin, Clarence, 291246 Pte.
Lewis, Thomas, 2718 Pte.
Lloyd, Arthur, 291098 Pte.
Lloyd, Samuel, 17884 Pte.
Lightfoot, James, 3746 Pte.
Lockett, George, 290167 Pte.
Lomas, Fred, 291096 L/Cpl.
Long, Samuel, 290150 Pte.
Lount, Alfred, 40790 Pte.
Lunney, Peter, 40847 Pte.
Lunt, Frank, 1261 Sgt.
Luscott, William, 291355 Pte.

Marsden, George, 67957 Pte.
Massey, Harry, 290993 Pte.
Mathers, Fred, 290020 Pte.
McHale, William, 290989 Pte.
Mellor, George, 2100 Pte.
Mercer, Rowland, 202032 Pte.
Millward, James, 1446 Cpl.
Mitchell, Charles, 290339 A/L/Sgt.
Morris, Edward, Thos., 20067 Pte.
Mottershead, John, 291044 Pte.

Naven, Thos. Edward, 291519 Pte.
Newman, Chas. William, 40448 Pte.

Nield, Harry, 1759 A/L/Cpl.
Nightingale, Charles, 1612 Cpl.
Nolan, John James, 49928 Pte.
Nunn, Bertie, 233(Pte.

O'Brien, William, 2612 Pte.
O'Connor, James, 291025 Pte.
Oldfield, Albert, 291382 Pte.
Oldfield, Frank, 291030 Pte.
Oldham, Joseph, 14525 Pte.
Oldfield, William Douglas Victor, 291440 Pte.
Ormes, Albert, 291217 Pte.
Owen, Wm. George, 1226 Pte.
Owens, Robert, 9623 Pte.

Palin, Samuel Herbert, 1277 Pte.
Parry, William David, 76578 Pte.
Pearson, Walter, 2322 Pte.
Pedley, Thomas, 1302 L/Cp!.
Peers, John, 202435 Cpl.
Pennington, Cromwell Nelson, 2630 Pte.
Peover, Frederick, 291169 Pte.
Pickering, Geo. Wm., 290091 Pte.
Pickford, Jos. Francis, 2757 L/Cpl.
Pomfret, Joseph Ellis, 291040 L/Cpl.
Pomfret, William, 2450 Pte.
Poole, William, 2404 Pte.
Postles, Luther, 290821 Pte.
Powell, George, 45 C.S.M.
Price, Chris. Llewellyn, 268302 Pte.
Prophett, Walter, 2719 Pte.

Ratcliffe, John Jos., 290824 L/Cpl.
Riddlesworth, Frank Dixon, 290515 Pte.
Ridgway, Thomas, 2371 Pte.
Roberts, Arnold, 241395 Pte.
Rowland, Hugh, 293167 Pte.
Rowarth, Ellis, 1667 L/Cpl.
Rowe, William, 2415 Pte.

Sadler, Alexander, 242864 Pte.
Sadler, Frank, 291112 Pte.
Sandbach, Fred, 291574 Pte.
Sant, William, 1835 Pte.
Savage, Thos. William, 290389 Pte.
Sellers, Charles, 290764 Pte.
Shaw, Hugh, 63075 L/Cpl.
Shaw, John, 2288 L/Cpl.
Sheen, John Allen, 21628 Pte.
Sherratt, Isaac, 290618 Pte.
Sherwin, John, 2836 Pte.
Silvester, Samuel Jas., 291197 Pte.
Skidmore, Frederick, 31858 Pte.
Smallwood, John, 2116 Pte.
Smallwood Joseph, 3446 Pte.
Snalan, Richard, 62490 Pte.
Sparkes, William, 240 Sgt.
Staniforth, John, 290356 Pte.
Stokes, Ernest George, 60403 Pte.
Street, Charles, 290741 Pte.
Stretton, Jas. Edmond, 20029 Pte.
Stringer, Alfred, 2826 Pte.
Stubbs, Frank, 290022 Pte.

Stubbs, Henry, 291113 Pte.
Stubbs, Thomas Louis, 446 Cpl.
Sutton, Joseph, 1589 Pte.
Swaine, James, 2112 Pte.
Swindells, John, 290174 Pte.

Taylor, Joseph, 113 Pte.
Tickle, Thomas, 291035 Pte.
Tomkinson, George, 1509 Pte.
Tomlinson, George, 65632 Pte.
Trueman, Herbert, 243645 Pte.
Trueman, Thomas, 291529 Pte.
Tuberville, George, 290894 Pte.
Turner, George, 290987 Pte.
Turner, Henry, 66637 Pte.
Turner, Rowland, 291081 Pte.

Varley, Wesley, 267022 Pte.
Varney, Harry Fredk., 51934 Pte.
Vickers, John, 291147 Pte.
Vigrass, Harry, 290625 Pte.

Vine, Joe, 1945 Pte.

Wall, Frederick, 52612 Sgt.
Walton, Frank, 2331 Pte.
Walton, Fred, 293193 Pte.
Walton, Joseph, 2752 Pte.
Warburton, James, 291520 Pte.
Wardle, George, 1479 Cpl.
Wardle, George, 1539 Pte.
Warhurst, Walter, 290458 Pte.
Warren, Harold, 2382 Pte.
West, William, 1016 Sgt.
Whalley, Herbert, 1531 Pte.
Whitehead, Alfred, 3103 Pte.
Whitelegg, Ernest Newton, 291532 Pte.
Whittaker, Walter Wm., 1819 Pte.
Wilkinson, Edward, 1266 L/Cpl.
Wilkinson, Harry, 2001 Pte.
Wilkinson, John, 2532 Pte.
Williams, Isaac, 2834 Pte.

Williamson, Harry, 291014 Pte.
Wilson, Jesse, 20646 Sgt.
Wilson, John Thomas, 50973 Pte.
Wood, Fred, 76584 Pte.
Wood, Wilson, 2841 Pte.
Woodall, Thomas, 243608 Pte.
Woodhouse, Walter, 3407 Pte.
Woodward, William, 268091 Pte.
Worrall, Harry, 290849 Pte.
Wright, Harold, 2728 Pte.
Wright, James, 290465 Cpl.
Wyatt, Charles, 291537 Pte.

2/7th BATTALION.

Brady, Alfred, 292925 Pte.
Oakden, Arthur, 4891 Pte.
Potts, Joseph, 3519 Pte.
Regnauld, Leslie James, 5876 Pte.
Sharpe, Henry Jonathan, 292641 Pte.
Sharpe, Hny. Jonathan, 292641 Pte.
Wootton, William, 4130 Pte.

Victory Marches

THE Colours of the 1st Battalion took part in the Victory March in Paris, July 14th, 1919. The Ensigns were: King's Colour, Lieut. E. M. Sidebotham; Regimental Colour, Lieut. E. G. Carr. The Escort was 10022 Sergt. Barnett, M.M., Corporal Hurd, M.M. and 10081 Pte. Davies. Oak wreaths were carried on the Colours, the only decoration of any kind among the whole mass of Colours. Many of the onlookers could be seen pointing out the wreaths to their friends. General Sir W. H. Anderson was present. The troops had a wonderful reception, and the British troops were easily second to " Les Poilus " in the popular favour.

On July 19th, the March was repeated in London. Our Colours still proudly carried their wreaths of oak, laurel wreaths being provided for the remainder. The reception was greater here, than in Paris. A barrage of fruit, chocolate and cigarettes was laid down during halts, while the troops were very hospitably entertained by the Marquis of Lincolnshire before the start. Corporal Bennett took the place of Corporal Hurd in the Escort.

Appendix III.

Note on the Medals of the Great War

"The 1914 Star."

In November, 1917, a Star in bronze was granted to all those who had served in France and Flanders between 5th August, 1914, and midnight 22nd-23rd November, 1914. No clasp was originally issued with this Star, the riband of which is red, white and blue, shaded and watered. (Army Order No. 350).

Obverse : Two crossed swords, surmounted by a Crown ; dates intertwined on a ribbon, within a wreath ; Royal Cypher at base.

Reverse : Plain, except for stamped name of the recipient.

In October, 1919, the issue of a clasp was sanctioned to those who had served under fire between the above-mentioned dates. (Army Order No. 361).

"The 1914-1915 Star."

In December, 1918, a Star in bronze was awarded to those who had served in the theatres of war between 5th August, 1914, and the 31st December, 1915. This decoration is identical, except for the date, with the " 1914 Star " but has no clasp. Those eligible for the " 1914 Star " do not receive the " 1914-1915 Star." (Army Order No. 20 of 1919).

"The War Medal."

In July, 1919, it was announced that this Medal would be issued to all those who had served overseas. The Medal is in silver ; the riband being orange centre, watered, with stripes of white and black on each side and with borders of Royal blue. (Army Order No. 266).

Obverse : Head of H.M. King George V. ; legend, Georgius V. Britt: Omn : Rex et Ind : Imp :

Reverse : Equestrian figure of St. George ; legend, 1914-18.

"The Victory Medal."

In August, 1919, this second Medal was granted, being in bronze. The riband is red in the centre, with green and violet on each side, shaded to form the colours of two rainbows. The design of the ribbon is the same as that issued by the other Allied Powers. (Army Order No. 301).

Obverse : A winged figure of Victory.

Reverse : Inscription, and dates, within a wreath.

An emblem of an oak leaf in bronze was authorized in January, 1920, to be worn on this riband, by those who had been " mentioned in despatches." (Army Order No. 3).

Honours Won by Individuals in, or serving with, The Regiment

ABBOTT, J. W., 11706. M.M.

ABERCROMBIE, D. Mention.

ABRAHAM, E. W. Mention.

ABRAHAMS, A. Mention.

ADAIR, H. S. Mention (4), D.S.O.

ADAMSON, E., 20225. M.M.

ADKINSON, R., 265375. M.M.

ADLER, S. M.C.

> During operations near Jenlain, 3rd Nov. 1918, on the occasion of an enemy withdrawal, after his Company Commander and other Officers had become casualties, he reorganized the company and pushed forward under intense shell-fire, though out of touch on both flanks, making ground, and capturing prisoners. He remained in command of his company for a considerable time after being wounded.

ADSHEAD, G. Mention.

> Promoted Brevet-Major.

ADSHEAD, M. S. M.C.

> During the operations in Sept., '18, while the Battalion was advancing, this officer galloped forward under exceedingly heavy shell fire to direct a company that had lost direction. Further, he worked with untiring energy throughout the day and night, performing many acts of gallantry for the advantage of his Battalion and setting a fine example to the men.
> Legion D'Honneur-Chevalier.

ADSHEAD, T., 16113. M.M.

ADSHEAD, T., 45761. M.M.

AHERN, W. P., 1109. D.C.M.

> After the enemy's trench had been captured, he organised and conducted carrying parties to bring up bombs and supplies, and generally consolidated the position gained.

AINSWORTH G., 32975. M.M.

AIREY, J., 26856. Mention.

AIREY, J. H.. 14780. D.C.M.

AITKEN, G., 17206. D.C.M.

> On the 25th Sept., 1915, near Festubert, he reached the enemy's parapet alone, and had returned for some distance when he heard the calls of a wounded man, who was near the point from which he had come. He at once returned to him, and crawled back to our trenches with the man on his back, a distance of about 200 yards, under very heavy fire, the wounded man being hit a second time.

ALLCOCK, L., 11519. M.M.

ALLEESON, A., 7652. M.M.

ALLEN, A., 11187. M.M.

ALLEN, F. Mention.

ALLEN, F., 52761. D.C.M.

> This warrant officer has rendered valuable assistance in obtaining information and taking responsible duties when officers have become casualties. He has proved himself to be a gallant and resourceful leader, and by his personal example has set up a high standard of efficiency among the non-commissioned officers and men of his company.

ALLEN, G. Mention.

ALLEN, T. W. Mention. M.C.

> As Battalion Intelligence Officer, he did fine work before and during the attack on the 14th October, 1918, East of Terhand. He laid a tape marking the assembly position under heavy fire. He collected much valuable information about enemy strong points before the attack. His example of pluck and endurance was invaluable and his good organisation of observers and runners greatly assisted in the success of the operations.

ALLMAND, A. J.   Mention (2).   M.C.
ALLUM, C. E.   Mention.   M.C.
AMBLER, R., 26670.   M.M.
AMBROSE, W. G.   Mention.   M.C.
AMES, J. B., 21393.   M.M.
ANDERSON, G. R. L.   Mention.
ANDERSON, W. H.   Mention (7).
    Promoted Brevet-Lieut.-Colonel; Colonel;
       Major-General.
    Legion of Honour.
    Russian Order of St. Stanislus.
    Croix de Guerre (Fr.)
    Order of the Sacred Treasure.
    Order of Christ.
    C.B.
    Portuguese Military Order.
ANDREW, E.   M.C.
ANDREWS, C. H., 263036.   Mention.
ANDREWS, C. R.   Mention.
ANGAS, L. L. B.   Mention (2).   M.C.
    In the action near Gheluwe on the 14th
October, 1918, he led the assaulting companies of the Battalion with marked dash and
gallantry. He not only reached the two
objectives given to the Battalion, but cleared
a position of the front of the Battalion on
the left as well. This fine action led to the
capture of some 150 prisoners and two field
guns.
ANKERS, E., 18061.   Mention.
ANTLIFF, G., 8312.   D.C.M.
    He has invariably performed his duties with
conspicuous zeal and ability, displaying the
highest courage and coolness under fire, and
setting a splendid example of devotion to
duty to all ranks with him.
APPLETON, F., 6029.   Mention.
APPLETON, T. S.
    Promoted 2/Lieut.
ARCHER, J.   Mention.
ARMITAGE, S.   12883.   Mention. M.S.M.
ARMSTRONG, R., 20277.
    Croix de Guerre (Bel.)
ARMSTRONG, S., 290134.   D.C.M.
    He has shown conspicuous gallantry
throughout the whole period, setting a
splendid example to his men. On a great
many occasions he has performed very

dangerous and arduous tasks under shell-
fire, and it was largely due to his fearlessness,
grit and determination, that the Battalion
never once failed to get supplies.
ARNFIELD, H.   Mention.
ASHBROOK, W. C., 10900.   Mention.   M.M.
ASHBY, G.   Mention (2).   C.B.
ASHLEY, H., W. 606.   M.M.
ASLATT, G., 18057.   M.M.
ASPDEN, E., 14343.   Mention.
ASPINALL, H., 13802.   M.M. and Bar.
ASTLE, S.   M.C.
    In a raid on the enemy's lines, his party was
help up for some time by hostile machine-
gun fire, but by his good leadership and
determination, he succeeded in reaching
his objective, captured a prisoner, and put
a large number of the enemy out of action.
He also destroyed an enemy dug-out in
spite of strong opposition.
ASTLEY-RUSSELL, F. D.   Mention.
ATHERTON, H. P., 10076.   M.M.
ATHERTON, S. E., 240391.   M.M.
ATKIN, H. A. W., 24714.
    Croix de Guerre (Bel.)
ATKINSON, A., 267604.   M.M.
ATKINSON, C. E., 16738.   M.M.
ATKINSON, H. N.   Mention.   D.S.O.
    Under a heavy fire from front and both
flanks he collected a few men and checked
the enemy, thereby facilitating the retire-
ment of his comrades.
ATKINSON, J., 45655.   M.M.
AUSTIN, J., 14691.   M.M.
AXON, E., 14418.   Mention.
AYRES, W., 52225.   M.M. and Bar.
BABINGTON, F., 23097.   M.M.
BACHUS, N.   Mention.
BACON, J. L. W.   D.F.C.
    During the last part of the operations, this
officer displayed marked gallantry and
determination, never hesitating to descend
to a low height to locate the position of
our troops, frequently in face of severe
hostile fire. On one occasion he carried
out four bombing raids in one day on an
objective seventy miles distant.

BAILEY, W., 290170.   M.M.

BAILEY, W., 49430.   M.M.

BAILEY, W., 17511.   Mention.

BAIRD, R., 39943.   M.M.

BAKER, A., 18921.   M.M.

BAKER, W. G., 263010.   M.S.M.

BAKER, W. H. G.   Mention.

BALL, W., 33525.   M.M.

BAMBER, H. L., 7426.   M.S.M.

BANCROFT, S., 14591.   Mention (2).

BAND, H., 558216.   M.M.

BANNISTER, W. H., 14748.   M.M.

BANNON, M., W/304.   M.M.

BARBER, F., 13771.   M.M.

BARBER, H., 12159.   M.M.

BARBER, J., 15817.   M.M.

BARBER, N. K.   M.C.

Previous to an attack he led several patrols, examining the enemy's wire, locating his working parties, and acquiring the necessary command of the ground. On one occasion, when in charge of a covering party, he went four times through heavy shell fire to locate a section of his party which had not received the order to withdraw. Throughout the operations he showed exceptional coolness, resource and devotion to duty.

BARFF, W. H.   Mention (2).   D.S.O.

He advanced practically alone under heavy fire to examine gaps in the wire. He displayed great courage and determination throughout, and, although severely wounded, continued to encourage his men.

BARKER, D., 18444.   M.M.

BARKER, R. G., 24978.   M.M.

BARNES, A., 49939.   D.C.M.

BARNES, E., 265978.   M.M.

BARNES, H., 14178.   M.M.

BARNES, J. A. L.   M.C.

He brought up his company under heavy shell and machine-gun fire. Later, during the advance, when he found himself in an isolated position, he held out against great odds and set a very fine example of coolness to his men.

BARNETT, E., 10022.   M.M.

BARNETT, V. G.   Mention.

BARNSHAW, H., 291323.   M.M.

BARROW, W. G.   M.M.

BARTLETT, C., 60369.   Mention.

BATCHELOR, W. H., 10/17804.   D.C.M.

He took command of a ration party at a critical moment, when the greatest confusion had arisen under heavy shell fire in a congested trench, reorganised the traffic, and, with the assistance of an N.C.O., restored order so that the relief which was in progress was not impeded. This had to be done under heavy and accurate shell and gas bombardment, in pitch darkness, rain, and on slippery ground. The initiative of this N.C.O. cannot be too highly praised.

BATHURST, W. J.   M.C.

During active operations, he sent in valuable reports, obtained by personal reconnaissance at great risk. Later, his company went through a village under a terrific fire from machine-guns. He showed remarkable courage on this occasion, and was dangerously wounded.

BATES, R., 268034.   M.M.

BATTERSBY, S.   M.M.

BAXTER, G., W/589.   Mention.

BAYLEY, A., 50159.   M.M.

BEADMORE, W., 20293.   Mention.

BEARCHILL, T. B., 266492.   M.M.

BEARD, A., 2206.   M.M.

BEARDOW, W., 9712.   M.M.

BEATTIE, J., 66246.   M.M.

Medaille D'Honneur.

BEAUMONT, N. E.   M.C.

He personally superintended the bringing up of rations under very heavy shell fire. The horses in the limber were hit, and he at once unloaded the rations and himself helped to carry them forward. He made four journeys with two men over very heavily shelled ground until all the rations had been got forward. But for his initiative and devotion to duty the troops in the line would not have been supplied.

BEAVON, T., 17899.   M.M.

BEAVON, W., 60891.   M.S.M.

BECKETT, W. E.   Mention.

BECKWITH, L. K., 35205.   Mention.

BELL, G., 200763.
Croix de Guerre (Fr.)

BELL, J., 14038.   M.M.
Medaille Militaire.

BELL, J., 291547.   M.S.M.

BELL, J. J., 639.   D.C.M.
On the 4th October, 1915, near Le Touquet,
while in charge of a wiring party, an officer
was wounded. Sergeant Bell, though under
a heavy rifle fire, the whole time, went to
his assistance, and with the help of another
man, carried him back into the trench.
On the 7th October, an enemy shell demolished the parapet of our trench and buried
a Corporal. Sergeant Bell at once went to
his assistance, and with the aid of another
man, dug the Corporal out, under a heavy
rifle fire all the time.

BELLEDONNE, L., 201650.
Croix de Guerre (Fr.)

BELLIS, J., 240948.   M.M.

BELLYOU, G., 20127.   D.C.M.
He has rendered exceptional service in the
front line, of a fearless nature, he has a most
cheerful disposition, and is of the greatest
value in inspiring his men. Whenever
patrol work had to be done he always
volunteered. He is at his best when danger
is greatest.

BENGOUGH, L.   Mention.   M.C.
Promoted Brevet-Major.

BENNETT, A., 9549.   M.M. and Bar.

BENNETT, J., 1295.   Mention.

BENNETT, W., 14605.   M.S.M.

BENNETT-DAMPIER, A. C. W.
Croix de Guerre (Bel.)

BENNINGTON, S., 58988.   M.S.M.

BENSON, R. H., 240758   Mention.

BENTLEY, T., 25401.   M.M.
Croix de Guerre (Fr.)

BENTLY, H. R.   Mention.   O.B.E.

BERKLY, M., 21163.   D.C.M.
He took part in a difficult reconnaissance
prior to an attack, and successfully kept the
direction of the adjoining troops during the
attack. He has carried out several valuable
reconnaissances and showed splendid courage and leadership on all occasions.

BERRY, J., 14544.   M.M.

BERTENSHAW, J., 16897.   D.C.M.
This N.C.O. in a counter-attack, organised the men round him and pushed
forward until, his position becoming untenable, he was ordered to withdraw, which
he did, personally carrying two wounded
men under fire. Later, when all the officers
had become casualties, he took command,
and held the position until relieved. His
example was excellent, and he acted with
coolness and determination.

BESWICK, W., 266767.   M.M.

BILLINGTON, E.   M.C.

BILLINGTON, J., 18440.   Mention.

BINNS, R. M., 52517.   M.M.

BIRCH, A., 967.
Serbian Gold Medal.

BIRCHALL, J. H., 18098.   Mention.

BIRD, H., 51483.   M.M.

BIRTWHISTLE, W., 13882.   Mention.

BISHOP, F.   Mention (2).   M.C.

BLACK, D., 3/26210.   Mention.

BLACKBURN, T.   M.C.

BLACKSHAW, G., 290325.   M.M.

BLACKWELL, L., 266284.   M.M.

BLACKWOOD, A. P.   Mention (3).   D.S.O.
He conducted a most successful raid on a
village in the enemy's lines, which resulted
in the capture of 55 prisoners, and heavy
casualties to the enemy. The success of
the enterprise was due to his forethought
and skilful handling of his command.
Order of St. Vladimir.
Star of Roumania.

BLAKE, P., 49736.   M.M.

BLAND, J.   M.C.

BLAND, S., 25055.   D.C.M.
On the night of 6th/7th December, 1915,
during a bombing attack on the Germans,
near Carnoy, as bayonet man he led the
assault with great dash. He bayoneted
one German, shot two more, and took one
prisoner. He was then wounded.

BLANTON, W., 9140.   D.C.M.
Near Moolenacker Farm in front of Ypres,
on 21st Feb., 1915, he went out to the rescue
of a wounded man lying in the open. Being

unable to move him, Pte. Blanton remained with the man till assistance arrived, during which time he was continually fired on.

BLEASE, E., 14524. M.M.

BLOOD, F. W. Mention.

BLOWEN, F. E. V. M.C.

BLYTHE, E., 200540. M.M.

BOAG, J., 11241. Mention.

BOARDMAN, J. A., 265123. Mention M.M. and Bar.

BODEN, G., 15525. M.M.

BOGER, D. C. Mention. D.S.O.

BONNER, W. H., 11005. Mention. M.S.M.

BONSALL, A., 302. M.C.

He assumed command of, and led his company with great courage and determination, capturing many prisoners. He set a fine example throughout.

BOON, D., 243696. M.M.

BOON, E., 28110. D.C.M.

During the capture of an enemy position, the first two waves of the attack were held up by a strong point. This N.C.O. initiated a flank attack and successfully put the strong point out of action, thus enabling our advance to proceed. His coolness and dash were most marked.

BOOTHBY, A., 290332. M.M.

BOSTOCK, W., 10763. M.M., D.C.M.

On 28th Sept., 1918, South of Neuve Chapelle, when entering the enemy line, he attacked the crew of a machine-gun post, killing two and capturing one. He then got his Lewis gun into action on a party of the enemy, who had made off.

BOSTON, F. C., 10074. Mention.

BOWCOCK, S., 14998. M.M.

BOWDEN, C., 34512. M.M.

BOWDEN, J., 14521. M.M.

BOWETT, R., 10174. D.C.M.

On the 5th May, 1915, on "Hill 60," owing to the telephone wires having been cut between the Battalion and the 15th Brigade Headquarters, a very critical state of affairs existed. Private Bowett carried important messages along the railway under a very heavy rifle, shell and machine-gun fire and through a badly gassed area.

BOWMAN, E., 51454. M.M.

BOWSHIER, T., 66333. M.M.

BOWYER, A., 8947. M.M.

BOYD, J. W., 291352. Mention.

BOYLE, J. E., 2268. Mention.

BRACE, W. H., 22053. D.C.M.

During operations, as C.O's. runner, he carried messages to all parts of the line. When the Adjutant, Signalling Officer and Assistant Adjutant became casualties, he did splendid work, and, though only a boy, knew exactly what was going on all along the line. He was twice blown off his legs during the day, close to his C.O.

BRADBURY, G. E. Mention.

BRADBURY, W., 14278. M.M.

BRADDOCK, H., 10/14882. Mention. Croix de Guerre (Bel.)

BRADLEY, A. Mention. M.C. To be Brevet-Major on promotion to Capt.

BRADLEY, T., 13376. M.M.

BRADY, J. Promoted 2/Lieut. M.C. During an attack he led a Battalion to their various objectives, which he consolidated with great skill and coolness. Previous to the attack he had distinguished himself greatly in a raid.

BRADSHAW, A., 29168. Mention.

BRADSHAW, W., 241042. M.M.

BRAITHWAITE, G. W., 28378. M.M.

BRAMHALL, H., 1531. M.M.

BRAMHALL, S., 240231. M.M.

BRAND, H., 265245. Mention. D.C.M.

As company sergeant-major and as regimental sergeant-major, this warrant officer, both in and out of the trenches, has proved himself a most courageous and reliable soldier. In operations when conditions were difficult, his disregard of danger and fine personal example were of great assistance.

BRANDON, H.A., 25197. D.C.M.

When his platoon was isolated on the flank of a position, he commanded it in a most gallant manner, after his officer had been wounded, and successfully extricated it under heavy machine-gun fire.

BRANDRETH, F., 49943. M.M.

BRASHAW, F. J., 9219. M.S.M.

BREEZE, J. E. Mention.

BRIARS, J. D., 27465. M.M.

BRIDGE, R., 15/19778. Mention.
Italian Bronze Medal.

BRICE, J., 27826. M.M. and Bar.

BRIGHT, J. E., 5189. Mention (2). D.C.M.
On repeated occasions during the Soissons operations, he organised and brought up the supply of ammunition to the battalion. He has always set a splendid example to all ranks of cheerfulness and devotion to duty.

BRINDLEY, T., 49007. M.M.

BRISCOMBE, J., 29190. Mention.

BRITAIN, H.
Croix de Guerre (Bel.)

BROAD, W., 12438. Mention.

BROADBENT, W., 49263. D.C.M.
During the attack on Wargnies Le Grand, Nov. 18, when his platoon was held up by heavy fire from a strong point, he led his section past the enemy flank and attacked with great dash, killing an officer and several of the enemy, capturing three machine guns and 10 prisoners. This enabled his platoon to reach its objective.

BROADHURST, F. 290620. M.M.

BROCKBANK, F., 267965. D.C.M.
During the attack he took command of his company and handled it with great success. Having reached his objective, he dug in and consolidated in an excellent tactical position, and, in spite of every effort of the enemy to regain it, he held it till relieved.

BROCKIE, J., 200384. M.M.

BROMLEY, C. E. Mention.

BROOK, W., 25986. M.M.

BROOKIN, J. J., 12282. Mention.

BROOKES, W., 12840. M.M.

BROOKS, H., 1787.
Medal of St. George, 4th Class (Rus.)

BROOKS, J., 52117. M.M.

BROOKS, R., 10527. Mention.
Croix de Guerre (Bel.)

BROOME, S. R. M.C.
Although under heavy fire, the orderly with-drawal of his company without loss and the quick establishment of a new line were due to his coolness. In the counter-attack, he kept his men well in hand and gallantly led them to the assault, during which he was badly wounded.

BROSTER, T., W/765. M.M. and Bar.

BROUGHTON, H. D. Mention.

BROWN, A. Mention.

BROWN, F., 21359. M.M.

BROWN, G. E., 35035. M.M.

BROWN, L. K. V. Mention.

BROWN, W., 67532. M.M.

BROWN, W. E. L. Mention. M.C.

BROWNE, B. S. D.C.M.
Near Vermelles he spent the whole night of 2nd/3rd October searching for, and carrying back, wounded who were lying between our own and the enemy's lines, which were only 200 yards apart. After daybreak, he carried back three more men under a very heavy fire. By his courage and ceaseless work, all the wounded in his area were brought in.

BROWNE, O. L. Mention.

BROWNE-CLAYTON, R. C. Mention (2).
D.S.O.
During five days of operations, he commanded his battalion with great coolness, and inspired his men with a fine fighting spirit.
Promoted Brevet-Lieut.-Colonel.
Order of the White Eagle.

BRUCE, J. Mention.

BRYAN, E., 61401. M.M.

BUCKLEY, A., 9497. M.M.

BUCKLEY, C. J., 52706. M.M.

BUCKLEY, G., 11413. D.C.M.
He led a bombing party with great determination and courage and took about 70 prisoners.

BUCKLEY, W., 8436. M.M. and Bar.

BURGESS, A., 290383. Mention.

BURKE, D., 67326. M.M.

BURN, L., 46203.
Croix de Guerre (Bel.)

BURNETT, A. Mention (2).

BURNETT, D.   M.C.

Very early in the attack he found himself the only officer left in his company, and 15 minutes later, hearing that the companies on both his flanks had lost their commanders, he visited each flank and took charge of the remnants of three companies. His personal example and exertions inspired all those under him with confidence.

BURNHAM, W., 20937.   Mention.

BURNS, J., 9816.   Mention.   D.C.M.

On 24th Aug., 1914, he voluntarily assisted to remove, under heavy fire, wounded men to a place of safety, he himself being wounded.

BURNS, J., 8935.   D.C.M.

On the 5th May, 1915, on " Hill 60," when, owing to the telephone wires having been cut between the Battalion and the 15th Brigade Headquarters a very critical state of affairs existed. Lance Corporal Burns carried important messages along the railway under a very heavy rifle, shell and machine-gun fire and through a badly gassed area.

BURNS, T. H., 19365.   D.C.M.

As a water cart driver, he kept the battalion supplied with water under circumstances of great difficulty. When his companion was wounded, he drove both carts alternately without interruption, and refused to be relieved.

BUSFEILD, J. A.   Mention (2).   D.S.O.

He led his company to the final objective without artillery support in the face of intense machine-gun fire, and inflicted heavy losses on the enemy. Though the enemy at once counter-attacked and completely outflanked his position, he held his ground with the greatest determination and skill.

BUSH, R. P.   M.C.

He personally superintended the establishment of a Lewis gun post and so held up the enemy for some hours and caused them heavy casualties. Later he carried a wounded non-commissioned officer to a place of safety. Throughout he inspired his men with confidence by his example, untiring energy and fearlessness under heavy fire.

BUSH, W., 39926.   D.C.M.

When a section leader, he took part in a successful counter-attack, which re-

gained lost ground, and he held on to the new position, against numerous attacks made by the enemy, throughout the day, at the end of which only Corporal Bush and one man remained of the thirteen originally composing the section, who then fought their way back to the company. Subsequently he collected the remains of the company and led it for four days.

BUTLIN, G. W., 57954.   Mention.

BUTTER, H., 26123.   D.C.M.

He continued to fire his Lewis gun until the enemy were within 50 yards of him and was the last man to leave the position.

BUTTERWORTH, H., 1312.   D.C.M.

He went to the assistance of a bombing party with his machine-gun, holding the position and accounting for a large number of the enemy. Later, although wounded, he continued to fire his gun until reinforcements arrived.

BYRNE, F., 201468.   M.M.

BYRNE, M.   16601.   M.M.

BYROM, W. H., 10154.   M.M.

CADDEN, B., 201802.   M.M.

CAIN, G. T., 8229.   M.M.

CAIN, J. S., 9550.
Croix de Guerre (Fr.)

CALLER, G., 39516.   Mention.

CALLF, A., 16006.   D.C.M.

On the 25th September, 1915, near Festubert, a shell set fire to a large bomb store in the trenches, which were very crowded at the time. Private Callf pulled a box of small arms ammunition, which was burning, from the back of the bomb store and carried it to a pool of water, a piece of shell being still in the box and too hot to remove.

CALVERT, W. H., 315008.   Mention.

CAMPBELL, R., 23156.   D.C.M.

As company runners to the officer holding an advanced post, Privates Campbell and Lowe repeatedly went backwards and forwards, carrying messages over open ground under artillery, machine-gun and rifle fire at 300 yards range. Their devotion to duty was fine.

CAPSTICK, H. P.   M.C., M.B.E.
Russian Order of St. Stanislas.

CAREY, A., 9955.   D.C.M.

As a stretcher bearer notably at Violaines, when, though warned that he would come under fire of a sniper at short range, he went out and fetched a wounded man ; also at Wulverghem where he brought a wounded man back from within 35 yards of the enemy and volunteered to bring another but was ordered not to do so.

CAREY, J., 9097.   Mention.

CARPENTER, A. G.   Mention.

CARROLL, F., 49380.   M.M.

CARROLL, J. G., 10757.   D.C.M.

During an attack across the open he led his men with coolness and with great success, and, although wounded continued to lead the way.

CARTER, F., 49340.   Mention.

CARTER, F. K. S., 265156.   D.C.M.

He seized a Vicker's gun from a team that had become casualties, took it in the open, and used it so effectively on the enemy that they fell back.   He did splendid service.

CARTER, J., 9/18580.   Mention.

CARTWRIGHT, A. H., 29189.   Mention.   M.S.M.

CARTWRIGHT, G. W., 2101.   D.C.M.

When the enemy had exploded a mine and blown up or buried an officer and several men, Private Cartwright volunteered to go down and investigate the crater.   He was under heavy and very close fire till he got right down into the crater.   He found some wounded men and returned twice under the same close fire, for food and water for them.   He brought back a wounded sergeant, and wished to return for a private, but was ordered to wait till dusk.   At dusk, although no longer on duty, he went out to help in further rescue.   His conduct throughout was very gallant.

CASEY, E., 139.   M.M.

CASS, J. F., 8197.   Mention.

CASSON, T.   M.C.

He led a raiding party into the enemy's trenches.   About eight of the enemy were killed and two prisoners were captured. The success was largely due to his fine leadership.

CATO, E. D., 29250.   Mention.

CATTERMOLE, A. H., 18089.   M.M.

CATTON, J. H., 11679.   Mention.

CAVEILL, W. H., 66016.   M.M.

CAVENEY, J., 290269.   M.M.

CAVEY, J. G., 7603.   M.M.

CHADWICK, H., 290818.   M.M.

CHAMBERLAIN, H. J., 8049.   Mention. Medal of St. George, 4th Class (Rus.)

CHAMBERS, J. W., 2343.   Mention.

CHANTLER, R., 7388.   Mention.

CHAPMAN, G. B., 52650.   M.M.

CHATFIELD, R., 7695.   M.S.M.

CHATTERTON, W.   M.C.

When in charge of a section of a captured position, which was counter-attacked by the enemy after heavy artillery preparation, he, with the utmost coolness, allowed the enemy to get within 50 yards of his position and then, by skilful use of a Lewis and a Vicker's gun, he drove them back, killing about 50 and capturing 20 of them.   On two occasions he showed great courage and resource during reconnaissances and brought back most valuable information under heavy shell fire.

CHEESMAN, F. W., 51248.   M.M.

CHESHIRE, J., 14972.   M.M.

CHOLMELEY, R. J.   M.C.

As Brigade Intelligence Officer, he spent five weeks in the front line previous to our attack, studying the enemy's system and acquiring information, which afterwards proved most useful.   His keenness in volunteering for every raid or patrol and his fearlessness and untiring energy in collecting information for his brigade have earned the unanimous appreciation and admiration of all commanding officers in his brigade.

CHORLTON, J. T.   M.C.

He led his platoon with great dash and determination in the attack, clearing all resistance and accounting for two hostile machine-guns which were attempting to hold up the advance.   Though wounded, he continued to carry on until he had to be assisted back.   His conduct throughout the operation was a splendid example to his men.

U

CHRISTIAN, J. E., 244415.   M.M. and Bar.

CHRISTIE, A. J.   Mention.

CHRISTIE, J., 10586.   Mention.   M.M.

CHURNS, E., 50749.   M.M.

CHURTON, H. L.   Mention.

CHURTON, W. A. V.   Mention (3).   D.S.O.

CLARE, H., 251.   Mention.

CLARE, H., 240018.   Mention.   M.S.M.

CLARK, E., 67547.   M.M.

CLARKE, A. C. B., 18113.   Mention.   M.M.

CLARKE, A. H., 290373.
> Croix de Guerre (Fr.)

CLARKE, B., 57824.   M.M.

CLARKE, H., 52562.   M.M.

CLARKE, J., 14025.   Mention.

CLARKE, J., 265169.   M.M.

CLARKE, M. F.   Mention (2).   D.S.O.

CLARKE, P., 10641.   Mention.

CLARKE, R., 18726.   M.S.M.

CLARKE, S. D., 240525.   M.S.M.

CLARKSON, A., 66312.   Mention.

CLAYSON, C. L., 57816.   M.M.

CLAYTON, J. A.   Mention.

CLEGG, N., 60534.   M.M.

CLEGG-HILL, THE HON. A. R..
>   Mention (3).   D.S.O.

CLIFFORD, W. R.   Mention.   C.B.E.

CLIST, L. F.   M.C.
> After all his Officers and C.S.M. were casualties, he led his company with the greatest dash to its objective, capturing two enemy field guns. He consolidated under a very heavy shell fire, and successfully resisted a strong counter-attack.

COATES, G., 50163.   M.M.

COATES, T., 51367.   M.M.

COBLEY, G. H., 678.   M.M.

COKER, W. T., 11370.   Mention.

COLE, G. W. J.   M.C.
> When a vigorous attack was launched by the enemy against the front held by his Company, he continually went up and down the line issuing clear orders and rallying his men. It was largely due to his fine leadership and example that the attacks were beaten off.

During the withdrawal he was wounded, being the last of the Company to leave the front line.

COLEMAN, J., 33532.   M.M.

COLEMAN, R. G., 267066.   M.M.

COLLIER, F., 1597.   M.M., D.C.M.
> He successfully laid a line under fire, enabling communications to be maintained with Battalion Headquarters at a critical time. He set a fine example of courage and coolness.

COLLIER, S.   M.C.

COLLIER, J., 33509.   M.M.

COLLINS, J., 10422.   D.C.M.
> During an attack he attacked an enemy strong point with one other man, killing all the garrison, and taking four machine-guns. He continued to do excellent work throughout the day.

COLLINSON, V., 19070.   Mention.

COLTON, E., 7385.   M.M.

COLVIN, H.
> Promoted 2/Lieut.

V.C.
> When all the officers in his company except himself—and all but one in the leading company—had become casualties and losses were heavy, he assumed command of both companies and led them forward under heavy machine-gun fire with great dash and success. He saw the battalion on his right held up by machine-gun fire, and led a platoon to their assistance. Second Lieut. Colvin then went on with only two men to a dug-out. Leaving the men on top, he entered it alone and brought up 14 prisoners. He then proceeded with his two men to another dug-out which had been holding up the attack by rifle and machine-gun fire and bombs. This he reached, and, killing or making prisoners of the crew, captured the machine-gun. Being then attacked from another dug-out by 15 of the enemy under an officer, one of his men was killed and the other wounded. Seizing a rifle he shot five of the enemy, and, using another as a shield, he forced most of the survivors to surrender. This officer cleared several other dug-outs alone or with one man, taking about 50 prisoners in all. Later he consolidated his

position with great skill, and personally wired his front under heavy close range, sniping in broad daylight, when all others had failed to do so. The complete success of the attack in this part of the line was mainly due to Second Lieut. Colvin's leadership and courage.

COMPTON, F., 9127. M.M.

COOK, F. W., 21139. D.C.M.

For two days he held an isolated post, after his officer was wounded, until the trenches were obliterated. He then saved his machine-gun, and with the remains of his garrison, fell back to the main trench. His sticking so long to his post aided much in the general defence of the position.

COOK, R., 10/13226. D.C.M.

During a hostile raid on our trenches, he showed great coolness and courage under heavy fire. He brought a machine-gun through the hostile barrage and rendered the greatest possible assistance.

COOK, W., 51369. M.M.

COOKE, H. M.C.

He led his company gallantly during the enterprise which took place north-east of Wulverghem on 20th/21st Sept., 1918. The success of the operations in which 14 prisoners and one machine-gun were captured was mainly due to the very gallant example which he set when leading his company forward, and to the care and forethought with which he trained and equipped it prior to the operation.

COOKE, H. M., 267789. M.S.M.

COOKE, R. J. Mention. O.B.E.

COOMBES, C. H., 241295. M.M.

COOPER, A. H. M.C.

Under continuous shelling and bombing, he cleared out forward railhead areas, serving a very large supply dump and the Army gun park.

COOPER, R. S. F. M.C.

During a raid on the enemy's lines, his Company became broken up while advancing at night over most difficult country. He showed great coolness in reorganizing the Company under fire, and successfully retrieved the situation and gained all his objectives.

COPE, C., 265982. M.M.

COPE, W. J., 1767. Mention.

COPELAND, J. A., 291245. M.M.

CORBETT, E. A., 531. Mention.

CORBETT, E. A., 240031. Mention. M.S.M.

CORDEN, B. W. M.C.

He organised and led a bayonet charge under heavy rifle fire, and took a position. He showed fine dash and good leadership.

CORFIELD, W. R. M.C.

He carried supplies by daylight to an isolated detachment, though heavily sniped. On another occasion he went out twice to recover the body of a sergeant who had been killed.

CORKER, F., 14830. M.M.

CORNING, D. P. M.C.

COSTELLO, A., 52545. M.M.

COTTON, H. W. S. Mention.

COTTRELL, F., 200539. Mention.

COULTER, P., 11056. Mention.

D.C.M. (S. African War), M.C.

Croix de Guerre (Fr.)

Bar to M.C.

On the 14th October, 1918, during the operations East of Terhand, he, by his bold initiative, effected the capture of 25 enemy and five machine-guns, and killed or wounded some 15 of the enemy. Accompanied by a non-commissioned officer, under cover of his Lewis gun, he rushed a pillbox, from which machine-guns were firing, and flung a bomb in. He accounted for 40 enemy and five machine-guns as above stated. He shewed fine courage and leadership.

COWAN, D., 265850. M.M.

COWAN, H. G. Mention. M.B.E.

Promoted to Brevet-Major.

Granted next higher rate of pay.

COX, A., 50586. M.M.

COX, W., 16429. Mention.

CRACKLES, C., 5297. Mention.

CRAVEN, J., 49864. M.M.

CRAVEN-ELLIS, W. Mention.

CREAN, C., 17742. M.M.

CREAN, J., 11827.
Croix de Guerre (Fr.)
D.C.M.

Although twice badly wounded himself, he repeatedly went forward, under very heavy rifle fire, to bring in wounded men, who had been driven out of the advanced trench.

CRIGHTON, J. W., 202278.   M.M.

CRITCHLOW, W. H. C., 9943.   M.M.

CROCKER, H. E.   Mention (4).   D.S.O.
Promoted Brevet-Lieut.-Colonel.

CROMPTON, C. H., 290098.   Mention.

CROOK, W., 200509.   M.M.

CROOKENDEN, A.   Mention (6).   D.S.O.
Croix de Guerre (Fr.)
Promoted Brevet Lieut.-Colonel.

CROPLEY, T., 17931.   M.M.

CROPPER, J., 1554.   M.M.

CROPPER, R. H., 61958.   M.M.

CROSBY, C. G., 3/27244.   M.S.M.

CROSBY, J., W/934.   M.M.

CROSBY, W., 50284.   D.C.M.

His company suffered severe casualties during a bombardment which preceded an enemy counter-attack. He took command of his platoon and by his coolness and example maintained the spirits of his men, and assisted in repelling the enemy's counter-attack.

CROSS, F. T., 24248.   M.M.

CROSS, W., 1262.   M.M.

CROSSLEY, H., 52281.   M.M.

CROSSLEY, J. D., 38368.   Mention.

CROTTY, R., 62921.   M.S.M.

CROWDER, F., 290392.   D.C.M.

His untiring industry and energy inspired all the Battalion runners to most successful efforts. He carried out his duties in a most capable manner under difficult conditions, and rendered valuable services to his Battalion.

CRUICKSHANK, G. N., 240477.   Mention.
M.M.

CRUTE, W.   M.C.

In the operations near Menin, he displayed most conspicuous gallantry and leadership in attacking pillboxes under heavy short-range machine-gun fire. He was responsible for the capture of 10 machine guns and 50 prisoners. Most of his men became casualties, but he pressed on till his objective was reached. He then led a patrol into Menin and sent back valuable information.

CUFF, B.
To be Brevet-Major.
Greek Military Cross.

CULLIMORE, J.   Mention (2).

CURBISHLEY, W., 14/24171.   Mention.

CURZON, R., 290650.   Mention.

CUTHBERTSON, W., 20842.   M.M., D.C.M.

He volunteered to patrol the company front, and obtained valuable information. Later, during the night, he again went out, and, though badly hit, succeeded in evading the enemy and crawling back with information which was urgently required. He set a splendid example.

DAKIN, E., 2887.   M.M.

DALE, E., 290394.   Mention (2).   D.C.M.

During the attack and occupation of an enemy position he remained for some 18 hours on duty, without a rest at the regimental aid post, in charge of the stretcher bearers. Throughout this trying period he set a splendid example of energy and devotion that was beyond all praise. It was very largely owing to his personal example that all cases were safely evacuated from this position.

DALE, R. V., 290431.   M.M.

DALY, J., 51035.   M.M.

DALZELL, THE HON. A. E.   Mention.

DANSON, J. R.   M.C.

DAVENPORT, C., 45598.   M.M.

DAVEY, G. H. J.   Mention.

DAVIDSON, F., 9466.   M.M.

DAVIDSON, J. H., 52252.   D.C.M.

When in charge of a Lewis gun section, although wounded, he continued to work his gun, not only supporting his own company but affording valuable assistance to another Brigade which had passed through them. He set a splendid example of courage and endurance under fire.

DAVIDSON, W., 13316.   Mention.   M.S.M.

DAVIES, A., 10815. Mention.

DAVIES, C., 21684. M.M.

DAVIES, D., 35312. Mention.

DAVIES, E., 14011. M.M.

DAVIES, G., 10111. Mention.

DAVIES, G., 202524. D.C.M.

He went over the open under intense fire and brought in a wounded comrade to safety. He showed great gallantry and self-sacrifice.

DAVIES, H., 23268. M.M.

DAVIES, H. C. E. M.C.

DAVIES, H. F. Mention.

DAVIES, J., 18086. D.C.M.

When a large gap occurred in the line, he at once filled the gap with his Lewis gun team. He also cleared a dug-out, capturing several prisoners.

DAVIES, J. A., 10124. Mention.

DAVIES, J. H. Mention.
O.B.E. (Military Division).

DAVIES, L. E. M.C.

In the attack on Beaurain and Le Cateau on the 23rd October, 1918, when all officers and 50 per cent. of the men of his company had become casualties, he took command of the remnants and reached the objective, shewing great determination and coolness under very heavy shell and machine gun fire.

DAVIES, R. H., 50573. M.M.

DAVIES, S., 15602. M.M.

DAVIES, S., 244202.
Mention. M.M. and Bar.

DAVIES, W., 13583. Mention (2).
Serbian Gold Medal.

DAWSON, T., 12728. Mention.
M.M., D.C.M.

When acting regimental sergeant-major, he was one of the last of the covering party left to cover the withdrawal of the battalion, and remained until the enemy were in the trench and both flanks exposed. He displayed great courage, and set a fine example to all ranks.

DAY, O. S., 7953. M.M.

DE LEROIS, H., 29012. Mention. M.S.M.

DEAN, J. H. E. M.C.

At Le Touquet salient on 29th Dec., 1915, he led a fighting patrol with great coolness and dash, obtaining a footing on the enemy's parapet and bombed their trenches for some forty yards, inflicting considerable loss. He was under heavy fire, but succeeded in withdrawing his patrol with the loss of one killed and nine wounded.

Bar to M.C.

Having gone through exceptionally desperate fighting with his battalion, in which it lost heavily in officers and men, he and another officer brought the battalion out of action on the following day, and were indefatigable in consolidating the ground gained and beating off every enemy counter-attack. Although the situation on the flank at one period was extremely critical, the battalion did not lose a yard of ground, largely owing to the personal example and fine leadership displayed by this officer and his comrade.

DEANE, P., 10325. Mention.

DEANE-DRUMMOND, J. D. Mention (4).
M.C., D.S.O. and Bar.

When in charge of divisional machine-guns, his personal example and fearlessness had a splendid effect on all ranks during an attack. He successfully took his machine guns through our barrage and prevented the escape of two hostile field guns.
Croix de Guerre (Fr.)

DEARDEN, F. M.M., M.C.

Near Bossuyt on the night of 29th—30th October, 1918, an attempt had been made to cross the river Escaut on a raft, but owing to enemy wire in the river this was not successful. He then swam across the river, thoroughly reconnoitred the enemy posts and brought back valuable information. This was done in face of considerable machine-gun fire. His cool courage and initiative was admirable.

DEARN, G., 2013. M.M.

DEE, S., 21814. M.M.

DEEPROSE, A. J., 40204. M.M.

DEMPSEY, P. J., 17137. D.C.M.

He attacked eight of the enemy single-handed, killing their leader, who was in the act of throwing a bomb. He set a very fine example of courage and promptitude to his men.

DENT, B. C.   Mention (2).

DENYER, H. F.   Mention.

DEVENEY, J., 14407.   M.M.

DEVON, W.   Mention.

DEWAR, H. E.   M.C.

DICKENSON, J., 29013.   Mention.

DICKSON, C.   M.C.

When in command of the British Sector of the Allied Mission at Omsk, he showed great courage and initiative behind the enemy's lines, and in dealing with superior enemy forces, by which the success of the Mission was largely secured.

DIGGLES, J. M.   Mention. M.C., Bar to M.C.

He showed marked courage and skill in assembling the Brigade previous to the assault. He set a splendid example throughout.
D.S.O.

DILLINGHAM, A., 52368.   Mention.

DISLEY, H., 29957.   M.M.

DIXON, A.   M.C.

Near Menin, Oct. 18, he went forward with the assaulting companies and established a forward report centre. Subsequently he carried his line from Battalion advanced H.Q. through Menin, under heavy shell and machine-gun fire.

DIXON, J., 291238.   D.C.M.

When in charge of ammunition and water convoys, he repeatedly took them up to the firing line under heavy fire. On another occasion he averted a stampede under sudden and unexpected artillery fire, and his coolness and ready presence of mind on all occasions inspired those under him with the greatest confidence.

DIXON, J. J., 44238.   M.M.

DIXON, T. R., 200854.   M.M.

DOBIE, E., 6521.   Mention.

DODD, F., 9/12401.   Mention.

DODD, H., 49482.   M.M.

DODD, J. W., 14719.   M.M.

DODD, W., 45029.   M.M.

DOLAN, J. F.   Mention. M.C. Croix de Guerre (Bel.)

DOLAN, T., 18878.   Mention.

DONE, J., 13384.   M.M.

DOOLEY, W. J. B., 8216.   M.S.M.

DOUGH, G. H. W.   Mention.

DOUGHTY, J. C., 240958.   M.M.

DOUGLAS, G. R. P.   Mention (2) M.C., O.B.E.
Order of St. Stanislas.

DOUGLAS, W., 19589.   M.M.

DOUGLAS, W., 10071.   Mention.

DOWNS, G., 7948

Near Ypres he continued to work his machine gun after the trenches on his left flank had been evacuated, thereby securing the general line from being broken. Has shown marked ability in machine gun work throughout the campaign.

DOWNS, J., 315313.   M.M.

DRIVER, T., 27012.   M.M.

DUDDLES, E. E., 50799.   D.C.M.

As a company stretcher-bearer he volunteered to go out and bring in a badly wounded officer. Later he continued to carry stretcher cases although he had been wounded in the right arm. Both these acts took place under intense enemy shelling, during which he displayed such complete disregard of danger as to encourage those men working with him.

DUDDRIDGE, S. M., W. 341.   M.M.

DUGDALE, A., 12130.   M.S.M.

DUKE, V. W. H.   Mention (3). M.C., O.B.E.

DUNBEBIN, W., 15795.   M.M.

DUNCAN, R., 201007.   M.M.

DUNN, S. L., 18025.   M.M.

DUTTON, F., 14439.   M.M.

DUTTON, F. F.   Mention. M.C.

When in command of a raiding party, in spite of the most determined opposition, he successfully extricated his command and inflicted heavy casualties on the enemy.

DUTTON, F. W., 1438.   M.M.

DYAS, J. R.   C.M.G.

DYER, A. J. L.   M.C.

DYKES, C. P., 50575.   M.M.

DYMOND, G. W.   M.C.

During an attack on the enemy's lines, the situation had become very obscure. He therefore went out with another officer in broad daylight under heavy fire and carried out a most difficult and dangerous reconnaissance, bringing back information of the highest value to his commanding officer. This officer has more than once greatly distinguished himself by his pluck and good work when on patrol.

EACHUS, N.   Mention (2).   M.C.
Greek Military Cross.

EAGLESON, J., 50087.   M.M.

EASTERBROOK, W. R.   M.C.

During an attack on the enemy defences, this officer was in command of the company, which, without artillery preparation or barrage fire, captured a substantial portion of the enemy's trenches which was screened by a belt of wire and a thick hedge. Under cover of rifle grenades and Lewis gun fire, he captured the objective and took two machine-guns. His leadership and example contributed to this successful result.

ECOB, E., 58115.   M.M.

EDGAR, J. J., 13270.   M.M.

EDGE, R., 19094.   M.M.

EDGE, W., 7415.   Mention (2).

EDMOND, H., 19366.
Croix de Guerre (Fr.)

EDWARDS, A., 11621.   Mention.

EDWARDS, G., 25294.   M.M.

EDWARDS, J., 14/18360.   Mention. M.S.M.

EDWARDS, R. A., 22218.   Mention.

EDWARDS, W. J., 9805.   Medaille D'Honneur.

ELLAMS, J., 291239.   Mention. M.M.

ELLICOCK, C., 26221.   M.M.

ELLINGTON, N. B.   Mention. M.C.

ELLIOT, W. G. R.   Mention (2).   D.S.O.

On 24th August, 1914, during a retirement, he ran back, picked up a wounded man and carried him 100 yards to safety under a hot fire, being himself shot through both ankles.

ELLIOTT, F., 23024.   M.M.

ELLIOTT, J. D., 16/20909.   Mention.

ELLIS, G., 302.   M.M.

ELLIS, G. D.   M.C.

He showed gallantry and resource in carrying out dangerous personal reconnaissances of machine-gun positions, with the result that his unit were able to successfully cope with them. He has been conspicuous for his energy and initiative in action.

ELLIS, J.   Mention.

ELLIS, W., 58411.   M.M.

ELSON, J., 50299.   M.M.

EMMENS, W., 19901.   M.M., D.C.M.

When laying out a wire during an attack with another N.C.O., he lost direction and met a party of 20 enemy with a machine-gun whom they attacked without hesitation their only weapons being one rifle and a signalling lamp stand. They captured the gun and brought back two prisoners. They then established communication with the captured position and maintained it under heavy fire.

ERLAM, H.   Mention.

ESSEX, G., 290493.
Croix de Guerre (Fr.)

ETCHELLS, G. H., 18846.   M.M.

EVANS, A. G., 49201.   M.M.

EVANS, D. C.   Mention.

EVANS, F., 200990.   M.M.

EVANS, J. C. O., 240029.   M.S.M.

EVANS, T., 6869.   M.M.

EVANS, T. C., 49149.   D.C.M.

During the advance N.E. of Gouzeancourt in Sept. 18, owing to severe casualties, he assumed command of a platoon and led them forward under heavy fire. On reaching the objective he took forward a patrol and located a machine-gun.

EVANS, W. D., 16530.   M.M.

EVANS, W. K.   Mention (8).   D.S.O., C.M.G.
Legion of Honour (Fr.)
Bar to D.S.O.

He led his battalion with great dash and initiative to their objective, capturing many guns and prisoners. He also repulsed strong hostile counter attacks, and showed great coolness and promptitude in rallying and reorganising troops who had been driven back through his line. His fine personal example saved a critical situation.

EVANSON, H., 200497.   Mention.

EVANSON, T., 243216.   M.M.

EYRE, J., 2935.   M.M.

EYRES, G., 36761.   M.M. and Bar.

EYRES, T., 52097.   Mention.

FABBY, C. E., 11/14274.   Mention.

FACEY, J. H., 72393.   M.M.

FAIRBANKS, W. H., 12425.   M.M.

FAIRBROTHER, J., 291391.   M.M.

FAIRCLOUGH, H. C., 49272.   M.M.

FAIRFAX, R. I.   M.C.

He was the only officer left with brigade transport, and volunteered to go up to the line with two limbers containing the rations of the whole brigade. After a journey of 15 miles, much of it under shell fire, he found his units and delivered their rations under the most difficult conditions. It was entirely owing to his initiative and determination that the units were supplied with rations.

Bar to M.C.

FAIRWEATHER, I.   Mention.

FALLOWS, P., 17501.   M.S.M.

FARENDEN, J. E., 29191.   M.S.M.

FARMER, F. W., 7234.   M.M.

FARRINGTON, H., 11/13905.   M.M.

FAULKNER, W., 16302.   M.M.

FAY, H., 19234.   D.C.M.

He worked a machine gun with only one man for three days and nights in the front line. He has set a splendid example throughout the operations.

FAYERS, C., 200882.   M.M.

FEARNLEY, A., 11134.   M.M.

FERNIHOUGH, N. T., 67360.   M.M.

FIANDER, C. W., 50229.   M.M.

FIDLIN, F.   M.M.

FINCH, L. H. K.   Mention (4).   D.S.O.

Bar to D.S.O.

Before an assault his battalion sustained considerable casualties. Undeterred by these losses, however, he drew up and re-

hearsed his plans for the assembly with the greatest care. During the assault the battalion sustained further heavy casualties, but this officer led the survivors with brilliant initiative and the utmost gallantry in an attack upon an enemy strong point, which he captured, killing or taking prisoners all the garrison. He then pushed his outpost line out and got into touch with battalions on his flank, making complete dispositions for his advance. He was badly wounded at the end of the day, having set a personal example of fearlessness and fine leadership, to which the excellent performance of his battalion was largely due.
Promoted Brevet-Major.

O.B.E.

FINDLAY, W. H.   M.C.

He was of great assistance to his C.O., repeatedly volunteering to undertake any difficult or dangerous work. On one occasion he guided a party of stretcher-bearers to some wounded men under heavy shell-fire.

FISH, J., 266171.   M.M.

FISHER, F. N., 243677.   M.M.

FISHER, J., 1232.   D.C.M.

When all the officers of his company had become casualties, he led the company to the attack and capture of a position, and by his determination and courage carried his men through a heavy barrage and consolidated his objective.

FISHER, J., 30656.   M.M.

FISHER, P. J., 1553.   M.M.

FISK, A. A.   Mention.

FITZPATRICK, J., 19552.   Mention.

FITZPATRICK, P., W/537.   M.M.

FLANAGAN, J. P., 11156.   M.M.

FLEMING, T. E., 10899.   Mention.

FLETCHER, J. W., 201483.   M.S.M.

FLETCHER, S., 14156.   D.C.M.

During an attack, he shot two snipers who were causing considerable casualties and successfully organised the remainder of two platoons for the final assault. He displayed the greatest coolness and devotion to duty the following night under an intense artillery bombardment.

FLUNDER, R. D. M.C.

He commanded a battalion during the operations near Menin on the 14th—16th October, 1918, with great skill and gallantry. His thorough organization and the perfect handling of his men at the start ensued success. The complete confidence which he inspired in his men contributed very largely to the success of the operations. Croix de Guerre (Fr.)

FLYNN, C., 1803. Mention.

FODEN, J., 29661. Mention.

FODEN, W. B. M.C.

During enemy attacks he showed great powers of leadership and contempt of danger under heavy barrage, encouraging his men, driving back hostile attacks, and inflicting heavy casualties on the enemy. Also he led a successful counter-attack.

FOLEY, G., 265378. M.M.

FOLEY, T., 7114. D.C.M.

On the night of March 7th, 1915, he went out in front of our trenches to bring in some stretcher bearers who had lost their way. Subsequently he went out three times under heavy fire to bring in wounded men, and although wounded more than once himself, he continued to carry out this duty.

FORESTER, E., 30654. M.M.

FORESTIER-WALKER, E. A. Mention.

FOSBROOKE, C., 52521. M.M.

FOSTER, H., 16587. Mention.

FOSTER, J. A., 18367. Mention.

FOSTER, J. W., 1146. M.M.

FOX, E., 29624. D.C.M.

Word having been brought in to the picquet line that the enemy was advancing in force, he took his Lewis gun out to the front, inflicting heavy casualties on the advancing waves, and materially helped to break up the attack. His action enabled the scouts to withdraw to the picquet line, and he maintained his position until ordered to retire, his conduct throughout being highly praiseworthy.

FOX, G. C., 3/28008. Mention.

FRANCE, L., 51531. M.M.

FRANCIS, G. E., 60553. M.M.

FRANCIS, J. W., 7724. Mention. French Medaille Militaire.

FRANCIS, W., 6140. M.S.M.

FRANCIS, W. A., 7278. M.S.M.

FRASER, H. M. Mention.

FRASER, H. R. D. M.C.

On two occasions, when direction was uncertain, he ran out by himself and with great courage remained standing in his forward position directing operations. By his gallant conduct the line was advanced in the face of intense machine-gun and rifle fire for a distance of 1,200 yards.

FRASER, L., 8530. M.M.

FREEMAN, N. Mention (2). M.C.

On the night of 2nd/3rd October, 1915, near Vermelles, the Germans advanced on the force and bombed our men out of their trenches, but Captain Freeman, who was holding the right of his trench, continued to hold his own, returning bomb for bomb, until the Germans were nearly all round him and he was in danger of being captured. Promoted Brevet-Major.

FREESTONE, A., 14423. Mention.

FREESTONE, E., 20600. Mention. M.M.

FRENCH, F., 15118. M.S.M.

FRITH, E., 13788. M.M.

FROST, M. M.C.

When his Company was being used up in reinforcing posts, he led a patrol from another Battalion with great daring and success. They killed many of the enemy and captured two machine-guns. On the way back he was seriously wounded.

FROST, R. Mention.

FROST, T. L. Mention.

FROST, W., 27464. D.C.M.

As leading bayonet man, he encountered several of the enemy single-handed and forced them to retreat with loss.

FUDGE, J. W., 25992. M.M.

FULLARD, W. H., 50105. M.M.

FULTON, G. K. Mention. D.S.O.

In handling his Battalion in a most skilful manner, he set a splendid example of courage and disregard of danger, and was indefatigable in arranging the Battalion dispositions, and personally supervising its movements. At all times when the situation was critical he was up in the front line encouraging the men and taking part in the fighting.

FULTON, S., 201207.　M.M.

FURNELL, T.　Mention.

FURNESS, W. V.　Mention.

GADD, A., 51157.　M.M. and Bar.

GAFFNEY, J., 10097.　M.M.

GALLAGHER, J., 10180.　M.M.

GALLAGHER, H. D.　M.C.

In leading his platoon against a position strongly held by the enemy, under cover of a bombardment of rifle grenades, he successfully led his men to the assault. During the whole day's operation he displayed exceptional powers of leadership and resource, and his example was largely responsible for the success of the attack at this part of the line.

Bar to M.C.

During a raid on an enemy strong point, the officer in command of the party had become a casualty. Lieut. Gallagher immediately took charge and rallied the men, whom he again led forward. The attack, however, proving unsuccessful, he collected the remnants of the party, and under very heavy fire, consolidated a forward post which had been taken, and held it. But for his gallantry and courage, the ground already won could not have been retained.

GALLIE, A. E.　M.C.

He assumed command of his company when the company commander had been killed, steadying his men under heavy shell fire and leading them gallantly throughout the attack. His coolness and personal courage were a fine example to the men.

GAMON, C. S.　Mention.

GARDINER, W., 65365.　Mention.

GARNER, H., 6397.　Mention.

GARNER, T. H., 8605.　Mention.

GARRATT, W., 7648.　M.S.M.

GARRATT, W. A.　M.C.

Noticing that two companies were held up by enemy fire at a time when delay might be fatal to success, he immediately dashed forward across open ground, swept by shell and machine-gun fire, and led them on. His fine example of courage and initiative was immediately responded to by the companies and the objective was captured.

GARSIDE, S., 14018.　M.M.

GATCLIFFE, A. C., 2137.　M.M.

GAY, R.

Promoted 2/Lieut.

GEE, C., 28404.　M.M.

GEE, F., 11674.　M.M.

GEE, W., 15018.　M.M.

GEORGE, A. H.

Croix de Guerre (Fr.)

GERRARD, J., 12177.　M.M., D.C.M.

During a counter-attack, he rushed forward and killed an enemy machine-gunner before he could open fire on his company. This action contributed greatly to the success of the attack.

GERRARD, G., 240101.　M.S.M.

GIBBONS, E., 17897.　M.M.

GIBBONS, J., 18775.　Mention.

GIBBS, T. C.　M.C.

As battalion intelligence officer, he continually visited the battalion frontage and the units on the flanks, obtaining information and carrying C.O's. orders. Later, with the C.O., he rallied the men and led them forward, in spite of a heavy fire of shrapnel shells and machine-guns. He set a fine example of courage and energy throughout.

GIBBS, W., 8973.　Mention.

GIBSON, J. H. L.　Mention.

GILBERT, R. B., 12493.　D.C.M.

During a counter-attack a number of the enemy were passed unseen, and opened fire on our troops from the rear. On his own initiative he went back, and single handed killed the whole of the enemy party. His performance was a splendid one, and throughout the whole of the operations his courage and determination were most marked.

GILBERT, W. J., 15667.　Mention.

GILES, A. J.   M.C.

He led his men in a counter-attack against positions which the enemy had just captured. On another occasion he did invaluable work with his platoon in an exposed position, when he held the enemy back until his company had withdrawn.

GILFOYLE, S. H., 200011. Mention. D.C.M.

This N.C.O. showed a very fine spirit and seemed to be actuated by the sole desire to get to close grips with the enemy, so much so that on several occasions he had to be restrained from exposing himself unnecessarily. He was one of the first to reach the enemy's position and was instrumental in capturing several prisoners.
Italian Bronze Medal.

GILL, A., 10494.   M.M.

GILLIAN, C., 268198.   D.C.M.

In a raid on the enemy's trenches, he led his party to the objective with great dash and determination in the face of strong opposition. He accounted for several of the enemy and destroyed a machine-gun. He set an admirable example to all.

GIROD, M.   Mention.

GLEAVE, H., 32533.   M.M.

GLEED, G. A.   Mention.

GLENNON, J., 26243.   M.M.

GLOVER, T., 9142.   M.M.
Croix de Guerre (Fr.)

GODBOLD, H., 24439.   M.M.

GOMM, F., 29572.   M.M.

GOODALL, J. R. S.   Mention.

GOODWIN, E. J. H.   M.M.

GOODWIN, J., 25126.   D.C.M.

When his party ran into an enemy working party of some 30 men, he scattered them with a bomb, thus enabling his officer and the other man to escape. He then killed one of the enemy and got away himself.

GOODWIN, J., 291495.
Decoration Militaire.

GOODWIN, J. H., 45127.   M.M.

GOODWIN, L., W/1079.   M.M.

GORTON, C. B.   M.C.

GORTON, J., 1185.
Italian Bronze Medal.

GOSS, H. J.   M.C.

He made a bold reconnaissance of a point, and later seized it with 15 men, hanging on till his company arrived. Two days later he did fine work in an attack after his two senior officers had been killed. He was himself wounded.

GOSSETT, A. B.   Mention (2).   C.M.G.

GOSSETT, F. J.   Mention.

GOUGH, A. P., 17080.   Mention (2).   D.C.M.

As regimental sergeant-major for the past 3½ years he has shown untiring zeal and energy in his efforts to maintain the efficiency of the battalion, thereby rendering most valuable assistance to his commanding officer, and by his courage, cheerfulness and resource under fire, he has set a splendid example to all ranks.

GOVER, W. W. B.   Mention (2).
Promoted Brevet-Lieut.-Colonel.
Serbian Order of the White Eagle.

GRACE, J.
Promoted 2/Lieut.

GRAHAM, A., 1948.   M.M.

GRAHAM, A. W.   M.C.

When his Battalion's objective was under heavy artillery fire, he collected a large number of men and led them to the final assault. He was the first into the enemy's position, inspiring great confidence in his men by his fine example of courage and fearlessness under fire and under difficult conditions.

GRAHAM, E. R. C.   Mention (9).
K.C.B.
K.C.M.G.
Star of Roumania.
Legion of Honour (Fr.)

GRANT, G., 7546.   Mention. D.C.M.

Single-handed he charged fourteen of the enemy, all fully armed, believing none of his own men to be near, and with assistance he succeeded in capturing the whole party. during another raid he displayed the greatest courage and determination when leading his men into all enemy posts encountered.
Promoted 2/Lieut.

GRAY, G., 20513.   M.M.

GRAY, W., 11436.   Mention.

GRAY, W. H., W/326.   M.S.M.

GREATBANKS, S.   M.M.

GREATRIX, J., 1255.   M.M.

GREAVES, F. H., 50053.   M.M.

GREAVES, T., 11238.   M.M.

GREAVES, W., 9172.   M.M.

GREEN, A., 290528.   Mention.

GREEN, E. T.   M.C.

In the attack near Fayet, Sept., 18, finding his platoon hung up by a hostile machine gun, he rushed the gun single handed and with the bayonet killed or put out of action the entire team and captured the gun. By the splendid act of gallantry he saved the lives of many and materially assisted the capture of the objective.

GREEN, L. E. M.   M.C.

Although his company suffered severe loss in the early stages of an attack he rallied his men, and by his personal and daring example led them to their objectives and held them against several counter-attacks. He was severely wounded.

GREEN, J. S., 19951.   M.M.

GREENALL, G., 16985.   M.M.

GREENHALGH, A., 53080.   D.C.M.

When with a few others he was mainly instrumental in delaying the advance of the enemy for some hours. Later, when the enemy gained a footing on one part of the spur, he displayed great courage and determination in the counter-attack, which drove the enemy from the position. Throughout the operations he set a good example to the men.

Bar to D.C.M.

After his commanding officer had become a casualty, he pressed home an attack on an enemy machine-gun, firing at close range. He set a splendid example of coolness and determination to his men, and successfully extricated his command from a precarious position, when his flanks were exposed to enemy machine-gun fire.

GREENWOOD, T., 201715.   M.M.

GREENWOOD, R. N.   Mention (2).   M.C.

GREG, A.   Mention.   C.B.E.

GREG, E. W.   Mention (2).   C.B.

GREGORY, A., 15958.   Mention.

GREGORY, A. E., 36834.   M.M.

GREGORY, F. C. Mention. D.S.O.

By the skilful handling of the Battalion under his command he kept the line intact throughout the whole action, and successfully supported the line on his left. On two occasions he organised counter-attacks and drove off the enemy with severe loss. Throughout the action he displayed leadership of a high order.

GREVILLE, DUDLEY.   M.C.

GRICE, C., 32508.   M.M.

GRIFFIN, J., 27649.   M.S.M.

GRIFFITHS, F., 2015.   M.M.

GRIFFITHS, R. H.   M.C.

In supervising the companies and leading them forward at critical times into new and better positions, when the troops on his left were driven back he rode out on his horse under heavy fire, collected them, and organized a line of defence, on which stragglers were collected and from which the O.C. was able to launch his counter-attack. He set a fine example of cheerfulness and courage throughout the operation. Croix de Guerre (Fr.)

GRIMES, T. F., 25774.   M.M.

GRIMSHAW, T., 49229.   M.M.

GROARKE, T.   M.C.

During the advance south west of Maubeuge in Nov., 18, he lost all his subalterns early in the operations when skilful leadership was most essential. Nevertheless in command of two companies, he seized the ridge overlooking the Sambre, afterwards moving across and holding the railway line three kilometres beyond.

GROVE, P. L.   Mention.

Croix de Chevalier (Fr.)
Promoted Brevet-Lieut.-Colonel.

GROVE, R. P.   Mention (2).   C.M.G.

GROVES, E. J.   Mention (3).   M.C., D.S.O.

He led his company to the final objective without artillery support in the face of intense machine-gun fire, inflicting heavy losses on the enemy and captured a large number of field guns. When the enemy counter-attacked and broke through on both his flanks, he carried out a skilful withdrawal and collected and reorganized scattered parties of other units under heavy machine-gun fire.

GROVES, J. E. G.. Mention (3). C.B.E.
Ordre du Merite Agricole.

GROWCOTT, T., 268204. M.M.

GUEST, 361158. Mention.

GUNN, T. B. M.C.
Serbian White Eagle.

GUTHRIE, R., 265428. M.M.

GWINNETT, W. E., 40339. Mention.

HACKING, G. S., 10797. M.M.

HACKNEY, G., 3/64003. Mention.

HACKNEY, T. W., 25281. M.M.

HADDOCK, J. W., 15802.
Croix de Guerre (Fr.)

HADFIELD, F., 34429. M.M.

HADFIELD, T., 34703. M.M.

HAGUE, F., 1098. M.M.

HALEWOOD, G., 200195. D.C.M.
In the neighbourhood of Kemmel on the night of 22nd September, 1918, he was one of a raiding party of one officer and eleven other ranks. After completing their mission, one Lewis gunner was missing; he at once, on his own initiative, went back and found him lying wounded. While carrying him back both of them were wounded, but he struggled into our lines, the man subsequently dying of wounds.

HALL, D. M.C.
He commanded the leading platoon of his company in an attack under heavy machine-gun fire, and handled his men with great courage, coolness and skill.

HALL, D., 11503. Mention. M.M.

HALL, R. L., 2680. M.M., D.C.M.
He led his men to the first objective with great gallantry. Later, although wounded, he continued to lead his men until exhausted.

HALL, R. M. Mention.

HALLOWS, H., 12931. M.S.M.

HALLMARK, B., 5601. Mention. M.C.

HALLWORTH, S., 11165. D.C.M.
He led a bombing party and bombed up

400 yards of trench, crossing 75 yards of open ground under machine-gun fire. He has always shown great initiative and coolness.

HALSALL, H. Mention.

HAMILTON, S., 12539. Mention.

HAMLETT, J. E., 26155. M.M. and Bar.

HAMMOND, W., 9268. Mention.

HAMMONDS, W. Mention.

HAMPSON, C. G. Mention.

HAMPSON, E., 17575. Mention.

HAMPTON, A., 60567. M.M.

HARBORD, E. R. M.C.

HARDEN, B., 63174. Mention.

HARDING, G. P. Mention. M.C.
On the night of 6th/7th December, 1915, in France, he led a bombing attack on the German trenches with great coolness and determination, although the mud rendered the advance almost impossible. He showed great personal bravery and himself threw bombs when the bombers were in difficulties. Several Germans were accounted for and one prisoner taken.
Bar to M.C.

HARDMAN, A. R., 67593. M.M.

HARDWICK, W. J., 58093. M.M.

HARDY, C. H. Mention.

HARKNESS, H. D'A. Mention.

HARLAND, H., 34944. M.S.M.

HARRATLY, J., 16277. M.S.M.

HARPER, L.
Albert Medal.
On 5th August, 1917, a melting pot, used for refining high explosives at an explosive factory, was being freed from a deposit of sediment which had accumulated. During the absence of Lieutenant Harper (one of the managers of the factory) a foreman attempted to break away the sediment, which was of a highly explosive nature, with an iron bar. The mixture fused, giving off fierce flames and thick fumes. On his arrival, Lieut. Harper at once crawled with a hosepipe underneath the pot, which was raised about three feet from the ground, and directed water at the flames immediately above him. It was not until five or six

hoses had been brought to bear on the pot for some time that the burning mixture was cooled down. Meanwhile there was imminent risk of an explosion, which would certainly have killed Lieut. Harper and must have involved other buildings near by, where twenty-five tons of high explosives were stored. Had such an explosion occurred, great loss of life and material damage must inevitably have resulted.

HARPER, S. A.   M.C.

He handled his men with great courage and ability. Later, although wounded, he superintended the consolidation of a new line and set a splendid example to his men.

HARRINGTON, H. N.   Mention.

HARRIS, G., 291159.

Croix de Guerre.

HARRIS, T., 18985.   M.M.

Medaille D'Honneur.

HARRIS, W. R., 19834.   M.M.

HARRISON, J., 19137.   M.M.

HARRISON, J., 49374.   D.C.M.

During an attack by our troops, Sergeant Harrison displayed coolness and courage of the highest order, and showed powers of leadership of remarkable distinction. When the platoon on his flank had lost all its officers and non-commissioned officers, Sergeant Harrison took command and with great dash captured a machine-gun, that was immediately turned on the retreating enemy. When the officer commanding the operations was killed, Sergeant Harrison took command of the whole line, handling his men with great ability, and, as often in past actions, showed the finest example to all ranks.

HARRISON, J. D., 7611.   M.M.

HARRISON, T., 40774.   M.M.

HARRISON, W., 268039.   M.M.

HARRY, A. E.   Mention.

HARTJE, H. G.   M.C.

HARTLEY, A. P.   Mention.   O.B.E.

HARTLEY, G. W. C.   Mention.

HARVEY, F., 293120.   M.M.

HARVEY, S., 7389.   D.C.M.

As signalling Sergeant, he carried on his

work single-handed with great courage and determination, thereby enabling the Battalion communications to be kept up.

HARVEY, S., 11842.   D.C.M.

He has persistently performed good work throughout, and has at all times set a splendid example.

French Medaille Militaire.

HASHIM, R.   M.C.

During operations near Jenlain on 3rd and 4th November, 1918, during an enemy withdrawal, he led his company in pursuit with great skill and made ground and captured prisoners, pressing forward in advance of the Division on his left. Afterwards, under intense shell fire, he reorganized his company and led them in another attack with complete success.

HASLAM, W. G.   M.C.

He assumed command of, and handled, his Battalion with great courage and skill, gained his objective and captured many prisoners.

HASSALL, A. B.   M.C.   Bar to M.C.

When temporarily . performing the duties of Brigade Major, he was of the greatest assistance to his brigade commander in organizing units. His untiring efforts and devotion to duty under fire materially assisted the movements of the brigade.

HASSELL, F. P.   Mention.

HASWELL, J. F.   Mention (2).

HATTON, J., 12102.

Medaille D'Honneur.

HATTON, J. F., 201334.   M.M.

HAWKESWORTH, W., 10689.   Mention.

HAWKINS, C., 8859.   Mention.

HAWKINS, H. C.   Mention.

HAWKSFORD, A. H., 1872.   Mention.

HAYES, R., 29109.   M.M.

Promoted 2/Lieut.

HAYES, S., 2048.   Mention.

HAYTER, R. J. F.   Mention (7).   D.S.O.
                              C.M.G., C.B.

Promoted Brevet-Lt.-Colonel and Colonel.

HAYWARD, W., 8334.

Greek Military Cross.

HAY, J. M.   Mention.

HAYES, R., 29109.   M.M.

HAYES-NEWINGTON, C. W.   Mention.

HAYWARD, W. T., 15215.
Croix de Guerre (Bel.)

HAZELL, R., 12053.   M.S.M.   M.M.
Croix de Guerre (Fr.)

HEALD, T. L. C.   Mention (2).   M.C.

HEAP, T.   M.C.

He took command of a raiding party after the officer in command had been killed early in the operation. He led his men to the final objective with great dash and determination, under heavy fire, and carried out the withdrawal in a most skilful manner. He showed splendid leadership and courage.

HEARN, J., 10440.   Mention.   M.M.

HEATH, A. S., 6502.   Mention.

HEATH, G. M.   Mention (3).   D.S.O.
Bar to D.S.O.

He went forward to obtain information during an attack. Though wounded, he succeeded in reaching the battalion, crossing an extended zone swept by heavy machine-gun and rifle fire. He obtained accurate information at a critical time and showed great courage and initiative.

HEATH, H., 241944.   M.M.

HEATH, W. H., 10079.   M.S.M.

HEATHCOTE, E., 15047.   M.M.

On 3rd July, 1916, at an attack on Thiepval, he was in charge of the Lewis guns of the battalion. The crew of both guns having been killed or wounded, he, although himself wounded earlier in the day, worked one gun alone and helped to beat off an enemy counter-attack.

HEATHCOTE-DRUMMOND-WILLOUGHBY, THE HON. C. S.   Mention (5).   C.B., G.M.G.

HEGARTY, J., 51539.   M.M.

HENSON, J., 12090.   D.C.M.

He rendered extremely valuable service to the battalion during May and June, 18. He was in charge of the battalion scouts and snipers and conducted several daring and very useful patrols. On one occasion he encountered an enemy post, and attacked it by himself, killing two of the enemy and dispersing the rest.

HENTHORNE, W., 33299.   Mention. M.S.M.

HERBERT, T., 3111.
Serbian Silver Medal.

HERBERT, T. O., 200969.   M.M.

HERON, E. S.   Mention.

HESELTINE, J., 35524.   M.M.

HEWITT, C. G., 240474.   M.M.

HEWITT, J., 27974.   M.M.

HEWITT, R. E., 240624.   Mention.

HEWSON, J., W/206.   M.M.

HEYES, H., 265501.   M.M.

HIGGINBOTTOM, C., 12478.   M.M.

HIGGINBOTTOM, C., 266396.   M.S.M.

HIGGINS, H., W/793.   Mention.

HIGGINSON, R., 12888.
Croix de Guerre (Bel.)

HIGGITT, J. R., 16330.   Mention.

HIGHAM, W. N., 201123.   M.M.

HIGNETT, H. N.,   Mention (2).

HILLMAN, F. W., 31782.   M.M.

HILLS, O. M.   M.C.

He went over with the first wave of his company and rushed the enemy's post, and organised the consolidation of the captured trench, though wounded. He set a splendid example to his men.

HILL-WOOD, S. H.   Mention.

HINE, E. J., 18029.   M.M.

HITCHEN, H., 12845.   M.M.

HITHELL, E., 1357.
Russian Medal of St. George (2).

HOAR, A. B., 20697.   M.M.

HOBSON, G., 265517.   M.M. and Bar.

HODDINOTT, T. I., 67389.   M.M.

HODGKIN, A. E.   M.C.

HODGKISON, E. G.   Mention.
Croix de Guerre (Fr.)

HODGSON, A., 52255.   M.M.

HODGSON, H. J.   Mention.   D.S.O.

HODGSON, M., 49402.   M.M.

HODSON, W.   Mention (2).   M.C.

He twice led his company to the assistance of another battalion when it was heavily attacked. He has displayed great powers of leadership and has set a fine example to his men.

D.S.O.

While in command of his Battalion, his coolness under heavy fire and his skilful disposition of his men greatly assisted in checking the enemy's advance.

HODSON, W. T., 28121.   Mention.

HOGARTH, W. E., 200204.   Mention. M.M.

HOLDEN, F., 265184.   M.M.

HOLDGATE, J., 15772.   M.M. and Bar.

HOLDING, G. H.   M.C.

In the operations South West of Maubeuge, in Nov., 18, during an advance, although ill, he performed must valuable work in maintaining the organization of the attacking line. After the objective had been captured, he cleared up the situation, which was obscure on both flanks by leading a patrol in the darkness and establishing communication.

HOLGATE, J. A.   Mention.

HOLLAND, F. W., 58052.   M.M.

HOLLAND, G., 265352.   M.M.

HOLLAND, J., 13604.   Mention. M.M.

HOLLAND, J.   M.C.

Under very heavy machine-gun and rifle fire, he collected and evacuated wounded from a ridge. He showed utter disregard for personal safety, and by his zeal and energy set a splendid example to those under him and saved many lives.

HOLLAND, J. F., 2204.   M.M.

HOLLAND, S., 265856.   M.M.

HOLLORAN, W. J.   Mention. M.B.E.

HOLMES, V. R.   M.C.

He led a patrol through enemy's wire and brought back valuable information. Two nights later, having marked down some wounded, he took out a party and brought in 15.

HOLLOWAY, H. C., 241030. D.C.M.

On 21st July, 1918, at Namirrue, he organized parties and materially assisted in putting out a serious fire caused by enemy shells, under a very heavy cross fire from machine-guns. It was mainly owing to the actions of this N.C.O. that the fire was prevented from spreading and rendering our position untenable.

HOLSGROVE, J., 32532.   D.C.M.

Although severely wounded, he carried on for five hours, encouraging his men, organizing bombing parties, and by his courage and determination contributed largely to the success of the operations.

HOLT, H., 203.   Mention.

HOLT, J. E., 50841.   M.M.

HOLYOAKE, 200610.   M.M.

HOOD, R. H., 16105.   M.M.

HOOLEY, J. A., 265180.   M.M.

HOOPER, R., 290255.   D.C.M.

At Gheluwe, on 14th Oct., 1918, and previously at Wytschaete Ridge, he showed great gallantry and devotion to duty in carrying out his duties as Signalling Sergeant, and by his example and conduct contributed greatly to the success of the operations. At Parcy Tigny in July 1918, and during the last two years, his skill in organizing and maintaining communications have proved invaluable.

HOPE, A., 290674.   M.S.M.

HORROBIN, J. A., 3/28034.   Mention.

HORSFIELD, E., 49979.   M.M.

HORSLEY, C. H.   M.C.

When commanding an assaulting company during an attack, his personal influence and fine leadership had a most inspiring effect upon his men, both before and during the attack, and he afterwards displayed the utmost energy and ability during the consolidation of the captured line.

Promoted 2/Lieut.

HORSLEY, R. C.   M.C.

During an enemy attack, he promptly got his guns into action and continued to fire throughout the bombardment, inflicting heavy casualties on the enemy. While withdrawing his guns with great coolness and ability, he was wounded in the head, but refused to let his men imperil their own safety by carrying him out, and lay there within 50 yards of the enemy till night. He set a splendid example of courage and devotion to duty.

HORTON, H., 49980.   M.M.

HOTCHKISS, J. E., 11710.   M.M.

HOUGH, I., 13774. M.M.

HOUGH, T. W., 16403. M.M.

HOUSE, J. T. M.C.

When in command of a trench mortar battery under heavy shell fire, he moved about, encouraging his men, who, when bombs had given out, continued to fight with rifles until ordered to withdraw. At all times he displayed great initiative, and his energy and pluck were a fine example to all ranks.

HOWARD, F., 4281 D.C.M.

HOWARD, W., 19489. M.S.M.

HOWARD, W., 7159. M.M.

HOWARTH, R., 265916. Mention.

HOWE, H. T., 51895. M.M.

HOWELL, J. A. Mention. M.C., D.S.O.

He showed great powers of leadership and resource in commanding his Battalion during an attack, and afterwards consolidated his position with great skill.

HOWELLS, W., 52605. M.M.

HUBBALL, G., 202138. M.M.

HUBBARD, H. V., 11866. D.C.M.

HUDSON, A., 45772. M.M.

HUDSON, G. E., 9809. M.M.

HUFFAM, R. E. M.C.

During an enemy attack he collected stragglers from other units, formed them into a company, and checked the enemy's advance until the arrival of fresh troops. He showed great determination and fine leadership.

HUGHES, A., 5742. Mention. M.S.M.

HUGHES, B., S/4791.

Croix de Guerre (Bel.)

HUGHES, C. G. E. Mention. O.B.E.

HUGHES, E., 6759. Mention.

HUGHES, G. W. M.C.

When commanding the right platoon on the right flank of an attack, he led his men with the greatest dash and determination to their objective, which was consolidated under heavy and continuous shell fire, and maintained against several determined counter-attacks. He also succeeded in securing his right flank by collecting and organizing scattered troops of other units into a fighting force. His personal gallantry throughout the day was an example to all.

Bar to M.C.

In Nov., 18, near Jenlain, when his company was held up by heavy machine-gun fire, he led his platoon forward with great dash into the village, outflanked the enemy and enabled the company to advance.

HUGHES, H., 24515. M.M.

HUGHES, J. L. J. Mention.

HUGHES, J. N. M.C.

Having captured an enemy position, he was at once subjected to heavy frontal and enfilade fire. He held on until dark, and then withdrew the majority of his men in safety. By his courage and coolness he undoubtedly saved many lives.

Bar to M.C.

He led his men to the attack with amazing dash and initiative. When his own and then another company commander were wounded, he took charge of the two companies, and controlled them with great ability, until he was seriously wounded. His example of leadership inspired all ranks.

HUGHES, W. R., 9655. M.M.

HULLEY, F., 290948. M.M.

HULLEY, H., 290347. Mention (2).

HULLEY, H., 290983. D.C.M.

As one of a Lewis gun team he behaved with the utmost fearlessness and gallantry in accompanying his leader, under heavy rifle and machine-gun fire. By his coolness and courage he greatly assisted in the effective fire of his gun at a critical moment.

HULME, J., 1036. M.M.

HUMPHREY, B., 292760. M.M.

HUMPHREYS, V. M.C.

In covering the retirement of his platoon, with his company sergeant-major he remained in a forward trench in face of the enemy advancing in vastly superior numbers, until the enemy had entered the trench on both flanks and until his platoon had taken up a new position in rear. Throughout he displayed great coolness under fire, and set a fine example.

HUMPHRIES, E., 316043. M.M.

HUMPHRIES, J. E., 24086. Mention.

HUMPHRIES, N., 36570.   M.M.

HUNT, F., 50527.   M.M.

HUNT, T. S., 51037.   M.M.

HUNT, W., 50125.   M.M.

HUNTER, F., 19554.   M.M.

HUNTER, W., 265704.   Mention.

HURD, J., 63845.   M.M.
  Decoration Militaire.

INCE, W., 200026.   M.M.

INGHAM, C. H., 11514.   Mention.

INGRAM, W., 16/20482.   M.M. D.C.M.
  During an attack his fearlessness and resolute conduct did much to inspire his section.
  Though wounded at the start, he carried on,
  capturing an enemy machine-gun and its
  team.

INMAN, D. S.   Mention (2).

INNES, W. R.   Mention.

INWIN, J., 1348.   Mention.

IRWIN, C.   Mention. M.C.

JACKSON, E. A.   Mention.

JACKSON, C. G., 36028.   Mention.

JACKSON, F., 2251.   M.M.

JACKSON, H., 11784.   D.C.M.

JACKSON, H., 242141.   M.M.

JACKSON, J., 1034.   M.M.

JACKSON, R., 5056.   Mention. M.S.M.

JACKSON, T. L.   M.C.

JACKSON, W. E., 17977.   Mention. D.C.M.

JACKSON-PAYNE, H., 554.   D.C.M.
  At Le Touquet salient on 29th December,
  1915, he was in charge of the right bombing
  party of a fighting patrol, and, though
  wounded in three places, persisted in continuing to throw bombs with the greatest
  coolness. He set a fine example to his
  men.

JAMES, A. W., 28002.   Mention.

JAMES, E., 240524.   M.S.M.

JAMES, E. J., 28040.   Mention.

JAMES, H., 20960.   M.M.

JAMIESON, H., 51251.   Mention.

JARBUCK, T. W., 29217.   Mention.

JARDINE, W. H., 34949.   Mention.

JARVIS, C. H.   M.M.

JEFFERSON, W., 11258.   M.M.

JENKINS, R. F.   M.C.
  On the 16th October, 1918, he led a patrol
  party of eight men who crossed the Lys
  canal on a temporary raft which only two
  men at a time could occupy, under heavy
  machine-gun and rifle fire. He maintained
  himself in face of machine-gun and minin-
  werfer fire on the enemy's bank until
  reinforced by a company of another
  regiment. He showed marked gallantry
  and dash.

JENKINSON, W. R.   Mention.

JERVIS, R. P.   M.C.
  He commanded the right platoon of the
  leading company in the attack on the " P "
  ridge on the 18th September, 1918. Immediately our barrage lifted off P 4¼ about
  thirty of the enemy dashed out of the dug-
  outs and commenced bombing. He led
  his platoon through the bomb barrage, and
  leaping into the trench, attacked the enemy
  with the bayonet. He personally killed a
  number of these, but was wounded in the
  face, when he shouted to his orderly to throw
  him out of the trench and carry on. He set
  a fine example of courage and determination
  to his command. He had already been
  wounded on four previous occasions.
  White Eagle 5th Class (Serbia).

JOHN, S. S.   Mention (2). M.C.
  During the fighting near Festubert on the
  25th September, 1915, after a retirement in
  the trenches had been ordered, Second Lieutenant John crawled out under heavy fire
  and assisted to bring in, in succession, a
  wounded officer and about twenty men of
  another regiment, thus saving many lives.
  He continued this gallant work throughout
  the day until he was utterly exhausted.
  This is not the first time that Second
  Lieutenant John has shown conspicuous
  courage.
  Greek Military Cross.

JOHNSON, A.
  Greek Military Cross.

JOHNSON, A., 290418.   Mention.

JOHNSON, A., 265240.   M.M.

JOHNSON, C.   Mention (2). M.B.E.
  Promoted Brevet-Major.

JOHNSON, E., 12944.   M.M.

JOHNSON, G., 40902.   M.M.

JOHNSON, G. S., 61007.

Croix de Guerre (Bel.)

JOHNSON, J. M. O.   Mention.

JOHNSON, O.   M.C.

JOHNSON, R., 200804.   M.M.

JOHNSON, T., 291354.   M.M.

JOHNSON, W. A., 57865.   D.C.M.

JOHNSON, W. H.   M.C.

He led his men splendidly against the enemy and accounted for several of them himself. He was badly wounded, but he set a fine example to his men on this as on all other occasions.

JOHNSON, W. H., 53550.   M.M.

JOHNSTON, E.

Promoted 2/Lieut.

JOHNSTON, H.   Mention (3).   D.S.O.

JOHNSTONE, W. D.   M.M.

JOLLEY, R. J.

Promoted 2/Lieut.

JOLLIFFE, A. H.   Mention.   M.C.

JOLLIFFE, C. E.   M.C.

JOLLIFFE, O.   M.C.

JONES, A., 1573.   Mention

JONES, A., 14979   M.M.

JONES, A., 17936.   M.M.

JONES, A., 240015.   M.S.M.

JONES, A. R., 200003.   M.S.M.

JONES, B. A. R.   Mention.   M.B.E.

Order of the Nile.

Croix de Guerre (Fr.)

JONES, D., 267946.   M.M.

JONES, D. T., 293124.

Croix de Guerre (Fr.)

JONES, E. G., 50089.   M.M.

JONES, G., 12212.   D.C.M.

When signal communication with Battalion H.Q. was being constantly cut by shell fire, he made, on his own initiative, five separate journeys to repair it. Later he laid a new line under very heavy fire and restored communications at a critical period.

Bar to D.C.M.

While in charge of battalion H.Q. signalling staff during an enemy attack, he went out

into the open under heavy fire, searching for ammunition and Lewis gun drums, which he carried into the trench. He also twice repaired his telephone wires, and found and brought into action a Lewis gun with which he inflicted heavy casualties on the enemy. He showed splendid courage and devotion to duty.

JONES, H., 44349.   D.C.M.

When a large gap occurred in the line, he at once filled the gap with his Lewis gun team. He also cleared a dug-out, capturing several prisoners. His initiative and promptness undoubtedly saved the situation.

JONES, H.   M.M.

JONES, H.   M.M.

Promoted 2/Lieut.

JONES, H., 265672.   M.M.

JONES, J., 9361.   M.M.

JONES, J., 19053.

Croix de Guerre (Fr.)

JONES, J., 3/25897.   M.M.

JONES, J. H., 200708.   M.M.

JONES, J. O., 19347.   M.C.

JONES, L. H.   Mention.

JONES, O., 33079.   M.M.

JONES, R., W/67.   Mention.

JONES, R., 266296.   M.M.

JONES, T., 16930.

French Medaille Militaire.

D.C.M.

He carried out the duties of C.S.M. with the utmost skill. During a very heavy bombardment all the officers of his company became casualties. He immediately took command, rallied and organised the men and greatly assisted the company on his left to beat off a vigorous counter-attack. He remained perfectly cool and cheerful throughout, and in the absence of an officer, sent back valuable information to Battalion Headquarters.

JONES, T. A., 11000.   V.C.

He was with his company consolidating the defences in front of a village, and, noticing an enemy sniper at 200 yards distance, he went out, and though one bullet went through his helmet and another through his coat, he returned the sniper's fire and killed him. He then saw two more of the enemy firing at him, although displaying a white flag. Both of these he also shot. On reaching the enemy trench he found several occupied dug-outs, and, single-handed, disarmed 102 of the enemy, including three or four officers, and marched them back to our lines through a heavy barrage. He had been warned of the misuse of the white flag by the enemy, but insisted on going out after them.

D.C.M.

This man went forward five times with messages through an intense barrage. He also led forward stragglers and placed them in positions. His fine example and utter fearlessness of danger were a great incentive to the men.

JONES, W.   Mention.

JONES, W., 10328.   M.M.

JONES, W. T., 200472.   M.S.M.

JORDON, R., W/4.   Mention.

JOULE, G., 11156.   M.M.

JOYCE, J. H., 25090.   M.M.

JOYCE, S., 25089.   Mention.

JOYCE, T. S., 301221.   M.M.

JOYNSON, W. A., 291062.   M.M.

JOYNSON, W. J., 34.   M.M.

KANE, V. W., 65648.   M.M.

KAY, H. D.   Mention. O.B.E.

KAY, J., 30636.   M.M.

KAY, R. L.   Mention. M.C.

KAY, W., 293140.   M.M.

KEAM, H., 14509.   M.M.

KEATING, J. H., 10516.   D.C.M.

During a bombing attack on the night of 6th/7th December, 1915, near Carnoy, when sent to reinforce a blocking party, which was in danger of being driven in, he rendered most gallant assistance, keeping the men together and with them repelling several counter-bomb attacks.

KEATING, W., 18570.   M.M.

KEENAN, H., 12377.   Mention. M.M.
Serbian Gold Medal.

KEGGAN, J. H., 996.   M.M.

KELLIE, A., 1688.   M.M.

KELLY, J., 10/17578.   M.M.

KELSALL, J., 266714.
D.C.M.

During the attack near Menin, on 14th October, 1918, he noticed that a machine-gun placed on top of a pill box was enfilading his company and checking the advance. He took his Lewis gun forward into an exposed position and engaged the enemy gun, putting it out of action. The following afternoon, while his company were consolidating their position, they came under direct fire from another machine-gun. He took his Lewis gun into a bedroom and engaged the enemy gun from the window, knocking it out. Throughout these operations his gallantry and initiative were most marked, and he did splendid work.

Medaille Militaire.

KEMP, J., 45955.   M.M.

KENNAUGH, W. E., 3/24893.   Mention.

KENNY, J., 52549.   D.C.M.

During a raid on the enemy trenches, he guided the raiding party across "No Man's Land," under very heavy fire. He showed a complete disregard of his own personal safety, and set a splendid example to all ranks.

KENYON, E. C.   Mention.

KENYON, W. J., 19864.   D.C.M.

This warrant officer, who has served in France with the battalion for over two years, has displayed great gallantry in action and conspicuous devotion to duty. Exceptionally cool under fire, his example has been of the greatest assistance to his company commander, to who he has proved a reliable support, no matter how bad the conditions.

KERFOOT, J., 265773.   M.M.

KERR, W., 11385.   M.M.

KIDD, C. B.   M.C.

He did remarkably fine work when his company was holding a position for many hours, from early morning till late at night, while heavily shelled. It was entirely due to his efforts that the men were kept together. He encouraged his men throughout the day, continually going up and down the trench. His conduct was splendid and he set a fine example.

KING, C. F.   Mention.   D.S.O.
M.C.

He led several bombing attacks and cleared out at great risk a bomb store which had been set on fire. All this happened after he had been wounded. He refused to leave his post till ordered.

Bar to D.S.O.

When in command of a Battalion, he organised the defence of a village, held it against heavy attacks, and over and over again led forward his small reserve to drive out bodies of the enemy who had obtained a temporary foothold. Throughout the subsequent withdrawal he was the life and soul of the defence, and his example and complete disregard of danger instilled the greatest confidence in his men.

KING, G. E., 241839.   Mention.

KING, H., 316298.   M.M.

KING, R.   Mention.

KILBOURN, A. S., 33887.   Mention.

KININMONTH, A. M.   Mention.

KIRK, R.   M.C.

When leading a patrol in the enemy's trenches, he shot three of the enemy in a dug-out, and skilfully withdrew his patrol without any casualties on finding that the alarm had been given.

KIRKBRIDE, T. C.   M.C.

During the operations east of Terhand, on the 14th October, 1918, he led his platoon to the attack with great gallantry and determination and dealt with the numerous strong machine-gun nests with success. His skilful handling of his command enabled the operations to be carried through with very few casualties. On arriving at his objective, he promptly set several captured machine-guns in order and placed them in position for use against the enemy.

KIRKHAM, O., 13102.   Mention.

KIRKHAM, S., 25779.   Mention.   M.M.

KIRKNESS, J. W., 15/23015.
Croix de Guerre (Bel.)

KIRTON, G. G.   M.C.

He led his company under very heavy fire to the final objective, and, though wounded, held it for an hour and a half, inflicting heavy casualties on the enemy and taking many prisoners. When he was nearly surrounded, and forced to withdraw, he gallantly brought his men back to the supports. His conduct throughout the operation was a splendid example to all.

KIRTON, J. W., 30788.   M.M.
Serbian Gold Medal for Valour.

KIVELL, H., 14494.   M.M.

KNIGHT, J., 1204.   Mention.

KNOWLES, J. A.   M.C.

He carried out several daring patrols and obtained valuable information previous to a raid. Later, he led a raiding party into the enemy's trenches with great gallantry.

KNOX, W., 31681.   Mention.

LALLY, J., 1188   D.C.M.

By his personal dash and fine leadership of his platoon during the capture of an enemy post, he gained his objectives and consolidated them under heavy fire. Afterwards he maintained his position against several determined counter-attacks.

LAMB, A., 1419.   M.M.

LAMB, C., 266229.   M.M.

LAMB, W., 29901.
Croix de Guerre (Fr.)

LAMBERT, 12677.   M.M.

LANDEN, H., 243063.   M.M.

LANGFORD, J., 36172.   M.M.

LANHAM, W., 34541.   Mention.

LARGE, W. E., 11330.   D.C.M.

For over two years, he has always rendered invaluable services during many active operations in personally supervising the taking up of rations, often under very adverse conditions, and has set a fine example to all ranks.

LATHAM, C.   Mention.

LATHAM, F.   M.C.

In an attack he led his platoon to their objective in the face of intense machine-gun fire. When his left flank was entirely in the air and the enemy were working round it in force, he saved the situation by his skilful dispositions and saved many casualties. His coolness and determination were of the greatest value at a critical time.

LATHAM, T.   Mention.

LAVIN, M., 9999.   M.M.

LAWRENCE, H. M.
Legion of Honour—Chevalier.

LAWRENCE, W. J., 290008.   Mention.

LAWTON, W. T., 201510.   M.M.
Medaille Militaire.

LAYCOCK, C., W/35.   Mention.

LEA, J., 33639.   M.M.

LEA, T., 16691.   M.S.M.

LEA, W. H., 52874.
Croix de Guerre (Bel.)

LEACH, A., 8648.   Mention.

LEACH, J. H., 34214.   M.M.

LEAH, A., 10176.   M.M.

LEE, A. V.   Mention.   M.B.E.

LEE, J.   M.C.
When commanding a raid his conduct throughout was of the highest order and a splendid example to his men ; it was entirely due to his fine leadership that the enterprise was successfully carried out.

LEE, J., 50270.   M.M.

LEE, H., 2197.   M.M.

LEE, R., 49991.   M.M.

LEECH, S. F.   M.C.
At Menin he took a patrol of four men by day to attempt to cross the river Lys. This he did under machine-gun and rifle fire and gained very valuable information as to the condition of the river banks.

LEES, J., 19847.   D.C.M.
When laying out a wire during an attack, with another N.C.O., he lost direction and met a party of 20 enemy with a machine-gun whom they attacked without hesitation, their only weapons being one rifle and a signalling lamp stand. They captured the gun and brought back two prisoners. They then established communication with the position and maintained it under heavy fire.

LEESON, B. E.   Mention.

LEETE, W. W.   Mention.   A.F.C.
Was employed as assistant instructor and acting flight-commander from 25th November, 1917, to 7th July, 1918. During this period Capt Leete gave a very great amount

of dual instruction of the highest quality. The many pupils who passed through his hands all reached a high standard of flying. By his unceasing hard work, exceptional keenness, and contempt of danger, Capt. Leete set an example which was undoubtedly of great moral value to his Station.

LEGH, A. H.   M.C.

LEICESTER, B.
Croix de Guerre (Fr.)

LEIGH, J., 10878.   M.S.M.

LEIGHTON, J., 265899.   M.M.

LEIVESLEY, G., 24381.   D.C.M.
When, his company was almost surrounded, he took charge of it in the absence of the officers, and conducted its withdrawal in a masterly manner, displaying much coolness under heavy fire.

LE MESURIER, H. F. A.   M.C.

LEONARD, C. E., 9353.   Mention.

LEONARD, E., 24589.   M.M.

LEONARD, H. V.   Mention.   M.C.
Croix de Guerre (Fr.)
Bar to M.C.
For two days this officer was in charge of his own and another Company, holding a detached position. While a hostile attack was on, the grass in front of the trench was set on fire. He, with another officer, went out and succeeded in extinguishing the flames. Later in the day he took the two companies forward in support of a counter-attack by tanks, which checked the advance of the enemy.

LEVINGS, W.   Mention.
Promoted 2/Lieut.
M.C.
During the operations near Moen and Autryve on 25th Oct., 18, he showed great courage and able leadership. His company was the first to reach its final objective in spite of heavy artillery and machine-gun fire, and during their advance took several prisoners. He sent back with great promptitude valuable reports regarding his positions and those on his flanks.

LEWIN, T., 33662.   Mention.

LEWIS, F., 7318.   Mention.

LEWIS, G., 25478. D.C.M. M.M.

On the night 2nd / 3rd October, 1915, near Vermelles, the Germans expected an attack by us, and the fire on both sides was very heavy, in addition to which flares were being constantly sent up. Pte. Lewis and Drummer Tucker were ceaseless in their efforts to bring in the wounded men, who were lying between our own and the enemy lines. On one occasion they were fired on by our own men, who were unable to distinguish who they were. They continued this work until after daylight, exhibiting marked courage.

LEWIS, H., 57898. M.M.

LEWIS, J. H. M.C.

LEWIS, T., 16903. M.M.

LEWIS, T., 290003. M.S.M.

LEWIS, W., 15061. M.M.

LEYLAND, G. F. Mention.

LIGHT, P. M.C.

LILBURN, H. P., 200019. M.M.

Medaille D'Honneur.

LINDLEY, F., 50615. M.M.

LINDOP, B. Mention. M.C.

LINFOOT, G. Mention (2). M.C.

At a critical moment, when the success of a strong raiding party seemed doubtful owing to very heavy casualties, he rallied them and brought them up supports, thereby dispersing the enemy and securing the success of the enterprise. Although wounded, and at one moment alone under heavy fire, his pluck and presence of mind enabled him to carry on.

LINFOOT, H. A. Mention (2). M.C.

He displayed great courage and determination when leading a night attack on the enemy lines. Under heavy shell fire he rushed an enemy machine-gun, which was captured mainly as a result of his own personal efforts. He then organized the consolidation of the position with the utmost energy and initiative.

D.S.O.

He was acting second in command of his Battalion and followed the attack with the rear companies. On arriving at the first objective whilst fighting was still in progress, he rushed a dug-out containing four machine-guns, capturing the guns and teams. He then moved along the line, under continuous shell fire and sniping, organising the first objective and the further advance. Throughout the action he sent back full and accurate information, and his example and leadership were of the greatest service.

Italian Silver Medal for Military Valour.

LINES, T., 10/16313. D.C.M.

With a few men he held a bay and built two blocks and held it successfully for two hours. He displayed great courage and determination throughout.

LINGARD, G. E., 10758. M.M.

LISLE, A. C. Mention.

LISTER, R., 878. M.M.

LITTLE, W., W/622. D.C.M.

During an attack, when only one man of his team was left besides his carrying party, he went forward with the infantry and did splendid work knocking out two hostile machine-guns. His services in his battery have always been invaluable.

LIVINGSTONE, J. O., 265475. D.C.M.

During ten days fighting this N.C.O., who had taken charge of the platoon when his officer was wounded, set a very fine example of courage, and disregard of personal safety, to his men. Throughout the operations, his coolness and cheerful demeanour under trying circumstances were remarkable. On one occasion he three times met heavy attacks of the enemy, whom he forced to retire with severe casualties.

LLEWELLYN, T. R., 67621. M.M.

LLOYD, A.

Promoted 2/Lieut.

LLOYD, F. L. Mention.

LLOYD, R. E., 11623. Mention.

LLOYD, T., 7296. D.C.M.

He succeeded in leading a party of pack animals, carrying ammunition, up to the firing line under heavy fire. He has rendered consistent good service throughout the operations, and has at all times performed his duties in a most efficient and satisfactory manner.

LOAKMAN, P. B. Mention. M.C.

LOCKETT, G. B.   M.C.

In the attack on Beaucamp on 27th September, 1918, in command of a company, he mopped up the valley west of the village, and part of the village itself, taking about 80 prisoners. Later he organized a section to deal with a machine-gun post in the village and under his guidance they captured the gun and killed four of the enemy with it. His determined courage, energy and leadership were a fine example to all.

LOCKETT, W.   M.C.

At Quennemont farm on 21-9-18, with a handful of men and a Lewis gun during the attack, he engaged an enemy party of one officer and a large number of men and four machine-guns and rendered invaluable service to the attackers by preventing the enemy surrounding them. The Battalion was eventually almost completely surrounded, but though continually threatened by superior numbers, he held on for over five hours and only withdrew when his own party consisted of himself and two men, both wounded, and his ammunition completely exhausted.

LOCKLEY, T., 1263.   D.C.M.

He took his machine-gun out in the open twenty-five yards to the right of the gun emplacement and opened fire on gaps cut in the enemy's wire. Being fired on by the enemy's artillery, he shifted his position, but was again fired on, six shells dropping close to him. He then withdrew.

LOFTUS, G., 9479.
Croix de Guerre (Fr.)

LOFTUS, J., 2767.   D.C.M.

He took charge of a party and lead them down an enemy trench, bombing and clearing the dug-outs. He set a splendid example throughout.

LOFTUS, W., 266075.   M.M.

LOMAS, A. J. C., 200725.   Mention.

LONG, H., 293129.
Medaille Militaire.
M.M.

For continuous good work whilst C.S.M. of a company. On several occasions he saved the situation by his coolness and handling of N.C.Os. and men near Pacry Tigny in July and August, 1918.

LONGTON, N., 34626.   M.M.

LOSCOMBE, A. R.   Mention (2).

LOWE, F., 15030.   M.M.

LOWE, P., 18978.   Mention.

LOWE, V., 21772.   D.C.M.

As company runners to the officer holding an advanced post, Privates Lowe and Campbell repeatedly went backwards and forwards, carrying messages over open ground under artillery, machine-gun and rifle fire, at 300 yards range. Their devotion to duty was very fine.

LOWES, W., 51774.   M.M.

LOWTH, C., 14634.   Mention.
Croix de Guerre.
D.C.M.

He showed exceptional judgment and dash in clearing parties of the enemy out of shell holes and gun emplacements during an advance. Throughout the operation he set a splendid example of courage to his men.

LUDGATE, J., 10790.   M.M.

LYELL, J.   Mention.

LYMAN, M. L., 32787.   Mention (2).

LYON, J., 316555.
Croix de Guerre (Bel.)

LYON, R., 5357.   M.M.

LYTHGOE, M., 16871.   Mention.

McNAUGHT, G. S.   Mention (2).   D.S.O.
Greek Military Cross.

MACAULEY, B., 35683.   M.M.

MACE, H., 39963.   M.M.

McARTHUR, W., 9/11900.   Mention.

MacCARTHY, F., 7085.   Mention.

On 15th September, 1914, at Missy Sur Aisne, volunteered to fetch ammunition under fire, and at night, at the imminent risk of being shot by both friend and foe, assisted 2nd Lieut. Atkinson to rejoin his Company.

McCORMACK, H., 2759.   M.M.

McCREARY, T., 8266.   Mention.

McCAFFERY, W. R.
Promoted Major.

McClellan, G., 15507. D.C.M.

He assumed command of, and led a bombing party with great courage and determination, capturing twenty-two of the enemy. He put a machine-gun out of action and killed the team.

McCrone, 8871. M.M.

MacDonald, 6912. D.C.M.

When a portion of a trench was blown in by a trench mortar and the garrison cut off. Later he went over the parapet, and carried in wounded men under heavy machine-gun fire.

McGachen, G. F. Mention. M.C.

As second in command of his Company, he led an attack in face of very heavy machine-gun and rifle fire, and took his objective.

McGivering, D., 15979. M.M.

McGowan, G. Mention (2). M.C.

McGrath, E. M.C.

When the battalion was forced to withdraw from its final objective by an enemy counter-attack, he went forward repeatedly to attend to the wounded under intense fire, and was the means of saving a large number who were in danger of falling into the enemy's hands. His coolness and disregard of danger were an inspiration to all ranks.

McGregor, C., 51812. D.C.M.

When the advance of the battalion was held up by the enemy machine-gun fire, he went out single-handed and killed the detachment and captured the machine-gun. His gallant action saved the battalion many casualties. Throughout the day he set a splendid example of courage and devotion to duty.

MacGregor, J., 51489. M.M.

McHugh, R., 15054. Mention. M.M.

McInnes, F. W., W/822. Mention.

McKay, F. H. Mention.

Promoted 2/Lieut.

Mackenzie, G. O. M.C.

On one occasion the tank he was in received three direct hits. Although twice wounded he continued to guide his section in spite of heavy shelling and successfully led the

attacking infantry to their objectives. Again, when his tank was disabled by shell fire, he joined the infantry and led a party to silence a hostile machine-gun.

McKerrow, W. H. Mention. M.C.

He performed his duties as adjutant with untiring energy and courage under heavy shell fire, visiting all posts, and by his fine example inspiring confidence in the men.

McLachlan, R. M., W/232. D.C.M.

He led his platoon under very heavy artillery fire to the attack. His leading was skilful and well timed, and he overcame all difficulties.

Maclean, G. H. M.C.

McNeil, G., 240612. M.M.

McNeil, S., 201075. M.M.

McNight, E., 21506. Mention.

McPhilemy, J., 50040. M.M.

McWhinnie, J. F., 9116. Mention.

Madden, H., 267958. M.M.

Maddock, J., 240600. Mention.

Croix de Guerre (Fr.)

Madeley, F. J., 45737. M.M.

Maguire, T., 15320. M.M.

Mahony, F. H. Mention.

Mahoney, J., 200452. Mention. M.M.

Mallalieu, J. R. M.C.

During a counter-attack, although wounded, he took forward parties to the front line under very heavy short-range machine-gun and shell fire. He took command of his company and continued to do most valuable work, until ordered to the field ambulance.

Maloney, A., 25250. M.M.

For carrying messages under heavy shell fire at Morval about 25th September, 1916.

Mandeville, J., 10313. M.M. D.C.M.

When commanding his platoon he led them with the greatest gallantry and skill, keeping up their spirits by his unfailing cheerfulness and personal example. He spent the whole of the following night in No Man's Land, searching for and successfully bringing in all our dead.

Manley, H. M.C.

During an enemy attack he made a reconnaissance, when the situation was very obscure, under heavy fire, and sent back most valuable information. Later, he successfully led his platoon in a counter-attack He did fine work.

MANN, H. C.   M.C.

He showed marked gallantry in the operations East of Courtrai in October, 1918. He attacked a farm with two men from a flank in face of heavy machine-gun fire and enabled the troops on the right to get forward and capture the farm.

MANSELL, W. H., 29542.   M.M.

MANTON, F., 1620.   M.M.

MARCH, W.   M.C.

On the 25th/26th September, 1918, at Pont De Nieppe, he acted with conspicuous gallantry and judgment in reconnoitring forward areas under heavy fire, whereby he was able to lead his platoon to the objective with very few casualties. He carried a wounded man himself a considerable distance under machine-gun fire to prevent him falling into the hands of the enemy. His disregard for danger and coolness had a most inspiring effect on his men.

MARCHANT, E. J., 25190.   Mention.

MARQUIS, E.   Mention.

MARRIS, O. C.   M.C.

At a moment when a gap occurred in our leading wave he promptly led his platoon up and filled it, thereby preventing our line from being broken. He accounted for eight of the enemy himself, and throughout the operations he continued to urge his men on by his own personal gallantry and cheerful example. He has frequently carried out daring patrols and reconnaissances.

MARSDEN, C. E.   Mention.

MARSDEN, G., 16453.   M.M.
D.C.M.

During an attack, he got into the enemy trenches and held out all day under heavy fire. Later, when several men had been buried by heavy shell explosion, he succeeded in digging out several under heavy fire.

MARSDEN, G. D.   M.C.

He took command of a company in a position which had become isolated owing to the unit on the flank being forced back and the position being subject to heavy enfilade fire. He consolidated the position and established a strong point, and by his courage and determination enabled the position to be held until the line had been re-established. He performed admirable work throughout the operations.

MARSDEN, J. R., 13293.   M.S.M.

MARSDEN, W., 16285.   M.M.
Greek Military Cross.

MARSH, C. F. W.   Mention.

MARSH, W., 15856.   M.S.M.
Croix de Guerre (Fr.)

MARSHALL, A., 18770.   Mention.   D.C.M.

Near Sari Bair, Gallipoli Peninsular, on 18th August, 1915, Sergt. Price and Private Marshall attended to wounded men under heavy fire.

MARSHALL, A., 29674.   M.M.

MARSHALL, R. D., 57882.   M.M.

MARTIN, G., 21281.   Mention.

MARTIN, J. W., W/116.   Mention.

MARTIN, W., 33567.   D.C.M.

He repaired his telephone wires and maintained communication during a heavy enemy barrage fire. When the enemy forced an entry into a front-line trench, entirely on his own initiative he immediately collected a supply of bombs, and alone cleared 100 yards of trench full of the enemy, killing twenty and wounding several more.

MARTIN-LEAKE, W.   Mention.
Promoted Brevet-Major and Brevet-Lieut.-Colonel.

MASON, J. D.   Mention.   M.C.

He led his company to their objective in the face of determined opposition. He personally led his bombers against enemy posts, accounting for many of them himself, and afterwards organized his company and consolidated the captured line with great promptness and ability. He has on all occasions displayed great gallantry under fire.

MATHER, T., 1073.   Mention.

MATHERS, A., 13184.   M.M. and Bar.

MATHEWS, A.   Mention.

MATTERSON, C. A. K.   Mention

MAUNDER, G., 2277.   M.M.

MAXWELL, E. C.   Mention (3).   M.C.
Promoted Brevet-Major.
Order of the Redeemer, Greek Medal for
    Military Merit.
Order of the White Eagle.
O.B.E.

MAY, C. A. C.   Mention.   M.C.
Greek Military Cross.

MAYBANK, J., 266836.   M.M.

MAYLOR, J., 21959.   M.M.

MAYLOR, J. H., 34541.   M.M.

MEACHIN, F. J., 8353.   D.C.M.
He led his platoon with great skill and dash
after his officers had been wounded, and
throughout the day he set an example of
cheerfulness and gallantry which did much
to encourage his men. He was invaluable
in reorganizing the company and making
good the ground gained.

MEAD, C. J.   Mention.

MEADOWS, A., 34537.   M.M.

MEARS, F., 17836.   Mention (4).
M.M. and Bar.

MEARS, T. 16734.   Mention.

MELLOR, J., 24036.   M.M.

MENNIE, J. B.   M.C.

MENZIES, F., 7977.   M.S.M.

MENZIES, W. H. W.   M.C.
On the 4th September, 1918, North-west
of Kemmel, he took his two trench mortars forward under heavy machine-gun fire,
and twice destroyed machine-guns which
were checking an advance from a flank.
When attacked and almost surrounded,
he managed to extricate his guns, with only
two men wounded.

MEREDITH, G. C.   M.C.
During enemy attacks he was acting second
in command, and obtained much useful
information which materially assisted his
commanding officer. Throughout, under
heavy machine-gun and rifle fire, he showed
contempt of danger, and rendered valuable
service to his battalion.
Bar to M.C.

METCALFE, H. L., 6936.   M.M.

MIDDLETON, T. H., 27422.   Mention.

MILEY, J., 203344.
Croix de Guerre (Fr.)

MILLER, A. W., 33602.   M.M.

MILLS, J. E., 14752.   Mention.   D.C.M.
For conspicuous good work and devotion
to duty throughout the campaign.

MILLWARD, J., 11670.   D.C.M.
When in charge of a section he led
his men with marked ability and coolness
under a heavy fire. His courage and devotion to duty have at all times been of the
highest order.

MILN, G. G.   Mention.   M.C.
He organized a piquet line, and commanding
outposts during a heavy attack by the
enemy. He never spared himself in his
duties, and by his brilliant powers of leadership and example of courage inspired the
greatest confidence in all his men (Captain Miln was killed in action almost immediately after winning his M.C.)

MILNE, J. R.
French War Cross with Palm.
D.F.C.
As a flying officer and flight commander,
Captain Milne has shown the greatest cool-
ness and determination, and has invariably
displayed qualities of leadership and com-
mand of a very high order.

MINSHALL, L., 12055.   M.M.

MINSHULL, G., 291488.
Croix de Guerre (Fr.)

MINSHULL, W., 49906.   M.M.

MIRAMS, W. E., 51232.   M.M.

MITCHELL, F., 265405.   M.M.   D.C.M.
At all times his conduct in action has been
worthy of praise. By his fearless disregard
of danger he rendered most valuable assistance to his company during critical operations.

MITCHELL, W. R., 241164.   M.M.

MILLER, W. V.   Mention.

MILLINGTON, J. C.
Promoted 2/Lieut.

MILLINGTON, L.   M.C.
He showed the greatest determination
when holding an advanced post during one

night and the whole of the next day, although heavily attacked by the enemy.

MILLS, E. J.   Mention.   O.B.E.

MILLS, R. W.   Mention (2).   M.C.

He commanded his company throughout the operations South-west of Cambrai, September, 1918, and was quick to seize opportunities to inflict loss on the enemy and to assist other troops. On 27th September, at Beaucamp, he pushed forward his company by covering fire, and rendered good service. On 28th September, he successfully attacked an enemy position held by machine-guns North of Gouzeaucourt. On 30th September, he led his company in a night attack on enemy trenches. Greatly owing to his conspicuously gallant and able leadership, the operation was successful. Owing to his careful arrangements and to his constantly collecting and reorganizing his company, fifty prisoners and a 7.7 m.m. gun were captured.

MOAT, G. W., 21769.   M.M.

MOFFAT, J., 200416.   M.M.

MOIR, A. R.   M.C.

During an attack he handled his company with great coolness and ability, capturing and holding all objectives with skill and deliberation. His services were of great value afterwards in reorganizing the battalion.

Croix de Chevalier, Legion of Honour.

MOIR, H. L.   Mention (3).   D.S.O.

He handled his battalion skilfully under most trying circumstances. On one occasion, although wounded in the side, he remained in command and was continuously under heavy fire, encouraging his men and supervising their movements. Later, he contributed largely to the success of operations by his courageous leadership.

Bar to D.S.O.

French Croix de Guerre with Palm.

MOLYNEUX, B.   M.C.

As scout officer, during the operations near Jenlain, November, 1918, when his battalion was attacking, he was continually backwards and forwards under very heavy artillery and machine-gun fire visiting platoons and assisting them to maintain direction. On one occasion he found a platoon, whose leaders had become casualties, pinned to the ground, took command, and with great courage led it forward.

MOLYNEUX, G., 15993.   M.M.

MOLYNEUX, G. W., 11002.   M.M.

MONTAGUE, G. R.   M.C.

During a determined enemy attack, when ammunition was urgently needed, he personally organised and supervised the carrying forward of stores and ammunition to the front line, in spite of a heavy enemy barrage. During the whole operations there is no doubt that the front line was kept supplied largely owing to his courage and powers of organization.

Bar to M.C.

During the operations near Moen on the 25th October, 1918, throughout the long advance of some 7,000 yards to the final objective, he acted as Adjutant, and under heavy fire performed his duty with great coolness. He went out under machine-gun fire to ascertain the latest situation in the front line and brought back very valuable information.

MONTAGUE-BATES, F. S.   Mention (2).   D.S.O.

Promoted Brevet-Lieut.-Colonel.
Legion of Honour.
Croix de Guerre (Fr.)

MOORE, G., 268111.   M.M.

MOORE, J., 13336.   D.C.M.

On the night of 6th/7th December, 1915, during a bombing attack near Carnoy, he was in charge of a " West " machine, and greatly assisted the attack by keeping up rapid fire. A lighted bomb dropped off the cap of the machine and would have caused many casualties, but Corporal Moore groped for it in the mud and had just time to throw it over the parapet when it exploded. This is not the first time he has been brought to notice for bravery.

MOORE, J., 6893.   Mention.

MOORE, J. R.   Mention.   M.C.

MOORE, L. A., 8498.   M.S.M.

MOORE, P., 13259.   M.M.

MOORES, A., 45751.   M.M.

MOORES, W., 290387.   M.M.

MORAN, J., 9539.
Italian Bronze Medal.

MORGAN, D., 39945.   M.M.

MORGAN, E.   M.C.

East of Marcoing on 31st October, 1918, he organized, and took out, a daylight patrol across the River Scheldt. He skilfully surprised a machine-gun post, capturing four prisoners and a light machine-gun, and, in face of intense machine-gun fire, obtained most valuable information of the enemy's positions. His courage and able leadership throughout were conspicuous, and his skill in a dangerous situation was most marked. He carried a wounded prisoner across a narrow plank over the river in spite of machine-gun fire.

MORGAN, J., 11003.   M.M.

MORGAN, S. F.   Mention.

MORGAN, T. H.   Mention.

MORLEY, A. L., 50830.   M.M.

MORLEY, F. P.   Mention.

MORRIS, A.   Mention.

MORRIS, B. F.   M.C.

During the attack on Beaurain, North of Le Cateau, on 23rd October, 1918, when the enemy barrage fell upon the company, he laboured indefatigably and exposed himself unsparingly. Later, when the right flank of the battalion was held up by heavy machine-gun fire, although severely wounded, he continued to direct operations from a shell hole, and by his fine example of courage inspired his men.

MORRIS, F., 50132.   M.M.

MORRIS, F. H.   M.B.E.

MORRIS, G. H., 53529.   M.M.

MORRIS, M., 27125.   M.M.

MORRIS, R. L., 49775.   M.M.

MORRISON, J. F., 240588.   M.M.

MORTLOCK, C., 266480.   M.S.M.

MORTON, E.   Mention.   O.B.E.
Promoted Brevet-Lieut.-Colonel.

MORTON, F., 24315.   M.M.

MORTON, R.   Mention (3).   M.C.
Greek Military Cross.

MORTON, R., 11892.   M.M.

MOSELEY, J. F., 253.
Italian Bronze Medal.

MOSES, M., 52861.   M.M.

MOSS, C.   Mention.

MOSS, C.   M.C.

He led his company with exceptional gallantry to its objective, which he reached in an hour, although continuously under fire, over a distance of 5,000 yards. He continued to lead his company against the enemy's support trenches, inflicting many casualties and materially assisting the success of the operation by his personal example and disregard of danger.

MOSS, F., 240083.   M.S.M.

MOSS, F. L., 200185.   M.M.
Medaille Militaire.

MOSS, L., 24095.   M.M.

MOSTYN, F., 1344.
Serbian Silver Medal.

MOTTERSHEAD, C., 290215.   M.M.

MOTTERSHEAD, H.   D.C.M.

He repaired wires and rescued several wounded men under intense fire, displaying great courage and determination. Later he rendered valuable assistance in reorganizing the position gained.

MOTTERSHEAD, J. A., 265414.   M.M.

MOUL, W. V.   Mention.

MOWBRAY, W. S., 19632.   Mention.

MOWLE, G. K.   Mention.   M.C.

He led his men with great dash in the attack, he was the first into the enemy's trenches, and immediately attacked the enemy with the bayonet. He afterwards reorganized his command and led them forward as a covering party. Throughout the day he showed great coolness and was at once on the spot where any danger was apprehended.

MULVANEY, J., 6308.   Mention

MUNNINGS, F. L., 20173.   M.M.

MURPHEY, H., 265596.   M.M.

MURPHY, D., 16040.   Mention.
Italian Bronze Medal.

MURPHY, J., 265663.   M.M.

MURPHY, J.   Mention.
Granted the next higher rate of pay.

MURPHY, W., 2344.   M.M.

MURRAY, F., 290127.   M.M.
MURT, J., 34011.   M.M.
MUSGRAVE, J. B.   M.C.

Immediately before an attack his company came under heavy barrage, and many casualties were caused. He went up and down through the barrage encouraging his men and setting them a splendid example. He then led his company successfully in the attack.

MUTCH, E., 16340.

Italian Bronze Medal.

D.C.M.

By his splendid example and complete disregard of danger, he gave invaluable help to his officer, and kept his men well together at a most trying and critical time. When his company was withdrawing he remained until the last, and issued orders for the covering fire. All this time he was working under heavy enemy fire.

MYCOE, A., 16260.   M.M.
NADEN, F.   Mention (3).   M.C.

He reorganized two companies and sent them forward to the final objective, thereby clearing up the situation at a critical time. He set a splendid example of coolness and courage.

Bar to M.C.

On several occasions during the operations, he went among the men, cheering them up, assisted the wounded, organized and took forward parties under heavy fire, regardless of danger to himself, and at all times was ready to render assistance in any way. He afterwards took over command of the battalion and brought them out. His conduct was magnificent throughout.

D.S.O.

When in temporary command of his battalion during an action, when the situation was obscure owing to the unit on his left having been held up, he made a thorough reconnaissance at great risk, and obtained valuable information. He then directed the attack of his battalion, capturing all his objectives. Throughout the day and the following days he went about under heavy shell and machine-gun fire, encouraging his men and directing the consolida-

tion. The skilful manner in which he handled a most difficult situation was a great factor in the success achieved.

Bar to D.S.O.

For three days he successfully kept the enemy out of a village, twice organizing counter-attacks after losing ground under constant and intense bombardments. It was largely owing to his personal gallantry and coolness that the village remained in our hands at the end of the enemy attacks.

NADIN, H., 50577.   M.M.
NAPIER, H. E.   Mention.
NARES, E. P.   Mention (3).   M.C.

When nearly all the officers of his battalion had become casualties he rendered invaluable service to his commanding officer in planning the assembly arrangements of his battalion, which subsequently took and held all its objectives in spite of having lost 60 per cent of its men. It was due to the example set by these two officers that the ground was maintained against many determined hostile counter-attacks, and after Major Nares had successfully established communication with other units on either flank, he was very severely wounded whilst returning to report to his commanding officer. His gallantry and devotion to duty deserved the highest praise.

Bar to M.C.

While commanding his battalion with great ability, he organized several attacks and counter-attacks, and maintained his position until practically surrounded by large forces of the enemy. When compelled to retire, he kept the battalion well in hand, and showed sound judgement in the selection of new positions. To be Brevet-Major.

NASON, E. R.   Mention.
NEEDHAM, J., 10543.   D.C.M.

On the 10th March, 1915, he volunteered to take a medical officer by daylight to attend to an officer who was reported to be bleeding to death in the trenches. Subsequently he assisted in an attempt to remove the officer by daylight, which proved impossible, but another attempt by night by Private Needham and the M.O. was successful, although the latter was wounded while getting the wounded officer away.

NELSON, G. E.   Mention.   D.S.O.

At a critical moment, when our advance was held up, he collected sufficient men to move forward and straighten the line. By his fine example and disregard for danger under heavy fire, he eventually led this line, which was composed of seven different units into the enemy's position.

NEWBY, R., 26483.   M.M.

NEWELL, F. W. M.   Mention (3).
D.S.O.   O.B.E.   M.C.
Ordre de la Couronne (Bel.)
Croix de Guerre (Bel.)

NEWTON, A., 8993.   M.M.

NEWTON, G., 51405.   M.M.

NEWTON, W. S., 15416.   M.S.M.
Greek Military Cross.

NICHOLS, E. B.   M.C.

Single handed he attacked, and captured, an enemy machine-gun, killing the two men who were firing the gun.

NICHOLSON, J., 29070.   Mention.

NICHOLSON, R.   M.C.

NICHOLSON, R. LE B.   M.C.

He led his company with great skill and dash to its objective, although under hostile fire from a flank. His company captured many prisoners.

Bar to M.C.

When his company was holding a sunken road, the enemy penetrated his right flank. He immediately organized a defensive flank, and held on to his position for several hours against repeated attacks accompanied by very heavy machine-gun fire until ordered to withdraw. He withdrew his company intact under cover of his Lewis gunners with very few casualties. He showed powers of command of a high order.

NIGHTINGALE, B., 51027.   M.M.

NINIS, F. A.   Mention.   M.C.

He led a raid against the enemy's trenches with great courage and determination.

NIXON, F., 8686.   M.S.M.

NIXON, W. H., 25828.   D.C.M.

On 1st October, 1915, near Vermelles, he threw bombs amongst the enemy during the whole day and night until he was the only one left out of the whole company. Private Nixon undoubtedly saved an officer's life on this day, by picking up a German bomb which was on the point of exploding close to him and hurling it back amongst the enemy.

NOBLE, A. F.   Mention.

NODEN, J. R., 10710.   Mention.   M.M.
Serbian Silver Medal.

NORMAN, C.   M.C.

NORMAN, R.   M.C.

He was in command of a party which carried out a raid on the enemy's lines. He personally led the party detailed for the demolition of a tunnel in the enemy's lines, and by his determination and good leadership successfully accomplished his task. He carried the preliminary training of the party, and the excellent results achieved were due to his efforts and personal example.

NORMAN, R. T.
Croix de Guerre (Bel.)

NORRIS, W. A., 8475.   Mention.   D.C.M.

On the 7th May, 1915, near " Hill 60," he voluntarily left a trench, crawled over an open space under an accurate fire from the enemy, and dragged in a wounded man. Later in the day he went out again, and brought in a wounded officer in spite of fire from numerous snipers.

M.M.

For bringing in wounded at Delville Wood, 19th August, 1916.

NORTHCOTE, P. M.   M.C.

NORTHROP, H., 13029.   M.M.

NORTON, T., 9163.   M.S.M.

NOTLEY, H., 9083.   D.C.M.

At Rue d'Ouvert, near Festubert, on 13th October, 1914, he behaved with the greatest gallantry during a period of 16 hours in the defence of a farm, in a very critical situation.

NUNN, C. P., 268164.   M.M.

NURSER, L., 57987.   M.M.

NYE, V. A.   Mention.
Medjidieh.

OAKLEY, J. E. E.   M.C.

OAKES, C.   Mention.

OATES, F., 33321.   Mention.   M.S.M.

OATTS, F. J.   M.C.

During a heavy bombardment by the enemy, he descended into a deep dug-out, which had been blown in and was on fire, to search for buried officers. Later, he gathered all the men he could find and held up an enemy attack for a considerable time.

O'CONNOR, P., 20767.   M.M.   D.C.M.

This N.C.O. in charge of a Lewis gun, attached to Company Headquarters, hearing that his company commander had been killed, rushed to the front, and, rallying the men, led them to attack a strong point. All his men becoming casualties, he went out and recovered the body of his officer, which was lying about forty yards from an enemy machine-gun in action. He showed great gallantry.

OFORD, A., 9290.   M.M.

OGDEN, E., 16097.   Mention (2).

OGDEN, G. H., 240124.   Mention.   M.M.

OGGIER, S. L., 34686.   Mention.

OLDFIELD, F., 10806.
Medaille Militaire.

OLDHAM, A., 10694.   M.M.

OLDMAN, R. D. F.   Mention (2).
C.M.G.   D.S.O.

OLLERENSHAW, S.   M.M.

O'NEILL, J., 10731.   Mention.

OPENSHAW, T. L., 3/33438.   Mention

ORME, A., 8421.   M.S.M.

OSTLER, J., 28352.   M.M.

OULTON, W. R.   A.F.C.

He has been employed in a squadron on Home Defence, and has taken part in defence against every hostile air raid there has been since March, 1917. Lieut. Oulton has shown great keenness and enthusiasm, has carried out his duties in an exemplary manner, and has given an excellent example to all others.

OWEN, L. W. G.   M.C.

Although wounded, he continued to command his company in an attack, and it was owing to his courage and determination that a strong point was captured with 50 prisoners and 14 machine-guns.

OWENS, E., 7788.   D.C.M.

At Ypres, on 16th November, 1915, he brought back under heavy fire from the enemy, only 80 yards away, an abandoned machine-gun, which had been left in a trench.

OWENS, E. W.   Mention.   D.C.M.

OXTON, J., 8425.   M.S.M.

PAGE, G., 11248.   Mention.

PAGE, W., 358390.   M.S.M.
Croix de Guerre.

PAKENHAM-WALSH, L. H.
Croix de Guerre (Fr.)

PALIN, A., 27253.   M.M.

PALIN, F., 26592.   Mention.

PALMEN, F. H.   M.C.

When in command of a company, and the troops on both flanks were forced back, he at once realised the situation, and withdrew his company to the support line, where he held the enemy. He then organized and led a successful counter-attack, regaining his original position and enabling the flanks to do likewise.

PAPWORTH, C., 59428.   M.S.M.

PARKER, H., 3/34667.   M.M.

PARKER, J., 13158.   Mention.   M.S.M.

PARKER, J., 19898.
Croix de Guerre (Fr.)

PARKER, H., 3/34667.   M.M.

PARKES, A., 290782.   M.M.

PARKHURST, R. G.   M.C.

He collected every available man near him and went forward, clearing the trench and capturing many of the enemy, at the same time joining up with three waves that had been reorganized, taking command and successfully leading them to their final objective.

PARKIN, L., 265031.   M.M.   M.C.

His dash and determination during the advance was responsible for putting several machine-guns out of action, thus clearing the way for the attacking waves. When all the officers of his company became casualties, he led the company in the most spirited manner and continued in command till they came out of action.

PARKIN, L., 717.   M.M.

PARR, C. J.
   Croix de Guerre (Fr.)

PARR, S., 290416.   Mention.   M.M.

PARRY, J. T.   M.C.
   When in command of 60 men to form a defensive flank guard to delay the enemy, he fearlessly exposed himself to encourage his men, and successfully commanded them until wounded. He set a splendid example of coolness to all.

PARSONS, W. S., 29548.
   Croix de Guerre (Bel.)

PARTINGTON, W.   Mention.   M.C.
   Italian Silver Medal for Valour.

PASCOE, W. H., 51175.   M.M.
PASSEY, G. A., 240211.   M.M.
PEACOCK, H., 240688.   M.M.
PEAKE, H., 58014.   M.M.
PEAKE, P., 290600.   M.S.M.
PEARCE, A., 9903.   D.C.M.
   For gallant conduct outside La Bassee in removing snipers (who were enfilading our trenches) from a house, and then holding possession of the house under heavy fire.

PEARSE, T. H. F.   Mention.   C.M.G.

PEARSON, B., 49014.   M.M.

PEARSON, C. E.   Mention

PEARSON, J., 13081.   Mention.   D.C.M.
   During a hostile attack on his post he was severely wounded, but refused to retire, making light of his wound, displaying the greatest courage, and setting a magnificent example to all ranks. On another occasion he voluntarily crossed 300 yards of open ground under heavy shell fire to assist a wounded man. His conduct throughout has been beyond praise.

PEARSON, J. H., 265538.   Mention (2).
   M.S.M.

PEMBERTON, A., 290788.   M.M.
PEMBERTON, C. A., 18525.   M.M.
PEMBERTON, J.   Mention (2).
PEMBERTON, J. A.   Mention (2).
   Croix de Guerre (Fr.)
   Order of the Nile.

PEMBERTON, R., 40276.   M.M.
PEMBERTON, T., 50001.   M.M.

PERFIELD, F., 290435.   Mention.
PERRIN, E. C.   O.B.E.
PERRIN, F., 50875.   M.M.
PHILLIPS, E., 17681.   M.M.
PHILLIPS, F., 34574.   M.M.
PHILLIPSON, T., 33623.   M.M.
PHYTHIAN, H., 8327.   M.S.M.
PICKERSGILL, J. H.   M.C.
   When Brigade Intelligence Officer, he performed invaluable service in reporting enemy movements and pointing out important landmarks, etc., to artillery and infantry observers. While thus engaged, he displayed great energy and disregard of personal danger.

PICKUP, C., 265482.   M.M.
PICKFORD, J., 291565.   M.S.M.
PIERCE, G., 875.
   Croix de Guerre (Fr.)

PILKINGTON, G. E.   Mention (2).
PIMBLOTT, W., 52661.   M.M.
PINNEGAR, W. C., 11062.   M.M.
PINQUEY, J. D.   M.C.
   This officer reached his final objective, reorganized his company under heavy artillery and machine-gun fire, and sent back valuable reports. When forced back with only four survivors, he reported at Battalion Headquarters and was sent to reorganize his men on a ridge, which the enemy were endeavouring to capture. He showed marked resolution throughout.

PITCHER, W., 26118.   M.M.
PLANT, H., 12050.   Mention.
PLATT, C.   M.C.
   He collected men from his own and other units and organized them as a consolidating party and dug in under heavy fire. He showed great initiative and skill in handling his men under very difficult conditions.

PLOWMAN, W. A.   M.B.E.
POCOCK, A. W.   Mention.
PODMORE, F. W., 11807.   Mention.   M.S.M.
POGSON, A.   Mention.
POGSON, L. V. J.   M.C.
   He led his company with great skill and determination throughout the operations.

W

He obtained valuable information before the attack. Later, he organized stretcher parties and carried out his work with great energy. He set a splendid example of coolness and initiative to his men.

POINTON, W. S., 6648.   M.S.M.

POLLIT, J., 13036.   M.M.
Greek Military Cross.

POLLITT, L., 1308.   D.C.M.
During the night of 24th March, 1915, he assisted in bringing into safety a non-commissioned officer and two men who were lying in the open under fire.
Russian Medal of St. George, 3rd Class.

POMEROY, H.   Mention (2).   M.C.

POOLE, R. W. F.   M.C.
In the attack on "P" ridge on the 18th September, 1918, he led his platoon forward under intense fire, and his coolness and contempt for danger inspired the greatest confidence in his command. He was wounded, but carried on, rallying his men until practically all had become casualties. Left wounded in the enemy lines, he succeeded in escaping under continuous fire from machine-guns and snipers, and was the last officer to leave the ridge. His courage and tenacity were splendid.
Legion D'Honneur Chevalier.

POTTER, H., 50437.   M.S.M.   M.M.

POTTS, R., 10733.   Mention.   M.M.

POTTS, S., 50793.   M.M.

POTTS, T., 265800.   M.M.

POWELL, G., 49087.   M.M.

POWER, K. F. M.   M.C.

POWER, P., 50109.   M.M.

POXON, S., 18315.   M.M.

PRATT, J. J., 242740.   M.M.

PRICE, J., 240874.   M.M.

PRICE, J. C., 200239.   M.M.

PRICE, T., 1687.   M.M.

PRICE, T., 10931.   Mention.   D.C.M.
Near Sari Bair, Gallipoli Peninsula, on 18th Aug., 1915. Sergeant Price and Private Marshall attended to wounded men under heavy fire.

PRICE, J., 27826.   M.M. and Bar.

PRICE, T., 200338.   M.M.

PRICE, W., 267859.   M.M.

PRIEST, E., 20518.   M.M.

PRIESTNER, W., 52699.   M.M.

PRINCE, C. W., 66328.   Mention.

PRING, F. J. H.   Mention (2).   M.C.
Bar to M.C.
He displayed great initiative and coolness under heavy fire, and it was entirely owing to his prompt action in turning the enemy's flank that the position was eventually captured.

PRITCHARD, T. E., 19131.   M.M.

PRYER, J. W., 200895.   M.M.

PUGH, E. A., 18282.   M.M.

QUARMBY, H., 266763.   M.M.

QUAYLE, H. E.   M.C.
During an attack on the enemy's lines the situation had become very obscure. He therefore went out with another officer in broad daylight, under heavy fire, and carried out a most difficult and dangerous reconnaissance, bringing back information of the highest value to his commanding officer.
Bar to M.C.
He led his company with great skill to their final objective. He showed not only great courage and contempt of danger, but a remarkable grasp of the situation, and the information and reports which he sent back were excellent. He organized and personally superintended the consolidation of the position, which was completed in spite of heavy enemy fire.

QUINE, S. L.   M.C.
He went out in exceptionally rough and stormy weather during an attack, and, flying very low over the enemy's batteries, reported and located those which were in action. By his courageous and determined efforts he assisted materially in clearing up the situation and enabled effective fire to be brought to bear on the enemy's batteries.

RACHUS, N.
Greek Military Cross.

RADLEY, O. A.   Mention.   M.C.

RANDALL, H. C.   Mention.

RANSOME, H. L.   Mention.

RANSOME, H. N.   M.C.

RATCLIFFE, D., 11572.   Mention.

RATCLIFFE, L., 3354. M.M..
Belgian Decoration Militaire.

RAYNOR, A. D.C.M.

READ, W. L. M.C.

READE, A. Mention. D.S.O. M.C.

READE, W. P. Mention.

REED, J., 20825. D.C.M. M.M.
During a very severe engagement he rallied the remnants of other platoons as well as his own, and, steadying them with his own cool and confident bearing he was able with this mixed forced to hold a gap in the centre of the line and assist the flanks that were sorely pressed.
He has been at the front for over two years, and his gallantry and cheerful courage have been an example to all ranks on many occasions.

REEKIE, A., 3461. M.M.

REES, J., 72067. M.M.

REEVES, J. M. Mention.

REGAN, T., 51532. M.M.

RETALLICK, R. T. D.S.O.
Near Kemmel, on the 20th September, 1918, while in charge of a raiding party of ten men engaged in bombing some dug-outs, he was severely wounded. In spite of this, he refused to be attended to until he had accomplished his task, in daylight, under rifle and machine-gun fire from both flanks. One of his party was killed and two wounded.

REYNOLDS, G., 12663. Mention (2).

REYNOLDS, H., 45372. M.M.

RHODES, A., 51540. M.M.

RHODES, A., 262161. M.M.

RHODES, W., 265576. D.C.M.
He led his platoon with the utmost skill and fearlessness, doing most valuable work and showing remarkable judgment and powers of leadership. He set a splendid example to his men.

RICH, W. S. Mention (2).

RICHARDS, C., 28234. Mention. M.M.

RICHARDSON, A. E., 203226. M.M.

RICHARDSON, G. W. Mention.

RICHARDSON, H., 28236. Mention.

RICHARDSON, R., 19204. M.M.

RICHARDSON, T., 25642. M.M.

RICHMOND, L. Mention.
Croix de Guerre.
D.S.O.
As Battalion Intelligence Officer he carried out many valuable reconnaissances before the attack on the " P " Ridge. He taped out the assembly positions of the leading battalion in Jackson's Ravine and carried out his duties with such skill that the assembly of the brigade proceeded in perfect order. After the attack had developed, he assumed command of a company which had lost its leaders and rallied them under intense fire. Later, under very heavy fire, he remained with his C.O. who had been mortally wounded. He showed marked courage throughout.

RIDDELL, G. A. Mention (2). M.C.

RIDDLES, A., 8805. M.M. and Bar.

RIDDLESWORTH, H., 50184. Mention.
M.S.M.

RIDING, F., 34581. M.M.

RIDING, W., 34597. D.C.M.

RIDLEY, J. H., 8857. Mention.

RILEY, H., 260232. M.M.

RILEY, J., 8/11222. M.M.

RILEY, W., 29184. Mention.

RILEY, W. D. Mention.

RISLEY, 201764. M.M.

RIVETT, E. Mention.

RIXON, J., 200530. M.M.

ROBBINS, J. L. Mention.

ROBERTS, A. E., 79110. M.M.

ROBERTS, F. D.C.M.
Promoted 2/Lieut.

ROBERTS, H., 58979. D.C.M.
When cut off from his battalion by an enemy counter-attack, he collected a few men and successfully withdrew them across a river and again forded the river to rejoin his battalion.

ROBERTS, J. F., 36717. M.M.

ROBERTS, T., 8824. M.M.

ROBERTS, W., 266497. Mention.

ROBINSON, A. M. G. Mention.

ROBINSON, C. C.   M.C.

In charge of two forward machine-guns West of Moeuvres, from the 22nd to 27th September, 1918, on three occasions when our post was driven in, he kept it and our approaches constantly under direct fire, denying it reinforcements from the enemy. His guns were at the time exposed to direct observation and heavy shelling from the enemy.

ROBINSON, F.   M.M.

ROBINSON, H., 12678.   M.M.

ROBINSON, J., 11107.   M.M.

ROBINSON, J., 13281.   M.M.

ROBINSON, J., 200676.   M.M.

ROBINSON, J., 32563.   M.M.

ROBINSON, J.   D.C.M.

He has shown at all times a devotion to duty and an example of courage which has inspired all men under him.

ROBINSON, J. C., 52301.   Mention.

ROBINSON, J. C., 52744.   M.M.

ROBINSON, R., 19794.   M.M.

ROBINSON, S., W/1094.   M.M.

ROBINSON, T., 437.   M.M.

ROBINSON, W., 24798.   M.M.

ROBINSON, W., 265278.   M.M.

ROBINSON, W. A., 29716.   M.M.

ROCHELLE, T. H., 266102.   M.M.

RODDY, E. L.   Mention.

ROEBUCK, F.

Promoted 2/Lieut.

ROGERS, J. W., 49219.   M.M.

ROGERSON, J., 200342.

Croix de Guerre (Fr.)

RONSON, G., 16529.   M.M.

ROSE, J. W., 19590.   Mention.   M.M.

ROSTRON, R.   Mention.

ROTHWELL, E. N.

Croix de Guerre (Bel.)

ROTHWELL, H., 290795.   M.M.

ROUSE, E.   M.C.

During the barrage in the attack on Moen in October, 1918, he was wounded, but for 3 hours led his company resolutely in the face of machine-gun and rifle fire and

advanced his line between 3,000 and 4,000 yards. Before being sent back to have his wound dressed, he gave the C.O. a very clear and accurate report of the situation.

ROWE, H. W. W.   M.C.

During a raid on the enemy's trenches, he was the first to enter the trench, and himself accounted for five of the enemy. He then organized the clearing of the trench with marked coolness and ability, with the result that heavy casualties were inflicted on the enemy.

ROWLEY, G.   M.C.

During a raid, his conduct throughout the whole of the operations was of the highest order, and it was due to his splendid leadership and personal example that the objective was reached after overcoming all opposition. He has previously done good work on similar occasions.

Bar to M.C.

Throughout eleven days' operations this officer showed exceptional powers of leadership and the greatest disregard of danger in reorganizing the line and encouraging the men during successive withdrawals. On one occasion he organized and led a counter-attack, inflicting severe casualties on the enemy, and reaching his objective.

ROWBOTHAM, G., 265434.   M.M.

ROXBY, J., 10049.   M.M.

ROYLE, H., 18306.   D.C.M.

Although severely wounded, he cleared the enemy trench and reorganized the position, and by his example and resource rendered most valuable service.

ROYLE, J. W., 240606.   M.M.

RUDD, T., 35220.   Mention.

Croix de Guerre (Bel.)

RUDDIN, L. G.   M.C.

He led his company with great dash and determination, sweeping aside all opposition and inflicting heavy casualties on the enemy. Though wounded he continued to lead his men to the final objective, until he had to withdraw exhausted. His conduct throughout the whole operation was a splendid example to all.

RUSHTON, A., 12264.   M.M. and Bar.

Promoted 2/Lieut.

RUTTER, E. C. V.   Mention.

RYALLS, H. D.   Mention.   D.S.O.

He held on to his position during a very heavy bombardment. Though he had suffered heavy casualties, and was attacked by strong forces of the enemy on both flanks, he handled his company and machine-gun with such skill that the attacks were repulsed with great loss.

RYAN, J.

Promoted Major

RYAN, L., 6938.   D.C.M.

When a portion of a trench was blown in by a trench mortar and the garrison cut off. Later he went over the parapet and carried in wounded men under heavy machine-gun fire.

SALMON, H. M.   M.C.

SALMON, J. D.   M.C.

SAMBROOK, G. A., 243237.   Mention. M.S.M.

SANDHAM, B., 268032.   M.M.

SANDS, J., 19479.   M.M.

SANKEY, P., 18059.   M.M.

SAUNDERS, J. P., 68217.   M.M.

SCARRATT, N.   M.C.

He took command of his company during an advance and led them forward to the final objective with great dash and skill. He handled his men with great ability, which contributed largely to the success achieved by his battalion.

SCHEERS, G., W/115.   M.M.

SCHOLES, A. H., 40930.   M.M.

SCOTT, 6024.   M.S.M.

SCOTT, R., 23378.   M.S.M.

SCOTT, R. M. L.   M.C.

SCOTT, W. H.   D.C.M.   M.M.

SEATON, J., 1637.   M.M.

SEATON, W., 266559.   M.M.

SECKER, E., 266451.   D.C.M.

SEDDON, F., 35000.   M.M.

SEELEY, J., 17550.   M.S.M.

SEGAR, F. E.   M.C.

Although wounded in an advance, he attacked a superior number of the enemy, and in hand-to-hand fighting with bombs and bayonet accounted for three of the enemy.

SELBY, G., 15592.   Mention.

SELLARS, E. F.   Mention.   M.C.

SENIOR, 13749.   M.M.

SERNBERG, C., 11792.   M.S.M.

SEVERS, J. J., W/86.   M.M.

SEYFERTH, C. A., 200897.   M.M.

SEYMOUR, C., 29348.   Mention.

SHACKLADY, T., 21987.   M.M.

SHACKLEY, A., 265921.   D.C.M.

He led a flank attack on the enemy and accounted for several of them himself with the bayonet. Throughout the operation his assistance was invaluable to his company commander, and his dash and determination cheered the men and set them a splendid example.

SHAKERLEY, W.   Mention.

SHAMBROOK, F. W., 27665.   M.M.

SHANKEY, P., 18059.   M.M.

SHANNON, J., 8653.   D.C.M.

For gallant conduct in continually conveying messages under shell and rifle fire.

SHAW, C. C.   Mention.

SHAW, E., 14983.
Medaille D'Honneur.

SHAW, F., 13622.
Italian Bronze Medal for Military Valour.

SHAW, F., 290892.   M.M.

SHAW, H. V.   M.C.

Whilst in command of a daylight patrol, he visited three hostile posts, and finding the first two unoccupied, he pushed on to the third, which he rushed, capturing six prisoners, gaining valuable information, and bringing back his patrol without casualties. His determined leadership and personal courage were deserving of high praise.

SHAW, M. A., 200068.   D.C.M.

He held an important position with his platoon under heavy shell fire, though without rations and water. He set a fine example of courage and initiative.

SHAW, P., 44192.   M.M.

SHAW, R., 11089.   M.M.

SHAW, R. L.   M.M.

SHAW, T., 11742.   M.M.

SHAW, T. C., 291196.   M.M.

SHAW, W., 17337.   D.C.M.

On the 25th September, 1915, near Festubert, when a retirement was ordered, he helped a wounded officer back to safety behind our parapet. He then heard that the officer whose servant he was, was wounded, and at once went out again to his assistance under an exceptionally accurate and heavy machine-gun and rifle fire, being himself wounded in so doing.

SHAY, F., 51456.   M.M.

SHEARD, J. W., 268012.   D.C.M.

As a runner he performed his duties in a gallant and fearless manner, on more than one occasion acting as a guide to reinforcements, guiding them to their positions during most critical periods. He went about continually under the heaviest bombardments, setting a splendid example. On one occasion he brought in a wounded comrade from an exposed position.

SHEASBY, J. H., 19381.
Croix de Guerre (Bel.)

SHELDON, P.   Mention (2).   M.C.

SHEPHERD, E. C., 51002.   M.M.

SHEPHERD, G. T., 51430.   M.M.

SHEPHERD, T., 6031.   M.S.M.

SHERLOCK, D. J., 30743.   M.M.

SHOOTER, W.   Albert Medal.

On April 8th, 1916, while bombing instruction was being given in a trench occupied by two officers, Sergt.-Major Shooter and a private, the private, who was about to throw a bomb from which he had withdrawn the safety pin, dropped it. Without giving any warning of what had occurred, he ran away. After about two seconds had elapsed Sergt.-Major Shooter saw the bomb. He could easily have escaped round the traverse, but in order to save the others he seized the bomb and threw it away. It exploded in the air before Sergt.-Major Shooter could take cover, wounding him. By risking his life he undoubtedly saved the two officers who were with him in the trench from serious or fatal injury.

SHORE, J. L.   Mention (2).   D.S.O.
Legion of Honour.

SIDAWAY, F. E.   M.C.

He commanded a company in the attack on "P" ridge on the 18th September, 1918. His company came under intense fire from machine-guns and trench mortars, and suffered heavy casualties, and he himself was wounded. He rallied his men under circumstances of the greatest difficulty, and led them forward with great determination until hit a second time. He set a fine example to all.

White Eagle, 5th Class, Serbia.

SIDDALL, J. W., 12485.   M.M.

SIDDALL, R., 267956.   M.M.

SIDDONS, J.   M.M.   D.C.M.

During the attack no information about the enemy forthcoming, Sergt. Siddons made his way through very heavy shell fire and gas up to the front line, returning with valuable information.

M.C.

When the enemy made a surprise attack on the position, he got a machine-gun into action, and with it materially assisted in the repulse of the enemy. During the next two days, while the enemy were attacking, he went along the line under heavy machine-gun and shell fire encouraging the men. Throughout the whole operations he showed leadership and determination of a high order.

SILLENDER, I., 52273.   D.C.M.

When in charge of a Lewis gun team, by his skilful and daring action, he killed and wounded a whole machine-gun team of the enemy which had been passed over in an emplacement and had opened fire on us from the rear. His prompt initiative saved several casualties.

SILVESTER, L.   Mention.

SIM, J., 51312.   M.M.

SIMMONS, J. A.   M.C.   Mention.

He led his company with great courage and initiative, himself accounting for several of the enemy. He set a splendid example to his men throughout the operations.

D.S.O.

During an attack he led his Battalion with find dash and leadership and gained his objective. Owing to both flanks being in the air he was obliged to order a withdrawal, which he covered together with 20 men. He eventually personally got in touch with his flanks and organized a defensive position. He displayed courage of a high order and set a splendid example to all.

SIMPSON, E., 265424.   Mention.   M.S.M.

SINGLETON, W. H., 2236.   Mention.

SKELSEY, 33076.   Mention.

SKELTON, J., 16919.   Mention.

SKERMERS, H., 265582.   M.M.

SKILLICORN, W., 240072.   M.M.

SKUSE, F. A., 265039.   M.M.

SLACK, T. R.   44125.   D.C.M.

He fired his machine-gun at point blank range and killed the whole of an enemy gun team, thereby enabling the clearing of the enemy front line to be successfully accomplished.

SLATER, W., 290747.
Croix de Guerre (Fr.)

SMALLWOOD, T. N.   M.C.

During four days' operations he was indefatigable in his efforts in maintaining communications between brigades and battalions, laying lines over difficult ground in trying conditions of mist, and making repairs under heavy shell and machine-gun and snipers' fire. It was entirely due to Lieut. Smallwood's courage, initiative and devotion to duty under circumstances of great difficulty that forward communication was maintained throughout the operations.

SMETHURST, H., 27760.   Mention.

SMITH, A., 7173.   Mention.   M.S.M., D.C.M.

He carried ammunitions to the trenches under very heavy shell fire. On another occasion he carried a wounded man under heavy shell fire to a place of safety.

SMITH, A., 26094.   M.S.M.

SMITH, A., 290733.   M.M.

SMITH, A. W., 10/13627.   D.C.M.

As Medical Officer's assistant, he endeavoured to rescue, under heavy fire, an officer who was lying wounded close to the enemy's lines. He finally succeeded in bringing in the body. He was himself wounded while assisting a wounded man to the aid post.

SMITH, C.   Mention.   M.C.

SMITH, D.   Mention.

SMITH, G. W., 50835.   Mention.

SMITH, C. H. P., 11828.   M.M.

SMITH, J., 8603.   D.C.M.

During the advance on Kemmel he led his platoon forward about 1,000 yards through difficult country full of machine-guns and snipers and remained in command for 8 hours after he was wounded, superintending consolidation of the line.

SMITH, J., 16861.   M.M. and Bar.

SMITH, J. D., 201205.   M.M.

SMITH, J. H., 7941.   D.C.M.

SMITH, J. P. G., 31679.   Mention.

SMITH, Ronald King.   Mention.   D.S.O., M.C.

SMITH, S.
Promoted 2/Lieut.

SMITH, S. H.   Mention (2).   M.C.

SMITH, T., 63744.   M.M.

SMITH, W., 290791.   M.M.

SMITH, W., 200249.   D.C.M.

SMITH, W., 244734.   M.M.

SMITH, W., 20501.   M.M.

SMITH, W. J.   M.M.

SMYTH, H.   Mention (3).   D.S.O.
Croix de Guerre.
Greek Medal for Military Merit.

SNOOK, A. G., 53233.   M.M.

SNOW, O., 28452.
Croix de Virtute Militara.

SOMERSET, F. R. A.   M.C.

At Le Touquet salient on 29th December, 1915, he was one of a successful fighting patrol which raided the enemy's trenches. Although shot through the right forearm and wounded in the head by a portion of a bomb, he remained at his post and continued to throw bombs till ordered to retire.

SOTMAH, F. A..   Mention

SOULS, A. W., 21683.   M.M.

SOUTHAM, W. A., 52584.   M.M.

SOUTHERN, J., 8726.   M.M.

SPARKS, R., 17971.   M.M.

SPARLING W. H.,   M.C.

He led his company in the attack with great courage and determination and captured his objective. He set a splendid example throughout.

SPEARING, J. G.

Promoted 2/Lieut.

SPEED, W., 14372.   M.M.

When in charge of a bombing party at Stuff Redoubt on the 9th October, 1916, he captured with his party 150 yards of trench and held it in spite of repeated counter-attacks.

SPENCE, C. H.   M.C.

While covering the advance of his battalion, he rendered very valuable service by bringing his guns into action on the flanks. He brought them up at great personal risk. He then went forward with the assault, and by his prompt action located and knocked out an enemy field gun.

SPENCE, E. E.   M.C.

He carried out his duties as transport officer with great determination under most difficult conditions and heavy shell fire. On two occasions, when several of his animals became casualties, his coolness and example were the means of saving the convoy, and his conduct was at all times a splendid example to his men.

SPENCER, A., 51735.   M.M.

Croix de Guerre (Fr.)

SPENCER, A. W., 44269.   M.M.

SPENCER, E., 60132.   Mention.

SPENCER, J. N., 51022.   M.M.

SPENCER, W., 7963.   Mention.

SPROULE, J. C.   Mention (4).   M.C.

Granted the next higher rate of pay.

Promoted Major.

SQUIRES, A.   M.C.

He led his platoon with great ability throughout an attack. When a withdrawal became necessary, owing to the position being outflanked, he secured the safety of the right flank of the battalion by the boldness and skill with which he pushed forward his Lewis guns, and inflicted heavy losses on the enemy. He set a splendid example to his men.

STAFFORD, F. S.   M.C.

During the action on 25th October, 1918, near Moen, after his company commander had been wounded, he led his company forward with fine courage and dash although his left flank was exposed. It was entirely due to him that his company reached its final objective some 7,000 yards from the start, and consolidated their exposed posts in the presence of the enemy, under heavy artillery and machine-gun fire.

STANLEY, J., 13162.   M.M.

STANSBY, H., 291330.

Croix de Guerre (Fr.)

STANWAY, W. H.   Mention (5).   M.C.
D.S.O.

When the enemy exploded a large mine which wrecked some 75 yards of our trench, and then attacked in force after bombarding the spot heavily, Captain Stanway at once took charge and, after the enemy had been driven off, with great skill and coolness organized the defences.

Bar to D.S.O.

He handled his Battalion in the attack with great courage and ability. He captured the position, inflicted much loss on the enemy, and took a large number of prisoners.

Promoted Brevet-Major and Brevet-Lt.-Col.

STAPLES, T. W. H., 31523.   Mention.

STELFOX, J.

Croix de Guerre (Fr.)

STEPHENSON, C.   Mention.

STEPHENSON, T., 33580.   M.M.

STEVENS, A. E., 7714.   M.M.

STEVENS, C., 58398.

Croix de Guerre.

D.C.M.

During a raid on a village in the enemy's lines, he led the first wave of his platoon and directed the bombing and searching of the houses with great skill, capturing several prisoners. Though wounded, he refused to leave his men, and set them a magnificent example of courage and resource.

STEVENS, N., W/308.   M.M.

STEWARD, C., 51083.   M.M.

STEWARD, H.   M.C.

During the operations near Menin on 14th October, 1918, he led his platoon with great courage and skill. In the mist and smoke, several strong points had been passed by the first waves, and he surrounded and captured these places, together with several prisoners. Having completed his task, he collected his men and filled up a gap in the line, establishing communication with the unit on his right.

STOCKTON, H., 291148.   M.M.

STOCKTON, E.

Croix de Guerre (Fr.)
M.C.

In the attack on " P " ridge on the 18th September, 1918, his platoon objective was on " P " 3, and reaching " P " 4 they came under intense fire from machine-guns, trench mortars and bombs. His platoon suffered heavy casualties, and he himself was wounded, but he rallied his men and led them forward with the greatest determination. Severely wounded a second time, he still carried on until compelled to give in through exhaustion and loss of blood. He showed splendid pluck and devotion to duty.

STOKES, J. C., 49705.   M.M.

STOLTE, W. G., 2310.   M.M.

STONE, A. B.   Mention.

STONE, J. T., 2329.   M.M.

STONEY, W., 202243.   M.M.

STOTT, H.   Mention.

STOTT, W.   M.C.

For bold reconnaissance work on the 21st September, 1918, near Wytschaete. He discovered a machine-gun post in a crater in front of the enemy line, and, organizing a party unobserved rushed the post, shooting one man, taking two prisoners, while the rest ran away.

STRACHEN, K. J., 50989.   M.M.

STRATFORD, G. F. F., 11324.   M.S.M.

STRETCH, J., 10565.   Mention.

STUART, E. M.   M.C.

STUBBS, A., 290763.   Mention.   D.C.M.

Throughout the advance against an enemy position, he was always well in front of his section, and at the final " run in," raced his company commander to the enemy trench. His splendid example greatly assisted in maintaining the advance.

STUBBS, A., 2785.

Serbian Cross of Karageorge.

STUBBS, R., 26541.   M.M.

STUTTARD, A., 6178.   M.M.

SUMNER, J. G., 2830.   Mention.

SUTCLIFFE, A. J.   M.C.   Mention.

SUTHERLAND, H. H.   Mention.

Promoted 2/Lieut.

SUTHERLAND, N.   M.C.

Having led his platoon to its objective with complete success, he personally went forward to reconnoitre another position, through heavy machine-gun and rifle fire, by his fine example and contempt of danger greatly rallying his party, who had become disorganized by hostile fire. Later, on being relieved, he refused to go back himself until he had clearly explained the situation to the relieving troops.

SUTTON, A., 7701.   D.C.M.

For conspicuous gallantry and devotion when a portion of a trench was blown up by a trench mortar and the garrison cut off. Later he went over the parapet and carried in wounded men under heavy machine-gun fire.

SUTTON, J. W., 265543.   M.M.

SWALLOW, P. A.   M.C.

When in charge of a forward post, which the enemy attempted to rush, he, by his gallantry and fearless example, prevented the enemy from breaking into the work. Though attacked on three sides, his coolness alone during a critical period saved the situation.

Bar to M.C.

On 3rd September, 1918, in front of Mont Kemmel, he led his company forward several hundred yards although unsupported by the company on his flank. He then went on in command of a daylight patrol, reaching a point far in rear of the enemy, from which he was able to count the garrison and number of machine-guns, and return without a casualty.

SWASH, J., 30344.   D.C.M.

During an attack, although nearly blinded with tear gas, he led his men most gallantly, cheering them on and rallying them at the final position. His party captured 30 prisoners and his work throughout the day was magnificent and set a splendid example to the men.

SWEENEY, F., 1647.   Mention.

SWIFT, W.   M.C.

During several days in operations, until he was wounded, in charge of the Battalion signals, he displayed the utmost courage and skill in maintaining communications with the rear and flanks, and it was mainly due to his untiring efforts that such communications was maintained throughout the operations. His splendid example under most trying conditions was an invaluable aid to his men.

SWINDELLS, G. H.   Mention (2).

Russian Order of St. Stanislas (3rd class).
Russian Order of St. Stanislas (2nd class).

SWINDELLS, J., 18916.   M.M.

SYKES, J., 52994.   M.M.

SYME, W. S.   M.C.

SYMONS, G. G.   M.C.

TAGGART, A. E., 33769.   M.M.

TAIT, J. A., 200431.   Mention.

TASKER, P. T., 9078.   D.C.M.

In action, whilst firing a Lewis gun, he noticed that the disabled 2.95-in. gun was being left, and attracted the attention of Lieut. Gardner to it, who went back for some men and dragged it out of the enemy's reach. Meanwhile Sergt. Tasker was keeping the enemy off with his Lewis gun, with which he undoubtedly did great execution. Lieut. Gardner and this N.C.O. were entirely responsible for saving the gun.

TAYLOR, A. J.   Mention.

TAYLOR, C., 9327.   Mention.

TAYLOR, F., 8776.   Mention.

TAYLOR, F. J.   Mention.

TAYLOR, G., 293136.   M.M.

TAYLOR, H., 14532.   Mention.

TAYLOR, J., 29379.   M.S.M.

TAYLOR, J. M., W/990.   M.M.

TAYLOR, T., 7/18016.   M.M.

TAYLOR, T., 52464.   M.M.

TAYLOR, T. B., 244412.   M.M.

TEDCASTLE, R.   M.C.

He showed fine determination and courage, although suffering much from a shell splinter and refused to leave his platoon until the engagement was over. He organized his men on the advanced line, and personally took several patrols forward to the enemy's position and obtained valuable information.

TELLETT, W., 16799.   M.M.   M.S.M.

TEMPLE, E. L. M., 24864.   D.C.M.

He organized attacks on machine-gun posts which were holding up the advance, and, until wounded, energetically assisted in leading the company to its final objective. His personal example of courage and determination was a great encouragement to the men.

TEMPLETON, R., 49579.   M.M.

THELWELL, J. J., 28445.

Croix de Guerre (Fr.)

THISTLETHWAITE, T. V. C.   Mention.

THOMAS, D. B.   Mention (2).   O.B.E.

THOMAS, D. R.   Mention.   M.C.

THOMAS, F., W/885.   M.M.

THOMAS, J. H., 16/20741.   Mention.

THOMAS, W. A., 11327.   D.C.M.

During an attack he set a splendid example to his men, leading them in the assault close to the barrage. When the trench had been captured he did splendid work in organizing the consolidation of the position.

THOMPSON, F., 8823.   D.C.M.

Near Ypres, on 4th March, 1915, he was wounded in the trenches, but refused to be taken away as he knew that his battalion was short of telephone operators. He remained there for 24 hours on duty till his company was relieved, and then was taken to hospital.

THOMPSON, H. J., 242367. M.M.

THOMPSON, J., 7001. Mention.

THORNLEY, 50540. M.M.

THORNTON, C. E., 14970. M.M.

THORP, H. O. C. Mention.

THORPE, A., 3/10735. Mention.

TICKLER, W. M. Mention (2). M.C.

When his company was held up by rifle and machine-gun fire, he held the line reached in spite of two determined counter-attacks and very heavy casualties. At dusk, when his left flank became dangerously exposed, he skilfully withdrew the remainder of his company.

Bar to M.C.

When his company was attacked by vastly superior numbers, he moved about in the open, encouraging and rallying his men. By his determination and courage, the attack was arrested and heavy casualties inflicted on the enemy.

TIERNEY, H., 25918. Mention.

TIMLIN, J., 265544. M.M.

TISSINGTON, C. F. M.C.

When in command of a party told off to construct a bombing block during an attack, he attacked, single handed, four of the enemy, killing two and wounding another. When wounded himself he refused to leave the captured trench until ordered to do so. He set a fine example of courage, dash, and promptitude to his men.

D.S.O.

During the operations before Zandvooide on 29th September, 1918, after securing the high ground in front as a jumping off point for other troops, he pushed forward his Lewis guns so as to neutralise enemy machine-guns when the attack was launched. Thanks to his pluck and initiative the attack made good progress.

TITLEY, J., 1589. M.M.

TITLEY, M. M. T., 265418. M.S.M.

TITTERTON, F., 45830. M.M.

TOD, A. G. W. Mention.

TOMLINSON, G., 291395. M.M.

TONGE, R. D. M.C.

He led his company forward amidst darkness, dust and gas, and captured twenty-five of the enemy with the aid of two of his men. His spirit and dash throughout the day was splendid.

TOOKER, H. W. M.C.

During an attack, he gained his objective, taking many prisoners and consolidating the position in the face of heavy fire. Later, he took command of the whole outpost line, and held it against hostile counter-attacks, after heavy gas bombardment.

TOPLISS, J. H., 52995. M.M.

TOWNSEND, A., 14312. Mention.

TOYNE, E. S., 3/28152. M.M.

Croix de Guerre (Fr.)

TRESTRAIL, A. E. Y. Mention (2).

D.S.O.

During the operations East of Terhand on the 14th October, 1918, he led his men to the attack in the most determined way, and when heavy hostile machine-gun fire was encountered from numerous strong-points, he got his men to surround them and either killed or captured the occupants. His marked gallantry, cheeriness and initiative were largely responsible for the objective being carried promptly.

TRICKEY, T., 52635. M.M.

TROBRIDGE, J., 8368. D.C.M.

When all the officers of his company became casualties, he took over command. Throughout the fighting he showed great courage, initiative and resource and was a fine example to his men.

Bar to D.C.M.

After all the officers of his company had become casualties he attained and held his objective until ordered to withdraw. His coolness and courage under very trying circumstances were most exceptional.

TROUGHTON-DEAN, G. R. Mention

Croix de Guerre (Fr.)

TRUEMAN, D., 6416. Mention.

TUCKER, L. H., 9088. D.C.M.

On the night 2nd/3rd October, 1915, near Vermelles, the Germans expected an attack by us, and the fire on both sides was very heavy, in addition to which flares were being constantly sent up. Drummer Tucker and Private Lewis were ceaseless in their efforts to bring in the wounded men who were lying between our own and the enemy lines. On one occasion they were fired on by our own men, who were unable to distinguish who they were. They continued this work until after daylight, exhibiting marked courage.

TURNER, A., 9/12405.   Mention.

TUNSTALL, J., 19400.   M.M.

TURNELL, G. B., 21396.   M.M.

TURNER, C. W., 8352.
     Croix de Guerre (Bel.)

TURNER, F., 24139.   Mention.

TURNER, H. M.   M.C.
     Croix de Guerre (Fr.)

TURNER, W., 14620.   M.M.

TURTON, R. D.   Mention.   C.M.G.
     To be Brevet-Colonel.

TWEMLOW, J., 10393.   Mention.   M.M.
     D.C.M.

As a stretcher-bearer he displayed the utmost fearlessness and devotion in bandaging the wounded under heavy fire ; also going out and personally rescuing the one survivor of a stretcher party, all of whom had been hit by snipers. His gallantry under fire has been most noticeable on many other occasions.

TWIGG, C., 16249.   M.M.

TYLER, F. W., 8546.   M.M.

UNWIN, A., 9901.   Mention.   D.C.M.

For consistent good work. He volunteered for many patrols, and has set a fine example to the men of his company.

URINOWSKI, W., 200235.   M.M.

UTLEY, F., 1585.   M.M.

VERNON, W. J., 240212.   Mention.

VIGORS, C. H.   Mention.   M.C.

After an intense and prolonged bombardment, the enemy attacked an isolated post, of which he was in command. He showed great courage and determination which resulted in the attack being repulsed, two prisoners captured, and heavy losses inflicted on the enemy.
     Croix de Guerre (Fr.)

VILLERS-STEWART, P. G.   Mention.
M.C.

VINCENT, H. E.   Mention.   M.C.

During the operations East of Terhand, on 14th October, 1918, without any staff to assist, he got orders out promptly, his instructions being always clear and short. During the attack he collected stragglers belonging to various units and put them in their own areas, thereby greatly assisting in the success and rapidity with which final objectives were reached.

VINCENT, T. C.   Mention.

WADSWORTH, W. J., 67456.   M.M.

WAGER, P. A., 7758.
     Italian Bronze Medal.

     D.C.M.

With the company headquarter details he covered the withdrawal of the company in face of heavy machine-gun fire. His courage and confidence did much to steady and encourage those around him in a difficult situation.

WAGSTAFF, R., 17544.   M.M.

WAIDE, E. F.   M.C.

During the attack East of Terhand in October, 1918, he set a fine example of gallant and determined leadership, in pushing on to his objective, maintaining excellent direction in spite of the mist. With but a few men he overcame resistance and although greatly outnumbered, made them surrender, taking 35 prisoners.

WALFORD, A. S.   Mention.

WALKER, A., 50707.   M.M.

WALKER, E., 19047.   M.M.

WALKER, E. E., 40778.   M.M.

WALKER, F., 59109.   Mention.

WALKER, F. E., 20588.   D.C.M.

During an advance the line was held up on two occasions by the machine-gun fire of the enemy. On each occasion he went out alone and bombed the machine-guns, accounting for the teams and capturing the guns. His courage and determination enabled his company to continue their advance and reach their objective. He set a splendid example of dash and initiative.

WALKER, F. S.,   Mention (2).   M.C.

WALKER, H., 243742.   M.M.

WALKER, H. S.
Croix de Guerre (Bel.)

WALKER, J., 14259. M.M.

WALKER, J. J., 15195. M.M.

WALKER, N. M.C.
As Brigade Intelligence Officer, he showed fine courage and initiative in making valuable reconnaissances under heavy shell fire. On one occasion, when the situation was obscure, finding exact location of all the troops, and bringing back very valuable information.

WALKER, S., 20730. M.M.

WALKER, T. Mention.

WALKER, T., 51583. D.C.M.
During the attack East of Terhand, on 14th October, 1918, he, with four others, came on a pill-box from behind which the enemy machine-guns were firing into the backs of our troops who had passed on without seeing it in the thick mist. On fire being opened with a Lewis gun, the enemy ran into the pill-box. He dashed forward, fired through the loophole, killing and wounding several men, and forcing the remaining eleven to surrender. This splendid action and dash in face of greatly superior numbers, was the means of saving heavy casualties to our troops.

WALKER, W. H., 50019. M.M.

WALKEY, C., 9719.
Croix de Guerre (Fr.)

WALL, L., 72280. M.M.

WALLEY, A., 15633. M.M.

WALLS, G. H., 49247. M.M.

WALSH, M., 3/25770. Mention.

WALSH, T., 9/11804. M.M.

WALTER, R., 10652. M.M.

WALTON, A., 1330. M.M.

WALTON, A. R. M.C.
At a critical period, and under heavy fire, he moved his company to the support of the front line, subsequently withdrew under close range machine-gun fire, and held up the enemy until ordered to withdraw again. Throughout the day he was an example of coolness and courage under most trying conditions.

WALTON, C., 2449. M.M.

WALTON, R. A., 2459. M.M.

WANT, A. M.S.M.

WARBURTON, J., 12555. M.M.
Promoted 2/Lieut.

WARD, J., 19304. D.C.M.
When only one officer was left with the company, he took charge of and reorganized two platoons, and by his personal example inspired his men to hold on under the most trying conditions, and when no officer was left, he took command of the whole company.

WARD, J. H., 200218. M.M.

WARD, P. M., 7180. M.S.M.

WARD, T. W., 61134. Mention.

WARD, W. A. M.C.

WAREHAM, G. E., 51107. M.M.

WAREING, W., 26174.
Greek Military Cross.

WARING, A., 31088. M.M.

WARING, G., 19172. M.M.

WARING, T., 200528.
Croix de Guerre (Fr.)

WARRENDER, B. F., 23292. M.M.

WARRINGTON, A., 11787. M.M.

WATKINSON, J. W., 1169. Mention.

WATSON, G. T. C. Mention.

WATSON, J. L., 49583. M.M.

WATSON, L. Mention.

WATSON, S. Mention (2). M.C. D.S.O.
Legion of Honour.

WATSON, S., 9570. M.M.

WALLS, G. H., 49247. M.M.

WATTS, E. D.S.O.
When nearly all the officers in his battalion had become casualties, he rallied the men and consolidated his position, working indefatigably. Next morning he led a bombing attack with great skill and courage. He set a fine example of pluck and endurance.

WATTS, H. O.B.E.

WATTS, L. W., 240527. M.S.M.

WEBB, D., 6458. D.C.M.
For gallant conduct and resource on many occasions whilst scouting, in obtaining

valuable information. Near Ypres he reconnoitred .the German positions, located a hostile gun, and killed a sniper who had been doing much damage.

WEBSTER, A. J., 28250.   M.M.

WEBSTER, A. T., 14883.   M.M.

WEBSTER, J., 1080.   M.M.

WEBSTER, W. A., 8120.   M.S.M.

WEEKS, W., 14684.   M.M.

WEIR, W. E., 24365.   Mention.   M.M.

WELSBY, W. H.   Mention.

WESTON, F., 240006.   M.S.M.

WESTON, F., 77.   Mention.

WESTRAY, C., 29568.
    Croix de Guerre (Fr.)

WHEELER, J., 51159.   M.M.

WHITBY, H., 44270.   M.M.

WHITE, A., 11323.   Mention.

WHITE, A., 24159.   M.M.

WHITE, A. S., 27349.   M.M.

WHITE, G. H., 691.   M.M.

WHITE, H., 16490.   M.S.M.

WHITE, H. P.   Mention (2).   M.C.

WHITE, I., 28260.   Mention.

WHITE, J., 50815.   M.S.M.

WHITEHEAD, T., 240176.   Mention. M.S.M.

WHITELEY, J., 21284.   M.M.

WHITELEY, R. F.   Mention.

WHITELEY, W., 5934.   M.S.M.

WHITELEY, W., 17/30666.   M.S.M.

WHITELOCK, N., 15/19646.   Mention.

WHITFIELD, J. F., 290655.   Mention. M.M.

WHITING, F., 5752.   Mention.   M.M.

WHITMORE, J., 290697.   M.M.

WHITNEY, S., 14714.   D.C.M.
    During an attack he showed great courage and determination, and was largely responsible for the capture and consolidation of the position. He set a fine example of coolness and devotion to duty.

WHITTAKER, F. N., 32953.   Mention (2). M.S.M.

WHITTAKER, W., 29108.   Mention.

WHYTE, B., 525.   M.M.

WIDDOWS, H., 52495.   M.M.

WIGGANS, W., 60482.   M.M.   D.C.M.
    While carrying messages to the front line under very heavy shell fire, the situation being at the time uncertain, and the outpost companies being almost surrounded. By his tenacity and courage in delivering these messages two companies were successfully extricated from a very precarious position.

WIGHTMAN, E.   M.C.
    When a wounded man was struggling towards our lines he was seen to collapse about forty yards off, apparently exhausted, this officer jumped over the parapet, and, although continuously fired at by the enemy, succeeded in bringing the man in on a stretcher by pushing it in front of him.

WILCOCK, J. F., 5587.   Mention. M.S.M.
    Croix de Guerre (Bel.)

WILCOX, S., 16704.   M.M.

WILDGOOSE, J., 52507.   M.M.

WILDING, R., 25119.   M.M.

WILKINSON, A., 200107.   Mention. D.C.M.

WILKINSON, A., 265042.   D.C.M.
    He was of great assistance in assembling his company for the assault under very heavy fire and led them forward in the attack, capturing the objective. Throughout the day his coolness and energy under very heavy shell fire were a fine example.

WILKINSON, F., 13186.   M.M.

WILKINSON, F. W., 20938.   M.M.

WILKINSON, H. M.   Mention (2).   M.C.
    He was acting Adjutant at a critical point in the battle when battalion headquarters was being surrounded, owing to the enemy having broken through on the flanks. He organized headquarters and manned a sunken road, and on receipt of orders, withdrew with great coolness under heavy rifle and machine-gun fire. He set a fine example to his men and sustained very little loss of life.

WILKINSON, J., 17589.   M.M.

WILL, N. G. H.   M.C.
    For seven days he commanded his company in an advanced position with the greatest

ability, under extremely bad weather conditions and continual heavy shelling. Under these trying circumstances his great coolness and cheerfulness set a fine example to his men. Taking command of his battalion a week later, in the absence of his Commanding Officer, he personally reconnoitred the whole of his sector (a line of battle outposts), although constantly exposed to hostile fire of every description. The valuable information which he obtained was absolutely essential for the successful co-operation of our artillery in repelling hostile counter-attacks.

WILLIAM, A., 32502. M.M.

WILLIAMS, G. H. M.C.

On the 27th September, 1918, near Baralle, his company was working with the Royal Engineers on the bridges across the Canal Du Nord and Agache River. When the situation was most confused he went forward and directed the work of carrying up bridging material under heavy machine-gun and shell fire. He also did good reconnaissance work of the forward areas both before and after the operations.

WILLIAMS, H., 18953. M.M.
Croix de Guerre.

WILLIAMS, H., 3/25316. Mention.

WILLIAMS, J., 21583. D.C.M.
He was four days almost isolated with his platoon under heavy fire, and set a fine example of courage and determination.

WILLIAMS, J., 275764. D.C.M.
At Sequehart, in October, 1918, he displayed great dash in leading his section against machine-guns and snipers, killing several of them himself. Later in the day, under heavy shell fire, he established two posts on an unprotected flank. During the heavy enemy counter-attack, he displayed a fine fighting spirit, holding back the enemy until he was almost surrounded.

WILLIAMS, J., 10728. M.M.

WILLIAMS, J. A., 12163. Mention.

WILLIAMS, P., 14885. M.M.

WILLIAMS, R., 67970. Mention.

WILLIAMS, W., 665. D.C.M.
At Le Touquet salient on 29th December,

1915, he was in charge of the left bombing party of a fighting patrol, displayed great coolness and bravery and kept his men well in hand while bombing the enemy's trenches.

WILLIAMS, W. A. M.C.
During an attack he led his company with great courage and determination, capturing an enemy field gun, and at once consolidated his objective. Afterwards he repulsed a strong enemy counter-attack, showing a splendid example of coolness under very heavy shell fire.

WILLIAMS, W. E. Mention (2). D.S.O.
Under very heavy artillery and machine-gun fire he organized his battalion, got into touch with troops on either side, and successfully held his position.
Promoted Brevet-Major.

WILLIAMSON, J. F., 240045. Mention.

WILLIAMSON, W., 268163. Mention.

WILLS, A. G. P. M.C.
He remained at his aid post under heavy shell fire for 18 hours without rest; by his gallantry and fine example; encouraging his bearers to work continuously, until the last case was safely evacuated.

WILSON, J.
To be 2/Lieut.

WILSON, J., 9/12895. Mention. D.C.M.
When in charge of five Lewis guns, he did excellent work, sometimes having to repair them under heavy rifle and machine-gun fire. It was due to his energy that none of the guns were out of action for more than ten minutes during three days' fighting, and that all were brought out of action in good condition.

WILSON, J. H. M.C.
He handled his section with great skill and courage. He took one of the gunner's places, and continued firing until he was wounded. Having had his wound dressed, he then took another gunner's place, and remained on duty until ordered to withdraw.

WILSON, T., 28251. Mention. M.M.
Serbian Gold Medal.

WILSON, V. L. M. M.C.
He showed great ability in leading his

platoon throughout the operations. His courage and coolness on all occasions have been most marked.

WILSON, W. A.

Promoted 2/Lieut.

M.C.

He led his company with great courage and initiative, capturing two lines of trenches. Later, he materially assisted in repelling an enemy counter-attack. He was severely wounded.

WILYMAN, T.   Mention.

WINDER, H., 51481.   M.M.

WINSTANLEY, W., 28794.   M.M.

WITHERS, K. S.   Mention.

WITNEY, J. H., 8955.   M.S.M.

WOLSTENHOLME, S., 2470.   M.M.

WOOD, A., 1517.   Mention.   M.M.

WOOD, F., 13849.   M.M.

WOOD, G.   Mention.   M.C.   O.B.E.

WOOD, G. H., 11325.   M.M.

WOOD, H., 14344.   M.S.M.

WOOD, H.   Mention (2).

WOOD, H., 10483.   M.M.

WOOD, W. A., 49109.   M.M.

WOODALL, C., 15209.   M.M.

WOODCOCK, F. T.   M.C.

He assumed command of the Company when all officers had become casualties, and maintained the defence for several hours in spite of an intense shell fire. He then withdrew with much skill and daring to a new position. Later, he assisted his Company commander in beating out a fire which had started in front of the trench, and was masking their fire.

WOODHEAD, F., 265322.   M.M.

WOODWARD, J., 266227.   Mention.

WOODWARD, S., 17858.   M.M.

WOODWARD, S. F., 19291.   M.M.

WOODIER, F., 8261.   D.C.M.

WOODYER, C. DE W.   Mention.   M.C.

WOODYER, H. M.   M.C.

During the operations before Wervicq, on 30th September, 1918, he pushed forward with his company, seizing the railway embankment, and, being unable to find the

company on his right, immediately formed a defensive flank and held on until the troops on his right came up. His courage and example inspired his men.

WOOLVINE, G. H., 8072.   M.S.M.

WORGAN, R. B.   Mention.

WORMINGTON, W. T.

Promoted 2/Lieut.

WORRALL, T. S., 15352.   M.M.

WORTH, T. H., 25796.   M.M.

WRENCH, A., 16026.   M.M.

WRIGHT, C.   Mention.   M.C.

He led his platoon with the greatest dash during an attack. Later, when in command of his company, he showed untiring energy and determination during the consolidation of his position, cheering his men to greater efforts.

WRIGHT, D., 9777.   Mention.

WRIGHT, H. B.

Croix de Guerre.

M.C.

He displayed great dash in all the counter-attacks carried out by the battalion, on one occasion rushing an enemy machine-gun and shooting the gunner operating it. He has done splendid work throughout the operations.

WRIGHT, J., 290465.   M.M.

WRIGHT, J. N., 290472.   M.M.

WRIGHT, N. G.   Mention.

WRIGHT, R. H. W., 10577.   M.M.

WRIGHT, W., 268094.   M.M.

WYATT, T., 7276.   Mention.

WYNNE, J. W., 7010.   D.C.M.

He bayoneted several of the enemy, and showed great energy in organizing working parties under fire. Later, he made daring reconnaissances, and was wounded.

YARWOOD, S., 13767.

Croix de Guerre.

D.C.M.

He commanded the left platoon in the attack on the " P " ridge on 18th September, 1918, and led his platoon with great dash on to its objective, overcame all opposition and used his guns against the machine-guns on Little Dolina. When the majority of his platoon had become casualties, he withdrew the remainder, personally carrying a wounded man to safety.

YATES, A., 13247.   Mention.   M.M.

YATES, J. W., 45867.   Mention (2). M.S.M.

YATES, W. Y.   M.C.

During a retirement he showed great skill and determination in maintaining his position with very few men in the face of heavy enemy attacks. In particular, one night he reorganized his men and parties of stragglers and dug in a line, and in spite of heavy shelling and machine-gun fire, repelled all enemy attacks for twelve hours until ordered to retire. He showed excellent leadership throughout.

YORKE, H. R.   M.C.

Owing to the troops on the left of the brigade failing to capture their objective their left battalion suffered heavy casualties. He was ordered to take forward his company to strengthen the left flank. Advancing all the time, under extremely heavy fire, he showed great skill in selecting his final position.

YORSTON, S.   M.C.

YOUNG, J.   Mention.

YOUNG, J. H. B.   Mention (2).   M.C.

During an advance he showed great ability and determination in organizing the operations of his company after his company commander had been wounded. He also did excellent work in bringing back valuable information through heavy shell fire.

D.S.O.

Near Jenlain in November, 1918, he led his company into a gap against determined opposition, capturing prisoners and securing the safety of his battalion. He then reorganized his company and led them in attack, securing his objective and capturing prisoners and machine-guns and mopping up Wargnies Le Grand.

YOUNG, W., 9246.   M.M.

Mobilization Period

1st BATTALION.

IMMEDIATELY before the Great War, the 1st Battalion was stationed at London-derry, where it formed part of the 15th Infantry Brigade. This Brigade, which belonged to the 5th Division, was commanded by Brigadier-General Count Gleichen, K.C.V.O., C.B., C.M.G., D.S.O.

The unrest in Northern Ireland had been causing considerable anxiety, and the possibility of Civil War in Ulster kept the thoughts of the 15th Brigade focussed on local problems, rather than upon the series of events on the Continent which culminated in the murder of the Arch-Duke Ferdinand at Serajevo.

By the end of July, however, the possibilities of a European War were obvious to all, but, on the 4th of August, just when it seemed likely that the crisis might be averted, telegraphic orders to mobilize electrified the garrison of Ireland, and automatically changed the perspective of the picture. Never was the King's health more fervently drunk than in the Officers' Mess that night. Many of those present honoured the toast for the last time ; none would have believed it had they been told that within three weeks, the Battalion would be decimated. Lieut.-Colonel D. C. Boger was in command, and Major B. H. Chetwynd-Stapylton was the Senior Major. Captain V. R. Tahourdin was Adjutant, and the four Companies were commanded by Captain A. J. L. Dyer, Captain J. L. Shore, Captain W. L. E. R. Dugmore and Captain E. Rae-Jones.

The mobilization scheme had been prepared with the greatest care and attention to detail, so the change over from a peace to a war footing worked smoothly according to the pre-arranged programme and was completed on the sixth day. August the 5th was the first day of mobilization and during the next three days drafts of Reservists arrived from the Depot totalling five hundred and fifty-six men. Many of these had seen only two or three years' colour service, and that as much as nine years previously. This accentuates the tenacity and courage they showed during the exhausting times which followed.

Three officers and fifteen N.C.Os. were despatched to Chester on August 7th to form a training cadre for new Battalions. Few realized, as yet, the magnitude of the struggle to which the nation was committed, and this lack of foresight in not retaining at home an adequate staff to assist in the formation and training of new units, soon produced a serious situation which took many months to rectify.

The Battalion entrained early on the morning of August the 14th in two specials. On arrival at Belfast, it detrained and marched to York Docks, whence it embarked with two Companies of the 1st Norfolks in the S.S. "Massillia." The ship sailed under sealed orders, which, when opened, revealed the destination as France.

2nd BATTALION.

The 2nd Battalion had been stationed at Jubbulpore, India, under the command of Lieut.-Colonel F. H. Finch Pearse. Major A. de C. Scott was 2nd in command, and the Company Commanders were Major A. B. Stone, Captain C. G. E. Hughes, Captain H. G. Turner and Captain G. Morton. Lieut. (now Colonel) H. G. Cowan was Quartermaster.

When ordered home, the Battalion travelled by train to Bombay. There it embarked in the S.S. " Braemar Castle," which, in company with thirty-eight other vessels all transporting troops, was convoyed by warships to England. It arrived at Devonport on Christmas Eve, 1914, which date, according to the optimistic prophets of August the 4th, should have been the last day of the war.

The Battalion then proceeded by train to Winchester, and went into camp some eight miles out from the city. Here tents were already pitched, but the site was a very pronounced slope of a hill and was an absolute sea of mud. The men remained there for ten days in appalling weather, cold, rain and snow. No facilities could be obtained for drying clothing or blankets, and the effect on the troops was very depressing. On the eleventh day, the Battalion was removed to Winchester and billeted in the Peter Symonds School, and in the County Girls' School, where, although the accommodation was very restricted, the men were at least able to dry their clothing.

Mobilization being concluded, the Battalion left Winchester by road, on January 16th, 1915, for Southampton, where it embarked in the S.S. " City of Chester " (which ordinarily was a cattle-boat) and sailed to Havre.

The Battalion coming direct from India, where it was at full strength, was made up of seasoned men, and having added to it Reservists, also seasoned men, it constituted a unit that for efficiency, discipline, morale, physical fitness and general appearance, must have rejoiced the heart of the officer who commanded it, as well as those who served in it.

3rd (SPECIAL RESERVE) BATTALION.

On mobilization in August, 1914, the Battalion assembled in Chester, drew its equipment and stores and proceeded to its War Station in Birkenhead.

Liverpool and Birkenhead together became " a Defended Port," and the Garrison, which consisted of four Special Reserve Battalions, was known as " Mersey Defences." The special duties of the Cheshires were to guard the Docks, and to occupy certain strategic positions in the Wirral and on Hilbre Island. The Battalion was under the command of Lieut.-Colonel E. T. Logan, D.S.O. Major G. W. C. May was 2nd in command, and Lieut. L. Bengough was Adjutant. The strength was about 16 officers and 500 rank and file, numbers which were very largely and rapidly augmented both by old trained soldiers, long since time expired, and by newly enlisted recruits.

Early in 1915, Colonel Logan was given command of the 15th Durham Light

Infantry. He took that Regiment out to France and was killed at Loos. Lieut.-Colonel Alex Greg, who was with the 3rd South Lancashires, and in command of the Dock Troops, took over the command in October 1915. Thus, he came back to the Battalion he had originally joined in the year 1890.

By this time, the Battalion had gone into new hutments at Bidston, retaining Gamlins Furniture Depot for Headquarters stores, recruits and the necessary training staff. At the end of 1915, the strength was over 3,000 men, and its ultimate maximum strength was just over 4,000. It is interesting to note that such was the elasticity of the organization of the Special Reserve that these huge numbers in no way upset the general procedure or interior economy of the Battalion. These numbers were by no means available at any one time for drafts, for, in addition to recruits, they comprised convalescent men and men awaiting discharge.

4th BATTALION.

The 4th, 5th, 6th and 7th Battalions formed the Cheshire Infantry Brigade, Welsh Division. It was under the command of Colonel E. A. Cowans, and Captain A. Crookenden was Brigade Major.

The staff of the 4th Battalion was as follows :—Lieut.-Colonel A. B. Hopps, T.D., was in command for the first month when he handed over to Major G. H. Swindells from the 7th Battalion. Major J. A. Pemberton was 2nd in command, Lieut (local Captain) H. R. Bently was Adjutant and Captain J. Ellis was Quartermaster.

The week-end before the outbreak of war, some 50 men were in camp near Eastham. But having been warned by Brigade to be prepared to mobilize, they returned to Birkenhead where a large crowd of men was clamouring to enlist.

The mobilization scheme provided for the local purchase of clothing, equipment and transport. Two officers were sent off early in the morning, with requisitions, and they did their job without a hitch, thus forestalling the Royal Engineers and Yeomanry who were doing the same thing. The transport was a queer sight. Every sort and condition of cart was requisitioned, including street watering carts ; the horses varied from hunters to heavy draft horses and the harness was all of civilian pattern and in various states of repair. A piece of waste ground near the Drill Hall became the transport lines. The only mistake occured over the feeding arrangements. As it would obviously be some time until rations could be drawn in the ordinary way from the Army Service Corps, it was arranged that for the first week a civilian Contractor was to supply food. But each day the number to be fed was hopelessly underestimated. Down Grange Road, long queues of men were waiting to enlist, and on the very first day over 80% of the Battalion turned up, although it had been expected that the men would not join in any large numbers until about the 3rd to the 5th day. This response to the order to mobilize was exceedingly creditable, especially as most of the men were clerks and cashiers, holding responsible jobs which they would have to hand over. Their new life now was to be a daily effort to break in new boots while out route marching.

On the completion of mobilization, the Battalion moved to Shrewsbury by train, on the 9th and 10th of August, in spite of a crop of scares that the Germans had landed, which threatened to change its destination. Here the men were billeted in the Midland Carriage Works, a most unfortunate choice of billets, as the works were infested with lice.

After a short training in Shrewsbury, the Battalion moved by route march to Church Stretton. The best that can be said of this march is that it was uniquely picturesque in its variety of transport, and other features. Here the camp was close to the railway along which passed a constant succession of trains carrying coal to the Fleet. The well-known trains full of Russians, their fur hats covered with snow, were said to have passed through the camp during the hours of darkness on August 27th and 28th.

The training went very smoothly, and showed that the Territorial Battalions were settling down in spite of every effort to upset them. Terrible uncertainty prevailed as to the fate of the 1st Battalion, and only the wildest rumours came through.

Training now began in earnest, till at the end of October, the Brigade was sent to Suffolk to dig great lines of trenches. No sooner had work begun than the 6th Battalion was ordered to France. The first train was scheduled to leave before the orders to entrain reached them, in billets 5 miles from the station.

Sudden orders for the Brigade to go to India brought the Battalions back to Northampton. Here men under age were placed on one side and the remainder fitted with drill clothing and tropical helmets; vehicles were given in and rifles taken away and passed on to Kitchener's Army. These were later replaced by Japanese rifles. On the evening of November the 14th, the weary staff who were not to accompany the Battalions to India met at dinner and planned their futures. On the 15th came orders cancelling the whole plan. Men were recalled by wire, transport was redrawn from Ordnance, and all ranks stood by, awaiting an immediate order which did not come. A state of tension existed until the 27th, when leave re-opened.

On December 7th, the Brigade moved to Stowmarket for more trench digging, where it remained until early in January. But even the digging was not allowed to continue in peace, for the trace and profile of the works were altered endlessly.

The next move was to Cambridge where the 2/5th and 2/6th joined the Brigade.

As the 5th Battalion had gone to France from Northampton soon after the 6th, it was now essential to bring the two second line Battalions up to the standard of the the others. So they received the benefit of the full attention of the Regular Staff, for which the other Battalions were devoutly thankful.

The 4th and 7th Battalions were at Royston and Baldock a good part of the spring.

On April 26th, Brigade Headquarters moved to Royston, and for the umpteenth time arranged training areas and classes. But maps and programmes had no sooner been drawn out, than the Brigade was ordered to Bedford. Here the 4th and 5th Welch took the places of the two second line Cheshire Battalions.

Early in July, the Brigade left England to disembark in the early dawn on a shingly beach which was said to be Suvla.

The 2/4th Battalion was raised in Birkenhead in September, 1914. Lieut.-Colonel A. B. Hopps, T.D., returned to command it. Major E. W. Morris was the Senior Major, and Captain H. Van Gruisen was Adjutant. It went to Aberystwyth until March 1915, when it moved to Northampton. Three months later, the Battalion went to Essex for a trenching course. In July it returned to Northampton, and within a month it was moved to Bedford, where it took over the billets vacated by the 1/4th Battalion.

The 3/4th Battalion was formed in July, 1915, under the command of Colonel F. W. Blood, V.D., T.D.

5th BATTALION.

The Headquarters of the 5th Battalion was at Chester. It was under the command of Lieut.-Colonel J. E. G. Groves, T.D., whose Adjutant was Captain (later Major) G. Adshead. Major C. E. Bromley was 2nd in command. Mobilized at Chester on August 5th, the Battalion went to Shrewsbury with the Cheshire Brigade. On going overseas in November, Major T. L. Fennell took over second in command, and Captain J. H. Davies became Adjutant.

The 2/5th Battalion was formed of officers and men who did not volunteer for service overseas. It was a Home Defence Battalion.

The 3/5th Battalion was formed later as a Reserve, and was really a Depot.

6th BATTALION.

The 6th Battalion is proud to think that it was the first Territorial Unit wearing the acorn to see active service. The men had been in Camp at Rhyl during the summer of 1914 under the command of Lieut.-Colonel A. J. Sykes, M.P., and were in a high state of efficiency when orders for mobilization were issued on August the 4th. The men of the 8 Companies turned up at their respective Drill Halls almost to a man. After medical inspection and a few days spent in filling up 200 vacancies in the rank and file, the Battalion left Stockport for Shrewsbury.

Before embarking for France early in November, Lieut.-Colonel G. B. Heywood took over the command, his two Majors being H. Hesse and R. Rostron. They arrived at Havre on November the 10th.

Recruiting for the 2/6th Battalion began in Stockport in September, 1914. This was placed under the command of Major G. H. Leah. It moved to Northampton when the 1/6th Battalion went abroad. Its subsequent moves were to Cambridge, Northampton again and then Bedford.

The 3/6th Battalion, under the command of Colonel H. Stott, was formed at the end of November 1914. It went to Aberystwyth, and later to Whittington Huts, Salop. The Burbage Silver Prize Band enlisted in this Battalion in a body.

7th BATTALION.

On mobilization at Macclesfield the 7th Battalion was under the command of Colonel E. W. Greg, T.D. Major (now Colonel) W. P. Reade, T.D., was Senior Major. Major H. Backhouse took the Battalion abroad with the Brigade in July 1915.

Second and third line Battalions were formed.

8th BATTALION.

The 8th Battalion, the first of the " New Army," was raised at the Castle, Chester, under the command of Captain H. S. Walker. It was composed entirely of men who joined up at once in their only clothes, many just off the street. The Grand Stand on the race-course was its Headquarters, and the men slept there as well. On August the 20th, the men entrained for Tidworth on Salisbury Plain. Here they were met in the dusk by Colonel H. F. Kellie, lately of the 1st Battalion, who marched them four miles to Shipton Bellinger, having drawn equipment of a sort from the station. Camp was pitched as well as 150 recruits (the Battalion !) could do it, and a meal of bread and tea, purchased from a grocer's cart, was issued, and thankfully eaten.

Men joined every few days, in drafts from Chester, the " first hundred thousand." Except for the first Company, the men had no uniforms, no equipment and no arms. New Army Officers joined in civilian clothes as they could not get uniforms. Lieut. Houston was appointed Adjutant, and ex-R.Q.M.S. T. Leigh (afterwards Captain) was Quartermaster.

At a later date, the Battalion moved from Tidworth to Chistleton, near Swindon, to help constitute the 13th Division. Training continued until the following summer. In July, the Battalion sailed from Avonmouth in H.M.T. " Ivernia," for Gallipoli, being then under the command of Lieut.-Colonel C. H. D. Willoughby.

9th BATTALION.

The 9th Battalion was formed out of the 8th about September the 15th. Lieut.-Colonel H. O. A. Harkness was the first Commanding Officer and Lieut.-Colonel W. E. Dauntesey acted as 2nd in command. Captain H. O. C. Thorp was Adjutant. The recruits were all men who had closed their businesses or handed over their jobs, and nearly all came with a change of clothes and a small bag. Training began, N.C.O. stripes were rigged up with pieces of tape and " Drill purposes " rifles were issued. When the weather broke the men suffered great hardship, for they were living under canvas, without tent boards, in a sea of mud. In spite of everything, they developed into a unit very quickly as a result of their amazing keenness. But there was ultimately a great deal of sickness, and they were moved into billets in Basingstoke.

" Kitchener's Blue " uniforms represented the next step, and not long after Christmas, khaki was issued.

The health of Colonel Harkness did not permit him to command in the field, so during the spring Colonel Dauntesey succeeded him, and a move was made to Andover.

On July 18th, 1915, the transport and machine guns sailed from Southampton for Havre. The main body followed from Folkestone the next day. They formed part of the 19th Division.

10th BATTALION.

About the end of August, 1914, the 10th Battalion, which consisted of 800 men all in mufti and with no change of clothes, was sent from Chester to Codford St. Mary. Lieut. (now Lieut.-Colonel) E. P. Nares went from the 8th Battalion as temporary Adjutant, and found himself in sole command for what he considers the most hectic fortnight of his life. A subaltern of less than 3 years' service, he was now to organize, administer and train a mob of civilians, under conditions of fantastic difficulty ! The " handing over " from Major A. S. Cooper, who had brought the men from Chester, took just two minutes. There was a nominal roll in duplicate of 800 men, but as the large majority of the names were Smith, Jones, Robinson and Brown, and they had no regimental or army numbers, this roll was not a great deal of use.

The next day Lieut. Nares fell in the whole Battalion (or as many of them as he could find) and organized them into Companies and Platoons. He chose provisional N.C.Os. purely from what they had been doing in civil life, and gave them one, two or three ribbons to tie round their arms. Even this ribbon he had to provide himself. This job took practically the whole day, and there was only time over to give an elementary lecture on camp sanitation, the necessity for which was very obvious after the first night.

The two following days resembled the break of the monsoon, and as the men had only the clothes they stood up in and one blanket, they had to stay in their tents. A few days later twelve large marine sergeants appeared, to the great relief of the Adjutant. Training then started in earnest, principally P.T. and elementary squad drill.

Officers now began to arrive, mostly from Public School O.T.Cs., among these being 2nd Lieuts E. F. Noble and J. A. Simmons, the latter (being) now Major Simmons, D.S.O., M.C. In due course, the Commanding Officer turned up, Colonel F. V. Whittall (Indian Army, retired). Majors L. Silvester, H. S. Marshall and P. L. Stevenson also joined up.

Training proceeded apace, and on September 26th, 1915, Colonel Whittall took his Battalion over to France.

11th BATTALION.

The 11th Battalion was raised at Chester Castle in Mid August, 1914, and sent to Codford under the command of Colonel Dyas. The Battalion turned into a field and found itself without tents, blankets or food. The Colonel and two or three officers went into Salisbury and bought what they could and presently rations were being drawn and a tent pitched for every twenty men. The men had been told to bring their oldest clothes. They sweated in these and had no change. To wash, they went down to the river, stripped, dipped and ran about to dry. Fortunately, the weather was good, but later heavy rain fell and the camp became water-logged. The training was largely dictated by one old Marine, a great stand-by, who tactfully taught the officers what they taught the men, until more adequate help arrived. Lieuts. Vickers and Kay from the O.T.C. knew a little drill, and Lieut. (now Major) C. F. Hill, an international footballer, had done a musketry course. Major Toller arrived, and as the drill improved, the clothing became so dilapidated that "Mr. Moses " was asked to supply more. A very motley crowd they were, in every sort and condition of civilian garment, not excluding bowler hats and shorts. Route marches with sticks instead of rifles, many hours of digging, night marches and football made the men very fit. But the hours were too long, the loads too heavy, and discontent spread. Conditions became worse with the approach of winter. Blankets were scarce, and the men were sleeping in mud. A neighbouring Battalion actually deserted, and one night serious trouble was narrowly averted. Lieut. Hill issued extra beer and persuaded the men to appoint spokesmen. Early next morning Colonel Dyas wired to Lord Kitchener, and the Battalion was moved by road to billets near Bournemouth. People were most kind on the way. Here strenuous training began again, lectures were given by wounded officers, old muskets were issued and the officers met in each other's billets to teach themselves tactics and strategy out of books bought privately.

The next move was to Flowerdown Camp, Winchester, where the first Divisional manœuvres were held. In June, the following year, the Battalion moved to Aldershot, where Colonel R. L. Aspinall took over the command. Major G. French was 2nd in command. Here they were inspected by Lord Kitchener and on September the 25th they sailed for Havre.

12th BATTALION.

The 12th Battalion was one of the many Battalions of the New Army raised at Chester during the first month of the war. Some six hundred men came from Stockport and district. Several veteran N.C.Os. and time-expired men were added to the strength, and early in September a move was made to Seaford in Sussex, Captain A. C. W. Bennett-Dampier being in charge. What training could be carried out without rifles or equipment was done. A fortnight later Colonel the Hon. A. E. Dalzell, C.B., took over command, and under him the Battalion gradually assumed a more military aspect.

Life under canvas during October was pleasant enough, but by November the Sussex mud began to make itself known. Roads became rivers of mud several inches deep. It was impossible to keep clean, and many a boot was left in the mud! So orders to prepare for a move to Eastbourne were welcomed. In Eastbourne the men were comfortably housed in magnificent billets in the best part of the town. The local people were not slow to appreciate the smartness of the 12th, and from the large number of photographs taken by request, the Battalion began to feel that Chester might look upon it as a worthy successor to the Regulars.

The Commanding Officer left to take over a Brigade. Major W. MacKay assumed command of the Battalion temporarily, but unfortunately his health gave out and Lieut.-Colonel Bennett-Dampier came back as Commanding Officer. It was now March, and one cold frosty morning at about 3 o'clock, the Battalion moved out of Eastbourne and entrained for Maidstone. Here much work was done on a trench system then being constructed for the defence of London.

In May, a march back to Seaford was made for a month's further training of a more intensive nature, and in July the Battalion went to Aldershot to fire a musketry course and complete itself for service overseas. Whilst at Aldershot, Lieut.-Colonel G. Capron, of the York and Lancaster Regiment, took over the Command. On September the 5th, 1915, an advance party of 3 officers and 108 men and transport sailed from Southampton for Havre. The next day the Battalion, as part of the 22nd Division, 25 officers and 823 men, followed from Folkestone to Boulogne.

13th BATTALION.

The 13th Battalion was raised at Port Sunlight on September 1st, 1914, as the result of an appeal by the late Lord Leverhulme to his employees. A thousand men at once volunteered for service—a staff of clerks was loaned from the offices of the factory, and medical examination and attestations were carried out at once.

• After a hearty send-off, the men were taken to Chester by ex-Sergeant-Major E. A. Brandon. They were joined there by 200 men from Wallasey recruited by the late Mr. Gershom Stewart, M.P. for the Wirral. Lord Leverhulme led them through the City to the Castle where they were put under the command of Captain Field. He took the " Wirral Battalion " (as it was called for some time) to Tidworth where several N.C.Os. from the Guards were waiting to help to get things into shape. Captain Field was promoted Lieut.-Colonel, and Sergeant Brandon Lieutenant and Quarter-Master. Major Reeves arrived as second in command, and Captain A. Wright was appointed Adjutant.

During its year of training, the Battalion moved to Codford, Bournemouth and Aldershot. As part of the 25th Division, it left Aldershot for France on September the 25th, 1915.

15th and 16th BATTALIONS.

In October, 1914, four miners walked from Durham to Birkenhead in answer to the call for recruits for the Regiment. Upon being medically examined it was found that these men did not come up to the required standard in height, although in every other respect they were healthy sturdy men, fired with patriotism. Mr. Bigland, M.P. for Birkenhead, thereupon obtained the special sanction of the War Office to recruit and raise a Battalion of "Bantams." The response was astonishing. Within a few days some three thousand men from all parts of the United Kingdom presented themselves for enrolment. Thus were formed the 1st and 2nd "Birkenhead Bantam Battalions," subsequently designated the 15th and 16th (Service) Battalions, The Cheshire Regiment. Within a few months a complete Infantry Division (35th "Bantam" Division) was raised under the command of Major-General Pinney.

On a cold bleak day in October, Lord Derby visited the assembled recruits and introduced Lieut.-Colonel C. E. Earle who was to command the 16th Battalion. Any man who had been a Cadet or a Boy Scout was made an acting N.C.O. on the spot. They were so keen to get into uniform that several purchased khaki privately. Those who could not afford to do so, removed strips of red baize from the seats of the Grand Stand of the Bebington Show Ground where they were quartered, and with these improvised puttees.

The 15th Battalion, commanded by Colonel H. W. K. Bretherton, was quartered in a High School in Rock Ferry. The kindness of the church workers here was most memorable. They stripped their own beds to provide hundreds of blankets for the men, and opened their hall as a canteen and reading room.

Both Battalions moved into camp at Hoylake, and in June, 1915, they moved to Masham on the Yorkshire moors, where they joined the 105th Infantry Brigade. Here Colonel F. Newell and Lieut.-Colonel R. Browne-Clayton took over command respectively of the 15th and 16th Battalions. Both these officers took their tough sturdy little men over to France, where they caused quite a sensation as they landed and were dubbed "piccaninni soldats." The 16th Battalion arrived on January 30th, 1916 and the 15th Battalion a month later.

14th and 17th BATTALIONS.

The 14th and 17th Battalions were both used as training and reserve Battalions. The former was raised in 1915, and was trained at Rhyl and at Whitchurch, and was under the command of Colonel Moss.

In September 1915 Major W. F. Austin took over command of the 17th Battalion.

18th to 22nd BATTALIONS.

The five Battalions numbered the 18th, 19th, 20th, 21st and 22nd, were all Labour Battalions. They were all raised before December, 1916. Their work consisted of making roads, laying sleeper tracks, digging trenches, barb-wiring, fixing machine-gun posts and building bridges, or, in fact, of any work of a heavy nature.

23rd BATTALION.

The 23rd Battalion was formed at Mundesley during the third year of the war. It was commanded by Lieut.-Colonel A. E. Churcher, and Major W. A. H. Vincent was 2nd in command. Captain W. A. Garratt was Adjutant, and the Hon. G. Kilpatrick was Senior Captain and Quartermaster.

The Battalion, comprising 36 officers and 1,015 men, sailed on May the 20th, 1918, from Dover to Calais.

24th BATTALION.

The 24th Battalion was for home service only. It was added to the Regiment towards the end of 1918.

1st GARRISON BATTALION.

The 1st Garrison Battalion was formed in August, 1915, and sent to Gibraltar. It was under the command of Colonel Loscombe. Major G. F. Chipman was appointed Camp Commandant, and Captain J. B. Bird, Camp Adjutant.

2nd GARRISON BATTALION.

The 2nd Garrison Battalion was raised in October, 1915, under the command of Colonel G. A. Ashby, C.B. Major K. J. Beardwood was appointed Adjutant, and Lieut. Gordon Quartermaster.

The composition of the Battalion was somewhat mixed, but the main part was composed of all ranks who in the earlier days of the war had become casualties. Men drawn from other units of the Cheshire Regiment were as far as possible made into " A " and " B " Companies. " C " and " D " Companies were largely formed of men from the South Lancashire and the Loyal North Lancashire Regiments.

Four large huts on Bebington Show Ground accommodated the men, but most of the officers had to be billeted outside. One of these huts blew down in a terrific gale which sprang up on New Years Day, 1916. Over 20 men were pinned beneath the fallen roof and injured, and to the great sorrow of the Battalion, 2 men were killed.

Light training, sport—in so far as the men's disabilities would permit—and plenty of good appetising food, well cooked and nicely served, soon brought the Battalion up to standard. The men were clean, smart and willing, though many individually were far from fit.

The Battalion was never Brigaded while in England. It was inspected twice and highly praised for steadiness and cleanliness. Embarkation orders were received early in March, 1916, and the Battalion sailed for Egypt.

3rd GARRISON BATTALION.

The 3rd (Home Service) Garrison Battalion was formed in November, 1915. It was sent to Ramsey, Isle of Man, under the command of Colonel H. O. A. Harkness,

INDEX

NOTE.—The total of 38 Battalions is made up by Young Soldiers Battalions.

Y

Lightning Source UK Ltd.
Milton Keynes UK
09 March 2011

168938UK00004B/6/A